S0-ARK-444

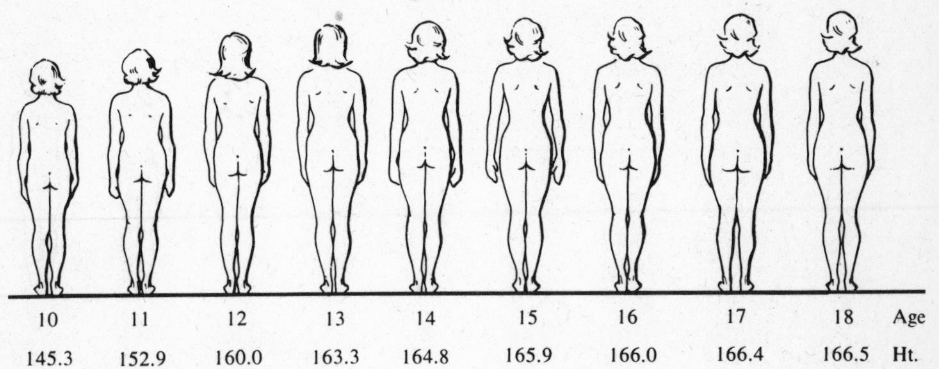
10 11 12 13 14 15 16 17 18 Age
145.3 152.9 160.0 163.3 164.8 165.9 166.0 166.4 166.5 Ht.

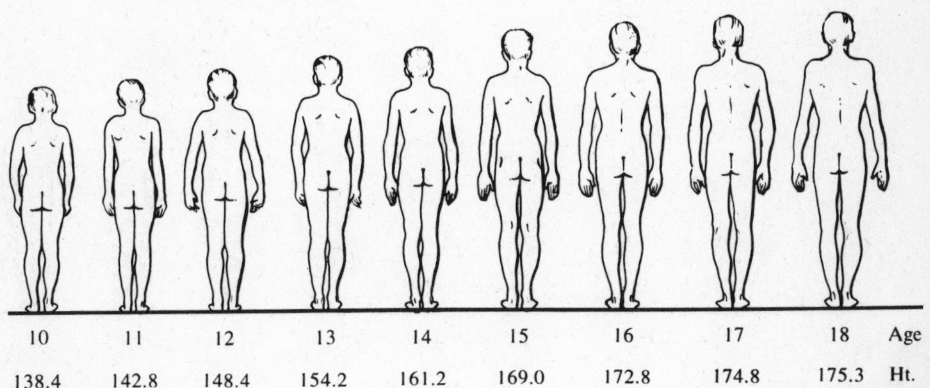
10 11 12 13 14 15 16 17 18 Age
138.4 142.8 148.4 154.2 161.2 169.0 172.8 174.8 175.3 Ht.

CHILDREN
Development and Relationships

CHILDREN
Development and Relationships

MOLLIE S. SMART and RUSSELL C. SMART

Department of Child Development and Family Relations
UNIVERSITY OF RHODE ISLAND

The Macmillan Company
Collier–Macmillan Limited, London

Seventh Printing, 1970

Library of Congress catalog card number: 66–25506

THE MACMILLAN COMPANY
866 THIRD AVENUE, NEW YORK, NEW YORK 10022
COLLIER–MACMILLAN CANADA, LTD., TORONTO, ONTARIO

Printed in the United States of America

To Laura

PREFACE

The purposes of this book are threefold: to give basic information to students preparing for professional work with children, to map out the field and kindle the interest of students planning to specialize in child development or child psychology, and to contribute to the reader's liberal education by adding to his knowledge of man.

The field of child development traditionally includes physical as well as psychological development. It also includes consideration of the family and culture in which the child grows up. The explosion of knowledge in recent years has discouraged some teachers of child development from venturing outside the field of psychology. We believe, however, that it is both valuable and possible to study the child as a physical and psychological being who lives in a family in a culture. We have included a minimum of physical growth material, all of which we consider important for understanding how the infant changes into a child and into an adult.

The framework of this book comes from two great men, Erik Erikson and Jean Piaget. Erikson, the Vienna-born psychoanalyst, and Piaget, the Swiss psychologist, have contributed deeply and broadly to the study of children. Their viewpoints fit together and complement each other in such a way as to delight the student of child development. They give a sweeping view of human growth, Erikson painting a far-reaching picture of personality development, Piaget illumining the growth of the mind. The work of both men can be studied on many different levels of difficulty. In an introductory book, we cannot hope to examine either in depth, our main purpose in using the ideas of Erikson and Piaget being to integrate the book. The multiplicity of research on children, especially on relationships, makes confusing reading unless some threads of consistent theory tie it together.

Another great man who has influenced our thinking is Lawrence K. Frank, who has been called the father of child development. Frank's understanding and creativity gave beginning and shape to the field of child development and to the dynamic developmental viewpoint. He continues to influence everyone in this field by integrating the past with the present and pointing forward to the future.

We are indebted to Raymond G. Kuhlen, who made valuable suggestions for improving the manuscript, and to Margaret Donaldson, who has stimulated our thinking. We are grateful for the assistance and encouragement of Louis Aikman and William Eastman. We express appreciation to those who helped with the preparation of the manuscript: Ruth West, Mary Fields, Cynthia Sheppard, Dorothy Burda, Ann Wilder, Susan Smith, John Smith, Ellen Smart, and Laura Smart.

M. S. S.
R. C. S.

CONTENTS

INTRODUCTION

The concept of stages of development is used commonly in both popular and scientific thinking. We follow both Erikson and Piaget in our use of *stages*. A stage is a period during which certain changes occur. The achievements of each stage are built upon the foundation of developments of previous stages. At each stage, there are certain kinds of problems to be solved. When the child succeeds, he can and does go on to tackle new problems and to grow through solving them. Each stage is named after activities which the child carries on during that period. Erikson's stages are named after activities involving the whole personality, Piaget's after intellectual activities. While there are not exact chronological ages to mark the beginnings and ends of stages, there are rough averages for landmarks. Figure 1 shows the usual ages for the duration of both series of stages. For each of Erikson's childhood and adolescent stages, there is a corresponding one in Piaget's series. Often it is possible to see a close relationship between the behavior patterns described by the two men. Sometimes the personality development taking place can be seen to be an essential result of the intellectual abilities and limits at that time.

The first chapter makes some general statements about development and relationships. The rest of the book is organized on an age-level basis in order to make children seem whole and real. We believe that a beginning student finds the subject matter more interesting when he can picture children as people. The disadvantage of an age-level organization is that the same topics have to be introduced in several different places. In doing this, we try not to repeat, but only to recapitulate enough to recall what has already been said. If a student wishes to study by topics rather than by age levels, he can do so by using the index.

Part I deals with the infant, from his conception to about two years of age. One stage of personality growth is almost completed during infancy, *almost* rather than *all,* because no stage of personality growth is ever entirely done. The development of the sense of trust is in its crucial period at this time, and

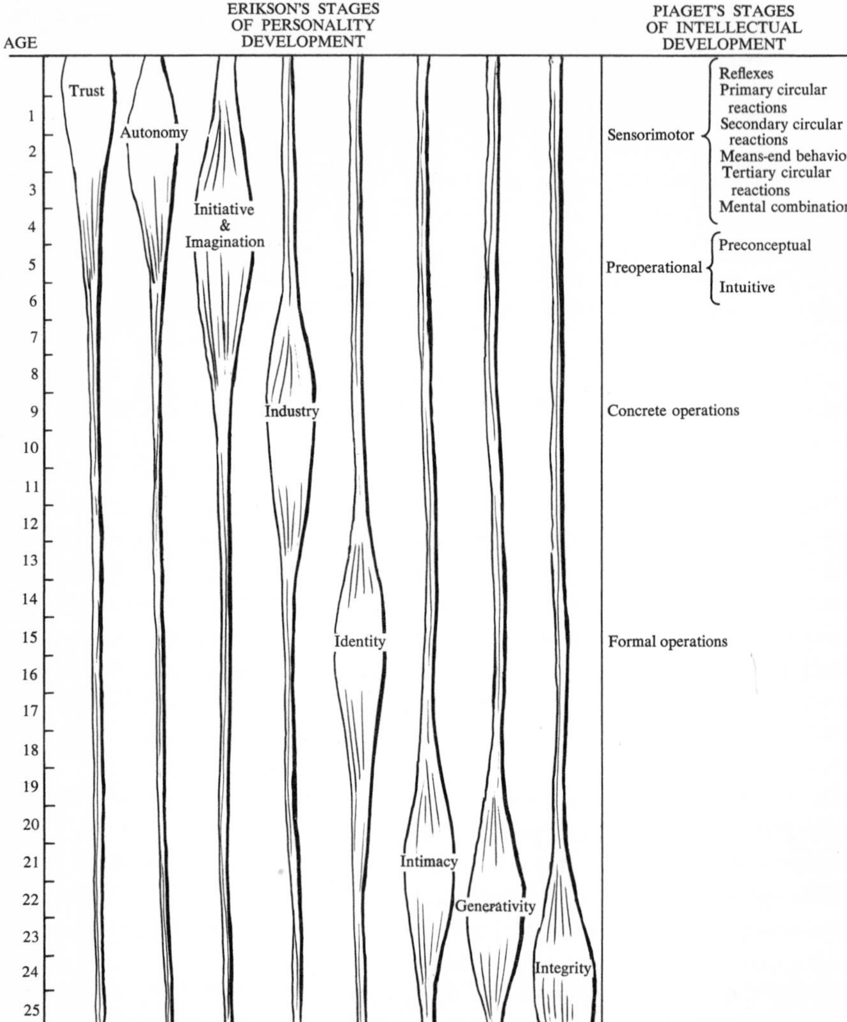

Figure 1. Schematic representation of Erikson's stages of personality development, with names of Piaget's stages of intellectual development placed at appropriate ages.

the resolutions of the problems of trust are the stuff of which infant personality is built. Infant intellectual growth comprises the sensorimotor period of intelligence, during which the child learns to control his movements in space and establishes the idea that objects are permanent. He comes to realize that he is an object in space, and an object among objects. These achievements contribute largely to his sense of trust, since he thus learns to expect certain regularities in the world, and he learns that he can count on himself to accomplish certain acts. During the last stage of the sensorimotor period of intelligence, the toddler becomes involved in a new stage of personality growth, the development of the sense of autonomy. Problems of autonomy occupy him for about the first half of the preschool period, which is considered in Part II of this book. The time from eighteen months to two years, when the child is called a *toddler,* is a transition period in both intellect and personality. Intellectually, the toddler enjoys the new ability to represent actions and objects to himself, through the use of mental images. He demonstrates that he can do so when he pretends and imitates. He can use very primitive foresight and planning. The growth of the sense of autonomy is facilitated by these new mental abilities, through which he begins to know himself as a person-among-persons. Growing physical powers and motor coordinations also contribute to his feelings of being an individual who can make decisions and who can succeed. His testing grounds and workshop include both objects and people. Through interactions with them, he develops in one direction or another. Our consideration of development and relationships therefore is very concerned with those interactions.

The child from two to six or seven, known as the preschool child, is the focus of Part II. *Preschool* is an accurate term in the sense that children are not required to go to school until the end of this period. It is a misleading term in its implication that education may not occur at this age. The preschool years are vastly significant for both personality and intellectual growth. With the problems of developing a sense of autonomy fairly well in hand by age three and a half, the preschool child comes to grips with the development of a sense of initiative and imagination. Although he thinks very concretely and cannot go beyond his own limited point of view in controlled thought, his imagination catapults him far and wide. Personality develops now through starting new activities, getting new ideas and through exploration of everything—places, people, language, objects, plastic materials. New experiences give him not only starting points for flights of fancy, but the wherewithal for building his primitive, concrete concepts of the world. Repeated experiences are necessary, too, since only through repeated encounters with classes of objects can he pull abstractions from them, and only through repeatedly checking his interpretations with other people can his thinking become socialized. Nor does he have to figure out everything for himself, through experience. Other people give him words with which to label his experiences, and then those experiences take on wider meanings, meanings which are valid in his culture. Other people show him how to feel in this or that situation, how to heal a hurt, how to see the funny side. They tell him what is important in life and how to get it. Although such messages often come through straight, they do not always do so. And often the behavior of the child is a language which adults find difficult to understand. One of the purposes of this book is to make the language of child behavior more comprehensible to adults. A second purpose is to aid adults in behaving in ways which have clear meaning to children.

The elementary school-child, considered in Part III, is quite different from the preschool child in body, mind and personality. He has the physical advantages of slow growth, well-developed motor coordinations and relatively few illnesses. His very admission to the world outside the family, the real world of school, proclaims that he is recognized as ready to go to work. Indeed, he is ready to give up much of the play which constituted his preschool business in order to learn the rules of his society and the fundamentals of being a worker. Personality growth requires the development of a sense of industry. He accepts a great deal of repetitive practice, even appearing to enjoy doing the same thing over and over. Not only does he strive to learn reading, writing and arithmetic, but much of his supposedly free time is spent practising motor skills and learning the rules of social and intellectual games. The school-age phase of intellectual development, the period of concrete operations, is marked by faster, more flexible and more accurate thinking. Instead of being limited by his own point of view, the school child can inquire and imagine himself into the places of other people, which he does in much of his social interaction. His broader backlog of experience and his previous achievements with concepts supplement his emerging ability to consider several aspects of the situation before coming to a conclusion. Satisfactory personality development results from interactions in which his physical and mental powers develop, in which he does learn the skills and rules which other children his age are learning and in which he gets the idea that he has performed satisfactorily. Since his field of interaction has broadened far beyond the family, people outside the family become increasingly important in contributing to success or failure, to a sense of industry or a sense of inferiority.

Part IV is concerned with adolescence, a time of life whose chronological age limits are very vague. A cycle of interrelated events begins shortly before puberty. If age 11 or 12 is considered as close to the beginning of adolescence, then most adolescents will be included. The end of adolescence is, of course, adulthood, however one defines it. The dominant personality problem is to develop a sense of identity. The intellectual stage typical of the period is that of formal operations, the same as it is for adults. The adolescent is faced with the problem of becoming a new, grown-up person who knows who he is, what he wants to become, what he could be and where he is going. He has to realize that he is the same person who used to be a certain child and that there is continuity in his life. At the same time, much is different, and many more changes will be necessary in the near future. He must get used to a rapidly changing body which probably does not look just as he would like it to look. New emotions are hard to deal with. Intellectual advances make true logical thought possible. Not only can the adolescent deal with the abstract concepts required by his school work, but he can think thoughts about how society ought to be, and what part he might play in bringing about all sorts of reforms. Often, even usually, the reality of his performance does not jibe with his plans and schemes. He has to work out a new identity in each area of his life, in study and work, in his family, with friends and sweethearts and in religion or what represents his relationship to all of reality. Another stage of personality development, the development of the sense of intimacy, is begun towards the end of adolescence, when the sense of identity is quite well established.

Figure 1 represents Erikson's stages of personality development and Piaget's stages of intellectual development, in order that their corresponding age levels can be noted. We conceive of each stage of personality development as a balloon which swells at the age level where its problems are most pressing. A thin tube, connected to each balloon, stretches throughout life to show that no stage is ever finished completely, no problems solved perfectly and finally. Problems of all types recur throughout life and are handled through interactions at the time of occurrence, determined by the personality already created and by the opportunities offered by the environment. Figure 1 shows the balloons and tubes separated. Since all life's problems and all aspects of development are closely related, we think also of personality as something like a rope, with the eight strands (the tubes of Figure 1) intertwined with each other. As one strand swells at its dominant time, the strains on the other strands are affected. The metaphor of the rope can also be extended by thinking of the personalities of a family's members as being intertwined ropes. When the parents' Generativity strands are becoming dominant, the infant's Trust strand is dominant. The two ropes fit smoothly together, indicating a complementary relationship between the personalities of infant and parents.

An Overview of Human Life and Growth

CHAPTER 1

All of existence is continuous and related. A search for beginnings and causes of life reveals psychological, physiological, biological, biochemical and physical structures built upon and of each other. Our topic is man as a human being, changing from single cell to an adult.

MAN'S PLACE AS A LIVING CREATURE

Although man is a very special kind of living creature, *homo sapiens,* the only species in the genus *homines,* he shares certain characteristics with all living creatures, even plants. Because he is an animal, he has certain qualities in common with animals. Because he is a chordate, a vertebrate, a mammal, in some respects he is like all chordates, vertebrates and mammals. Some understanding of man's more general characteristics is essential to an appreciation of his human qualities. We are not here going to define living creatures, plants, animals and man. We simply want to show some important ways in which all of these are the same, other ways in which animals are alike and still other characteristics that belong to man alone.

All Living Creatures Are Thus

THE SURROUNDINGS OF LIVING CREATURES AFFECT THEM. In order for an organism to grow from a seed into a plant-with-seeds, in order for a unicellular creature to split into two creatures like its former self and in order for a fertilized ovum to become a man, there must be certain conditions of warmth, chemicals, water and light. If the environment is too hot or too cold, the growth of the seed will not be the same as if the temperature had been in the middle range. Its growth will vary with differences in the chemicals supplied and differences in moisture. Amount of light and wavelength composition of light will also influence the plant's growth. For the best kind of growth, the temperature, chemicals, water and light must vary only within certain definable limits and in certain relationships to each other. For example, a drought in the spring with unseasonably high temperatures retards the growth of shrubs and may even damage the plants permanently. So also do animals, including man, have certain limits within which life and growth are possible. When temperatures and nutrients go above or below ideal points, growth is affected adversely, and finally life itself.

Sometimes an environmental condition will vary so as to affect a living creature in one benign way or another. Putting limestone in the soil around a hydrangea will turn the flowers pink. Aluminum sulphate will make the flowers blue. Similarly, a person with naturally curly hair will have ringlets in a moist atmosphere in contrast to mere waves under ordinary conditions of humidity.

LIVING CREATURES AFFECT THEIR SURROUNDINGS. Man is very obvious in his effect on his world, changing natural elements into cities and paintings, scrap heaps and missiles. Plants change their environments more quietly and steadily. A tree draws water and nutrients from the soil. Its leaves cut off so much light from its base that grass grows sparsely. Plants exhale water and oxygen. You may not notice the oxygen on a hot, sunny day, but you can perceive the difference in comfort between the shade of a canvas umbrella and that of a tree. Water vapor makes the difference. Thus all living creatures make their changes in the world by affecting physical, chemical and biological processes.

INTERACTIONS OCCUR BETWEEN LIVING THINGS AND THEIR ENVIRONMENTS. Every organism and its environment have dynamic, reciprocal relationships [13]. Affecting each other and being affected by each other, neither can be understood without the other, nor can either be what it *is* without the other. The cool air under the tree does not exist without the tree, nor would the tree exist without air.

An interesting interaction between plants and landscape can be seen in coastal areas where conservation projects are carried out. A beach which was washed away by a hurricane now stretches smoothly into the Atlantic, backed by sand dunes built by plants. The plants were dead Christmas trees stuck into the sand and then reinforced by living plants which, finding nutrients and moisture enough in the sand, sent down a network of tough roots, which held the sand in the dunes.

More remarkable even than the building of beaches is the interaction of the human baby with his environment, his family. A human baby grows into a human child as he lives in a human family, calling forth maternal and paternal responses from two adults whose behavior could not be parental if he were not there. Although an individual is commonly thought of as being bounded by his skin, it is often more fruitful to consider him as existing in an organism–environment field. It is a dynamic field in which interactions are taking place.

All Animals Are Thus

THEY ARE ACTIVE. Animals move; plants stay put. Creatures more complex than single-celled animals have parts which expand or contract, allowing the organism to change its environment. If a seed sprouts in noxious surroundings, its growth will be stunted or warped; if an animal finds itself in a bad situation, it can move to a new source of food, to escape an enemy or find a mate.

AN ANIMAL HAS A NERVOUS SYSTEM. Energy received in the form of stimuli from the environment triggers the release of energy as muscle movements. In forms of animal life above the most primitive, the nervous system is divided into a sensory part, which receives the stimuli and transmits impulses toward the center of the body, a motor part, which sends impulses resulting in action and a central part, which processes and transmits impulses.

Only Man Is Thus

ZOOLOGICALLY. Man has important unique features, three in terms of structure and one in terms of growth. These characteristics underlie the sociological difference between man and other animals.

Man has a hand with an opposable thumb, permitting him to manipulate objects precisely and to make and utilize tools which act as extensions of his body. Speech structures, together with the large association areas in the cerebral hemispheres, make possible language, symbolic verbal representation of experience. Comparing one species with another, the more highly developed the cerebrum, the more important is learning in the development of behavior patterns.

Man's long growth period and his relative immaturity at birth also differentiate him from other animals. These characteristics are important because they occur in conjunction with the highly developed cerebral hemispheres. Enormous potentiality for complexity results from the combination of hemispheres, plasticity, a long time for growth and learning and a brain with tremendous capacity for learning.

PSYCHOLOGICALLY. Through thought, language and imagination, man deals with aspects of reality which are unknown to other animals. Although some higher animals form concepts, abstractions and generalizations, and some animals and birds even speak a few words, their performances in these areas never improve beyond what man can do as a baby. A child can put words together, to transmit meaning through symbols. Even though he may combine words in unique ways, other people can understand their message. He invents verbal symbols that stand for objects and actions, classes of objects, classes of actions and classes of classes. Only man can communicate with people widely separated in time and space, since only he has a written language, a graphic representation of the verbal symbols. Using the written symbols, he makes permanent records of the objects he perceives, the actions he has taken and the ideas he has produced.

When man cannot solve a problem directly, through controlled thought, he may succeed through imagination, a flexible, free-wheeling, distinctly human kind of intellectual activity. Imagination is essential to creativity, the human function which some scholars regard as man's apex of behavior [18].

Man's learning capacity in the newborn period appears to be below that of rats and rabbits [4]. In its vast immaturity, the human brain seems at first unready to learn quickly through experience, in contrast to the brains of animals who mature and learn quickly but learn relatively little during a lifetime [8, 20, 26, 39].

Because of his highly developed nervous system, man has a greater capacity than other animals for rich and varied feelings. The autonomic nervous system, which functions in emotional states, operates similarly in man and other animals. Man's cerebrum, however, elaborates intricate relationships between emotion-producing stimuli and behavior resulting from emotions. Emotion-producing stimuli are abundant and complex, due to the exciting social and intellectual environment which man creates for himself.

Relative immaturity at birth plus a lengthy childhood and adolescence make it possible and necessary that man be a social animal, dependent on interrelationships with other people. From his dependency on another human being, a baby develops patterns of social behavior. The human mother, having to devote so much of her time and energy to her infant and young child, needs the protection and nurturance of others. In most cultures, the father of the child is expected to meet the needs of the mother in relation to the child, as well as much of her need for social–emotional relations with other human beings.

SOCIOLOGICALLY. Man is the only creature who has invented cultures—learned, transmissable patterns of life. This achievement has been possible because of the combination of hand, speech, generalizing ability and a long life span in which to use these assets. Not only does man make objects by which he changes and controls his environment, but he also teaches his offspring how to do so. Because he writes, human beings living after his death can know accurately what he knew and how he lived.

Man not only teaches his offspring how to make objects like those he made but he also teaches appropriate ways of using the objects. He teaches the younger generation the proper ways of dealing with human beings. He communicates wisdom concerning values of human experience. From written records left by each generation, succeeding generations can choose goals valid for them.

VARIETIES OF INTERACTION BETWEEN THE INDIVIDUAL AND HIS WORLD

The individual starts his existence as a bit of hereditary material with a glob of environmental material. Interaction between the bit and the glob produces a rapidly changing creature who interacts with more and more of his environment, changing it and being changed by it. When the individual assimilates some of his environment to himself, as he does when he takes in food, he changes that portion of his environment. In the process, he himself is changed; he accommodates to the environment.

Beyond the first moment of his existence, from conception onward, the individual is the product of continuous interactions between himself and his environment. Therefore, to say that a certain structure, attribute or ability is either inherited or acquired is inaccurate. Hereditary expressions and environmental expressions never occur independently of each other.

The processes of change by which a baby becomes a man are going on all the time, but from one moment to the next, most of them are unnoticed. They are as natural as breathing, which is itself an ongoing interchange between a living body and the earth's atmosphere. Some of the unnoticed interactions seem to result chiefly in maintaining the status quo of the organism. Others produce gradual changes which can be detected by periodic observations, such as measuring a child's height every birthday. Some interactions are very obvious, through effects on the organism, the environment or both, such as when Bobby eats his dinner and Katie has an emotional outburst.

Equilibration

The possibilities for interaction are infinite. In order to think about them and study them, it is necessary to put them into some categories. Equilibration is a useful way of describing many of the varieties of interaction between the individual and the world.

HOMEOSTASIS. Homeostasis is a balance which the organism maintains within itself during the processes of living and as environmental influences affect its internal conditions. Since the balance is continually upset and recreated, through a complex of interactions, it can be called a dynamic equilibrium. Through activities that are mostly unconscious, the individual keeps his blood sugar at a definite level, his water content within a given range, his oxygen content just so. Breathing and heart beat speed up or slow down from their average rates to restore disturbed balances. The mechanisms of homeostasis regulate sleeping and waking states, activity and rest. Pressures and depleted tissues may register consciously as felt needs, leading to such purposeful interactions with the environment as eating, drinking and eliminating.

Looming large in the life of a newborn infant, the problems of homeostasis dwindle throughout infancy and childhood. By about three months of age basic physiological processes are well controlled. At any time throughout the life span, however, when the balance is seriously threatened, when biological demands become crucial or urgent, the individual drops his higher-order activities, such as giving a lecture or playing tennis, in order to restore the balance within his body.

Little is known about the processes by which the homeostatic mechanisms develop in the young infant. It is likely that by stimulation and reaction the neural and glandular tissues gradually reach a state where they function more and more smoothly. After about three months of life outside the uterus the structures involved are formed and operating at a level close to those that will continue at least until senescence. Looked at from one point of view, it is possible to say that the organism has "learned" how to act. Looked at from another, it is possible to say that the organism has "matured." (Learning will be discussed later in this section.)

PSYCHOLOGICAL EQUILIBRIUM. The idea of homeostasis has been expanded into one of equilibrium as applied to perceptual and intellectual spheres [21, 33]. It can even be used in thinking of social relationships. Equilibration means the achieving of a state of balance or dynamic equilibrium, but not necessarily maintaining that new balance. Equilibration includes selecting stimuli from the world, seeking this or that kind, more or less, paying attention to some of them and using some in more complex mental operations. When you consider all the sounds, sights, tastes and other perceptions available, it follows that a person could not possibly attend to all of them at once. There must be ways of selecting stimuli and avoiding or reducing psychological conflict [2, p. 6]. In Walter's words, ". . . there are mechanisms within the brain which act like traffic cops for information and actually damp down and modify the action of the receptors themselves. It has been shown that the information which is allowed to reach the brain from the outside world is a function of its novelty and significance. The level of the receptor itself, the actual eye or ear, is cut down, as though the central nervous system were to say: 'I'm not interested in what you're sending me' " [51, p. 109]. What Walter is describing is very much akin to homeostasis of physiological functions, the maintenance of satisfactory internal conditions.

SCHEMA. A schema is a pattern of action and/or thought. A baby develops some schemas before he is born and has them for starting life as a newborn. With simple schemas, he interacts with his environment, working toward equilibration. He achieves equilibrium over and over again, by using the schemas available to him at the moment.

Change, Growth and Development

If homeostasis were the only process among human resources, there would be no progression of structure or function. The organism would return to its original state after internal or external change. But while maintaining internal physiological balance the body grows bigger and becomes more complex. The infant and child become capable of new and more intricate behavior.

The human being, from infancy onward, seeks food when he is in a state of disequilibrium nutritionally. In the very beginning each disequilibrium and each seeking can be thought of as a new experience. Some of the food restores the nutritional equilibrium, and some is used for growth or additions to the organism. The new cells then become part of the mass which has to be maintained thenceforth in a state of equilibrium, and the cycle begins again. The schema of taking in milk lasts for a long time, and eventually becomes changed and expanded into other food-intake schemas.

Faced with a problem, a person is in a state of disequilibrium which makes him feel tense and dissatisfied. Solving it, he creates a new state of equilibrium which brings a feeling of relaxation. The baby pushes himself forward to grasp a toy that is out of reach. The four-year-old makes a mailbox which is necessary for his game of postman. The first-grader sounds out a new word. Each child reduces a feeling of tension as he creates a new equilibrium. The equilibration (achievement of new balance) makes him into a slightly different person from what he has been, a person who can move forward a bit, a person who has made his own mailbox and can therefore make other things, a person who can read another word. Thus equilibration is a way of describing behavior development. New and more complex behavior occurs as it is demanded by the person's relationship with his surroundings.

For many years, philosophers and psychologists have expressed the conviction that man is impelled to seek new experience. Much intellectual and perceptual activity is inexplicable in terms of survival, but seems to be done for its own sake. Such activities are called play, recreation, self-expression, "fooling around," travel, exploration, research. The force has been called a wish, a drive to explore, appetite for change. The problem has been how to locate and explain the force. Activity is intrinsic in living tissue [23]. Brain cells are no exception. Even in sleep, brain waves continue to register in electroencephalograms. There is probably an optimal level of stimulation (which we would expect to vary with states of the organism) below which increases in stimulation are rewarding (reinforcing) and above which decreases in stimulation are rewarding. Studies on perceptual isolation in both humans and animals have shown that when stimulation is cut down below a certain level, subjects make great effort to get sensory variety [21]. In addition, there are other kinds of positive and negative forms of exciting stimulation. Sexual stimulation without completion is sought by college men and women as well as rats. Eating has been shown to be reinforcing even when it does not reduce hunger. Electrical stimuli applied to animals' brains have demonstrated pleasant excitement in some areas and unpleasant excitement in others.

When a person's schemas are adequate to deal with the situation in which he finds himself, he reacts automatically. For example, the response of a hungry breast-fed baby of three months would be quite automatic when offered his mother's breast. A ten-year-old would automatically answer the question "What is two times two?" When the schemas are not quite adequate to the situation, the child uses what he has, changing them slightly into actions which do solve the problem. For instance, the baby would change his behavior sufficiently to cope with a bottle and the ten-year-old with "$2x = 4$. What does x equal?" The change which takes place at the same time within the child is the development of a new behavior pattern or schema. A pleasant feeling of curiosity and satisfaction accompanies successful adjustments to demands for new behavior.

A person feels uneasy when he encounters a situation in which his resources are very inadequate. In order to provoke uneasiness, the problem must be somewhat similar to those which a person can solve, but not similar enough for him to succeed with. Such a problem for the baby mentioned might be a cup of milk. For the ten-year-old it might be an equation such as $5x - 49/x = 20x/5$. If the situation is so far removed from a person's past experience that his schemas for dealing with it are extremely inadequate, then he will have no reaction to it. He will not notice it. He will not select from the environment the stimuli which would pose the problem. The baby will not try to drink out of a carton full of cans of milk. The child won't attempt to solve $xY - x5 - 144 = 1062 + 2300$.

Familiar objects in unfamiliar guise produce unpleasantness, uneasiness or even fear. (Chimpanzees are afraid of the keeper in strange clothes, an anesthetized chimp, a plaster cast of a chimp's head. Human babies are afraid of strangers.) In order to be frightened or to get the unpleasant feeling, the subject must first have residues of past experience with which to contrast the present experience. Thus does incongruity arise, with its accompanying unpleasant feeling tone. If the individual can cope with the situation successfully, he achieves equilibration and its accompanying pleasant feeling tone. Stimuli preferred and chosen are those that are slightly more complex than the state of equilibrium that the individual has already reached. Thus he moves on to a new state of equilibrium [34].

Learning and Maturation

These minute changes in behavior as the individual becomes aware of incongruities between his schemas and his perception of his environment are the processes of learning. They are analogous to the minute changes in cell structure, number and distribution which occur as the body grows. Both occur as a result of interaction with the environment. Both occur at the same time as the organism engages in internal activities which keep it operating at a satisfactory level.

Because of the importance of learning in the existence of human beings, it has been studied extensively, not only as it occurs in human beings, but also in many other animals. As a result of these many investigations, a good deal is known about the conditions which promote learning, particularly the learning of simple behavior. Learning experiments are still an important subject of experiments in psychological laboratories. Learning is defined as having occurred when there is a relatively permanent change in behavior as a result of practice. It is never directly observable, but is only inferred to have happened from observations of changes in behavior. When the subject in an experiment is able to repeat without error a list of nonsense syllables, the experimenter considers that the subject has learned the list. By using a number of subjects and varying the conditions of the learning, the experimenter is able to relate the speed of learning with the conditions. By using animals, particularly white rats, experimenters are able to control more precisely than would be possible with human subjects the conditions which are related to changes in behavior. Although it is not permissible to apply the results of animal learning experiments directly to learning by human beings, there are certain laws of learning which hold in the various kinds of learning.

One way in which learning is divided is in terms of the motives for learning. Simple learning takes place when primary drives motivate the organism. Primary drives are physiological (hunger, pain, sex, for instance). Classical conditioning is simple learning. A neutral stimulus is paired with one which evokes a response. The classic situation is a buzzer paired with food, which evokes salivation in a hungry dog. After a certain number of pairings, the buzzer alone evokes salivation. Learning through reinforcement is basically learning through reward and punishment. Although it is plain enough that rewarded responses tend to be repeated and punished responses to drop out, it is not always easy to figure out which events will be rewarding and which punishing. Motivation is complex, but necessary to understand in order to use reinforcement effectively.

Complex learning takes place when the individual is motivated by acquired drives and/or rewards. The complicated things which people want and work for, such as chocolate ice cream cones, a low golf score and money, become important through learning and in turn influence other learning. Most of the human learning which concerns parents and teachers of children is complex.

People learn from each other, especially children from adults. Imitation begins in the first year. So does discrimination between the self and others. Most important in facilitating truly human learning is language as a mediator. Towards the end of infancy, man begins to learn in a way that is vastly different from the ways in which animals learn. Through language, responses are established rapidly and easily, without need for consistent repetition and reinforcement. Opposite responses can be established quickly, without having to go through a process of extinguishing the first one. Responses can be made to sequences and to abstract ideas.

IMPRINTING AND PRIMARY SOCIALIZATION. Research on birds, animals and man has shown that in all social species studied there is a short period early in life when the individual establishes positive relationships, typically with certain members of his own species, and later establishes avoidance responses for certain other creatures. Goslings will follow the first moving, sound-emitting object they see after hatching. Ordinarily, of course, this object is their mother. This simple mechanism of attachment was first called *imprinting*. Goslings under nine weeks of age will pay no attention to an eagle unless their mother warns them. At a signal from her, they will look at their enemy. At nine weeks, however, a gosling who has never seen an eagle and who has not even been warned will react intensely to the sight of one [50]. The fact that no experience is necessary for either the following or the avoidance reaction and the fact that imprinting must take place at a very specific time in the young creature's life leads to the conclusion that maturation is a strong factor.

Imprinting is a very specific kind of interaction between an individual and his environment. Because the term may give the impression that the environment stamps the individual, instead of implying an interaction, the phenomena of early attachment have been called *primary socialization* [38]. This term signifies some of the processes by which the infant first becomes attached to his mother and then to other appropriate people and then is prevented from having relationships with inappropriate people.

MATURATION. Imprinting is considered to be unlearned [29, p. 49], since it does not meet all the criteria for learned behavior. It appears in full form when the organism is subjected to an appropriate stimulus. Some reflexes have similarities to imprinting in that they appear in full form after very little opportunity for practice. In the human being, for instance, the pupillary reflex appears soon after birth and quickly attains adult speed [20]. Its appearance has been said to be due to maturation. Buttoning, cutting with scissors, and climbing were shown by a classic study to have large maturational components [22]. Two groups of nursery school children were matched with respect to age, sex, mental age and skill in buttoning, cutting with scissors and climbing. The first group received training in these activities for twelve weeks. The second group was trained during the thirteenth week. At the end of the thirteenth week the two groups were equal in performance, presumably due to the control group's becoming mature to such an extent that with one week's practice its members could do as well as those children who had been taught for twelve weeks.

Thus there is a time factor in processes of maturing. When behavior patterns depend largely upon maturation, their development cannot be hurried much. Nor can they be retarded much, except by very drastic methods. In these ways maturing of behavior resembles maturing of the body, a series of events which take place with great uniformity and under widely contrasting environments. This obvious similarity in growth patterns suggests a close connection between physical growth and mental growth. Recent advances in neurology have revealed some of the connections [11]. There is a definite sequence of maturing of the nerve tissue in the cerebral cortex which has been carefully mapped for the first two years of life. Certain areas of the cortex function during specific kinds of behavior. When the timetable of appearance of the various schemas in human infants is compared with the timetable of maturation of areas of the cortex, a certain approximation between the two schedules appears.

Some authors refer to maturation the processes of change which are relatively independent of experience and to learning the changes which take place as results of experience. It is difficult to find any behavior pattern which could be called the result of pure maturation. Even the schemas present at birth, the reflexes, have most likely been developed prenatally through processes of interaction [23]. The environment within which the reflexes develop is so universal, however, that it is easy to forget about its existence and its role. It is only when an exception appears, that an almost-universal environment is noticed. For instance, the motor sequence in children, the progress from lying down to creeping, standing and walking, is generally considered due to maturation. But change the ordinary human environment to an abnormal one, where the baby must always lie on his back, and creeping does not appear [9]. The more uniform an environmental situation is for all members of the species, the more will interactions with it be attributed to maturation.

In light of the difficulties encountered in isolating changes in structure and function which are genetically determined, uniform for all individuals and appearing without any possible prior experience, it has become apparent that the use of this term with this meaning should be discarded. Maturation is still a usable word when it is applied to the process of becoming more mature, without reference to genetic or environmental determinants.

PRINCIPLES OF GROWTH AND DEVELOPMENT

The terms *growth* and *development* are often given slightly different meanings, but we are using them synonymously, to mean increased amount or complexity, or both, in structure or function, or both. "He has grown" may mean simply "He has become taller." Or it may mean "He has become more like a man in body structure than he used to be." The process of growing from child to adult involves becoming bigger, taller and heavier. It means changes in bodily proportions. It means changes in structure and functioning of organs and systems.

The terms *growth* and *development* were borrowed from the physical field, but they are commonly understood in connection with mental and personality characteristics. One can say, "He has grown mentally," or "He has developed mentally." The statement means "He is now functioning on a more complex intellectual level." Or one can speak of growth of personality and development of attitudes. Listening in on second grade and fifth grade classrooms in the same school building will reveal differences in subject matter interests and in mode of thinking.

Growth or development can be shown to have taken place either by comparing younger and older individuals at the same moment of time or by comparing the same individuals at two different points of time. When the measures of some characteristic of a number of individuals are averaged by age groups, the averages of the successive age groups show what growth has taken place. If each individual is measured only once, that is, if there are different people at each age, the study is *cross-sectional*. If the same individuals are measured at each successive age, the study is *longitudinal*. If some individuals do not remain available for continued study and new ones are added, the study is called *mixed longitudinal*. In a cross-sectional study, growth status at each age is investigated, and inferences regarding growth are drawn from *differences* between any groups. *Change* in status from age to age can be inferred only if the individuals at the two ages can be assumed to be comparable in all relevant ways. In a longitudinal study both growth status at each age and change in status from age to age can be investigated more precisely, because the same individuals are involved and actual growth patterns are established for individuals.

There are a number of generalizations about growth which are more apparent with respect to physical growth but which, as far as research can show, are also true for psychological growth. We will elaborate on 10 such statements about growth at this point, some of them with subheadings, and return to them where appropriate throughout the volume.

1. *Continuity*

Children grow all the time, not in fits and starts. Tanner [48, p. 14], a British authority on physical growth, uses the analogy of a train on its way from one station to another to explain the curve for growth in height from birth to maturity, the child's growth being a form of motion. Although this train may slow down or pick up speed, it does not stop. At the turn of the century crude measurements and statistics gave rise to the erroneous idea, which persisted for some time, that children grew for a while in height, then in width and then again in height. The refined measurement methods of today show continuous growth to be the case.

How well does this principle apply to mental growth? A common way of thinking about psychological development is in terms of stages, as though not being able to read, for example, were entirely distinct and separate from being able to read. In this example, it is not hard to picture growth as continuous, the process of focusing the eyes, shading into complex eye movements, learning to understand words and to speak being gradual, learning to appreciate books through a series of experiences with them, noticing printed words, asking about them, receiving answer after answer, recognition of name tags and signs, recognition of some words in books and then more and more words.

Perhaps this list of processes involved in learning to read does not seem like a series of discrete steps. Rather these steps are more like forms of motion flowing along and into one another. One cannot really be sure, because every method of testing and describing psychological growth requires looking at it in small pieces.

There is widespread interest in linking mental processes to their physical foundations in the body. Advances in neurology and in the field of computers have resulted in increased understanding of what happens in the human brain, but the neural processes underlying thinking, problem solving and creating are not clear. If, however, brain tissue grows in accordance with the same principles of growth which apply to other tissues, then brain growth is continuous. The psychological growth corresponding to it would presumably also be continuous.

In his studies of perception in young children, Piaget found no discrete steps but rather stages, which flowed into one another through continuous development [50, p. 12]. Considering problem solving and the development of methods for it, it is all too easy to think of growth occurring in steps. Often a solution is reached suddenly and quickly, after a long period of inactivity or trial and error. It is likely that the underlying process is continuous, however. Probably cell assemblies mature continuously. Fusion and integration of assemblies would occur continuously, but only after a certain amount of integration has taken place would a new kind of problem solving happen. Piaget describes such stages of development as successive equilibrium states.

2. *Variation of Rates*

Rates of growth vary from one individual to another, and they vary within one individual. An organism grows at varying rates, from one time to another. The organs and systems grow at varying rates, at different times. There is a sex difference in rates and terminals. Various group differences can be shown. It is no wonder that comparisons of growth require facts obtained by highly controlled methods.

(a) AN ORGANISM AND ITS PARTS GROW AT RATES WHICH ARE DIFFERENT AT DIFFERENT TIMES. Using Tanner's analogy of the train, consider the Dehra Dun Express, a train which runs between Bombay and Delhi. Because of the principle of continuous growth, we'll have to pretend that it does not stop at any stations along the way. It slows down from its cruising speed to 10 miles an hour when it crosses a bridge over a flood at Surat and to 15 miles an hour going through the city of Baroda. On the wide open plains of the Rajasthan Desert, it goes up to 50. The Dehra Dun's motion through space from Bombay to Delhi is like a child's growth in height from birth to maturity in that both have times of high velocity, low velocity and varying rates between high and low.

If attention is focused on groups of parts of the body, the Dehra Dun Express will have to be broken into four smaller trains, each with the power to propel itself to Delhi, which represents the size at maturity. Bombay is size at birth. Each train runs on its own track, parallel to the tracks of the other trains. One train represents weights of neural type of tissue (the nervous system, its coverings, and the eyes); one, lymphoid tissue (the thymus, lymph nodes, intestinal lymphoid masses); another the weight of the whole body (and also the respiratory, digestive, muscular and skeletal systems, the kidneys, spleen, aorta and pulmonary trunks); and the fourth, the genital type of tissue (testes, ovaries, and so on). The 20 hours each train takes to reach Delhi represents the 20 years during which the average individual matures.

The neural train starts off at a great rate, outdistancing all the others, reaching the halfway mark in less than three hours and covering 90 percent of the distance to Delhi in six hours. It runs very slowly for the following six hours and at a snail's pace for the last eight. The lymphoid train starts out fast and runs almost as fast as the neural train, overtaking it at the place where the neural train has achieved 90 percent of the distance to Delhi. It looks as though the brakes won't work, or the engineer has his signals mixed, for the lymphoid train arrives in Delhi at the seventh hour and does not slow down a whit and rushes right through the city. After racing beyond Delhi for five hours, it reverses its direction and backs up to meet the other trains at the twentieth hour. The general train has the most even trip, starting off rapidly, gradually slowing down to cruising speed, spurting between the twelfth and sixteenth hours and gliding quietly into the station 20 hours after it left Bombay. The genital train dawdles over half the time, then puts on steam and zooms along even faster than the lymphoid train was going when it overshot Delhi. All trains meet at Delhi at the twentieth hour. Delhi represents 100 percent of average adult weight of these four divisions of the human body. Figure 1–1, which represents the growth velocities of four types of tissue, also corresponds with the rates of speed of the four trains.

The train analogy illustrates each type of tissue with its own rates of growth, differing from one another in speed of progress toward maturity. It reflects

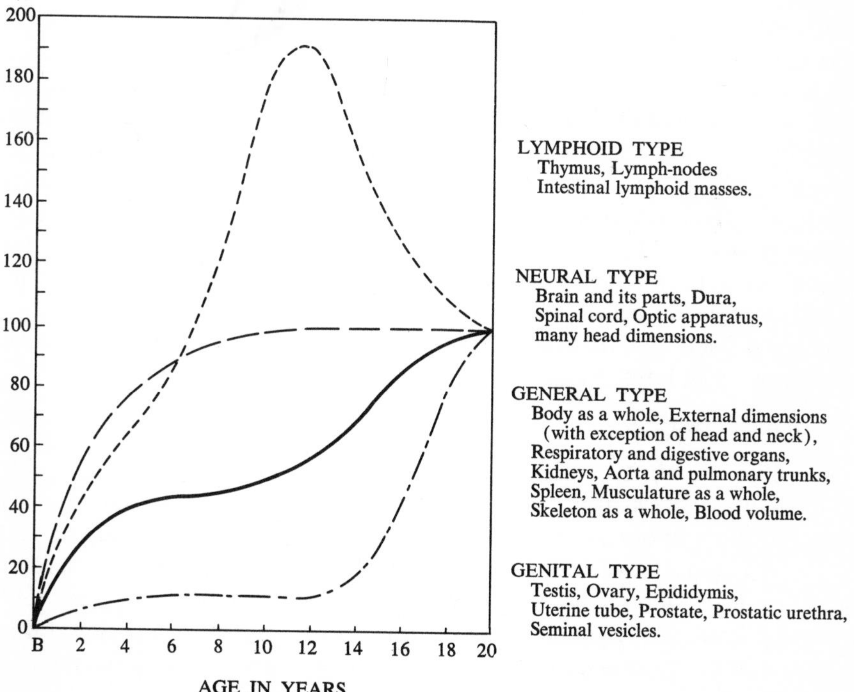

Figure 1–1. Growth curves of the body as a whole and of three types of tissue. Values at each age are computed as precentages of values for total growth. (Reproduced by permission from J. A. Harris, C. M. Jackson, D. G. Paterson, and R. E. Scammon, *The Measurement of Man.* Minneapolis: University of Minnesota Press, 1930.)

how a child differs from one age to another in terms of the maturity of his systems in relation to each other.

(b) RATES OF GROWTH VARY FROM ONE INDIVIDUAL TO ANOTHER. Three trains which run between Bombay and Delhi, the Frontier Mail, the Dehra Dun Express, and the air-conditioned De Luxe, represent three people on their way from birth to maturity. The Dehra Dun takes 20 hours and represents a child who grows at an average rate. The De Luxe is like a fast grower, whizzing through in 18 hours. The Frontier Mail, like a slow grower, takes 24 hours to Delhi. Thus the overall velocity of motion in the trains, or growth of the children, differs from one to the other.

The trains vary also in their slow and fast times. The Frontier Mail runs faster than the Dehra Dun up to the city of Baroda but very much more slowly on the Rajasthan Desert. Similarly, one child will have a faster spurt in height at preadolescence than another child will.

The time of reaching sexual maturity is only one growth measurement. When one considers the tremendous number of points one might take in the countless aspects of human growth and the infinite number of growth characteristics one might delineate, it is easy to see how every individual is unique in his pattern of growth.

(c) THERE ARE SEX DIFFERENCES IN RATES OF GROWTH. Early in fetal life, girls show evidence of maturing faster than boys, especially in skeletal development, one of the best, if not the best, indicators of general physiological maturity. At birth, girls are four weeks ahead of boys skeletally. Boys' skeletal development is about 80 percent of that of girls' from birth to maturity [48, p. 43]. Girls are ahead of boys in dentition, as measured by eruption of permanent teeth. Although sex differences in height and weight before the preadolescent growth spurt are very slight, favoring boys, sexual maturity and its antecedent growth spurt occur in girls about two years before they do in boys. Therefore, there is a period of about two years when girls are taller and heavier than boys. At all ages, girls are more mature physiologically.

3. *Individual Differences in Terminals*

It is obvious, yet it is essential in understanding growth, to recognize that for different people maturity comes at different points. You have only to walk down the street to observe that some people grow until they are over six feet tall, others stop at five feet and most people stop in between. Measurable mental growth stops at different times for different individuals too. The average girl reaches height and weight terminals before the average boy. Little is known about mental growth terminals and less about sex differences in mental growth.

4. *Dynamic Interrelations in Growth*

It would be surprising if different measures of growth were not related to each other. A tremendous number of studies have probed into the question of interrelationships of growth-controlling and regulating mechanisms.

Olson [31] developed a system of considering all measures of growth together in his concept of the child-as-a-whole. He took measures of height, weight, dentition, skeletal development, strength, intelligence, reading and social maturity. Each measure was translated into an age value. For example, a child has a height age of six when he reaches the average height for six-year-olds. The average of all the age values is the *organismic age,* a figure which represents the growth of the child as a whole. Olson found organismic age to be a stable measurement over a period of time, much steadier than any single measurement, suggesting a balancing tendency within the organism. Another of the interrelationships demonstrated was that between rate of growth and social and emotional problems. Problems tended to appear when growth rate slowed down or when growth became disorganized, or vice versa. (See Figure 1–2.)

In a group of boys 6 to 18 years of age, abrupt changes in height were shown to be associated with abrupt changes in IQ but not coinciding in time [32]. Physical and psychological disruptions were related to each other and

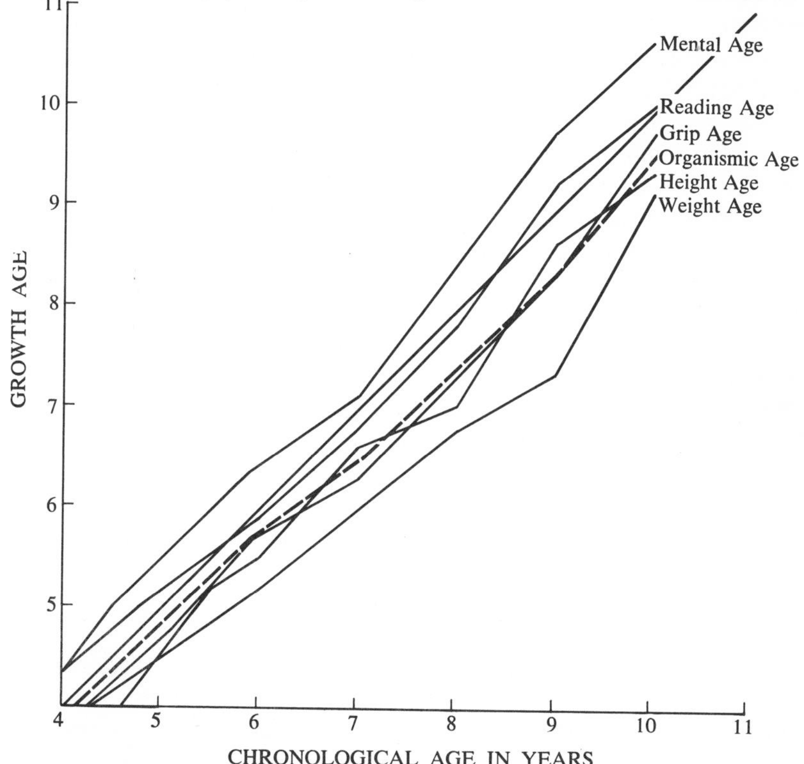

Figure 1–2. Growth of a child from 4 to 10 years of age, plotted by Olson's method, showing consistently average growth. ("Concepts of Growth—Their Significance to Teachers," by Willard C. Olson and Byron O. Hughes. From *Childhood Education,* October 1944, Vol. 21, No. 2. Reprinted by permission of the Association for Childhood Education International, 3615 Wisconsin Avenue, N.W., Washington, D.C. 20016.)

to disturbances in the environment. Boys from broken homes and from families where parental relations were strained showed more fluctuation in rate of increase of height and IQ than did boys from normal homes.

Correlations between measures of growth can be between measures in the same field (physical–physical, mental–mental, and so on), or in different fields (physical–mental, mental–emotional). Skeletal development, assessed by X rays of the wrist, is at present the best indicator of physiological maturity [50], although if body proportions could be quantified and scaled in some manageable way, this might prove even more useful. Eruption of teeth is another indicator of general bodily maturity. Fat thickness in childhood is also a measure of general physiological maturity [15]. Sexual maturity and eventual height can be predicted with good accuracy from measurements of skeletal maturity. A general factor of bodily maturity operating throughout the growth period influences the child's growth as a whole, including his skeleton, teeth, size, physiological reactions and possibly intelligence. Influencing factors of more limited scope operate independently of the general factor and of each other. One of these limited factors controls baby teeth, another permanent teeth, another the ossification centers in the skeleton and probably several others involved with the brain. This is why various measures of physical growth have low positive correlations with each other. If there were only one controlling factor, then the different measures would presumably all correlate highly or even perfectly with one another [48].

Studies of the relation between physical and mental growth show a small but consistent positive correlation, bearing out the hypothesis of a general factor which influences all growth processes. This relationship has been studied from age six and a half onward, comparing the mental ages or academic achievement, or both of early-maturing youngsters with those of late maturers [1, 10, 27, 42, 43, 47]. A study of children at the extremes of distributions of mental traits showed gifted boys to be significantly ahead of retarded boys in measures of physical growth [27]. A small positive correlation between mental ability and size is also found in adults [36, 37]. As an example of the relationships between growth and personality, there is good evidence that early maturers feel more adequate and more comfortable about themselves than do late maturers [25, 30].

5. *Differentiation and Integration*

From large global patterns of behavior, smaller, more specific patterns emerge. Later the small, specific patterns can be combined into new, complicated, larger patterns. For example, a photographic study of human beginnings shows an eleven and a half weeks' fetus reacting to being stroked on the right cheek [16, p. 25]. The fetus contracted the muscles of his neck, trunk and shoulder, causing his whole body to bend away from the stimulus and the arms and hands to move backward. When a newborn infant is stroked on the cheek he turns toward the stimulus, pursing his lips and opening his mouth when his lips touch something. Thus he shows a new, specialized response pattern which involves a small part of his body instead of the whole. As he grows older, the rooting response changes and becomes integrated with other behavior patterns. Instead of turning toward food when he is touched near the mouth, he turns toward the breast or bottle when he sees it. His hands come to play in guiding food toward his mouth. Later he uses a knife and fork. He is integrating behavior patterns of eyes and hands with the rooting pattern, forming a smoothly functioning whole.

Examples can also be taken from purely intellectual fields, such as mathematics. There is a stage of maturity at the end of infancy when a child knows *one, two* and *a-lot-of*. At five, he has differentiated *three* and *four* out of *a-lot-of*. By six, numbers up to ten have true meaning. Using these differentiated concepts, he next combines them in addition and subtraction to form new and more complicated concepts. Conceptual differentiation and integration are at work as the student moves up through algebra and geometry into higher mathematics. There remains an undifferentiated sphere where each person stops in his progress in mathematics.

6. *Normative Sequence*

The sequence of motor development has long been noticed and understood as one of the ways of nature. "A child must creepe ere he walke."

As the structures of the body mature in their various sequences, they function in characteristic ways, provided that the environment permits appropriate interaction. The resulting behavior patterns appear in an orderly sequence. Sequences have been described for locomotion [40], use of the hands [19], language [28], problem solving [17], social behavior [5] and other kinds of behavior. During the decade of the thirties, the bulk of research in child development was normative, delineating sequences of development and designating average ages for the patterns observed. The classic viewpoint, exemplified by Gesell, stressed normative sequences as an unfolding. While some lip service was paid to the necessity of an environment, development was thought of largely as an inner process. Today interaction between organism and environment is recognized as basic to development. The change in viewpoint has come about to some extent because of the broadening of areas of child study to include a variety of cultures, at home and abroad. Although child development continues to occur in orderly sequences, exceptions can be found [9]. Hence normative sequences cannot be considered as universal, but must be understood as occurring in particular kinds of environments.

7. *Developmental Direction*

Certain sequences of development take place in certain directions, in reference to the body. The motor sequence takes two such directions, cephalocaudal (head to tail) and proximodistal (midline to outer extremities). Like all animals, the child grows a relatively large, complex head region early in life, whereas the tail region or posterior is small and simple. As he becomes older, the region next to the head grows more, and finally, the end region grows. Coordination follows the same direction, the muscles of the eyes coming under control first, then the neck muscles, then arms, chest and back and finally the legs. The motor sequence illustrates the proximodistal direction by the fact that the earliest controlled arm movements, as in reaching, are large movements, controlled mostly by shoulder muscles. Later the elbow is brought into play in reaching, then the wrist and then the fingers.

8. *Epigenesis*

Growth takes place upon the foundation which is already there. New parts arise out of and upon the old. Although the organism becomes something new as it grows, it still has continuity with the past and hence shows certain consistencies over time. Through interactions with the environment, the organism continues to change throughout life, being at each moment the product of the interaction which took place in the previous moment between organism and environment. A toddler's body results from interactions of a baby's body with food, water and air. A baby's personality grows epigenetically first through establishing a sense of trust through constructive interactions with people and the world. Then, with a personality firmly based in trust, he tackles a toddler's problems and interacts with people and things so as to achieve a sense of autonomy. The epigenesis of personality continues well into adulthood, perhaps throughout life. The epigenesis of the intellect is described in Piaget's works. New and more complex schemas (ways of acting and thinking) develop from the interaction of existing schemas with the environment. Much of this book is concerned with the ways in which the various kinds of development and relationships result from the epigenesis which occurs when the child interacts with the world.

9. *Critical Periods*

There are certain limited times during the growth period of any organism when it will interact with a particular environment in a specific way. Imprinting is an example (see pages 14–15). The result of interactions during critical periods can be especially beneficial or harmful. The prenatal period includes specific critical periods for physical growth. The first three months are critical for the development of eyes, ears, and brain, as shown by defects in children whose mothers had German measles during the first trimester of pregnancy. Apparently those organs are most vulnerable to the virus of German measles when they are in their periods of rapid growth.

Experiments on vision with human and animal infants reveal critical ages for the development of visual responses, times when the infant will either show the response without experience or will learn it readily [12]. If the visual stimulus is not given at the critical age (as when baby monkeys are reared in darkness), the animal later learns the response with difficulty, or not at all.

Personality development also shows critical periods [6]. One such period is that of primary socialization, when the infant makes his first social attachments and then distinguishes strangers from familiar members of his species [35, 38]. Much has been written about the critical nature of the time from six to eighteen months of age, when basic trust develops [44, 45, 46]. A warm, close relationship with a mother figure is held to be essential among the experiences which contribute to a sense of trust.

10. *Optimal Tendency*

An organism behaves as though it were seeking to reach its maximum potential for development in both structure and function. Even though growth is interrupted, such as in periods of inadequate food supply, the child (or organism) makes up for the lean period as soon as more and better food is available, returning to his characteristic pattern of growth. Only if the deprivation is very severe, or if it occurs throughout a critical period, will he show permanent effects from it. During the deprivation period, the organism adapts by slowing growth and cutting down on the use of energy.

All sorts of adaptive arrangements are worked out when there are interferences with the normal course of development, as though the child is determined to reach his best potential by another route when one is blocked. The child with poor eyesight seeks extra information from his other senses. Babies with a tendency toward rickets drink cod liver oil freely if permitted to, selecting their own diets from a wide variety of simple foods [7]. "Every breach in the normal complex of growth is filled through regenerative, substantive, or compensatory growth of some kind. . . . Insurance reserves are drawn upon whenever the organism is threatened. . . . Herein lies the urgency, the almost irrepressible quality of growth" [16, p. 165].

This principle has been recognized as working in physical realms as well as organic, where there seems to be a self-stabilizing or target-seeking property of certain systems [49]. Faced with such phenomena, it is difficult to be purely scientific, for surely here is a subject for philosphical consideration.

SUMMARY

Man, the human animal, shares important characteristics with other forms of living things. Factors in the environment affect each individual's growth and behavior. The existence of each individual has some effect on his surroundings. Therefore there exists a continuous series of transactions between each person and his milieu. Like all animals, each human being is structured to be active in his setting and to receive stimulation from it. Although in many ways human sense organs are similar to those of other animals, the human brain, particularly the cerebrum, is more highly developed and specialized than in other animals. The human being is able to form abstract concepts, based on the sensations he receives, and to develop symbols which stand for the concepts. In conjunction with his vocal apparatus, each individual is capable of uttering words, one kind of symbolic representation of objects and events. Language thereby becomes a tool for interacting with the environment both in reality and imaginatively. Unique human structure, the prehensile hand with thumb in opposition to the fingers, is another means by which each person interacts with his surroundings. The relative immaturity of the human being at birth, the relative lack of inborn behavior mechanisms and the relatively tremendous potential for learning bring about the long infancy and childhood during which each individual is dependent upon adults. The dependency of the young human being necessitates a family group, some form of which exists in every human society. From all these human characteristics comes the human capacity to develop and pass on to succeeding generations a culture, the way of life of a group of people. An important part of each way of life is the values which determine the ends and means of each individual's life.

Since the individual and his environment are continually interacting, nothing that an individual is or does can be said to be wholly hereditary or wholly acquired. Maturation and learning, interactions which produce change in the individual, and equilibration, which maintains the existing state, are the names given classes of interactions. The maintenance of physiological equilibrium of the organism is called homeostasis. It has to do with the chemical content of the blood and with other internal biological balances. Although the biological equilibrium is constantly changing, there is a balance of conditions toward which the organism is constantly tending. The principle of homeostasis has been extended to cover perceptual and intellectual activities. Such psychological equilibration, instead of constantly tending to return to an optimal state, results in a new state of balance if the forces disrupting the original state are not too great. Psychological growth is therefore seen as the gradual change of psychological structures, or schemas, as the human being becomes aware of differences in his environment and changes his behavior to accommodate to those differences. Since the individual cannot be aware of all aspects of his setting at the same time, there is selectivity within the organism as to what sensations are registered and reacted to. Intellectual activity and its forerunner, perception, seem to be related, when biological maintenance is in relatively good equilibrium, by a tendency of the individual to seek for and react to slightly new or different sensory and intellectual stimulation. Slightly incongruous situations lead to pleasant feeling tone and activity. Too great incongruity leads to unpleasant feelings and avoidance.

Changes in the body and in behavior which occur as time passes can be considered as due to maturation or learning or a combination of both. Since very few, if any, changes can be said to be completely free of environmental influences, maturation in a pure form rarely if ever can be distinguished in human structure or function. However, each kind of learning of which the human being is capable cannot take place before the individual has reached a certain level of maturity.

Studies of growth and development are carried out either by comparing people of different ages with one another or by comparing the same individuals with themselves at different ages. Both methods yield generalizations which summarize knowledge about the changes that take place with the passage of time. Growth is continuous although the average rate of growth varies in its various aspects and from time to time. Individuals of the same sex differ in their rates of growth. There are sex differences in rates of growth. Some individuals grow for a longer period of time than others and reach higher levels of growth. The many aspects of growth are interrelated.

Organs and behavior develop through the differentiation of specific entities out of larger parts and through the integration of the specifics into larger and more complex wholes. There are sequences of development which are, for the most part, invariant for all children. These sequences show up particularly in the direction of growth from head to tail and from the midline of the body to the extremities. Structures and functions arise from interweaving and combination of parts. For many if not all kinds of growth there are periods which are critical in the sense that any hindrance to growth occurring at that time disrupts the timetable and rate of later growth. In spite of disturbances of growth, however, there is a tendency for each organism and its parts to reach a level which is optimum for it.

REFERENCES

1. Abernethy, E. M. Relationships between physical and mental growth. *Mono. Soc. Res. Child Devel.*, 1936, **1**:7.
2. Berlyne, D. E. *Conflict arousal and curiosity*. New York: McGraw-Hill, 1960.
3. Bowlby, J. *Maternal care and mental health*. Geneva: World Health Organization, 1951.
4. Brackbill, Y. Experimental research with children in the Soviet Union. *Am. Psychol.*, 1960, **15**, 226–233.
5. Buhler, C. *The first year of life*. New York: Day, 1930.
6. Caldwell, B. M. The usefulness of the critical period hypothesis in the study of filiative behavior. *Merrill-Palmer Quart.*, 1962, **8**, 229–242.
7. Davis, C. M. Self-selection of diet by newly weaned infants. *Am. J. Dis. Child.*, 1928, **36**, 651–679.
8. Dennis, W. Is the newborn infant's repertoire learned or instinctive? *Psychol. Rev.*, 1943, **50**, 203–218.
9. Dennis, W. Causes of retardation among institutional children: Iran. *J. Genet. Psychol.*, 1960, **96**, 46–60.
10. Douglas, J. W. B. Communication to *Soc. Study Hum. Biol.*, 1960. Cited in Tanner [48].

11. Eichorn, D. H., & Jones, H. E. Maturation and behavior. In G. S. Seward & J. P. Seward (Eds.), *Current psychological issues.* New York: Holt, 1958, pp. 219–224.
12. Fantz, R. L. The origin of form perception. *Sci. Am.,* 1961, **204,** 66–72.
13. Frank, L. K. *Individual development.* New York: Doubleday, 1955.
14. Freeman, F. N., & Flory, C. C. Growth in intellectual ability as measured by repeated tests. *Mono. Soc. Res. Child Devel.,* 1937, **2:**2.
15. Garn, S. S. Fat thickness and developmental status in childhood and adolescence. *J. Am. Medic. Assoc.,* 1960, **99,** 746–751.
16. Gesell, A. *The embryology of behavior.* New York: Harper, 1945.
17. Gesell, A., & Thompson, H. *The psychology of early growth.* New York: Macmillan, 1938.
18. Gutman, H. The biological roots of creativity. *Genet. Psychol. Mono.,* 1961, **64,** 417–485.
19. Halverson, H. M. An experimental study of prehension in infants by means of systematic cinema records. *Genet. Psychol. Mono.,* 1931, **10,** 107–286.
20. Hebb, D. O. *The organization of behavior.* New York: Wiley, 1949.
21. Hebb, D. O. Drives and the CNS. *Psychol. Rev.,* 1955, **62,** 243–254.
22. Hilgard, J. R. Learning and maturation in preschool children. *J. Genet. Psychol.,* 1932, **41,** 31–56.
23. Hunt, J. McV. Experience and the development of motivation: some reinterpretations. *Child Develop.,* 1960, **31,** 489–504.
24. Jones, M. C., & Bayley, N. Physical maturing among boys as related to behavior. *J. Educ. Psychol.,* 1950, **41,** 129–248.
25. Jones, M. C., & Mussen, P. H. Self-conceptions, motivations, and interpersonal attitudes of early- and late-maturing girls. *Child Devel.,* 1958, **29,** 492–501.
26. Kessen, W. Current research in the psychological development of infants. Speech at Merrill-Palmer Conference on the Contribution of Research to the Teaching of Infant Development, February 16, 1962.
27. Ketcham, W. A., Relationship of physical and mental traits in intellectually gifted and mentally retarded boys. *Merrill-Palmer Quart.,* 1960, **6,** 171–177.
28. McCarthy, D. *The language development of the preschool child.* Minneapolis: Univer. of Minnesota, 1930.
29. Mednick, S. A. *Learning.* Englewood Cliffs, N.J.: Prentice-Hall, 1964.
30. Mussen, P. H., & Jones, M. C. The behavior-inferred motivations of late- and early-maturing boys. *Child Devel.,* 1958, **29,** 61–67.
31. Olson, W. C. *Child development.* Boston: Heath, 1959.
32. Peskin, H. Possible relations of growth and maturity to early psychic experiences. Paper presented at meetings of The Society for Research in Child Development, April 1963.
33. Piaget, J. The general problems of the psychobiological development of the child. In J. M. Tanner & B. Inhelder (Eds.), *Discussions on child development,* Vol. 4. New York: International Universities, 1960.
34. Sackett, G. P. Effects of rearing conditions upon the behavior of rhesus monkeys (Macca Mulatta). *Child Devel.,* 1965, **36,** 855–868.
35. Schaffer, H. R., & Emerson, P. E. The development of social attachments in infancy. *Mono. Soc. Res. Child Devel.,* 1964, **29:**3.

36. Schrieder, E. Taille et capacités mentales: étude experimentale et statistique d'une correlation apparément "simple." *Biotpol.*, 1956, **17,** 21–37. Cited in Tanner [49].
37. Scott, E. M., *et al.* A psychological investigation of primigravidae: II. Maternal social class, age, physique, and intelligence. *J. Obst. Gynaec. Brit. Emp.*, 1956, **63,** 338–343. Cited in Tanner [49].
38. Scott, J. P. The process of primary socialization in canine and human infants. *Mono. Soc. Res. Child Devel.*, 1963, **28:**1.
39. Sherman, M., & Sherman, I. C. Sensorimotor responses in infants. *J. Comp. Psychol.*, 1943, **5,** 53–68.
40. Shirley, M. M. *The first two years: a study of twenty-five babies* (two volumes). Minneapolis: Univer. of Minnesota, 1931.
41. Shuttleworth, F. K. Sexual maturation and the skeletal growth of girls age six to nineteen. *Mono. Soc. Res. Child Devel.*, 1938, **3:**5.
42. Shuttleworth, F. K. The physical and mental growth of girls and boys age six to nineteen in relation to age at maximum growth. *Mono. Soc. Res. Child Devel.*, 1939, **4:**3.
43. Simon, M. D. Body configuration and school readiness. *Child Devel.*, 1939, **30,** 493–512.
44. Spitz, R. A. Hospitalism: an inquiry into the genesis of psychiatric conditions in early childhood. *Psychoan. Stud. Child.*, 1945, **1,** 53–74.
45. Spitz, R. A. Anaclitic depression. *Psychoan. Stud. Child.*, 1946, **2,** 313–342. (a)
46. Spitz, R. A. Hospitalism: a follow-up report. *Psychoan. Stud. Child.*, 1946, **2,** 113–117. (b)
47. Stone, C. P., & Barker, R. G. Aspects of personality and intelligence in postmenarcheal and premenarcheal girls of the same chronological age. *J. Comp. Psychol.*, 1937, **23,** 439–455.
48. Tanner, J. M. *Education and physical growth.* London: Univer. of London, 1961.
49. Tanner, J. M. The regulation of human growth. *Child Devel.*, 1963, **34,** 817–847.
50. Tanner, J. M., & Inhelder, B. (Eds.). *Discussions on child development,* Vol. 1. New York: International Universities, 1953.
51. Walter, G. In J. M. Tanner & B. Inhelder [50].

Robert J. Izzo

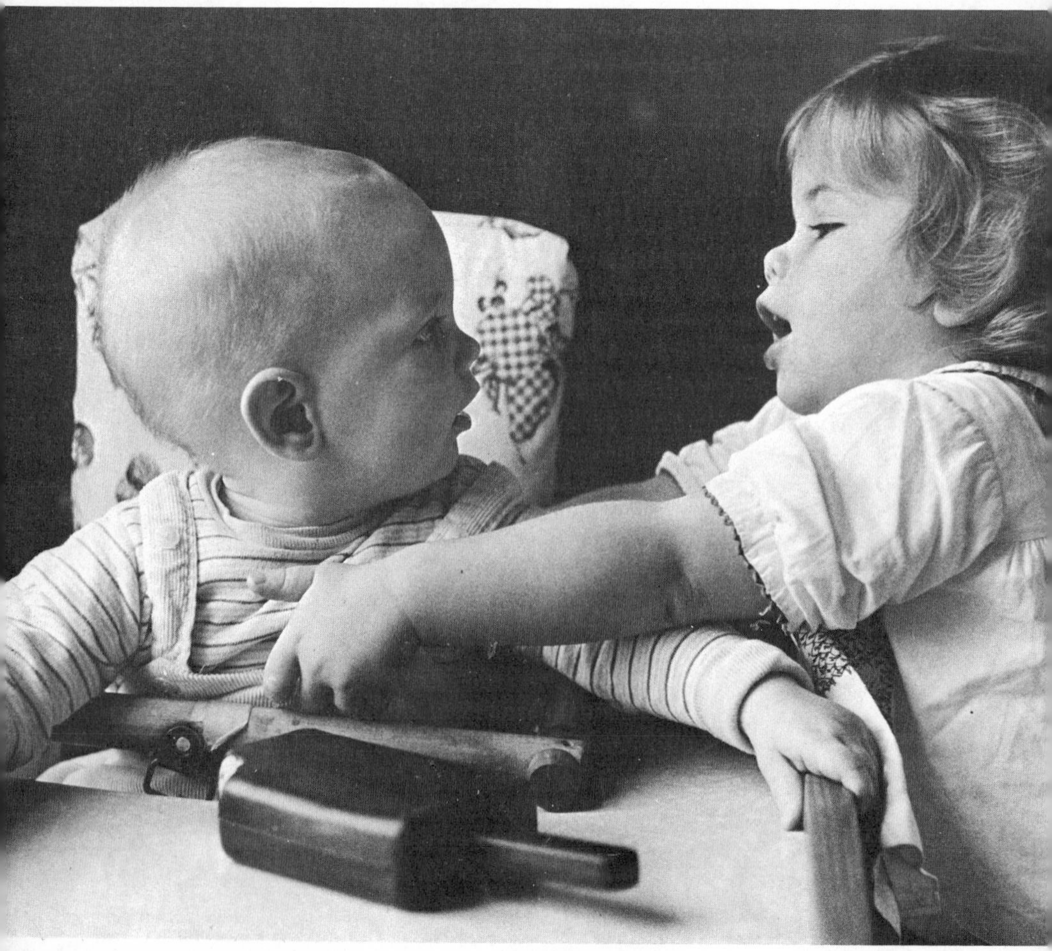

PART I

Infancy

Introduction

In the brief period of two and a half years, the human being develops from a speck of fertilized ovum into a real person who can walk, talk, make decisions and build relationships. Never again will he grow as fast as he grows during his first weeks of existence. Never again will he have such a wide range of potentialities and possibilities for development.

The dynamic interplay and interdependence of mother and baby is punctuated by the dramatic crisis of birth, when the relationship of the two must be reorganized on a different level. Both physical and emotional interaction continue while a new dimension is added. Cognitive stimulation and intellectual development occur in the give and take of mother and baby and also in the participation of other people in the infant's expanding social world. Although he does not speak his first recognizable words until near the end of the first year, the baby prepares for this achievement throughout the early months in a remarkable interweaving of motor, sensory, social and emotional experiences. The end of infancy is marked by his use of language for both communication and thinking.

The infant takes an active role in influencing his environment, at first through an impressive repertory of reflex behavior which is gradually modified and reorganized on more complex levels. The new baby makes his family into a different family, its members into new people. The development of the infant's sense of trust goes hand in hand with the development of a sense of generativity in his parents.

The first chapter in this part of the book deals with prenatal life and birth from the standpoints of both the baby and mother, stressing the natural mechanisms which promote the safety and well-being of both.

Chapter 3 is concerned with the newborn and his adjustment to life. The next two chapters deal first with the baby's physical, motor, intellectual and emotional development and then with care and guidance in relation to healthy development.

Prenatal Life and Birth

CHAPTER 2

The individual's first relationship is as a baby inside his mother. As an embryo and then a fetus, he influences his mother and is influenced by her. The mechanisms of the mutual influences have been revealed only sketchily, but research in this area is full of promise. The stress in this chapter will be on the physical and psychological development of the baby, explained in the light of the mother's development and the mutuality of the two individuals.

STAGES OF PRENATAL DEVELOPMENT

From Fertilization to Implantation

The time when the baby can begin depends upon ovulation. At about the middle of each menstrual cycle (the thirteenth or fourteenth day of a 28-day cycle), a mature ovum reaches the middle of the Fallopian tube in its journey from the ovary to the uterus. If the ovum is penetrated by a spermatazoon, the nuclei of both cells fuse. Fertilization is now complete and a zygote has been produced (see Figure 2–1).

The zygote divides into two cells, the two into four, the four into eight, and so on, creating in nine months about seven pounds of baby from a speck that was barely visible. The two-cell stage has been observed 36 hours after fertilization and the eight-cell stage after about 60 hours. The divisions that occur in the first three or four days are subdivisions and add no mass to the fertilized egg, which is now called a morula (from the Latin for *mulberry*). After drifting down the Fallopian tube, the morula floats in the uterus for a day or two before "burrowing" into the soft lining of the uterus on the seventh or eighth day. It digests away the surface of the lining to expose the deeper cells, in which it becomes implanted.

None of these events can be felt by the mother, not even implantation. Her offspring is well settled into her body before she has any indication of his presence.

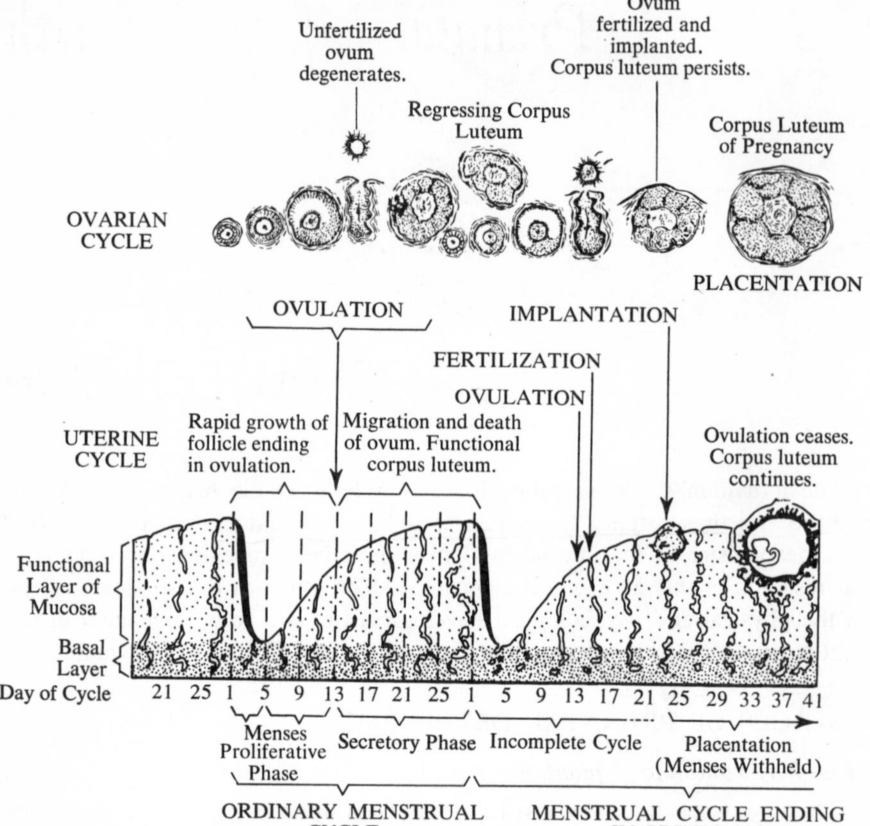

Figure 2–1. Changes taking place in the ovary and uterus during an ordinary menstrual cycle and during the beginning stage of a pregnancy. (Modified from Schroder in B. M. Patten *Human Embryology,* 2nd edition. Copyright 1953. McGraw-Hill Book Company. Used by permission.)

The Embryo

The individual is called an embryo during the time that the various organs and tissues are being differentiated and formed, from the end of the second week to the end of the second month. Mosslike villi extend from the embryo into the blood spaces of the maternal uterus, forming a means of exchanging body fluids. Protective and supportive membranes, the chorion and amnion, take form. The amniotic sac enclosing the embryo begins to fill with fluid.

The head comes first in the developmental timetable. The head of the embryo is one half of its total length; of the newborn, one quarter; of the adult, one tenth. These ratios illustrate the principle of developmental direction, described in Chapter 1, which holds for lower animals as well as for man and

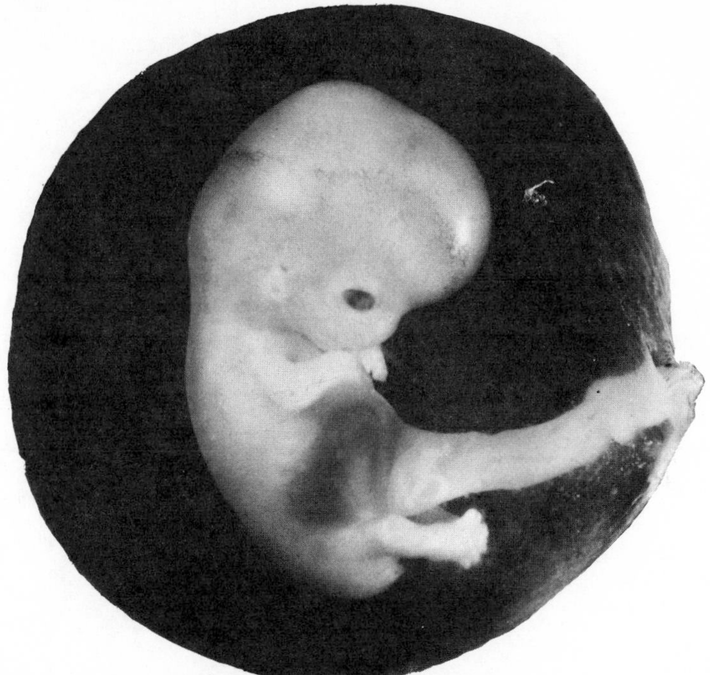

Figure 2–2. The embryo at seven weeks. This photograph is about four times life size. Notice the human looking face, with eyes, ears, nose and lips. The arms have hands, with fingers and thumbs. The legs have knees, ankles and toes. (By courtesy of the Carnegie Institution of Washington.)

for function as well as for structure—that is, *development proceeds from anterior to posterior.*

The 18-day embryo has the beginning of a heart, which begins to beat at the end of the third week. By four weeks the embryo, 2.5 millimeters long, has a system of blood vessels connected with the heart and two tubes which are the beginnings of the gastrointestinal tract and the cerebrospinal canal. He has eyeballs with lenses, pits which will be parts of the nose, semicircular canals, a primitive kidney, lung sacs, and limb buds. Figure 2–3 shows some of these structures.

Development is very rapid during the second four weeks. During this time the embryo comes to look a little like a human being. The internal organs develop to the point where some of them can function. Nerves and muscles grow and develop. The muscles, smooth as well as striated, contract feebly. While muscular movements probably occur before eight weeks of age, the first observed response to a stimulus was at eight and a half weeks. A photograph of a 25mm fetus showed it contracting the long muscles of the neck and trunk after being stroked across the right cheek with a hair.

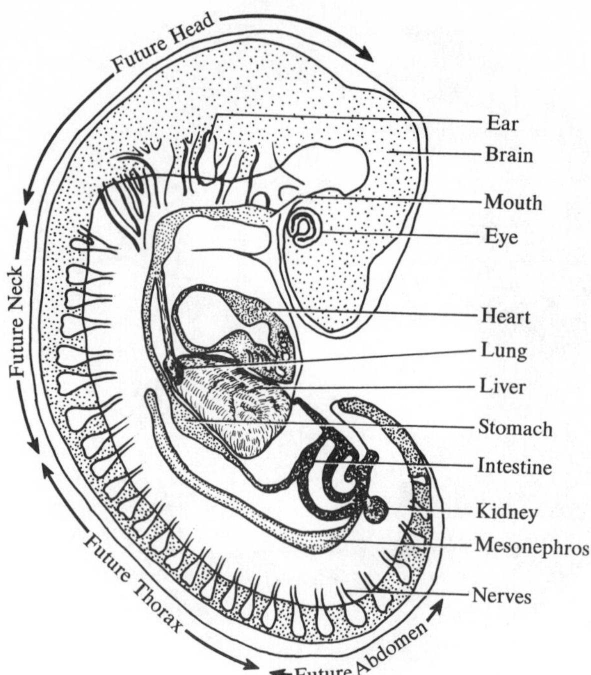

Figure 2–3. The month-old embryo has the foundations of many organs and systems. (Reproduced by permission from M. S. Gilbert, *Biography of the Unborn.* Baltimore: The Williams & Wilkins Co., 1938.)

The Fetus

At eight weeks, the embryo has reached 350 times his original size. Since he is now recognizable, at least to the practiced eye, as a human being, a new name is applied. From the end of the eighth week until he is born, the baby is called *fetus* instead of *embryo*. Complete with face, neck, arms, legs, fingers, toes, some calcification of his bones, functioning internal organs and muscles, the fetus is ready to build upon the basic form that has been laid down.

Development during the third month includes differentiation between the sexes, the tooth buds and sockets for the temporary teeth, the vocal chords and, of course, growth in size and complexity. The third and fourth months are a time of tremendous growth in size; six or eight inches are added to his length. At four months the fetus has reached half of what its length will be at birth. At six months the vernix caseosa, formed from skin cells and a fatty secretion, protects the thin, delicate skin. The skin is red and wrinkled until subcutaneous fat is deposited under it, during the last three months of prenatal life. The fetus swallows, makes breathing movements, secretes enzymes and hormones, digests, and secretes urine. He makes hiccuplike movements and is thought to suck his thumb. All of these functions indicate the maturing of the nervous system.

In describing the postural development of the fetus, Gesell [14, p. 62] warns the reader not to think about the textbook pictures and preserved specimens that he has seen, since these convey an image of the fetus as stiff, crumpled, confined and sedentary, instead of free-floating as he is in the first half of the fetal period, and possessing enough space for movement even during the second half. The inch-long eight-weeks fetus is enclosed in a two-inch amniotic sac where the only force exerted on him is that of gravity. Gesell pictures him in various orientations, prone, supine, oblique, contracting the muscles of one side of the trunk and neck, flexing the head and shoulder to the side contracted, the arms moving passively with the shoulder, rotating the rump.

By twelve weeks the head extends when the trunk flexes, the rump flexes more rapidly and one arm moves farther back than its opposite. To a lesser degree, the legs also move independently of the trunk and asymmetrically, suggesting the beginning of alternating movements. Thus the anterior portion shows more behavior than the posterior portion, illustrating again the principle that development proceeds from anterior to posterior. Another principle specified in Chapter 1 is demonstrated also, namely that *development proceeds through differentiation and integration*. The generalized movement of the fetus at eight weeks, when the limbs move along with the trunk, is differentiated to a unit of movement in which arms and legs are independent of the trunk but coordinated with it.

The fetus is 16 to 20 weeks old when his mother first feels him moving, like a butterfly inside her. Already he has a large repertory of movements which includes blinking, sucking, turning the head and gripping, and a wide variety of movements of limbs, hands and feet. The last half of prenatal life is a period of preparation for birth and independent living. Most important is the maturing of the nervous system, which must organize and coordinate all the other systems. The establishment of breathing, the most precarious step into the outside world, will be determined largely by the condition of the nervous system. Table 2–1 shows the timing and the details of prenatal physical development.

STAGES OF MATERNAL DEVELOPMENT AND EXPERIENCE

Since the zygote is free-floating and self-contained for about a week, the mother has no reactions to pregnancy until after implantation.

Symptoms and Diagnosis

Failure to menstruate is usually the first symptom of pregnancy, although it is not a conclusive symptom. Absence of menses can be due to a variety of reasons, including age, illness and emotional upset; menstruation during the first two or three months of pregnancy is possible. Breast changes may

TABLE 2–1

Summary table showing development during embryonic and fetal life.

Age in Weeks	*Crown-Rump Size in Inches*	*Body Form*	*Skin and Appendages*	*Mouth*	*Alimentary System*	*Breathing Apparatus*	*Urinary System*
2.5	1/16	Flat embryonic disc	Single layer of cells		Continuous with yolk-sac		Embryonic bladder present
3.5	3/32	Cylindrical	Single layer of cells	A definite pit Membrane ruptures	Pharynx broad and flat Intestine present Bud of liver present	Groove in pharynx "Gill clefts" forming	First kidney present
4	3/16	Body flexed into C-shape Limb buds present	Single layer of cells	Jaws and tongue beginning	Pharynx, esophagus, stomach, intestine, liver, gall bladder, pancreas begun	Trachea and paired lung buds present Larynx a slit	First kidney degenerated Second kidney flourishing Third kidney begins
5	3/8	Nasal pits present Tail prominent	Epidermis two cells thick	Jaws develop-ing	All above developing Intestine loops Cecum begun	Bronchial buds forming	Second kidney reaches limit Ureters begin
6	1/2	Head dominates Limbs recognizable Face forming	Milk (nipple) lines indi-cated	Lips and gums forming Salivary gland buds	Stomach changes position Intestine elongating Rectum	Bronchi subdividing	Urethra forming

7	¾	Face and neck form Digits beginning Back straightens Tail regressing	Mammary glands forming	Right and left palate folds forming	Stomach in final shape and position Anus opens	Lung "lobes" indicated Larynx developing Nasal conchae appear	Third kidney developing Urethra opens
8	15/16	Body evenly rotund Fetal form attained	Continuing development	Continuing development	Intestinal villi forming Liver very large	Lungs glandlike Nostrils plugged	Continuing development interrelated with genitalia
10	1⅝	Head erect Limbs molded	Nail folds show Epidermis thickens Facial hair follicles forming	Palate folds fusing	Continuing development	Nasal passages forming	Kidneys secreting urine Bladder develops
12	2¼	External genitalia (sex) distinguishable	Epidermis 3 cells thick Dermis distinct	Milk tooth buds form Palate fused	Bile secreted Muscle in intestine	Conchae formed Lungs acquire definite shape	Bladder becoming muscular
16	4 7/16	Face human Body growing faster than head	Body hair, sweat, and sebaceous glands appearing	Hard and soft palates differentiated	Stomach and intestinal glands forming Feces collecting	Nasal sinuses developing	Kidneys attain more typical shape
20–40 (5–10 months)	6¼–13¾	Fetus lean wrinkled, red (5, 6, and 7 months) Fat collecting, body rounding (8–10 months)	Fetal wax present Nails developed Hair shed between 7 and 10 months	Permanent tooth buds form	Canal parts all developed	Faucial and pharyngeal tonsils typical; nostrils open	Kidney tubules form until birth, then cease

TABLE 2–1 (*Continued*)

Age in Weeks	*Circulatory System*	*Skeletal System*	*Muscular System*	*Sense Organs*	*Nervous System*	*Endocrines*	*Reproductive System*
2.5	Blood islands in yolk-sac Cardiac plate present	Notochordal plate present			Neural groove		
3.5	Blood cells and vessels present Heart formed and beat begins	Notochord a rod	Mesenchyme segmenting	Optic and auditory plates present	Neural groove closing	Thyroid indicated in pharynx	
4	Chief arteries and veins formed Heart 2-chambered	Primitive vertebrae mass about notochord	40 pairs of mesenchymal segments present	Middle ear beginning Optic and auditory apparatus developing Olfactory plates arise	Neural tube closed Primary brain and paired nerves formed	Hypophysis begins	
5	Vessels extending Heart septa forming Spleen begins	Condensation of mesenchyme in positions of future bones	Primitive muscle masses in head, trunk, and limbs	Eyes and ears developing Olfactory pits form	5 brain vesicles Cerebrum bulging Nerves extending		Genital ridges present
6	Blood cells forming in liver Heart acquires its definite external form	First cartilage First indications of skull bones	Segmentation gone Premuscle masses coalescing	Eyes at 160°	Brain bending as result of growth Nerves extending Meninges forming	Thymus forms Parathyroids forming	Sexless gonads developing

7	Vessels, heart, and spleen developing	Cartilage formation more general	Muscles assuming final shape and positions	Continuing development	Cerebral hemispheres enlarging	Further development Suprarenals begin	
8	Lymph sacs present	First ossification centers	Fetus capable of movement	Eyes converging External, middle, internal ears formed Taste buds forming	Cerebral cortex and olfactory lobes differentiated	Continuing development	Testes and ovaries distinguishable
10	Lymphatic system developing	Continuing cartilage and bone formation	Lower trunk muscles developing	Iris, ciliary body and lacrimal glands forming	Spinal cord attains its internal structure	Pancreatic tissue forming	Ducts of the opposite sex degenerating
12	Blood cells forming in bone marrow Vessels become muscular	Notochord degenerating Upper bones well outlined	Smooth muscle in viscera	Retinal layers forming	Brain attains definitive shape Nerves developing	Thyroid attains typical shape	Uterus, sperm ducts, prostate Seminal vesicles
16	Blood cells form in spleen Heart muscle developing	Most bones outlined Joints forming	Fetal movements can be detected through maternal body wall	Eye, ear, nose approaching final form General receptors forming	Cerebrum covers other brain parts Cerebellum developing	Continuing development	Testes in position for descent Vagina formed
20–40 (5–10 months)	Blood cells forming more in marrow and less in liver Some fetal blood vessels close (10)	Some ossification	Lower trunk muscles take typical form	All sense organs partially developed All functioning at birth except ear	Continuing development	Continuing development	Testes descend between 7 and 9 months

Source: Elizabeth Lee Vincent and Phyllis C. Martin, *Human Psychological Development*. Copyright © 1961, The Ronald Press Company. Reprinted by permission.

announce pregnancy. Fullness, tingling and hypersensitivity may occur even before the first missed period.

Nausea or queasiness may begin when the first period is overdue. For those who are nauseated, the common pattern is morning queasiness, which disappears gradually in about eight weeks. Guttmacher [16], an obstetrician with wide experience, says that fewer than half of pregnant women nowadays are nauseated, whereas the majority suffered from the symptom a generation ago. Fatigue and the need for extra sleep, frequent during the early months of pregnancy, probably represent a protective mechanism for facilitating physical changes. Frequency of urination is another early symptom.

The physician can diagnose pregnancy through laboratory tests soon after the first missed period. The classic and conclusive signs are hearing the fetal heartbeat, feeling fetal movements and seeing the fetal skeleton in an X ray, all possible between the sixteenth and twentieth weeks.

Physical Changes

The whole body is affected by pregnancy. The first stage seems to be one of reorganization. The middle stage is normally one of smooth functioning, when the mother feels and looks blooming, settles into her job of supplying the fetus. Later stages involve more preparations for the birth process.

It is very advantageous to begin pregnancy with a normal, healthy, well-nourished body. For example, if the mother has a good supply of calcium already stored in her bones, she will be more likely to keep herself and her baby well supplied with calcium than will a mother with inadequate stores, even though both have a good diet during pregnancy. Similarly with nitrogen retention and hemoglobin level, a healthy condition in the beginning makes it easier to maintain good levels through pregnancy [34, 35].

A bulletin of the National Research Council [38] underlines the importance of prenatal and preconceptional nutrition by describing the practices of some historic and primitive peoples. It was common in ancient civilization to provide special diets not only for pregnant women but also for girls for a time before marriage. In some cultures, even husbands-to-be have their diets supervised.

REPRODUCTIVE SYSTEM. The uterus grows in weight from two ounces to over two pounds, in capacity from a half teaspoon to four or five quarts. Muscle fibers grow to 10 times their former length. The preparation of the muscular layer of the uterus is extremely important, since it will open and retract the cervix, help to push the baby out and form ligatures to cut off the blood vessels supplying the mucosa. The mucosa (the lining) provides the spot where the morula implants and takes part in forming the placenta. It provides a mucus plug to close the entrance to the uterus. The cervix, or neck of the uterus, softens as its muscle fibers diminish in number and size, connective tissue grows thinner and blood supply increases. The vagina increases in length and capacity as its muscle fibers hypertrophy, connective tissue loosens and more blood is supplied. All perineal structures, the tissues surrounding the birth canal, are loosened, becoming more distensible. Vaginal secretions increase in quantity and in bacteriocidal action.

The breasts increase in size due to an increase in mammary gland tissue and an increased blood supply.The pigmented area darkens. From the fourth month on, colostrum, a clear yellow fluid, is excreted from the nipple.

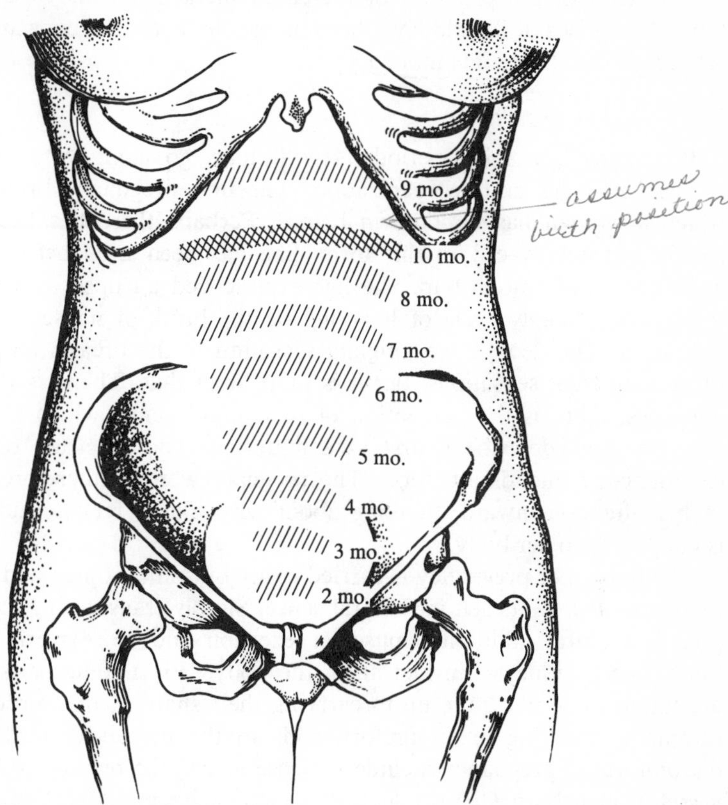

Figure 2–4. The tremendous expansion of the uterus is suggested by this drawing, showing the height reached by the uterus at each successive month of pregnancy. (Reproduced by permission from J. B. DeLee and J. P. Greenhill, *Principles and Practices of Obstetrics*. Philadelphia: W. B. Saunders Company, 1947.)

CIRCULATORY SYSTEM. The blood vessels supplying the uterus elongate, dilate and become tortuous. The blood volume increases by one fifth, but has a progressively lower specific gravity and lower hemoglobin count. Although this condition is not true anemia, good hygiene is important in order to prevent anemia. Because of the changing specific gravity, the ordinary balance of fluids in the lymph system and certain veins may be upset. Balance is encouraged by breathing movements and muscular activity and upset by inactivity and gravity. When too much blood accumulates in the vessels of the legs and the perineal and anal regions, drainage is helped by reversing the force of gravity, resting with the feet up.

SYSTEMIC FUNCTIONS. Changes in the hormonal balance occur. Pregnancy affects various glands, including the thyroid, parathyroid, pituitary and suprarenals. Metabolism is increased and improved after the third month. The capacity to store essential elements increases. The kidneys must work harder to take care of the products of increased metabolism and excretion of the fetus. The pelvis of the kidney dilates to double its former capacity. Sweat and sebaceous glands become more active.

Psychological Aspects

Pregnancy is a crisis period. New feelings go along with the pervading physical changes and reorganization. The first pregnancy brings sensations which a woman has not known before. Perhaps there has been something like it, but not exactly in this form. She has been tired before, but not so eager for an afternoon nap. She has experienced an upset stomach, but not the consistent daily cycle of hovering on the brink of nausea and then conquering it. The deep, alive, tingling sensation in the breasts may remind her of premenstrual sensations, but it is more than that. Then, as the pregnancy advances, there is the perception of fetal movements, which is like nothing else. She may describe it first as a fluttering. The spectrum of new bodily experiences demands attention. The pregnant woman, therefore, turns some of her attention inward, thinking about what she is feeling and about what is happening to her body.

The burden of pregnancy is carried easily by some women and not so easily by others. It is a burden in a literal sense. Simply transporting 15 to 25 extra pounds requires additional muscular exertion and more work done by the lungs, heart, kidneys—in fact all of the body. When some parts of the body are found to be not quite up to carrying their share of the burden, their performance, resulting in discomfort, adds to the perceived burden. Common discomforts of pregnancy include varicose veins(the bulging of loaded blood vessels), heartburn (the product of the stomach's imperfect functioning) and shortness of breath (resulting from a squeezed thorax). Such discomforts may be slight or severe, depending on such physical factors as bodily structure, nutrition and fatigue. Medical care and good hygiene help to alleviate the difficulties. The woman's reactions to pregnancy are also the product of her culture and of her own personality.

Little girls are taught what to anticipate as they look forward to growing up and having babies of their own. Their mothers set example when carrying baby brothers and sisters. Overheard conversations are influential. So are glances, nuances and conversations which stop in midair as the child approaches. If mothers tell their children that pregnancy and birth are simple, natural and beautiful and yet the children hear them exchanging stories with their friends which depict these processes as frightening and agonizing, they will surely not accept the first version confidently. Children also give each other information and misinformation. They may read news items and see films and television which contribute to their attitudes towards pregnancy and childbirth. The reality of the situation is not lost on those looking forward to pregnancy. They notice how pregnant women are regarded in their culture. Today, pregnant women go everywhere, wearing pretty clothing, frankly suited to their expanding shapes. They are obviously acceptable at parties, in church, on the beach and in many jobs. Fifty years ago, a birth was called a "confinement." Pregnant women were supposed to go into relative seclusion. Another aspect of today's reality is the comparative ease and safety with which human reproduction occurs. Because of medical knowledge and techniques, drugs, nutrition and health care, girls do not hear very often about women dying in childbirth or of their being almost frightened to death. They do hear, however, of children being born with physical and mental defects. They may be even more aware of these children than their grandmothers were, since there are more of them around. Modern medicine, although doing marvels to correct defects, keeps increasing numbers of defective children alive. Pregnant women commonly fear that their children will not be normal [17].

The personality of the expectant mother plays a large part in her reactions to pregnancy. If she has coped successfully with the problems of identity and has a marriage in which her sense of intimacy has developed, then, most likely, she welcomes parenthood with a feeling of confidence and happy anticipation. Nobody is unshakable in his self-concepts, and nobody has perfect communication and sharing with another. Therefore, even the healthiest pregnant woman will have occasional doubts about herself, her potential as a mother and her ability to run the more complicated family which will result from the birth of her baby. The woman who had difficult problems before her pregnancy is likely to find life harder now. The demands upon her would understandably increase fears about sex, modesty, physical adequacy, and family difficulties. The women who assume a "sick" role when pregnant tend to be those who are unhappy and insecure in their marriages and in life in general [37].

A pregnant mother's emotions are understandably affected by whether she wants the pregnancy or not. A study [26] of couples' reactions to first pregnancies showed considerable initial upset in those who had tried to avoid pregnancy. Those mothers who had planned their pregnancies decreased in emotional upsets during the first three months. Both groups settled down to almost-normal emotional levels for the last six months. Mothers who had done no planning at all in regard to pregnancy increased in upsets as pregnancy progressed. Figure 2–5 shows the emotional changes in women, grouped as to attitude toward pregnancy.

THE EXPECTANT FATHER. A man can contribute to the well-being of his unborn child through the help and support he gives to his wife. Feeling vulnerable as she does, her confidence in him as provider and protector is constructive in making her relaxed and secure. She appreciates reassurance that

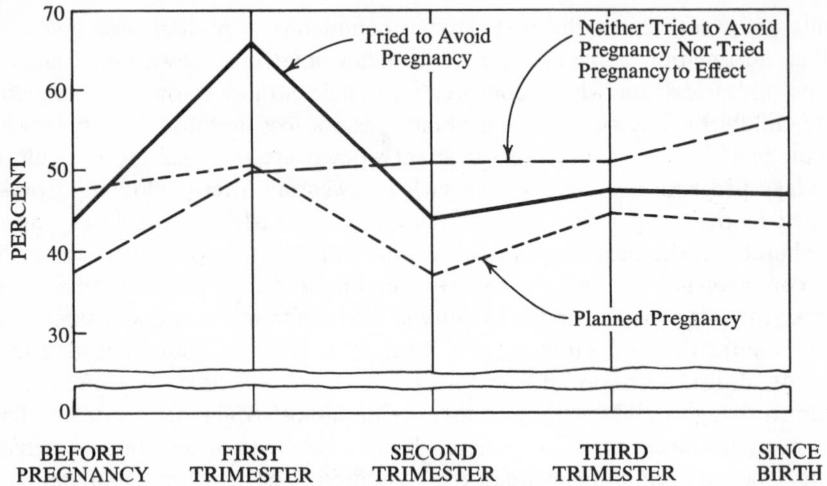

Figure 2–5. Emotional reactions to pregnancy of mothers who had planned the pregnancy, those who had tried to avoid pregnancy and those who had done no planning. (Reproduced by permission of the authors and The American Sociological Association from S. B. Poffenberger, T. Poffenberger and J. T. Landis, "Intent Toward Conception and the Pregnancy Experience," *American Sociological Review,* 1952, **17,** 616–620.

she is still attractive in spite of her increasing girth and decreasing agility. She may want some sympathy for the aches, pains, annoyances and limitations on activity. If she has fears about the pain of delivery and the well-being of the baby or fears about her competence as a mother, she may seek reassurance from her husband. A mature man, who has coped successfully with his own personality growth, can give his pregnant wife a great deal of comfort through his understanding, sympathy and confidence. Many men, even while trying to be supportive, find the role of expectant father a very difficult one to play [3].

With a first pregnancy, the natural turning inward of the woman's attention may constitute the first time in the marriage when the husband feels displaced in her thoughts. He may realize that the worst is yet to come, when the infant will require a great deal of the time and attention which used to belong to him. He may feel deprived sexually, since the doctor may limit intercourse in early pregnancy, probably forbidding it during the last few weeks. The father will probably feel added financial responsibility, since a new baby costs something even before birth and then costs more and more as the years go by. New, larger, costlier living quarters may be indicated. The thoughts of college expenses may cross his mind. If the pregnancy is an unwanted one, especially if it threatens the mother's health and the family's solvency, then the expectant father is likely to feel strong guilt.

The husband may find himself being the main, or even only, emotional support of his pregnant wife. When a young couple move to another part of the country, leaving family and friends behind, they are dependent, at least for a while, on the resources which they have as a pair. In contrast, an extended family offers vast aid and support to a pregnant woman. If not already living with the older generation, the young woman may go home to her mother's house, where she is surrounded with affectionate care until after her baby is born and adjusted to life. Or her mother may come to her, taking authoritative command of what is considered woman's affairs, thus relieving the young father of much of the burden which he would have to carry in a nuclear family consisting of husband, wife and child.

In order to fill in some of the emotional and technical gaps created by the change from extended to nuclear family life, some communities offer education for childbirth. Such education is done for example, by the Maternity Center in New York and the Merrill-Palmer Institute in Detroit. Pregnant mothers, with the permission of their doctors, learn about the changes taking place within themselves, how delivery takes place, how to care for themselves and how to care for their babies. Fathers go to classes which focus on what they want to know, what is happening to mother and baby, their own hereditary contribution, what they can do psychologically, and something about infant care and development. Through discussions, both parents clarify their own feelings and share with other expectant parents. Thus they derive much of the security offered in other cultures by experienced family members, while they enjoy the added advantage of applying knowledge from modern research.

PRENATAL INFLUENCE

The question of whether and how a woman could influence her unborn baby is one which has intrigued people since the dawn of history. Some societies have maintained that specific thoughts and experiences could mark the baby in specific ways, such as the notion that if a rabbit ran across the pregnant woman's path, she would bear a baby with a hare lip, or if she squashed a strawberry, her baby would have a red birthmark. Less specific, but just as unfounded is the notion that by listening to good music and viewing great paintings, a woman could confer talent upon the child within her. As scientific knowledge about pregnancy and birth became widespread, more and more people realized that the baby's blood system was separate from the mother's, exchanging nutrients and products of excretion through membranes, but not exchanging blood. As the old superstitions, such as those of the hare lip and strawberry mark, were swept away, many people got the idea that nutrition was the *only* prenatal influence. Although nutrition is of great importance, there are indeed additional ways in which an unborn baby can be affected through its mother.

Nutrition

The woman who starts her pregnancy in good nutritional condition is fortunate, since she can thus provide the optimal environment for her baby right from the beginning. A nutritional defect is difficult to correct when the demands upon the body are increased by pregnancy. The very fact of being well-nourished shows that the woman has established a pattern of eating an adequate selection of foods in amounts suited to her. She will not have to change her ways of eating other than to increase the amounts slightly as pregnancy advances. Although the supplementing of prenatal diets is a common custom, over 1,800 lower-income women, who received no supplements, did as well as the average American woman as to complications of pregnancy and birth and condition of infants at birth and afterwards [21]. The diets of these women were varied and included the basic foods, milk, eggs, green and yellow vegetables, citrus fruits and other fruits. While the average woman in this group got along well, there were those who had difficulties. The underweight group had more premature births. The overweight group had more stillbirths and much more toxemia, a dangerous metabolic disturbance. This study did not indicate that nutrition is unimportant but rather that a wide range of nutrition can produce healthy mothers and babies and that in a large group of low-income mothers, many can obtain the necessary nutrients. Since women apparently vary quite widely in their nutritional needs, it seems all the more important for every pregnant woman to have the individual guidance supplied by a physician supervising her pregnancy.

Studies on extreme conditions show what can happen when that wide range of safety is violated. Wars and other disasters have provided famine conditions under which the effects of serious nutritional deficiencies could be studied. Toward the end of World War II and immediately afterward, the birth weight of babies was reduced in parts of Holland, Germany and Russia [8, 30]. Studies of mothers showing certain kinds of deficiencies give further evidence of the importance of keeping within the limits of safety. Starvation with protein depletion is associated with underweight babies and probably with neurological defects, such as mental deficiency and cerebral palsy [18]. The effects of improving an inadequate diet were demonstrated by Canadian physicians who supplemented the diets of half of a group of nutritionally deficient pregnant women [9]. The experimental group of mothers (those with improved diets) had fewer cases of anemia, toxemia, miscarriages and premature births. Their average length of labor was shorter. Their babies were in better condition at birth and were healthier infants than those of the control group. Another way of focusing on the problem of poor prenatal nutrition was to examine the histories of stillborn infants, infants who died in the first few days of life, prematures and babies with congenital defects [4]. Almost all of the mothers of these infants had had very poor diets during pregnancy.

Physicians usually limit the amount of weight gain that they allow their pregnant patients, since toxemia is related to excessive weight gain. There is also the consideration that extra fat laid down during pregnancy will have to be lost afterward if the mother is to regain her figure and ideal weight. Sometimes pregnant women take all this to mean that the less they gain the better. Therefore, it is well to point out the risk involved in limiting the diet too severely [42]. In the effort to cut calories, certain essential elements may be eliminated or at least skimped. The baby may or may not be able to get what he needs, depending on which elements are lacking. An old and erroneous notion is that the baby is able to draw his requirements from the mother's body no matter what she eats. The baby's blood has a higher level of concentration of iron, ascorbic acid and vitamin B 12 than does the mother's blood, but the mother's blood can be higher in iodine and vitamins A and E. In other words, if there are shortages of iron, ascorbic acid and B 12, the baby will take them at the expense of the mother. In the case of iodine and vitamins A and E, however, the mother will get them before the baby does.

Let us sum up the practical knowledge gained from studies of prenatal nutrition. The majority of pregnant women eat fairly adequate diets, but a minority have nutritional deficiencies. Requirements vary from one woman to another and there are a variety of ways in which requirements can be met. When deficiencies occur, they can harm either mother or baby but they are likely to harm both. Dietary deficiencies can contribute to premature and otherwise abnormal births, stillbirth, death within the first few days of life, congenital defects, small size and illnesses during infancy. The importance of adequate, individualized prenatal care is emphasized by the role of nutrition in assuring the health and safety of mother and baby.

Sensory Stimuli

It has long been known that the fetus responds to a wide variety of tones and to loud and sudden noises with increased motor activity and heart rate. Although this behavior has been studied in detail [32], it is not known whether there are any lasting effects from stimulating the unborn baby in this way. Probably every baby receives some loud and sudden stimuli before birth, when his mother drops a pot in the kitchen, at a concert, in heavy traffic, when a siren blows, and so on. Mothers report that their fetuses do react to such noises by moving. The baby can be conditioned during the last two months of pregnancy to give a startle response. In one study, the primary stimulus, a loud noise, was paired with a vibrotactile stimulus (an electric doorbell with the gong removed). The latter called forth no fetal response when originally applied to the mother's abdomen, but after 15 or 20 trials with the loud noise, the vibrotactile stimulus alone elicited a startle response [33].

The mother's heartbeat may be an important source of prenatal sensory stimulation. It is an intermittent, repetitive, auditory stimulus which the infant receives during his whole prenatal life, or at least from the time when his hearing apparatus is mature enough to receive sounds. Other repetitive, intermittent stimuli come from the mother's breathing, but these are tactile and kinesthetic stimuli, due to pressure changes. Stimuli from pressure changes also occur when the mother moves her body, but these changes are neither continuous nor rhythmic, as compared with stimuli from heartbeat and breathing [12].

The following chapter includes a description of experiments with babies and toddlers, using a heartbeat sound. Because the sound was found soothing to infants and children, it seems worth while to consider what meaning it may have prenatally. The heartbeat sound has the criteria of an imprinting stimulus being intermittent and repetitious and occurring early in the life of the organism, before it experiences fear [27]. Later, when the organism is exposed to fear, it is reassured by the stimulus to which it has been imprinted. Thus it seems quite possible that the unborn baby interacts with his environment in such a way that the rhythms of sounds and pressures prepare him for coping with some of the difficulties he will encounter after he is born, Seeking to comfort his distress and express their love, his parents and other people will hold him in their arms and walk with him or rock and jiggle him. The resulting sounds and pressures will reassure him, perhaps because he was imprinted prenatally to such stimuli.

Maternal Emotions

Fetal behavior has been studied at the Fels Institute for several decades. Emotional disturbances in the mother have been shown to be associated with high activity in the fetus [31]. Infants of mothers who had suffered emotional upsets during pregnancy were likely to show frequent irritability, excessive crying and gastrointestinal disturbances, such as regurgitation, dyspepsia, and diarrhea. These difficulties are thought to be of autonomic origin and to be caused by intrauterine conditions.

Further evidence of the significance of maternal emotional upset comes from a study of factors connected with birth difficulties and infant abnormalities. A highly anxious group of mothers was found to experience more complications of delivery and things wrong with their babies [7]. The connection between maternal emotions and fetal upset is made through several steps, but it can be explained in physical terms [23, pp. 192–193].

The nervous and endocrine systems communicate through the blood. An experience of the mother is registered in her cerebral cortex from which impulses pass to the thalamus, hypothalamus and into the autonomic nervous system. The autonomic system acts on the endocrines, which pour their products into the blood. The blood takes the products of the endocrines to the placenta, through which some of them pass to the fetal blood and to the nervous system of the fetus.

Another explanation is suggested by Salk's [27] explorations with a gallop heartbeat rhythm and a very fast heartbeat. The newborn infants who had quieted to the sound of a normal heartbeat showed an immediate increase in crying and disturbance to these unusual heartbeats and also to a hissing sound which the machine accidentally developed. A frightened or disturbed pregnant mother could be expected to show variations from the normal pattern of heartbeat and breathing. Her baby then might be disturbed by the resulting tactile, auditory and kinesthetic stimuli. Either by themselves, or added to the effects of the endocrines in the blood, these stimuli could be a significant prenatal influence. Proof of their influence awaits further research.

Another indication of the importance of babies' prenatal experience is a conclusion which Pasamanick and Knobloch [24] state as a result of their research on brain-injured children. They say, "Except for a few hereditary clinical deficiencies and for exogenous injury to neural integration, behavioral variation does not seem to be the result of genetically determined structural origin." They consider the possibility that individuals at conception may be very much alike in potential for intellectual development. Individual differences in level of performance would then be due largely to differences in experience.

If an unborn baby can suffer from his mother's extreme emotional upset, then could the opposite be true? What happens to the fetus whose mother has an unusually happy, safe, secure time? At birth, is he different from babies whose mothers have had an average or disturbed pregnancy? American research has not yet dealt with this question. Since there are no controlled experiments to report, definite answers cannot be given. However, observations by a French nurse in Africa are suggestive. Working under the World Health Organization, Geber [13] tested over 300 babies in Uganda. She found them to be consistently advanced in psychomotor functions, as compared with European and American babies. This finding has been confirmed by other observers of African babies [1, 2, 11]. The acceleration in development was greatest at birth, then gradually decreasing. From the first day, the children could hold their heads steady when drawn into sitting position, an achievement of the European child at about six weeks. The average Uganda baby sat alone at four months, stood alone at eight and walked at ten. Some individuals achieved these coordinations earlier. Language, problem solving and personal-social development were likewise two or three months advanced over European standards. Since the babies were born developmentally accelerated, the reason for their condition must be in something that happened before birth. Geber suggests that the reason for the infant acceleration is the way in which pregnancy is conducted. She describes it thus:

> The arrival of a baby is always looked forward to with great pleasure (sterility is thought to be a calamity) and is not a source of anxiety for the future. The mother is in no way upset by her pregnancy and is active up to the moment of delivery. The unborn child is the chief object of her life, especially as she believes that any other interest may have an adverse affect on him [13, p. 194].

Perhaps the idyllic pregnancy thus described provides an environment in which the baby can develop maximally. The multiplicity of research on harmful influences makes one aware of all that can go wrong in prenatal life, without giving much indication of what can result when all goes well. A happy, relaxed pregnancy may be just as important for the baby as it is for the mother. It makes sense, then, for the father and other family members to be especially understanding, considerate and affectionate with the expectant mother, not only for her sake, but also for the baby's. This is not to say that the pregnant mother cannot safely deal with everyday problems and work, but only that she benefits from having the general tone of her life a positive one.

Physical and Chemical Agents

It has been known for a quarter of a century that massive X ray doses are lethal or seriously damaging to the unborn child. After World War II, effects of atom bomb radiation on children who had been in utero at the time included increased anomalies and morbidity [25, 43].

Many drugs taken by the pregnant mother can affect the baby, some apparently temporarily and some drastically and permanently. Quinine can cause deafness. Smoking causes an increase in fetal heart rate. In a study [29] on 7,499 patients, premature birth was shown to be twice as frequent among smoking mothers as among nonsmoking mothers. The more cigarettes smoked daily by the pregnant mother, the more prematurely the baby was likely to be born. Heavy doses of certain barbiturates produce asphyxiation and brain damage. The tranquilizer, thalidomide, resulted in thousands of tragic births in Germany, England and Canada, where its prenatal use produced babies lacking limbs or with limbs in early stages of embryonic development.

Since extremely noxious and dangerous stimuli and agents cannot be used experimentally on human beings, a great deal of research is being carried on with animals to find out exactly how radiation and drugs affect them. It has been shown that the stage at which the agents are administered is important in determining the extent of injury and that within certain ranges of stimuli, the stage is more important than the strength [39]. These findings are an example of the growth principle of *critical periods,* described in Chapter 1.

Rats have been subjected to various-sized doses of X rays and different drugs in order to explore the effects which these noxious agents, given prenatally, might have upon growth, health and behavior [40, 41]. It was possible to induce behavior changes without any measurable physical changes, thus showing that the brain had been specifically affected. Behavior changes included decreases in activity and emotionality, increases in activity, emotionality and seizures, resistance to seizures, and increases in learning speed. Delayed effects of radiation were demonstrated by results of prenatal X rays which did not show up until old age. Such findings, like results from all animal research, cannot be applied directly to human beings. They can be taken as indications of how similar mechanisms *may* work in man, awaiting further proof from actual observation of human beings.

Infections and Rh Factor

German measles is probably the best known of the diseases which, when contracted by the mother, can damage the fetus. If German measles occurs during the first eight weeks of pregnancy, the baby has about one chance in three of being damaged. Some other diseases dangerous to the fetus are. syphilis, smallpox, chickenpox, measles, mumps, scarlet fever, tuberculosis and malarial parasites.

About one pregnancy in 200 results in some disturbance from incompatibility between the blood of mother and baby. When the mother's blood is Rh negative and the fetus' blood is Rh positive, there is one chance in 10 that the infant will have some of his red blood cells destroyed. The way it happens is that the fetus produces antigens which go through the placenta into the mother's blood. Her blood then makes antibodies which go back through the placenta to the baby's blood stream. Results include miscarriage, stillbirth, death after birth, brain damage, jaundice and anemia.* Adequate prenatal care requires a blood test which will detect negative Rh. The physician discovering it would then determine the husband's blood type and learn the chances of incompatibility arising between fetus and mother. Taking into account the finding that the danger from Rh factors increases with each baby after the first, he would be ready to cope with symptoms likely to arise. Much can be done to alleviate the condition immediately after birth or even before birth.

Age of Mother

The only time a woman of 35 is considered elderly is when she is having her first baby. In this case, she is called, by the medical profession an "elderly primipara," a logical term in light of the fact that the childbearing period is more than two thirds over. At 35 and older, the average length of labor is increased beyond the overall average by an hour and a half and the risk to mother and baby is increased slightly. Guttmacher says that the additional risk is so slight that no woman over 35 should be deterred from having a first baby [16]. As long as she gets good obstetrical care, there is no cause for worry beyond the ordinary hazards of having a baby. The possibility of mis-

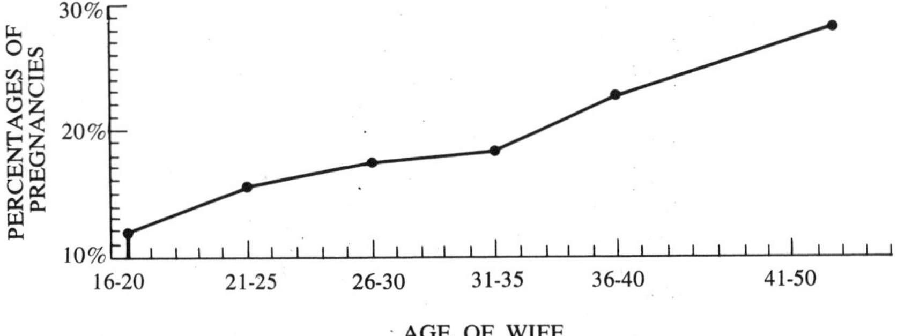

Figure 2–6. Likelihood of miscarriage increases with age of mother. (Reprinted with permission of The Free Press from *Marriage* by R. O. Blood. Copyright © 1962 by The Free Press of Glencoe.)

* This account follows Montagu [23].

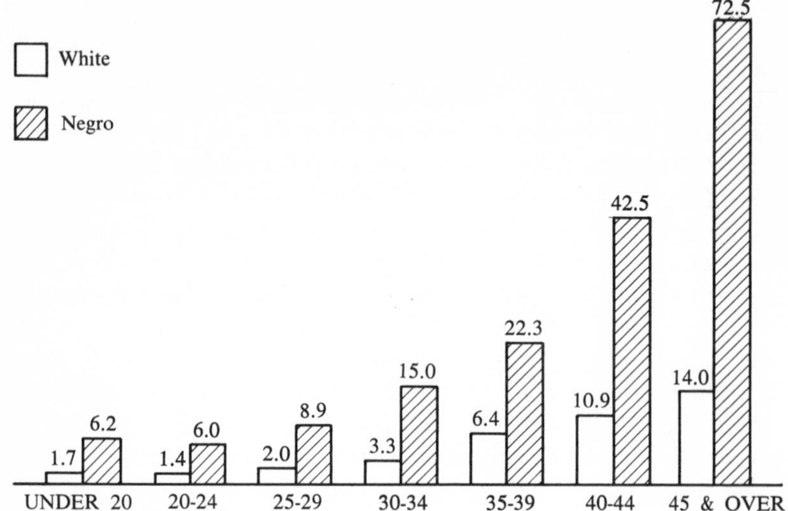

Figure 2–7. Number of maternal deaths for each 10,000 live births, given for Negro and white women (United States, 1959), by age. (Reproduced by permission from data from Table 1, *Statistical Bulletin,* Metropolitan Life Insurance Co., September 1961.)

carriage rises with age, with a sharper increase after 35, as can be seen from Figure 2–6. Maternal mortality, by age and race, is shown in Figure 2–7. Note that the hazards of age are enormously increased if the woman is a Negro, but only slightly increased if she is white. These figures reflect the depressed economic conditions under which many Negroes live.

THE BIRTH PROCESS

The developments described in the chapter thus far occur in the course of about nine months. The obstetrician names the delivery date on the pregnant woman's first visit, by adding 280 days to the first day of her last mentrual period. He will warn her, though that this date is an approximation. Only 4 percent of women deliver on the 280th day; 46 percent deliver within a week of that date and 74 percent within two weeks of it. Being born and giving birth are physical crises for the two most concerned. The crises are emotional, also, for the two and their family. Thus birth must be understood in various contexts.

The Processes and Stages of Labor

Labor is the work that the mother does in giving birth. Three distinct stages can be described. *The first stage,* requiring the major portion of the duration of labor, is the opening of the cervix or neck of the uterus. It begins with rhythmic uterine contractions, usually felt as pains. The two types of muscular forces working to enlarge the cervical openings are indicated in Figure 2–8. The uterus resembles a pear-shaped balloon whose walls are made of very strong muscle fibers. The fibers contract, exerting about 30 pounds of pressure on the fluids surrounding the baby. The membranes enclosing the fluids press on the tiny opening in the lower end of the uterus. After the membranes break (the mother cannot feel this) the baby presses on the opening. At the same time another set of muscle fibers, which surround the tiny opening, are relaxing to allow the opening to enlarge. As these muscular processes continue, the tissues of the cervix are pulled back into the general roundish shape of the uterus. When the cervix is completely dilated the diameter of the opening is about four inches.

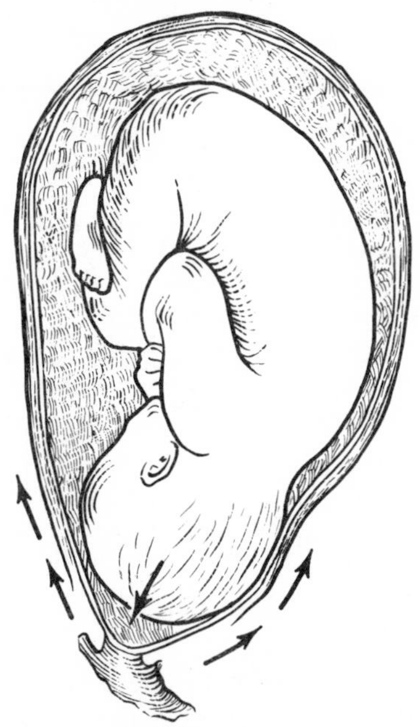

Figure 2–8. The baby during the first stages of labor. Uterine contractions push him downward while the muscle fibers surrounding the opening are pulled upward by the upper segment of the uterus, thus enlarging the opening. (Reproduced by permission from J. P. Greenhill, *Obstetrics,* 13th edition. Philadelphia: W. B. Saunders Company, 1965.)

The muscular processes of the first stage of labor are involuntary. The only way in which a woman can influence them is through relaxation. Although it is still a debatable subject, it is commonly believed that general bodily relaxation, due to absence of fear, plus confidence, hastens relaxation of the muscle fibers surrounding the cervix; fear and tension are thought to increase their resistance to stretching and to result in pain. One of the purposes of education for childbirth is to induce this kind of relaxation.

The second stage lasts from the time that the cervix is completely open until the baby emerges from his mother. For a first baby this stage requires an hour and a half on the average; for the second, half as long. The uterus continues to push the baby out. The mother adds a bearing down action to it, pushing with her diaphragm, but involving her whole body. (See Figure 2–9.) Although she bears down spontaneously, without teaching or conscious

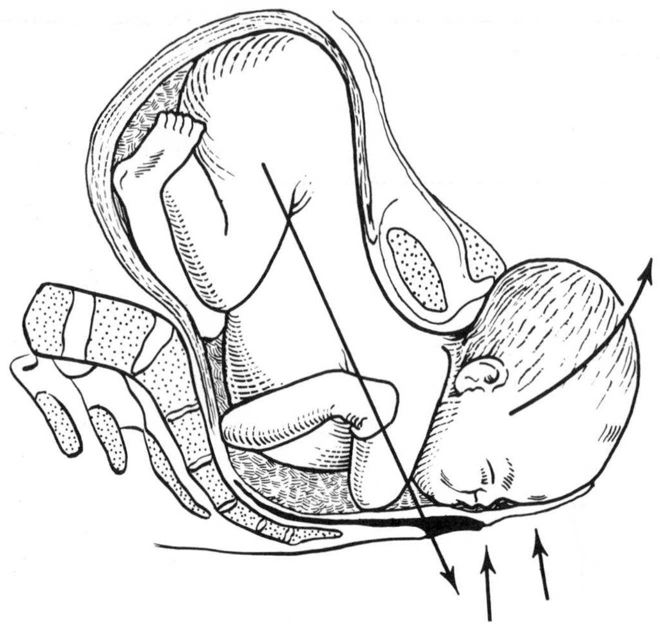

Figure 2–9. The baby during the second stage of labor. The mother's bearing-down action, pushing with her diaphragm, adds to the uterine forces pushing the baby out. (Reproduced by permission from J. B. DeLee and J. P. Greenhill, *Principles and Practices of Obstetrics.* Philadelphia: W. B. Saunders Company, 1947.)

thought, a great deal of this activity can be placed under conscious control. Education for childbirth includes teaching the mother to breathe, relax and bear down in a manner calculated to facilitate the natural labor processes. The confidence factor is just as important in the second stage as in the first in promoting control and either eliminating pain, reducing it or making it more bearable. The *third stage* is the expelling of the placenta and membranes. It lasts only a few minutes.

When women discuss the length of labor with each other, they often mark its beginning with the trip to the hospital. Or the beginning may be considered the time when labor contractions become severe. To be accurate, labor length has to be measured from the time of the first contraction to the moment when the placenta and membranes are completely expelled. Therefore, the average figures for length of labor may look formidably long to the woman who takes her neighbor's experience as the norm. For a first baby, half of the women in a study of nearly 15,000 cases took less than 11 hours; half took more. The commonest length of labor was seven hours. Women who had already had at least one baby had shorter labors, half under approximately six hours, half over, with the commonest length of labor four hours. A few babies are born after only two or three contractions, involving no pain. About one in 125 has a first labor under three hours, while one in 14 requires less than three hours for a subsequent labor. Labors lasting over 30 hours happen once in 8–10 cases of first babies and once in about 33 cases after the first [16].

When a normal birth is impossible or dangerous, the baby may be delivered by Caesarian section, a procedure of cutting the mother's abdomen and uterus to remove the baby and then, of course, the placenta. Although this surgical procedure used to be very dangerous, it now carries relatively slight risk. A Caesarian section is much safer for mother and baby than a difficult forceps delivery or a breech birth through a narrowed pelvis [16]. Although there is no limit to the number of Caesarian births one patient can have, each repetition means that the scar in the uterus is stretched by the pregnancy and hence runs a small risk of rupturing. Many physicans recommend sterilizing with the third Caesarian operation.

Emotional Aspects

The culture in which she has grown up will set the broad outlines of a woman's attitude toward labor. The Judeo-Christian tradition, for example, builds up considerable expectation of pain and tears. According to Mead [36, p. 28] ". . . in some African tribes, women are expected to shriek, scream, writhe and go through the most terrific expressions of agony, and all the little girl children are brought along to watch, so they will know how to have a baby. In other societies, women are enjoined to the greatest stoicism, and to utter a single cry would be to proclaim yourself not a woman, and again the little girls are brought along to see that they behave like this."

Education and specific experiences are important in setting the mother's expectations of pain and danger and her confidence in her own abilities. The ways in which she handles the fear and pain involved will depend not only on herself, however, but on the support and help she receives during labor. Her husband, the hospital staff and, most of all, the doctor have important emotional functions. Directly connected with the mother's fear or confidence, tension or relaxation, pain or easiness, is the amount and type of anesthetic she will receive. A woman who feels confident and in command of herself and who also feels trust in the help she is receiving, will most likely need a minimum of drugs. The terrified patient will seek a maximum, including amnesiacs. (Abnormal physical conditions may require maximum use of drugs, too.)

A famous obstetrical event in the animal kingdom pointed up the life-and-death aspects of emotions during labor. A live baby elephant was delivered successfully at the Portland (Oregon) Zoo, after months of anxious waiting and speculation as how to avoid the fiascoes of past elephant reproduction in captivity. One of the innovations which may have spelled success was the presence of several female elephants in the labor pen. These "aunties" were warmly and actively concerned with the mother, even massaging her with their trunks. In contrast to the frantic concern of isolated elephants-in-labor, this mother conducted herself with calm efficiency.

To return to the human mother, the crowning emotional experience is, of course, the joy in receiving her baby, the result of her labors. Or so it is for many women, especially those who can and do choose to be conscious during the delivery. Case histories of successful "natural childbirth" experiences always make a very big point of this moment. Personal accounts of natural childbirth can be found in popular magazines. Many mothers who meet their babies for the first time upon awaking from heavy sedation and anesthetics admit, at least to themselves, that this was not a tremendous experience. Taken from a first-person account [5] the following excerpt contrasts the experience of traditional American childbirth with one of natural childbirth conducted by the famous Dr. Read:

> I did as he said and, unbelievable but true, I felt no pain, not even discomfort, for the first four or five hours.
>
> Dr. Read insists that no woman in labor be left alone for more than a few minutes during this first phase. He is in favor of the husband's being there until the actual delivery, and at times allows him to be present even then. So there I lay in my pleasant room, my husband with me and Dr. Read coming to see me at frequent intervals.
>
> Finally, after one of his periodic examinations, Dr. Read said, "You are doing wonderfully. It won't be long now." I happened to look at the clock and realized I'd been at the hospital for ten hours! I had a flash of panic. I grabbed the doctor's hand and asked if something was wrong. The next contraction started as I was clutching his hand tightly, and immediately I felt pain, real pain. Dr. Read said quite sharply: "Breathe deeply now, lie still, relax. Everything is going beautifully. Don't give up now." By great effort I made myself relax and the pain faded away.
>
> After about three more hours I suddenly felt a very long and strong contraction, and asked my husband to get Dr. Read. When the doctor came, I had another long contraction and sensed that the dreary waiting was over. The doctor confirmed my suspicions and had me wheeled into the delivery room. Again I had a second's panic as I remembered my former experience. But by now I knew the end was not far. I felt I could stand anything.
>
> Dr. Read took my hand and gave me instructions: "Now your perpendicular muscles are getting to work, and in this you can and must help. When you feel a contraction coming, take a deep breath, hold it, and bear down as hard as you can. If I say stop, let your breath out and relax completely until you feel the next contraction coming."
>
> I could now feel the baby moving down with each contraction. Each time the nurse would ask, "Do you want some gas?" and I'd say, "No, thank you." Finally I said, "Don't bother me. Can't you see I'm busy?"
>
> Between contractions I lay relaxed and limp, my physical forces regaining their strength, my mental forces wide-awake. After a particularly big push

> Dr. Read said, "Ah, shoulder first; that's why it's been so long." Just then came another contraction, and with the most glorious sensation of achievement I felt my child slide into the world.
>
> The doctor said, "I want you to be the first to shake hands with your little girl." I took my baby's petal-soft hand, and she opened her mouth and yelled at me. I had wanted a boy, badly, but now I loved that wee, ugly thing in a way that astonished me.
>
> That was my experience: the first birth agonizing, undignified, with no feeling of love for the child for quite a few days; the second birth natural, unfrightening, with an unsurpassable flood of love to end a really wonderful experience. It was not painless, but the pain was bearable.*

As far as anyone knows, there is no connection between exultation after childbirth and later successful parenthood. There is interest in exploring this topic through research which could reveal such a connection [36, p. 35].

The emotional aspects of childbirth for mother, baby and family and the importance of psychological preparation and support are not widely appreciated. The people who come to understand the significance of it often come to embrace it as a cause. The International Childbirth Education Association is "a federation of groups and individuals interested in family-centered maternity and infant care." This group spreads information through conferences, literature and films.

The Baby During Labor

Being born is a difficult and risky experience which has claimed the attention of philosophers and psychiatrists, as well as physicians and lay people. The great obstetrician, DeLee, believed that babies suffered pain while being born. The fact that babies give little evidence of a skin pain sense in the early postnatal days is not proof that the global experience of birth is without trauma.

The fetal heartbeat responds to each uterine contraction by speeding up, slowing down and then speeding up again. As labor progresses, the fetal heart beats more slowly. When the baby is in danger, his heart beats very fast, slowly, or irregularly. During a strong uterine contraction, the fetal blood cannot get oxygen from the placenta. The increasing concentration of carbon dioxide stimulates the respiratory center and hence the beginning of breathing after birth. Amniotic fluid and mucus escape from the baby's air passages during expulsion of the baby, due to compression of his chest. After the first gasp of air, a sneeze or cough expels more of the fluids. The head adapts to birth by a flattening of the face and forehead and an overlapping of the bones of the skull. The asymmetry usually disappears within a week.

The emotional significance of the birth experience is a matter of conjecture. Some schools of thought hold that birth has a lasting psychological influence, while others maintain that the organism is too immature to record experience

* Reprinted by permission from "The Most Glorious Experience" by Bimbetta Coats, *The Reader's Digest,* May 1950.

meaningfully. There is no question but that birth is a critical physical experience and no argument with the fact that the newborn needs adequate physical care if he is to survive.

Injuries from Abnormal Conditions of Childbearing

The wonderful protective and adaptive resources of both mother and baby result in most infants being born intact. A minority of babies suffer from conditions existing prenatally and during the birth process. Such damage can result in fetal death, stillbirth, death soon after birth, cerebral palsy, epilepsy, mental retardation, behavior disorders and perhaps speech and reading disorders [19]. The dangerous conditions include complications of pregnancy such as toxemias and bleeding, premature birth, difficult, prolonged or precipitate labor, malpresentation, general anesthetic and major illnesses of the mother.

Research is revealing increasingly the milder aspects of birth injury. A study of infants who had suffered oxygen deprivation during birth, contrasting them with normal babies during the first five days of life, showed the traumatized infants to be significantly less sensitive to pain stimulation and visual stimulation, less integrated in motor behavior patterns, more irritable and more tense and rigid muscularly [15]. Another study on infants who suffered oxygen deprivation at birth showed them to differ intellectually from normal children at age three. The oxygen-deprived children averaged 8 points lower in IQ and did less well on tests of concept formation [10].

Children born prematurely have a greater chance of having neurological and behavior defects [6, 20]. The greater the prematurity (as estimated by birth weight), the greater the chance of neuropsychiatric disorders in the child. A study [28] on prematurely born infants and preschool children revealed this syndrome: keenly aware of sounds and sights, poor speech, persisting longer in baby talk, poor motor control (choppy, slap-dash, spilling, clumsy, lunging gait, poor posture), overactive or sluggish, slow in bowel and bladder control, poor emotional control, shy, dependent, extremes of attention span, interest in artistic expression.

The ways in which prematurity is associated with defects are complex. First, the neurological and behavior disorders associated with prematurity may be the results of the same prenatal disorders which caused the baby to be born early. Second, the immature condition of the prematurely born baby makes him less able to stand the stresses and strains of birth and postnatal life. Third, he is treated differently from full-term babies. Kept in an incubator and extrasanitary environment, he is deprived of normal skin contacts and other stimulation. He is probably not breast-fed and may not even be able to seek, find and suck his food. Later on, the anxiety surrounding his early days may evoke special handling from his family, encouraging dependency.

Incidence of Abnormalities

Most seriously malformed fetuses are spontaneously aborted (miscarried). Miscarriage can be looked upon as nature's way of insuring normal babies, since about four fifths of spontaneous abortions are of abnormal embryos and fetuses. In live births, minor abnormalities occur to one in 60. Serious abnormalities, causing stillbirth or early death, happen once in about 225 cases [16]. When hereditary defects are present in a family, then the risks of having a baby with such defects can be predicted [22]. Table 2–2 shows the

TABLE 2–2

Table for calculating chances of inheriting various birth defects when those defects are present in parents and/or siblings.

Disease or Defect	*Approximate Frequency Among Newborns or Morbid Risk*	*Risk for Sibs Parents Unaffected %*	*Risk for Sibs One Parent Affected %*	*Risk for Children One Affected Parent %*
Anencephaly	1:1,000	1	—	—
Chondrodystrophy	1:10,000	0.01	50	50
Cleft palate alone	1:2,500	2–12	17	7
Congenital cataract with idiocy	1:50,000	15	—	—
Congenital clubfoot	1:1,000	3	10	10
Congenital luxation of the hip	1:1,500	5	10–15	10
Convulsive disorders (Grand Mal)	1:300	2–4	—	3–6
Diabetes mellitus (appearing before age 50)	1:200	15–20	—	10–15
Harelip or Harelip combined with cleft palate	1:1,000	4	14	2
Hydrocephaly	1:1,000	1	—	—
Imbecility or feeble-mindedness (unspecified)	1:100	13–18	30–40	30
Malformations of the central nervous system	1:200	3	—	—
Manic-depressive psychosis	1:100	15	15	15
Microphthalmus or anophthalmus with idiocy	1:100,000	10	—	—
Mongoloid idiocy	1:700	1–4	—	—
Pyloric stenosis	1:250	5	—	—
Schizophrenia	1.0–1.5:100	10–15	10–15	10–15
Spina bifida	1:1,000	1	—	—
Strabismus	1:50	10	17	—

Source: Reprinted by permission from H. G. Hammons, *Heredity Counseling.* Copyright © American Eugenics Society Inc.

frequencies of various defects in the general population and in families where parents and/or siblings are affected. A couple wishing to know their chances of having a normal baby, given certain hereditary conditions in their family, can consult a heredity clinic.*

* Names and addresses of heredity clinics can be obtained from the American Eugenics Society, Inc., 230 Park Avenue, New York, N.Y. 10017.

TABLE 2–3

Perinatal mortality rates by sex and color, showing recent decreases in rates.

	Average Annual Death Rates Per 1,000 Live Births					
	Males		*Females*		*Percent Decrease*	
Period of Death	*1962–63*	*1952–53*	*1962–63*	*1952–53*	*Males*	*Females*
			White			
Perinatal Deaths*	31.9	35.4	26.0	28.9	10	10
Fetal	14.4	16.7	13.2	15.2	14	13
Early neonatal	17.5	18.7	12.8	13.7	6	7
			Nonwhite			
Perinatal Deaths*	54.0	59.3	44.5	48.0	9	7
Fetal	28.7	33.8	24.7	27.9	15	11
Early neonatal	25.3	25.5	19.8	20.1	1	1

* Fetal deaths with a period of gestation given as 20 weeks or more or not stated, and deaths occurring in the first week of infancy.

Note: Excludes New Jersey for 1962–63.

Source: Basic data from Reports of Division of Vital Statistics, National Center for Health Statistics. Reprinted by permission from *Statistical Bulletin*, Metropolitan Life Insurance Company, May 1965.

Table 2–3 shows perinatal mortality rates and recent decreases in these rates. *Perinatal* refers to the period between the twentieth week of prenatal life and the end of the first week after birth. The table shows the survival advantages of being white and female. Higher death rates for nonwhite fetuses and newborns reflect the depressed economic situation of Negroes and other colored people. The causes of deaths during the first week after birth are seen in Table 2–4.

The Importance of Good Obstetrical Care

This brief sketch of what can go wrong in pregnancy and childbirth serves to emphasize what a physician does to promote the safety and normal development of the mother and baby. He gives the mother general directions as to nutrition, rest and hygiene, carefully prescribes drugs, watches signs and symptoms which predict trouble, treats disorders before they become serious, plans and prepares for the safest kind of delivery. Education and preparation for childbirth are for the benefit of the baby, even more than for the emotional and physical comfort of the mother, since they can influence the type and amount of anesthetic needed and perhaps the quality and duration of labor [37].

TABLE 2–4

Causes of death during the first week after birth.

Cause of Death	*Death Rate Per 1,000 Live Births*							
	White				*Nonwhite*			
	Males		*Females*		*Males*		*Females*	
	1962–63	*1952–53*	*1962–63*	*1952–53*	*1962–63*	*1952–53*	*1962–63*	*1952–53*
All Causes	17.5	18.7	12.8	13.7	25.3	25.5	19.8	20.1
Congenital malformations	2.0	2.2	1.7	1.8	1.5	1.4	1.1	1.1
Circulatory system	0.9	1.0	0.6	0.6	0.7	0.7	0.5	0.5
Certain diseases of early infancy	15.0	15.8	10.7	11.4	22.5	21.5	17.6	17.0
Birth injuries	2.5	3.4	1.7	2.3	2.8	3.7	2.0	2.5
Intracranial and spinal injury	0.7	1.3	0.4	0.8	1.1	2.0	0.7	1.3
Other birth injury	1.8	2.1	1.3	1.5	1.7	1.7	1.3	1.2
Postnatal asphyxia and atelectasis	4.6	4.5	3.2	3.0	6.5	5.3	5.1	4.2
Pneumonia of newborn	0.4	0.4	0.3	0.3	1.1	0.9	0.7	0.6
Disorders arising from maternal toxemia	0.2	0.1	0.1	0.1	0.3	0.2	0.2	0.1
Erythroblastosis	0.5	0.7	0.5	0.6	0.2	0.4	0.1	0.2
Immaturity unqualified and other diseases of early infancy	6.7	6.7	4.9	5.2	11.7	11.1	9.4	9.4
All other causes	0.5	0.7	0.4	0.5	1.4	2.6	1.1	2.0

Note: Excludes New Jersey for 1962–63.

Source: Basic data from Reports of Division of Vital Statistics, National Center for Health Statistics. Reprinted by permission from *Statistical Bulletin*, Metropolitan Life Insurance Company, May 1965.

SUMMARY

Fertilization occurs in the middle of a menstrual cycle, when a spermatazoon penetrates a mature ovum. After subdividing for three or four days, the fertilized egg implants itself in the lining of the uterus. Differentiation of the organs and tissues takes place during the first two months of life, during which time the baby is called an embryo. Fluid fills the aminotic sac, which encloses and protects the baby. Recognizable as a human being, the baby is called a fetus when he reaches eight weeks of age. Further differentiation of organs and tissues takes place along the basic form which has been laid down. The organs begin to function. The fetus moves freely and performs many reflex acts. The head end is better developed than the tail end, both physically and functionally.

Pregnancy can be diagnosed through laboratory tests soon after the first missed menstrual period. The mother's awareness of pregnancy may occur even before this time, or it may be delayed until much later, depending upon the symptoms she experiences. The first trimester of pregnancy is a time of physiological reorganization which usually involves fatigue. New feelings and emotions go along with the pervasive bodily changes which affect all the systems. Adjustment to pregnancy is affected by physical and psychological preparation for it, by the natural resources of the mother and by the care and experiences she has during pregnancy. The small, nuclear family tends to place the main burden of emotional support upon the husband.

Infant and mother are affected by the nutritional state of the mother when the pregnancy is begun, as well as by the adequacy of nutrition throughout the pregnancy. Since mothers vary considerably in their needs, individual nutritional guidance is very desirable. Serious nutritional deficiencies are associated with complications of pregnancy, labor and delivery and with defective development of the baby.

Babies respond prenatally to loud sudden sounds by moving, often in sudden movements which are probably similar to the startle response of the newborn. Maternal emotional disturbance, also, is associated with high activity in the fetus. Emotional well-being of the mother probably contributes to the emotional well-being of the baby. Prenatal influence also occurs through physical, chemical and biological means. X rays, beyond a certain level, are damaging and even lethal. Many drugs, such as quinine, certain barbiturates and tranquilizers, will damage the unborn baby. Cigaret smoking is associated with premature birth. Many diseases, such as measles, are likely to damage the embryo or fetus. Incompatability between the mother's blood and the baby's blood will, under certain conditions, harm the baby. Certain risks to mother and baby are increased when the mother is in the later years of childbearing.

Birth is a physical and emotional crisis for the mother, baby and family. Labor, the work which the mother does in giving birth, consists of three stages. The first stage, the opening of the cervix, is accomplished by muscles which are not under voluntary control. The confident, secure mother can probably help the process by relaxing. The second stage, pushing the baby out, is partially involuntary and partially controllable by the mother. Education for childbirth prepares her to function here. The third stage, a brief process, is the expelling of the placenta. The duration of labor varies considerably, the most common length for a first labor being seven hours, and for subsequent labors, four hours. A Caesarian birth is safer for mother and baby than is a difficult natural delivery.

The mother's emotions and her experience of pain during labor are determined to some extent by what she has been taught to expect. Education for childbirth can be a very positive influence, "Natural childbirth" uses education, emotional preparation and support during labor.

The baby is equipped with mechanisms for adapting to the birth process. Some of his responses to this process prepare him for beginning to breath. A few babies are injured at birth and others are damaged prenatally. Premature birth is associated with neurological disorders. Hereditary defects account for some abnormalities. Most seriously malformed fetuses do not live to full term. Good obstetrical care includes prenatal supervision and education as well as skilled help to the mother and baby during labor and delivery and afterward.

REFERENCES

1. Ainsworth, M. D. Personal communication. April 1963.
2. Bayley, N. Comparisons of mental and motor test scores for ages 1–15 months by sex, birth order, race, geographic location, and education of parents. *Child Develop.*, 1965, **36,** 379–411.
3. Bibring, G. L. Some consideration of the psychological processes in pregnancy. *Psychoan. Stud. Child.*, 1959, **14,** 113–121.
4. Burke, B. S., Beal, V. A., Kirkwood, S. B., & Stuart, H. C. The influence of nutrition during pregnancy upon the condition of the infant at birth. *J. Nutrition,* 1943, **26,** 569–583.
5. Coats, B. The most glorious experience. *Reader's Digest,* May 1950.
6. Dann, M., Levine, S. Z., & New, E. V. The development of prematurely born children with birth weights or minimal postnatal weights of 1,000 grams or less. *Pediat.*, 1958, **22,** 1037–1053.
7. Davids, A., DeVault, S., & Talmadge, M. Anxiety, pregnancy, and childbirth abnormalities. *J. Consult. Psychol.*, 1961, **25,** 74–77.
8. Dean, R. F. A. The size of the baby at birth and the yield of breast milk. Studies of undernutrition, Wuppertal, 1946–1949. *Special Report Series, Medical Research Council,* 275. London: Her Majesty's Stationery Office, 1951.
9. Ebbs, J. H., Tisdall, F. F., & Scott, W. A. Influence of prenatal diet on mother and child. *J. Nutrition,* 1941, **22,** 515–526.
10. Ernhart, C. B., Graham, F. K., & Thurston, D. Relationship of neonatal apnea to development at three years. *Arch. Neurol.*, 1960, **2,** 504–510.

11. Falade, S. *Le dévéloppement psychomotor du jeune Africain originaire du Sénégal au cours de sa primière année.* Paris: Foulon, 1955. Cited in Geber [13].
12. Frank, L. K. Tactile communication. *Genet. Psychol. Mono.,* 1957, **56,** 209–225.
13. Geber, M. The psychomotor development of African children in the first year, and the influence of maternal behavior. *J. Soc. Psychol.,* 1958, **47,** 185–195.
14. Gesell, A. *The embryology of behavior.* New York: Harper, 1945.
15. Graham, F. K., Mantarazzo, R. G., & Caldwell, B. M. Behavioral differences between normal and traumatized newborns. *Psychol. Mono.,* 1956, **70,** 20 & 21, Numbers 427 & 428.
16. Guttmacher, A. F. *Pregnancy and birth.* New York: Viking, 1957.
17. Hamilton, E. Emotional aspects of pregnancy: an intensive study of fourteen normal primiparae. Unpublished doctoral dissertation. New York: Teachers College, Columbia Univer., 1955.
18. Hepner, R. Maternal nutrition and the fetus. *J. Am. Med. Assoc.,* 1958, **168,** 1774–1777.
19. Kawi, A. A., & Pasamanick, B. Prenatal and paranatal factors in the development of childhood reading disorders. *Mono. Soc. Res. Child Devel.,* 1959, **24:**4.
20. Knobloch, H., Rider, R., Harper, P., & Pasamanick, B. The neuropsychiatric sequelae of prematurity: a longitudinal study. *J. Am. Med. Assoc.,* 1956, **161,** 581–585.
21. McGanity, W. J., *et al.* The Vanderbilt cooperative study of maternal and infant nutrition: VI. Relationship of obstetric performance to nutrition. *Am. J. Obst. Gynec.,* 1954, **67,** 501–527.
22. Metropolitan Life Insurance Company. Perinatal mortality decreasing. *Stat. Bull.,* 1965, **46,** 5–8.
23. Montagu, M. F. A. *Prenatal influences.* Springfield, Ill.: Charles C Thomas, 1962.
24. Pasamanick, B., & Knobloch, H. Epidemiologic studies on the complications of pregnancy and the birth process. In G. Caplan (Ed.), *Prevention of mental disorders in children.* New York: Basic Books, 1961, pp. 74–79.
25. Plummer, G. Anomalies occurring in children exposed in utero to the atomic bomb in Hiroshima. *Pediat.,* 1952, **10,** 687–693.
26. Poffenberger, S., Poffenberger, T., & Landis, J. T. Intent toward conception and the pregnancy experience. *Am. Soc. Rev.,* 1952, **17,** 616–620.
27. Salk, L. Mother's heartbeat as an imprinting stimulus. *Trans. N.Y. Acad. Sci.,* Ser. II, 1962, **24,** 753–763.
28. Shirley, M. A behavior syndrome characterizing prematurely born children. *Child Devel.,* 1938, **10,** 115–128.
29. Simpson, W. J. A preliminary report on cigarette smoking and incidence of prematurity. *Am. J. Obstet. Gynecol.,* 1957, **73,** 805–815.
30. Smith, C. A. Effects of maternal undernutrition upon the newborn infant in Holland. *J. Pediat.,* 1947, **30,** 229–243.
31. Sontag, L. W. Significance of fetal environmental differences. *Am. J. Obstet. Gynecol.,* 1941, **54,** 994–1003.

32. Sontag, L. W., & Richards, T. W. Studies in fetal behavior: I. Fetal heart rate as a behavior indicator. *Mono. Soc. Res. Child Devel.,* 1938, **3**:4.
33. Spelt, D. K. The conditioning of the human fetus in utero. *J. Exptl. Psychol.,* 1948, **38,** 338–346.
34. Stearns, G. Human requirements of calcium, phosphorus and magnesium. In *Handbook of nutrition: a symposium.* Philadelphia: Blakiston, 1951.
35. Stearns, G. Nutritional state of the mother prior to conception. *J. Am. Med. Assoc.,* 1958, **168,** 1655–1659.
36. Tanner, J. M., & Inhelder, B. *Discussions on child development,* Vol. 3. New York: International Universities, 1958.
37. Thomas, H., & Roth, L. G. *Understanding natural childbirth.* New York: McGraw-Hill, 1950.
38. Toverud, K. U., Stearns, G., & Hoobler, I. M. *Maternal nutrition and child health: an interpretive review.* Washington, D.C.: National Academy of Science, National Research Council, 1950.
39. Werboff, J. Prenatal factors determining later behavior. In *The teaching of infant development.* Detroit: Merrill-Palmer Institute, 1962.
40. Werboff, J., Broeder, J. D., Havlena, J., & Sikov, M. R. Effects of prenatal X-ray irradiation on audiogenic seizures in the rat. *Exptl. Neurol.,* 1961, **4,** 189–196.
41. Werboff, J., Goodman, I., Havlena, J., & Sikov, M.R. Effects of prenatal X-irradiation on motor performance in the rat. *Am. J. Physiol.,* 1961, **201,** 703–706.
42. Wishik, S. M. Speech at *Advances in Nutrition* symposium. Univer. of Pittsburgh, 1958.
43. Yamazaki, J. N., *et al.* Outcome of pregnancy in women exposed to the atomic bomb in Nagasaki. *Am. J. Dis. Child.,* 1954, **87,** 448–463.

The Newborn

CHAPTER 3

Of all species of infants, the human has farthest to go from birth to adulthood. Born in a very immature condition, he eventually becomes the most complex of creatures. In fact, if his behavior patterns were more biologically preset and determined that they are, he would not have as great possibilities for development as he does have. His brain has almost unlimited potentialities for learning and creating.

Human relationships, as well as human development, owe their variety and complexity partly to the immaturity of the human infant. If children could take off on their own like mice and lions, there would be no brothers and sisters to fight and love, no grandparents, aunts, uncles, cousins, no family at all. This immaturity was and is a necessary condition for humanity. Sometimes it is thought of as a disadvantage for the infant to be able to do so little for himself at birth. Actually the infant can do everything he needs to do in order to survive and grow. Although immature, he is competent to handle the situation in which he first finds himself, provided his mother cooperates with him.

The neonatal period is used here to mean approximately the first month of extrauterine life. It has been defined in various terms, sometimes as the period from birth until the umbilicus is healed. Although the neonatal period is short in time, it is significant because it is the beginning of life as a separate organism. Great are the changes and adaptations which take place in this brief interval. The neonate has been studied more intensively than older infants, not only because the period is important, but also because subjects are more available. Many pieces of research are oriented around the lying-in period simply because it is easy to study the babies then and difficult to see them later [14].

EQUIPMENT AND FUNCTIONING

Appearance

Neonates look strange to most people because new infants are rarely seen. Since they change quickly in looks, the normal appearance at two or three months is the one which comes to mind when most individuals think of a young baby.

The average newborn baby has a reddish, wrinkled skin which soon approximates the color that the skin will be for the rest of life. The wrinkles smooth out toward the end of the first month, as more and more fat is laid down beneath the skin. Immediately after birth the waxy vernix caseosa covers the skin for about eight hours. The head is often elongated and bumpy, perhaps with one particularly large bump, the result of molding during birth. The head gradually resumes its normal shape, with possibly the trace of a bump or two remaining. It is quite easy to see some of the six fontanelles, the soft spots in the brain case where membranes connect the bony parts of the skull. The nose, formed of cartilage, is often pushed out of shape temporarily by the birth process.

The eyes, smoky blue for the first month or two, change gradually to their permanent color. They are large in proportion to the rest of the face, since the cranial part of the head is much more fully developed than the rest of the head. Here is an illustration of the principle of developmental direction: *development proceeds from anterior to posterior*.

Hair may be abundant or scanty, perhaps covering the head and scattered around the body, especially on the back. The body hair disappears and often the scalp hair, too. Very often the permanent head hair is a different color from that at birth.

Size and Proportions

The average birth weight for American babies is 7½ pounds, with the average for boys about three ounces more than that for girls. Average length is 20 inches, with boys a fraction of an inch longer than girls. The size of babies varies with many factors, including race, socioeconomic status, age of the mother and birth order.

Body proportions, compared with those at later ages, show a large head, small trunk and very short, undeveloped legs. The legs are bowed and drawn up, making them look even smaller than if they were stretched out .

*Physiological Functioning**

The change from being a water-born parasite to being an air-born independent individual is a complex one, although one which the newborn is ready to make. An example of his fitness to adapt is that he can stand degrees of

* This account follows Breckenridge and Murphy [10].

oxygen deprivation which an adult could not tolerate. The crucial change is in respiration; and this is begun as he emerges. It may take a day or two for the amniotic fluid and mucus to drain completely from the baby's breathing apparatus. Breathing is irregular, rapid and shallow, involving the abdomen more than the chest. The neonate is often a noisy breather, wheezing and snuffling in a fashion which can be alarming to first-time parents.

Breathing reflexes are coordinated with and activated by the oxygen-carbon dioxide balance. The amount of air a baby breathes is regulated thus. Coughing, sneezing and yawning are all reflexes with important survival value. Coughing and sneezing clear the air passages and lungs. Yawning gives a quick gulp of air when needed suddenly. The essential change in circulation follows immediately the change in respiration. Only a small quantity of blood goes to the lungs before birth, since it flows to the placenta to exchange products. After birth, blood is forced into the lungs and the circulation to the placenta cut off by the closing of the opening which leads from the fetal heart to the placenta. Another important change in the circulatory-respiratory combination is that the lungs expand gradually in the first two weeks. During that time, the blood includes 1 to 2 million more blood cells than it does immediately after the lungs are fully expanded.

The newborn changes from taking nutrients in through the placenta to taking food into the mouth and stomach. Hunger contractions and rooting, sucking and swallowing mechanisms, are present at birth. The small lower jaw and the fat pads in the cheeks are equipment for sucking. The mother's breasts supply first colostrum, a highly specialized food adapted to the newborn's needs, not available (as yet) from bottles. The breasts supply milk from the second or third day, regulating its composition and quantity to the maturity of the baby. Thus a delicately balanced nutritive relationship continues to exist between the mother and baby after birth.

The first material evacuated from the colon is meconium, the material accumulated before birth from cellular breakdown, intestinal secretions, bile, mucus and material swallowed with the amniotic fluid. After three days, the stools assume a character which depends on the type of food, those of breast-fed babies differing noticeably from those of bottle-fed babies in appearance and exceeding them in number. The kidneys excrete small quantities of urine before birth. Frequency of urination increases after the second day to an average of around 20 times a day, with a wide range of individual differences.

The newborn has a higher metabolic rate than the adult, but lower than the preschool child's. Immediately after birth, the temperature drops two to five degrees and then rises to 98 to 99 degrees after about eight hours. Since mechanisms for maintaining a stable body temperature are immature, the neonate's temperature is unstable. Premature babies' temperatures are even more unstable than those of full-term infants. Heat loss is great through the baby's comparatively large surface, which is poorly insulated because skin and fat layers are thin. In hot climates or when wearing too-warm clothing, he suffers from the heat because he can neither sweat nor shiver in mature ways.

The newborn shows little diurnal change in temperature [41]. Thus the newborn gets along best in a controlled temperature, with clothing and bedding carefully regulated to maintain a steady temperature.

Although all the nerve cells of the brain are present before birth, many are not mature enough to function in the newborn. Careful examination of the cells [44, pp. 71–96] suggests that no cortical function is possible at birth, although the spinal cord and the brain below the level of the cortex have mature cells. During the first month, many cells in the motor cortex mature, especially those in the areas controlling the upper trunk, back and upper arm. By three months the level of maturity suggests that simple vision and hearing occur on a cortical level, but that interpretation cannot take place. The behavior patterns of the newborn, listed below, are witness to the capacities and scope of the neural areas below the cortex.

Inventory of Behavior Patterns

Motor behavior, crying, sleeping and excreting can be observed, whereas sensory perception has to be inferred from other behavior. A list of types of neonatal motor behavior follows [17].

EYES

1. Opens and closes lids both spontaneously and in response to stimuli.
2. Pupils widen and narrow in response to light. Narrow upon going to sleep. Widen upon waking. Widen with stimulation.
3. Following moving stimulus. Also jerky movements.
4. Oscillatory movement.
5. Coordinate, compensatory movements when head is moved quickly.
6. Coordinated movements.
7. Convergence.
8. Eye position in sleep frequently upward and divergent, as in adults.
9. Tear secretion (unusual).

FACE AND MOUTH

1. Opens and closes mouth.
2. Lips: licks, compresses, purses in response to touch.
3. Sucks.
4. Smiles.
5. Pushes material from mouth.
6. Yawns.
7. Grimaces, twisting mouth, wrinkling forehead.
8. Retracts lips, opens mouth to touch. Turns lower lip.

THROAT

1. Cries. Sometimes sobs.
2. Swallows, gags to noxious stimuli or touch at back of throat.
3. Vomits.
4. Hiccoughs.
5. Coughs, sneezes.
6. Coos. Holds breath.

HEAD

1. Moves upward and backward when prone, especially to stimuli.
2. Turns face to side in response to touch. Turns from side to side when prone or when hungry or crying.
3. Head shudders to bitter stimuli.
4. Moves arms at random. Arms slash when crying.

TRUNK

1. Arches back.
2. Twists, squirms. When head rotates, shoulders and pelvis turn in same direction.
3. Abdominal reflex in response to needle prick as stimulus.

REPRODUCTIVE ORGANS

1. Cremasteric reflex (testes raised when inner thigh stroked).
2. Penis erects.

FOOT AND LEG

1. Knee jerk reflex.
2. Achilles tendon reflex.
3. Leg flexes. Plantar flexion accompanies leg flexion (reverse of adult response).
4. Leg extends in response to gentle push. May support some of weight on first day.
5. Protective reflex (if one foot or leg is stimulated, the other pushes against source of stimulation).
6. Kicking, usually during crying.
7. Stepping movements, when held upright with feet against a surface.
8. Toe usually extends when sole of foot is stroked.

COORDINATE RESPONSES

1. Resting and sleeping position: legs flexed, fists closed, upper arms extended.
2. Back arches from head to heels often during crying or when held upside down.
3. Backbone reflex (the side that is stroked or tickled bends in concave direction).
4. Tonic neck reflex or "fencing position" (head turned to the side, facing an extended arm, the other arm bent up near the head).
5. Springing position (when held upright and forward, arms extend forward and legs are brought up).
6. Stretches, shivers, trembles.
7. Startle response (Moro reflex).
8. Crying and mass or general movements.
9. Creeping movements when prone.
10. When held upright and rotated around vertical axis, arms and legs are extended in the direction of the rotation.
11. Body jerks to loud noises.*

* Reprinted by permission from W. Dennis, "A Description and Classification of the Responses of the Newborn Infant," *Psychological Bulletin,* 1932, **31,** 5–22.

Display Behavior

Extensive as this inventory of responses is, it gives no picture of the baby as an interacting individual. A person experiencing a real infant will, however, have interpretations of and reactions to his behavior. For example, when the baby yawns, the other person is likely to have the feelings that go with yawning, sleepiness, and perhaps yawning in response. Lorenz [29, pp. 76–79], the ethologist, discusses the language of animals as something shared by man but minimized and degenerated as word language developed. Animals display behavior unintentionally which transmits meaning to members of the same species. For example, when a jackdaw flies up into the air, the others in the flock know whether he is going to light on a nearby branch or take off on a long flight. They pay no attention to the former, but in the latter case, they join him promptly. The giving and receiving of sign stimuli by human beings is at present receiving the attention of psychologists. Here we can only point to the existence of such phenomena and speculate that they may be of greatest importance in infancy, when people are in a prelinguistic stage. We wonder about individual differences, too. Is Baby *X* more gifted in display behavior than Baby *Y?* Is Mother *X* the same as Mother *Y* in her perception of display behavior? And what about the display behavior of mothers and the sensitivity of infants to it?

Patterns of Coping with the World

There is much that the infant can do to adapt himself to the world and to adapt it to him, even though his nervous system is too immature to use the higher brain centers in solving problems. Using the sensorimotor schemas that he has, he begins to accommodate to extrauterine life and to assimilate changes into his repertory of behavior. He moves through states of equilibrium and disequilibrium, using his repertory of behavior to create new states of equilibrium. Crying and food-seeking behavior are his main methods of effecting direct changes in his environment. Through these two vigorous activities, he immediately enters into a relationship with his mother or caretaker which is idealized by the term *mutual regulation,* a dynamic equilibrium between two people.

Crying usually occurs in response to stomach contractions, cold, loud noises and other intense stimuli. Many, probably most, adults interpret crying as an indication that the baby needs something done for him. In the 1930's, however, many people were convinced that crying did not have such a simple meaning, after all. For a decade or so, crying between four-hour feeding periods, when stimuli from cold (wet diapers) and pain (open pins) could not be inferred, was interpreted as useful exercising of the lungs or a deplorable attempt to control the adult. The results were some stern, mechanical methods of infant care. Aldrich and his associates [2, 3, 4, 5], studying the crying of newborn babies, found that increased and improved nursing care reduced the incidence and duration of crying. It took the combined and concentrated efforts of many professionals to make a cultural change in the interpretation of infant crying, especially in regard to "spoiling" or getting the upper hand with adults. The Cornelian Corner [31], an association of pediatricians, psychiatrists, nurses, obstetricians, and others, was a prime force in affecting this cultural change. The famous Dr. Spock [42] was another. *Parents' Magazine* printed articles with titles such as "Spoil That Baby." The American culture became reoriented to accept crying as a mode of communication.

Crying is generally recognized as an indication that the infant is seeking a change in the condition of his environment. As crying differentiates into various kinds of sounds during the early weeks, the parents or caretakers come to attribute different meanings to the sounds, such as this means "pain," that means "hunger," and yet another cry means "fatigue."

Tracking, seeking and *sucking* are part of the repertory of the newborn. This behavior is sometimes called the "rooting reflex"; when the cheek is touched, the infant moves his head toward the source of the touch, his mouth open. The newborn is likely to show the rooting reflex after several touches on his cheek rather than after the first stimulus [8]. When touched above the lip, the baby opens his mouth wide and moves his head from side to side. When touched on the lip, he purses his lips or pouts [36, 37]. The first two movements are obviously useful for finding the nipple. The third may cause erection of the nipple, making it easier to grasp and suck. (It is intriguing to speculate on the lip-pursing reflex as the progenitor of kissing).

The sucking reflex occurs in response to anything in the mouth and, when the infant is very hungry, to stimuli to other parts of the body. Well-coordinated sucking most likely depends on a pattern of stimuli delivered to the infant's mouth. Although ordinarily the breast provides these stimuli, there are breasts which fail to supply the necessary stimuli due to some of the tissues not being sufficiently protractile [22].* In such a case, the baby is apathetic about sucking. If offered a bottle (which does go farther back in his mouth, thus stimulating the sucking reflex), he is likely to take it more enthusiastically than he does the breast. Infants vary in the strength of their sucking movements and in how well they coordinate sucking, breathing and swallowing. While the shape of the breast has something to do with this variation, there are probably other reasons, too. Strength of sucking varies during a feeding period and changes from one period to another, probably with intensity of hunger. The breast adapts its milk production to the length and strength of sucking on it.

Thus does the infant take an active role in finding and securing food, first by crying, then by turning toward the source of tactile stimulation, preparing the nipple to give milk and then actively withdrawing the milk from the breast, probably stimulating the breast to give more or less. The roles of the infant

* This condition can be noticed during pregnancy. It is usually possible to correct it then.

and mother are completely complementary, requiring the meshing of two people's activity. The first few days of life are often crucial in establishing successful breast feeding. In addition to failures resulting from inadequate breasts are those which arise because of the baby's having trouble breathing. Sometimes it happens that his upper lip gets pushed over his nostrils, due to the way in which he is placed at the breast. Then he has to fight for air, a frightening experience to him. After only one or two such experiences, he may reject the breast and yet eagerly accept the bottle [22].

Defense mechanisms are not all so clearly adapted to the world as are crying, feeding and breathing. Some authors, such as Aldrich [1], muse upon the value of these mechanisms in the history of the species. The baby withdraws from painful stimuli, blinks to a bright light, shivers when cold, resists restraint. The Moro or startle reflex, a response to a sudden loud noise or sudden loss of equilibrium, consists of stiffening the body, throwing the arms up and out then forward and toward each other, plus crying. The Darwinian reflex is a strong grasp upon anything placed against the palm of the hand. These two reflexes are called "defense mechanisms" because they might be, or might have been historically, useful for warding off threats and for clinging to a protector. Some of the defensive reflexes are pictured in Figure 3–1.

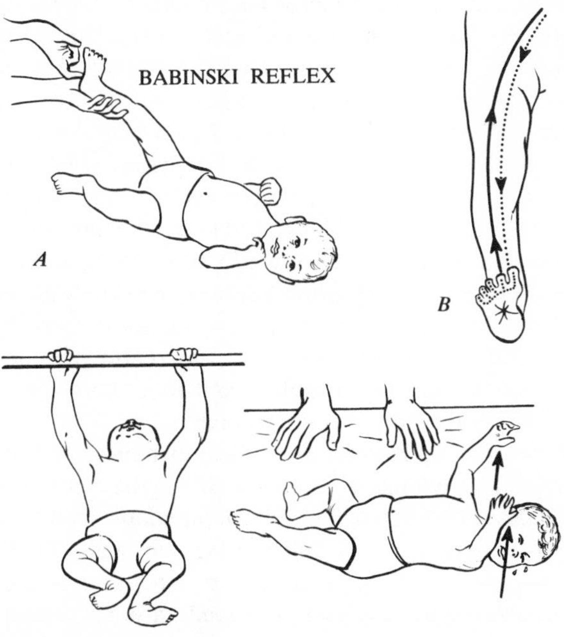

Figure 3–1. Some of the reflex behavior of the newborn, known as defense mechanisms. (Reproduced by permission from Elizabeth Lee Vincent and Phyllis C. Martin, *Human Psychological Development.* Copyright © 1961 The Ronald Press Company.)

Lois Murphy has studied many children longitudinally (over a period of time). Careful observation has led her to consider control of stimulation a defensive coping device [32, pp. 300–301]. Within the first month, the baby selects what he is going to look at and how long he will regard it [19]. Perhaps he can do the same with other senses, such as controlling the amount of stimulation he gets from his own bodily movement. Murphy also suggests that the child's basic coping orientation takes place very early in life, most likely beginning with early experiences of success or failure in obtaining food and comfort.

Relating to the World Through Perception

Although physiological functions occupy most of the newborn's energy, and his first active approach to the world is a foray in search of food, some of his activity is that of taking in sensory data and processing it. The mysterious question "What is the world like to a baby?" is just as intriguing today as it was to the experimental child psychologists of the twenties and thirties. Although there is still widespread investigation of all the sensory processes, the role of the skin senses is of special significance.

TACTILE SENSES. Skin and vestibular (inner ear) senses are highly developed before birth, having functioned prenatally longer than the other senses. Sensations from lips, mouth and other orifices are included in tactile sensations. The skin, being the locus where the individual is in physical contact with his environment, is the place where much interaction occurs. To name the sensations heat, cold, pressure and pain tells a minimum about tactile experience. Animal experts and clinical experience with infants have led to the conclusion that tactile stimulation is essential for normal development [15, 16]. Patting, caressing, cuddling, carrying, rocking, changing position, washing, drying—all these activities seem to be soothing and to promote well-being in babies. There is a connection between the skin and sympathetic nervous system [20]. Animal experiments have led to an hypothesis that early perceptual stimulation of mammals affects the central nervous system, producing animals which learn better, utilize their food more efficiently and show less reaction to stress than do average animals.

Frank [20], an inspired theorist in the field of human developments, points out that the regular, rhythmic stimulation which the fetus receives from his mother's heartbeat is translated through the amniotic fluid to all of his skin. After birth, the baby lying in a crib receives no such stimulation, but the baby carried by a person does, especially so if he is in skin-to-skin contact. Mead [30] and others [16, 21] have also made a point of the importance of skin contacts.

Frank goes on to explain how tactile experience is the basis for getting meaning from other sensory experience, for personality development and for interpersonal relationships. Sounds and sights derive their meaning initially from experiences of touch. The concept of his own body, where it stops and where the rest of the world begins, mother and other people, the objects which make up the rest of the world, are all discovered and understood first through tactile senses with some help from vestibular senses.

Touching another person involves two people. It is the simplest and most fundamental kind of relationship. Touching is communication, since two people perceive each other. The feeding behavior described above is to the infant a primary-touch relationship. The communication may well involve emotion, since along with each person's perception may go a feeling tone. By simply being the other person in a touch relationship, the baby profoundly affects his world in the form of his mother and others who care for him. The tender feelings which well up from holding a baby are the energizers of much mature adult work and development.

HEARING. Although it has long been known that the fetus, and of course the neonate, can hear, it used to be thought that the infant's sensory world was a "buzzing, blooming confusion." Unless he showed a startle reaction, which he did to loud, sudden sounds, a baby gave no indication that one sound or another made any difference to him. Since a baby can neither understand language nor speak, it is difficult for adults to conceive of sounds which could be meaningful to an infant, and of ways in which infants' responses to sound could be observed and measured. Research is showing, however, that the neonate can make fine discriminations and that certain sounds are very meaningful in his existence.

The human heartbeat as a significant sound has been studied by Salk [39] by playing a tape recording in a hospital nursery. One hundred and twelve newborn babies were in the group exposed continuously to a heartbeat recording and 102 in a control group. Although there was no significant difference in food intake between the two groups during the first four days of life, they differed significantly in weight gain. The experimental group averaged a gain of 40 gm and the control group lost an average of 20 gm. Table 3–1 shows both groups' weight change in terms of birth weight. They differed in amount of crying too. During the heartbeat sounds, one or more of the nine babies in the nursery cried 38.4 percent of the time, whereas the crying lasted 59.8 percent of the time in the control situation. The author concluded that the heartbeat sound was comforting (anxiety-reducing). Further experimentation showed that it was the normal heartbeat sound which soothed the infant, not just any sort of heartbeat. The newborns were exposed to a galloping heartbeat and to one of 128 beats per minute, instead of the normal 72. Both recordings were quickly followed by increased crying and restlessness. Then something went wrong with the normal recording and a hissing sound was emitted along with the 72 beats per minute. The experimenter did not take the next logical step of altering the 72 beats only slightly, because he feared that it might harm the babies.

Two studies show that newborn infants can make fine distinctions in pitch. In a Russian experiment [9] on learning, a baby's sucking movements were charted along with sound stimuli on a revolving drum. When a sound occurred, the sucking movements stopped, but when the sound was repeated, the baby gradually shortened the time during which he made no sucking movements. After enough repetitions of sound of one pitch he continued to suck when it was played. When a sound of different frequency was played, the baby stopped sucking again, thus showing that he could discriminate it from the first sound. In an essentially similar experiment [11], a tone was sounded repeatedly until the infant stopped giving any motor response. Then a note of different pitch was sounded. Many babies gave motor responses and increased their heart rates.

VISION. That the newborn baby can see is shown by a great variety of research [35]. Intense and sudden stimulation elicit responses in eyelids, neck, circulation, respiration, and the whole body, as in the startle reflex. Some eye fixation occurs on the first day. Within the first few days head turning follows a visual stimulus. The infant probably can see differences between colors.

TABLE 3–1

Weight changes in newborn babies who have been exposed to heartbeat sounds.

Group	Birthweight (gm.)	Weight			
		Gained		No Change or Lost	
		N	%	N	%
Experimental (exposed to heartbeat sound)	2510–3000	27	72.9	10	27.1
	3010–3500	32	71.1	13	28.9
	3510 and over	12	60.0	8	40.0
	Total	71	69.6	31	30.4
Control (*not* exposed to heart-beat sound)	2510–3000	11	37.9	18	62.1
	3010–3500	19	40.4	28	59.6
	3510 and over	7	19.4	29	80.6
	Total	37	33.0	75	67.0

Source: Reprinted by permission from L. Salk, "Mother's Heartbeat as an Imprinting Stimulus," *Transactions of the New York Academy of Sciences*, Ser. II, 1962, **24**, 753–763.

Using an apparatus which makes it possible to measure how long an infant looks at either of two visual stimuli, Fantz [19] has shown that infants under one month of age can perceive stripes one eighth inch wide at a distance of ten inches, a visual angle of slightly less than one degree. The infants looked at complex patterns, such as a checkerboard and bullseye more than they looked at simple patterns, such as a square and circle. Of all patterns shown, a human face elicited more interest (that is, time spent) than any, especially in the youngest babies. When given a choice between a flat representation of a face and a spherical one, the infants looked longer at the latter. Thus it has been demonstrated that neonates see more than they have been given credit for and that not only do they have better visual acuity than people used to think, but they are selective as to what they regard. It is reasonable to conclude that the newborn infant can pick out from the world a human face, the object which has more significance for his survival and well-being than anything else.

COORDINATION OF VISION AND HEARING. Although coordination of vision and hearing has not been thought to be part of the neonate's repertory, recent studies show that newborn babies have some of this ability. During her first ten minutes after birth, one baby turned her eyes in the direction of a sound. A toy cricket clicking on one side or the other elicited eye movements half of the time. Most of the eye movements were in the direction of the click [45]. A controlled study done on 64 normal newborn infants confirmed the conclusion that neonates can discriminate location of sound source [26]. Vision and hearing become better coordinated as the child learns through experience.

TASTE. Taste is functional in the fetus as well as the newborn, although it seems to develop with age. Infants accept sweet solutions and tend to reject those that are salty, bitter or sour.

SMELL. Smell has been investigated, using strong odors and evoking avoidance reactions in infants. During the first few days of life, the infant quickly becomes more sensitive to chemical nasal stimuli [28]. Although it is worth knowing that the sense receptors do function at birth, it would be important to discover what role, if any, smell plays in the life processes of the infant, such as the significance of odors from his mother and other people who care for him. Unfortunately, relevant research has not been done. However, it is known that man has a less developed sense of smell than have most other animals. He therefore receives less information about the environment through this sense modality than he does through sight and hearing, for instance. Because of the technical difficulties of investigating the sense of smell, there is less knowledge about it than about the other senses. It may be that perceptions of odors are important to human development in ways that have not been investigated and are not understood.

PAIN. Adults would like to know whether a newborn baby feels pain, and if so, what causes pain and how severe it is. Since crying and withdrawal movements are the only indications of pain an infant can give, these reactions have been studied in connection with certain kinds of stimulation. It has long been known that neonates do not cry much when circumcized, especially if given something sweet to suck during the operation. Gastrointestinal upsets, however, result in a great deal of crying. The baby seems to be more sensitive to some kinds of threats than to others and to be able to escape or avoid some more than others [32]. Early research on pain in young infants used pin pricks as stimuli, noting how many were necessary before the baby made some withdrawal response [35]. The more modern method is to use mild electric shock up to a level where a withdrawal action is observed. The stimulus can thus be measured exactly. The experiments show that pain sensitivity increases

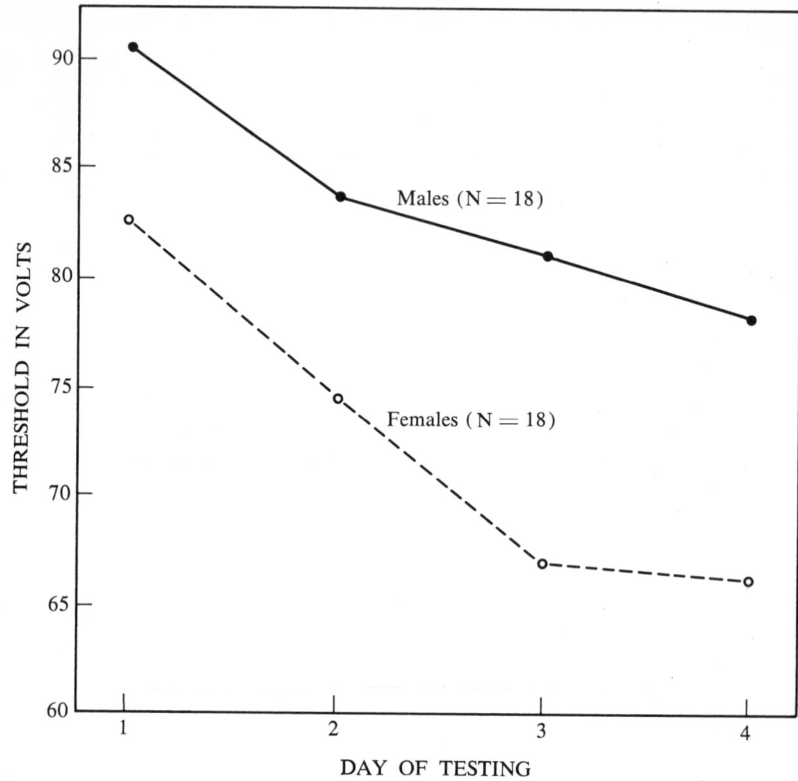

Figure 3–2. Responses to electrical stimulation during the first four days of life, showing decrease in volts required to elicit response. (Reproduced by permission from L. P. Lipsitt and N. Levy, "Electro-tactual threshold in the neonate," *Child Development,* 1959, **30.** Copyright © 1959, The Society for Research in Child Development, Inc.)

steadily during the first few days of life. Figure 3–2 shows the decrease in volts required to elicit a reaction of the toe during the first four days. A sex difference was found, as well as an age difference, with girls showing more sensitivity than boys, a result in keeping with the generally greater maturity of girls at birth [27].

Stable Individual Differences in Neonatal Behavior

There are certain obvious differences in babies which are nonetheless important, such as sex, weight, length, color and hair. Common observation and research [13, 24, 40] show that babies differ in amount of spontaneous activity. In other words, some babies are very quiet, some very active, and the rest are in between. The question of basic constitutional differences is of theoretical and practical importance, because it is really the problem of what heredity contributes, what environment gives and how the two interact. How much is given at birth? How fixed is it? Investigations on differences in physiological functioning and behavior, and their constancy, are beginning to fill in the blanks opposite these questions.

The amount of hand–mouth contacting is a measure that shows stable differences from one newborn to another [25]. Differences have been found in heart rate, level of arousal, depth of sleep, tactile sensitivity and strength, oral integration (largely concerned with sucking and rooting) and similarity to fetal position [6, 27, 38]. When 30 neonates were tested systematically with four different stimuli, and rated as to reactions, consistent individual differences were found [7]. A soft tone, a loud tone, a cold disk and a pacifier were used to stimulate the infants. Some responded vigorously to all situations, some moderately and others mildly. Not only were the babies different from each other in the vigor of their responses, but they tended to stay in the same position, relative to one another, from the second day of life to the fifth. Another area in which stable individual differences have been observed is in the pattern of states shown by newborns during the lying-in period [12]. *State* refers to levels of consciousness, tension or arousal, including being awake, asleep, drowsy or alert. The infants studied showed consistency in the patterns of states which they maintained. People who have seen many new babies will tell you that some are easily startled while others are more placid. This common observation has been substantiated on 50 babies in the first week of life [11]. Some showed little and some showed much response to a stimulus of a given tone and intensity. With the same stimulus repeated, some infants adapted quickly, showing no response after the first few stimuli; others continued to respond with the same intensity.

RELATIONSHIPS AND EXPERIENCES

The meaning of his relationships and the success of his experiences depend upon *what the infant is seeking*. Much of his behavior can be explained in terms of *homeostasis,* maintaining a state of physiological equilibrium in the organism. Tension is reduced and balance restored by food seeking, sucking, and swallowing, through breathing, moving and having baths and dry diapers. If imprinting does occur in human beings, as for instance, Salk [39] thinks it does with heartbeat sounds, then receiving imprinted stimuli becomes another tension reducer. To achieve and maintain a state of equilibrium also requires a certain level of sensory stimulation—enough but not too much of the various kinds. Equilibrium is continually being disturbed and restored in a new state. The general state of equilibrium is made up of a number of substates. In its striving for equilibrium, the organism (or baby or adult) gives preference to some substates over others. There is probably a central mechanism which mediates between the various states, increasing and directing the baby's activity towards restoring and creating equilibrium [43]. For example, a certain degree of fatigue takes precedence over a certain degree of hunger and over a certain level of desire for sensory stimulation. As states of equilibrium are continually disturbed and created, changes occur in the organism's structure and behavior. These changes are growth and development.

Personality development is going on while the newborn is reducing his tensions and maintaining homeostasis. The sense of trust is the crucial aspect of personality growth at this time and for at least the first year of life. Erikson [18, p. 249] writes of the feeling of goodness which comes when the baby is helped to achieve homeostasis. The world must seem like a good place to be and the people in it trustworthy when he is fed before he is overwhelmed by hunger, when he is kept at a comfortable temperature and when he receives a satisfactory amount of sensory stimulation. As he is allowed and assisted to use his various competencies in different situations, his feeling of trust increases, and his personality develops in a healthy direction. In the following section, some of his relationships and experiences are examined in the light of personality development.

Feeding

If rooting, pursing the lips, grasping, sucking and swallowing result in ingesting food, then the disequilibrium of hunger is reduced. Such restoring of equilibrium occurs promptly in most non-Western societies. The practice in most American hospitals is to feed babies on a four-hour schedule, either taking them to their mothers to be breast-fed or given bottles or feeding them by bottle in the nursery. The four-hour interval was established long ago from observations that babies' stomachs tended to empty in four hours and that, therefore, many babies were ready for food in approximately four-hour intervals. The custom continues because hospitals run on schedules, and even for those who doubt the value of the four-hour feeding plan, there is the rationalization that the lying-in period is so short that it does not matter. If homeostasis were the only goal involved, then it really would not matter. The fact that babies live and gain weight would be justification enough. In actual practice, the baby's early experiences even in the first few days, may determine whether he is fed by breast or bottle [22].

The four-hour schedule takes no account of the baby's competency in seeking and securing food. Nor is it concerned with his states of hunger and arousal. He may be sleeping when mealtime comes; whereupon he is wakened and offered food. Or he may have cried, rooted and sucked for an hour beforehand. In neither situation does he gain confidence in his ability to get food, nor in the world as a place where food is available for the seeking. The rooming-in plan which operates in some hospitals takes account of this aspect of feeding. Developed along with natural childbirth, *rooming-in* is an arrangement whereby the mother gets well acquainted with her baby in the hospital. Although there are variations in the procedures, the essentials are thus. The baby stays in the room with his mother for a large portion of the time, in a bassinette beside her bed, or in an arrangement which can be swung over her bed. She can pick him up and care for him if she wishes. A nurse, or nurse's helper, shows her the techniques of baby care and does it for her if she does not feel like doing it herself. When the mother wants to sleep or rest, the baby is taken into another room and cared for by the nurse. The mother is able to get to know her infant as an individual, to begin interacting with him, to find the ways of caring for him which bring most satisfactory results and to feed him at the times which seem most appropriate. A good beginning with breast feeding can make all the difference between success and failure. In the rooming-in arrangement, the mother is likely to receive interested, informed instruction from a nurse who is skilled at helping newborn babies and their mothers to cooperate in breast feeding. With such assistance, the baby is likely to grasp the nipple in such a way that it will stimulate an adequate sucking reflex and he will avoid the pitfall of getting his nose blocked by his lip. The mother has an excellent chance to feel and be successful from the beginning.

If rooting, pursing the lips and grasping results in breast feeding, the chain of results differs from what happens when the result is bottle feeding. Colostrum is different from milk and human milk is different from cows'. Breckenridge and Murphy [10, pp. 210–217] give an excellent account of lactation and the nutritional differences between cow's milk and human milk. The tactile sensations from breast and bottle are different, the breast being warm, more flexible and responsive to a sucking movement which differs from the sucking required by a bottle. Taste is different, too, not only because of the differences in human and cow's milk, but because the breast gives a low concentration of fats at first and a larger amount of cream at the end. Tactile and olfactory sensations from the mother's body are likely to be more intense in breast feeding because the baby is closer to her skin.

Of greatest importance in the feeding situation (granted that food is obtained) is the fact that it is a relationship between two people. When working in harmony, the baby's mouth and the mother's breast together perform an act. Two people contact each other and cooperate. The feelings that accompany the act promote personality development in both. The baby's feelings of trust and confidence are enhanced by successful use of all his equipment for getting food. The accompanying sensory stimulation, especially tactile, not only reduces tension but also promotes growth and mental organization. The mother's parental sense is enhanced and she grows at the level appropriate for her, if all goes well. (The parental sense or sense of generativity is one of the adult stages of personality development, during which the individual becomes involved in promoting the well-being of the next generation.)

Inability and/or unwillingness to breast-feed is widespread in Western culture. In substituting bottles for breasts, it is important to imitate the psychological situation as well as the nutritional. In other words, holding and cuddling during feeding may be as important as getting the formula right. However, research has not demonstrated any clear-cut difference, either physical or psychological, between breast-fed and bottle-fed babies [23].

Holding, Cuddling, Rocking, Changing Position

Stimulation to the skin, muscles and ear senses seems to create states of equilibrium in the young baby, as everyone knows if he has tried these means of soothing crying. The "good feeling" which accompanies tension reduction doubtless occurs here. Crying is probably the only way in which a newborn can indicate this kind of disequilibrium, unless his general restlessness also signifies it. Although he may gain some equilibrium on his own through moving his body, he does not have a very handy method of getting someone to hold him. If his cries or if his wriggles result in his being picked up, rocked and carried, then surely he gets one more assurance that the world is a place where he can find comfort and satisfaction.

An experiment on neonates demonstrates different kinds of behavior resulting from different ways of handling infants [34]. An attempt was made to continue after birth a type of stimulation similar to prenatal stimulation. Mothers were instructed to hold the infant in fetal position, firmly wrapped in a blanket, in close contact with the mother's body. After breast feeding in this position, the mother was to rock the baby very gently. The nurses gave similar care. The control group was on regular hospital routine, with bottle feeding by the mothers. The control group cried significantly more than the experimental group, especially when no external instigation was present. Although the authors rule out the difference between bottle and breast feeding as the source of the difference in crying, it is possible that breast feeding did contribute to the greater satisfaction of the experimental group. At any rate, it is safe to conclude that rocking and breast feeding resulted in less crying than did minimum handling and bottle feeding. Table 3–2 shows the difference between the two groups of babies.

TABLE 3–2

Newborn babies who were given extra holding, rocking and breast feeding, compared with control group.

	(N = 10, each group) Nonmothered		Mothered			
Variable	*M*	*SD*	*M*	*SD*	*t*	*p*
Age at end of study (in days)	4.33	.65	4.61	.45	.99	
Handling (av. min./hr.)	3.15	.56	11.02	.84	24.51	.01
Crying (av. min./hr.)	5.42	.56	3.37	.32	9.51	.01
Prefeeding, unknown stimulus	1.95	.64	1.23	.53	2.72	.05
Postfeeding, unknown stimulus	.42	.34	.27	.18	1.18	
Between feedings, unknown stimulus	2.34	.33	1.08	.29	9.13	.01
External stimulus	1.31	.40	1.18	.48	1.31	
Vomits (av. no./hr.)	.02	.01	.01	.01	.66	
Sleep (av. min./hr.)	43.47	1.80	41.83	2.81	1.84	

Source: Reprinted by permission from L. Ourth and K. B. Brown, "Inadequate Mothering and Disturbance in the Neonatal Period," *Child Development*, **32**:2, Table 1, p. 292. Copyright © 1961, The Society for Research in Child Development, Inc.

Although breast feeding is confined to mothers (and wet nurses), anybody can hold and cuddle a baby. A good feeling comes from meeting his needs, restoring his equilibrium and helping him to grow. What is more, when two people touch, both get tactual stimulation, and the person who holds a baby gets a sensory and emotional satisfaction from the way his arms, chest, neck and cheeks feel. Perhaps his own heartbeat is reflected back from the baby's body, giving mutually satisfying stimulation. It is in this situation that the newborn baby begins to build relationships with his father, grandparents, brothers and sisters.

In some cultures, babies are frequently held close to their mothers. Americans tend to leave the baby in his crib or playpen unless he indicates a need for care. Each culture has its own way of handling infants and supports it with theories about what is good for them. Some babies are strapped to cradleboards, others swing in hammocks, some are kept vertical, others horizontal. These different methods of handling produce different kinds and degrees of stimulation in the infants. Presumably, different kinds of development would occur in different cultures, and they do. Life and culture are too complex, however, to show a one-to-one relationship between any kind of infant care and a "piece" of adult behavior.

Bathing, Dressing and Other Physical Care

The film *Four Families* [33] shows the activities involved in the physical care of babies in four different cultures. Although the babies are older than newborns, the point is still valid that many different experiences can go under the name of "bath," and that many of those experiences symbolize a cultural attitude toward children. We (the authors) would like to report a personal cross-culture experience which highlighted for us the different sets of sensations possible in American and Indian bathing. Laura, our 10-year-old, having fallen in love with the nightwatchman's baby, reported that Umersingh didn't like the way his mother bathed him because he always cried and kicked hard when she put him upside down on her legs, splashed water over him and rubbed him with her hand. Laura brought Umersingh home for baths in our washbasin, where he never cried, and moved his legs in the most gentle, relaxed way. "Ummy prefers American baths," she concluded. The uniformly warm temperature of our washbasin, in contrast to splashed water which cooled quickly, was probably one point in our favor. Also, having his whole body submerged must have been a more satisfying tactual stimulus than merely being wet. The buoying quality of the water, too, would give muscular stimulation. Our bath was more prolonged, with much sudsy washing, which must have felt smooth, slippery and soothing. Even so, Umersingh might have preferred the Japanese bath shown in *Four Families* if he could have compared it with American bathing. The Japanese grandmother took the baby into the bath with her, thereby adding all the tactual delights of (and to) her own skin.

Dressing symbolizes and defines attitudes toward the skin and toward

By Permission of the Editors of *Look*, Copyright © 1958, Cowles Communications, Inc.

THE HIPPOPOTAMUS

This is the skin some babies feel
Replete with hippo love appeal.
Each contact, cuddle, push, and shove
Elicits tons of baby love.

Courtesy of The University of Wisconsin

THE CROCODILE

Here is the skin they love to touch
It isn't soft and there isn't much,
But its contact comfort will beguile
Love from the infant crocodile.

Ylla from Rapho Guillumette

THE ELEPHANT

Though mother may be short on arms,
Her skin is full of warmth and charms
And mother's touch on baby's skin
Endears the heart that beats within.

Courtesy of The Zoological Society of London

THE RHINOCERUS

The rhino's skin is thick and tough,
And yet this skin is soft enough
That baby rhinos always sense,
A love enormous and intense.

Figure 3–3. Dr. Harry Harlow wrote these verses for his famous article "The Nature of Love," which was originally his presidential address to the American Psychological Association. While Dr. Harlow would be the last one to claim scientific accuracy for the verses, he used them, and we use them here, as an imaginative way of bringing home a truth about human babies. The skin senses are important in normal development. (Reprinted by permission from H. F. Harlow, "The Nature of Love," *American Psychologist,* **13,** 677–678. Copyright © 1958, American Psychological Association.)

From *All About Snakes,* by Bessie M. Hecht.

THE SNAKE

To baby vipers, scaly skin
Engenders love 'twixt kith and kin.
Each animal by God is blessed
With kind of skin it loves the best.

activity. The kind and amount of stimulation and activity possible depends to a large extent on how the baby is clothed. Exposed to the same conditions, a swaddled baby will not get much stimulation, and a naked baby would have greater opportunities for satisfaction and growth. When the surrounding temperature is not ideal, tension reduction is achieved by adding or subtracting clothing and coverings in such a way that the infant's temperature is regulated most comfortably.

Other kinds of physical care can be pleasurably stimulating, such as massage and hair brushing, or of doubtful outcome, such as putting black around the eyes and swabbing the nose. Insofar as the baby's actions initiate care that brings tension reduction, his sense of trust probably increases. Likewise, relationships which bring tension reduction and certain kinds of stimulation are also trust-promoting.

SUMMARY

The newborn baby is usually red, wrinkled, blue-eyed and bumpy-headed. He has a large head, a small trunk and very small, bowed legs. His first big adjustment is to establish breathing with his lungs. The next demand upon him is to secure food through his mouth, which he does by using a complex of reflex mechanisms. He is very limited in his ability to regulate his body temperature.

Many different motor coordinations, involving all parts of the body, can be observed in the neonate. Through crying and food seeking, he effects environmental changes, many of which involve relationships with his mother. Mutual regulation occurs between mother and baby, especially in the realm of breast feeding, where milk supply and strength of sucking become adapted to each other. First experiences in obtaining food and comfort may be influential in patterning the ways in which the infant copes with other problems.

A child probably tries to maintain the level of stimulation which is optimal for him. Tactile and inner ear senses, highly developed before birth, are very important to the infant. Animal experiments show that early tactile experiences promote growth and learning. Human mothers and babies communicate to a great extent through touch. The neonate can hear, even making fine discrimination in pitch. The sound of the human heartbeat probably has significance for him. The newborn responds to visual stimuli, selecting what he regards, and showing preference for a human face and for complex patterns as compared with simple ones. Taste and smell receptors function. Pain sensitivity in the skin increases during the first few days of life. Infants vary considerably in the intensity and selectivity of their responses to stimuli.

Many or most of the neonate's efforts are directed toward maintaining and restoring states of physiological equilibrium. Growth and development occur as new states of equilibrium are achieved. Presumably, comfortable feelings and healthy personality growth accompany optimal maintenance of equilibrium. A sense of trust grows as the baby is fed, comforted and stimulated satisfactorily and as he plays some part in bringing about these experiences. Flexible, mutually regulated feeding practices contribute to the sense of trust. Mothers and infants can be helped to establish a satisfactory feeding relationship by a rooming-in arrangement in the hospital. This plan includes expert education given by the nurses. Comfortable feelings, stimulation and relationships are also built through other aspects of physical care, including holding handling, dressing and bathing.

REFERENCES

1. Aldrich, C. A., & Aldrich, M. M. *Babies are human beings.* New York: Macmillan, 1954.
2. Aldrich, C. A., Sung, C., & Knop, C. The crying of newly born babies: the community phase. *J. Pediat.,* 1945, **26,** 313–326. (a)
3. Aldrich, C. A., Sung, C., & Knop, C. The crying of newly born babies: early period at home. *J. Pediat.,* 1945, **27,** 428–435. (b)
4. Aldrich, C. A., Sung, C., & Knop, C. The crying of newly born babies: individual phase. *J. Pediat.,* 1945, **27,** 89–96. (c)
5. Aldrich, C. A., Sung, C., & Knop, C. The crying of newly born babies: follow-up study after additional nursing care had been provided. *J. Pediat.,* 1946, **28,** 665–670.
6. Bell, R. Q. Relations between behavior manifestations in the human neonate. *Child Devel.,* 1960, **31,** 463–478.

7. Birns, B. Individual differences in human neonates' responses to stimulation. *Child Devel.,* 1965, **36,** 249–259.
8. Blauvelt, H. H. Capacity of a human neonatal reflex to signal future response by present action. *Child Devel.,* 1962, **33,** 21–29.
9. Brackbill, Y. Experimental research with children in the Soviet Union. *Am. Psychol.,* 1960, **15,** 226–233.
10. Breckenridge, M. E., & Murphy, M. N. *Growth and development of the young child* (7th ed.). Philadelphia: Saunders, 1963.
11. Bridger, W. H. Sensory habituation and discrimination in the human neonate. *Am. J. Psychiat.,* 1961, **117,** 991–996.
12. Brown, J. L. States in newborn infants. *Merrill-Palmer Quart.,* 1964, **10,** 313–327.
13. Brownfield, E. D. An investigation of the activity and sensory responses of healthy newborn infants. Unpublished doctoral dissertation, Cornell Univer., 1956.
14. Caldwell, B. M. Assessment of infant personality. *Merrill-Palmer Quart.,* 1962, **8,** 71–82.
15. Casler, L. Maternal deprivation: a critical review of the literature. *Mono. Soc. Res. Child Devel.,* 1961, **26:**2.
16. Casler, L. The effects of extra tactile stimulation on a group of institutionalized infants. *Genet. Psychol. Mono.,* 1965, **71,** 137–175.
17. Dennis, W. A description and classification of the responses of the newborn infant. *Psychol. Bull.,* 1934, **31,** 5–22.
18. Erikson, E. H. Identity and the life cycle. *Psychological Issues,* **1,** 1. New York: International Universities, 1959.
19. Fantz, R. L. The origin of form perception. *Sci. Am.,* 1961, **204:**5, 66–72.
20. Frank, L. K. Tactile communication. *Genet. Psychol. Mono.,* 1957, **56,** 209–225.
21. Geber, M. The psychomotor development of African children in the first year, and the influence of maternal behavior. *J. Soc. Psychol.,* 1958, **47,** 183–195.
22. Gunther, M. Infant behavior at the breast. In B. M. Foss (Ed.), *Determinants of infant behavior.* Vol. I. New York: Wiley, 1961, pp. 37–44.
23. Heinstein, M. I. Behavioral correlates of breast-bottle regimes under varying parent-infant relationships. *Mono. Soc. Res. Child Devel.,* 1963, **28:**4.
24. Irwin, O. C. The amount and nature of activities of newborn infants under constant external stimulating conditions during the first ten days of life. *Genet. Psychol. Mono.,* 1930, **8,** 1–92.
25. Kessen, W., *et al.* Selection and test of response measures in the study of the human newborn. *Child Devel.,* 1961, **32,** 7–24.
26. Leventhal, A. S., & Lipsitt, L. P. Adaptation, pitch discrimination and sound localization in the neonate. *Child Devel.,* 1964, **35,** 759–767.
27. Lipsitt, L. P., & Levy, N. Electrotactual threshold in the neonate. *Child Devel.,* 1959, **30,** 547–554.
28. Lipsitt, L. P., Engen, T., & Kaye, H. Developmental changes in the olfactory threshold of the neonate. *Child Devel.,* 1963, **34,** 371–376.
29. Lorenz, K. Z. *King Solomon's ring.* New York: Crowell, 1952.
30. Mead, M. Babies in primitive societies. *Child Study,* 1947, **24,** 71–73.

31. Moloney, J. C. The Cornelian Corner and its rationale. In M. J. E. Senn (Ed.), *Problems of early infancy.* New York: Josiah Macy, Jr. Foundation, 1947, pp. 17–26.
32. Murphy, L. B. *The widening world of childhood.* New York: Basic Books, 1962.
33. National Film Board of Canada. *Four families.*
34. Ourth, L., & Brown, K. B. Inadequate mothering and disturbance in the neonatal period. *Child Devel.,* 1961, **32,** 287–295.
35. Pratt, K. C. The neonate. In L. Carmichael (Ed.), *Manual of child psychology.* New York: Wiley, 1954, pp. 215–291.
36. Pratt, K. C., Nelson, A. K., & Sun, K. H. *The behavior of the newborn infant.* Ohio State Univer. Studies, Contrib. Psychol. No. 10, 1930.
37. Prechtl, H. F. R. The directed head-turning response and allied movements of the human baby. *Behavior,* 1958, **8,** 212–242.
38. Richmond, J., & Lipton, E. L. Some aspects of the neurophysiology of the newborn and their implications for child development. In L. Jessner & E. Pavenstedt (Eds.), *Dynamic psychopathology in childhood.* New York: Grune & Stratton, 1959.
39. Salk, L. Mother's heartbeat as an imprinting stimulus. *Trans. N.Y. Acad. Sci.,* Ser. II, 1962, **24,** 753–763.
40. Schaefer, E. S., & Bayley, N. Maternal behavior, child behavior, and their intercorrelations from infancy through adolescence. *Mono. Soc. Res. Child Devel.,* 1963, **28:**3.
41. Smith, C. A. *The physiology of the newborn infant.* Springfield, Ill.: Charles C Thomas, 1959.
42. Spock, B. *The commonsense book of baby and child care.* New York: Duell, Sloan and Pearce, 1946.
43. Stagner, R. Homeostasis, need reduction and motivation. *Merrill-Palmer Quart.,* 1961, **7,** 49–69.
44. Tanner, J. M. *Education and physical growth.* London: Univer. of London, 1961.
45. Wertheimer, M. Psychomotor coordination of auditory and visual perception at birth. *Science,* 1961, **134,** 1692.

Emerging Resources for Coping with the World

CHAPTER 4

The drama of the first two years of life involves the change from horizontal to vertical, from sedentary creature to runner, from crybaby to speaker, from vast dependency to a large measure of autonomy. The changes are comparable to the changes from prenatal to postnatal life, and much more visible and comprehensible. Although the newborn comes equipped for maintaining his body processes, his behavior is largely subcortical, controlled by lower brain centers and not those basic to thinking and consciousness. As the cerebral cortex matures, behavior rapidly becomes more complex and flexible. Reflex activity is suppressed and/or integrated into larger coordinations that have some conscious control. For example, the area of the motor cortex controlling the arms matures before the area that controls the legs. At three or four weeks, the legs are at their peak of making reflex crawling movements, while the arms, inhibited by cortical control, do not make many reflex movements. The interpretation and use of sensory perception is thought to follow the order of maturing of the cerebral cortex, with vision more advanced than hearing during infancy. Active, like all living creatures, and with powers emerging, like all developing creatures, the infant deals more and more effectively with the world, the people in it and himself.

DIRECTIONS IN PERSONALITY DEVELOPMENT

Infancy encompasses the first critical period in personality growth and part of the second. The development of the sense of trust comes first, laying the groundwork for a feeling of security throughout life. The development of a sense of autonomy is central to personality growth from about a year and a half to three and a half or four years of age. Most of the infant's behavior and experiences can be understood in the light of these two achievements in personality development.*

Trust

Successful growth during the first year results in a well-established sense of trust. Begun with the first experience of securing food and skin stimulation, the growth of trust continues through experiences with things, other people and the self. The good feelings from tension reduction, repeated consistently in good physical care, make the baby confident that he will be fed when hungry, dried when wet, rocked when restless and stimulated when bored. He is confident also that he can do something toward initiating these satisfying experiences.

People, largely mother, are part of the good-feeling experiences and come to stand for the whole. Thus the four-month baby, crying from hunger, stops crying and even smiles when he sees his mother or hears her footsteps, trusting that she will feed him.

Appreciation of the permanence of objects is a basic ingredient of the sense of trust. Through his interactions with the world during his first year and a half, the baby comes to know that things exist even when he is not perceiving them. As will be described in greater detail later in the chapter, the first 18 months is the sensorimotor period, in Piaget's series of stages. The two essential achievements of this period are a realization of the permanence of objects and the organization and control of his movements in space. These two achievements go along together. As the baby controls the movements of his body, he deals with the objects of the world, seeing and feeling them, noticing them appearing and disappearing, understanding that events can take place when he is not watching. He comes to trust the world to have certain kinds of order in it, to be dependable. He also comes to know his own powers and how to use them, a beginning of the sense of autonomy.

Establishing trust also involves learning that mother (and others) exists even when she cannot be seen, and that she will come again and again. The game of peek-a-boo dramatizes mother's disappearance and reappearance. In playing it, the infant lives and relives the frightening situation which has a happy ending, enjoying it throughout the months when trust is growing. As he learns that mother continues to exist apart from him, he also learns that he exists apart from her. His sense of self begins perhaps from this knowledge and certainly grows as he explores his own body. Fingering his hand and watching it move yield one complex of sensations; fingering the blanket gives another. Reaching, grasping, securing, releasing, touching, mouthing—all tell him what is himself, what are other things and what he can do, or what he can trust his body to do with the world. As a good feeling goes along with the accumulation of knowledge of his body, his power, the objects outside himself, and other

* This account follows Erikson [12, pp. 247–254] and Witmer and Kotinsky [52, pp. 8–15].

people, then the sense of trust grows. Mistrust arises from discomfort, disappointment, anxiety, inability to explore, discriminate and cope with the world.*

Autonomy

In the beginning or early months of the second year, the baby who trusts himself and the world is ready to concentrate on the next stage in personality growth, the development of autonomy. Able to move himself from one place to another, able to pick up, manipulate and reject toys, able to say a few words, able to feed himself some foods, able to "hang on" for a while when he feels the urge to eliminate, he has many choices to make. He feels autonomous as he makes choices freely and wholeheartedly. He gets the feeling "What I do is all right" and a companion feeling, "There are many things that I can either do or not do."

Me do is the keynote phrase of the age from 18 months to two and a half. Everyone knows how determined two-year-olds are to do things in their own ways at their own times. The doing and the choosing are the means of growth, for these are the ways in which toddlers test themselves, other people and the world in order to establish themselves as creatures who function independently and adequately.

Choosing involves taking or leaving, holding on to or letting go. When the child discovers, through active testing, that there are many places where he can choose and live comfortably with his choice, then he feels good about himself. He can decide whether to take a proffered hand or not, whether to play with the truck or the bunny, whether to have a second serving of applesauce or not, whether to sit on grandma's lap or stand on his feet. He also needs restrictions that are clear and firm, in order to prevent him from making choices that are beyond him. Frustration and consequent anger are frequent even in older infants who are guided with skill and understanding. Temper outbursts increase in the latter part of infancy, as the child tests himself to find out what he can do and tests his parents and his world to find out what they will let him do. Each successful encounter and choice adds to his sense of autonomy. Shame and doubt arise when disaster follows choice-making and also when the child is not allowed to make enough choices. Shame, doubt and inadequacy (lack of autonomy) lead to extremes of behavior—rebellion or oversubmissiveness, hurling or hanging on tight.†

* The period of development of trust is the *oral stage* in psychoanalytic theory. The mouth is the site of the most important experiences, feeding and the love relationship associated with feeding. Pain from teething is associated with biting and cruel, harsh experiences. In many psychoanalytic writings the skin senses and other senses, too, are greatly overshadowed by the significance of the mouth.

† The period of autonomy is the anal stage in psychoanalytic theory. The central problem is dramatized by the idea of the anal sphincters which open or shut, hanging on or letting go. Depending on the child's experiences with bowel control and control by other people, his personality takes on characteristics like suspicion or confidence, stinginess or generosity, doubt and shame or autonomy and adequacy.

In longitudinal studies of children, the beginnings of autonomous behavior have been seen even in early infancy, especially in the ways in which infants defended themselves from unwanted experiences [36, pp. 226–227, 302]. Babies differed in how often and how vigorously they protested over feeding, rejected foods and ended the meal. They differed in ways of rejecting stimulation and being moved. For instance, some babies of three or four months stiffened their back and legs when adults were performing unwelcome procedures, while other relaxed and went limp. The first reaction resembled taking a stand, even before the child could literally stand up, whereas the second was more like passive resistance. As soon as infants can move around, some will crawl, pull or stretch to get away from an unpleasant situation, and others will push the adult away, kick, fight or protest against her.

Infants in the study were shown to differ in how much stimulation they accepted and sought and in how they reduced unwelcome stimulation. One little girl of 28 weeks went to sleep at the moment when three observers came to record her behavior, as though she could not accept such a concentrated dose of attention. Some children were hyperalert to sights and sounds, and others seemed to shut out many of them. Thus while the peak age for concern with autonomy is between 18 months and three or four years, some attempts at autonomous behavior occur much earlier.

PHYSICAL AND MOTOR DEVELOPMENT

Development and change are rapid during the first two years of life. This period, as well as the preschool years, is a time when illness is relatively frequent and careful physical care is consequently very worthwhile. Respiratory infections are the most frequent type of physical difficulty, with gastrointestinal upsets second in frequency [49]. Figure 4–1 shows the number of occurrences of various kinds of illnesses in a group of children between birth and two years of age.

After the first month, more or less, a baby really looks like a baby, like babies in ads and photograph albums, like other babies in the neighborhood —chubby, skin pink and white, golden, brown, or whatever it is destined to be, bumps smoothed out and nose in shape. New coarser hair comes in during infancy, replacing the fine black hair of the newborn (if he had it) and showing more and more the color it is going to be. Compared with an older child, a baby has a large forehead, large eyes, small nose, small chin and plump cheeks. His hands and feet are chubby and his abdomen round; his delicate skin looks soft and fragile.

Changes in shape and proportion continue along the lines charted prenatally, the head regions being most developed, the trunk and legs beginning to catch up, the center of gravity high in the trunk but descending. Birth weight is doubled by four or five months and tripled at a year. Height is doubled by about two years. Thus the child starts life as a slender neonate, fills out to a round, plump infant during the first year, and then in the second

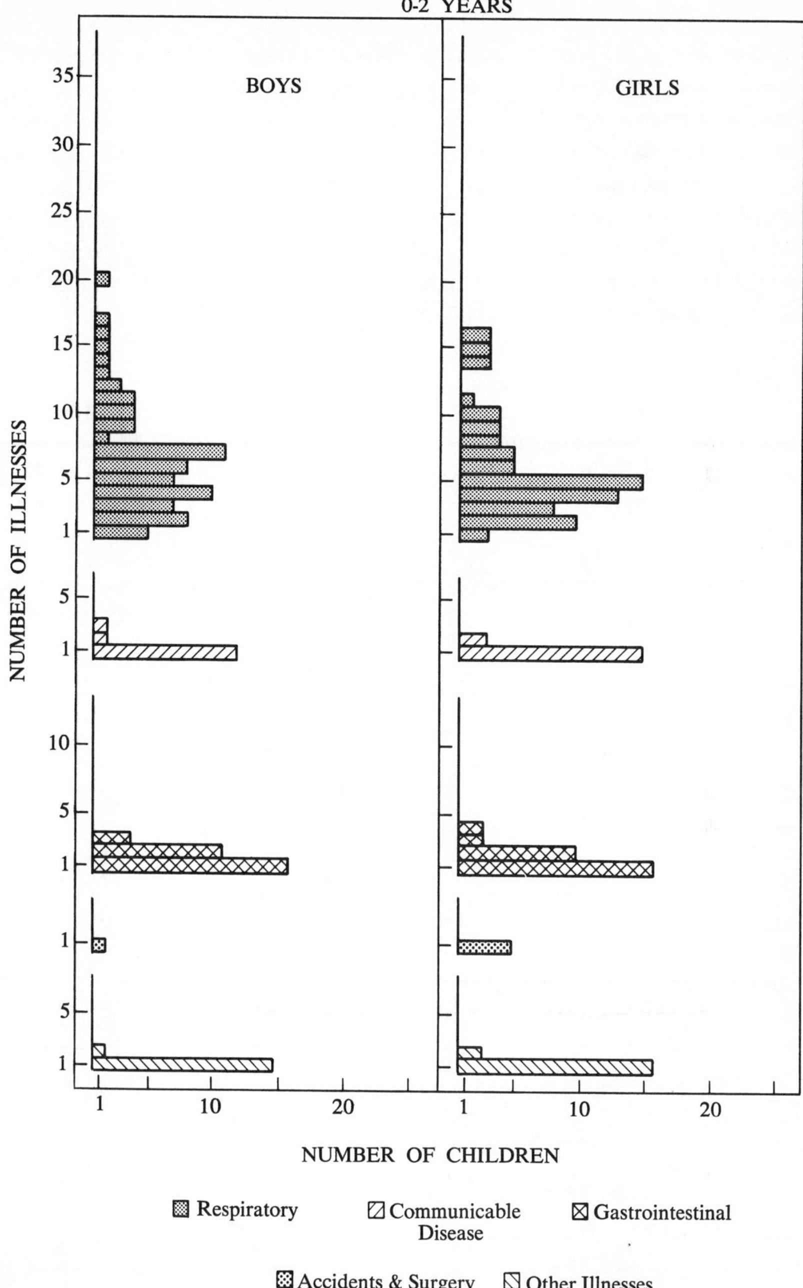

Figure 4–1. Respiratory infections are by far the greatest cause of illness in infancy. (Reprinted by permission from I. Valadian, H. C. Stuart and R. B. Reed, "Studies of Illnesses of Children Followed from Birth to Eighteen Years," *Monographs of The Society for Research in Child Development,* **26**:3, Figure 21. Copyright © 1961, The Society for Research in Child Development, Inc.)

year, he again becomes more slender, continuing this trend into middle childhood. Height and weight percentile tables (Tables 4–1 through 4–4) can be used to compare a baby with others the same age and sex.

Babies differ in appearance, from one to another; the older they are, the more obvious the differences. They differ, of course, in coloring, facial features, amount and type of hair, height and weight. They feel different, too. Firm muscles and good muscle tone give a solid impression, in contrast to the softness of slacker muscles or abundant fat. The baby's reactions to being held also add to the impression, according to whether the infant holds himself erect, pushes away or yields to the arms which hold him.

Teething

Almost as obvious as children's increase in height and weight is the appearance of teeth. A baby's toothless grin, the single tooth of a slightly older baby, the gaps left in the row of teeth between the shedding of the first incisors and

TABLE 4–1

Height percentile table for boys from birth through age two.

	Length in Inches						
Age	3%	10%	25%	50%	75%	90%	97%
Birth	18¼	19	19½	20	20½	21	21½
1 mo.	19¾	20¼	20¾	21¼	22	22¼	23¾
2 mo.	21	21½	22	22½	23	23½	24
3 mo.	22½	22¾	24¼	23¾	24¼	24¾	25
4 mo.	23½	23¾	24¼	24¾	25¼	25¾	26
5 mo.	24¼	24½	25	25½	26	26½	27
6 mo.	24¾	25¼	25¾	26	26¾	27¼	27¾
7 mo.	25½	26	26¼	26¾	27¼	28	28½
8 mo.	26	26½	27	27½	28	28¾	29¼
9 mo.	26½	27	27½	28	28¾	29¼	30
10 mo.	27	27½	28	28½	29¼	29¾	30½
11 mo.	27½	28	28½	29	29¾	30¼	31
12 mo.	28	28½	29	29½	30¼	30¾	31½
13 mo.	28½	29	29½	30	30¾	31¼	32
14 mo.	29	29½	30	30½	31¼	31¾	32½
15 mo.	29¼	29¾	30¼	31	31½	32	33
16 mo.	29¾	30¼	30¾	31½	32	32½	33½
17 mo.	30¼	30½	31¼	31¾	32½	33	34
18 mo.	30½	31	31½	32¼	33	33½	34¼
19 mo.	31	31½	32	32¾	33¼	34	35¼
20 mo.	31¼	31¾	32½	33	33¾	34½	35½
21 mo.	31½	32	32¾	33¼	34	34¾	36
22 mo.	32	32½	33	33¾	34½	35	36½
23 mo.	32¼	32¾	33½	34	34¾	35½	36¾
24 mo.	32½	33	33¾	34½	35¼	36	37¼

Source: From *Growth and Development of Children*, 4th edition, by Ernest H. Watson and George H. Lowrey. Copyright © 1962, Year Book Medical Publishers, Inc., Chicago. Used by permission of Year Book Medical Publishers.

the coming of the permanent incisors—these are familiar landmarks in development. The near universality of the presence, early or late, of teeth in children, taken with their appearance and displacement, make the growth of teeth seem a likely source of information for assessing the maturity of children at any age. An added advantage would certainly be that no special instruments are necessary for determining which teeth have erupted at any moment.

Actually, the appearance of the deciduous teeth appears not to be related to skeletal development. Data from the Fels Research Institute reveal that the mean times of eruption of the deciduous teeth in the right and left side of the mouth were practically identical [46]. As for differences between the upper and lower jaw, the lower central incisors came earlier and the upper lateral incisors appeared earlier than the lower. Otherwise the differences in the mean times of eruption of the teeth in the two jaws were not significantly different. The mean ages for boys and girls for eruption of the various deciduous teeth as reported in this study are given in Table 4–5, page 102.

TABLE 4–2

Height percentile table for girls from birth through age two.

	Length in Inches						
Age	*3%*	*10%*	*25%*	*50%*	*75%*	*90%*	*97%*
Birth	18½	18¾	19¼	19¾	20	20½	21
1 mo.	19¾	20¼	20½	21	21½	22	22½
2 mo.	21	21½	21¾	22¼	23	23¼	23¾
3 mo.	22	22½	22¾	23½	24	24¼	24¾
4 mo.	22¾	23¼	23¾	24¼	24¾	25¼	25¾
5 mo.	23½	24	24½	25	25½	26	26½
6 mo.	24	24½	25	25¾	26¼	26¾	27
7 mo.	24½	25¼	25¾	26¼	27	27½	27¾
8 mo.	25¼	25¾	26¼	27	27½	28	28½
9 mo.	25¾	26½	27	27½	28¼	28¾	29¼
10 mo.	26¼	27	27½	28	28¾	29¼	29¾
11 mo.	26¾	27¼	28	28½	29¼	29¾	30½
12 mo.	27	27¾	28½	29¼	30	30¼	31
13 mo.	27½	28¼	29	29½	30¼	30¾	31½
14 mo.	28	28½	29½	30	30¾	31¼	32
15 mo.	28¼	29	29¾	30½	31¼	31¾	32½
16 mo.	28¾	29½	30¼	31	31¾	32¼	33
17 mo.	29	29¾	30¾	31¼	32¼	32¾	33½
18 mo.	29½	30¼	31	31¾	32½	33¼	34
19 mo.	30	30½	31½	32¼	33	33¾	34½
20 mo.	30¼	31	32	32½	33½	34¼	35
21 mo.	30½	31¼	32¼	33	33¾	34¾	35½
22 mo.	31	31¾	32¾	33¼	34¼	35¼	36
23 mo.	31¼	32	33	33¾	34½	35½	36¼
24 mo.	31½	32¼	33¼	34	35	35¾	36¾

Source: From *Growth and Development of Children*, 4th edition, by Ernest H. Watson and George H. Lowrey. Copyright © 1962, Year Book Medical Publishers, Inc., Chicago. Used by permission of Year Book Medical Publishers.

The sequence of eruption of the deciduous teeth is not the same for all children. In this respect the eruption of teeth is similar to the appearance of the epiphyses of the bones in the hand and the carpal bones. In the Fels data, the most usual sequence was the same as the sequence of the mean times of eruption for the whole group. When most of a child's teeth appeared later than the average there were more variations from the common pattern of eruption. (The same principle holds for the appearance of the bones in the wrist—when ossification is delayed, then there is wider variation from the common sequence of bone development.) A principle of growth is involved here. When an event interferes with the normal course of growth at a critical period for one organ or tissue, that part of the body is delayed in development; parts of the growth sequence normally occurring later may not be interfered with. In the case of teeth (and bones of the hand and wrist), the situation might be figuratively viewed thus: If one tooth (or bone) is delayed for any reason, the next tooth (or bone) pushes ahead, impatient to appear on

TABLE 4–3

Weight percentile table for boys from birth through age two.

	Weight in Pounds						
Age	*3%*	*10%*	*25%*	*50%*	*75%*	*90%*	*97%*
Birth	5¾	6¼	7	7½	8¼	9	10
1 mo.	7½	8½	9	10	10½	11½	13
2 mo.	9	10	10½	11½	12	13¼	14¾
3 mo.	10½	11	11¾	12½	13½	14½	16¼
4 mo.	11¾	12½	13¼	14	15	16¼	18
5 mo.	13	13¾	14¼	15	16½	17¾	19½
6 mo.	14	14¾	15½	16¾	18	19¼	20¾
7 mo.	15	15¾	16¾	18	19	20¾	22¼
8 mo.	15¾	16¾	17¾	19	20½	22	23½
9 mo.	16½	17¾	18¾	20	21½	23	24½
10 mo.	17¼	18¼	19½	20¾	22½	23¾	25¼
11 mo.	18	18¾	20¼	21½	23¼	24½	26¼
12 mo.	18½	19½	20¾	22¼	23¾	25½	27¼
13 mo.	19	20	21¼	22¾	24½	26	27¾
14 mo.	19½	20½	22	23¼	25	26½	28½
15 mo.	19¾	21	22½	23¾	25½	27¼	29½
16 mo.	20¼	21½	23	24¼	26	27¾	30¼
17 mo.	20¾	21¾	23½	24¾	26½	28½	31
18 mo.	21	22¼	23¾	25¼	27	29	31½
19 mo.	21½	22¾	24¼	25¾	27½	29½	32¼
20 mo.	22	23¼	24¾	26	28	30	33
21 mo.	22¼	23½	25	26½	28½	30½	33½
22 mo.	22½	24	25½	26¾	28¾	31	34
23 mo.	23	24¼	26	27¼	29¼	31½	34½
24 mo.	23¼	24¾	26¼	27¾	29¾	32	35

Source: From *Growth and Development of Children*, 4th edition, by Ernest H. Watson and George H. Lowrey. Copyright © 1962, Year Book Medical Publishers, Inc., Chicago. Used by permission of Year Book Medical Publishers.

schedule; the delayed part has to wait for a gap in the line before it can rejoin the procession, perhaps even until more than one part has kept its appointment.

Establishing Regularity of Basic Processes

The body must stay within certain physical and chemical limits if it is to stay alive. In order to function optimally, it must stay within narrower limits. Homeostasis, the maintenance of steady states within these limits, is accomplished by integrated control of the nervous and endocrine systems. During the first three or four months of life, the mechanisms of homeostasis become more and more efficient. The baby settles down to an easier, more automatic supporting of life processes, his energies freed for a wider variety of activities.

Temperature regulation is one of the vital homeostatic processes. A certain constancy has to be kept in spite of heat loss and heat production. The baby regulates his temperature more adequately after the neonatal period than he

TABLE 4–4

Weight percentile table for girls from birth through age two.

	Weight in Pounds						
Age	*3%*	*10%*	*25%*	*50%*	*75%*	*90%*	*97%*
Birth	5¾	6¼	7	7½	8	8½	9½
1 mo.	7	8	8½	9¾	10¼	11	11¾
2 mo.	8¼	9½	10¼	11	11¾	12½	13½
3 mo.	9½	10¾	11½	12¼	13	13¾	14¾
4 mo.	10¾	12	12¾	13¾	14½	15½	16½
5 mo.	11¾	13	13¾	14¾	16	17	18¼
6 mo.	12¾	14	14¾	15¾	17¼	18½	19¾
7 mo.	13½	15	16	17	18½	20	21¼
8 mo.	14¼	15¾	16¾	18	19½	21¼	22½
9 mo.	14¾	16¼	17½	18¾	20¼	22	23½
10 mo.	15½	17	18¼	19¾	21¼	23	24¾
11 mo.	16	17½	19	20½	22	23¾	25¾
12 mo.	16½	18	19½	21	22½	24½	26½
13 mo.	17	18½	24¼	21¾	23¼	25¼	27½
14 mo.	17½	19	20¾	22¼	23¾	25¾	28
15 mo.	18	19½	21¼	22¾	24½	26½	28¾
16 mo.	18½	20	21¾	23¼	25	27	29½
17 mo.	18¾	20½	22¼	23¾	25½	27½	30
18 mo.	19¼	21	22½	24¼	26	28	30¾
19 mo.	19½	21½	23	25	26½	28¾	31¼
20 mo.	20	21¾	23½	25½	27	29¼	32
21 mo.	20¼	22¼	23¾	25¾	27½	29¾	32½
22 mo.	20¾	22¾	24¼	26¼	28	30½	33
23 mo.	21¼	23	24¾	26¾	28½	31	33¾
24 mo.	21½	23½	25¼	27	29¼	31¾	34½

Source: From *Growth and Development of Children*, 4th edition, by Ernest H. Watson and George H. Lowrey. Copyright © 1962, Year Book Medical Publishers, Inc., Chicago. Used by permission of Year Book Medical Publishers.

TABLE 4–5

Average ages (in months) of eruption of deciduous teeth for boys and girls.

	Boys	*Girls*
Central Incisors		
Lower (*L* 1)	7.3	7.8
Upper (*U* 1)	9.1	9.6
Lateral Incisors		
Lower (*L* 2)	13.0	13.8
Upper (*U* 2)	10.4	11.9
Canines		
Lower (*L* 3)	19.3	20.2
Upper (*U* 3)	18.9	20.1
First Molars		
Lower (*L* 4)	16.2	15.6
Upper (*U* 4)	16.0	15.7
Second Molars		
Lower (*L* 5)	25.9	27.1
Upper (*U* 5)	27.6	28.4

Source: Reprinted by permission from M. Robinow, T. W. Richards, and M. Anderson, "The Eruption of Deciduous Teeth," *Growth*, 1942, **6**, 127–133.

does in the beginning. For example, the sweat glands become active at about a month of age. Even with temperature regulation improving, infants and young children are still highly susceptible to temperature fluctuation. Bodily temperature is likely to shoot up with active exercise, crying, emotional upset or rise in surrounding temperature [3]. Bodily temperature responds readily to chilling. Infants and young children, when suffering from infections, usually

TABLE 4–6

Average body temperature of infants and children.

	Temperature		*Standard Deviation*	
Age	*F.*	*C.*	*F.*	*C.*
3 months	99.4	37.5	0.8	0.4
6 months	99.5	37.5	0.6	0.3
1 year	99.7	37.7	0.5	0.2
3 years	99.0	37.2	0.5	0.2
5 years	98.6	37.0	0.5	0.2
7 years	98.3	36.8	0.5	0.2
9 years	98.1	36.7	0.5	0.2
11 years	98.0	36.7	0.5	0.2
13 years	97.8	36.6	0.5	0.2

Source: From *Growth and Development of Children*, 4th edition, by Ernest H. Watson and George H. Lowrey. Copyright © 1962, Year Book Medical Publishers, Inc., Chicago. Used by permission of Year Book Medical Publishers.

show higher temperatures than do older children. Table 4–6 shows the average temperature throughout infancy and childhood. Note that while the average temperature at three months is 99.4, about one third of babies this age have temperatures above 100.2 or below 98.6. At six months, two thirds of infants have temperatures between 100.1 and 98.9. The corresponding range at one year is 100.2 to 99.2. Thus average temperature decreases and individual variations decrease as the infant grows into childhood. Individual differences continue to exist, though, and it is important to realize that an occasional child has an unusually high (or low) temperature which is normal for *him* [51].

Heat production increases with age throughout the growth period. The younger the child, the more he is likely to vary from the average and also to vary with himself from time to time [30]. Table 4–7 shows heat production from birth to adulthood. The larger the body, of course, the greater the absolute amount of heat produced. Taken in terms of heat production per unit of body weight, however, the six-month baby produces more heat than anybody. Heat production builds up from birth to six months and then tapers off to adulthood.

Considering what is known about temperature in children, it can be seen that good care includes protection against extremes of temperature and supervision which helps the child to regulate his own temperature. During about the first year a temperature between 68° and 72° is recommended [3, p. 159]. When the baby can run around, 65° to 68° is a good temperature for him. Adequate clothing helps to keep temperature at an optimal level while also providing flexibility. Since infants and young children produce such large amounts of heat, they are likely to become overheated through

TABLE 4–7

Heat production by age, weight and body surface.

Age	*Weight, Kg*	*Heat/24 Hr*	*Heat/Sq M/Hr*	*Heat/Kg/Hr*
2 days	3.45	162	32.1	1.91
5 days	3.34	150	30.5	1.88
6 mo.	5.40	353	40.0	2.75
10 mo.	9.37	479	37.7	2.12
2½ yr.	11.5	585	51.9	2.20
5 yr.	15.5	720	52.4	2.01
9 yr.	22.0	898	44.9	1.70
10 yr.	30.6	1,065	41.3	1.43
14 yr.	40.2	1,300	39.2	1.35
18 yr.	65.6	1,700	32.8	1.08
Adult	70.0	1,400*	35–40.0*	1.00*

*Average figures.
Source: From *Growth and Development of Children*, 4th edition, by Ernest H. Watson and George H. Lowrey. Copyright © 1962, Year Book Medical Publishers, Inc., Chicago. Used by permission of Year Book Medical Publishers.

active play or when wearing heavy clothing. They will show discomfort by a flushed face, perspiration and perhaps irritability.

Respiration changes considerably during the first year. The rate slows down to about half what it was at birth. After one year, it continues to become slower. Breathing becomes deeper, too. At birth, the diaphragm does practically all of the work in breathing. The chest gradually comes into play during infancy, but thoracic breathing is not well established until the end of the preschool period [51]. A young baby's breathing sounds harsh, irregular and shallow. Gradually his breathing becomes more regular and less noisy as he changes toward thoracic breathing, as his chest grows and as the tissues covering his chest thicken and insulate the sounds.

The timing of eating, sleeping and eliminating becomes regularized. By three or four months, even the baby who has made his own schedule (fed when hungry, allowed to sleep until he wakens) eats and sleeps at fairly predictable times. The newborn sleeps 16 or 17 hours a day, nearly all of the time when he is not eating and receiving physical care. He tends to waken every four or five hours [37]. From one to three months, the infant stays awake for longer periods, shortening the average number of hours of sleep to 15. From this time until six months, he gradually stays awake more in the daytime and sleeps longer at night. Studies of brain waves show real sleep patterns at around three months and not before, suggesting that during the first three months, there is little difference between sleeping and waking [30, p. 171]. During the second year, most babies sleep through the night and take one or two naps during the day. Some time during this year, the second nap tends to drop out, with one nap continued until age four or five.

As eating and sleeping become regularized, bowel movements also tend to do so. After the neonatal period, the average number of stools per day is two to four for the breast-fed baby and one to three for the bottle-fed [3, p. 221]. Wide individual differences occur, however. By six months, one or two stools a day are most usual. About half the two-year-olds have bowel movements at predictable times and half are unpredictable [45].

Feeding Behavior

Feeding is one of the essential ways in which a baby deals with his world. In describing an individual, a family, a culture, or even homo sapiens, it is important to tell what food is used, how it is obtained and how it is prepared. "Man might be defined as a being who uses cooking and eating utensils" [17]. Foods become endowed with meanings and even become symbols, ways of communicating. (Rice is an almost universal fertility symbol at weddings, coconuts mean good luck in India, wine is a Christian symbol for blood.) The culture into which an infant is born is organized to offer him certain foods in certain ways with certain meanings attached. Within the opportunities and limits which he encounters, he develops ways of obtaining food and eating it, as well as ways of thinking and feeling about food.

In *Feeding Behavior of Infants,* Gesell and Ilg [17, pp. 36–41] devote a section to the history of nursing implements and techniques. They show pictures of artificial baby feeders, including the Roman clay boat, the French cow's horn, the English bubbly pot and pap boat, metal nipples, chamois nipples and modern glass and rubber equipment. They tell of such practices as pigeon feeding, in which the mother or nurse chewed food before putting it in the baby's mouth, and soothing teething discomfort with hare's brain or dog's milk. When faced with these historic practices or with some of the customs reported by modern anthropologists [34], one is struck by the adaptability of infants' feeding behavior.

In studying what infants actually do in the feeding situations, the constructors of infant tests utilize as "test items" the motions that children go through. As you read through Table 4–8, you can see how the baby grows steadily in capability. By the end of the second year, he can chew well and can use the basic implements and utensils—cup, spoon and plate. He can seek and find food and obtain and reject it through the use of words. *All gone, more, drink,* and similar expressions, are powerful symbols through which he can control many important events.

NURSING. Babies ordinarily begin their feeding histories by sucking milk from breast or bottle or both. Weaning is the taking away of breast or bottle and substituting a cup for drinking. The effects of variations in methods of feeding, on both baby and mother, have been the subject of much speculation. Breast feeding has been espoused as a cause, especially by groups interested in "natural childbirth" and other psychological aspects of the mother–baby relationship. The meshing of roles of mother and infant is a powerful argument for the value of breast feeding. As the previous chapter has shown, the newborn

TABLE 4–8

Normative sequence of development of patterns of feeding behavior.

FIRST QUARTER: 0–12 WKS.

On Presentation

Tongue surrounds lower half of nipple well (6 wks. ff.)
Hands are usually fisted (4–8 wks.)
Regards breast or bottle eagerly (10 wks. ff.)
Hands contact each other on chest (12 wks. ff.)

During feeding

Hands open as feeding progresses (4–10 wks.)
Regards mother's face prolongedly (8–12 wks.)
Expels gas during feeding as well as at end of feeding

On Satiety

Falls asleep
Face brightens (2–4 wks.)

Developmental Items

Looks at faces (4 wks.). Smiles (8 wks.). Coos (12 wks.)
Head predominantly rotated when supine (tonic-neck-reflex) (4–12 wks.)

TABLE 4-8 (*Continued*)

SECOND QUARTER: 16–24 WKS.

On Presentation

Mouth poises to receive nipple (16 wks. ff.)
Mouth poises to receive spoon (20 wks. ff.)
Grasps and draws bottle to mouth usually with assistance, but hands release as soon as nipple is inserted (10–26 wks.)

During Feeding

Tongue holds nipple firmly producing strong suck (16 wks. ff.)
Tongue projects after spoon removed, thereby ejecting food involuntarily (16–20 wks.)
Coughs and chokes both with milk from bottle and solids (16–20 wks.)
Strong hand to mouth response as nipple or spoon is removed (16–24 wks.)
Slumps in sitting in high chair (16–26 wks.)
Makes smacking noises with lips (22 wks.)

On Satiety

Expels gas easily and usually spontaneously in sitting position
Fusses or cries after solid food (16–24 wks.)
Throws head back or turns to side
Brings hands to mouth (16–24 wks.)
Ejects food with tongue projection (18–24 wks.)

Developmental Items

Holds head steadily erect in supported sitting position (16 wks.)
Closes in with both hands to grasp rattle held near him (20 wks.)
Looks at rattle held in hand (20 wks.). Turns head to sound (24 wks.)
Reaches for object on sight and grasps it (24 wks.)

THIRD QUARTER: 28–36 WKS.

On Presentation

Vocalizes eagerness as regards bottle, dish, cup, or when placed in chair (28–34 wks.)
Impatient and eager as sees mother preparing dinner (28–36 wks.)

During Feeding

Removes food quickly from spoon (28 wks. ff.)
Draws in lower lip (28–32 wks.)
Smacks or presses tongue against palate (28–36 wks.)
Bounces on mother's lap (28–36 wks.)
Hands reach for dish out of reach (32 wks.)
Chokes easily when drinking from cup (32 wks. ff.)

On Satiety

Keeps mouth tightly closed (28 wks. ff.)
Razzes (sputtering with tongue and lips) (32–36 wks.)
Bites on spoon, nipple, or rim of cup (32 wks.)
Hands become more active, grasps spoon, dish, cup or bottle (28 wks. ff.)
Plays with feeding utensil (28 wks. ff.)
Grasps feet in supine position (32 wks. ff.)

Developmental Items

Transfers object held in one hand to other hand (28 wks.)
Sits alone, without support (32 wks.)
Vocalizes da-da or similar syllables (36 wks.)

FOURTH QUARTER: 40–52 WKS.

On Presentation

Grasps bottle and bring to mouth (40 wks. ff.)
No approach with hands on cup or spoon (40 wks. ff.)
Manifests eagerness or impatient fussing if mother is slow in presenting food (44–48 wks.)

During Feeding

Demands play object (40 wks. ff.)
Approximates lips adaptively to rim of cup (40 wks. ff.)
Drinks fairly continuously, 4–5 swallows or more (40 wks. ff.)
Spills from corners of mouth as drinks (40–44 wks.)
Pokes with index finger at nipple and food in dishes (44 wks. ff.)
Chews well (44 wks. ff.)
Finger feeds small pieces of food from tray (46 wks. ff.)
Rubs spoon back and forth on tray (50 wks. ff.)

On Satiety

Ejects food with tongue projection (40 wks. ff.)
Razzes (40 wks. ff.)
Pulls self to standing position (40 wks. ff.)
Pivots in sitting position (44 wks. ff.)
Throws bottle to floor (44 wks. ff.). Hands bottle to mother (48 wks. ff.)

Developmental Items

Pokes at small objects with index finger (40 wks.)
Grasps small objects with well defined thumb opposition (44 wks.)
Cruises (48 wks.). Walks with support (52 wks.)

SECOND YEAR: 12–24 MOS.

On Presentation

Demands to have dish on tray (14 mos. ff.)
Demands to help feed self (15 mos. ff.)
Grasps cup with both hands (15 mos. ff.)
Goes to hgh chair as he sees dinner being prepared (16 mos. ff.)
Asks for meal with single word, such as "eat" (18–21 mos.)

During Feeding

Tilts up too rapidly with wrist rotation (15–17 mos.)
Turns spoon upside down or sideways as he brings it to mouth (15 mos.)
Spills to a marked degree (15–17 mos.)
Lowers cup to tray deftly (16 mos. ff.)
Fills spoon by inserting point into food (16 mos. ff.)
Spills to a moderate degree (17–22 mos.)
Chews meat well (18 mos.)
Finger-feeds discrete objects of food (18–20 mos.)
Places food in spoon with free hand, then lifts spoon to mouth (19–21 mos.)

On Satiety

Shakes head "no" (13–17 mos.)
Hands dish or cup to mother (15 mos. ff.)
Shakes head and says "no" (18 mos.)
Says "all gone" or "no more" (18 mos. ff.)

Developmental Items

Hands over and releases objects (12 mos. ff.)
Says two "words" or more (12 mos. ff.)
Builds a tower of two blocks (15 mos.)
Climbs (18 mos.). Talks jargon (18 mos.)
Turns pages of book (18 mos.)
Names a familiar picture (21 mos.)
Uses words in combination (2 years)

Source: Reprinted by permission from A. Gesell and F. Ilg, *Feeding Behavior of Infants* (Philadelphia: Lippincott, 1937), pp. 142–144.

baby's reflex activity is adequate for finding the nipple, stimulating it and withdrawing milk. The mother's reactions and the baby's can mutually regulate one another, the baby taking what he needs, the mother supplying it. Human milk is biochemically suited to human infants. In the early weeks after birth, the baby's sucking stimulates the mother's uterus to contract and hence fosters return to normal size and structure. On the other side of the ledger is the fact that many mothers do not produce enough milk to sustain their babies, and that some women do not wish to nurse their babies, no matter what their milk supply.

Little is known about the long-term results of different nursing situations, although a recent study [21] gives some insight into this question. The behavior of 47 boys and 47 girls was studied from birth to 18 years of age, through mothers' reports, interviews with mothers and children, ratings and projective tests. The mothers' personalities were studied, rated and related to their children's experiences and behavior. The results did not show any difference between bottle-fed and breast-fed children, nor did they indicate any relationship between method of feeding and health. (This is not to say that no differences existed, but only that no differences were demonstrated by this research.) The study did show that nursing became important in connection with other factors in the child's life. The mother's stability and psychological warmth were the key factors in the significance of breast feeding. Boys nursed by a warm mother for a long time had few behavior problems; boys fed by a cold mother for a long time on either breast or bottle had the largest number of behavior problems. For girls, a different set of relationships appeared. A short nursing period was most favorable when the mother was stable; a long nursing period was associated with few behavior problems when the mother was unstable. When mothers were cold, daughters showed fewer behavior problems if bottle-fed than if breast-fed. Thus nursing experience is important within context, its significance depending upon the sex of the child and the psychological warmth and stability of the mother. These findings raise serious doubts about the wisdom of any person or group trying to promote a particular technique of feeding without regard for the individual mother–infant relationship.

WEANING. Emerging resources include new ways of eating. Instead of getting all of his food as liquids which he sucks, the baby learns to bite and chew solids and to drink liquids from a cup. This particular changeover is called weaning. Weaning is also used sometimes to mean any gradual change from immature to mature behavior. In all contexts, weaning usually involves some pushing and encouraging of the child toward more mature behavior. The timing and techniques of weaning are related to personality development of the child and to cultural prescriptions.

Modern Americans are advised by their authorities to wean gradually. The Children's Bureau, The Child Study Association and Dr. Spock all recommend gradual substitution of the cup for the bottle or breast. In addition to being gradual, the mother is usually warned that the baby needs extra loving and attention when he is being asked to give up a familiar way of eating.

Americans usually wean babies during the first year. The Children's Bureau publication written for parents of minimal reading level says, "Take your time with weaning. Breast-fed babies can be weaned directly and gradually to a cup after about 6 months old. Bottle-fed babies usually like to suck the bottle a little longer" [5].

The stress on gradualness and gentleness is consistent with what is known about personality development during the first year. While developing his sense of trust, it is most helpful for the baby to be assured that the world and the people in it can be trusted. Traumatic experiences and major readjustments to life are injurious to the sense of trust and hence to the establishment of the foundations of a healthy personality.

An example of another cultural setting shows how weaning can be crucial to the sense of autonomy, rather than to the sense of trust, when weaning occurs at a time that is critical for the sense of autonomy. A group of Zulu babies were studied before, during and after weaning, which occurred between 15 and 24 months, at the average age of 19 months [1]. The day of weaning was a serious event, fixed months ahead. Bitter juice of the aloe was put on the mother's breast while the child watched and then the breast was offered to him throughout the day. A charm was put around his neck, to help him in various ways. On the day of weaning, all but one baby refused the breast after the first encounter with the aloe juice. Behavior changes followed a definite pattern of disintegration, followed by integration on a higher level. During the first two hours, the toddlers became more negativistic, aggressive and fretful. They sucked their fingers and other objects. Some performed stereotyped actions. After the first day, relationships changed with everyone in the home. With their mothers, they first alternated attacking and ignoring, then tried to gain attention by illness, clinging, fretting and crying and finally paid little attention to them, showing no anger and behaving with increasing independence. Sudden increases in mature behavior included helping with housework, imitating others, using new words, talking more distinctly, leaving home more often and showing hospitality. Children also became more aggressive and mischievous, spilling water, playing with fire and wasting food. Eating patterns changed, with preferences for adult food and greatly increased appetite.

These behavior changes can be seen as contributing to a growing sense of autonomy. Normal development during the second year, especially the latter half of the second year, involves establishing oneself as a separate individual. All of these six changes in behavior indicate increased independence, power in decision making, differentiation and reorganization. The weaning experience apparently precipitated the second stage of personality growth. Thus the method of sudden weaning, conducted differently and timed differently, had a very different result from weaning conducted American-style. Both methods of weaning can be seen to be functional in regard to the stage of personality growth during which they are conducted.

SELF-REGULATION OF DIET IN INFANCY. Of great practical significance is the question of how competent the child is to select the quantity and quality of his food. "Does the baby know how much he ought to eat?" and "Does the baby know what is good for him?" are questions which have long been debated by parents, doctors, nurses and teachers of young children. The classic experiment of Clara Davis [7, 8, 9] gives information as to choices infants can make under a certain set of conditions. Davis took a group of newly weaned babies and gave them complete freedom to choose their diets from a variety of simple, natural, unmixed, unseasoned foods, including fruits, vegetables, milk, eggs, meat, whole-grain cereals, salt and cod liver oil. At first a baby tended to sample all of the food on his tray, but later on, he was likely to settle down to a smaller selection of foods. Sometimes an infant would go on a "jag" and eat five eggs at a sitting or drink a large amount of cod liver oil. No child suffered a digestive upset from such a spree. At the end of the experiment, all subjects had grown well, were in good health, and some in better nutritional condition than at the beginning. An analysis of their 36,000 meals showed that the infants had balanced their diets perfectly. Davis [9] paints a vivid word picture of the babies:

> . . . Before meals hands and faces are washed and when the dietitian comes in and says, "The trays are ready," all who can walk join in an eager rush to the dining room, the nurses carrying the others. Bibs are tied on and, as the trays are brought in, the smaller babies often show their eagerness for food by jumping up and down in their chairs, and trying to reach the trays before they are set down on the tables. Yet, once started, they eat with an evident absence of strain, without hurry and without dallying and with poise and complete satisfaction, knowing that they may have all they want of everything. Sometimes they fall asleep while eating as their eyes close like nursing babies. This almost pagan joy of eating reminds one of young animals or the accounts of the eating of primitive peoples. Since they feed themselves with their hands the babies rapidly become independent, and by the time they are fifteen or sixteen months old the nurses' functions are reduced to moving dishes that the child cannot reach and seeing that empty ones are refilled, so that one nurse seated between their tables can attend to two infants. From the age of twenty months on all the babies thus far have been able not only to feed themselves entirely, but to rearrange their dishes on the tray to suit themselves and to hold up empty ones to attract attention when they wish them refilled. These older ones have only waitress service, no nurse sitting beside them. When a baby is through eating, he gets down or is helped down and leaves the dining room whether the others have finished or not.*

Thus research showed that human beings, at least as infants, have in common with animals the ability to choose the kind of food they need and to eat the amounts they need for adequate growth and maintenance. Even though Davis first reported her research in 1928, it has taken a long time

* From C. M. Davis, "Self-Selection of Food by Children," *Am. J. Nursing,* 1935, **35,** 403–410. Reprinted, with permission, from the *American Journal of Nursing,* May 1935.

to spread the news. Even more difficult is the problem of putting it into practice in our culture. What mother *can* provide cafeteria service while keeping her toddler away from all contact with candy, soft drinks, ice cream and other snack foods, as well as the dishes she prepares for the other members of the family who like stew, salad and pie?

What happens at mealtime is significant not only for physical growth but for personality development too. Trust grows as the baby learns he can count on satisfying meals turning up as he feels a need for food. Early autonomous activity includes the defensive actions of dribbling, drooling, not accepting, not swallowing, compulsive repetitious acts, using substitute oral comfort, such as sucking fingers, blanket or pacifier [36, p. 305]. Seeking, finding and taking in food are positive kinds of autonomous acts. As Davis has shown, infants of about a year of age can be very autonomous in choosing what to eat, how much to eat and how to eat it. The possibility that children have good nutrition while being autonomous in the selection of foods requires, as in the Davis experiment, not only that they be allowed their selections but also that all of the choices available to them be foods that are nutritionally valuable in themselves. Chocolate bars and lollipops, pies and doughnuts, were not on Davis's menus.

Locomotion

The baby's world expands and stimulation increases greatly when he learns to move from one place to another. Much maturation and learning go on before the infant actually creeps, crawls or hitches.

Growth of the parts of the brain concerned with locomotion is evident as the baby progresses through the locomotor sequence. The motor region of the cortex is maturing at a faster rate than other regions. The cerebellum, concerned largely with balance and posture, grows slowly during the first few months and rapidly in size and complexity between 6 and 18 months [15]. The sequence of motor development is shown in the silhouettes presented in Figure 4–2. Here is shown progression from fetal position to walking—in 15 months.

The following items from the Griffiths scale of locomotor development gives more details of the stages of locomotion, showing the order in which they normally occur [19, pp. 140–142].

FIRST YEAR

FIRST THREE MONTHS

1. Lifts his chin up slightly when lying in the prone position.
2. Pushes with both feet against the examiner's hands.
3. Holds his head erect for a few seconds.
4. Lifts his head well up when lying prone.
5. Kicks his feet vigorously when put to lie down.
6. Is active in his bath, kicking his feet, etc.
7. Lifts his head up slightly when in the dorsal position.
8. Can roll from side to back.

Figure 4–2. The sequence of motor development, with ages at which the average baby achieves each coordination. (Reprinted by permission from M. M. Shirley, *The First Two Years: A Study of Twenty-Five Babies,* Vol. II: Intellectual Development, Copyright © University of Minnesota Press, Minneapolis, 1933.)

SECOND THREE MONTHS

9. His back is firm when held in the sitting position.
10. Lifts his head and chest up when lying prone.
11. Holds his head erect continuously.
12. Lifts his head and shoulders when in dorsal position.
13. Can roll from one side right over to the other.
14. Plays with his toes.
15. First crawling reaction: pushes on hands, draws up knees, etc.
16. Sits with slight support—for example, can be left sitting among pillows in pram or cot.

THIRD THREE MONTHS

17. Can roll over from back to stomach or from stomach to back.
18. First stepping reaction: (a) moves feet alternately as if dancing when held up.
19. Tries vigorously to crawl, using both hands and feet (Crawling II).
20. Sits alone for a short while.

21. Stepping reaction: (b) feet now go definitely one in front of the other.
22. Can turn himself around when left lying on the floor (Crawling III).
23. Can be left sitting on the floor.
24. Crawling IV: makes some progress, forward or backward.

FOURTH THREE MONTHS

25. Stands when held up.
26. Sits well in a chair.
27. Can pull himself up from crawling or sitting, by grasping the furniture.
28. Can stand holding on to furniture.
29. Crawling V: creeps on hands and knees, or gets about freely by some other method—for example, bear walk.
30. Sidesteps around inside cot or playpen, holding on to railings.
31. Can walk when led, adult holding one or both hands.

SECOND YEAR

FIRST THREE MONTHS

32. Climbs onto a ledge or step when crawling.
33. Can stand alone.
34. Walks alone, at first unsteadily.
35. Can kneel on floor or chair. Balances in this position.
36. Climbs the stairs, climbing up but not yet down.
37. Likes to walk pushing a pram, or toy horse, or other toy.

SECOND THREE MONTHS

38. He now trots about well.
39. Can stoop to pick up a toy without overbalancing.
40. Climbs into a low chair.
41. Can walk backward.
42. Likes to walk pulling a toy on a string.

THIRD THREE MONTHS

43. Can climb stairs, up and down.
44. Can jump. Child gives a little jump when standing if pleased, etc., with both feet off floor together.
45. Runs. This is not a trot now but a definite running.
46. Can now *walk* upstairs, no longer on hands and knees, holding adult's hand, etc.
47. Climbs and stands up on a chair.

FOURTH THREE MONTHS

48. Can jump off a step, both feet off the ground together.
49. Can seat himself at a table, placing chair first.
50. Walks up and down stairs; has abandoned climbing, but holds adult's hand or banisters.
51. Can kick a ball.
52. Can be trusted on stairs alone.*

* Reprinted by permission from Ruth Griffiths, *The Abilities of Babies* (London: University of London Press Ltd., 1954), pp. 140–142. Copyright © 1954, University of London Press Ltd.

The locomotion of the first year is creeping, of the second year, walking. Each of these ways of getting around in the world can be traced from early beginnings. Considering creeping, you can see its beginning in the early attempts to raise the head when the baby is in prone position. Most babies do this momentarily at one or two months, gradually lifting their heads higher and for longer periods of time. Although some babies actually make progress by crawling during their first weeks, this reflex-like movement fades out, leaving infants stationary until they develop the more purposive kind of creeping movements. Although maturation plays a major role in the achievement of creeping, anyone who has watched a baby go through the final stages before creeping is likely to conclude that a great deal of effort and trial and error go into developing this coordination. For instance, the *swimming stage* is one in which the baby perches on his abdomen, does a completely ineffectual frog kick and moves his arms at cross purposes as often as not [47]. Any progress at this point is likely to be backward and slight. Shortly afterward comes a stage when babies try out a variety of methods, such as using the stomach as a pivot, hitching by means of head and feet, shoulders and feet or buttocks and hand, making a bridge by standing on toes and hands and scooting backward. Although some infants retain idiosyncratic ways of creeping, most do it in the usual style, which is shown in Figure 2.

Basic to walking are holding the head and shoulders erect, sitting, making stepping movements and standing. Even in the first trimester, most infants resist with their feet when held in standing position. Gradually more and more of the baby's weight is borne by his feet. Stepping movements (while held) begin in what looks like dancing, standing on the toes, lifting one foot and then the other and putting them down in the same place. Later come putting one foot down ahead of the other, and bouncing. Before they can pull themselves up into standing position, most babies can stand hanging onto helping hands or to the rail of a playpen. Some children, however, learn to pull up before they can remain standing [16, p. 39; 21, p. 147].

Most children learn to walk during the first trimester of the second year. Parents often think that their baby really could walk if he would, since he gets around so quickly and easily with one hand held or with just one hand on a piece of furniture. The stage of cruising or walking with help seems to be a period of perfecting walking skills and gaining confidence before setting out independently. Walking is unsteady at first, gradually improving with maturing and practice. Maturation includes a change in proportions and posture, as well as neuromuscular development. The toddler has short legs, a long trunk, large head and abdomen and consequently a center of gravity high in his trunk. In order to balance himself better, he spreads his feet, walking on a broad base. As his proportions change toward those of childhood, he can afford to place his feet closer together. By the second half of the first year, he can run, covering territory at least twice as fast.

Locomotion includes climbing, too, which looks much like creeping, but begins in the second year, usually in the first trimester. Climbing further enlarges the infant's scope of activities, giving him the run of all the floors of his home and access to the sofa, chairs, tabletops, cupboards, drawers.

Because the world expands so enormously with sitting, creeping, walking, running and climbing, there are a multitude of opportunities for the sense of autonomy to grow. So many choices to make! So many ways in which to test oneself! So many avenues to discovery of powers and limits on powers! It can be very heady or even overwhelming.

Manipulation

Through the use of his hands, the baby reaches out into the world, finds out about it and changes it. He cannot interact much with his hands until he can sit up, although he does make a beginning in the early weeks. The first trimester is a time of contacting objects with eyes more than with hands, following moving objects in several directions. The grasping reflex, present at birth, is strong for the first three months and loses its automatic quality before the first half year. At first the grasping reflex consists of grasping anything that is placed against the palm. Gradually the child becomes able to grasp objects that he touches with his hand, first in a fumbling way and then more and more deftly. At the same time that he is starting to grasp what his hand contacts, around the end of the first trimester, he also looks at his hands and glances at the objects he holds [15].

A photographic study [20] of the development of reaching and grasping show how grasping changes from a primitive sequence of palm and fingers to a precise coordination of thumb and forefinger. As can be seen in Figure 4–3,

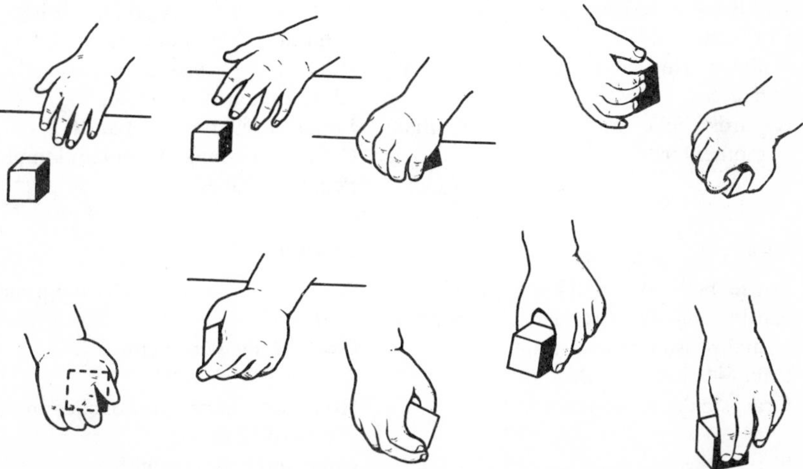

Figure 4–3. Stages in the development of grasping. (Reprinted by permission from H. M. Halverson, "An Experimental Study of Prehension in Infants by Means of Systematic Cinema Records," *Genetic Psychology Monograph,* **10,** 107–286. Copyright © 1931, The Journal Press.)

coordination of thumb and forefinger occurs when a baby picks up a pellet or a crumb. When the baby can look and grasp, he also takes the object to his mouth, where he examines it further with his lips, gums and tongue.

In a description of the sequence of development in eye–hand coordination, the principle of differentiation and integration stands out. Early grasping is an all-out event, with both arms active and the whole body straining. On the Gesell test, 12 weeks intervene between this kind of approach and a one-handed grasp. Transferring objects from one hand to another comes at the same time as one-handed grasp. Here is the beginning of the differentiation that is basic to human manipulation. One hand does one thing while the other does something else and the two are integrated, working toward one goal. In the course of differentiation and integration, one hand becomes the preferred hand, to be used as the leader in manipulation.

A list of items from the Gesell test [16] shows the sequence in which manipulation and its mental concomitants develop.*

4 weeks

Hand clenches on contact.
Drops immediately.
Regards ring and rattle in line of vision only.
Follows ring moving from side to midline.

8 weeks

Follows ring moving past midline.
Looks at hand holding the ring.
Retains rattle briefly.

12 weeks

Holds rattle actively, glances at.
Contacts cup.
Follows ring moving through 180 degrees.
Regards cube and cup more than momentarily.

16 weeks

Ring—retains, regards, brings to mouth; free hand to midline.
Ring, rattle—regards immediately.
Ring, etc., arms activate.
Looks at test table or hands.
Cube, cup—looks from hand to object.
Pellet—regards.

20 weeks

Rattle, bell—two-handed approach.
Rattle, ring—grasps near hand only.
Visual pursuit of lost rattle.
Cube—holds, regards another.
Grasps cube on contact.

24 weeks

Ring, rattle, cube, bell—approaches, grasps.
Grasps cube with palm.
Retains rattle.
Holds one cube, approaches another, regards a third.
Cube and bell to mouth.

* From A. Gesell and C. Amatruda, *Developmental Diagnosis.* Copyright 1941, 1947 by Arnold Gesell (New York: Hoeber, 1951). Reprinted by permission of Harper & Row, Publishers, Incorporated.

28 weeks

Cube—grasps with thumb and palm.
Pellet—rakes with whole hand.
One-handed approach and grasp.
Holds cube, grasps another.
Shakes rattle, bangs bell.
Transfers cube, ring, bell.

32 weeks

Grasps second cube, holds prolongedly.
Retains two as third cube presented.
Pellet—rakes, tries scissors prehension.
Holds cube, regards cup.
Pulls string to secure ring.

36 weeks

Grasps third cube.
Hits, pushes cube with cube.
Cube against cup.
Pellet and bottle—approaches bottle.
Manipulates string.

40 weeks

Crude release of cube.
Grasps pellet with thumb and forefinger.
Plucks string easily.
Matches two cubes.
Touches cube in cup.
Index finger approach to pellet.
Pellet and bottle—regards, grasps pellet.
Bell—grasps by handle, shakes.

44 weeks

Removes cube from cup.
Imitates putting cube into cup without release.
Points at pellet through bottle.
Regards and pokes clapper of bell.
Approaches string before ring.

48 weeks

Plays with cubes in sequence.
Pellet and bottle—takes pellet only.
Removes round block from formboard easily.
Neat pincer grasp of pellet.

52 weeks

Tries to build tower of two cubes.
Releases one cube in cup (demonstrated).
Tries, fails, to insert pellet in bottle.
Dangles ring by string.
Looks at round hole in formboard.

56 weeks

Cube into cup (no demonstration).
Drawing—imitates scribble.
Formboard—inserts round block.
Grasps two cubes in one hand.

15 months

Tower of two.
Six cubes in and out of cup.
Incipient imitation of stroke in drawing.
Places round block (no demonstration).
Adapts to turning formboard.

18 months

Throws small ball.
Turns pages, two or three at a time.
Tower of three or four cubes.
Ten cubes into cup.
Dumps pellet out of bottle.
Spontaneous scribble.
Imitates stroke in drawing.
Piles three blocks onto formboard.

21 months

Tower of five or six.
Imitates pushing train with cubes.
Places two or three blocks in formboard.
Retrieves ball out of box.

24 months

Tower of six or seven.
Aligns two or more cubes for train.
Imitates *V* and circular stroke in drawing.
Turns pages of book singly.
Inserts blocks after formboard rotated.
Inserts square block into box.

Reading over this list of accomplishments, you can see how the baby gradually learns to release objects from his hands, a task more difficult than grasping. Notice how long it is between the first releasing of the cube and the time when he can put a pellet into a bottle.

Note also how he gains in the ability to use objects and to use more than one object at a time. Here are the early stages of man's ability to use tools. You can see him as an infant, hitting a cube against a cup, choosing between bottle and pellet, considering the details of a ball and using a pencil on a paper.

INTELLECTUAL DEVELOPMENT

The infant experiences people, objects and himself as he interacts with his environment. He explores through his sensory and motor resources, making some changes in the objects and people he contacts, changing himself as he receives sensory data and processes them. He communicates with people, rapidly improving his techniques for doing so. As he refines his methods of communicating, he is also developing a tool of thinking.

Cognition

Cognoscere, Latin for *to know,* gives rise to the term *cognition,* one of man's most human activities. By *cognition* is meant the individual's becoming acquainted with the world and the objects in it, including himself. He comes to understand relationships between objects and between himself and the world, by taking in information through his senses and processing it. While cognition is of great practical use from day to day and from moment to moment, man cognizes just for fun in addition to cognizing for necessity. The toddler's flow of "Wazzat?" the curiosity of the preschool child, the drive of the research scientist—all reflect a certain amount of wanting to know for the sake of knowing. Cognition goes on during most of what is called play in infancy. While using all of his resources for dealing with the world, the infant is also cognizing and developing cognitively.

KNOWING THE WORLD. According to Piaget [24] cognitive development takes place in stages that can be distinguished by achievements. Each stage prepares the way for the stage that follows it. The major stages can be divided into substages. The first major stage, the period of sensorimotor intelligence, lasting 18 months or more, has six substages.

The achievement of the infancy stage in cognition is to come to know one's immediate environment as permanent objects and background, separate from oneself. *Permanent* means that the object (bottle, mother, rattle, and such) continues to exist even though it is moved, hidden or placed in a new relationship with other objects (such as mother in a party-going hat). All the parts of an object (such as the nipple on a bottle) must be known to exist even when they cannot be seen.

Understanding some facts about movement is a part of coming to know permanent objects. A child has to find out that when an object is moved, it can be put back again, that when it turns around, it can be turned in the other direction, that when an object is moved away, he can reach it by a path other than the one taken by the object, in fact by many different paths.

Starting with the resources he has for dealing with the world, the baby uses them to develop new patterns of action. For example, he integrates thumb-sucking with grasping and grasping with looking at his hand. The result is a behavior pattern of grasping an object, looking at it, bringing it to the mouth and examining it. Using this method of exploration many times with toys, bottles, clothing and other objects, the infant makes progress toward the conviction that objects are permanent. Other behavior patterns, involving seeing, smelling, tasting, hearing, touching and manipulating, are used in getting knowledge of the world. Locomotion, moving from place to place, gives the baby chances to map out the space in which he lives, getting to truly cognize it and himself as an object in space.

As experience with reality shows his existing resources to be inadequate or insufficient, the baby develops new ones through changes or improvements in what he has. When the child falls only slightly short of being adequate to cope with an experience, his feeling tone is pleasant and interesting. Growth is stimulated. When he is very inadequate in dealing with the experience, the child is frightened and tries to withdraw [22].

Piaget has described six substages of the period of sensorimotor intelligence,* the period during which the infant establishes basic knowledge of the world. The substages are:

I. *Simple reflexive action*. The schemas of the neonatal period are the reflex movements described in Chapters 2 and 3 and a general mass activity. During this stage, various abilities, such as the sucking reflexes, improve and consolidate. The baby can neither reach for an object nor search for it. There is no indication that he cognizes objects as separate parts of the environment or as distinct from himself.

II. *Primary circular reactions*. Neonatal behavior patterns begin to change through maturation and experience. The baby learns to bring his hand to his mouth and to suck on it, most likely his thumb. He touches his hands together and fingers them, looks at his hands and at objects grasped by his hands. Objects grasped by the hands are carried to the mouth. He looks at an object

* Follows Flavell [13, pp. 85–121].

making a noise. He does not know what he can cause and what takes place independent of his own actions.

III. *Secondary circular reactions.* The baby develops ways of prolonging interesting events. When a change in the environment results from his actions, he is likely to repeat those actions. He reaches for the toy suspended from his crib, hits it, watches it move and hits it again.

He still does not search for an object that has disappeared, suggesting that he still does not conceive of it as existing permanently. However, if all but a small part of an object is covered, as when his bottle sticks out from under his blanket, he recognizes it and can recover it. If an object is made to disappear slowly, he follows it with his eyes and continues tne movement of his eyes in the direction in which the object went. If, however, it is jerked away, or quickly screened, he does not look for it. One of Piaget's experiments with his son, Laurent, showed that the baby did not even miss the bottle when it was hidden quickly. Just before a feeding time, when Laurent was hungry, Piaget showed him his bottle, whereupon Laurent cried. Piaget quickly hid the bottle and Laurent stopped crying. This sequence was repeated several times. When Laurent could see a small portion of the bottle, he cried harder than ever [38, p. 30].

Another interesting aspect of substage III, evident in Laurent's behavior, was failure to realize the existence of the nipple if it did not show. When he saw a small portion of the bottle but not the nipple, he tried to suck the bottle itself, but when the nipple was visible, he turned the bottle around so that he could suck the nipple. Thus he cognized the bottle as a suckable object, but unless he could see the nipple, he did not deal with the bottle as an object with a specialized suckable portion. Thus in this stage, objects are becoming endowed with permanence, but the process is not complete.

IV. *Coordination of secondary schemas.* Secondary circular reactions become coordinated with each other to form more complex schemas. The new schemas are used definitely as means to ends. This is the earliest age at which the baby shows intention in a definite and unmistakable way. For example, hitting is not just for the sake of hitting, but in order to grasp a new object. Piaget tells how Laurent, at nine and a half months, pushed his father's hand and at the same time pulled on the toy which Piaget was holding [39, p. 219].

There is true searching for a vanished object, although still not complete appreciation of the object's permanence. Piaget describes how his daughter Jacqueline searched for a toy parrot. First, Piaget covered it with his hand. Jacqueline raised his hand and grasped the parrot. Piaget slowly took the toy away from her, hid it under a rug and put his hand on her lap, on the spot where the parrot had first been. Jacqueline raised his hand and looked under it for the parrot. This process was repeated three times [38, p. 51].

V. *Tertiary circular reactions.* Instead of merely prolonging or reproducing interesting events, the baby tries to produce new events. He experiments to see what will happen. He appears definitely curious, looking for new experience.

Now the baby looks for a vanished object in the place where it disappeared instead of in the place where he last found it. He demonstrates increased understanding of movements of objects by following a trajectory and looking at its end and by throwing something back of himself and turning around in the other direction to look for it.

Throwing and dropping toys are common kinds of play at this age, as the infant examines movements of objects, disappearance and reappearance, building his understanding of the permanence of objects. Piaget watched Laurent using various methods of letting a tin can fall from his hands and then dropping a chunk of bread first as a whole and then in the form of crumbs. Later Laurent dropped toys from different positions.

VI. *Invention of new means through mental combinations.* Instead of having to go through a series of sensorimotor explorations and trials, the child can find solutions mentally. He begins this stage by representing objects and actions to himself. Probably the first kind of representing is to act it out. Piaget's daughter, Lucienne, illustrated this behavior when she was trying to get a little chain out of a match box. She looked at the small opening, not knowing how to open it wider, then opened and shut her mouth several times, each time opening it wider [39, pp. 337–338]. After a few quiet moments, she used a new technique to open the box with her finger. Lucienne's opening of her own mouth was a symbolic act, representing the opening of the box, which she desired. This stage, in coping with problems, is midway between trying out solutions in action and thinking them out. When problems are solved by thinking, without any action, the child is representing objects and actions to himself by symbols which are entirely within. He thinks of ways of acting and tries them out by thinking. He can think of objects which are not present, of past events and of events which might happen.

The toddler shows his new powers by imitation and pretending and insightful problem solving. When he imitates a past event, he shows that he has a mental image of it. When he pretends, he uses a mental image of a behavior pattern to act out that pattern in a new situation. Feeding a doll, he uses his mental image of his mother's behavior, acting it out at his little table. The achievement of imitation, pretending and insightful problem solving marks the completion of the stage of sensorimotor development. As with all the stages outlined by Piaget, the average age for beginning and ending a stage is not placed exactly but approximately. The sensorimotor stage, according to Piaget, ends at around 18 months. Gesell [16, p. 71] places imitation and pretending at two years, which is probably closer to the age at which most children achieve these feats.*

Ordering and classifying, cognitive behavior which develops noticeably during the next stage of intellectual development, can be observed in its very

* Piaget's observations on sensorimotor activity were on his own children, who were most likely very advanced in development. The importance of Piaget's work lies in his revealing the ways in which intelligence grows. Gesell contributed information on norms.

beginnings during infancy. Gesell mentions the one-year-old's sequential play with cubes as being a preliminary to ordering and counting, and his looking at a round hole while holding a matching block as being incipient perception of geometric form [16, p. 65]. Between 12 and 24 months, infants will do some sorting and grouping when presented with an array of two different kinds of objects, such as four clay balls with four yellow cubes [44]. Sorting and grouping activity increased with age between 12 and 24 months.

KNOWING THE SELF. Only a small beginning in self-cognition can be made in infancy, but it is essential. To know reality means to know that you are an object distinct from other objects, including background and people. One of man's unique features is the ability to stand off and look at himself, himself as an individual and himself as related to the rest of the world.

Although one may recognize a human being as an organism-in-a-field, as an individual intimately bound up with and interacting with his environment, the common definition of a baby's or a man's boundary is his skin. For most practical purposes, he stops where his skin stops. When a baby fingers his hands, bites his toes, lets his hand fall on his chest, when he watches these actions with his eyes, feels them with both hands, with mouth and toes, with chest and hand, he is coming to know his body. He is cognizing his body, or building an inner image of it. The sensations which come from within, largely gastrointestinal, add to the image. At first, the baby probably does not make a distinction between his own body and his mother's. Psychoanalysts say that gradually he realizes their separateness as he experiences wanting the breast and not getting it. There are additional experiences of separation from the mother—being alone instead of seeing her, feeling the tactile pleasure of her arms and face and hearing her voice. These separations also define his being from his mother's.

The body image surely grows in clarity as the infant finds out which events in the world are caused by him and which are not. In fact, the two are reciprocal. It is only around four months of age that the baby seems to make a dim connection between one of his actions and an event, such as hitting the cradle gym and seeing it swing. He gradually cognizes the interaction of his body with the rest of the world, and as he does, he knows his body better.

PARENTS' CONTRIBUTION TO SENSORIMOTOR DEVELOPMENT. Although not always recognized as such, mothers and other family members are teachers in that they help babies to know the world and to deal with it.

It is not with the aim of education that a mother picks up her baby, cuddles, pats, strokes and kisses him, murmurs words of baby talk and sings a lullaby to him. She really is teaching, however, if teaching is considered to include the offerings of opportunities for development and learning. Picking Billy up gives him a great rich field of perception—touch sensations on the skin of his body and head; muscle sensations as his muscles are pressed by his mother's hands and as he moves himself; inner ear stimulation as his head swings up from a horizontal to vertical orientation and the balance mechanisms operate; a completely different visual world, full of varied objects instead of walls and ceiling; for his hands to feel, his mother's clothing, her firm shoulder, soft neck and hair; against his cheek, her warm cheek and lips; her voice to listen to. His cognition, his knowing of the world, proceeds through sensory experiences, these and others. Picking Billy up is only one small act among the many educational acts his mother performs. She props him up, too, so that he can see the world from this angle. He looks at his hands, at toys his mother puts in his lap, at his hands contacting the toys. Babies of three or four months who have had normal opportunities (for American culture) strain to sit up and show by their pleasure in being propped that this is a welcome experience. A frequent change of position prevents fatigue and enriches the sensory field. Here is one place where resident grandparents and older brothers and sisters can add to a baby's education, since mothers often have many duties in addition to baby teaching, and many fathers are absent all day.

When sitting and grasping schemas are sufficiently developed, the normally experienced infant enthusiastically accepts and examines all objects that come his way. For example, here is part of a half hour's observation of an eleven-month-old baby.

> George pulled himself to his feet and stood watching his mother for a few minutes. He moved around the rail of the playpen by putting one foot out to the side and bringing the other up to it. . . . He squealed, tried to hurry and fell down. . . .
>
> Mrs. MacIntyre gave George a cardboard box with a ball in it. George pounced on the ball and dropped it . . . he crept after it and then put it back in the box. He took it out, dropped it, crept after it, and so on, going through the whole process four times. He sat and watched the adults for a minute. Then he picked up a stuffed cat by the tail. His fingers slipped up and down the tail. He squeezed the cat and touched the fur. He poked its eyes and pulled the whiskers. A red ribbon and bell around the cat's neck came in for a share of fingering and pulling. George dropped the cat and pulled himself up.
>
> George sat down and picked a string of brightly colored beads out of his toy basket. He looked at several of the beads and poked at them with his finger. He shook the string and put it round his neck. Then he tried to get it off by pulling down. The beads worked down over his arm. George roared until his mother pulled them off. He put them on again immediately. . . .
>
> George beat on the saucepan and lid with the spoon, gnawed the spoon, put the lid on the saucepan with a bang, removed the lid. He thumped the pan on the lid and the lid on the pan, put the spoon in the pan and the lid on his head. He put the ball in the saucepan [48, pp. 122–123].

Thus a baby sought and found many sensations. Visual sensations were combined with touch, giving varieties of shape, texture, size and color. Touch sensations came from his hands, lips, gums, tongue, knees, feet and buttocks. He elicited sounds. Active as George was, he could not have experienced such a wealth of sensations had the toys and play materials not been present in his environment. Due to his mother's planning, management and constant care, he had the wherewithal to educate himself.

Several studies have demonstrated the importance of sensory stimulation during the sensorimotor period. Both the amount of stimulation and quality of stimulation of the baby by the mother have been found highly related to the baby's IQ [53]. By *quality* is meant the appropriateness of the stimulation to the child as an individual and to his developmental level. A study done in infant welfare clinics in England, where 90 percent of young children are served by such clinics, related babies' sensory and motor development to their mothers' ways of caring for them [2]. The infants who received maximum stimulation were farthest ahead on the tests of sensory and motor achievement.

Most dramatic of studies of sensorimotor stimulation are those done in the most drastic of settings, consisting of infant institutions in Iran. The effect of sensorimotor experience on IQ was demonstrated by a comparison between subjects from a well-baby clinic and a group from an institution where babies were kept in cribs with covered sides [11]. The latter could see nobody but the caretakers, and those only rarely. Bottles were propped for feeding. Caretakers picked the babies up only for physical care. Words and caresses were very rare. When tested on the Catell Infant Scale, the control group had an average IQ of 102; the institution group, 68. The institution babies had had practically none of the experiences which would give them a fair chance on the test. The test requires that babies over two months be held on an adult's lap for many of the items. The institution babies had not sat on laps, and therefore had not had the sensory perceptions and the consequent cognitive development that stem from lapsitting. Such restricted children would not have a fair chance in real life situations, either. The second study [10] compared the babies in the institution just described with infants in another institution. In Institution I, where the infants lay in cribs with covered sides, they remained in the cribs until they were able to pull themselves to sitting, when they were placed on pieces of linoleum on the stone floor. There were no toys. Bottles were propped in the beds. Baths were given on alternate days. The control group was from Institution III, where babies were held in arms while fed, placed prone, propped to sit, put in playpens on the floor and given plenty of toys. Both groups were tested on five motor items.

Table 4–9 shows their achievements. Children in Institution III were much superior to those in Institution I, although the former did not equal the performance on home-reared children (as reported in the norm given on pages 111, 112 and 113. Although all normal, American home-reared children sit alone by nine months and nearly all walk alone by two years, among the children in Institution I less than half could sit alone before age two. Only 8 percent could walk before age three.

Children in Institution I were thus severely retarded in motor development.

TABLE 4–9

Motor achievements of babies in two contrasting institutions in Iran.

	Percent of Group Passing Each Test			
Institution	*I*	*I*	*III*	*III*
N	*50*	*40*	*20*	*31*
Age Range	*1.0–1.9*	*2.0–2.9*	*1.0–1.9*	*2.0–2.9*
Sit alone	42	95	90	100
Creep or scoot	14	75	75	100
Stand holding	4	45	70	100
Walk holding	2	40	60	100
Walk alone	0	8	15	94

Source: Reprinted by permission from W. Dennis, "Causes of Retardation Among Institutional Children: Iran," *Journal of Genetic Psychology*, **96**, 46–60. Copyright © 1960, The Journal Press.

They also showed differences in mode of locomotion. Almost all who could progress did it by scooting, whereas those in Institution III progressed by creeping. The author reasons that the babies scooted because they had never been placed in positions where creeping and preparation for creeping were possible. They rarely, if ever rolled from supine to prone in their cribs because the cribs were very small and the mattresses soft. In contrast, a child in Institution III, often prone in bed and on the floor, could raise his head, push with his arms, raise his chest, pull his arms and legs beneath his body and thus practice creeping. Thus delayed walking, as well as delayed creeping, can result from denying a child the prone position. The child who creeps can go to the playpen rail or a piece of furniture and pull himself to his knees. He may walk on his knees. Soon he pulls himself to his feet. He then is in a position to practice walking while hanging on, and this he does, in the normative sequence for Americans, for two or three months.

The data assembled by a number of investigators have been summarized to show that rate of intellectual growth is influenced in infancy by the number of new objects and events experienced. The more varied the experience the more the child seeks new experiences [23, pp. 148–149]. That is, the more curious he becomes. Thus children who have had few toys and other stimulation become apathetic, as do institutional children who have had limited space and opportunities to explore.

Communication

Communication gradually takes on a conscious and purposeful quality, overlaid upon the subcortical feeling and tactual experiences and behavior displays of the newborn. The baby cuddles and snuggles in ways that spell love and affection to adults. Perhaps to the baby it means simply a good feeling or a feeling of warmth and closeness. It is a relationship which a baby can choose or reject, since even during the first half of the first year, he will sometimes snuggle close, relaxing and melting his body to conform with the adult's, while at other times he will stiffen and push his body upright. During the second year, to cuddle or not to cuddle is a choice that the baby prefers to make. While he wants and needs loving arms and a hospitable lap, it is important to him to take it or leave it according to how he feels at the moment. He cries and shoves the gushing auntie who snatches him up to hug and kiss him at an inappropriate time, communicating to her clearly.

Stroking, patting and hugging develop out of early cuddling. Kissing probably comes from the pursing reflex of feeding. During his first two years, the baby takes into himself the acts of love he has experienced, the gestures by which his family have symbolized their love for him. He gives them back, and the expression of love becomes more of a true communication.

Children in the second year often communicate purposefully with their hands, pulling another person to show him something, pushing him away, putting a hand over a mouth that is saying what the child does not want to hear, pointing at food, toys and wet pants. Such language of the hands can be very effective in transferring ideas, even without a single word. Insofar as they achieve what the baby wants, these methods of communicating are, to him, adequate ways of coping with the world.

Vocal communication begins with crying and develops out of it. Frequency of crying during the early days of life shows a positive correlation with intelligence scores at three years and a suggested relation to speech [29]. Crying remains in everyone's repertory of communication as a way of showing distress. Gesell [14] states that month-old babies give different cries for hunger, pain and discomfort. Not all parents or research workers can interpret so early the meaning of different cries, if there truly is a difference. However, some time during the early months, infants do give cries which, coupled with other cues, communicate various meanings to parents, depending no doubt on both the infant and the adult and their expressiveness and sensitivity.

Speech. The great human invention, spoken language, is of vast significance as a method of communication. "The child may begin as a parrot, imitating what others say, but he will end as a poet, able to say things that have not been said before but which will be grammatical and meaningful in his community" [4].

Even though the first real word is normally uttered toward the end of the first year, all of infancy is a period of preparation for talking. Maturation of the nervous system, the respiratory system and the organs of eating are all basic to language development. In fact, language is intimately related to all the maturation and learning that take place in the child.

Association of language development and other aspects of growth. Irwin's [25, 26, 28] investigations of language development revealed the order in which consonants and vowels appeared and their relative use at various ages throughout the first two and a half years of life. During the first two months, about four vowel sounds are heard in noncrying vocalization. The earliest vowels are those made in the front part of the mouth. A new vowel sound appears about every two months during the first year. The first consonant, *H,* is associated with gasping and crying. The early consonants are those made in the back of the throat, and the labials and dentals are the last to come.

The sounds made at the earliest stages of development are based on movements similar to those used in sucking and swallowing. It is only after breathing and eating and physiological equilibrium are established that the infant coos and plays vocally. Progress in language seems to be associated with postural development, too. "Talking back," or responding vocally to a human face and/or voice, first occurs at two or three months, the time when the baby holds his head erect. The babbling stage, when a syllable is repeated, as in *ga-ga,* begins at about seven months, when the infant is first sitting up. Nasal sounds spurt at this age, probably because the upright posture facilitates them. The first words, at about a year, occur at the same time as learning to stand alone [33]. Table 4–10 summarizes the time of emergence of various speech patterns.

The year-old baby covers a lot of territory under his own powers of locomotion, whether it be creeping or walking with support or even independent walking. A rush of new experiences stimulates the learning of new words. A single word at this point stands for a whole experience, often an emotionally toned one. *Car* might mean, "Here we are, going for a ride in the car, seeing the wide world and having such an exciting time together." *Bobby!* could indicate, "I see my big brother coming in. He is going to pick me out of the playpen and we'll roughhouse a bit on the floor. It will feel delightful."

Other events connected with the mouth are probably of great importance in language development. It is during the time that the teeth are erupting, 6 to 28 months, that the labial and dental sounds are established. The connection with early sucking and swallowing has been mentioned. Spoon and cup feeding and swallowing solids are associated with the babbling period. At ten months, most infants handle solids well, eating a variety of them and chewing some chipped foods. At this time also, considerable vocalizing occurs in the feeding situation [33].

UNDERSTANDING OF LANGUAGE. Communication is a reciprocal process; language must be understood as well as spoken. The understanding of what other people say is more advanced than the ability to express oneself in words, as you can see in yourself by the many words which you understand yet never use in speech. At eight or nine months, Gesell's [18, p. 144] normative babies listened to and adjusted to selected words. Between 9 and 12, they responded to *bye-bye,* adjusted to commands and adjusted to inhibitory words. One word, however, was the most usual vocabulary at 11 months and two words at 12 months. It is generally agreed that there is another function of speech, that of talking to oneself, although authorities disagree as to whether it begins in infancy. A Russian psychologist [50] thinks that inner speech starts later, as an ingrowth of egocentric speech, or expressing thoughts aloud to nobody

TABLE 4–10

Landmarks in language development and the ages at which eight major studies place the appearance of these behavior patterns.

Behavior	*Age in Months* 0–6	6–12	12–18	18–24	24–30
First noted vocalizations	xxxxxxxxxx				
First responds to human voice	xxxxxx				
First cooing	xxxxx				
Vocalizes pleasure	xxxxxxx	x			
Vocal play	xxxx				
Vocalizes eagerness and displeasure	xx	x			
Imitates sounds		xxxxxxxxx			
Vocalizes recognition		xx			
Listens to familiar words		xxxx			
First word		xxxxxxx	xxxx		
Expressive sounds and conversational jargon		xxxxxx	xxxxxxxxxxxxxxx		
Follows simple commands		xxx	xxxxx		
Imitates syllables and words		x	xxxxxxx		
Second word			xxxxx		
Responds to "no" and "don't"			xxxxxxxxxxxxxx		
First says more than two words			xxxxx		
Names object or picture				xxxxxxxxxxxxx	
Comprehends simple questions				xx	
Combines words in speech				xxxxxx	x
First uses pronouns					xxxxx
First phrases and sentences					xxxx
Understands prepositions					xxx

Source: Data from McCarthy, "Language Development in Children," in L. Carmichael (ed.), *Manual of Child Psychology* (New York: John Wiley & Sons, Inc., 1946), pp. 406–581. Reprinted by permission of the publishers.

in particular. He suggests that a portion of thought consists of thinking in silent language, while another part of thought does not use language.

Expressive jargon, a kind of speech used in the middle of the second year, is not communication in the sense of expressing ideas through words. The youngster sounds as though he were really talking, but none of it makes sense because there are no real words in it, rather like double-talk. There are rhythm rises and falls and feeling in the sounds. Expressive jargon is probably an expression of feeling for the child, perhaps of ideas, and it may be intended as a contact with another person.

Autonomy and Language

The ability to communicate with language must surely facilitate the sense of autonomy. For instance, saying "drink" can produce water at one's lips or "out" can transform the whole environment from indoors to outdoors. The extension of the child's powers and control is enormous. As it dawns upon him that everything has a name, that verbal symbols exist and that he can use them, he must have a surge of satisfaction over his expanded powers. One can imagine next a push to discover just how much he can do with these symbols, words, in both understanding and controlling the world and the people in it, including himself.

The End of Infancy

By the end of the sensorimotor period, the child has gone about as far as a creature can go without true language. Here is where other animals stop in their mental development, but man takes a great leap forward. *Words come to stand for things and actions.* Instead of having to go through sensory and motor acts, words can be manipulated in a twinkling. One doesn't even have to be where the problem is. He can think and talk about things which are remote in time and space. *Words are combined.* Here is what makes man's speech truly different from the utterances of birds and animals. He can combine words in ways which he has not even heard before, to mean something which has the same meaning for his listener. No wonder that, for many students of human nature, this intellectual leap marks the end of infancy, since it transforms the individual into a very different kind of person.

Parents' Contribution to Language Development

Language education is another activity which goes on spontaneously for normal infants in normal homes, with the mother taking the lead as teacher. The mother and others ordinarily talk to the baby in affectionate tones while they are feeding, bathing, changing diapers, picking up, cuddling and otherwise taking care of the baby. There is also the conversation of the household which forms a background and punctuation marks in an infant's experience.

Students of human nature have long pondered on how infants learn to speak. Imitation and reinforcement of meaningful sounds by parents are understandable enough as contributing to the learning of language, but they do not explain why the child tries to imitate. The structure of the organs of speech and spontaneous exercising of them in vocal play are also understandable as part of the process. Research on language and personality disorders has led to an appreciation of the mother's essential role in language development. Slowness in starting to talk, defective articulation and stuttering are all associated with certain kinds of disturbed parent–child relationships [32].

Several studies shed light on the process of learning to talk, showing how it is related to the infant's experiences in the family. Infants vocalized more when adults smiled at them than when they looked with solemn faces at the babies [43]. A psychologist noted that his 10-weeks-old infant made an average of four sounds per three-minute period under ordinary circumstances. When the father said "Hello" every 10 seconds, the baby averaged 18 sounds per three-minute period [31]. An experiment on influencing sound production used subjects of lower socioeconomic status between 13 and 30 months of age [27]. Their parents were given picture-story books and encouraged to read to the toddlers. At the end of the experimental period, the stimulated children were producing significantly more sounds than a control group. A study conducted in an institution compared the behavior of babies who had many caretakers with that of babies who were cared for by only one person [42]. From six to eight months of age, the experimental infants had the attentive care of one person for seven and a half hours a day. They became more socially responsive than babies on the regular routine. At 18 months of age, after they had settled down in adoptive homes, the infants were tested again. The only significant difference between experimental and control groups was that the former vocalized more. The "quality of stimulation," mentioned before [53] as significant, probably operated here. One caretaker would be more likely than many caretakers to offer stimuli appropriate to the child as an individual.

These studies offer convincing proof that the infant's early experience with people's talking have definite effects on his own language behavior. One theory [35] suggests that sounds become associated with mother and with the experiences of comfort and stimulation which her presence brings. When the baby hears himself make a sound like mother makes, he feels comforted and happy, just as he does in her presence. Thus he stimulates himself to make more noises like mother makes. "Words are reproduced if and only if they are first made to sound good in the context of affectionate care and attention." This theory has been born out by a study in which the sound production of infants was shown to be related to the warmth and amount of vocalization of their mothers [40]. On visits to the infants' homes, records were made of their sound production, including crying as well as cooing. Correlations between infant vocalization and mother vocalization and between infant vocalization and mother warmth increased with age.

An authority on language development spells out the ways in which the mother–child relationship influences the baby's learning to speak [33].

"Whether she welcomes or dreads the child's arrival; whether she feels adequate to care for him; whether she is tense, worried and uncertain in everything she does for him; whether she is happy and talks to him as she goes about her tasks or pushes the baby carriage; whether she is silent and preoccupied while giving mere physical care, or is impersonal and allows the child to vegetate most of the time are the kinds of things which are important in determining whether his language development will thrive, or be stunted and distorted in some unfortunate way."

Another student of language development [6, p. 86] points out how passive language is learned in a context of feelings and actions, by simple association. "When the adult says, 'Come here,' he holds out his hands to receive the child. When he says, 'Now you give it to me,' he reaches out for the toy; and when he says, 'Now I'll give it to you,' he hands it back. When the baby makes off with the parent's slippers, the adult cries, 'Where are my slippers? Bring me back my slippers.' When the parent pretends not to see the baby, he says, 'Where's Bobby? Where's Bobby?' and elaborately pantomimes the business of looking for him; when he finally finds him, he announces, 'There he is!' "

Thus the early stages of learning to talk are deeply emotional as well as intellectual and motor. Language is embedded in the total mass of experience, affected by a multitude of factors. The emotional qualities of maternal care and family life are basic to speech.

SUMMARY

The sense of trust grows as the baby has successful experiences in seeking and finding food, comfort and stimulation, as he gains more and more control of his body and as he comes to realize that certain regularities and permanencies exist in the world. He develops trust in his mother and in other key people as they repeatedly interact satisfactorily with him.

The sense of autonomy grows rapidly during the second year, as the baby realizes his power as a maker of choices. He knows himself as a person who can decide which action to take, to do or not to do, to hold on or to let go. Healthy personality growth results not only from experiencing himself as choosing, but upon an accompanying conviction that what he does is generally all right and acceptable. The negative feelings typical of this stage are doubt and shame, feelings which occur when the child has too few opportunities for choosing and also when his choices are disastrous.

Physical development is rapid during infancy, with changes occurring in appearance and proportions. The deciduous teeth erupt. The basic physiological processes of respiration and temperature control become regularized, along with the timing of eating, sleeping and elimination. Feeding behavior matures as the infant learns to hold his food, to sit up, to drink from a cup, to chew and to control situations by talking. Although no specific technique of feeding has been shown to have definite results, the emotional context of feeding is significant. Weaning, the substitution of cup for breast or bottle, can be conducted and timed in various ways. When offered a wide variety of simple foods, year-old babies choose adequate diets. Many of the infant's autonomous acts occur in feeding situations.

Progress in locomotion takes place in a regular sequence of achievements. Creeping is perfected during the first year, walking during the second. The sense of autonomy grows as the child gains upright position and as he becomes more and more mobile, enlarging the scope of his interactions and his possibilities for choice making. Manipulation also develops through a regular sequence, increasing the baby's competence in exploring his environment, changing it and understanding it.

Cognition is the activity of coming to know and understand. Cognitive development takes place in a sequence which stretches throughout infancy, childhood and adolescence. The infant first interacts with his environment through reflex patterns. Then he adapts and combines these patterns to enlarge his repertory. He comes to realize that objects and people continue to exist even when he cannot see them. He experiments, trying out different kinds of actions in order to see their results. Finally, he imitates and pretends, representing objects and actions to himself mentally. As he cognizes the environment, he also comes to know himself more clearly, as an object which is distinct from the rest of the world. He also realizes his mother as a creature distinct from himself and from everything else. Cognitive development is promoted by a mother and other members of the family who offer the baby a rich variety of experiences.

The acquisition of language extends the child's powers, encouraging growth of the sense of autonomy. The baby discovers that words stand for objects and actions, and that everything has a name. Language learning takes place in the context of family communication, the baby experiencing other people talking to each other as well as direct interaction with his mother and others. The process is deeply emotional as well as cognitive and motor.

REFERENCES

1. Albino, R. C., & Thompson, V. J. The effects of sudden weaning on Zulu children. In W. Dennis, *Readings in child psychology*. Englewood Cliffs, N.J.: Prentice-Hall, 1963, pp. 128–148.
2. Blank, M. Some maternal influences on infants' rates of sensorimotor development. Speech at meeting of The Society for Research in Child Development, April 12, 1963.
3. Breckenridge, M. E., & Murphy, M. N. *Growth and development of the young child* (7th ed.). Philadelphia: Saunders, 1963.
4. Brown, R., & Berko, J. Word association and the acquisition of grammar. *Child Devel.,* 1960, **31,** 1–14.
5. Children's Bureau. *Your baby's first year*. Washington, D.C.: Government Printing Office, 1962.
6. Church, J. *Language and the discovery of reality*. New York: Random House, 1961.

7. Davis, C. M. Self-selection of diet by newly weaned infants. *Am. J. Dis. Child.*, 1928, **36,** 651–679.
8. Davis, C. M. Self-selection of diets. *The Trained Nurse and Hospital Review,* 1931, **86:**5. Cited in C. A. Aldrich & M. M. Aldrich, *Feeding our old-fashioned children.* New York: Macmillan, 1941.
9. Davis, C. M. Self-selection of food by children. *Am. J. Nursing,* 1935, **35,** 403–410.
10. Dennis, W. Causes of retardation among institutional children: Iran. *J. Genet. Psychol.,* 1960, **96,** 46–60.
11. Dennis, W., & Najarian, P. Infant development under environmental handicap. *Psychol. Mono.,* 1957, **71:**7.
12. Erikson, E. H. *Childhood and society.* New York: Norton, 1963.
13. Flavell, J. H. *The developmental psychology of Jean Piaget.* Princeton: Van Nostrand, 1963.
14. Gesell, A. *Infancy and human growth.* New York: Macmillan, 1928.
15. Gesell, A., *et al. The first five years of life.* New York: Harper, 1940.
16. Gesell, A., & Amatruda, C. *Developmental diagnosis.* New York: Hoeber, 1951.
17. Gesell, A., & Ilg, F. *Feeding behavior of infants.* Philadelphia: Lippincott, 1937.
18. Gesell, A., & Thompson, H. *The psychology of early growth.* New York: Macmillan, 1938.
19. Griffiths, R. *The abilities of babies.* New York: McGraw-Hill, 1954.
20. Halverson, H. M. An experimental study of prehension in infants by means of systematic cinema records. *Genet. Psychol. Mono.,* 1931, **10,** 107–286.
21. Heinstein, M. I. Behavioral correlates of breast-bottle regimes under varying parent-infant relationships. *Mono. Soc. Res. Child Devel.,* 1963, **28:**4.
22. Hunt, J. McV. Experience and the development of motivation: some reinterpretations. *Child Devel.,* 1960, **31,** 498–504.
23. Hunt, J. McV. *Intelligence and experience.* New York: Ronald, 1961.
24. Inhelder, B. Some aspects of Piaget's genetic approach to cognition. In W. Kessen & C. Kuhlman, Thought in the young child. *Mono. Soc. Res. Child Devel.,* 1962, **27:**2.
25. Irwin, O. C. Infant speech: equations for consonant-vowel ratio. *J. Speech Dis.,* 1946, **11,** 177–180. (a)
26. Irwin, O. C. Infant speech: vowel and consonant frequency. *J. Speech Dis.,* 1946, **11,** 123–125. (b)
27. Irwin, O. C. Infant speech: effect of systematic reading of stories. *J. Speech Hear. Res.,* 1960, **3,** 187–190.
28. Irwin, O. C., & Chen, H. P. Infant speech: vowel and consonant types. *J. Speech Dis.,* 1946, **11,** 27–29.
29. Karelitz, S., Fisichelli, V. R., Costa, J., Karelitz, R., & Rosenfeld, L. Relation of crying activity in early infancy to speech and intellectual development at age three years. *Child Devel.,* 1964, **35,** 769–777.
30. Kelley, V. C., & Bosma, J. F. Basal metabolism in infants and children. In I. McQuarrie (Ed.), *Brennemann's Practice of Pediatrics,* Vol. I. Hagerstown, Md.: W. F. Prior, 1957.
31. Lewis, M. M. *How children learn to speak.* New York: Basic Books, 1959.

32. McCarthy, D. Language disorders and parent-child relationships. *J. Speech Dis.*, 1954, **19,** 514–523.
33. McCarthy, D. Language development. In N. E. Wood (Ed.), Language development and language disorders: a compendium of lectures. *Mono. Soc. Res. Child. Devel.*, 1960, **25:**3, 5–14.
34. Mead, M. Research on primitive children. In L. Carmichael (Ed.), *Manual of child psychology*. New York: Wiley, 1954, pp. 735–780.
35. Mowrer, O. H. Hearing and speaking: an analysis of language learning. *J. Speech Dis.*, 1958, **23,** 143–151.
36. Murphy, L. B. *The widening world of childhood.* New York: Basic Books, 1962.
37. Parmelee, A. H., Schultz, H. R., & Disbrow, M. A. Sleep patterns of the newborn. *J. Pediat.*, 1961, **58,** 241–250.
38. Piaget, J. *The construction of reality in the child.* New York: Basic Books, 1954.
39. Piaget, J. *The origins of intelligence in children.* New York: Norton, 1963.
40. Rebelsky, F. G., Nichols, I. A., & Lenneber, E. H. A study of infant vocalization. Speech at meeting of *Society for Research in Child Development,* April 12, 1963.
41. Rheingold, H. The measurement of maternal care. *Child Devel.,* 1960, **31,** 565–575.
42. Rheingold, H., & Bayley, N. The later effects of an experimental modification of mothering. *Child Devel.,* 1959, **30,** 363–372.
43. Rheingold, H., Gerwitz, J. L., and Ross, H. W. Social conditioning of vocalizations in the infant. *J. Comp. Physiol. Psychol.,* 1959, **52,** 68–73.
44. Ricciuti, H. N. Object grouping and selective ordering behavior in infants 12 to 24 months old. *Merrill-Palmer Quart.,* 1965, **11,** 129–148.
45. Roberts, K. E., & Schoelkopf, J. A. Eating, sleeping, and elimination: practices of a group of two and a half year old children. *Am. J. Dis. Child.,* 1951, **82,** 121–152.
46. Robinow, M., Richards, T. W., & Anderson, M. The eruption of deciduous teeth. *Growth,* 1942, **6,** 127–133.
47. Shirley, M. *The first two years: a study of twenty-five children. Vol. I. Postural and locomotor development.* Monograph Series, 7. Minneapolis: Univer. of Minnesota, Institute of Child Welfare, 1933.
48. Smart, Mollie & Russell. *Living and learning with children.* Boston: Houghton Mifflin, 1961.
49. Valadian, I., Stuart, H. C., & Reed, R. B. Studies of illnesses of children followed from birth to eighteen years. *Mono. Soc. Res. Child Devel.,* 1961, **26:**3.
50. Vygotsky, L. S. *Thought and language.* Boston: Massachusetts Institute of Technology, 1962.
51. Watson, E. H., & Lowrey, G. H. *Growth and development of children* (4th ed.). Chicago: Year Book, 1962.
52. Witmer, H. L., & Kotinsky, R. *Personality in the making.* New York: Harper, 1952.
53. Yarrow, L. J. Research in dimensions of early maternal care. *Merrill-Palmer Quart.,* 1963, **9,** 101–114.

Relationships with People

CHAPTER 5

The baby is active in building relationships with people, just as he is active in the world of things. His very arrival causes changes in the world, especially in the people responsible for his care. Their interaction with each other and with him is the basis of social, emotional and personality development. The baby's family is already anchored in a cultural framework which will direct and limit all of their interactions. The values and attitudes that influence parental behavior are understandable in their cultural context [27]. Before discussing actual parent–child relationships, this chapter will deal with some of the influences on relationships which come from different sources.

FACTORS INFLUENCING RELATIONSHIPS

Three main types of influences are basic to the building of a baby's relationships with people and hence to his social and emotional development. The culture, the family and the infant himself, all play essential roles in initiating, limiting and guiding interactions. Although these three influences are the main ones, they do not constitute an exclusive list. There are other factors, such as climate, which might conceivably have some bearing on the question.

Culture

Culture influences the infant by drawing the outlines of his parents and structuring his relationships with other people, especially relatives. This function is mentioned first because of the importance of parents to babies. It is only one small aspect of culture, however, and all those other aspects also influence the infant. The language he hears determines what he will speak and to a large extent, how he will think. The food he receives affects not only his life and growth but his preferences. His house, furniture, clothing, grooming equipment and medicine all bear relation to his health, posture, activity and attitudes. Toys, art and music are vital in his cognitive and emotional life.

Even the more distant aspects of culture, like government and law, have effects, though indirect ones, on infants.

Ideals of behavior are pictures of how roles *ought* to be performed. What is a good husband? A good wife? A good child? A good employer? Sometimes a culture presents a detailed word picture of an ideal, as did Judaism in Proverbs and Hinduism in the Laws of Manu. Ideals of childrearing techniques are part of a culture and are parts of the parental role and of the roles of other people concerned with children. These ideals hold up "right" punishment, rewards, regulations and other methods of influence. In a simple, stable society, most parents treat their children in the ways that they themselves were treated as children, and these ways coincide rather well with the ideals. Ideal patterns are expressed in the folklore and art. To spank or not to spank, to wean early or late, to toilet-train or to let the child train himself—these and similar questions are not really questions to parents who live in an unchanging culture.

In a rapidly changing culture, such as the United States, parents and grandparents often conflict over child care. Parents cannot rely comfortably on custom to give them definite directions on childrearing, since many different and changing directions are available. The same is true of other changing societies, which include a fair share of the world. When actual behavior differs widely from the ideal pattern, then conflict and confusion result.

Ideals for childrearing come in profuse variety in the United States as influenced by social class, ethnicity, region, religion and other factors. Some attempts have been made to clarify the ideal role through pamphlets, books and articles giving advice to mothers. Although the publications of the Children's Bureau do not carry religious authority, as do the Book of Proverbs, the Laws of Manu and the Koran, they do reflect the ideals of the culture. One investigator [43] studied nine editions of the Children's Bureau publication *Infant Care,* spanning about 40 years. She found progressive changes in recommendations for parents, especially in the degree of severity with which the good mother was supposed to cope with various kinds of behavior in her infant. Changes in delineation of the mother's role stemmed from changes in conceptions of baby nature, in fact, of human nature. In 1914, the good mother was urged to be vigilant and relentless in her battle against the child's sinful nature, stamping out thumbsucking and masturbation. In the thirties, the mother must not permit the baby to dominate her. During the forties, the mother was advised to be nonchalant in distracting her baby from thumbsucking and masturbation, since he would be almost equally interested in toys and exploration. Since 1950, naturalness (of both mother and baby), within limits, has been stressed [42].

Social philosophers and scientists have related changes in conceptions of human nature and the consequent changes in parent and child roles to broader changes in the culture. For example, childrearing was considered in the context of fathers' occupational orientation [29, 32]. Fathers' occupations are, of course, related to the economic and technological aspects of a culture. Changes in childrearing practices, such as those described above, were found to be due, not to the whimsies of "experts," but to more general social changes.

Social Class: A Cultural Influence

Although social class is by no means the only sociological variable important to parent–child relations, it is one which has been studied extensively. An accumulation of evidence indicates a real difference in the way children are brought up in the middle class, as contrasted with the working class. Middle-class parents tend to be warmer, to use more love-oriented discipline and to be more permissive as to demands for attention from the child, sex behavior, orderliness, aggression, bedtime and obedience. Working-class parents use more physical punishment, shouting and ridicule, and they tend to be more restrictive [4]. What is more, these differences have changed over time [11]. Before World War II, working-class mothers, in contrast to middle-class mothers, did more breast feeding and more self-demand feeding, weaned children later and toilet-trained them more leniently. After World War II, these trends were reversed, probably due to the middle-class mothers' being in closer touch with the advice of experts and more readily influenced by it. The changes which took place in the concepts of child nature were transmitted faster to middle-class mothers than to working-class mothers by pediatricians, the Children's Bureau, magazine writers and other parent educators. At present, there is some indication that class differences in child training are diminishing [11]. Table 5–1 shows some contrasts in childrearing between the upper-middle and the upper-lower class. In each case of differences, the higher-status families tend to be more permissive and less restrictive. A recent

TABLE 5–1

Social class differences in methods of infant feeding.

	Upper Middle	*Upper Lower*	*t*	*p*
Percent who breast-fed child	43%	37%	—	
Average length of breast-feeding (for those breast-fed)	2.8 mo.	2.6 mo.	—	
Age of beginning weaning	10 mo.	9½ mo.	1.42	
Age at completion of weaning	12½ mo.	13½ mo.	2.48	<.02
Severity of weaning 1 = mild 9 = severe	4.9	4.9	—	
Scheduling of feeding 1 = complete self-demand 9 = rigid schedule	5.1	4.6	1.62	

Source: E. E. Maccoby, *et al.*, "Methods of Child-Rearing in Two Social Classes," in C. B. Stendler (Ed.), *Readings in Child Behavior and Development* (New York: Harcourt, Brace & World, 1964), Table 1. Reprinted by permission of Eleanor E. Maccoby.

TABLE 5–2

Social class differences in toilet training.

	Upper Middle	*Upper Lower*	*t*	*p*
Age of beginning bowel training	$11\frac{1}{4}$ mo.	$10\frac{3}{4}$ mo.	.88	
Age of completing bowel training	$19\frac{1}{4}$ mo.	18 mo.	1.85	
Severity of toilet training* 1 = mild 9 = severe	3.8	4.6	4.05	<.01

* This scale takes into account training for both bowel and bladder control.
Source: E. E. Maccoby, *et al.*, "Methods of Child-Rearing in Two Social Classes," in C. B. Stendler (Ed.), *Readings in Child Behavior and Development* (New York: Harcourt, Brace & World, 1964), Table 2. Reprinted by permission of Eleanor E. Maccoby.

TABLE 5–3

Social class differences in training for control of aggression.

	Upper Middle	*Upper Lower*	*t*	*p*
Permissiveness: aggression toward other children 1 = not at all permissive 9 = completely permissive	5.1	4.6	2.46	>.02
How much parent encouraged child to fight back if attacked 1 = never 8 = strongly encouraged	4.2	4.3	—	
Permissiveness: aggression toward siblings 1 = not at all permissive 9 = completely permissive	4.7	4.5	—	
Permissiveness: aggression toward parents 1 = not at all permissive 9 = completely permissive	3.6	2.8	3.84	>.01
Severity of punishment for aggression toward parents 1 = no punishment 8 = severe punishment	5.3	5.8	3.47	>.01

Source: E. E. Maccoby, *et al.*, "Methods of Child-Rearing in Two Social Classes," in C. B. Stendler (Ed.), *Readings in Child Behavior and Development* (New York: Harcourt, Brace & World, 1964), Table 4. Reprinted by permission of Eleanor E. Maccoby.

TABLE 5–4

Social class differences in restrictions and demands upon children.

	Upper Middle	*Upper Lower*	*t*	*p*
Amount of restriction of use of fingers at table 1 = no restrictions 9 = high restrictions	4.6	5.1	3.11	<.01
Pressure for conformity with table standards and restrictions 1 = no pressure 9 = high pressure	4.7	5.2	3.23	<.01
Restrictions: care of house and furniture 1 = few restrictions 9 = many restrictions	6.3	6.6	2.16	<.05
Pressure: neatness and orderliness 1 = no pressure 9 = high pressure	5.5	5.9	2.93	<.01
Strictness about bedtime 1 = not at all strict 9 = very strict	5.4	5.5	—	
Strictness about noise 1 = not at all strict 9 = very strict	4.5	4.9	2.29	<.05
Sex role differentiation: (mother's expectation for child to be "masculine" or "feminine") 1 = no differentiation 9 = high differentiation	5.0	5.4	1.66	
Restrictions: physical mobility (How far away from the house may the child go alone?) 1 = no restrictions 9 = high restrictions	4.5	4.8	1.88	
Keeping track of child 1 = rarely checks 9 = constantly checks	4.3	4.8	2.37	<.05
Extent of demand for instant obedience 1 = no demands for obedience 9 = child must obey instantly	5.0	5.0	—	
How far is child expected to go in school 1 = grade school 9 = graduate school	6.4*	4.3*	11.4	>.01
How important is it for child to do well in school 1 = unimportant 9 = very important	5.1	5.9	3.4	>.01

* A score of 6.4 on this scale means that the mother says she expects the child to go through college, and states no reservations about it. A score of 4.3 means that she feels he certainly should finish high school, and may go to college if he wants to badly or if he shows unusual abilities.

Source: E. E. Maccoby, *et al.*, "Methods of Child-Rearing in Two Social Classes," in C. B. Stendler (Ed.), *Readings in Child Behavior and Development* (New York: Harcourt, Brace & World, 1964), Table 5. Reprinted by permission of Eleanor E. Maccoby.

TABLE 5–5

Social class differences in techniques of discipline.

	Upper Middle	*Upper Lower*	*t*	*p*
If no trouble at table, what does mother do? 1 = always praise 8 = never praise	3.9	4.4	2.04	<.05
If children play well together, what does mother do? 1 = always praise 8 = never praise	4.0	4.3	1.33	
Frequency of use of isolation 1 = never used 9 = very often used	5.7	5.5	—	
Extent of use of withdrawal of love (rating) 1 = never used 9 = very often used	4.1	4.5	1.64	
Proportion of scolding statements involving withdrawal of love* 1 = low proportion 9 = high proportion	6.4	6.0	4.5	<.01
Extent of use of reasoning 1 = never used 9 = very often used	5.0	4.8	1.22	
Extent of use of reward 1 = never used 9 = regularly used	4.6	4.9	.89	
Can child earn money? 1 = yes, regular earning system 9 = money not used as reward	3.8	3.8	—	
Extent of use of praise 1 = never used 9 = very often used	4.8	4.8	—	
Extent of use of ridicule 1 = never used 9 = very often used	3.6	4.0	2.28	<.05
Extent of use of deprivation of privileges 1 = never used 9 = very often used	4.6	5.1	2.02	<.05
Extent of use of physical punishment 1 = never used 9 = very often used	3.9	4.8	4.84	<.01

* The mother was asked to fill out a checklist of possible remarks which could be made in scolding a child, indicating which of the remarks she made often, occasionally, or never. Some of the statements were considered indicative of withdrawal of love, such as "Go away—I don't want to look at you until you can smile." Others were not so relevant to withdrawal of love, such as "That wasn't a very smart thing to do." Total scores were based on the number of withdrawal of love statements the mother used, minus the number of other types of statements she used.

Source: E. E. Maccoby, *et al.*, "Methods of Child-Rearing in Two Social Classes," in C. B. Stendler (Ed.), *Readings in Child Behavior and Development* (New York: Harcourt, Brace & World, 1964), Table 6. Reprinted by permission of Eleanor E. Maccoby.

study, based on observations of mothers with children, finds lower-class mothers to be more coercive with their children than middle-class mothers and also indicates a progressive change over time in which the general trend is for mothers to be less coercive [41].

A new dimension in class differences is emerging from studies on culturally deprived children. Contrasting the very poorest children, those who live in crowded slums, with middle-class children, there appears a difference in stimulation. Quite possibly the young infant reaps the benefit of extra stimulation during his first year of life, when he lives in a room with several other people. The many sights and sounds and perhaps more frequent handling may give him a richer environment than the middle-class baby [26]. As soon as he begins to move around, the situation reverses in regard to opportunity for intellectual growth. During the second year, he irritates adults by getting in the way. Frustrated and tired, adults do not respond helpfully, especially in verbal areas. Fewer objects are available as playthings. Membership in a very low socioeconomic stratum, then, may give the baby a slight initial intellectual advantage before subjecting him to progressive deprivation.

Family

The infant's family translates the broad culture into a unique specific family culture which the baby experiences directly. The ideals, goals, beliefs and customs of his family affect the way in which the baby is received and cared for. Suppose he is a fourth child born to a family where every child is a welcome gift from God. In contrast, suppose he is a fourth child born to a family where two children are considered the ideal number. Consider a family which holds that a baby is born wicked and must be trained to be good; that the infant must learn early who is boss; that crying exercises the lungs. Then consider a family which holds that infants have a right to happiness and that children cannot learn anything until they reach the age of reason, at six or seven.

Family customs are important in the experience of infants. Many rural Dutch babies ride in boxes on their parents' bicycles, enjoying the stimulation of sun and wind, getting the feel of balancing, watching the Van Gogh-like landscape change before their eyes. Many English babies loll and crawl on the green grass of Kensington Gardens, watching the swans and the fountains, accompanied by parents, brothers and sisters who play and relax. Indian babies who live in joint families have constant companionship and immediate attention to their cries. Others, who live in small families, are left alone or inadequately tended by small children for long periods when their mothers must carry water.

In these ways, and in other ways, does the family determine the experience of its babies. Cognitive, emotional and social growth are thus influenced.

The composition and stage of development of the family affect a baby [10, pp. 53–78]. For example, it is well known that the first born carries a different burden from subsequent babies and that, in fact, each order of birth has its own assets and liabilities. Being a twin is very different from being a singleton. It makes a further difference which kind of twin you are, a monozygotic or dyzygotic, like sex or unlike, and which sex [28].

Family to most American readers means parents and children, but even in America millions of children live in families which are otherwise. A parent is absent, a grandparent is present or other relatives are present. The composition of the family can make a big difference in the amount of stimulation a baby receives. Many people in the house, especially children, make for noise, excitement, handling, play and variety of contacts.

Stage of development refers to a way of looking at family life as cyclic. Each stage has its own characteristics. A typical way of naming the stages is: (1) beginning, (2) childbearing, (3) preschool, (4) school-age, (5) teenage, (6) launching, (7) middle-age, (8) old age, and (9) broken.

It is possible for a baby to be born to a mother when the family is in any one of the stages from (2) to (6) or (7). Infants born in the early stages come to families oriented toward living with babies. Home, furnishings, schedules, menus and pace are suited to young children. Those who come later are likely to be swept into activities appropriate for older children or teenagers, such as camping trips and Scout meetings, or perhaps they will be left out frequently as the family goes off to meetings and parties and engages in conversation too mature for the youngest.

Emotional climate is a summary term for all the feelings that exist in the home. Love and tenderness are known to be essential ingredients for healthy growth. The love which parents and children have to offer to their baby depends somewhat on all of the relationships in the family. General tension and disturbance comes through to the baby, not in a mysterious way, but through his various senses, just as perception of love also comes through his senses. Hence the emotional climate of the home is a global factor which has significance for the infant.

The basic factors in emotional climate are the parents' love for each other, their adjustment to one another and their personality maturity in regard to taking on parent roles. Relationships with their own parents also influence the mother and father, since they themselves are children as well as parents. Not only do the parents act in the light of their past experiences as children, but they are affected by present and changing relationships with their own parents [38]. Furthermore, parents react emotionally to such strains as money troubles and inadequate housing. Big crises and joys and small irritations and pleasures all register in the emotional climate of the home, from which the baby receives stimuli.

Infant's Characteristics

The baby himself plays a big part in determining the course of relationships with people. Some of his effects are obvious, others subtle.

According to whether the newborn is a boy or a girl, the baby is immediately placed in some categories and removed from others. The infant's sex determines many of the feelings, attitudes and actions of people. Cultures and families vary widely in the ways in which they interpret and value sex roles. The Shah of Iran divorced a wife he loved (or so the newspapers said) because she bore him no sons, even though she produced daughters. His duty to perpetuate his line, for the good of his country, was a value above and beyond love for his wife. Imagine the welcome a son would receive in such a family and the disappointment which would mount with the birth of each daughter! Followers of religions like Hinduism and Confucianism want sons in order to carry out religious duties toward ancestors and to assure their own religious fulfillment. Therefore the birth of the first son is an occasion of boundless joy and relief from anxiety. Sons are less essential in the West than in Asia. Many Americans prefer daughters. Religion and property are not involved and daughters are considered easier to bring up. Americans may try not to form a sex preference before a baby is born, realizing that it makes for better relationships to be happy with their offspring no matter which sex it is.

Mothers tend to treat boys and girls differently in the nursing situation according to Murphy's observations [30, pp. 346–347]. "Come and get it" typified the attitude toward boys, who were permitted considerable autonomy in establishing their own rhythms and in starting and stopping. "Mother knows best" was the key to the prevalent attitude toward girls, indicating that they were supposed to conform and fit into the mother's way of doing. Mothers tended to hover over girls, to fiddle with their clothing and to give them a great deal more tactile stimulation than boys received. Given less opportunity to move, to explore and to choose, restricted in expression and yet stimulated, girls must discharge more emotion inward. Here could be the foundation of feminine passivity and masculine activity. Or perhaps it is only an emphasizing and elaborating of genetically determined characteristics. Whichever explanation be the right one, the fact remains that the baby's sex influences the mother's way of handling the baby and her relationships with her infant. And from such differential treatment begins the sex typing of the child.

Appearance can make a difference in how a baby is accepted and regarded. Although this statement is more in the realm of common belief than scientific fact, it is important if true. Not only is the matter of beauty or good looks involved here, but of an appearance that suggests something significant to the parents; a family resemblance causing pride or the expectation that the new baby will act like Uncle Joe or like his big brother; fragility, including delicate handling, or sturdiness, inciting rough play; a characteristic thought to predict a personality trait, such as red hair indicating temper or a weak chin indicating weak character.

Behavior of the baby has an immediate and continuing impact. From a study of the first six months of life and the relation between the mother's behavior and the infant's, this story illustrates how different behavior calls forth different responses from the family [45]. Two boy babies of the same age were placed in one foster home. Jack was passive and quiet, slept a great deal, showed little initiative and little response to social approaches. George was vigorous and active, showing much initiative and response. By seven weeks of age, there was a difference in the way the foster mother referred to the babies. George was "George" and Jack was "the other one." By three months, the mother complained openly that "the other one" slept too much and did nothing. The whole family wanted to feed George. Nobody wanted to feed Jack. Jack's bottle was propped more often than George's. George was often found in the middle of a family activity, while Jack stayed in the playpen, apart from the general stream of action. With two infants the same age and same sex in the same family at the same time, it is apparent that to an unknown degree the difference in their care and experience was initiated by the babies themselves.

The relationships of the baby with his family depend upon all the people involved and how their personalities fit together. It is conceivable that another mother would have preferred Jack to George, a mother who wanted a quiet baby with little initiative and vigor. Certainly, adults vary in how much they approve of characteristics such as ease and vigor in expression of needs and self-assertion in response to coercion. Some even call the latter stubbornness, and if they do, it is likely to be in disapproving tones. The baby's search for autonomy dominates his second year. The strength with which he pursues it is significant in his family relationships. The parents' attitudes towards his search for autonomy are just as significant.

GUIDANCE AND SELF-CONTROL

In their efforts to regulate what a baby does and when, where and how he does it, parents are guided by what they believe to be good for the baby and good for the rest of the family and by their own needs. "Good for the baby" involves what is good for him now and what will help him to grow into the right kind of child, adolescent and adult. "Good for the rest of the family" means considering all the other people in the home and even some beyond the home, perhaps grandparents. Parents "own needs" includes those that they recognize as existing and also needs of which they are unaware or only dimly aware. Guidance means influencing a child toward some kinds of behavior and away from others. Through guidance, the youngster learns not to do this but to do that, and to do it in certain ways at certain times. He learns self-control. The behavior influenced by parental guidance includes thinking and feeling as well as overt action.

Our main purpose is not to give directions on how to bring up children, because this book is concerned with what actually happens and why it happens. *How to* schedule, discipline, toilet-train and do the many other things which parents must do is covered by that master parent-educator, Dr. Spock [37], and by the usually reliable Children's Bureau [40], as well as by many others. Occasionally we list a few practical suggestions which stem from research.

Scheduling and Its Products

Family life has many rhythms. The fitting of small rhythms to one another and into larger wholes is a dynamic process. The ways in which infant and family adapt to one another have important outcomes for both.

The term *mutual regulation* is perhaps more apt than *scheduling* to describe what happens in a home with a young baby. Since the newborn baby cannot wait for food and comfort, the family has to adjust pretty much to *his* rhythms if he is to be kept comfortable and helped to feel that the world is worth trusting. After two or three months, however, a baby can wait briefly for food and attention. With the development of physiological stability, some confidence and some interest in sensorimotor exploration, he can begin to fit into some of the rhythms of the family. Perhaps he'll sit happily on Daddy's lap for five minutes while Mother finishes her dessert, even though he is hungry. In another month or two, the baby can eat larger meals and can last for longer times between meals. Although he may have some preference as to mealtimes, a mother can fit them into convenient times by gradual change and planning the staying qualities of meals and snacks.

In the matter of sleeping, too, a baby accommodates himself more and more to family rhythms as he matures and as he is guided to do so. In the beginning, sleep follows eating and waking brings a demand for food. Gradually he stays awake for longer periods and sleeps for a longer time at night, when the rest of the family sleeps. In societies where babies are always with other people, going to bed when the family goes to bed, and sleeping when sleepy during the day, there is no problem of scheduling sleep. American life, especially middle-class American life, is tightly scheduled. Infants have to have naps and go to bed early in order to get enough sleep and also in order for their mothers to get their housework and other jobs done. Parents tend to feel that they need some free, quiet hours without children present, in the evening. Thus getting the baby to go to sleep at certain times often comes to be a problem. It is usually solved by exerting pressure on the baby's own changing rhythms, waking him from previous sleep in time to have him need sleep appropriately, timing meals, arranging baths, play and outings to induce just enough fatigue.

Babies often come to resist being put to bed, sometimes because they are put to bed when they really are not tired and sleepy. An infant may feel mistrust and lack of confidence in the family who is overeager to get him out of the way. Fears and excitement can prevent and disturb sleep. Sometimes the most careful attention to schedules and emotional security is not enough, and a tired baby cries when put to bed. The mother may then decide to impose the limits by leaving him in bed.

Scheduling includes planning baths, toileting and dressing at times that fit both the family and baby. Times for play of different kinds and in different places, walks and rides, visiting and receiving guests—all are part of planning for the baby's well-being and for family living. Thus the family, especially the mother, structures the infant's life in time and space, in terms of maintaining his life, stimulating his development and building relationships with him.

Physical well-being hinges on a schedule that fits the baby. Health and optimal growth require adequate nutrition, rest and exercise. It takes careful planning and management to see that the baby gets all of these while family living goes on to everyone's benefit. What the baby seems to want at the moment is not always what is best in the overall picture, at least as viewed by the adult. A toddler may want to get into the thick of a game with his kindergartner sister and her friends, not realizing that the results for him would be great excitement, frustration and fatigue. Or he may be hungry and yet refuse to come in for lunch just because it feels so good to be climbing outdoors.

Cognitive development results from good scheduling, too. For the baby too young to sit up by himself, a frequent change of position and scenery is necessary for giving him mental food (visual and tactual stimulation). When he enlarges his own sphere of operations, first by sitting, then by creeping and walking, his family can still enlarge the scene for him by moving him to different rooms and different furniture and taking him places. Scheduling does not mean that the mother has to pick the baby up at 9 and 11 but rather that she carry on a plan of household activity which includes a change of scene and action for the baby at fairly regular intervals. Her management of his toys has a bearing on mental growth, too. He benefits from some system of rotating toys, so that he gets only a few at a time and frequent changes. Thus a schedule can assure a steady flow of stimulation.

Emotional health is fostered by a suitable schedule. When the infant's physical needs are met before they become overwhelming, he is spared anxiety and frustration. He enjoys the good feeling of trust. Regular holding and cuddling further build up his sense of trust, allaying fears and anxiety and stimulating his senses. Because he trusts, he learns to wait and hope and thus to cooperate as a family member.

Restricting Movement and Exploration

Parents everywhere set limits on their infants' behavior. If they did not, there would be no more babies, since babies creep and toddle right into danger, whether it be off the platform of a house built on poles over the sea or under a station wagon parked in the driveway. There are always dangers to be kept from exploring fingers and mouths, too—a dung fire in the corner, incense burning before a household god, an electric socket. Little fingers and mouths have to be prevented from destroying precious objects, such as a threaded loom, a clay water pot or a piece of Steuben glass.

Cultures vary widely in whether babies are expected to learn self-control from the limits placed on their behavior. In some societies, keeping the baby safe is just that and no more. Somebody is expected to look out for him during his early years to see that he does himself no harm. But in many societies, including the American culture, keeping safe is, of course, a prime motive, but a variety of other aims makes for a wide range of practices.

As Duvall [16] has noted, one may distinguish two types of parental roles, the traditional and the developmental. Developmental parents want children to be healthy, happy, well-adjusted, cooperative, loving and intellectually growing; traditional parents want children to be clean, orderly, obedient, respectful, industrious and dependable. The latter aims will logically result in more restrictive handling of young children.

That such is likely true was demonstrated by an investigation of the family life of permissive (developmental) and restrictive (traditional) parents living in the same housing project in units with identical floor plans [5]. The permissive parents had more cluttered homes, more damaged possessions, more noise and more disruptions, and it was more difficult to impose limits on their children, even though the limits were more lenient than those of traditional parents. But even so, the permissive parents showed less annoyance and disturbance, being possibly more relaxed about it all than restrictive parents. The acceptant attitudes were attributed to their deep convictions that the freedom they offered was right for children, to their attitude that possessions were expendable and meant for family use rather than to impress visitors and to the adaptations they made for young children. Probably the permissive parents behaved as they did because of greater personal security and other personality factors, as well as because of personal beliefs and convictions. How do families vary in the degree to which they restrict their infants and young children? Some answers are given in the results of a study by Sears and associates [36] on 397 families, divided almost equally between middle class and working class. Not one of these mothers admitted to placing no restrictions on children. Only 6 percent reported "few" restrictions. Thirty percent were "moderate," allowing wide freedom in certain parts of the home, and 50 percent imposed "considerable" restriction. Thirteen percent were "very restrictive," requiring children to treat all parts of the house very carefully. Sears sees the whole complex of the mother's permissiveness-strictness as pertinent to personality development. From the standpoint of the toddler's developing sense of autonomy, the permissiveness or strictness of the family determines how many choices he will be allowed to make, how successful he will be in the choosing, and how often he will feel "I can decide" and "What I choose is all right."

Some confirmation of the importance of autonomy in infancy for later personality development is offered by a longitudinal study on infants and their mothers [30]. During the infancy period, the mothers of the babies were observed and rated on how much autonomy they permitted and how much they tried to control their children. For example, would the mother let the baby decide when he had had enough to eat, or would she try to get him to take more? When the children reached preschool age, they were rated on a number of personality characteristics, and these ratings correlated with the mothers'

TABLE 5–6

Relationship between autonomy permitted by mother in infancy and personality characteristics of preschool-age boys.

Correlation Coefficient	*Personality Characteristic*
.614	Capacity to maintain internal integration
.571	Ability to limit or fend off excessive stimulation
.511	Resistance to discouragement
.610	Ability to mobilize energy to meet challenge or stress
.784	Sense of self worth
.646	Clarity in sex role
.700	Separation (differentiation of self and others)

Source: Reprinted by permission from L. V. Murphy, *The Widening World of Childhood* (New York: Basic Books, 1962). Copyright © 1962, Basic Books, Inc.

autonomy-control behavior. Significant correlations were found, showing that there were relations between the mothers' behavior during infancy and the children's preschool behavior. Table 5–6 shows the size of correlations between mothers' permission or autonomy and characteristics of preschool-age boys. Another study indicates that boy babies and girl babies react differently, in terms of their intellectual development, to opportunities for autonomy and the degree of control given by their mothers [3].

Adaptations in the home which make possible the permission of wide limits include the provision of spaces where little damage can result from play and exploration. Fussy, breakable objects can be put away. Furniture can be upholstered or slip-covered in tough, washable fabrics. Floors and draperies can be of relatively indestructible materials. A baby can creep in this kind of room without hurting himself or anything else. A toddler can climb, explore, run his cars and push a doll carriage. The permissive mother will have a bathroom arranged so that a toddler can climb steps in front of the washbasin and there enjoy freedom with water play. She arranges to have some cupboards in the kitchen where young children can go to pull out pots and pans and perhaps put them back again.

Toilet Training

Here is a kind of restriction which requires the child to bring a reflex activity under conscious control, and which, according to some writers, has far-reaching effects upon personality. Freud, for example, saw toilet training as the important influence on such traits as orderliness, messiness, stinginess and generosity, but at least one empirical study has failed to show such specific relationships [25].

All societies impose some toilet regulation on children. Sears' study of chil-rearing practices gives details on how it is done in the United States. A few mothers began training when the child was under five months, 41 percent began between five and nine months and 30 percent began between 10 and 14 months [36]. Seven months was the average length of time it took to complete bowel training, but there was a range from a few weeks to a year and a half. The later the training was begun, the less time it took.

Punishment and scolding did not decrease the length of time required but did increase the amount of upset in babies whose mothers were relatively cold and undemonstrative. Severe training had no upsetting effect when mothers were warm in their relationships with the child. The time of beginning training was related to upset, with both early (before six months) and late starters (15 to 19 months) more disturbed than those who began between 6 and 10 months. Children trained after 20 months tended to learn quickly and to have little upset. Figure 5–1, taken from an earlier study, shows how much more quickly a child is likely to learn bladder control when his training is started late. Achievement curves for two twins show the slow progress made by Hugh, who began at approximately seven weeks. By two years, Hugh's training was almost complete and Hilton's was begun. Almost immediately, Hilton did as well as Hugh.

The facts in the above paragraph cannot be taken uncritically as a guide to toilet training. At first glance, it would seem logical to say, "Let every mother wait until 20 months to toilet train her baby." More is involved here than the age of the baby, mainly the personality of the mother. The Sears study also showed that mothers who were high in sex anxiety tended to begin training early. (Perhaps because sex and toileting are connected in the minds of many people, in addition to sheer amount of extra work entailed in laundry,

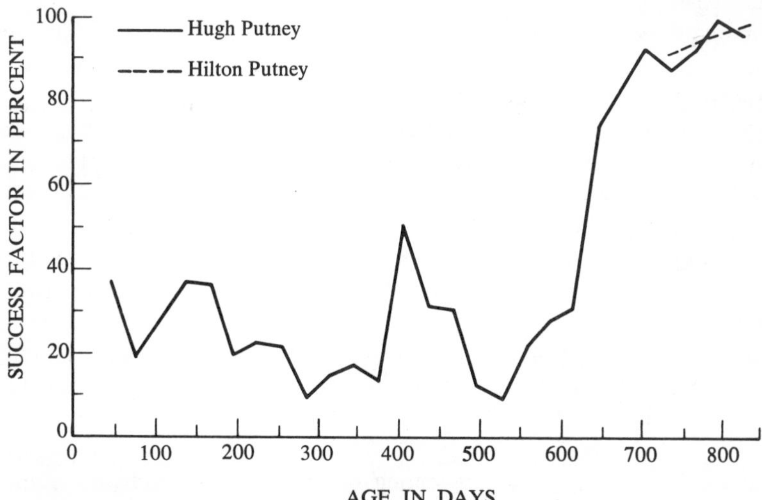

Figure 5–1. Records of toilet training of twins, one of whom started early and one late. (Reprinted by permission from Myrtle B. McGraw, "Neural Maturation as Exemplified in Achievement of Bladder Control," *The Journal of Pediatrics,* **16:**580, 1940, The C. V. Mosby Company, St. Louis, Missouri.)

there is a desire to get it over with quickly in those mothers with high sex anxiety.) Anxiety cannot be reasoned away. It is a real part of the person. If a mother has strong feelings that she should begin toilet training early, she may have a healthier relationship with the baby by training him early than by forcing herself to wait.

Restricting Sex Activity

Infants are sensitive to sexual stimulation, showing signs of relaxation and pleasure when the genital areas are touched. Newborn boys have erections of the penis. Both boys and girls learn to stimulate their genitals during infancy, through the process of exploring their bodies.

Although some societies permit expression of infant sexuality, Americans and many Europeans take a stern attitude toward it. Having investigated how American mothers brought up their children from birth to five years, Sears [36] describes four major techniques that mothers actually used in order to control sexual stimulation and expression:

1. *Preventing stimulation.* Modesty training, to prevent development of sexual interests, began in early infancy in some families. The mother kept a diaper on the baby at all times, wrapped him in a towel quickly after his bath, hurrying to get him dressed. Although children might be bathed together when very young, the practice was stopped when they showed any interest in each other's genitals. Parents kept themselves modestly covered. Assuming that masturbation might result from irritation, mothers kept their babies very clean, using oil and powder regularly.
2. *Changing stimulation.* Distraction was a favorite technique. The mother moved the child's hands away from his genitals and gave him something else to do with them, such as playing pat-a-cake.
3. *Borrowed sanctions.* The mother might simply say, "Stop that. It isn't nice," but she was more likely to add a reason that was not quite accurate, such as, "It's dirty." Or she might ask, "Are you itchy?" or "Do you have to go to the toilet?"
4. *Avoiding labels.* Many families used no terms for sexual organs and activities; others used vague terms, like "down there"; and still others said baby words, such as "wee-wee." The implication is that if the child has no term for an organ or action, he won't notice it. One mother said, "I think it is very important for them to hardly realize any difference between different parts of their body."

Some notion of the variation among parents as to restrictiveness and permissiveness about nudity and masturbation can be obtained from Table 5–7. Although percentages pile up on the nonpermissive end of the scale, substantial differences exist. The results of this study are interesting in light of the recommendations to parents which have been made for many years in regard to sex education. Parent educators have long believed that it was wise to use the names of organs and functions and to permit babies to explore their bodies. Reasons for this point of view include promoting cognition (increased knowledge of the world, a clear body image) and laying a foundation for good sexual adjustment as an adult.

TABLE 5–7

Variations in family practices regarding sex restrictions.

Permissiveness for Child's Going Without Clothes Indoors	%
1. Not permissive. Must be clothed always. Nudity not nice.	30
2. Slightly permissive	14
3. Moderately permissive. May go nude briefly (to and from bathroom).	16
4. Quite permissive. Some restraint.	23
5. Entirely permissive. Child nude when he wishes.	13
Not ascertained	4

Permissiveness for Masturbation	%
1. Not permissive. Consider wrong, harmful	25
2. Slightly permissive. Wouldn't like it.	24
3. Moderately permissive. Must not let it become a habit.	28
4. Quite permissive. Expect some, worry if too frequent.	13
5. Entirely permissive. Natural. No effort to stop.	5
Not ascertained.	5

Source: Tables "Permissiveness for Child's Going Without Clothes Indoors" and "Permissiveness for Masturbation" from *Patterns of Child Rearing* by Robert R. Sears, Eleanor E. Maccoby and Harry Levin. Copyright © 1957 by Row, Peterson and Company. Reprinted by permission of Harper & Row, Publishers.

Nobody knows whether minimizing sexual stimulation in the first years of life will suppress sexual activity before marriage. Whatever the rational aspects of the situation may be, it is likely that the restrictive parents act more from what they *feel* to be right than from having thought it out objectively.

Sears points out that sex training differs in an important way from the other kinds of inhibitory training a mother does. When she asks her child to give up his bottle and his diapers, there are more mature forms of behavior to replace babyish ways. With sexual behavior, there is nothing to do but to stop it. Thus minimizing sexual stimulation, with the hope of preventing it, is realistic, *when the parent's aim is control through suppression.*

EMOTIONAL ASPECTS

Relationships with people always have feeling tones. Emotional development occurs through interaction of the individual with the rest of the world, to a large extent with the people in the rest of the world. Although the newborn seems to express only distress or no emotional tone, within a few weeks he appears to have both negative and positive emotions, *distress* and *delight,* as

Bridges [9] has called them. Illustrating the principle of development stated earlier, that *development proceeds through differentiation and integration,* the general emotions distress and delight become differentiated into more specific emotions. Figure 5–2 represents this process during infancy, suggesting how one general emotional state becomes 11 different emotions. We shall discuss here three of the emotions which have greatest significance for the infant and his relationship with people—love, fear and anger. Of these, the discussion of love warrants much more space than the others.

Love and Attachment

Hardest to define, impossible to agree upon, *love,* for our present purposes, means delight in being with, desire to be with and desire for contact and response from another person. Perhaps we should add to this list the budding of a desire to give to the other person, not just for the purpose of eliciting a response. Probably this dimension of love is noticeable toward the end of infancy.

The strength of the mother's love was defined, measured and correlated with infant behavior in a longitudinal study done at the University of Cali-

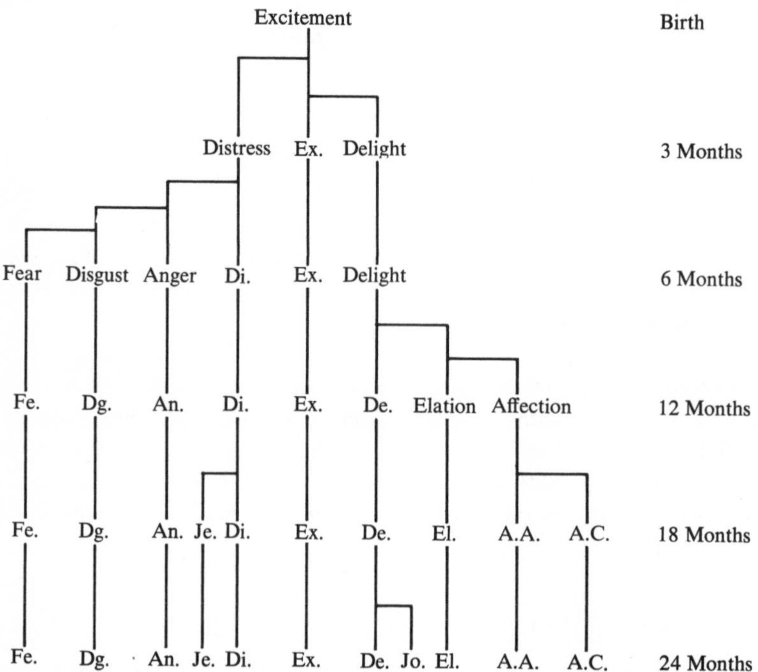

Figure 5–2. Bridges' schematic representation of the differentiation of emotion from general excitement in the newborn to 11 types of emotion at two years. (Reprinted by permission from K. M. B. Bridges, "Emotional Development in Early Infancy," *Child Development,* **3,** 324–341. Copyright © 1932, The Society for Research in Child Development, Inc.)

fornia [33]. Using the data from many observations and ratings of maternal behavior, a factor analysis showed the existence of two dimensions of behavior, autonomy–control and love–hostility. Although the first did not show clear relationships to infant behavior, the second did. Tests which tapped the mother's feeling of love and hostility could predict, to a very small degree, the baby's behavior. In other words, small, significant correlations were found between certain maternal measures and certain infant measures. One of the mothers' rating scales which tapped hostility, for example, used these questions: Does she often comment on how much extra work or trouble the child is? Does she tend to overlook the needs of the child? Babies were rated on seven point scales on these characteristics: degree of strangeness, shy to unreserved; activity, inactive to vigorous; speed of movements, slow to rapid; responsiveness to persons, slight to marked; amount of positive behavior; irritability, or tendency to be sensitive to and react to stimulation; emotional tone, unhappy to happy. Mothers' love behavior was found positively related to babies' happiness, positive behavior and calmness, especially between 10 and 36 months. Correlational studies such as this one tell nothing about whether the mother's love caused the babies' happiness or if the babies' being happy and behaving positively caused the mothers to love them. Although an educated guess would be that the reaction was reciprocal, the results do not permit a definite conclusion.

Because *love* has so many different meanings, it is fruitful to use more precise terms rather than the word *love* in discussing the love between a baby, his family and friends. In employing the more exact terminology, we indicate no callousness towards that mysterious emotional relationship, but rather a warm interest in understanding it better. It is harder to discover what happens in normal family relationships than it is to study what happens in disturbed relationships, judging from the numbers of studies available. One review of research on maternal deprivation comments on about 90 studies [45], another on 268 [13]. There are, however, a few recent studies which reveal much about how the infant builds relationships with other people. The concept of attachment is the key to the infant's social and emotional relationships.

ATTACHMENT. An infant is attached to another person when he shows pleasure in being with, desire to be with, desire for contact with and response from another person. Attachment can be noticed most readily when a baby is separated from his object of attachment, since he protests and tries to restore contact with the person. Human babies, as well as all young animals, tend to seek the proximity of certain members of the species and to avoid others [35]. The avoidance function will be discussed later, in the section on fear. This section is concerned with attachment behavior, how it occurs and what influences it.

An orderly sequence of behavior basic to attachment can be outlined [1, 2, 7]. From birth, of course, the infant cries, signaling a need for change in conditions. Before the infant shows any signs of preference for a particular person, he attends selectively to the human face or to a fascimile of it (as mentioned on page 80), beginning at about five weeks. The smile is not the result of associating the face with nursing but a response to the face itself [35]. Expressing friendliness, the smile has throughout life the function of social stimulation. In the beginning of smiling, then, the infant smiles to everything that looks like a human face. Until around five months of age, he smiles at everybody, but by approximately six months, he is becoming selective, smiling only at familiar people, and most of all at his mother or other people with whom he is making attachments. He also vocalizes selectively, "talking" more to his attachment object. Another sign of beginning attachment which occurs as smiling becomes selective, or possibly before, is differential crying. The baby cries when held by someone other than his mother and stops when she takes him. The next step is to watch the object of attachment, as when the baby keeps his mother in view even though he is in someone else's arms. Then comes a definite indication of attachment, crying when the specific person leaves and not crying when other people do. Figure 5–3 shows the intensity with which infants at various ages protested being left by anybody and by attachment objects. The curve for "indiscriminate attachment" shows that

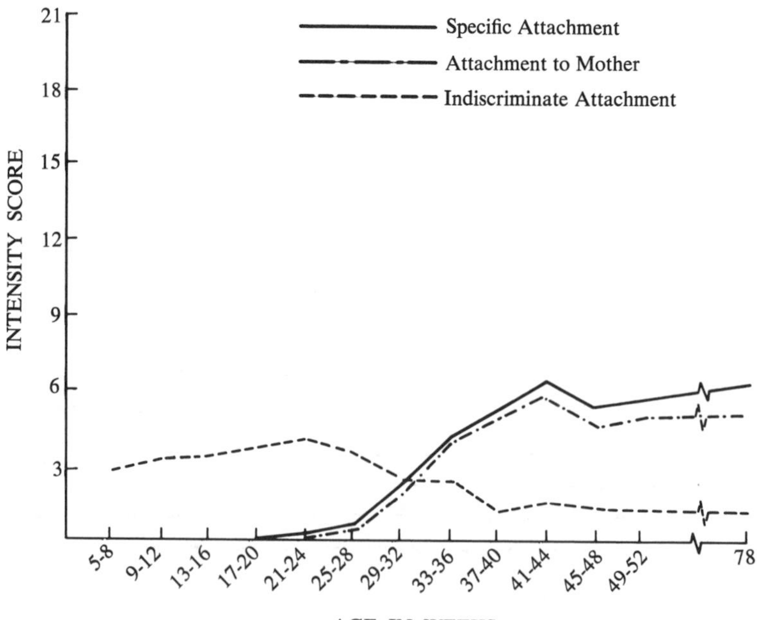

Figure 5–3. Development of infants' attachments to the mother, to other persons and to people-in-general, shown in terms of strength of protest at being left. (Reprinted by permission from H. R. Schaffer and P. E. Emerson, "The Development of Social Attachments in Infancy," *Monographs of The Society for Research in Child Development,* **29:**3. Copyright © 1964, The Society for Research in Child Development, Inc.)

babies as young as two months may protest when social stimulation is withdrawn but that it takes a maturity of seven or eight months to cry for attention from specific individuals. Other indications of attachment include clinging, scrambling over the mother and exploring her person, burying his face in her lap, following the attachment object as soon as he can creep, lifting arms, clapping hands and crowing in greeting [27]. Attachment behavior is not confined to close physical contacts. Vision and hearing, vocalizing and gestures, are used for keeping and making contact, as the infant widens the environment in which he operates. As sensorimotor competency increases, the baby can allow his mother to go farther away, since he is able to contact his attachment objects over a wider area.

Attachment has been studied longitudinally in 60 babies, focusing on the infant's protest at being separated from the objects of attachment [34] and at the strength of his crying or whimpering at the ending of a contact between him and the other person. The situations were everyday, ordinary occurrences, such as being left alone in a room, being left in his pram outside a store and being put down from arms or lap. Using these criteria, it was found that half of the specific attachments, including attachments to the mother, occurred most often between 25 and 32 weeks. A few occurred earlier and the rest later,

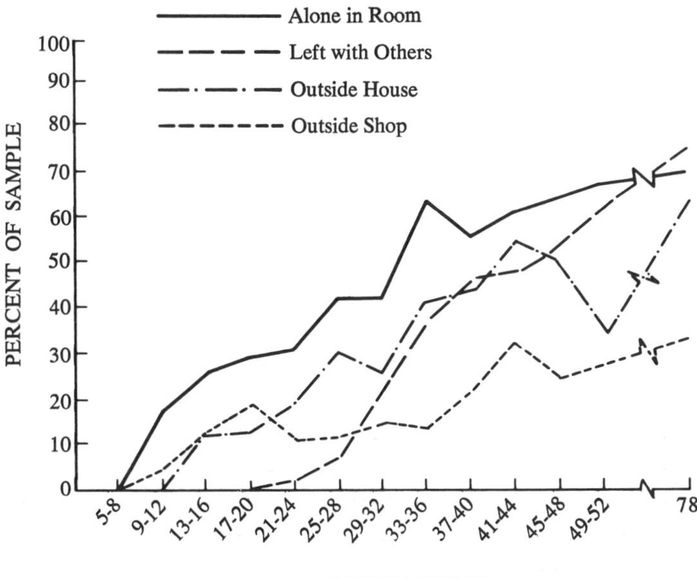

Figure 5–4. Percent of babies protesting being left alone in room, contrasted with percent protesting being left alone outside a shop. Interesting stimulation makes separation from attachment object much more acceptable. (Adapted from H. R. Schaffer and P. E. Emerson, "The Development of Social Attachments in Infancy," *Monographs of The Society for Research in Child Development,* **29**:3. Copyright © 1964, The Society for Research in Child Development, Inc. Used by permission.)

between 32 and 78 weeks. An attachment to a specific object was not a slow, gradual development, but rather a quick emergence, taking place in a month or less. Individuals showed variation from time to time in strength of protest over separation. Interesting stimulation made separation much more tolerable, as shown by the frequent acceptance of the mother's absence when she parked the pram outside the shop, on a busy street, in contrast to the protest which occurred on being left alone in bed. Figure 5–4 shows the difference between these two situations. Pain, illness, fatigue and fear led to intense protest and strong seeking of the mother's presence. When the attachment object returned from an absence, the infant was more demanding of attention, as when the father came in after work. A temporary change in social stimulation, such as the visit of an attentive relative, also brought increased demands on the mother after the period of extra stimulation had ended, but this demand was only temporary.

Often, but not always, the infant becomes attached to one person before he forms attachments to several. Often, but not always, the first person is his mother. Table 5–8 shows the objects of attachment at various ages. It will be noted that the mother soon comes to share the baby's affections with other people, the father most of all, but fairly often grandparents, siblings and other relatives and friends.

In an effort to find out why some infants were more intensely attached than others, certain aspects of the mothers' behavior were investigated. No relation was found between attachment and methods of feeding, weaning and toilet

TABLE 5–8

Identity of attachment objects: Percentage of subjects forming specific attachments according to identity of object at successive age period.

	Lunar Month Following Age at Onset in First Year						
Identity of Object	*1st*	*2nd*	*3rd*	*4th*	*5th*	*6th*	*18 Months (CA)*
Mother (sole object)	65	53	32	50	47	17	5
Mother (joint object)	30	35	54	43	50	77	76
Father (sole object)	3	9	7	2	0	5	4
Father (joint object	27	23	42	29	44	59	71
Grandparent (sole object)	2	0	0	0	0	0	0
Grandparent (joint object)	9	12	14	12	10	29	45
Other relative (sole object)	0	0	0	0	0	0	2
Other relative (joint object)	5	5	5	14	10	18	16
Friend or neighbor (sole object)	0	0	2	0	0	0	0
Friend or neighbor (joint object)	3	7	7	9	3	12	26
Sibling (sole object)	0	0	0	0	0	0	2
Sibling (joint object)	2	5	7	7	7	12	22
Other child (sole object)	0	0	0	0	0	0	0
Other child (joint object)	3	5	14	7	3	12	14

Source: Reprinted by permission from H. R. Schaffer and P. E. Emerson, "The Development of Social Attachments in Infancy," *Monographs of The Society for Research in Child Development*, **29**: 3, Table 8. Copyright © 1964, The Society for Research in Child Development, Inc.

training. The amount of time a mother spent with her baby had only a very small relationship to his attachment. When several people helped the mother to take care of the baby, he was somewhat less likely to show strong attachment to her. One variable which showed a definite relationship to attachment was that of maternal responsiveness. Intensely attached infants usually have mothers who respond quickly to their indications of need. It is not clear, however, which is cause and which is effect. It may be that intense attachment results from the interaction of a strongly demanding infant with a very responsive mother. Another significant variable was the amount of interaction initiated by the mother, the strongly attached babies having highly stimulating mothers. These findings are confirmed by another study in which the most firmly attached babies were likely to have mothers who were very involved with their infants and responsive to them [2].

The number of attachments made by a baby depended largely on availability of people to whom he could attach himself. A good candidate for attachment is responsive and stimulating. Simply being present is not enough. If the social setting includes siblings, relatives, neighbors or friends who often play with the baby, then he is likely to make wide attachments. There was no evidence to show that the strength of mother–infant attachments had any bearing on whether he formed many or few additional attachments. This study indicates the wisdom of studying the infant's social development in terms of his family and social setting and not only in relation to his mother. Although many studies to date have concentrated on mother–child relationships, few include the broader picture.

Unusual infant-mother situations. Much research has been concerned with what happened to babies who were not brought up by mothers who stayed home and played the roles expected of American middle-class women. The practical implications of this question are far-flung. What about mothers holding jobs? What about adoption laws? What about Communists? And so on.

Although studies of orphanage children generally show them to be retarded in some aspects of development, the question of stimulus deprivation confuses the issue [13]. Therefore, let us see what deprivation of the mother does in some other situations. The children who spent their infancy in college home-management houses were babies who received excellent physical care and wide stimulation from many students and several faculty members. The subsequent personality development and academic achievement of some of these children were studied after the children had spent several years as adopted children, living in regular families [18]. The experimental group was compared with a control group of children who had been born into their families and who matched the experimental subjects in age, sex and intelligence. No difference between the groups was shown in school achievement, anxiety and social adjustment. A test of personal adjustment favored the control group, suggesting that the children who had had multiple mothering were at a slight disadvantage emotionally.

Children in the kibbutzim (cooperative communities) of Israel are interesting in regard to multiple mothering, because they see their own mothers only briefly and periodically, while another woman and her assistants take care of them otherwise. A group of kibbutz-reared babies were found to score lower than home-reared on the Griffiths scale, especially in the area of personal-social development. However, by age 10, the kibbutz-reared children surpassed the home-reared Israeli ones on tests of intelligence and competency [31]. It might be expected here that the children would be slower in forming attachment to their mothers, due to less contact with them. One would also expect the nature of the attachment to be different, less intense, while attachment to nurse, teachers and peers would also be different from that of home-reared children. Considering the demands of life on a communal farm, it is not surprising that a communally reared child, by age 10, would be better able than a home-reared child to cope with the tasks facing him. Similarly, observations of communal rearing of Russian children reveal no ill effects from multiple mothering [8].

In families of the European-American middle-class type, the mother does most of the baby care, relieved by few, if any, helpers. In this situation an intense relationship naturally develops. The situation is different in western lower- and upper-class families and in joint families, where several or many adults may take care of the baby and have warm relationships with him. Even in large families where a baby is exposed to many people, it takes a certain level of maturity to distinguish between those he knows and those he does not know and a certain amount of progress in attachment behavior in order to care who people are. Mead [39] describes how, in villages she has studied, a baby will be brought up with 30 or 40 people around him all the time and yet at eight or nine months, he suddenly rejects all but the 20 or so who have been taking a lot of care of him. A "stranger" from four houses down the street can be very frightening. Mead observes that children cared for by the mother only have more fear of people (and less acceptance) than those cared for by several or many people. She thinks that the adult adjustment of the latter is easier, but points out that the result of one kind of upbringing fits into one culture, the other into another.

Taken all together, the studies on multiple mothering seem to amplify Mead's conclusion. If multiple mothering is a normal part of the culture, then it seems to work well in preparing the child to fit into that culture. If multiple mothering is not, then the child may experience some ill effects from it.

Another point of view from which to study the mother–infant relationship is to find out what happens when they are separated. Extensive research on infants separated from their mothers has indicated that when a baby is separated from his mother after the attachment is firm, which means after about six months, he becomes disorganized and disturbed [6]. A study [44] of the impact of maternal environment on children under six months showed that when a baby was changed from one foster mother to another, he was likely to show blunted social responses, increased tension, disturbance of routines, physiological disturbances and developmental regression. The severity and pervasiveness of the disturbance increased with increasing age from 3 to 12 months. At three months, only a few showed any disturbance; at four months, 50 percent did; at six months, 86 percent were disturbed; and at seven months, all of the infants showed upset upon being moved. When the relationship with the first mother was a close one, the immediate disturbance on separation was more severe; when the relationship between infant and mother was superficial, disturbance was milder.

Long-term effects of separation were studied through a follow-up of 20 adults who had been preschool children in London during World War II [20]. Their parents had placed them in residential nurseries. The young adults were studied by means of interviews, projective tests, interviews of their parents, reviews of medical and social agency files and nursery school records. The subjects were rated on feeling life, inner controls, relationships with people, role performances and intellectual functioning. The findings showed relatively normal adjustment, with most of the group not significantly different from a normal population. Adjustment varied, however, with the type of nursery, the age at which the child was placed, and his family experiences before and since. The year-olds fared the worst, the two-year-olds the best and the three-year-olds were in between. That the Twos adjusted better than the Threes seems to be out of line with findings on attachment behavior. The authors have two explanations: the Threes were beginning the Oedipus phase of parent–child relationships and were also more able to understand and misinterpret reasons for their placement; since many of the families were so troubled that they had a disorganizing effect upon their children, the children who entered the nurseries at two were exposed to less damage from their families than those who came at three. Further inquiry into the families led to this tentative conclusion: ". . . parents who voluntarily place a child in the first year of life, even though in a socially sanctioned program and in a time of national crisis, often have limited or distorted feeling lives and relationship capacities for caring for their children."

Thus the study shows that separation cannot be studied apart from the child's whole life experience. It affirms the plasticity of human personality. Most important, the authors conclude that "early childhood separation and preschool residential care, at least from about age two on, are not themselves *sufficient* antecedents to a seriously troubled or troublesome young adulthood."

Another report from Britain [15], this one on 5,000 children, underlines the necessity of studying separation within the life context of the child. It was found that children separated from their parents for one month or more showed at five years more nightmares, nail biting or thumbsucking than children who were not so separated, but only if the children were away from home during the period of separation. The effect was the same whether the children were in hospitals or in the home of friends or relatives. The same was true for the children's scores on mental ability and school achievement at 8 and 11 years of age and on teachers' reports of their work. As at 5 years, the effects showed only if the preschool separation had involved leaving home. Another finding was that the children of manual workers showed little, if any, effects of separation, whereas children of professional and administrative workers were heavily handicapped by a period of separation away from home if it occurred before the age of two years.

If the mother's admission that she did not want the baby indicates lack of love, the study done in Brussels is pertinent here [17]. Interviewing mothers within a few days after the birth of their babies, the question was asked, "Did you want to have a baby at the time when your child was born?" Later, from age 4 weeks to 3 years, the 215 unwanted babies were compared with a control group of wanted babies. Significant differences indicated that the desired children had fewer allergies, fewer emotional disturbances, less hostility, and better motor and intellectual development.

Implications of Infant Experience for Later Behavior. Clinical work with human beings sometimes suggests a connection between infant experiences and later sexual behavior. Although appropriate experiments with human beings are not feasible, Harlow has done dramatically suggestive research with macaque monkeys. Testing baby monkeys with substitute mothers, he found that they spent more time with warm, rocking, cloth-covered surrogates than with stationary wire surrogates, even if wire mothers gave milk. At this time, he reported that as far as the experimenter could observe, the baby monkey's attachment to a cloth mother was as strong as for a real mother and that the security he gained from a cloth mother was as great as from a real mother [22]. However, when the cloth-mothered babies grew to maturity, neither males nor females were interested in mating. The females who were impregnated and gave birth did not take adequate care of their babies. They were ". . . helpless, hopeless, heartless mothers, devoid, or almost devoid of any maternal feeling" [23].

Thus the monkey's experience as an infant deeply affected her performance as a mother. Deprived of a normal infant–mother relationship, she could not later take part in a normal mother–infant relationship. Although it cannot be asserted that human beings would behave in exactly these ways under the same circumstances, there is a likelihood that similar mechanisms would operate.

Little attention has been paid in recent years to what infants do when they are together, although the investigators of the nineteen thirties were interested in this topic. They observed that babies did indeed interact with each other, from about five months onward. Fighting over toys seemed to be at a peak between 9 and 14 months, with personal aggression increasing with age. Cooperation in play was observed at about nine months, increased with age and increased considerably at 19 months. Recent research [21] has produced a refinement in methods of observation and a film showing infant interaction [12]. Present-day interest in the attachment process in infancy leads to investigating the baby's love relationships other than those he has with his mother. Curiosity in this area has achieved a great impetus from Harlow's [24] discoveries on the nature of infant–infant love in monkeys.

Harlow had demonstrated that monkeys brought up with surrogate but inanimate mothers grew up to be abnormal. (See above.) He also found that babies raised with normal mothers but without the company of other babies showed later behavior abnormalities, as far as sex and play were concerned. In order to analyze contributions of mothering and of peer companionship to normal development, he tried raising babies with surrogate mothers, giving them daily time in a playroom with their peers. Although they did not play as much with peers during their first year as did infants with real mothers, these monkeys developed normal play patterns and normal social-sex behavior in their second year. Their behavior became just as mature as that of monkeys raised with real mothers and peers. Another experiment involved putting four babies in a cage together, with no mother at all, but with regular opportunities for playroom play. Although their infant behavior was somewhat abnormal (they clutched each other a great deal), they showed mature social-sex patterns at one year. These monkeys are shown in the photographs on these pages (Figure 5–5).

Figure 5–5. Motherless monkeys are somewhat abnormal as infants, but through living and playing with peers, grow up to be fairly normal adults. (Courtesy of Harry F. Harlow.)

From these experiments and others, Harlow [24] concludes:

1. The mother–infant relationship is significant, especially in facilitating infant–infant interaction.
2. Infant–infant interaction under optimal conditions may fully compensate for lack of mothering. The infant–infant affectional system may be "the *sine qua non* for later adjustment in all spheres of monkey life."

Nobody knows whether seriously deprived human infants would get a comparable beneficial result from playing together. The same situation could not even occur for humans, even if such experimentation were possible, since they are still immobile at the age (or even at the comparable point in the life span) when little monkeys are racing, chasing, climbing, swinging, scuffling and playfully biting each other. Although there are some slight indications that preschool social play can help children to recover intellectually from early deprivation [14], it is not feasible to experiment with human beings in such a way as to show a relationship between mother–infant experience and adult sexual behavior. Animal experiments give hints, guides and suggestions but not blueprints on human behavior mechanisms. Harlow's experiments on monkey infant–infant relationships suggest that the peer relationships of young human beings may be extremely valuable and important in assuring normal growth and in compensating for some deprivation in other areas of life. As for discovering the age at which peer play would have maximum benefits or where its absence would be most serious, the monkey experiments are of little help.

Fear

Everyone knows how fear feels—stomach turning over, heart racing, mouth dry, skin perspiring, thoughts concentrated on how to get away from the situation in which he is. It is not too hard to see fear reactions in other people, if they are at least six months of age. When does fear begin, how does it feel and how does it show? These are questions which have received various answers by psychologists.

Loss of support and intense stimuli, including pain and loud noises, were once thought to be the primary inducers of fear in infants, even in newborn infants. Other fears were thought to result from conditioning or association with primary fear-inducing stimuli. Although this kind of explanation accounts for many of the fear reactions of infants, it does not quite explain the fear of strangers, which seems to be a normal development at about six months, nor does it always account for fear of the dark. One way of looking at the fear of strangers is this: unfamiliar sights and people are frightening, but only after the baby has had time and opportunities for building up a set of familiar images and expectations. Strangers can look strange only after some people have become familiar. The most frightening sights are those which are just a little bit different from familiar ones, especially where expectations of important human beings are not quite fulfilled. Susan, on her six-month visit to the doctor, kept looking at her mother with a distressed expression as she sat in the car seat beside her. Susan cried as her mother bent over to undress her in the doctor's office. "Why don't you take your hat off?" asked the pediatrician. As soon as the hat came off, Susan stopped crying and smiled at her mother. The hat must have made her mother into a stranger, a person who looked almost right, but not quite right.

Fear of strangers becomes meaningful when viewed in the sequence of attachment behavior described on page 156. Positive attachments to the mother and other important human beings are built up, and then discrimination against others is developed. In the previously mentioned study [34] of attachment in infancy, 77 percent of babies were found to show their first fear of strangers about one month after they showed the beginnings of specific attachments. A similar kind of developmental sequence can be seen in all social animals. "Certain behavioral processes will promote positive contact with living objects, normally members of the same species, and certain other processes will prevent such contacts as the animal grows older" [35]. Thus fear can be thought of as a protective mechanism which develops with maturation and learning. Fear of being left alone and fear of the dark probably have a large hereditary, maturational basis. It would be very dangerous for a young, wild primate to be left alone, especially in the dark. His fears and protestations would have real survival value. What meaning does this have for human parents? If they think of such fears as natural outcomes of development in infancy, then they will expect to provide comfort and reassurance if such fears are aroused and to be patient until children grow beyond them.

What meaning does such a concept of human fear have for the medical profession and for parents faced with illness of children? Since hospitalization and medical treatment usually involve pain and behavior patterns inadequate for the occasion, fears are likely to be provoked even in people who are not in the stage of life when fear of the dark and fear of strangers dominates. For infants and young children, then, a hospital experience is likely to pile fear upon fear. Adequate care will include extreme caution in hospitalizing children at the time when such fears are dominant, plus the full use of the natural antidote to such fears.

The antidote to fear is the presence of someone or something to which the immature creature is attached. Harlow [22] demonstrated this fact with his baby monkeys who had become attached to wire, cloth-covered artificial mothers. When placed in a strange room, the little monkey cowered, crouched, rocked, sucked and clutched his own body. With the surrogate mother there, the baby clung to her, ventured forth to explore the objects in the room, clung again and explored again, as though he neutralized his fear by contacting her, and derived continued reassurance by seeing her in the room.

Human parents show understanding of the principle demonstrated by Harlow when they stay with their children during times of stress or when they make themselves available for the children to contact. They also give a child a favorite toy or blanket to tide him over a strange situation. A baby will creep or toddle toward new situations, strange toys or people when he can return periodically to the people to whom he is attached. Often a look or a word is contact enough. It does not always have to be a touch, although tactile contact seems to be most reassuring and holding closely in the arms the most reassuring of all. Attachment and fear are thus articulated to promote survival of the infant and to permit exploration and growth.

Practical Suggestions for Preventing and Dealing with Fears in Infancy

1. Avoid separations of the baby from his attachment objects excepting for brief periods. Since mothers are sometimes necessarily absent, it is wise to encourage the building of other attachments, which the infant is likely to do with anyone who responds to him and who offers interesting stimulation.
2. Avoid separations and frightening experiences especially at the time when fear of strangers is developing and at its peak. Hospitalization and painful treatments are best postponed if possible. If such experiences are essential, keep the child with a person to whom he is attached. If the parent is powerless to provide this safeguard to emotional well-being, then provide an object to which the child is attached, preferably an object belonging to a person to whom he is attached. For example, his mother's purse might serve.
3. Introduce the infant gradually to new situations, so as to prevent fears arising from sudden stimulus changes.
4. Provide new situations and gradual changes along with reassurance, so as to help the child tolerate novelty and cope with newness.
5. Use reconditioning, when appropriate. A fear of a specific object or situation may be overcome by experiencing it along with something pleasant and comfortable. For instance, if a baby is afraid of water, he might come to like it by being put in a small amount of warm water with attractive toys.

Anger

Anger is the distress that accompanies being restrained or blocked in progress toward some sort of fulfillment. Anger involves lashing out rather than withdrawing as in fear. The crying and bodily activity of infants under conditions of bodily tension, such as hunger, look like anger. They seem to be reacting similarly to children and adults who are known to be angry. During the first year, babies learn to use anger for solving some of their problems, to a greater or lesser degree, depending on how successful it is. Some anger expressions seem to be only release of emotional energy.

During the second year, when the desire to establish autonomy is strong, interference with choice making is likely to bring angry resistance, crying, screaming, kicking, perhaps hitting, throwing and biting. For establishment of a sound sense of autonomy, a baby grows by having many experiences in successful choice making and few in choosing activities where he cannot succeed.

Goodenough's comprehensive and classic study, *Anger in Young Children,* describes and analyzes 1,878 anger outbursts of children in the first eight years of life [19]. Since the observations were recorded by parents, the cases were necessarily selected from families where parents were unusually cooperative and intelligent. As can be seen in Figure 5–6 there was a marked peak in anger outbursts during the second year and then a rapid decline. Little sex difference appeared in infancy, but during the preschool period, boys had significantly more outbursts than girls. At all ages, however, differences between individuals were greater than differences between the sexes.

Anger behavior changed with age. Most of the outbursts during the first three years involved display or undirected energy. Such behavior included crying, screaming, stiffening the body, throwing self on floor, stamping, jumping up and down. With age, such primitive bodily responses tended to be replaced with more directed, less violent, more symbolic expressions. The duration of outbursts changed very little, however.

Physical factors were influential. Outbursts occurred more often before mealtimes than at any other times of day. Children showed more outbursts when ill, even with slight colds or constipation. Outbursts were more frequent

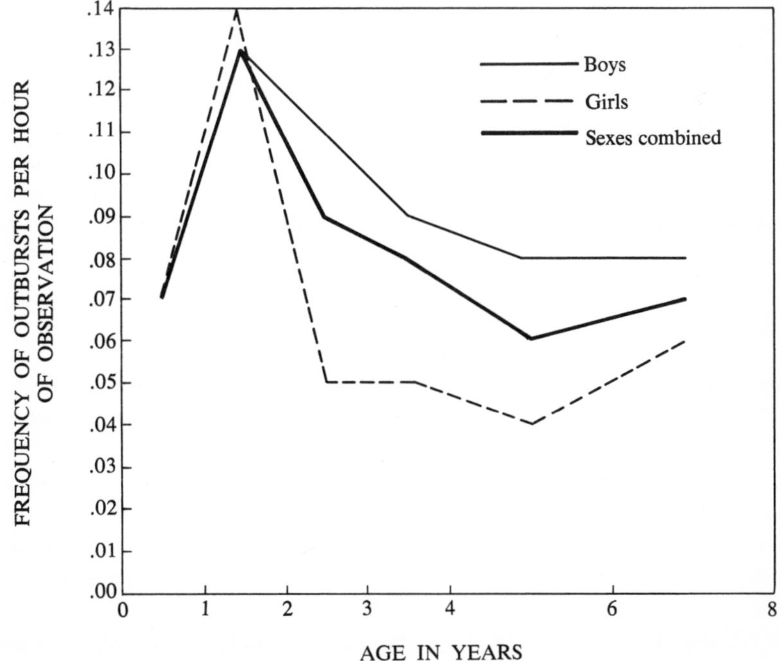

Figure 5–6. Frequency of anger outbursts by age and sex. (Reprinted by permission from F. L. Goodenough, *Anger in Young Children*. Copyright © 1931, University of Minnesota.)

among those who had recovered from one or more fairly serious illnesses than among children who had not been ill.

Many psychological factors were shown to be significant. Children who were being toilet-trained showed more outbursts on days following bed-wetting than on days following dry nights. The more adults in the home, the more likely was a child to have anger outbursts. When parents shifted from one method of control to another, the child tended to have more outbursts. "Giving the child his own way" was reported more often for children who had many outbursts than for those who had few.

Goodenough comes to this conclusion: ". . . the control of anger in children is best achieved when the child's behavior is viewed with serenity and tolerance, when the standards set are within the child's ability to achieve, and when these standards are adhered to with sufficient consistency to permit the child to learn through uniformity of experience, without such mechanical adherence to routine that the child's emotional or physical well-being is sacrificed to the demands of an inflexible schedule. However, when departures from the established schedule are made, they should be determined by a recognition of the needs of the child and not simply by the convenience or mood of the adult in charge. Self-control in the parents is, after all, likely to be the best guarantee of self-control in the child."

Hostile aggression is a type of anger expression which will be discussed further in Chapter 9, in relation to the preschool child. The roots of hostile aggression may lie in the infant–mother relationship [36, pp. 221–226]. Since it so often happens that the mother answers the baby's calls after he has become angry through frustration, he learns to be aggressive with his mother. She reinforces his angry behavior because she follows it with satisfactions. He also learns that he can either do or not do what she wants him to do. He learns that it hurts her when he does not do what she wishes. If he repeatedly perceives hurt in the other person as he achieves his ends (overcomes his frustrations), then hurting another person may become pleasant to him.

SUMMARY

The culture into which a child is born determines the limits of his opportunities for physical, cognitive and social development. Role prescriptions and ideals for childrearing, although clear in simple, stable societies, are often confusing in a rapidly changing culture. In the United States methods of childrearing change relatively fast. A variety of attitudes and methods exist at any one time, varying with such factors as economic level and stage of family development. The infant himself is active in determining how people respond to him.

Scheduling or timing is basic in the care and guidance of infants. The needs of all family members have to be balanced and adjusted in mutual regulation, taking special account of the baby's immaturity. At the same time that the family takes care of the infant's requirements for food, rest, exercise and cleanliness, they also build relationships and attitudes. Intellectual development is influenced through all experiences, as well as during play and stimulating interactions. Infant care also includes restrictions, many of which are applied in order to insure safety and health, others of which exist for the purpose of making life comfortable for other family members. Especially during the stage of development of the sense of autonomy, healthy growth requires clear, firm, minimal restrictions, within which the child can operate freely. Toilet training is accomplished more quickly when begun later, rather than earlier, in infancy. The mother's personality, especially her warmth or coldness, is a factor in success. In toilet training, the mother requires the child to substitute a more mature form of behavior for an immature pattern. In restricting sex activity, however, the mother asks the child to give up an activity without substituting for it.

Emotions become differentiated as the child develops. Love, a term with many implications, has been studied in the context of attachment. An infant shows attachment to another person when he shows desire for the presence, contact and response of that person. Attachment is shown by selective smiling and vocalizing and by crying at separation from the attachment object. The mother is usually the first attachment object, the father the second. Babies tend to select responsive, stimulating people as objects for their affection. Intense infant–mother relationships are frequent in cultures where the mother has little help with the care of her baby. When separated from the mother to whom he is firmly attached, the baby shows disturbance and disorganization. Separation and other love-deprivation experiences have to be interpreted in the life context of the child. Experiments with monkeys suggest that play with peers may compensate somewhat for deprivation in infant-adult affectional relationship.

Fear of strangers develops soon after the first attachments are formed. Fears may also result from intense and painful stimuli, from strange situations and from being alone in the dark. In coping with fear-provoking situations, an infant, like all people, only more so, gains courage and reassurance from the presence of a person to whom he is attached.

Anger involves tension and attack in connection with a blocking situation. Anger outbursts occur most frequently during the second year, when the child is very eager to make choices and yet lacks experience and skills necessary for independent successful action. Parents can minimize young children's anger outbursts by meeting their physical needs before tensions become acute and by maintaining firm, consistent, yet reasonable control.

REFERENCES

1. Ainsworth, M. D. Patterns of attachment behavior shown by the infant in interaction with his mother. *Merrill-Palmer Quart.*, 1964, **10,** 51–58.

2. Ainsworth, M. D. The development of infant-mother interaction among the Ganda. In B. M. Foss (Ed.), *Determinants of infant behavior, II*. London: Methuen, 1963, pp. 67–112.
3. Bayley, N., & Schaefer, E. S. Correlations of maternal and child behaviors with the development of mental abilities: data from the Berkeley growth study. *Mono. Soc. Res. Child Devel.,* 1964, **29:**6.
4. Becker, W. C. Consequences of different kinds of parental discipline. In M. L. Hoffman & L. W. Hoffman (Eds.), *Review of child development research*. New York: Russell Sage Foundation, 1964, pp. 171–208.
5. Blood, R. O. Consequences of permissiveness for parents of young children. *Marr. Fam. Living,* 1953, **15,** 209–219.
6. Bowlby, J. *Child care and the growth of love*. London: Penguin, 1953.
7. Bowlby, J. The nature of the child's tie to his mother. *Int. J. Psychoan.,* 1958, **39,** 1–24.
8. Brackbill, Y. Experimental research with children in the Soviet Union. *Am. Psychol.,* 1960, **15,** 226–233.
9. Bridges, K. M. B. Emotional development in early infancy. *Child Devel.,* 1932, **3,** 324–341.
10. Brim, O. G. *Education for childrearing*. New York: Russell Sage Foundation, 1959.
11. Bronfenbrenner, U. Socialization and social class through time and space. In E. E. Maccoby, T. M. Newcomb, & E. L. Hartley (Eds.), *Readings in social psychology*. New York: Holt, 1958, pp. 400–425.
12. Brown, J. L. *Peer group interaction in the first year of life*. (Film shown at meetings of *The Society for Research in Child Development,* Berkeley, 1963.)
13. Casler, L. Maternal deprivation: a critical review of the literature. *Mono. Soc. Res. Child Devel.,* 1961, **26:**2.
14. Dennis, W., & Najarian, P. Infant development under environmental handicap. *Psychol. Mono.,* 1957, **71:**7.
15. Douglas, J. W. B. Social class and the effect of maternal deprivation in early childhood. In A. Merminod (Ed.), *The growth of the normal child during the first three years of life,* Vol. 7. New York: Modern Problems in Pediatrics, 1962.
16. Duvall, E. M. Conceptions of parenthood. *Am. J. Sociol.,* 1946, **52,** 202–203.
17. Emery-Hauzeur, C., & Sand, E. A. Enfants désirés et non désirés. *Enfance,* 1962, **2,** 109–126.
18. Gardner, D. B., Hawkes, G. R., & Burchinal, L. G. Noncontinuous mothering in infancy and development in later childhood. *Child Devel.,* 1961, **32,** 225–234.
19. Goodenough, F. L. *Anger in young children*. Minneapolis: Univer. of Minnesota, 1931.
20. Haas, H. S. Long-term effects of early separation and group care. *Vita Humana,* 1963, **6,** 34–56.
21. Haas, M. B., & Harms, I. E. Social interaction between infants. *Child Devel.,* 1963, **34,** 79–97.
22. Harlow, H. F. The nature of love. *Am. Psychol.,* 1958, **13,** 673–684.
23. Harlow, H. F. The heterosexual affectional system in monkeys. *Am. Psychol.,* 1962, **17,** 1–9.

24. Harlow, H. F., & Harlow, M. K. Social deprivation in monkeys. *Sci. Am.*, 1962, **207**:5, 136–146.
25. Hetherington, E. M., & Brackbill, Y. Etiology and covariation of obstinacy, orderliness and parsimony in young children. *Child Devel.*, 1963, **34,** 919–944.
26. Hunt, J. McV. The psychological basis for preschool enrichment. *Merrill-Palmer Quart.*, 1964, **10,** 209–248.
27. Hunt, R. G., & Winokur, G. Some generalities concerning parental attitudes with special reference to changing them. In J. C. Glidewell (Ed.), *Parental attitudes and child behavior*. Springfield, Ill.: Charles C Thomas, 1961, pp. 174–187.
28. Koch, H. L. Twins and others. *Am. Psychol. Assoc.*, 1962.
29. Miller, D. R., & Swanson, G. E. *The changing American parent*. New York: Wiley, 1958.
30. Murphy, L. B. *The widening world of childhood*. New York: Basic Books, 1962.
31. Rabin, A. I. Behavior research in collective settlements in Israel. *Am. J. Orthopsychiat.*, 1958, **28,** 577–586.
32. Riesman, D., *et al. The lonely crowd: a study of the changing American character*. New Haven: Yale Univer., 1950.
33. Schaefer, E. S., & Bayley, N. Maternal behavior, child behavior and their intercorrelations from infancy through adolescence. *Mono. Soc. Res. Child Devel.*, 1963, **28**:3.
34. Schaffer, H. R., & Emerson, P. E. The development of social attachments in infancy. *Mono. Soc. Res. Child Devel.*, 1964, **29**:3.
35. Scott, J. P. The process of primary socialization in canine and human infants. *Mono. Soc. Res. Child Devel.*, 1963, **28**:1.
36. Sears, R., Maccoby, E. E., & Levin, H. *Patterns of child rearing*. Evanston, Ill.: Row, Peterson, 1957.
37. Spock, B. *Baby and child care*. New York: Pocket Books, 1957.
38. Stringer, L. A., & Pittman, D. J. The unmeasured residual in current research on parental attitudes and child behavior. In J. C. Glidewell, *Parental attitudes and child behavior*. Springfield, Ill.: Charles C Thomas, 1961, pp. 167–173.
39. Tanner, J. M., & Inhelder, B. *Discussions on child development,* Vol. II. New York: International Universities, 1954.
40. U.S. Children's Bureau. *Infant care*. Washington, D.C.: Government Printing Office, 1963.
41. Waters, E., & Crandall, V. J. Social class and observed maternal behavior from 1940 to 1960. *Child Devel.*, 1964, **35,** 1021–1032.
42. Wolfenstein, M. The emergence of fun morality. *J. Soc. Issues,* 1951, **7,** 15–25.
43. Wolfenstein, M. Trends in infant care. *Am. J. Orthopsychiat.*, 1953, **33,** 12–130.
44. Yarrow, L. J. Maternal deprivation: toward an empirical and conceptual re-evaluation. *Psychol. Bull.*, 1961, **58,** 459–490.
45. Yarrow, L. J. Research in dimensions of early maternal care. *Merrill-Palmer Quart.*, 1963, **9,** 101–114.

Peter J. Izzo

PART II

The Preschool Child

Introduction

Chronological age does not define the exact span of years of this period of life. Our discussion of infancy ended at about two years of age, or when the child had completed the growth of sensorimotor intelligence and had begun to use language for communication and thinking, when he had done the major work on establishing his sense of trust and was busy with the problems of establishing a sense of autonomy. With these achievements in intellectual and personality growth, he begins the preschool period. As he progresses through this stage, towards the school age, he works to perfect new coordinations of his maturing body. He builds his mind through coping with certain types of intellectual problems and his personality through further development of the sense of autonomy and then through the development of a sense of initiative and imagination. Interactions with the world of objects and people continue to be the means through which growth takes place and learning is accomplished. The chronological ages at which the various achievements can be noted vary from one child to another. To say, for example, that a certain type of thinking ends at seven is not to say that all children under all circumstances achieve a certain mode of thinking but only that the majority of children in a certain culture have done so.

Piaget places the end of one stage of intellectual growth at about seven years. Erikson places the end of the main concern with the sense of initiative at about seven. Many educational systems throughout the world recognize seven as a nodal age, a time when the child is appropriately occupied with learning the tools of his culture, whether they be reading, writing and arithmetic or work such as hunting, fishing and child care. Therefore, in our consideration of the preschool child, we often include the six-year-old, even though, strictly speaking, the American six-year-old is a schoolchild, required by law to attend school.

Asserting his individuality, testing the limits of himself, his family and his world, pushing out into that world, the preschool child is building his mental structures in complex and wondrous ways. His business is play, a widely varied activity through which he develops his body, personality, intelligence and emotions. He is the psychologist's darling, because he reveals his inner self so fully. As a baby, he could not tell what he was thinking and feeling. As a school-age child, he won't tell. And as an adolescent, he either won't know or will tell only his friends. Not only does the preschool child *tell* through his words and his behavior, he also delights adults by his mistakes in reasoning and interpretation. Preschool thinking has some of the appeal which baby diminutive proportions have. It is "cute." What adult's heart would not be melted by the two-year-old who, widening her blue eyes at a tug pulling three barges on the river, commented, "Choo-choo going fwimming." Or by this three-year-old's observation, "Ephalanuts wash with just water; people wash with water, too, and soap for rinsing." Preschool thinking has surprise qualities, too. Think of the jolt received by the six-foot-three father whose nursery school child commented, "Teachers are bigger than mummies and daddies, even bigger than daddies."

Much research has been done on preschool children, largely because of their availability. Many institutions of higher learning run nursery schools, where young children are offered opportunities for growth and learning in a setting where scientists can learn from the children. As Chapter 8 will show, ongoing research indicates increasingly the importance of the preschool years for basic education. The term *preschool* may not be quite appropriate when schools for young children become more and more available.

The first chapter in this section, Chapter 6, deals with personality development, physical maturing and bodily coordination. The next two chapters are concerned with intellectual growth and its nurture, one chapter dealing with cognitive and language development, the other with imagination and the stimulation of development through education. Since the preschool period is dominated by the development of the sense of initiative and imagination, this aspect of growth is given special emphasis in the present section of the book.

Personality and Body

CHAPTER 6

No longer a baby, the preschool child interacts with an expanding world of people and things. Although physical growth is slower than it was during infancy, he is still growing faster than he will in the years which follow this period. Personality development is dramatic, as he moves from infantile concerns to the stage which gives color and focus to the preschool years.

DIRECTIONS IN PERSONALITY GROWTH

Two threads dominate the fabric of personality growth during the preschool years, the sense of autonomy and the sense of initiative. If all has gone well during infancy, a firm sense of trust is established by now. Further satisfactory experiences strengthen it, although shreds of mistrust are also present throughout life. Upon the foundation of a sense of trust, the child builds his sense of autonomy, and upon trust and autonomy, his sense of initiative. The success of his preschool interactions determine the adequacy of the sense of initiative and imagination which he builds.

Autonomy

The sense of autonomy blossoms as the child of two or thereabouts experiences the power of doing and deciding that comes with his wealth of budding abilities. Walking freely, although in a jerky trudging style, running a bit stiffly, climbing, bear-walking, knee-walking, galloping, riding a kiddy car, he has many independent modes of locomotion to exploit and choose from. The house and yard are for exploring. His hands easily do his bidding in reaching, grasping, letting go, throwing, turning, pulling, pushing. Toys to manipulate, tools that extend the powers of his hands, milk bottles with clothes pins, Daddy's old hat, Mummy's old purse, crayons and paper, sand and water, mud—all give him choices and successes. "Shall I play with it or not? . . . I'll do what I want with it. . . . What I do is all right."

Talking brings control over both the self and others and a corresponding strengthening of the sense of autonomy. The average increase in vocabulary from 18 months to two and a half years is from 22 to 446 words [36]. Four hundred and forty-six words represent a great many things, ideas, activities and people brought into the child's orbit of influence. He has made the discovery that everything has a name and that when he can say the name, he can exert some control over the thing.

Even headier is the power to cooperate with people or not. If you ask a two-year-old, "Do you want to go outdoors?" the chances are that he'll say *no.* Even though he really would like to go out, he gets tremendous momentary satisfaction out of deciding thus. If you say, "We're going out now," he'll most likely trot along happily, the decision having been kept out of his hands. Similarly with helping him finish a job that is too hard, like putting his rubbers on, it is better to do it than to ask, "Shall I help you?" There are many opportunities for choosing and deciding, even when adults limit them. The child decides whether to kiss, hug and give other endearments, whether to finish his dinner and whether to urinate on the toilet or in his pants. The last decision mentioned, the question of toileting, is the one which, to the psychoanalysts, symbolizes the whole stage of developing autonomy. It is indeed an area where the sternest of parents has a hard time forcing the child and where the child can retain his autonomy under severe pressure. In the normal course of events in Western society, the child exercises autonomy as he brings his sphincters under control and takes on the toileting patterns approved by his family.

The opposite of a healthy sense of autonomy is a sense of shame and worthlessness. These negative feelings creep in when the youngster cannot choose enough and act independently enough, when the results of his choices and actions are disastrous and when adults use shaming as a method of control. Because the young child is vulnerable to shaming, adults may use it as a discipline technique, not realizing its dangers for personality development [11, pp. 251–254]. When a person is ashamed, he does not want to be seen or noticed. The use of shaming as a technique of control does not promote good behavior but rather defiance and trying to get away with doing what one wants to do. Another unfortunate outcome of poor guidance of autonomy is compulsive repetition of certain acts, a stubborn exerting of power. This type of behavior is probably the source of conforming rigidly to rules as written, in contrast to flexible interpretation of meaning.

> Outer control at this age, therefore, must be firmly reassuring. The infant must come to feel that the basic faith in existence, which is the lasting treasure saved from the rages of the oral stage, will not be jeopardized by this about-face of his, this sudden violent wish to have a choice, to appropriate demandingly, and to eliminate stubbornly. Firmness must protect him against the potential anarchy of his yet untrained sense of discrimination, his inability to hold on and to let go with discretion. As his environment encouraged him to "stand on

his own feet," it must protect him against meaningless and arbitrary experiences of shame and of early doubt [11, p. 252].

Initiative and Imagination

Just as development of a sense of autonomy dominates the early part of the preschool period, the sense of initiative is the central theme of the latter part. Personality growth is never in a straight line. There is always some backing up and reworking of old problems. Even with a firm sense of trust, there are frights over Mother's being away too long or strangers threatening. Even with a strong sense of autonomy, a child occasionally asserts it in a temper tantrum, a refusal to eat or a toilet "accident." Little threads of problems run through life as imperfections in trust and autonomy, demanding attention and solutions.

Now at four years or so, the sense of initiative claims the center of the stage. The child is pushing vigorously out into the world, seeking a wide range of information about it, about people and what they do, about what he himself can do. Grasping a piece of reality, like Mother's high heels and handbag, Daddy's briefcase or a doctor's kit, he creates the experience he wants, trying on the role of a mother or father or doctor, contemplating what these adults do, imagining how it would be if he himself were doing it. Building a store with cartons, he becomes a storekeeper. He paints a picture. He creates a new world in a stream bed. It is at this stage that children put beans in their ears and stir eye shadow into cold cream. If the child's seeking is successful, then he finds a wide variety of things he can do, make and create, with the approval of his family and other adults. If he succeeds, he continues as an older child and adult to look for new ideas, solutions, answers, reasons, creative experiences. Imagination will be discussed in greater detail in Chapter 8, where its development will be related to cognitive growth and where both these functions will be seen as integrated in play, which is the business of the preschool child. Aggression, also, is a function of the sense of initiative, since aggression involves pushing out into the world and attacking. Since aggression is also involved with anger, its discussion will be postponed until Chapter 9, which deals with emotional development and control.

Conscience develops at this time, regulating initiative and imagination. The child takes the voice of his parents into himself, saying what he may do and what he may not do. When he does not obey it, he feels guilty. Sometimes he even feels guilty for his thoughts and wishes which run counter to the commands of his conscience. His vigorous imagination can easily hit or kill people who oppose him or it can, more deviously, create a bear or a wolf to eat the annoying people. The bear may get out of control and threaten the child himself, especially in a dream. Conscience development will be considered further in the framework of parent–child relationships.

Thus do the forces of creativity and social control struggle in the person of a young child, producing dreams of beauty and fright, glimpses of new worlds of achievement, the constriction of guilt. The establishment of a healthy sense of initiative means that the child can interact vigorously under the control of a conscience that is strong enough but not too punishing.

Activity and Passivity in Relation to the Sense of Initiative

While the expression of initiative includes pushing out, exploring and making beginnings, being active is also an aspect of initiative. To be passive is to behave in a way that does not express initiative. Therefore, it is worth noting what has been found about activity and passivity in the early years of life. Individual differences in activity have been observed even in infancy, as well as during the preschool years, indicating that the beginnings of initiative can often be seen before the full flowering of the sense of initiative [29, pp. 342–354]. Differences were seen in motor activity and in sensitivity to the environment. Motor differences included those in total amount of activity and those in ways of using the body. For example, some babies were very active with their arms and legs, whereas others turned and rolled more. Some moved quickly, others slowly, some mildly, some forcefully. They varied in the distribution and length of periods of quiet and activity. Some children seemed to keep quiet in order to think. The children in the study also differed in the external forces that were brought to bear on their activity. For example, some mothers encouraged activity more than other mothers did. Some children had medical problems which required them to be more quiet than children who had no such restraints [29, p. 5].

Another approach to the understanding of activity was through a longitudinal study which followed children from birth to maturity [21]. Passivity was defined as the tendency to acquiesce to or withdraw from frustrating situations, instead of dealing with them actively. The opposite of passivity, then, sounds very much like the sense of initiative. Passivity was found to be a highly stable personality characteristic during the first 10 years of life. Another characteristic studied was dependence, defined as the child's tendency to seek affection, help and company of female adults, usually his mother. The opposite of dependency also sounds like an aspect of initiative, since initiative includes independent action. Dependency was found to be a moderately stable personality characteristic during the first 10 years of life [21, pp. 50–54].

Achievement in Relation to the Sense of Initiative

During the preschool years, when the development of the sense of initiative dominates life, it seems more important to get things started than to finish them. Planning, undertaking, exploring, pushing out and attacking are all of the essence of this period. Achieving (finishing jobs, doing well) becomes much more important during the stage which follows, the period of the development of a sense of industry. Since preparations for each stage of personality development are made during preceding stages, some of the foundations for later achievement can be studied during the preschool years. The young child has experiences which affect his efforts, persistence and expectations of himself in regard to excellence. As the youngster pushes forward to explore and to try new activities, his parents take certain attitudes toward what he is doing. Some hold high standards of excellence for their children; others hold lower standards. Some push children to do well; others let children do more as they will. Some give children a large measure of independence; others control children tightly. There are steps in between each of these pairs of extremes. Research shows that achievement motivation and behavior are affected by experience during the period of development of the sense of initiative and even more in the years which follow [5].

Nursery school children tried longer and harder in difficult tasks after being trained by being given tasks of gradually increasing difficulty and by being praised for achievement and persistence [22]. A child was likely to persist when adults made demands that he was able to fulfill and to put forth little effort when adults asked too much or too little of him [46]. Observations of the same children at home and at school showed certain children to be consistently interested in achievement-oriented play [6]. The mothers of these children tended to reward their achievement efforts and their seeking of approval and to ignore requests for help. These children in contrast to those less interested in achievement were less dependent upon adults for help and for emotional support.

The ways in which parents treat preschool children have definite effects upon their achievement behavior at later ages. At age 8 to 10, boys with high achievement needs and high achievement ratings, as contrasted to low achievers, had mothers who had demanded more independence, maturity and achievement of their sons and who also had rewarded them liberally for fulfilling the demands [45]. In other words, the mothers' demands and rewards during the preschool years were related to the children's achievement during the elementary-school years. Figure 6–1 shows the number of demands for mastery and independence made between the ages of 1 and 10 on high-achieving and low-achieving boys. The development of achievement motivation becomes increasingly important during the early school-age period. An extensive body of research on achievement will be reported in Part III, which deals with that age level.

SEX DIFFERENCES IN INITIATIVE. Common observation indicates that boys explore the world more vigorously than do girls. Any teacher of young children will agree that in general, boys are harder to control than girls. A study of dependency shown by children in the nursery school demonstrated greater dependency behavior in girls than in boys [17]. The previously mentioned longitudinal study on dependence and passivity showed a sex difference in the stability over time of the characteristics dependence and independence [21]. Between the ages of 3 and 14, girls were stable in this characteristic, but boys were not. That is, a girl tended to remain at the same level of independence, as compared with girls her age, but a boy was likely to change his degree of

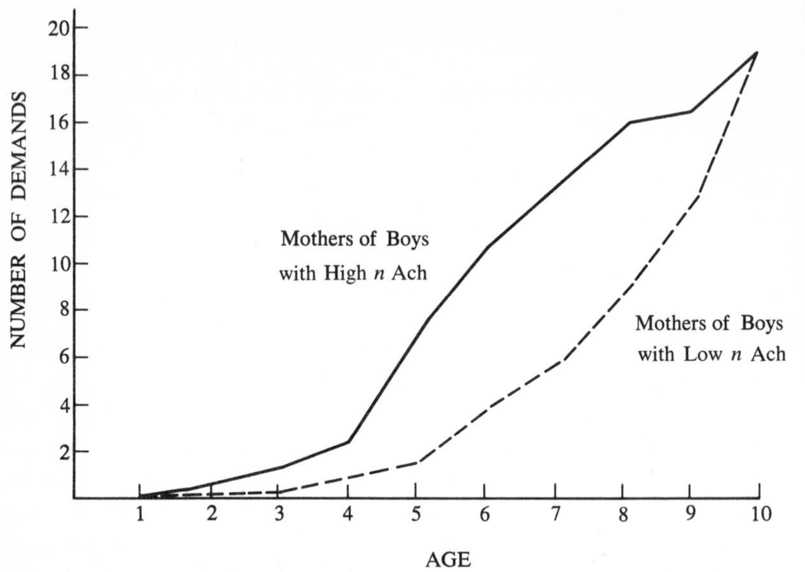

Figure 6–1. Demands for mastery and independence made by mothers of boys with high need for achievement and by mothers of boys with low need. (Reprinted by permission from M. R. Winterbottom, "The Relation of Need for Achievement to Learning Experiences in Independence and Mastery," in J. W. Atkinson (Ed.), *Motives in Fantasy, Action and Society*. Princeton, N.J.: Van Nostrand Co., 1958. Copyright © 1958, Van Nostrand Co.)

independence in relation to his age group. The authors reasoned that the culture is permissive for dependence or independence in girls, but for boys, expectations of independence are usually enforced when they enter school. Therefore, a girl could follow the course of her early choice as to degree of independent behavior, but a boy who had been dependent as a young child would have to switch.

The vigor with which the preschool child interacts with the world can thus be traced back to his infancy and forward into childhood and adolescence. Genetic and constitutional factors, experiences with food and mother, the culture impinging through the mother, and physical problems—all these are basic to the development of initiative.

PHYSICAL CHARACTERISTICS, EXPERIENCES AND THEIR IMPLICATIONS

Although much more independent than infants, preschool children are able to operate independently only within circumscribed areas. The protective and nurturing roles of parents are understood best in the light of the young child's physical characteristics.

Growth Rates

HEIGHT AND WEIGHT. Growth in height is not so fast as it was during infancy. The growth rate decelerates slowly throughout the preschool period. At two years, a child has added 75 percent of his birth length to his height [3, p. 279]. At four years, he has added 100 percent to it. Thus the second two-year period of life sees only one third as much gain in height as do the first two years. Rate of weight gain follows a slow deceleration from two to three years and a gradual acceleration from three to five. Birth weight is quadrupled by two and a half, showing the rapid rate for weight gain in infancy. Between two and five, the weight gain is less than the amount gained during the first year of life, showing the slower rate at which weight is gained in the preschool period as contrasted with infancy [3, p. 285].

Sex differences in height show up in these early years, girls progressing faster toward maturity than boys. The same is true of weight; girls are farther along toward their mature weights than are boys of the same age. However, during the preschool period, boys are slightly heavier and taller than girls, on the average, since their eventual heights and weights are greater.

TISSUES AND PROPORTIONS. Rates of growth change for various tissues, as well as for height and weight. The growth of fat and muscle is especially interesting, because of the consequent change from babylike to childlike appearance. Fat increases rapidly during the first nine months of life, decreases rapidly in thickness from nine months to two and a half years, and decreases slowly until five and a half. At five and a half, it is half as thick as at nine months. Thus does the chubby baby grow into a slender child. Muscle tissue follows a different pattern, growing at a decelerating rate throughout infancy and childhood, lagging behind other types of tissue growth until the puberal growth spurt. (See Figure 6–2.)

Sex differences show up in tissue growth, too. Boys have more muscle and bone than girls; girls have more fat than boys. Of course, there are individual differences, too, in all aspects of growth. Individual differences in amount of fat are greater than sex differences.

Bodily proportions change due to differential growth rates of various parts of the body. The principle of developmental direction is illustrated here by the growth which takes place in a cephalo-caudal (head to tail) direction. Development is at first more rapid in the head end of the body, with the tail end reaching maturity later. At age two, the head is still large in relation to the trunk and legs. The abdomen sticks out, since a relatively short trunk has to accommodate the internal organs, some of which are closer to adult size than is the trunk. Thus the toddler is top-heavy. The head itself grows according to the same principle, with the upper part closer to completion than the lower part. A large cranium and a small lower jaw give the characteristic baby look to a two-year-old's face. These proportions, plus fat, result in the diminutive nature of immature creatures which adults find emotionally appealing. Ameri-

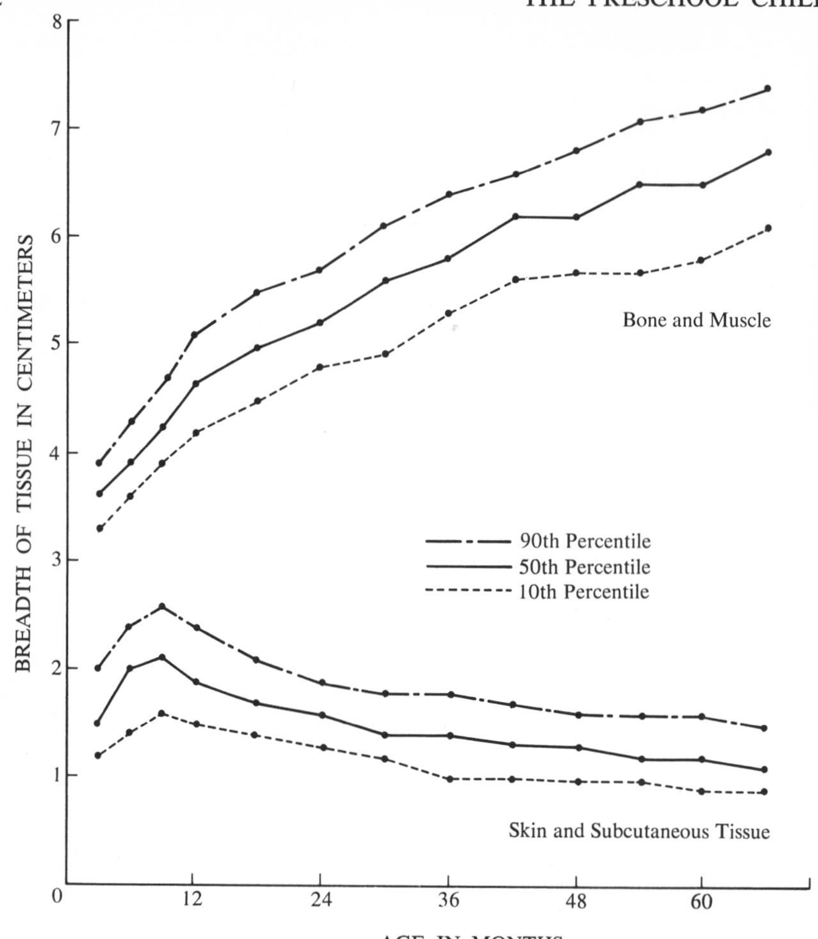

Figure 6–2. Rates of growth of bone and muscle tissue and of skin and fat. (Reprinted by permission from M. E. Breckenridge and M. N. Murphy, *Growth and Development of the Young Child,* 7th edition. Copyright © 1963, W. B. Saunders Company.)

cans call baby humans, puppies, kittens and other animal infants cute. Germans add *chen* to their names and French *ette*. As the legs, trunk and jaw grow in relation to the head, the baby loses his "cute" or diminutive look. This is what happens to the human baby between two and five years of age. By the time he starts to kindergarten or first grade, his proportions more nearly resemble those of the children in the rest of the grades than they resemble his preschool brothers and sisters at home.

Bones of preschool children have their own qualitative characteristics as well as proportional. The younger the child, the more cartilage there is in his skeletal system and the less the density of minerals in the bones. The joints are more flexible; the ligaments and muscles are attached more tenuously than in an older child. Thus it is easier to damage young bones, joints and muscles by pressure and pulling and by infections. The skeletal system is very responsive to changes in environment that produce malnutrition, fatigue and injury [3, p. 298].

The brain is more nearly complete, as to total weight, than the rest of the body. By three years, the brain is about 75 percent of its adult weight and by six years almost 90 percent. At age five the total nervous system is one twentieth the total weight, in contrast to the adult nervous system, which is one fiftieth the total weight [43, p. 138].

The fact that there is relatively little increase in brain weight at this time does not mean that brain development is not proceeding rapidly. There is every reason to believe that during the preschool period, there is a continuous increase in the number, size and complexity of connections between cells in the cortex and in connections between the different levels of the brain [40, pp. 82–84]. Evidence strongly suggests that Piaget's successive stages of cognitive growth occur as the cortex matures and becomes progressively organized.

The patterning of brain waves shown by electroencephalograms shows characteristic changes during the preschool period [42]. The delta rhythms prominent in infancy decline and the theta rhythm reaches its peak of frequency in the preschool period. Although not a great deal is known of the significance of brain waves, it has been observed that the time of the rise in frequency of the theta rhythm is associated with the time of the rise in frequency of temper outbursts. Specific incidents of temper outbursts were associated with immediate, specific increases in theta waves.

Of the special senses, *vision* and *taste* are noteworthy in the preschool years. The macula of the retina is not completely developed until about six years, and the eyeball does not reach adult size until 12 or 14 [43]. The young child is far-sighted because of the shape of the eyeball. Estimates for visual acuity, taken from several studies [9] are: at two years, 20/100 to 20/40; at three, 20/50 to 20/30; at four, 20/40 to 20/20; at five, 20/35 to 20/25; at six, 20/27. Thus even at six years of age, the estimated acuity is not yet 20/20. Investigations of the ways in which children use their visual mechanism show that they function in immature ways during the preschool years [12].

Taste buds are more generously distributed in the young child than in the adult, being scattered on the insides of the cheeks and the throat as well as on the tongue. The ear, too, is significantly different in the young child because of the Eustachian tube which connects the middle ear with the throat. The tube is shorter, more horizontal and wider in the infant and preschool child than in the older child and adult.

The internal organs show various immaturities, with implications for child care. For example, the stomach, at four to six years, has less than half the capacity of the average adult stomach. Calorie requirements at that age, however, are more than half as great as that of an active adult. The shape of the stomach is straighter than in older children and more directly upright than an infant's or older child's. Thus it empties rather readily in either direction. The lining of the digestive tract is easily irritated by seasonings and roughage. The respiratory system matures sufficiently during the preschool years to establish the adult type of breathing, combining abdominal and chest movements. However, air passages are relatively small at this time and the lymphatic system prominent so that tonsils and adenoids are at their maximum size.

Methods of Assessing Growth

A child can be compared with other children his age, to find out whether he is larger or smaller than they are. He can be compared as to height and weight and as to height and weight in relation to each other. In order to

TABLE 6–1

Height percentile table for boys from age 2½ through age 5½.

	Length in Inches						
Age	*3%*	*10%*	*25%*	*50%*	*75%*	*90%*	*97%*
2½ yr.	34¼	34¾	35½	36¼	37	38	39¼
3 yr.	35¾	36¼	37	38	38¾	39½	40½
3½ yr.	37	37¾	38½	39¼	40¼	41	42
4 yr.	38½	39	39¾	40¾	42	42¾	43½
4½ yr.	39½	40¼	41	42	43¼	44¼	45
5 yr.	40¼	41¼	42¼	43¼	44½	45½	46½
5½ yr.	41½	42½	43¾	45	46¼	47¼	48

Source: From *Growth and Development of Children*, 4th edition, by Ernest H. Watson and George H. Lowrey. Copyright © 1962, Year Book Medical Publishers, Inc., Chicago. Used by permission of Year Book Medical Publishers.

TABLE 6–2

Height percentile table for girls from age 2½ through age 5½.

	Length in Inches						
Age	*3%*	*10%*	*25%*	*50%*	*75%*	*90%*	*97%*
2½ yr.	33¼	34	35¼	36	37	38	39
3 yr.	34¾	35½	36¾	37¾	38½	39¾	40¾
3½ yr.	36¼	37	38	39¼	40¼	41½	42½
4 yr.	37½	38½	39½	40½	41½	43	44¼
4½ yr.	38½	39¾	40¾	42	43	44¾	45¾
5 yr.	40	41	42	43	44¼	45½	46¾
5½ yr.	41¼	42½	43½	44½	45¾	46¾	48

Source: From *Growth and Development of Children*, 4th edition, by Ernest H. Watson and George H. Lowrey. Copyright © 1962, Year Book Medical Publishers, Inc., Chicago. Used by permission of Year Book Medical Publishers.

discover his speed of growth, measurements must be taken more than once. His speed of growth can then be compared with that of other children. Height–weight–age tables represent the most common instrument used for making such assessments of growth. Tables 6–1, 6–2, 6–3, and 6–4 give for each age and sex the heights and weights which are at seven points on a percentile scale [43, pp. 70–73]. For example, four-year-old David is 40 inches tall and weighs 34 pounds. Table 6–3 shows that he weighs less than 75 percent of children his age, whereas Table 6–1 indicates his height to be above that of 75 percent of children. These figures suggest that David is slim, but they tell nothing about his body build. Width is taken into account by another type of table [31], combining age, height, weight and width. This rather complicated table has been little used for practical purposes. Another method of assessing growth is by means of a special record form on which repeated

TABLE 6–3

Weight percentile for boys age 2½ through age 5½.

	Weight in Pounds						
Age	*3%*	*10%*	*25%*	*50%*	*75%*	*90%*	*97%*
2½ yr.	25¼	26½	28½	30	32¼	34½	37
3 yr.	27	28¾	30¼	32¼	34½	36¾	39¼
3½ yr.	28½	30½	32¼	34¼	36¾	39	41½
4 yr.	30	32	34	36½	39	41½	44¼
4½ yr.	31½	33¾	35¾	38½	41½	44	47½
5 yr.	34	36	38½	41½	45¼	48¼	51¾
5½ yr.	36¼	38¾	42	45½	49¼	53	56½

Source: From *Growth and Development of Children*, 4th edition, by Ernest H. Watson and George H. Lowrey. Copyright © 1962, Year Book Medical Publishers, Inc., Chicago. Used by permission of Year Book Medical Publishers.

TABLE 6–4

Weight percentile for girls age 2½ through age 5½.

	Weight in Pounds						
Age	*3%*	*10%*	*25%*	*50%*	*75%*	*90%*	*97%*
2½ yr.	23½	25½	27½	29½	32	35½	38¼
3 yr.	25½	27½	29½	31¾	34½	37½	41¾
3½ yr.	27½	29½	31½	34	37	40½	45¼
4 yr.	29¼	31¼	33½	36¼	39½	43½	48¼
4½ yr.	30¾	33	35¼	38½	42	46¾	51
5 yr.	33	35½	38	41	44½	48¾	52¼
5½ yr.	35	38	40¾	44	47¼	51¼	55½

Source: From *Growth and Development of Children*, 4th edition, by Ernest H. Watson and George H. Lowrey, Copyright © 1962. Year Book Medical Publishers, Inc., Chicago. Used by permission of Year Book Medical Publishers.

measurements are entered. The Wetzel Grid [44] is a well-known example of this method. The Grid can be used to indicate the child's body type as obese, stocky, good (average), borderline, fair or poor and to compare a child with other children in height, width, body volume and rate of growth. The child can be compared with himself at any time in the past. Growth can be seen as even or uneven. The Wetzel Grid is used by physicians for supervising health and growth.

Skeletal Age

Another way of assessing growth is to measure the maturity of the skeleton, by means of X rays. Early in prenatal life the precursors of most bones appear as cartilage. (The bones of the upper part of the skull develop from membranous tissue.) The cartilage is gradually replaced by bone beginning in the sixth week after fertilization. From this time until the individual is in his twenties bone is being laid down, starting from centers of ossification which appear in highly uniform places in each cartilage. Ossification takes place in the cells through a process of formation of organic salts of calcium and phosphorus. Each center of ossification appears in a fairly uniform order. Bones grow in width or diameter by the addition of bony material on the outer surface of the bone underneath the periosteum (a membrane which surrounds the bone). Long bones grow longer by the addition of ossified materials at their ends. During the growth period, therefore, any given bit of bone is overlaid by later ossified material, not replaced by it.

In long bones another ossification center appears at the end of the cartilage which forms the model of the growing bone. This separate piece of bone is called the epiphysis. The cartilage between the epiphysis and the shaft of the bone (the diaphysis) appears to become thinner and thinner as growth proceeds. Eventually, in normal human beings the epiphysis and diaphysis fuse into one piece of bone, and lengthwise growth in that bone ceases. Just as the timetable of the appearance of centers of ossification is fairly regular for the individual, so the fusion of epiphyses and diaphyses follows a time pattern [32]. As each piece of bone grows, its size and shape changes in a systematic fashion which varies relatively little from one person to another.

All of these changes in bony tissue can be followed in X rays of the bones. The cartilaginous material is transparent to X rays; the ossified material, opaque. Most of the studies of skeletal development have been done using X rays of the left hand and wrist. The developed film is compared with standard illustrations in order to match it as closely as possible to one of them. The skeletal status of a child is expressed in terms of skeletal age, which corresponds to the chronological age at which the children on whom the standards were based usually attained that same degree of skeletal development [14]. Mental age, which is to be discussed in the next chapter, is a similar derived measure of development and is defined in much the same way as skeletal age.

Bone growth as a record of health. X rays of the hand yield information about the quality of a child's growth. Lightly mineralized bones may be due to insufficient intake of calcium, or insufficient metabolism of calcium, or both. An X ray film may therefore yield supplemental information concerning the nutritional status of a child. Some kinds of illnesses and other traumatic events in the child's life may result in bands of increased density of the bone at the growing end of the long bones [14, p. 19]. If they occur, they become permanent records of disturbances in the body's metabolism during that period of the child's life.

The principle of critical periods (Chapter 1) is apparent in the disruption of the orderly sequence of appearance of ossification centers during illness [14, p. 18]. If there is a disturbance in the calcium metabolism, such as occurs during illnesses, at the time when an ossification center is due to appear, its appearance may be delayed until a later time, even until after the appearance of the next scheduled center. When this happens, an X ray film taken subsequently, even perhaps several years later, will show imbalances in the development of individual bones and centers of ossification. Since the age of the bones that are present can be judged from their appearance, it becomes possible to make a judgment as to the time of the crisis and about how severe was the impact on the skeleton (and presumably the total organism). Later X ray examinations can tell at what point the child has made complete recovery.

Feeding the Young Child

Timing. Because a small child's capacity is limited while his needs for growth-promoting and protective foods are great, his nutritional program merits careful planning. Menus and timing are both important. Although feeding a new baby when he cries for food contributes to the early building of a sense of trust, the preschool child benefits from a structured program, including regular mealtimes that fit his stage of maturity. If the child comes to meals hungry but not famished and exercised but not exhausted, he is likely to take in adequate nutrients. For most American children, it works out well to have three meals a day, with a snack in the middle of the morning and another in the middle of the afternoon. The snacks can be adjusted in time, quality and quantity to make the youngster appropriately hungry at family mealtimes. Even though it may work out well in other cultures to let children eat when and and what they choose, this custom is not likely to meet the growth needs of American preschool children. For one reason, casual snacks are all too prone to be long on carbohydrates and fats and short on proteins, minerals and vitamins. With his limited capacity for intake and high need for growth-promoting foods, a preschool child cannot afford to eat many empty calories (foods devoid of proteins, minerals and vitamins). For another reason, eating and sleeping can be tied together in rhythms which assure adequate sleep for the young child. Insufficient sleep leads to fatigue which depresses the appetite.

Nutrients. The Food and Nutrition Board of the National Research Council regularly publishes recommended allowances of food elements for people of all ages [10]. Table 6–5 shows the recommended allowances for nutrients for young children. A food guide is useful in giving foods and amounts in terms of daily requirements.

Figures are not to be taken completely literally. Individuals vary in the amounts they need and in the amounts they eat from one day to another and from one meal to another. If the foods offered are chosen along the lines of this plan, most preschool children will take what they need from it.

Sensory aspects. Taste sensitivity varies from one individual to another, in preschool children as well as in older children and adults. An investigation [23] of preschool children's thresholds for the basic tastes, salt, sweet, bitter and sour, showed degrees of sensitivity to all four tastes to be highly correlated. Preschool children tended to be at the extreme ends of the scale for tasting bitter. That is, they either tasted it or they did not, whereas for sweet, salt and sour, they could be arranged into groups of high, medium and low sensitivity. The number of subjects reporting that they were always hungry for meals increased as taste sensitivity decreased. Breakfast was the meal most enjoyed, in contrast to teenage girls, who have been found to enjoy breakfast least.

Nutritionists recommend variety in the textures of foods which make up a meal. A combination of crisp, chewy and soft foods is usually enjoyed [39]. Common observation, as well as research [8], shows that preschool children often accept a raw vegetable in preference to the same vegetable cooked. Such a preference may be based on flavor as well as texture. None of the foods liked best by preschool children contained anything gritty or stringy [23].

Taste is not the only sense involved in eating. Sensations of touch come from fingers as well as mouth when young children eat. They often want to feel the slipperiness of gelatin and spaghetti, the crinkliness of lettuce and the cloudlike softness of a soufflé. Bright colors and color contrasts are thought to be effective in making meals attractive to children as well as to adults. Young children prefer lukewarm food to hot food [3, p. 229]. The sense of smell doubtless plays an important part in enjoyment of eating.

Emotional aspects. Emotional surroundings can enhance or depress appetite. Conversely, hunger disposes the child toward anger outbursts, as seen in Chapter 5. Excitement and upset conditions cause the stomach to stop its movements. To eat with the family may be too stimulating for a young child, or it may add to his happiness and feelings of belonging, depending on what goes on at the family table. Whatever the arrangements, the preschool child has the best chance of eating an adequate diet in an atmosphere that is calm and pleasant.

Avoiding problems. The year between two and three is a time when eating problems often begin. Because the rate of growth has slowed down appetite is likely to be smaller. Parents, remembering the joyous abandon with which their baby waded into his food, may worry when they see that the same

TABLE 6–5

Recommended amounts of nutrients for children of average height and weight.

	Weight		*Height*											
	kg	*lb*	*cm*	*in*	*Calories*	*Protein*	*Calcium*	*Iron*	*Vitamin A*	*Thia-mine*	*Ribo-flavin*	*Niacin Equiva-lents*	*Ascor-bic Acid*	*Vita-min D*
Children														
1–3 years	13	29	87	34	1300	32	0.8	8	2000	0.5	0.8	9	40	400
3–6 years	18	40	107	42	1600	40	0.8	10	2500	0.6	1.0	11	50	400
6–9 years	24	53	124	49	2100	52	0.8	12	3500	0.8	1.3	14	60	400

Source: *1963 Recommended Dietary Allowances*, NAS-NRC Pub. No. 1146. Copyright © 1964, National Academy of Sciences, Food and Nutrition Board. Reprinted by permission.

child at two and a half toys with his food and fusses over what he will eat and what he will not eat. Urging and forcing at this point often prolong and complicate the problem. Eager to exercise his autonomy, the two-year-old wants to choose and decide for himself. It is satisfying to decide to eat a small serving and then to ask for more or to refuse it; it can be very annoying to have too large an amount presented, especially if poked at you in spoonfuls. If the child can do it himself, his sense of autonomy is enhanced. He can make progress with a spoon and even more with his fingers if given foods that are easy to pick up. Custard and soup are easier to drink than to spoon up. The young child profits from all arrangements which facilitate self-help and from wide limits within which to do it himself. He does need limits, though, for healthy development of the sense of autonomy. The child suffers, as well as the family, when he is allowed to throw his applesauce on the floor or to grab the food from his neighbor's plate. It is important for him to feel that what he does is all right, and for him to have that feeling, his behavior has to be acceptable to the people around him.

Planning for Sleep and Rest

Sleep is a protective function which allows for repair and recovery of tissues after activity. Cognition is more adequate and emotional life more positive under conditions of enough sleep.

In the neonatal period, it is hard to differentiate exactly between sleeping and waking. During infancy, sleep patterns become more definite, influenced by night and day and by family activity rhythms. During the second year a common pattern is two naps a day and an all-night sleep. One nap is more usual between two and five and after that, no nap. In some cultures, an afternoon nap is normal for everybody, adults as well as children.

By the end of the preschool period, according to one study [7], the average child slept 11¼ hours in 24. Children varied widely, however, in hours of sleep, consistency of patterns, distribution of sleep between night and day, soundness of sleep and effects of various influences on sleep.

How much sleep is enough? This is a very difficult question to answer with scientific evidence or even to answer in a home situation. A practical way for adults to judge whether children are getting enough sleep is to use as criteria such signs as: ready to get up in the morning, good appetite, emotional relaxation, cheerful, agreeable, warm skin with good color, bright eyes, good posture, activeness in play, curiosity, enthusiasm.

Pediatricians have commented that mothers often find it more difficult to let children establish their own sleep patterns than to let them regulate their own feeding [3, p. 263]. In recent years, almost everyone has seen preschool children who stay up in the evening until they fall asleep or express a wish to go to bed. It came as a surprise to us to note a survey of bed-going practices which showed that only 7 percent of the children in the study had no specified bedtime [34, p. 296]. More in line with our casual observations was their

finding that 49 percent of the families were mild in enforcing the bedtime limitations that they had in mind. Whether permissively reared children get enough sleep is a difficult question to answer because of the problem of defining *enough* sleep. In countries such as Italy and India, where babies and preschool children go out in the evening with their parents, falling asleep here and there on a friend's sofa or an extra chair at a concert, we have not noticed the most obvious signs of fatigue in children. Young children seemed to sit around more than Americans, but in a relaxed, not tense, way. Extra sitting around might be due to more relaxed adults, fewer toys and less stimulating conditions rather than to lack of sleep.

AVOIDING PROBLEMS. In the United States, even if not in some other cultures, children benefit from parental supervision which makes regular sleep and rest a part of their lives. At developmental periods when certain influences disturb sleep, guidance is appropriate. For instance, toward the end of the first year, when strangers are recognized as strange and frightening, it is important for babysitters to be well acquainted with the baby, in order to prevent fright when he wakens from sleep. In the latter part of the second year and for some time after that, when motor activities are thrilling and the sense of autonomy is at a crucial stage of growth, a child may find it very hard to accept bed and sleep. Here is where a routine and careful guidance can prevent sleep problems from getting established. It is easiest to go to bed and to sleep after a period when stimulation has been cut down (that is, excitement minimized), a regular series of steps toward bed (such as washing, tooth brushing, story, putting teddy bear in bed), and an affectionately firm parent has indicated that sleep is imminent. Dreams are likely to be disturbing, because they are not clearly distinguished from reality. Reassurance after a fright or disturbance is conducive to sleep, as long as it is calm, confident and given in the child's room. Parents who make a big entertainment production out of the incident, or who take the youngster into their bed, usually rue the night. The reassurance, in these instances, comes to be a goal in itself.

Illness and Accidents

PREVENTION. Maintaining life and health in young children is no simple matter for parents, even in the favored environment of western civilization. (In some parts of the world, the odds are against an infant's surviving.) Preventive care means taking a young child regularly to a physician or to a well-baby clinic, where he is immunized against diseases, assessed as to growth and health and his mother given advice as to nutrition, physical care and attention to defects. Dental care is necessary from the preschool period onward.

Promotion of health and growth through routines of feeding, sleep and activity have been discussed. Parents also have the jobs of promoting community health measures, supervising general hygiene in the home, nursing ill children and keeping children from injury. Although most of the serious childhood diseases are preventable through immunization and many of the lesser illnesses are preventable through home hygiene, there are still many respiratory disturbances and some gastrointestinal illnesses which are common in preschool children. The immaturity of the systems involved makes them prone to infections and disturbances. As shown in Figure 6–3, the peak period for all illnesses, with respiratory ailments predominating, is the time from two to six.

ACCIDENTS. Accidents kill more children age 1 to 14 than any individual disease [26, 27]. A study by the Metropolitan Life Insurance Company showed that in the United States 29 percent of the deaths of boys between one and four and 25 percent of deaths of girls were caused by accidents [28]. Motor vehicles ranked first as a cause of accidents. Other types of accidents were pedestrian, drowning, falls, burning, firearms and poisons. Supervision of children outdoors is thus seen to be vital—not only telling them what not to do but watching them and keeping them out of the way of traffic, water and other hazards. Making and keeping the home safe for young children requires constant planning and vigilance.

Another Metropolitan Life Insurance study [27] showed that about 25 percent of the annual deaths from accidental poisoning in the United States were deaths of children between one and four years of age. The agents of death were chiefly aspirin and other salicylates, petroleum products, lead and household pesticides. The obvious implications are that safety of preschool children requires keeping them away from many substances of common use in the home. Saying *no* is not enough at this age. Since preschool children

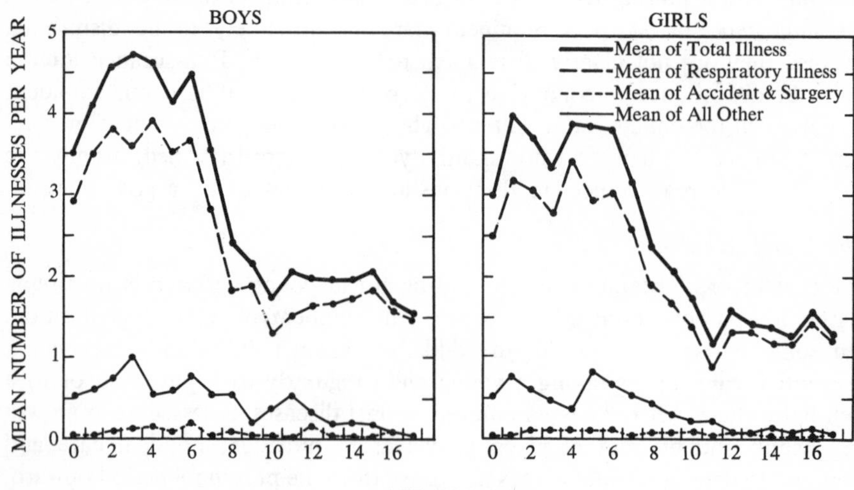

Figure 6–3. Incidence of illnesses and certain types of illnesses in boys and girls. (Reprinted by permission from I. Valadian, H. C. Stuart, and R. B. Reed, "Studies of Illnesses of Children Followed from Birth to Eighteen Years," *Monographs of The Society for Research in Child Development,* **26:**3, Figure 13. Copyright © 1961, The Society for Research in Child Development, Inc.)

tend to be good climbers, the problem of where to keep poisons out of their grasp is an important one to solve.

Studies on children over six indicate that accident-proneness is associated with stereotyped patterns of impulsively discharging anxiety through motor activity [26]. Preschool children tend to be impulsive in motor acts anyway. While the anxiety is the primary place to focus for prevention, it may also be worth helping preschool children to act less impulsively.

PSYCHOLOGICAL CARE OF ILL AND INJURED CHILDREN. It is frightening to be hurt or sick—frightening to anyone, but especially to a preschool child. Pain itself can be frightening as well as unpleasant. Reduced to a lower level of autonomy, he is disturbed at not being able to control himself and the environment as efficiently as normally. His thinking and his actions are less adequate for coping with the world.

Reassurance from parents makes the pain and fright possible to bear, just as Mother's presence in a disturbingly new situation gives a young child courage to explore. The most reassuring parent is one who combines sympathy with the calm expectation that balance and normalcy will be restored in due time. The ill or injured child is comforted and strengthened by having the limits of his activity redefined appropriately. For instance, "You are going to stay in your bed, but you can move around it all you like. I'll give you this box of toys to play with now. After your nap, you can choose a story for me to read to you." If toys and activities require less effort than his normal top speed, then he can still feel satisfied with what he achieves.

Hospital care for young children has been slowly undergoing a revolution, sparked by the research of Bowlby [2] and Spitz [37, 38] and pushed along by writers such as Robertson [33]. Gradually doctors, nurses and parents are accepting the evidence that it is damaging for children between six months and three years to be separated from their mothers, and that even after three years of age, separation may be harmful. Some hospitals now permit and even encourage parents to stay with their young children so as to give them the emotional support which they need every day but all the more when they are ill. Visiting rules have been liberalized in many places, too. There is still much to be learned about the problem, still a big educational job to be done in adapting hospitals to children's emotional needs.* Unfortunately many medical personnel still interpret a young child's stony silence as good adjustment and the flood of tears released by his parents as evidence that parents are bad for him.

PARENTS AS SOURCES OF PHYSICAL DANGER. Parents are the second most frequent cause of physical injuries to children, ranking second to motor vehicles [16]. So states a horrifying report on child-beating. This source of danger to children has received little publicity until fairly recently, since nobody likes to admit that parents can be so hostile toward their children. The authors of

* An illuminating film: *A-Two-Year-Old Goes to the Hospital* (British National Health Service and World Health Organization).

this report strongly suspect that child-beating inflicts many more injuries on children than do even motor vehicles, but that most parental violence is not reported. They estimate that for every child brought to the hospital with positive evidence of parentally inflicted damage, 100 such cases remain undetected. (Parents who batter their children are in dire emotional turmoil. They seriously need psychiatric help.)

MOTOR DEVELOPMENT

Watch a group of preschool children playing. The first impression is of constant motion. Closer inspection reveals some children sitting looking at books, others squatting in the sand box and one or two in dreamy silence beside the record player. The younger the child, the shorter the interval during which he is likely to stay put. Carrying out simple motor acts, he tends to finish quickly. In contrast, the older preschooler weaves simple acts together into more complicated units which take longer to perform. To crawl through a piece of culvert, for instance, takes only a minute and to crawl through several times takes only five, whereas to make that culvert into the Holland Tunnel and to use it as such may take half the morning.

The Developmental Sequence

The chart of motor behavior Table 6–6, drawn from several sources, shows how development between two and five results in a child who moves and manipulates more like an adult than he does like the toddler he used to be. Having worked through stages of using a spoon and fork, holding a glass and pouring from a pitcher, he can feed himself neatly without having to try very hard. He can even carry on a conversation at meals. He can cut and fold paper. From imitating a circular stroke at two, drawing a vertical line at three and copying a square with some accuracy at five, he is poised on the brink of learning to write. The two-year-old, to whom walking steadily, running and climbing are thrilling achievements, advances through walking tiptoe, hopping, jumping, tricycling, agile climbing and stunting to the graceful age of five. Skipping, hopping skillfully, running fast, he looks into an exciting future of skating, swimming and riding a two-wheeler. Balls, the toys beloved by babies, children and adults, are used with increasing maturity [15, 20, 25].

INDIVIDUAL DIFFERENCES. One child differs from another in the speed with which he progresses through a sequence of behavior patterns. Individual differences in rate of motor development were apparent in 152 children between three and seven years, who were tested for skill in cutting and tracing a straight line [24]. Although these skills showed fairly high correlations with age (.63 for cutting and .70 for tracing), two of the 50 youngest children ranked in the upper third in cutting and two in tracing. Four of the 49 oldest children ranked in the bottom third in cutting and four in tracing. We have seen four-year-olds who could swim and ride bicycles and six-year-olds who

TABLE 6–6

Some landmarks in motor development during the years from 2 to 6, from basic normative studies. The item is placed at the age where 50 percent or more of children perform the act. (Initials in parentheses refer to sources. See footnotes.)*

	Age Two	*Age Three*	*Age Four*	*Age Five*
EYE-HAND	Builds tower of 6 or 7 blocks (GA) Turns book pages singly (GA) Spoon into mouth without turning (GA) Holds glass in one hand (GA) Imitates circular stroke (GA) Puts on simple garment (GA)	Builds tower of 9 blocks (GA) Makes bridge of 3 blocks (TM) Catches ball, arms straight (MW) Spills little from spoon (GA) Pours from pitcher (GA) Unbuttons, puts shoes on (GA) Copies circle (TM) Draws straight line (TM)	Cuts on line with scissors (GI) Makes designs and crude letters (GI) Catches small ball, elbows in front of body (MW) Dresses self (GI)	Folds paper into double triangle (TM) Copies square (TM) Catches small ball, elbows at sides (MW) Throws well (G) Fastens buttons he can see (GI) Copies designs, letters, numbers (GI)
LOCOMOTION	Wide stance, runs well (GA) Walks up and down stairs alone (GA) Kicks large ball (GA) Descends large ladder, marking time (MW) Jumps 12″ (MW)	Walks tiptoe (GA, B) Jumps from bottom stair (GA, B) Stands on one foot (GA, B) Hops, both feet (MW) Propels wagon, one foot (J) Rides tricycle (GA) Descends long steps, marking time, unsupported (MW) Jumps 18″ (MW)	Gallops (G) Descends small ladder, alternating feet easily (MW) Stunts on tricycle (G) Descends short steps, alternating feet, unsupported (G)	Narrow stance (GI) Skips (G, MW) Hops on one foot, 10 or more steps (MW) Descends large ladder, alternating feet easily (MW) Walks straight line (GI)

* Sources:

B —Bayley, N. "Development of Motor Abilities During the First Three Years." *Mono. Soc. Res. Child. Devel.*, 1935, **1**.
GA —Gesell, A. and Amatruda, C. A. *Developmental Diagnosis* (New York: Hoeber, 1941).
GI —Gesell, A. and Ilg, F. L. *Child Development* (New York: Harper, 1949).
G —Gutteridge, M. V. "A Study of Motor Achievements of Young Children." *Arch. Psychol.*, 1939, No. 244.
J —Jones, T. D. *Development of Certain Motor Skills and Play Activities in Young Children*, Child Development Monographs (New York: Teachers College, Columbia University, 1939), No. 26.
MW—McCaskill, C. L. and Wellman, B. L. "A Study of Common Motor Achievements at the Preschool Ages." *Child Devel.*, 1939, **9**, 141–150.
TM —Terman, L. M. and Merrill, M. A. *Stanford-Binet Intelligence Scale* (Boston: Houghton Mifflin, 1960).

spilled their food consistently. Children differ also in speed, power and accuracy of their muscular coordinations, as witness the "natural athletes" who throw and catch balls efficiently in the preschool years. They differ, too, in balance and grace. When reading a chart that shows average development for various ages, it is important to keep in mind that this is a summary of a group of children and that it does not picture any one child as he is.

SEX DIFFERENCES. Boys have been found superior on steps, ladders and ball activities, while girls were better at hopping and skipping [25]. The latter can be confirmed by observing a kindergarten in the fall, where there are almost sure to be several little boys who merely run or gallop while the other children skip. Sex differences were found as early as two years of age, when French children were given Gesell tests similar to those mentioned in the

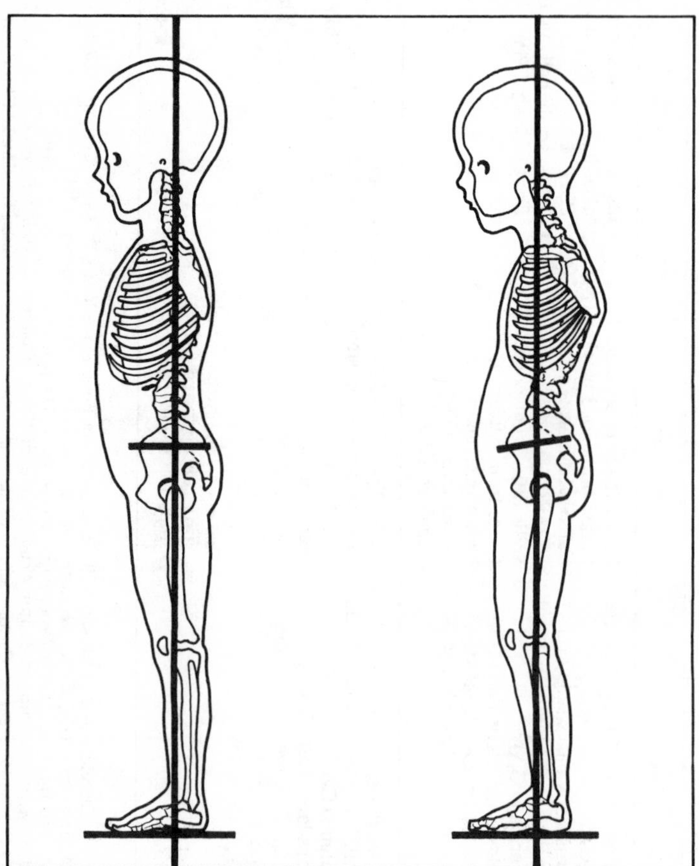

Figure 6–4. The child on the left shows good posture, the child on the right, poor posture. The first child's body is arranged symmetrically about a line that passes through his center of gravity. The head and chest are high, chin in, abdomen in, shoulder blades in, curves of back small and knees straight. (Figure 4.3 on page 90 of *Good Posture and the Little Child,* Children's Bureau Publication 219. Washington, D.C.: U.S. Government Printing Office, 1935.)

preceding chart of motor development. Boys were superior to girls on motor tests [41, p. 48].

A recent conference [41], involving authorities from various disciplines, focused, in part, on the origins of all sorts of sex differences. It was noted that even by two years, boys and girls have had sex-type experiences which influenced the ways in which they move and the toys which they prefer. Psychoanalytic interpretations were offered, linking male bodily structure to the greater activity and intrusiveness of boys and female to the girlish penchant for quiet play with soft, cuddly toys and for enclosing objects. Different cultures were described as patterning motor behavior in different sex-appropriate ways, some stressing masculine, some feminine, and some maximizing sex differences, some minimizing them. In all but extremely rare exceptions, however, boys are more exploratory in their play than are girls, more interested in mechanics and in experimentation.

Posture

Posture is the way in which the whole body is balanced, not only in sitting and standing, but also in play and rest. Posture is neuromuscular behavior, just as surely as bouncing a ball and drawing a circle are. Parents and teachers rarely make great headway when they try to get children to stand up straight or otherwise consciously improve their posture according to standard ideas of what good posture is. The ways in which a child stands, sits and moves are the results of a dynamic interplay of forces which cannot be controlled by holding his head up or throwing back his shoulders. This is not to say that good posture is unimportant in its influence on health, growth and efficiency of movement. It is very important indeed, but it is achieved through good muscle tone and healthy skeletal development, as well as through general physical and mental health. Figure 6–4 illustrates good and poor posture in the preschool child.

Breckenridge and Murphy [3, p. 313] distinguish five important factors when considering body dynamics:

1. *Gravity*. The body is most efficient motorwise if it is arranged symmetrically about a line that passes through the center of gravity (see illustration). The center of gravity drops in the trunk as the child's proportions change, and the lower it is, of course, the easier it is for him to maintain his balance in the upright position. The transverse line in Figure 6–5 shows the location of the center of gravity in the body from birth to adulthood. During the years from two to five, the center of gravity drops from just above the umbilicus to just below it [30, p. 89].
2. *Muscles and bones*. Good tone is important in all muscles. If opposing pairs of muscles are unequal in pull, faulty balance between them results in poor posture.
3. *Stage of development*. We have already mentioned that the young child has flexible joints, due to looser attachment of ligaments and muscles. Also, his center of gravity shifts downward, causing him to adjust gradu-

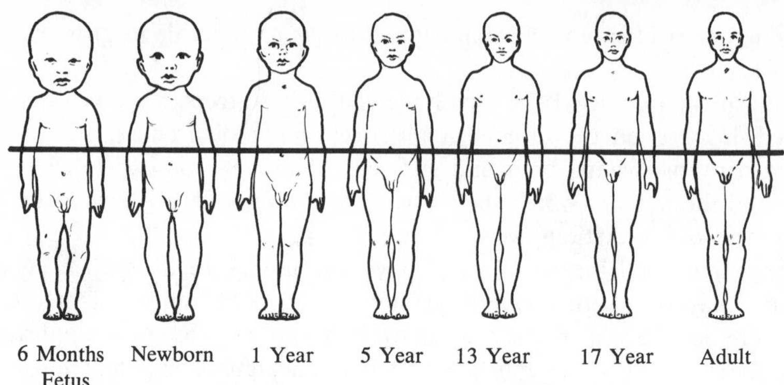

Figure 6–5. The horizontal line shows the center of gravity which changes its location in the trunk as body proportions change. (Reprinted by permission from C. E. Palmer, "Studies of the Center of Gravity in the Human Body," *Child Development,* **15,** Figure 7. Copyright © 1944, The Society for Research in Child Development, Inc.)

ally to the change. Standing on a wide base at first, in order to maintain his balance, the young child toes out and takes much of his weight on the inner part of his feet. The arch is protected with a fat pad at this point, and it makes him look as though he had flat feet. Knock knees and lordosis (small of back curving in excessively) are so common in the preschool period as to be considered normal. These conditions usually improve with age.

4. *Individual differences.* There is no one best posture for all, since a child's body dynamics are individual. A stocky child must balance his body in one way, a thin child in another. Varieties of proportions will have their own dynamics.
5. *Environmental influences.* The child's whole regime affects his posture. Obviously, nutrition determines what materials build and maintain his body, and hence is one key to the efficiency with which the body can operate and balance itself. Rest and fatigue, with their intimate connection with nutrition, nerves and muscles, play a big role in determining posture. Activity is essential, too, for developing coordination, maintaining muscle tissue and promoting its growth. A variety of equipment and opportunities for large-muscle play is hygienic. Shoes, clothing and furniture all have roles to play in promoting or hampering the dynamic coordination which is ideal for a given child.

The child's own personality is expressed in his posture, both his general attitudes towards himself and the world and his specific ups and downs. Sometimes a sagging, slumping body is the first indication that something is wrong. A handicap, such as blindness or deafness, often leads to a characteristic posture. A beautifully balanced body is one indication of a healthy child.

The influences of culture on posture can be seen as early as the preschool years. Mead [41, p. 40] gives illuminating examples from three different cultures. In Bali, girls of two and three walk with a "pregnant" posture because there is much teasing about pregnancy. A girl is told that she is probably pregnant and older people will often hit her on the abdomen, asking, "Got a baby in there?" Among the Iatumul, it is almost impossible to tell boys and girls apart, even with moving pictures, because they are dressed like girls, and all move like girls. Among the Manus, Mead could not tell the little girls and boys apart because they were all dressed like boys and moved like boys.

Physical Fitness

The past decade has seen the arousal of interest on a nationwide basis in the topic of physical fitness of children. School-age and college young people have been the subjects of most of the surveys and efforts at improvement. Most authorities on preschool children take the point of view that preschool children will take appropriate exercise in play if they are given a healthy general program which includes opportunities for using outdoor space and wide variety large-muscle play equipment. Tests of physical fitness on nursery school children have shown a wide range of results, however [35]. While some children scored the maximum on tests of muscular strength and flexibility, others could pass none and most scored between the two extremes. Since these children had rich opportunities for motor play, other factors must have accounted for their differences. In fact, the study indicated relationships between healthiness of personality and muscular strength and flexibility. Further study has confirmed the relationship between body flexibility and personality, as expressed in a test which explores the child's concept of his body [13].

Hand Preference

By two years, most children show a preference for the right hand, a few for the left and a few seem to have little preference. During the next three years, the hand preference becomes more firmly established, and established in more children. Thus hand preference is a developmental trait, a trait which increases with increasing maturity. While there are probably genetic foundations to laterality, social learning also influences hand preference. Figure 6–6, based on data from several investigators, shows how right-handedness increases with age. Note that the preschool years are the time when the greatest increase in established preferences occurs.

Studies on hand preference use an index of handedness derived from sampling a variety of activities. The formula for the index of dominance is $\frac{R - L}{R + L}$. (R is right hand, L is left hand.) Thus +1 would be complete right dominance and −1 left dominance. Figure 6–7 shows the distribution of such handedness indices for 44 nursery school children [18] who took part in

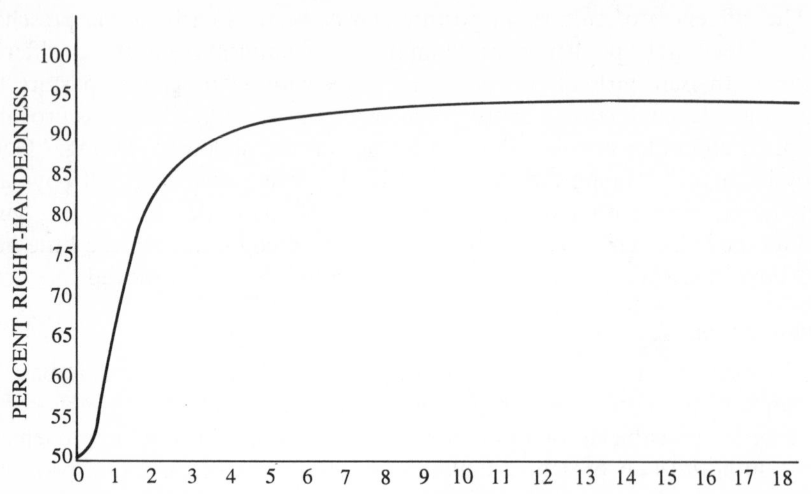

Figure 6–6. A steady increase in right-handedness takes place during the preschool years. (Reprinted by permission from G. Hildreth, "The Development and Training of Hand Dominance: II. Developmental Tendencies in Handedness," *Journal of Genetic Psychology,* **75,** 221–254. Copyright © 1949, The Journal Press.)

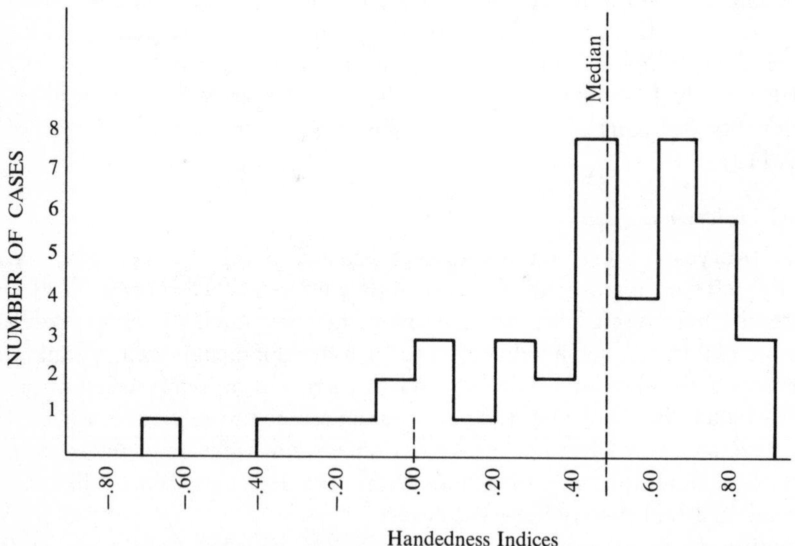

Figure 6–7. Distribution of handedness in nursery school children. Zero indicates no preference, +1 extreme right-dominance, −1 extreme left-dominance. (Reprinted by permission from G. Hildreth, "Manual Dominance in Nursery School Children," *Journal of Genetic Psychology,* **72,** 29–45. Copyright © 1948, The Journal Press.)

experiments to determine hand preference and who were also observed eating and playing. For example, hand preference was noted while the child ate with silver, ate with his fingers, threw a ball and drew with crayons. The lowest indices for hand preference were found while children ate with their fingers. Random observations for spontaneous acts also gave indices close to zero. About 11 percent of the children showed dominant left-handedness.

Sex differences are small but consistent. All studies concerned with such differences show a greater incidence of left-handedness and ambidexterity in boys. The difference may be due somewhat to social conditioning, since girls engage in more hand play than boys and are more amenable to training.

Stuttering and handedness have long been thought to be associated. Low left dominance or partially converted dominance has been shown to occur in stutterers more than in the general population. Which is cause and which effect, or whether either is cause or effect, is not definitely established. Stuttering tends to occur first at three or four years, the age when hand preference is being established ordinarily. It has been found that when manual dominance is established, stuttering tends to disappear, at least at this age [18]. The left-handed person incurs many disadvantages in addition to possible speech disturbance. In a world designed for right-handed people, he has to adjust to scissors, golf clubs, classroom chairs, table settings and countless other arrangements which are awkward for him. There are certain prejudices against left-handers, although feelings against them vary from time to time and from culture to culture.

The present permissiveness in childrearing makes for less pressure on children whose behavior deviates from that of the majority. When adults subscribe to an "unfolding" theory of child development, they take the attitude that left-handedness is natural to some children and that therefore it is better to let them be. The point of view in this book is that behavior patterns are developed through interaction of the child with the environment, and that since the environment can be controlled to a large extent, behavior patterns can be influenced. Since hand preference is definitely a behavior pattern which becomes established, not one which is given at birth, it is reasonable to expect that experience will influence it. Observation shows that this is the case. Conclusions drawn from a number of studies suggest that it is easy to establish right-handedness in children between one and three through training them in the use of eating implements and through other arrangements of the environment which favor the use of the right hand [19]. It is possible that left-handedness becomes established because a parent, seeing the child use his left hand for eating, reaching or throwing, thinks that the youngster prefers his left hand, while the child is still in an immature stage of having no true preference. The parent then treats the child as though he were left-handed, placing his spoon in the left hand, putting his cup at the left, handing objects to his left hand, and so on. Soon the child actually does prefer the left. Another possibility is that with a parent paying no attention to which hand he uses, the left becomes established purely by chance. If teaching and learning are important factors in establishing right-handedness, then permissiveness for choosing a preferred hand would increase the incidence of left-handedness. During the years from 1913 to the present, the incidence of left-handedness has indeed gone steadily up [19]. Table 6–7 shows results from studies in different decades.

TABLE 6–7

Incidence of left-handedness in schoolchildren over three decades.

Author	*Year*	*Percentage of Children Writing with Left Hand*
Hildreth	1932	2.2
Hildreth	1937	4.1
Hildreth	1941	6.2
Carrothers	1945	8.2
Belmont & Birch*	1963	10.0

* In addition to writing as a criterion of handedness, this study also used ball throwing, turning a doorknob and cutting with scissors.

Source: Data from Belmont and Birch [1], Carrothers [4] and Hildreth [19].

The question of hand preference is a significant one during the elementary-school years, when its reference to writing is obvious. Further discussion of this topic occurs in the section on the school-age child.

SUMMARY

Two stages of personality development occur during the preschool period: the development of the sense of autonomy, during the early years, and the development of the sense of initiative, from about three years to six or seven years. The sense of autonomy is promoted by clear, firm guidance which permits successful decision making within the limits it imposes. The opposite of a sense of autonomy includes feelings of shame and doubt. Initiative and imagination grow as the child explores the world of people and things, as he imagines himself into a variety of roles and activities and as he successfully seeks reasons, answers, solutions and new ideas. Conscience develops, along with guilt, requiring a balancing with initiative for adequate personality development. Beginnings of initiative can be seen in infancy, when children differ in activity and passivity. During the preschool years, differences in achievement behavior represent differences in the sense of initiative. Parental encouragement of achievement behavior at this age is likely to have lasting effects. The sense of initiative results from the interaction of a variety of influences, including genetic, constitutional, cultural and familial.

Physical growth is slower than it is in infancy. The rate of growth in height decelerates slowly during the preschool years. Although boys are slightly larger than girls, girls are closer to maturity than boys. Appearance and proportions change from the chubby, babylike configuration to the more slender, childish pattern, due to changes in amount and distribution of fat, as well as growth of muscle and skeletal tissues. Evidence of changes in the nervous system is more in terms of function than of size and structure. The structures of vision are immature. Taste buds are more numerous than in the older child. Characteristic shape, position and structure make for significant differences, as compared with older children, in the preschool child's middle ear, digestive system and respiratory system.

Assessment of growth is most often done in terms of a child's height and weight, which are compared with a standard derived from measurements of a large number of children. Or the present status may be evaluated according to a record of past growth. Growth can also be judged from skeletal development. X rays of the bones provide information on the health history of the child, as well as on his present status.

Adequate nutrition requires appropriate timing of meals, as well as nutrients. Since fatigue depresses appetite, health care includes careful guidance of rhythms of eating and sleeping. Eating problems are avoided by such guidance plus attention to the physiological, sensory and emotional aspects of preschool children's eating and by recognition of his eagerness for autonomy. Sleep problems, also, are avoided by appropriate timing, nonstimulating bed-going routines, reassurance in frightening situations and gentle firmness.

Many illnesses and accidents are preventable by planning, guidance, careful arrangement of the environment, hygiene, immunizations and medical supervision. Preschool children are especially vulnerable to illness—to respiratory ailments most of all and then to gastrointestinal upsets. Accidents rank high as causes of death and injury to preschool children. Frightened by illness or injury, a young child is reassured by the presence of a loved person, especially if that person is calmly sympathetic.

Motor development proceeds through a fairly stable sequence of patterns. Individual children differ in speed of sequential development as well as in quality of performance, as shown in speed, power and accuracy. In many, but not all, motor performances, boys excel girls. Posture, or body balance, expresses health and influences it. Young children vary in muscular strength and flexibility. Hand preference is established in most children during the first five years of life. Right-handedness increases with age. Left-handedness and ambidexterity occur more often in boys than in girls. Although genetic influences probably play some part in the establishment of hand preference, evidence suggests that most children can be taught, during the early years, to be right-handed.

REFERENCES

1. Belmont, L., & Birch, H. G. Lateral dominance and right-left awareness in normal children. *Child Devel.*, 1963, **34,** 257–270.
2. Bowlby, J. *Child care and the growth of love.* London: Pelican, 1953.

3. Breckenridge, M. E., & Murphy, M. N. *Growth and development of the young child* (7th ed.). Philadelphia: Saunders, 1963.
4. Carrothers, G. E. Left-handedness among school pupils. *Am. School Board J.,* 1947, **114,** 17–19.
5. Crandall, V. Achievement behavior in young children. *Young Children,* 1964, **20,** 77–90.
6. Crandall, V. J., Preston, A., & Rabson, A. Maternal reactions and the development of independence and achievement behavior in young children. *Child Devel.,* 1960, **31,** 243–251.
7. Despert, J. L. Sleep in preschool children: preliminary study. *Nerv. Child,* 1949, **8,** 8–27.
8. Dudley, D. T. Effect of methods of vegetable preparation on choices and amounts eaten by nursery school children. Unpublished Master's thesis, Iowa State Univer. Cited by Korslund [23].
9. Eichorn, D. H. Biological correlates of behavior. In H. W. Stevenson, J. Kagan, & C. Spiker, *Child psychology.* The sixty-second yearbook of the National Society for the Study of Education, Part I. Chicago: Univer. of Chicago, 1963, pp. 4–61.
10. Engle, R. W. 1963 recommended dietary allowances. *J. Am. Dietetic Assoc.,* 1964, **44,** 91–94.
11. Erikson, E. H. *Childhood and society.* New York: Norton, 1963.
12. Gesell, A., Ilg, F. L., & Bullis, G. E. *Vision.* New York: Hoeber, 1949.
13. Gollerkeri, S. B. Relationship between body image and muscular fitness of preschool children. Unpublished Master's thesis, Univer. of Rhode Island, 1963.
14. Greulich, W. W., & Pyle, S. I. *Radiographic atlas of skeletal development of the hand and wrist* (2d ed.). Stanford, Calif.: Stanford Univer., 1959.
15. Gutteridge, M. V. A study of motor achievements of young children. *Arch. Psychol.,* 1939, **244.**
16. Gwinn, J. L., Lewin, K. W., & Peterson, H. G., Jr. Roentgenographic manifestations of unsuspected trauma in infancy. *J. Am. Med. Assoc.,* 1961, **176,** 926–929.
17. Hicks, S. E. Dependence of children on adults as observed in the nursery school. Unpublished Master's thesis, Pennsylvania State Univer., 1962.
18. Hildreth, G. Manual dominance in nursery school children. *J. Genet. Psychol.,* 1948, **72,** 29–45.
19. Hildreth, G. The development and training of hand dominance: II. Developmental tendencies in handedness. *J. Genet. Psychol.,* 1949, **75,** 221–254.
20. Jones, T. D. The development of certain motor skills and play activities in young children. *Child Devel. Mono.,* New York: Teachers College, Columbia Univer., 1939.
21. Kagan, J., & Moss, H. A. *Birth to maturity.* New York: Wiley, 1962.
22. Keister, M. E. The behavior of young children in failure. *Univer. Iowa Stud. Child Welf.,* 1937, **14,** 27–82.
23. Korslund, M. K. Taste sensitivity and eating behavior of nursery school children. Unpublished Master's thesis, Iowa State Univer., 1962.
24. Lueck, E. Ability of young children to execute tracing and cutting tasks. Unpublished Master's thesis, Iowa State Univer., 1962.

25. McCaskill, C. L., & Wellman, B. L. A study of common motor achievements at the preschool ages. *Child Devel.*, 1938, **9**, 141–150.
26. Marcus, I. M. *et al.* An interdisciplinary approach to accident patterns in children. *Mono. Soc. Res. Child Devel.*, 1960, **25**:2.
27. Metropolitan Life Insurance Company. The frequency of accidental poisoning. *Stat. Bull.*, 1960, **41**:3, 8–10.
28. Metropolitan Life Insurance Company. Accidents: a major killer. *Stat. Bull.*, 1961, **42**:2, 6–7.
29. Murphy, L. B. *The widening world of childhood.* New York: Basic Books, 1962.
30. Olson, W. C. *Child development.* Boston: Heath, 1959.
31. Pryor, H. B. Width-weight tables (revised). *Am. J. Dis. Child.*, 1941, **61**, 300–304.
32. Pyle, S. I., Stuart, H. C., Cornoni, J. & Reed, R. Onsets, completions and spans of the osseous stage of development in representative bone growth centers of the extremities. *Mono. Soc. Res. Child Devel.*, 1961, **26**:1.
33. Robertson, J. *Young children in hospitals.* New York: Basic Books, 1958.
34. Sears, R. R., Maccoby, E. E., & Levin, H. *Patterns of child rearing.* Evanston: Row, Peterson, 1957.
35. Smart, R. C., & Smart, M. S. Kraus-Weber scores and personality adjustment of nursery school children. *Res. Quart.*, 1963, **3**, 199–205.
36. Smith, M. E. An investigation of the development of the sentence and the extent of vocabulary in young children. *Univer. Iowa Stud. Child Welf.*, 1926, **3**:5.
37. Spitz, R. A. Hospitalism: an inquiry into the genesis of psychiatric conditions in early childhood. *Psychoan. Stud. Child.*, 1945, **1**, 53–74.
38. Spitz, R. A. Hospitalism: a follow-up report. *Psychoan. Stud. Child.*, 1946, **2**, 113–117.
39. Sweeny, M. E., & Breckenridge, M. E. *How to feed children in nursery schools.* Detroit: Merrill-Palmer School, 1951.
40. Tanner, J. M. *Education and physical growth.* London: Univer. of London, 1961.
41. Tanner, J. M., & Inhelder, B. (Eds.) *Discussions on child development,* Vol. 3. New York: International Universities, 1958.
42. Walter, W. G. Electroencephalographic development of children. In J. M. Tanner & B. Inhelder, *Discussions on child development,* Vol. 1. New York: International Universities, 1953, pp. 132–160.
43. Watson, E. H., & Lowrey, G. H. *Growth and development of children* (4th ed.). Chicago: Year Book, 1962.
44. Wetzel, N. C. *Instruction manual in the use of the grid for evaluating physical fitness.* Cleveland: NEA Service, 1941.
45. Winterbottom, M. R. The relation of need for achievement to learning experiences in independence and mastery. In J. W. Atkinson (Ed.), *Motives in fantasy, action and society.* Princeton: Van Nostrand, 1958, pp. 453–494.
46. Wolf, T. H. The effect of praise and competition on the persisting behavior of kindergarten children. Monograph Series, **15.** Minneapolis: Univer. of Minnesota, Institute of Child Welfare, 1938.

Intellectual Development

CHAPTER 7

This chapter and the next concern the preschool child's intellectual development, and the measurement and stimulation of that development. Thinking, concept formation, intelligence and language make up the subject matter of this chapter. Imagination and stimulation of development are the focus of the next. Thought, language and imagination interweave and overlap as cognitive growth proceeds. Language provides symbols for thinking and also socializes thought, through interaction with other people. Children talk to others and talk to themselves. Young children talk out loud to themselves. Imagination or fantasy, an unfettered kind of thought or inner life, expresses emotion and complements controlled thought. Fantasy is both inner language and, on occasion, outer language. It is dreams and artistic expressions. Sometimes fantasy is equated with egocentric thought, because both are the means of pleasure seeking rather than truth seeking. Although fantasy is not limited by reality and does not purposefully deal with reality, it sometimes achieves solutions to problems which controlled thought cannot solve. An adult may "sleep on" a problem and awaken with the solution. A child may work through his problems in dramatic play or with dolls. The role of controlled thought is widely appreciated in children's education and development, but fantasy is little understood. Adults tend to dismiss it as a whimsical activity which will pass with time. Some schoolteachers deplore it as a waste of time; others see it as one of the keys to understanding children's thoughts and emotions.

Other keys are available for unlocking the mysteries of children's minds. Tests and experiments are used to investigate cognitive processes and factors which influence them. Observations are made under controlled conditions and the results analyzed. Children are rated by adults who have certain bases for agreeing or disagreeing with statements about their behavior. Results of tests, experiments, observations and ratings are treated statistically so as to extract generalizations from them and then those generalizations are tested for significance. Knowledge gained from research is then applied, in the case of cognition, by educators. The last part of the following is concerned with some recent developments in preschool education which stem from new knowledge of cognitive development.

THOUGHT PROCESSES AND CONCEPTUAL DEVELOPMENT

The intellectual landmark of the end of infancy is the completion of the period of sensorimotor intelligence, a phase of cognitive development discussed in Chapter 4. At this point, the child has achieved two major feats, the control of his movements in space and the notion of object constancy. He realizes that an object continues to exist even when he does not perceive it. Sensorimotor intelligence links successive perceptions and movements, with brief anticipations and memories. It does not take a large, sweeping view. ". . . Sensorimotor intelligence acts like a slow-motion film, in which all pictures are seen in succession but without fusion, and so without the continuous vision necessary for understanding the whole" [33, pp. 120–121].

From the end of the sensorimotor period to about age seven, thinking has certain characteristics which are more sophisticated than what has gone before, but naïve in comparison with later thinking. During the preschool years, of course, the child progresses towards more complex thinking. To describe his progress in stages is not to imply that he remains the same throughout the years included in a given stage.

*Characteristics of Preschool Thinking**

1. The young child cannot think from any point of view except his own, and he does not realize that he is limited in this fashion. His thought is centered on one perspective, his own. An example of centered thinking in an adult makes this limitation more clear, because it is obviously inappropriate for adults.

MRS. A: My, what a charming accent you have, Mrs. B. I think it is so quaint the way you say "two-dooah Foahd cah" for "two-door Ford car." I'd just love to have an accent like yours.

MRS. B: Your own accent is interesting, Mrs. A. I've never heard anyone say "ca-ow" for "cow," as you do.

MRS. A: Why, *I* don't have an accent. In Ohio we speak perfectly normally.

Mrs. A could not consider her own speech from Mrs. B's point of view, nor could she hear Mrs. B's speech from her point of view or from that of anyone but herself. In addition, she could not comprehend that there existed

* In Piaget's terms, the stage of preoperational thought. This stage begins at around 18 months or two years and ends at around seven. During these years, the child becomes less egocentric as his thought processes become more flexible, more controlled and less dominated by his perceptions and his wishes.

other points of view. She was centered in her own and could not move off or decenter.

The preschool child characteristically has but a dim awareness of his psychological self in relation to the rest of reality even though he knows that his body is a separate and distinct object among other objects. He cannot realize himself as experiencing. He does not know that his thoughts and actions make up a part of the situation in which he is. He has little objectivity, or relativism, which means looking from another person's point of view, from another angle in space or time, or imagining how it would be if you were somewhere else. This is not to say that the preschool child cannot step into the role of someone else. He can do it very well indeed, but when he does it, he loses himself. He cannot stand off and view himself from the angle of somebody else, but he can become the other person. He can do through fantasy, in taking the role of another, what he cannot do through controlled thought. Through neither fantasy nor controlled thought, however, can he see both points of view at once and weigh them.

2. Perceptions dominate the young child's thinking. He is greatly influenced by what he sees, hears or otherwise experiences at a given moment. Literally, seeing is believing. The static picture is what he believes. He does not pay attention to transformations or changes from one state to another. What he perceives at any one time is, however, only part of what a more mature person would perceive. Carolyn, the two-year-old who remarked, "Choo-choo going fwimming," was beholding on the river a large object, followed by several similar, rectangular objects, which did in fact resemble a train. The pointed prow of the tug, the decks, the small size, the absence of wheels—all these features did not indicate to her that this object was not an engine, although they would have done so to an older child. If Carolyn saw these aspects of the tug, she ignored them. She also ignored past experiences which would have been brought to bear on the situation by a more sophisticated observer. Nobody has seen a train moving itself on anything but a track. Carolyn's thinking was not flexible enough to watch the tug and barges, think of trains and how they run, compare this event with past observations of trains and then come to a conclusion based on both present and past. Another illustration of the dominance of perception is the ease with which young children can be fooled by a magician. Although the older members of the audience reject the evidences of their senses because they reason on the basis of past experience, the preschool children really believe that the magician found his rabbit in the little boy's coat pocket and that the card flew out of the air into the magician's hand.

One of Piaget's famous experiments is done by pouring beads from one glass container to another glass, taller and thinner than the first. When asked whether there are more or fewer beads in the second glass, the child answers either that there are more, because the level has risen, or that there are fewer, because the glass is narrower. The child centers on either height or width, unable to take both into consideration at the same time. In contrast, a child who had reached the next stage of thought, the period of concrete operations, would reason with respect to both relations and would deduce conservation. His perceptions would be placed in relation instead of giving rise to immediate reactions [33, pp. 130–131].

Perception becomes more flexible, "decentered," with increasing maturity [9]. Children between 4 and 12 were tested with cards containing at least three ambiguous figures apiece. The first card showed a butterfly with a face in either wing. The score was for number of spontaneous perceptions. The number of perceptions increased with both age and IQ. Four-year-olds typically saw a butterfly but no faces, whereas children nine and up ordinarily saw the butterfly and both faces. A few of the preschool children with high IQ's gave responses much like those of sixth graders. Thus, with intellectual growth, children became less rigid perceptually, less tied to the first perceptual response made in the given situation.

3. Reasoning at this age is from the particular to the particular rather than from general to particular. Piaget [34, p. 231] tells how Jacqueline, age 34 months, ill with a fever, wanted oranges to eat. Her parents explained to her that the oranges were not ripe yet, they had not their yellow color and were not yet good to eat. She accepted the explanation until given some camomile tea, which was yellow. Then she said, "Camomile tea isn't green, it's yellow already. . . . Give me some oranges!"

Thus she reasoned that if camomile tea was yellow, so were oranges. She went from once concrete instance to another, influenced by the way she wanted things to be.

4. Preschool thinking is relatively unsocialized. The young child feels no need to justify his conclusions and if he did, he would not be able to reconstruct his thought processes so as to show another person how he arrived at his conclusions. He takes little notice of how other people think, sometimes even ignoring what they say when he is talking. He begins to adjust his thinking to that of other people only as he becomes aware of himself as a thinker and as he grows in power to hold in mind several aspects of a situation at a time. Through years of interaction with other people, discussing, disagreeing, coming to agreements, the child gradually adopts the ground rules necessary for logical thinking.

Concepts of Classes

Certain recurring experiences are realized as having similar or identical aspects. When the child applies a word to a group of objects or events, he shows that he has a concept of it. He may very well have a concept of it before he indicates that he knows a word for it, but at least when he has the word, he has the concept. The first concepts are concrete, tied to definite objects or events. Through repeated experiences, especially those verbalized by other people in certain ways, the child develops abstract concepts. The concepts he builds will always be affected by the people around him, through the give and take of social living. For example, most children acquire the abstract concepts *red* and *black*. Figure 7–1 shows how a group of American preschool children increased in their successes on tests of matching and naming colors. Living in a culture which uses abstract color names, these children

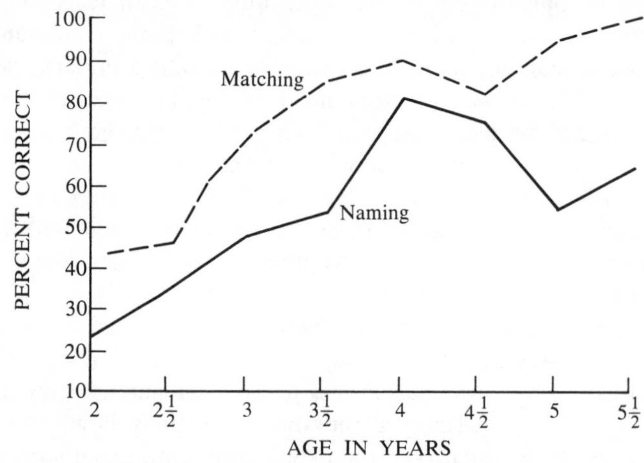

Figure 7–1. Age increases in ability to match colors and ability to name colors. (Reprinted by permission from W. M. Cook, "Ability of Children in Color Discrimination," *Child Development,* **2,** Figure 3. Copyright © 1931, The Society for Research in Child Development, Inc.)

were in the process of acquiring abstract concepts of color, as shown by naming. In New Pomerania, however, red is always tied to the concrete experience of blood, since the word *gab* means both, "red" and "blood." The word *kott-kott* means both "crow" and "black." Even more concretely tied to perception is the Brazilian Indian word *tu ku eng,* which is used for any and all of these colors: emerald green, cinnabar red and ultramarine blue. *Tu ku eng* is also a parrot which bears all three colors. Thus green, red and blue are not only bound up with the parrot but also with each other [52, pp. 234–241].

Several experiments have been devised to find out how children will classify (group) objects spontaneously when not given labels to aid in abstraction. The role of perception in concept formation can thus be seen more clearly. In the first experiment [20], children between three and five years were asked to choose from a group of red triangles and green circles the figures which were the same as another figure. The other figure was either a green triangle or a red circle. (See Figure 7–2.) The younger children chose quickly, without hesitation, usually on the basis of color rather than form. With increasing age, form more often became the basis of choice. Another experimenter [8], using what was essentially the same situation, found that when faced with the choice between form and color as a way of grouping, the older children often showed concern over the ambiguity of the choice. These experiments show how the perceptual processes in young children are almost automatic in grouping certain elements and that when a grouping is formed, it predominates over other possible groupings.

Further research dealing with the use of categories shows that the salience of various concepts is related to age during the preschool years [21]. Children between three and a half and six and a half years of age were given systematic choices in how to group a collection of toys. It was possible to classify the toys in terms of color, size, number, form, analytic characteristics (such as having four wheels or two arms) or sex type (for girls or for boys to play with). In general, the children found it easier to use color, number, form and size for classifying toys than to use analytic concepts or sex type. There were age differences in the use of color, size and form, the younger children using color and size more easily than form, the older ones using form more easily than color and size. It was suggested that although six-year-olds are capable of classifying by color and size, form has greater significance for them, because they are learning to read and write, tasks in which form is very important.

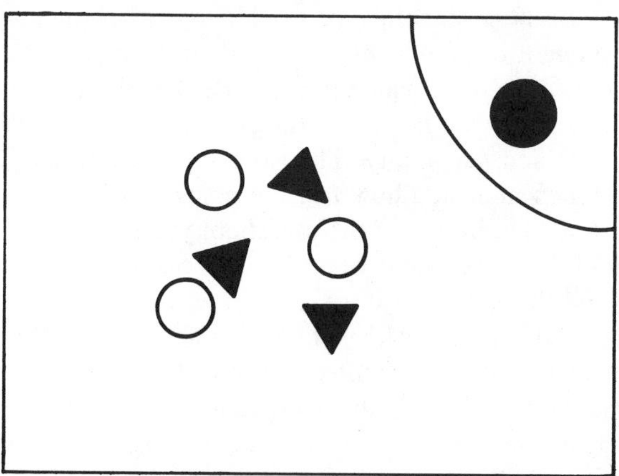

Figure 7–2. An ambiguous situation. Matching can be done by either form or color. (Reprinted by permission from H. Werner, *Comparative Psychology of Mental Development.* New York: International Universities Press, Inc., 1957. Copyright © 1957, International Universities Press, Inc.)

A third experiment [14] demonstrates the gradual elaboration of classifying which takes place with growth. Children were given forms of several shapes and colors and told to put them into groups. The first step in ordering is to put the objects into groups of either form or color. The young child (78 percent of three-year-olds and 33 percent of four-year-olds) was unable to arrange the objects further even after the examiner set an example. In step 2, most six-year-olds made subgroups by form after having grouped all the objects by color. In step 3, still another subgrouping was made. That is, after arranging the objects into colors, and into forms within the color groups, the child then ordered them according to size. Step 4, characteristic of the adult, involves taking more than one category into account at a time. In order to do this, the person has to abstract the categories completely. He has to be able to consider form, color and size entirely apart from the objects in which he perceives them. This process is a freeing of thought from sensory perception. No child under eight achieved it unaided. Thus preschool children are ordinarily dominated by their perceptions and unable to deliberately select or reject a category as a way of ordering.

Sensory, motor and emotional experiences all enter into the early building of concepts. Young children often group together things that they have experienced together, as did the child who used *quack* to mean duck, water and all other liquids and the child who used *afta* to mean drinking glass, pane of glass, window and what was drunk out of the glass ([52, p. 226]. The experience of the family group is often used in ordering objects which have no claim to family membership other than belonging in a category. For example, two-year-old Dickie called two half-dollars *daddy* and *mummy,* a quarter *Dickie,* and a dime *Baby*. Children frequently take into account physical qualities such as heaviness, clumsiness, pliability or prickliness, when naming objects. The name itself is thought to be part of the object, and language can express such qualities. Two children who made up a language used the word *bal* for *place*. The longer the vowel was held, the larger the place. *Bal* therefore meant village, *baal,* town and *baaal,* city. The word *dudu* meant go. The speed with which it was spoken indicated how fast the going was [52, p. 261].

A concept of *all* is built during the preschool years. In the early part of this period, the child does not know whether a succession of objects which look alike are one and the same object or a series of objects. Jacqueline, two and a half, walking in the woods with her father, was looking for slugs (snails). Catching sight of one she commented, "There it is." Seeing another, several yards away, she cried, "There's the slug again." Piaget took her back to see the first one again and asked if the second was the same or another. She answered "yes" to both questions. Jacqueline had no concept of a class of slugs [34, p. 225]. A two-year-old ordinarily has the concept of "another" when it is a case of wanting a cookie for each hand, or asking for more. The difference between cookies in the hands and slugs on Jacqueline's walk is that the two cookies are present at the same time, whereas the slugs were seen in succession.

A step beyond Jacqueline's dealing with a concept of slugs was shown by Ellen, at three and a half. Looking up at the blue Michigan sky surrounding her, she asked, "Is our sky at camp joined onto our sky at home?"

Thus Ellen showed that she realized that the sky in New York state and the sky in Michigan were either the same thing or of the same order of things. By asking, she was trying to develop the appropriate concept.

Adults often wonder why young children accept a succession of streetcorner Santa Clauses as Santa Claus. The reason is seen above, in the child's uncertainty as to whether similar objects constitute an individual or a class. Through experience and discussion, the child builds concepts of *one, some* and *all.* At first, *all* means that he perceives in a given situation. The toddler, listening to his bedtime story about Sleepyboy taking off his clothing, gets up at the mention of Sleepyboy's shoes and points out the shoes of everyone in the family. This early form of generalization is a *plural concept.* It is less mature than a concept of *all shoes,* which begins at around five. This stage was demonstrated in an experiment where each child was shown two series of trays. The trays in the first series contained: a dog and a bird, a dog and a pig, a dog and a cow, a dog and a sheep. Although every child could recognize that this tray had a dog, and that tray, and the other tray, few children under five could express the fact that all the trays contained dogs [14].

Time Concepts

The earliest experiences of time are most likely those of bodily rhythms, states which recur in regular patterns, such as hunger, eating, fullness. Interactions with the environment impose some patterns on bodily rhythms, calling them by such names as breakfast, nap time and bath time. Other early experiences which form the basis of time perception include dealing with a succession of objects, such as filling a basket with blocks; taking part in an action which continues and then stops, such as pushing or pulling a wheeled toy; hearing sounds of varying lengths; perceiving repetitions of stimuli in patterns, such as music and dance, or even rhythms of patting which a parent might do to a child in his arms.

In early childhood, time is not "an ever-rolling stream" but simply concrete events, embedded in activity. Time and space are not differentiated from each other, nor are they until beyond childhood. Having no overall, objective structure, time is largely the way that the preschool child feels it or wants it. Adults can appreciate this quality when they consider how long 10 seconds can be under the dentist's drill and how brief a hit Broadway show can be. Or, looking back at events such as your first formal dance or first trip alone, the vivid scene is as yesterday. Accepting the objective nature of time, the dental patient "knows" that the drilling was really only 10 seconds, the audience admits that the show lasted for two and a half hours and the adult realizes that his solitary trip to Grandpa's was 10 years ago.

Time is structured differently by different cultures, groups and individuals. A Balinese child must learn to orient himself within several simultaneously running calendars. An Eskimo gets a concept of night and day as varying dramatically from season to season, whereas to an Indonesian, night and day are very stable. Minute-conscious Americans are scheduled throughout the days, weeks and years, equipped with abundant watches, clocks, timers and calendars. The ages at which American children replace egocentric time concepts with objective ones are not necessarily those of the other children in the world. In fact, in primitive time systems, nobody detaches time concepts from the concrete activities in which they are embedded, such as milking time, apple blossom time or the year that a certain field was planted with yams. Emotional experiences may divide time into lucky and unlucky periods. Although western civilizations have attained considerable objectification of time, there are still many time structures based on personal, emotional and spiritual experience—spring, holy days, vacation, mourning period, anniversaries. A child's concepts will be molded by the time concepts he encounters in other people—his family, friends and teachers. As he checks his notions with theirs, he gradually changes his private, egocentric (self-referred) ones to generally held concepts.

Time concepts of children between 18 and 48 months were studied by both observation and questioning for two consecutive years in a nursery school [1]. All the children in the school were used both years, and all spontaneous verbalizations involving or implying time were recorded. The results show the trend of development in time concepts throughout the preschool period, although since the subjects ranged from high average to very superior intelligence, the age levels at which concepts occurred must be considered as applying to children of above-average intelligence. Note, they do show the trend of development in time concepts from egocentric to objective:

18 months: Some sense of timing, but no words for time.

21 months: Uses *now.* Waits in response to *just a minute.* Sense of timing improved. May rock with another child, or sit and wait at the table.

2 years: Uses *going to* and *in a minute, now, today.* Waits in response to several words. Understands *have clay after juice.* Begins to use past tense of verbs.

30 months: Free use of several words implying past, present and future, such as *morning, afternoon, some day, one day, tomorrow, last night.* More future words than past words.

3 years: Talks nearly as much about past and future as about the present. Duration: *all the time, all day, for two weeks.* Pretends to tell time. Much use of the word *time: what time? it's time, lunchtime.* Tells how old he is, what he will do tomorrow, what he will do at Christmas.

42 months: Past and future tenses used accurately. Complicated expressions of duration: *for a long time, for years, a whole week, in the meantime, two things at once.* Refinements in the use of time words: *it's almost time, a nice long time, on Fridays.* Some confusion in expressing time of events: "I'm not going to take a nap yesterday."

4 years: Broader concepts expressed by use of *month, next summer, last summer.* Seems to have clear understanding of sequence of daily events.*

Another study [40] traces the development of time concepts from egocentric to objective by showing how children learn to use a clock. When asked what time events in their day took place, a quarter of four-year-olds, a tenth of five-

* Reprinted by permission from L. B. Ames, "The Development of the Sense of Time in the Young Child," *J. Genet. Psychol.,* 1946, **68,** 97–125.

year-olds and no six-year-olds either recited their schedules or used words like *morning* and *early*. Numbers, either unreasonable, approximate or correct, were used by the rest of the children.

Space Concepts

The young child's concepts of space, like his concepts of time, are derived from bodily experience. He gets sensations from within his body and from his interactions with the rest of the world. During the sensorimotor period, he looks, touches, mouths and moves to build concepts of his body and other objects. During the period of preoperational thought, space is still egocentric, related to the child's body, his movements and perceptions. Four-year-old Laura named a certain tree "the resting tree" because she often sat under its cool branches for a few minutes on her way home from kindergarten. The land where the "resting tree" is located was the "resting place," and the family who lives there was "the resting tree people."

Space concepts were studied in nursery school children in the same way in which the time study, reported above, was conducted [2]. The order of appearance of verbalized concepts of space is thus shown. As in the time study, the ages given are for children who measured above average on intelligence tests.

1 year: Gestures for *up* and *down*.
18 months: Uses *up, down, off, come, go*.
2 years: Big, all gone, here. Interest in going and coming.
30 months: Many space words are rigid, exact ones: *right, right here, right there, right up there*. Words were combined for emphasis and exactness; *way up, up in, in here, in there, far away*. Space words used most: *in, up in, on, at*.
36 months: Words express increased refinements of space perception: *back, corner, over, from, by, up on top, on top of*. A new interest in detail and direction: tells where his daddy's office is and where his own bed is, uses names of cities.
42 months: Next to, under, between. Interest in appropriate places: *go there, find*. Interest in comparative size: *littlest, bigger, largest*. Expanding interest in location: *way down, way off, far away*. Can put the ball *on, in, under* and *in back of* the chair.
48 months: More expansive words: *on top of, far away, out in, down to, way up, way up there, way far, out, way off*. The word *behind*. Can tell his street and city. Can put a ball in front of a chair. Space words used most: *in, on, up in, at, down*.*

Primitive languages contain many space words which refer to the body or its motion and location in space. So does everyday (nonscientific) English in such words and expressions as groundwork, sky-high, eye-level, handy, back-

* Reprinted by permission from L. B. Ames and J. Learned, "The Development of Verbalized Space in the Young Child," *J. Genet. Psychol.*, 1948, **72**, 63–84.

side, neck and neck. When asking directions from the man-in-the-street, how often does one get an answer such as, "Follow Elm Street for half a mile and then turn right onto Route 4"? Not very often. It is much more likely to be, "You know where the Mobil gas station is down past the cemetery? No? Well then, go to the second stop light and turn kitty-corner to the Catholic Church. You can't miss it." *You can't miss it* is almost inevitable at the end of a set of directions so firmly rooted in concrete experience. The person giving such directions is doing it so much from an egocentric standpoint that he cannot imagine anyone finding the route less clear than it is in his own mind.

The child's progress toward objective space concepts depends not only upon his bodily experiences, moving through space and perceiving objects, but also upon the concepts which adults offer him. Although it is necessary to have experience and to internalize it, the child also checks his interpretations with

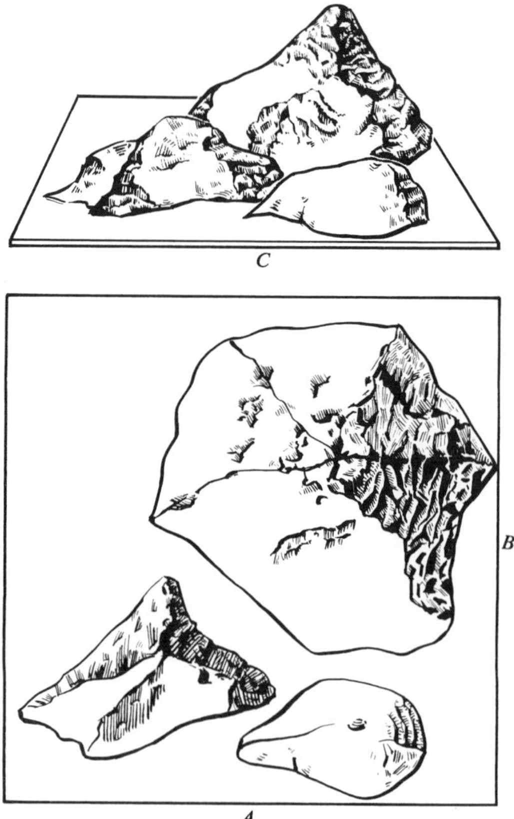

Figure 7–3. Model of mountains, as seen from different viewpoints, used in testing children for egocentric concepts. (Adapted from J. Piaget, and B. Inhelder, *The Child's Conception of Space*. London: Routledge & Kegan Paul Ltd., 1948. Copyright © 1948, Routledge & Kegan Paul Ltd. Reprinted by permission of the publishers.)

those of other people. Thus he comes eventually to have an idea of space existing independently of his perception of it.

Piaget [36, p. 211] demonstrates egocentric space concepts by his mountains test. Three mountains are placed on a table, as in Figure 7–3. A doll is placed first at one side of the table, then at another and another. The child is asked to choose from pictures or cutouts what the doll would see in the various positions. A child under seven or eight shows no understanding of the problem. He cannot conceive of the mountains as looking different from the way in which he is viewing them, because his space concepts are still tied to his own perceptions. All he can do with the problem is to attribute his own view to the doll. (This childish immaturity in spatial thinking is reminiscent of the trouble adults have had in conceiving of the world as round, the sun as the center of the solar system and the solar system as part of the Milky Way.)

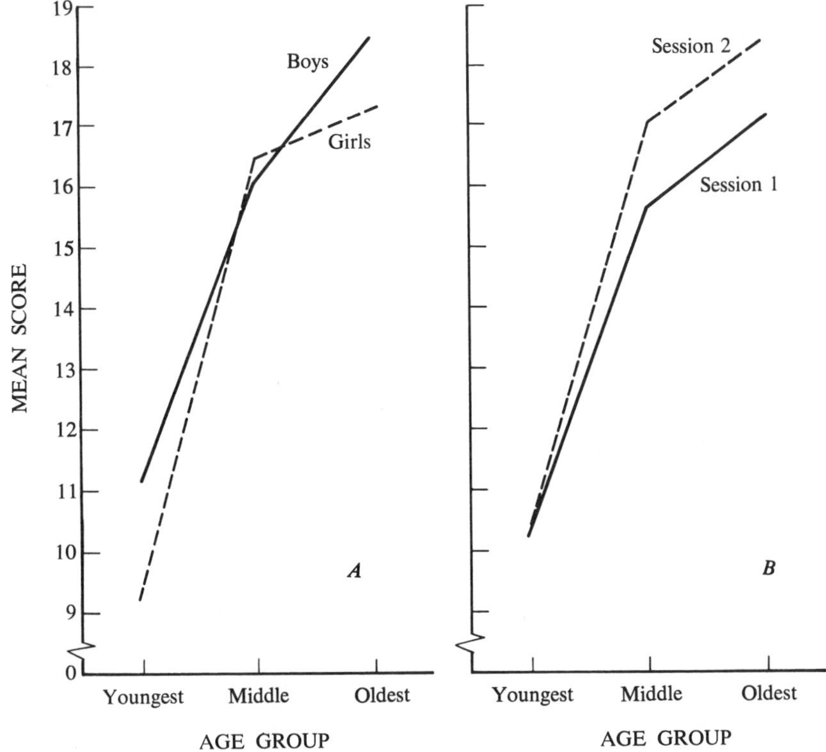

Figure 7–4. Scores of children between three and six on a test of ordering in space. The figure on the left shows mean scores of boys and girls on two testing sessions, indicating significant increases with age for ability to order space. The figure on the right shows scores on two tests, two weeks apart, indicating significant increases over a two-week period. (Reprinted by permission from J. Gottschalk, M. P. Bryden, and M. S. Rabinovitch, "Spatial Organization of Children's Responses to a Pictorial Display," *Child Development,* **35,** Figure 1, p. 813. Copyright © 1964, The Society for Research in Child Development, Inc.)

The ordering of space by preschool children has been studied in terms of their methods of dealing with columns and rows of pictures [1]. Children between three years, three months and six years, three months were tested in two sessions two weeks apart. The child was given a card with rows of pictures of 20 familiar objects and asked to name all the pictures and to report "I don't know" for unfamiliar ones. The order and direction used were noted. Responses were scored for organization, one point being given each time the picture named was adjacent to the one named previously. As Figure 7–4 shows, scores increased very significantly with age and also increased with the same groups over a two-week period. Therefore, as children grew older, they applied more order to the way in which they dealt with objects in space, as though they realized increasingly that they could be more efficient if they organized their behavior.

Number Concepts

Like concepts of time and space, number concepts are rooted in early concrete experience. The toddler does not have to count at all in order to choose the plate containing four cookies rather than the plate with two cookies. A configuration of objects, up to five or six, can be grasped perceptually without true number concepts being employed. A larger group may be seen as complete or not because every object is known as an individual. For instance, a two-year-old (like the others)in a family of eight realizes that eldest brother is absent, not because he has counted and found only seven members present, but because he does not see a certain individual who is often part of the family configuration. The development of perceptual discrimination of numbers of objects was demonstrated in a study of children between three and seven years [22]. The children were asked to discriminate 10 marbles from smaller groups of marbles, to match a group of marbles varying in number from 2 to 10 and to select larger and smaller groups of marbles as compared with a group of four. Figure 7–5 shows the results of the tests. Perceptual discrimination of number improved steadily, with number discrimination developing first, then number matching and then group matching. A score of 10 would indicate exact matching, which would involve true counting and comparison. Note that the average scores reached in this period were approximately eight, seven and six, suggesting that the discrimination was indeed done on a perceptual, not conceptual, basis.

When a child counts objects and tells accurately that there are seven apples or seven blocks, he has a concrete number concept, a more exact way of dealing with numbers of objects than does the child who discriminates on a perceptual basis. An abstract concept, in contrast to a concrete one, is not involved with apples or blocks but with seven. Many experiences with seven of this and seven of that occur before seven becomes free from objects and stands alone. As has been shown with concepts of classes, time and space, the preconceptional period is a time when thought is quite concretely and

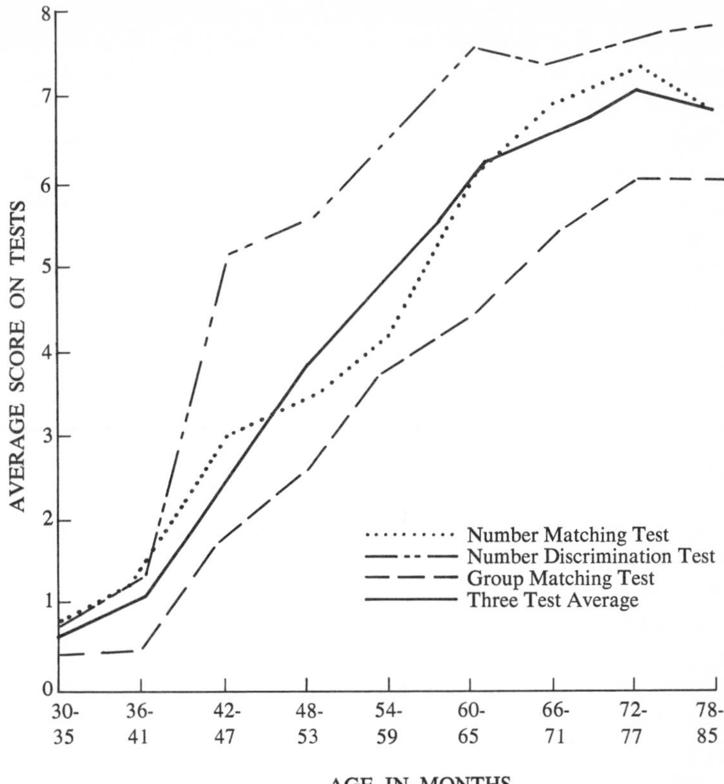

Figure 7–5. Improvement between ages three and seven on tests of matching numbers, discriminating numbers and matching groups. (Reprinted by permission from L. Long, and L. Welch, "The Development of the Ability to Discriminate and Match Numbers," *Journal of Genetic Psychology,* **59,** 377–387. Copyright © 1941, The Journal Press.)

specifically tied to personal experience. During this period, however, thought becomes progressively freer.

Certain primitive number concepts illustrate the stage of preconceptual thought. Werner [52, pp. 289–290] tells of cultures where a different type of number name is used for each of seven classes of objects: indefinite and amorphous; long, round or flat; human being; boats; and measures. He tells of a language in which *nakua* means 10 eggs and *nabanara* 10 baskets, a language where 10 baskets are *bola* and 10 coconuts *koro*. Being partially fused with the objects to which they refer, the names of numbers have to change as the objects change. A step toward abstraction is shown in the language where *lima,* the word for *hand,* is also the word for *five*. The use of the body as a natural number schema is found in primitive cultures and in children, and alas, in an occasional college student. Number systems based on 5 or 10 obviously have their roots in the human hand. Werner [52, p. 29], says, "At the beginning, no schema is an abstract form purely mathematical in significance; it is a material vessel in which the concrete fullness of objects is poured, as it were, to be measured."

A relationship has been shown at least in retarded children, between the ability to articulate the fingers and the development of number concepts. Each child was asked to point, with eyes closed, to the finger touched by the examiner. A group showing high ability in number concepts made almost no errors, whereas a group with mathematical disability showed many errors [52, p. 296].

Children who grow up in cultures using abstract number systems must go through the primitive stages of enumeration, but they are offered the abstract concepts to grasp when they are able to do so. (Or, unfortunately, they may have the abstract concepts pushed at them before they have built the conceptual bases which underly them.) Three developmental stages in number conception were described for 72 children between four and seven years: (1) Preconceptual. Number is responded to in purely perceptual terms. When the arrangement of objects is changed, it may change perception of number. (2) Individual numbers are responded to in conceptual terms. The verbal terms are very helpful here in achieving concepts. (3) Relationship among the individual numbers is understood [53].

Perceptual dominance can be demonstrated in young children's quantification by some of Piaget's tests [31, pp. 49–50]. For example, the child is given a number of flowers and the same number of vases and asked to place a flower in each vase. Then the examiner takes out the flowers and puts them in a bunch. He spreads out the vases and asks, "Are there more flowers or more vases?" The child under seven or eight usually says that there are more vases. If the vases are bunched up and flowers spread out, he is likely to say that there are more flowers. He bases his answer on the perception of the moment. The flowers, in a bunch, cover less area than the vases spread out. Therefore he concludes that there are more vases. Instead of recalling his experience of matching flowers to vases, and reasoning that the quantities must be equal, he is so dominated by what he sees that he is not free to use concepts.

Being able to count is no guarantee of being able to cope with a situation similar to the flowers test. Children between five and nine, all of whom could count beyond six, were asked to place a rubber doll in each of six little bathtubs, which were placed side by side [18]. Upon questioning, the child agreed that there were the same number of dolls and tubs. Then the experimenter asked him to remove the dolls and place them in a heap. Answers to the questions as to whether there were more dolls or more bathtubs usually brought the answer that there were more bathtubs.

An objective number concept involves knowing that the number of objects is the same, no matter how they are arranged. ...... = ::: = :..: The difference between five-to-six-year-olds and seven-to-seven-and-a-half-year-olds in regard to this kind of understanding is demonstrated by this experiment [23]. Children were given two groups of four beans to represent eight sweets. Four sweets were to be eaten at mid-morning and four more at teatime. Then two more sets of four were presented, and the children were told that these represented sweets to be eaten the following day, when only one was to be eaten in the morning and the remaining three would be eaten with the four teatime sweets. While the children watched, three sweets were taken from the group and added to the other group of four. Thus the children had in front of them two sets, one being 4 + 4 and the other 1 + 7. The experimenter then asked each child if he would eat the same number of sweets on each day. The younger children said no, that 1 + 7 was either larger or smaller than 4 + 4. The older children gave the correct answer promptly. Questioning showed that they understood the equivalence of the sets and the compensation occurring in the change. The children under seven demonstrated inability to weigh more than one factor at a time and their centering on what they first perceived. They compared either 1 or 7 with the 4's. The older children, having considerable freedom from perceptual dominance, could consider the several aspects of the situation in relation to one another.

Cardinal number concepts are built from putting objects into groups or classes and then abstracting out the number. Ordinal number concepts come from putting objects in series and then abstracting out the order. Classifying and seriation are therefore both essential activities in building number concepts. Piaget [35, p. 156] maintains that classification and seriation are necessarily learned simultaneously, since the processes are complementary. Below about five years, a child cannot make a series of objects, as of dolls of increasing size, but between five and six, he does so. At this point, he has great difficulty in finding the correct place for an object which has been omitted from the series, but at around seven, he can do this task easily. At seven, he is sufficiently freed from the perception of the dolls to conceive at the same time of the first doll being smaller than the second and the second smaller than the third.

Causality Concepts

The idea of universal laws is absent in primitive and childish thinking. What explanations are given tend to be in concrete and personal terms. Egocentrism in regard to causality occurs at the same time and for the same reasons as egocentrism in concepts of space, time and number.

The events of the outer world are closely linked with the child's inner world and his needs. During the preschool and school years, causality becomes less subjective. It can be followed through three stages of subjectivity. At first events are explained in terms of the child's own feelings and actions or in terms of people close to him or perhaps in terms of God. Although he does not consider all events to be caused by his own action, as he did in the sensorimotor period, he understands causes as forces resembling personal activity. "The peaches are growing on our tree, getting ready for us to eat." "The moon comes up because we need some light in the night." The next step toward maturity is to see natural events as caused by forces contained in themselves or by vague agents called *they*. "The radish seed knows it is supposed to make a radish." Increasing sophistication of thought decreases egocentrism, and the child begins to see causes as impersonal. For instance, heavy things sink and light things float. Progress in understanding cause is from concrete toward abstract. At first, explanations are merely descriptions of events. QUESTION: "What makes a sailboat move?" PETER: "My daddy takes me out in our sailboat. Mummy goes and Terry goes. Daddy starts the motor and we go chug, chug, chug down the pond."

The idea of universal, impersonal causes is beyond even the stage of childhood thinking and is not achieved by naïve adults. The concept of chance is related to the concept of necessity. Both require some logical or formal thought. Young children's explanations tend to be diffuse and inconsistent. Several events are explained by several different causes instead of by a unifying cause. Piaget [31, p. 137] gives these accounts of conversations of an adult with two five-year-old children, Col and Hei, dealing with the concept of floating:

> COL: Rowing boats stay on the water because they move. —ADULT: And the big boats? — They stay on the water because they are heavy.
>
> ADULT: Why does the boat (a toy) remain on the water? — HEI: It stays on top because it's heavy. . . . The rowing boats stay on top because they're big.— Fifteen days later Hei says, on the contrary, that boats stay "because they're not heavy." But comparing a pebble with a plank, Hei again says: "This pebble will go to the bottom because it isn't big enough, it's too thin." Finally Hei says that a stone goes to the bottom because "it's stronger" (than the wood).— And the boats, why do they stay on top?— Because the water is strong.

These children give different, and what look like conflicting, explanations of events which an adult would unify under universal laws of floating. The children are showing their inability to consider several factors at one time and their consequent inability to come to general conclusions.

Achievements in Thinking During the Preschool Period

In all areas of thinking, the preschool child increases in speed and flexibility. Strongly dominated by perception in the early years, he moves toward greater control of his thinking. His earliest concepts of classes, space, numbers, time and causes are rooted in concrete, personal experience, gradually becoming more objective and abstract as he has more experience, especially interactions with other people, who check his thoughts and conclusions.

INTELLECTUAL DEVELOPMENT AS REVEALED BY STANDARDIZED TESTS

Many tests of intelligence have been invented, each according to the concept of intelligence defined by its creator. Binet, who with Simon, developed the first standardized intelligence tests, considered three different capacities as constituting intelligence—the ability to understand directions, to maintain a mental set and to correct one's own errors [29, p. 349]. Terman [43], whose revisions of Binet's tests have had the greatest influence on modern intelligence testing, thought of intelligence as the ability to think abstractly and use abstract symbols in solving problems. Thorndike [45], who accepted a concept of intelligence as comprising problem solving through use of abstract symbols, defined three dimensions of intelligence: altitude, breadth and speed. Altitude referred to difficulty of problem, the more intelligent person being able to solve the more difficult problem; breadth meant the number of tasks a person could do; speed, of course, referred to how fast problems were solved. Thorndike considered altitude the most important of the three attributes of intelligence. Guilford [12, 13] thinks of intelligence as consisting of many different abilities, possibly 120, about 80 of which are already known. He stresses creativity as a component of intelligence.

Measurement of Intelligence

Many tests have been designed to measure preschool intelligence, the best known of which is the Stanford–Binet, a derivative of Binet and Simon's original tests. The Stanford–Binet yields a single mental age score, from which an intelligence quotient, the IQ, is computed. Although the Stanford–Binet can be given to most two-year-olds, it is often easier to interest them in tests which have more manipulative materials and which involve more sensory stimulation, such as the Merrill–Palmer Test [42] or the Gesell Test [10]. Advantages of the latter type include the adaptability of the scoring to the child's refusing some items and the fact that more than one score can be obtained from each of these tests. The Merrill–Palmer can be scored for verbal and nonverbal items and the Gesell for four areas of development, called motor, adaptive, language and personal social. Merrill–Palmer scores can be expressed as percentiles, standard deviations or IQs. Gesell scores are expressed as developmental quotients. The Wechsler Intelligence Test for Children [50] is favored over the Stanford–Binet by some examiners for elementary-school age children. The Wechsler can also be used for preschool children. Like the Merrill–Palmer, the Wechsler yields verbal and nonverbal scores.

Mental age (MA) is a construct conceived by Binet. A child's MA is found by comparing his test performance with the average performance of a large number of children. Binet gave a large number of tests to a large number of children, found the ages at which most children passed each test and arranged the tests in order of difficulty. This procedure is essentially the one which has been followed in constructing intelligence tests since then. To show how the MA is found, take, for example, a child who passes the items passed by the average eight-year-old. The child's MA is eight. If his chronological age (CA) is also eight, then he is like the average child his age. If, however, his CA is six, he has done more than the average. If his CA is 10, he has done less.

Intelligence quotient (IQ) is a construct originated by Stern, a German psychologist. IQ is a ratio of CA to MA, which has been found to be fairly constant. IQ is found by dividing MA by CA and multiplying by 100. 100 MA/CA = IQ.

IQ As an Expression of Rate of Growth

The intelligence quotient is a measure of rate of growth in mental age, although the convention of multiplying by 100 obscures this fact. A child who at the age of 70 months earns a score of 77 months of mental age has grown since birth at the average rate of 1.1 months of mental age for each month he has been alive. His IQ is 110. Similarly, a child who has a score of 63 months of mental age at the chronological age of 70 months has progressed at the average rate of .9 months of mental age for each month. His IQ is 90. If both children continue to grow at the same rate, their IQ's will stay the same. If, however, both children grow 12 months in mental age during the next 12 months (at the rate of 1.0 for each month), their IQ's at that point will be different at the time of the second test. The first child will earn an IQ of 108 and the second 91. This is true because for each test the IQ expresses the average rate of growth since the child was born.

IQ As a Measure of Brightness

The common concept of IQ is as a measure of quality or strength of intelligence. The higher the IQ, the brighter the child and the more capable he is of doing good work at school.

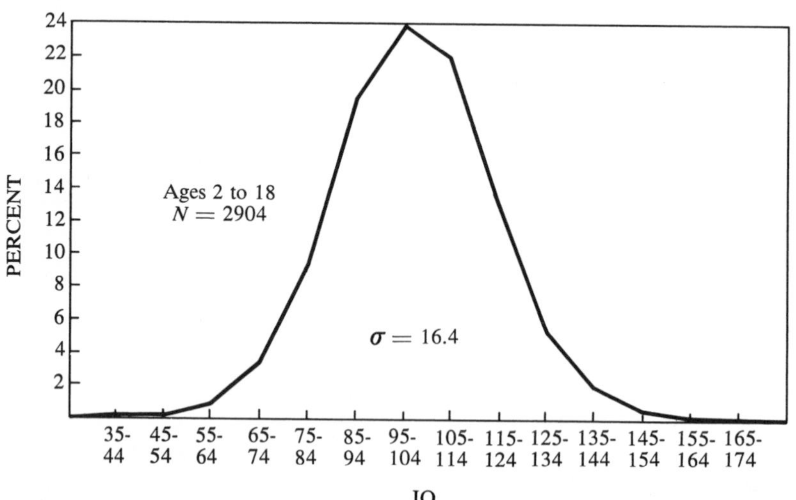

Figure 7–6. Distribution of Stanford-Binet IQ's in the population on which the test was standardized. (Reprinted by permission from L. M. Terman, and M. A. Merrill, *Measuring Intelligence*. Boston: Houghton Mifflin Company, 1937. Copyright © 1937, Houghton Mifflin Company.)

In the example above, the child who has been growing at the rate of 1.1 months of mental age for each month of chronological age for 70 months is brighter than the child who had been growing at the average rate of .9 MA months per chronological month. A child 50 months old who for those 50 months has been growing at the 1.1 rate (and IQ of 110) is just as far above the average 50-month-old child as the 70-month child with the same rate. Assuming that he will continue at the same rate for the next 20 months, by the time he is 70 months old, his mental age will be 77 and his IQ will still be 110.

TABLE 7–1

Distribution of IQ's in children tested in the standardization of the Stanford–Binet test in 1937.

IQ	*Percent*	*Classification*
160–169	0.03	
150–159	0.2	Very superior
140–149	1.1	
130–139	3.1	Superior
120–129	8.2	
110–119	18.1	High average
100–109	23.5	Normal or average
90–99	23.0	
80–89	14.5	Low average
70–79	5.6	Borderline defective
60–69	2.0	
50–59	0.4	Mentally defective
40–49	0.2	
30–39	0.03	

Source: Reprinted by permission from L. M. Terman and M. A. Merrill, *Stanford-Binet Intelligence Scale* (Boston: Houghton Mifflin Company, 1960). Copyright © 1960, Houghton Mifflin Company.

Distribution of IQ's

Figure 7–6 and Table 7–1 show how IQ's were distributed in the 1937 Stanford–Binet [44]. *Average* includes 79.1 percent of the population. *Defective,* with 8.23 percent, is a little smaller than *superior,* with 12.63 percent, although the most inferior categories match the most superior in size.

Another way of showing how IQ's are distributed is to tell how often a given IQ occurs in 100 cases, or in the case of extreme IQ's, how often in 1,000 or 10,000. Table 7–2 expresses IQ's thus.

Errors of Measurement

Errors are likely to affect any test through less-than-perfect presentation and scoring, through the subject's not performing at top capacity and through poor conditions of testing, such as noise or discomforts. The standard error

TABLE 7–2

Frequency of occurrence of common and uncommon IQ levels.

The Child Whose IQ is:	*Is Equalled or Excelled by*
160	1 out of 10,000
156	3 out of 10,000
152	8 out of 10,000
148	2 out of 1,000
144	4 out of 1,000
140	7 out of 1,000

The Child Whose IQ is:	*Equals or Exceeds (%)*	*The Child Whose IQ is:*	*Equals or Exceeds (%)*
136	99	99	48
135	98	98	45
134	98	97	43
133	98	96	40
132	97	95	38
131	97	94	36
130	97	93	34
129	96	92	31
128	96	91	29
127	95	90	27
126	94	89	25
125	94	88	23
124	93	87	21
123	92	86	20
122	91	85	18
121	90	84	16
120	89	83	15
119	88	82	14
118	86	81	12
117	85	80	11
116	84	79	10
115	82	78	9
114	80	77	8
113	79	76	8
112	77	75	6
111	75	74	6
110	73	73	5
109	71	72	4
108	69	71	4
107	66	70	3
106	64	69	3
105	62	68	3
104	60	67	2
103	57	66	2
102	55	65	2
101	52	64	1
100	50	63	1
		62	1

Source: Reprinted from *Supplementary Guide for the Revised Stanford-Binet Scale, Form L*, by Rudolph Pintner, Anna Dragositz, and Rose Kushner with the permission of the publishers, Stanford University Press. Copyright 1944 by the Board of Trustees of the Leland Stanford Junior University.

of measurement has been calculated for various ages and IQ ranges [44]. For practical purposes, *five* is the standard error. In interpreting any IQ, then, ±5 should be added to the figure. If Mary's measured IQ is 107, there are 68 chances in 100 that her "real" IQ lies between 102 and 112. There are 95 chances in 100 that Mary's IQ lies between 97 and 117.

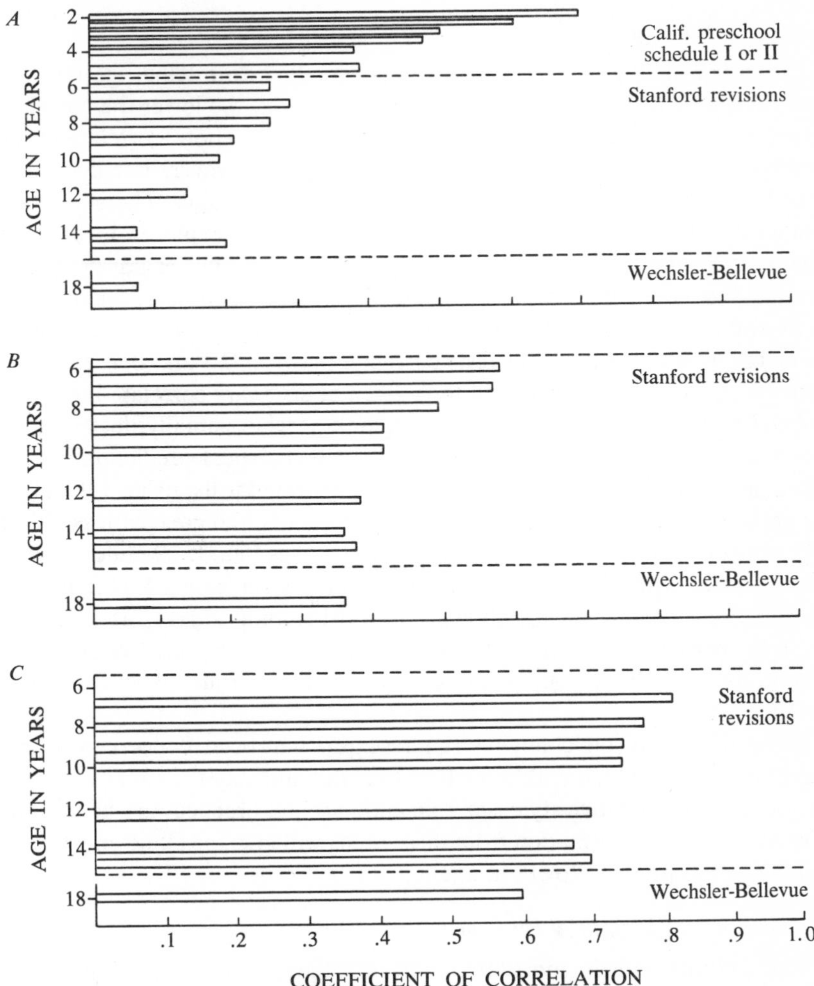

Figure 7–7. Coefficients of correlation between scores of mental tests given to children at three age levels and tests given to the same children at later dates. *A:* Tests on children 21 months old are correlated with subsequent tests given at ages 2 to 18. *B:* Tests on children three years old are correlated with subsequent tests given at ages 6 to 18. *C:* Tests on children six years old are correlated with subsequent tests given at ages 7 to 18. (Adapted from M. P. Honzik, J. W. Macfarlane, and L. Allen, "The Stability of Mental Test Performances Between Two and Eighteen Years of Age," *Journal of Experimental Education,* 1948, **17,** pp. 309–324. Used by permission of the journal.)

The standard error must be used when comparing the IQ's of two children and also when comparing two tests on one child. In the first case, the difference between IQ's must be at least 10 before a real difference can be said to exist. When tests on the same child are compared, the difference between the two tests must be ten or more before a real change in growth rate is indicated.

Predicting Intelligence

Preschool intelligence tests correlate positively with intelligence tests given later. The longer the interval between tests, however, the lower the correlation. Infant tests, especially those given in the first year, show correlations close to zero with tests at age five [3]. By three years, however, intelligence tests have some predictive value, and by six, considerable value. The stability and predictive value of intelligence test scores have been explored in a study in which 252 children were tested repeatedly at specified ages between 21 months and 18 years. Figure 7–7 shows how tests given at 21 months, three years and six years, respectively, correlate with tests given in succeeding years up to 18. Note that three-year tests correlate between 0.3 and 0.4 with tests at both 14 and 18 years of age, and tests given at six years correlate between 0.6 and 0.7 with those at 14 and 18 [16]. A look at what actually does happen to individual IQ's is helpful in understanding why statistical prediction has to be within large ranges. In another study [39] of repeated tests, using 140 subjects, the greatest gain in an individual case was 58 points, the greatest loss, 32. The following distribution of mental growth patterns was found: 29 children showed even growth, with IQ staying about the same, as in case 64 (Figure 7–8); 16 increased steadily in IQ, showing upward-sloping curves, as in case 58; seven decreased, as in case 139. Sixteen decreased during preschool and grew evenly during school age, as in case 133. Thirty-four were classified as irregular.

Since this study on changing IQ, research has been concerned with the conditions under which children's IQ's rise, fall and stay the same. Personality characteristics, cognitive style, sex role and parental practices are being studied in relation to IQ. Information from these areas will give the clinician some basis from which to predict growth in intelligence.

Organization of Measured Intelligence

The abilities which constitute adult intelligence have been studied and delineated by several investigators, using factor analysis. Thurstone [46] identified these factors in intelligence: *space,* the ability to visualize objects; *number,* facility with simple arithmetic; *verbal comprehension,* dealing with verbal concepts and reasoning; *word fluency,* ability to produce appropriate words; *memory,* storing and retrieval of experiences and concepts; *induction,* finding principles; *deduction,* use of principles in problem solving; and *flexibility and speed* of thought. Thurstone [47] has devised tests for measuring "primary mental abilities" in children as young as five, the tests being grouped into motor, verbal, spatial, perceptual and quantitative categories.

Two factor analytic studies [15, 37] have been done on existing test data from preschool children, revealing three principal factors, called sensorimotor alertness (prominent before two years), persistence (outstanding at two to four

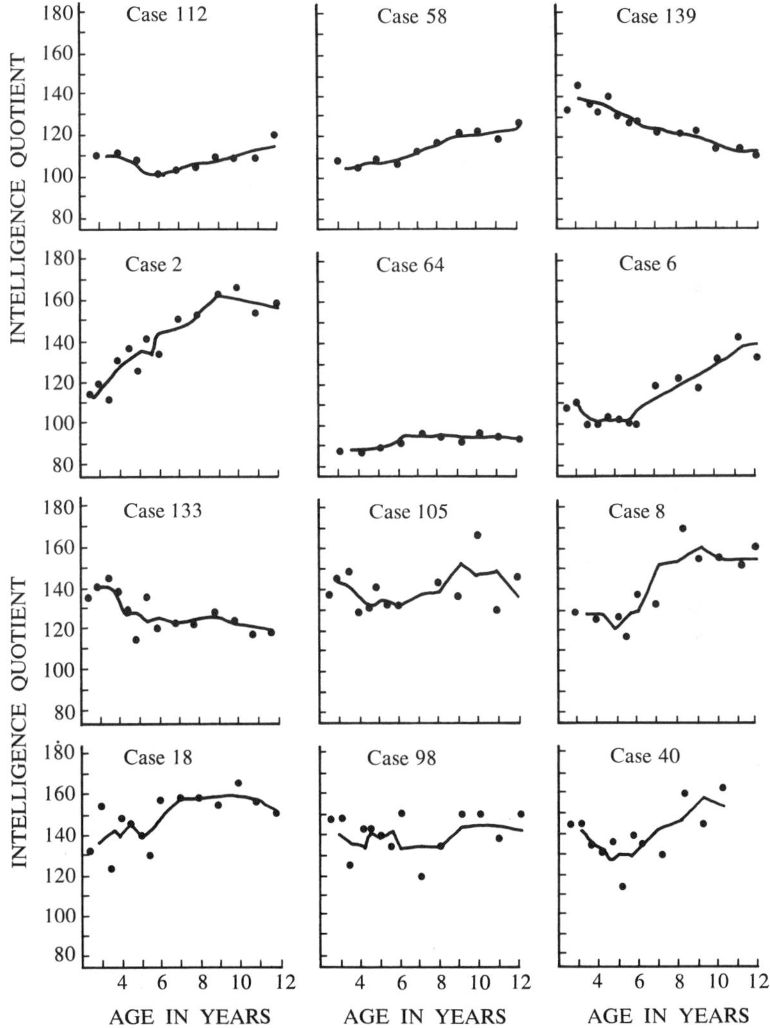

Figure 7–8. Examples of individual records of IQ's from 2 to 12 years of age, illustrating variation in mental growth patterns. (Reprinted by permission from L. W. Sontag, C. T. Baker, and V. L. Nelson, "Mental Growth and Personality Development: A Longitudinal Study," *Monographs of The Society for Research in Child Development,* **23,** Figure 1. Copyright © 1958, The Society for Research in Child Development, Inc.)

years) and verbal reasoning (rising rapidly throughout the preschool period). Figure 7–9 shows the waxing and waning of these three factors, Another investigator [17] found six factors for three- and four-year-olds on the Merrill–Palmer Test: willingness to cooperate, persistence, finding relations, fine motor coordination, perceptual speed and space. Two other factor analytic studies of test results from six-year-olds [27] and from two-, four- and six-year-olds [26] yielded these factors: eye–hand psychomotor, perceptual, speed, linguistic

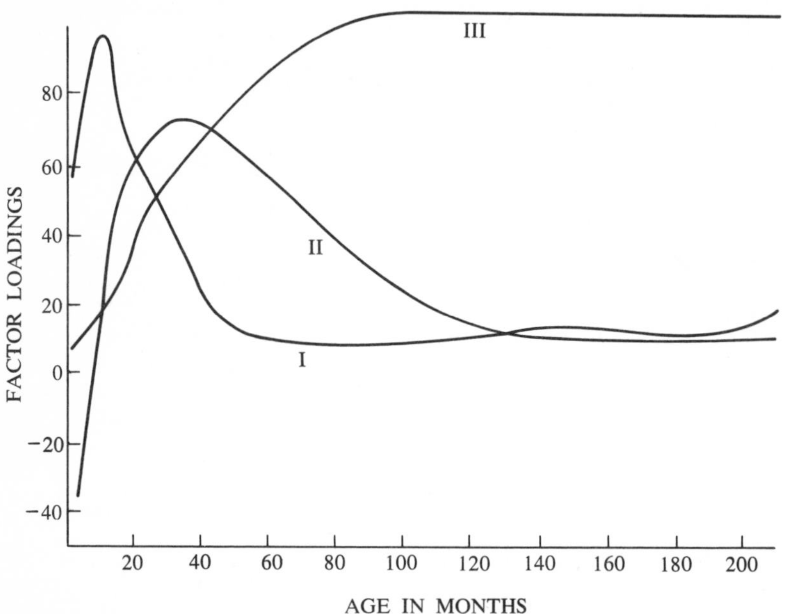

Figure 7–9. The rise and fall of three intelligence factors which show considerable change during the preschool years. (Reprinted by permission from P. R. Hofstaetter, "The Changing Composition of 'Intelligence': A Study in Technique," *Journal of Genetic Psychology,* **85,** 159–164. Copyright © 1954, The Journal Press.)

ability, and figure reasoning. The results from these factor analyses give some indication of the composition of measured intelligence. Because of differences in procedures the results of the studies are not in complete agreement, but at least a sensorimotor factor, a factor of perceptual speed, one of verbal fluency and one of dealing with spatial relations seem to be common to them. Bayley [4] sees intelligence as ". . . a complex of separately timed developing functions . . . with the more advanced . . . functions in the hierarchy depending on the maturing of earlier, simpler ones."

LANGUAGE DEVELOPMENT

Language supplements the tactile link between the young child and other people and supplants that link in many of the child's relationships with others.

Language is a vital tie between past, present and future, both for the individual and for groups of people. The rapid acquisition of language by the preschool child, shown by increase in vocabulary (see Table 7–3) and development of grammatical structures is intimately related to the development of autonomy and initiative, to the growth from egocentric thought to objectivity and to social relationships. And it is also closely related to general intelligence, vocabulary being one of the best single measures.

TABLE 7–3

Vocabulary during the preschool years.

Age in years	1	1½	2	3	4	5	6
Number of words	3	22	272	896	1540	2072	2562
Gain in words		19	269	624	644	532	490

Source: Data from Smith [38].

Fusion of Thought and Language

The linking of thought and speech marks the beginning of the period of preoperational thought. During the sensorimotor period, children think and reason, but they do it slowly and concretely, in terms of the experience of the moment. Higher animals do the same kind of thinking and reasoning that infants do. They also make sounds which have meaning. Baboons use 18 different sounds meaningfully. Some animals can recognize a few words which stand for people, objects and actions.

Intellectual development receives a big impetus when thinking and speech come together in the discovery that everything has a name. The average timing of the discovery is between 18 months and two years, when the vocabulary increases from around 20 words to almost 300 words. Over 600 words are added annually for the next two years, and then the rate of vocabulary increase drops somewhat.

After discovering that everything has a name and that names are very handy in thought and deed, the toddler concentrates on learning as many names as possible. He also invents names, as did a boy of 16 months, who called *yoyo* all portable things with handles and *gogo* all yoyos with lids [49, pp. 34–35]. In a similar vein, a little girl called all drinkable liquids *gaggle-gaggle*. A pair of twins, before using any regular words, said *ee-ee* to each other to call attention to an interesting change in the environment and *aw-aw* when they wanted an exchange of toys. Similarly, a more involved invention of names was noted [14, p. 249] in two boys, four and six, playing with blocks. One did the building while the other handed blocks to him, and together they invented the following names for the blocks: Big Thin Window, Little Big Thin Window, Big Stone, Little Stone, Big Knups, Little Knups, Big Peppermint, Little Peppermint.

At about the time when children discover that everything has a name, they think that a name is an intrinsic part of the object. Preschool children say that the names come from the objects or that they were made with the things themselves. When Piaget [32, p. 536] asked a young child how people knew that the sun was called the sun, he got this answer, "They saw it was called the sun because they could see it was round and hot."

This notion is strong throughout the period of preconceptual thought and in the thinking of primitive people. To know the name, then, is to have some control over the object. The idea persists beyond the preschool period. The power of names is implied in the cancellation games which schoolchildren play. For instance, Dorothy Levin, contemplating Harry Rogers, wonders if he would make a good husband for her. She puts their names down, one above the other, and cancels the letters. With the remaining letters she recites a stage of courtship for each: like, love, courtship, marriage, like . . . Aha! The magic contained in their names together could get Dot and Harry to the "like" stage only. No marriage! Many if not most adults show some lingering belief in the power of words when they react emotionally to a curse.

Language As a Tool of Cognition

One of the important differences between the infant and preschool child is the latter's verbal control of learning. When the child can attach labels to objects and processes, then he can generalize more readily. It is easier to discover principles and act according to them. For example, here is a situation which distinguishes between children in the stage of preverbal learning and those who use verbal mediation in learning [19]. The experimenter hid candy under the smaller of two boxes, presenting the boxes in random arrangement until the child learned to pick up the smaller box. Then a new set of boxes was used in the same way, with the candy under the smaller one. In the second set, the larger box was about the same size as the smaller box in the first pair. The child who had learned to choose according to a specific-sized box would choose the larger from the second set, but the child who had used verbal mediation (saying to himself or aloud something such as "The candy is under the smaller box") would choose the correct one promptly. The third phase of the experiment used two equal-sized boxes, one bearing the picture of a mouse, the other an elephant. The child who had learned the task by verbal mediation immediately knew that the candy was under the mouse, since he had a concept of smallness as indicating location of candy.

The more a child learns through verbal mediation, the more resources he has available to tackle new problems and learn new material. The more words he learns, the more readily he stores his experiences as memories. The more memories he stores, the more available is past experience for use in thinking and problem solving. Hence the acquisition of language is an integral part of cognitive growth. The child who does not acquire adequate verbal symbols and who does not use them in thinking becomes retarded intellectually.

Egocentric Speech

Much but not all of the speech of preschool children expresses their wishes, needs, intentions and experiences without regard for any effect that the comments might make on the listeners. The other person's thoughts, feelings, needs, wants and *comments* are not taken into account [30]. Piaget calls this type of speech egocentric. By this term, he refers to the fact that the young child is limited to and centered on his own point of view, not that he is selfish. His thought processes are not sufficiently flexible to permit him to consider what the other person is experiencing. Egocentric speech is like a monologue, even when it is broken by remarks from other people. When two people carry on egocentric speech at the same time, it gives a very disjointed result. Stone and Church [41, p. 146] give this intriguing example of a collective monologue by two four-year-olds in the Vassar nursery school:

JENNY: They wiggle sideways when they kiss.
CHRIS: (*vaguely*) What?
JENNY: My bunny slippers. They are brown and red and sort of yellow and white. And they have eyes and ears and these noses that wiggle sideways when they kiss.
CHRIS: I have a piece of sugar in red pieces of paper. I'm gonna eat it and maybe it's for a horse.
JENNY: We bought them. My mommy did. We couldn't find the old ones. They were in the trunk.
CHRIS: Can't eat the piece of sugar, not unless you take the paper off.
JENNY: And we found Mother Lamb. Oh, she was in Poughkeepsie in the trunk in the house in the woods where Mrs. Tiddywinkle lives.
CHRIS: Do you like sugar? I do, and so do horses.
JENNY: I play with my bunnies. They are real. We play in the woods. They have eyes. We *all* go in the woods. My teddy bears and the bunnies and the duck, to visit Mrs. Tiddywinkle. We play and play.
CHRIS: I guess I'll eat my sugar at lunch time. I can get more for the horses. Besides, I don't have no horses now.

Children's utterances are not all easily classified as to egocentricity. We were witnesses to a puzzling performance by a four-year-old. He made the round of the living room telling the same thing to each person. He told it to his mother in Hindi, to his father in Bengali, to us in English and to the other guests in Gujerati. In a very sociable and multilingual family, the child had got the idea that different people speak in different ways and that if he was to be understood, he had to use certain words with certain people. The content of his speech was still concerned with his own thoughts, feelings and experiences. He was not interested in hearing about other people's points of view, and yet he took those viewpoints into consideration without realizing that he did so.

Socialized speech, in contrast to egocentric, involves an exchange with others, through asking and answering questions, commenting on what the other person has said, giving him information which has some pertinence. Piaget noted that egocentric speech decreased and socialized speech increased with age, showing a real change in proportion at the end of the period of preoperational thought.

Vygotsky [48, pp. 16–24], disagreeing with Piaget's contention that egocentric speech simply dropped out with increasing maturity, devised experiments to reveal its function. He put children in what appeared to be quite free situations. Just as the child was getting ready to draw, for instance, he would discover that he had no paper or that his pencil was not the color he needed. In such frustrating situations, the proportion of egocentric speech doubled, in comparison with Piaget's figure for children that age and also in comparison with Vygotsky's findings for children under nonfrustrating circumstances. (His own figure for egocentric speech in normal circumstances was slightly lower than Piaget's.) The child would say such things as: "Where's the pencil? I need a blue pencil. Never mind, I'll draw with the red one and wet it with water; it will become dark and look like blue."

Vygotsky maintains that egocentric speech is not a mere accompaniment of activity but a means of expression, a release of tension and a true instrument of thought, in finding the solution to a problem. He showed developmental changes in the use of egocentric speech. In the younger child, it marked the end of an activity, or a turning point. Gradually, it shifted to the middle and then to the beginning of an activity, taking on a planning and directing function. He likens this process to the developmental sequence in naming drawings. First, a little child names what he has drawn; a few months later, he names his drawing when half done; later, he announces what he is going to draw before he does it.

Vygotsky suggests that egocentric speech is a transitional stage between vocal and inner speech, which is a kind of thought. Egocentric speech, he says, "goes underground."

Culture and Language

What could be more obvious than the fact that children speak the language into which they are born, the *mother* tongue? It is not always appreciated, however, that the language shapes the child's thinking and that the mother tongue traces cognitive pathways which are extremely persistent. Mead [25] tells of finding Samoan influences in the speech of an American 12-year-old who had begun to talk in Samoa. The great respect of Indian children for their parents is no doubt fostered by the frequent use of the ending *ji* which is added to *father* and *mother,* as well as to the names of revered people such as Gandhi. ". . . language conveys to the individual an already prepared system of ideas, classification, relations—in short, an inexhaustible stock of concepts which are reconstructed in each individual after the age-old pattern which previously molded earlier generation" [33, p. 159]. As the child grows up, he takes from the stock of concepts what he can use at the time.

Growth Trends in Structure of Language

A few pages earlier, vocabulary growth was shown in Table 7–3. Rapid growth during the preschool period is also seen in other aspects of language development, such as sentence length, grammatical structure and articulation of speech. A summary of a large number of studies on sentence structure, errors and grammatical use of parts of speech shows that trends toward maturity continue throughout childhood [24]. The most noticeable changes, however, take place during the preschool period, in fact by about three years of age.

SENTENCE LENGTH. The first type of sentence is a single word. (This stage has been discussed in Chapter 4, in the section on language in infancy.)

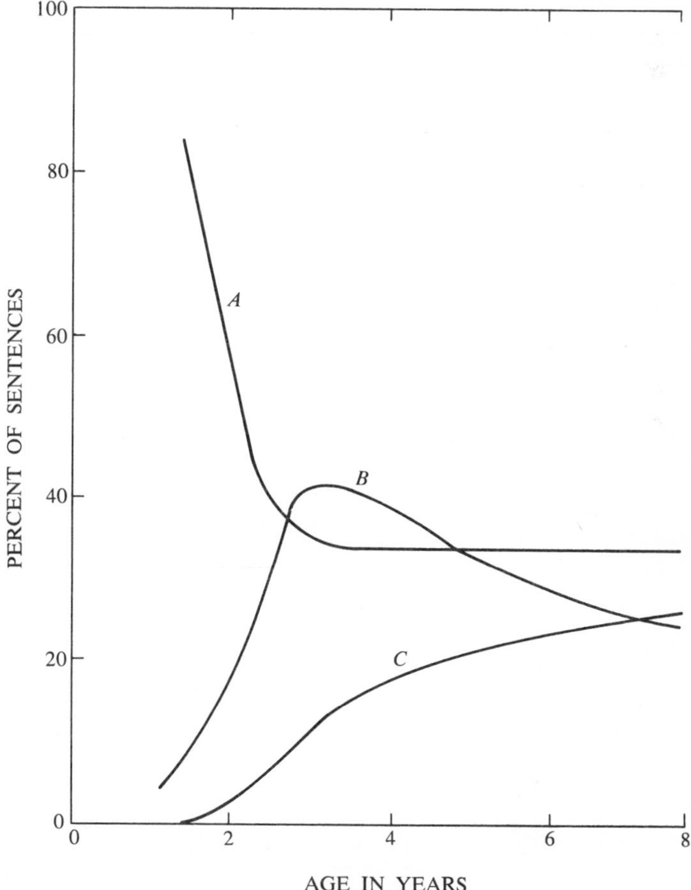

Figure 7–10. Frequency of use of different types of sentences in childhood. Curve *A* shows sentences that are functionally complete but grammatically incomplete. Curve *B* shows simple sentences. Curve *C* shows sentences that are more elaborate than simple sentences. (From G. A. Miller, *Language and Communication*. Copyright © 1951. Used by permission of McGraw-Hill Book Company.)

The second stage, the early sentence, typical of age two, lasts for a period of four to seven months. The early sentence includes a preponderance of nouns. Lacking articles, it has few auxiliary and copulative verbs and few prepositions and conjunctions. The third stage of sentence formation produces sentences of about four words. Figure 7–10 shows proportions of the types of sentences at various ages. Only one or two sentences out of 50 are compound or complex. The following story told by a two-year-old includes second-stage and third-stage sentences:

> Me tell story about angleworm. One time go angleworm. Little girl pick up angleworm. Know dat? Angleworm cry. Angleworm lie down pillows. Angleworm go sleep pillow. Two pillows. Two angleworms. Angleworm wake up.

The fourth stage of sentence formation appearing at about age four, yields sentences of six to eight words in length and more complex structure. This story illustrates the fourth stage:

> The first Christmas was Jesus' birthday and Santie Claus did come. And I was afraid of him. And after that I was happy that I played with my toys.

An analysis [51] of the presleep utterances of Anthony, a two-and-a-half-year-old boy provides, among other interesting data, information about the number of words in the sentences he used. Figure 7–11 shows that Anthony used two-word sentences most and three-word sentences almost as often. Figure 7–12 shows percentages of various sentence lengths in his talking. Estimates of the mean length of utterance are given in Table 7–4 for 13

TABLE 7–4

Estimates of lengths of utterance and some of the grammatical forms used by 13 young children.

Name of Child	*Age in Months*	*Mean Number Morphemes**	Be *in Progressive*	*Modal Auxiliaries* will *or* can
Andy	26	2.0	no	no
Betty	31½	2.1	no	no
Charlie	22	2.2	no	no
Adam	28½	2.5	no	no
Eve	25½	2.6	no	no
Fanny	31½	3.2	yes	no
Grace	27	3.5	yes	yes
Helen	30	3.6	yes	yes
Ian	31½	3.8	yes	yes
June	35½	4.5	yes	yes
Kathy	30½	4.8	yes	yes
Larry	35½	4.8	yes	yes
Jimmy	32	4.9	yes	yes

* Mean count from 100 consecutive utterances.

Source: Reprinted from R. Brown and C. Fraser, in U. Bellugi and R. Brown (eds.), "The Acquisition of Language," *Monographs of The Society for Research in Child Development*, **29**: 1, Table 13. Copyright © 1964, The Society for Research in Child Development, Inc.

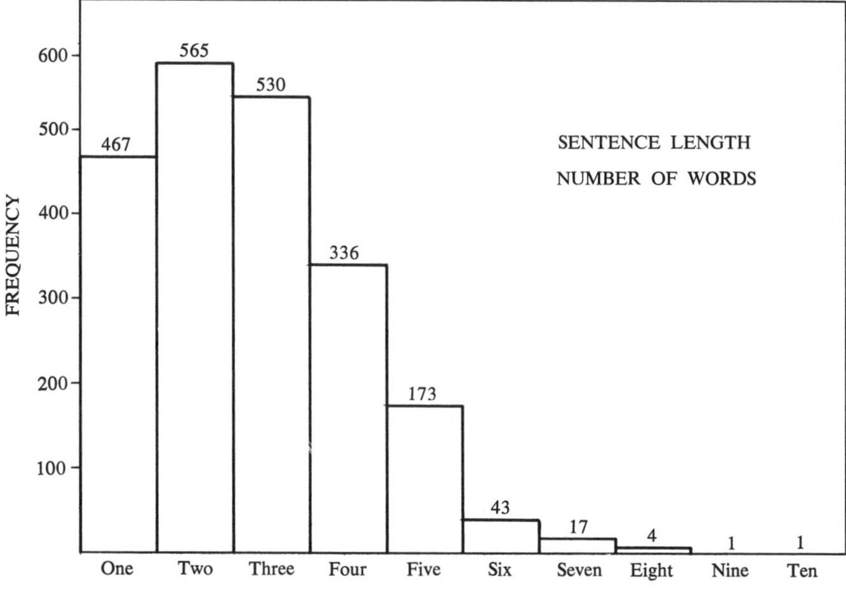

Figure 7–11. Frequency of sentences of various lengths used by one little boy in spontaneous presleep talking. (Reprinted by permission from R. H. Weir, *Language in the Crib*. The Hague: Mouton & Co. N.V., 1962.)

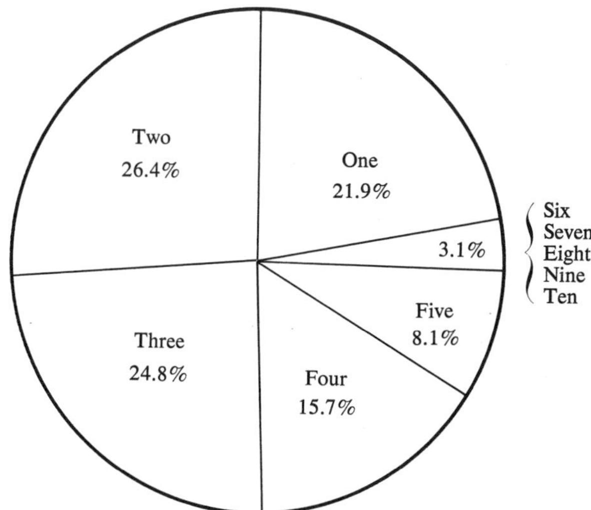

Figure 7–12. Presleep utterances of Anthony divided as to length of sentences, showing relative frequency of use. (Reprinted by permission from R. H. Weir, *Language in the Crib*. The Hague: Mouton & Co. N.V., 1962.)

children, ranging in age from 26 to 32 months, showing, with age, a steady increase in length of utterance [5].

GRAMMAR. From their very first attempts to put words together, children do so according to rules or customs. The rules they use in the beginning are not, of course, those of adults. Studies of children's speech suggests that the child reduces adult speech and the rules which govern speech to simpler forms [7]. When words are first combined, the resulting sentences are sometimes called *telegraphic speech.* In comments such as "See doggie," "Mommy come home," and "Go car," only words carrying necessary information are used. However, these sentences can be understood, because the order of the words is correct. Even though the young child reduces sentences to the barest essentials, he usually preserves the word order, an extremely important dimension of English grammar.

Another example of the ways in which children simplify adult grammar is the childish tendency to produce regular inflections. Children and adults were shown a picture of a man swinging something above his head and told: "This is a man who knows how to gling. He glings every day. Today he glings. Yesterday he—?" Adults hesitated and offered *gling, glang, glung* and even *glought;* children confidently replied, "Glinged." Syntax, the ordering of words, reaches mature form before morphology, the structuring of the words themselves, not only in English, where syntax is very important and morphology less important than in a highly inflected language, but also in other languages, where children's progress has been carefully studied [51]. There is considerable evidence that the various aspects of grammar are learned in a fairly consistent order. For example, plurals were made by adding *s* before irregular forms were used. Every one of 18 children said *mans* before he used the word *men* [5].

How does the child go about learning his grammar? Recent studies [6, 28, 51] give some insight into how the child tackles this task. He will begin by imitating a form as used by adults. After he generalizes or makes a rule from it, he applies the rule and thus produces a new combination [5]. The role of adults, especially the mother, is seen in records which show verbal interchange between mothers and children who use telegraphic speech. For example:

CHILD: Go car.
MOTHER: Bobby and Mommy are going in the car.
CHILD: Go in car.

The mother expanded the child's utterance, whereupon the child reduced the mother's expansion in his imitation of her, and yet added to his first utterance.

The young child plays with words in two main ways, sometimes combining these two approaches in the same utterance. He plays with sounds and with the words themselves; he learns to use the language for expressing ideas and communicating. The former function, sometimes called the poetic function, is illustrated by the following quotation from Anthony: "Look at those pineapple

. . . in a pretty box . . . and cakes . . . what a sticks for cakes . . . for the click." Learning to use language correctly, Anthony practices and drills himself in sounds, words and syntax. The records of his bedtime talks show systematic manipulations of language which often resemble the grammars written for the study of a foreign language [51]. The following excerpt is an exercise in noun substitution: what color—what color blanket—what color mop—what color glass. Noun modifiers are explored in this sequence: there's a hat—there's another—there's hat—there's another hat—that's a hat. A verb substitution pattern occurred thus: go get coffee—go buy some coffee. Negatives are practiced: like it—don't like it— like it Daddy. He holds a question-and-answer dialogue with himself: There is the light—where is the light—here is the light. Some of Anthony's verbalizations have a large element of sound play in them, such as: train—Anthony can see the plane—plane—plane—see bubble—bubble's here—bubbles—flowers—bed flowers. Sometimes he comments on his achievements: one two three four—one two—one two three four—one two three—Anthony counting—good boy you—one two three.

One of the important revelations of Anthony's bedtime talks is the self-motivated nature of his language learning. Nobody was responding to him with praise or criticism. Nobody was answering his expressed needs. Nobody was even listening, as far as he knew. Anthony's exploratory combining of words and his persistent drilling must have been for the reward of increased competence. Motives for other aspects of his language activity were probably sensory and expressive pleasure in the sound play and a seeking for understanding of experience, which will be discussed later.

SUMMARY

Thinking, language and imagination are intimately associated with one another in such a way that each is necessary to mental life. The preschool (or preoperational) stage of thought begins when infant thinking ends, with grasping the idea of the permanence and constancy of objects and also when the child has achieved control of his own movements in space. From this time until about seven years of age, thinking is dominated by the perceptual experiences of the moment. Thought is centered, since the preschool child finds it extremely difficult to consider how any situation looks to another person. He feels no need to justify his thinking to anyone else. As he moves through the preschool years, his thinking becomes increasingly flexible, less centered and less dominated by perception. Concepts are at first embedded in concrete experience, becoming more and more abstract as the child has more experiences in grouping objects, dealing with time, space and numbers, experimenting with processes. The process of abstraction is aided by the abstractions offered by language. Both language and concepts are learned through interactions with people, where the child checks and rechecks his accuracy, eventually achieving socialized thought.

Tests measure certain aspects of intelligence, each test being designed to measure intelligence as defined in a certain theory. Mental age is a score found by matching a child's test performance with that of the average child and noting the age at which the average child succeeded. Intelligence quotient (IQ) is the ratio of mental age to chronological age, a ratio which has some constancy through the years. IQ can be used to express rate of mental development and brightness or quality. Measured intelligence has been analyzed statistically into factors which wax and wane at various ages.

Language develops rapidly in the second year of life, speeding up thought and also making it more precise and flexible. The use of verbal symbols makes problem solving much more efficient. Since the preschool child is centered on his own point of view, his speech reflects this fact. As he gradually increases, through social interaction, in his ability to take into account the viewpoints of other people, he continues to talk to himself as an aid to problem solving and planning and directing his activities. Through social interaction, he also comes to possess and use the concepts with which his culture organizes experience. He also progresses toward the use of adult structure in language, increasing the number of words, refining his use of grammar and speaking in longer, more complex sentences.

REFERENCES

1. Ames, L. B. The development of the sense of time in the young child. *J. Genet. Psychol.,* 1946, **68,** 97–125.
2. Ames, L. B., & Learned, J. The development of verbalized space in the young child. *J. Genet. Psychol.,* 1948, **72,** 63–84.
3. Anderson, L. D. The predictive value of infancy tests in relation to intelligence at five years. *Child Devel.,* 1939, **10,** 203–212.
4. Bayley, N. On the growth of intelligence. *Am. Psychol.,* 1955, **10,** 805–818.
5. Bellugi, U., & Brown, R. (Eds.) The acquisition of language. *Mono. Soc. Res. Child Devel.,* 1964, **29:**1.
6. Brown, R., & Berko, J. Word association and the acquisition of grammar. *Child Devel.,* 1960, **31,** 1–14.
7. Brown, R., & Fraser, C. The acquisition of syntax. In U. Bellugi & R. Brown (5), pp. 43–98.
8. Descoeudres, A. Le développement de l'enfant de deux à sept ans. 1921. Cited in Werner [52].
9. Elkind, D., & Scott, L. Studies in perceptual development: I. The decentering of perception. *Child Devel.,* 1962, **33,** 619–630.
10. Gesell, A., & Amatruda, C. S. *Developmental diagnosis.* New York: Hoeber, 1947.
11. Gottschalk, J., Bryden, M. P., & Rabinovitch, M. S. Spatial organization of children's responses to a pictorial display. *Child Devel.,* 1964, **35,** 811–815.
12. Guilford, J. P. The structure of intellect. *Psychol. Bull.,* 1956, **53,** 267–293.
13. Guilford, J. P. Intelligence: 1965 model. *Am. Psychol.,* 1966, **21,** 20–26.

14. Hazlitt, V. Children's thinking. *Brit. J. Psychol.,* 1929, **30,** 20. Cited in Werner [52].
15. Hofstaetter, P. R. The changing composition of "intelligence." A study in T technique. *J. Genet. Psychol.,* 1954, 159–164.
16. Honzik, M. P., Macfarlane, J. W., & Allen, L. The stability of mental test performance between two and eighteen years. *J. Exper. Educ.,* 1948, **17,** 309–324.
17. Hurst, J. G. A factor analysis of the Merrill-Palmer with reference to theory and test construction. *Educ. Psychol. Measmt.,* 1960, **20,** 519–532.
18. Hyde, D. M. An investigation of Piaget's theories of the development of the number concept. Unpublished doctoral dissertation, Univer. of London. Cited in Lovell [23].
19. Jensen, A. R. Learning in the preschool years. *J. Nursery Educ.,* 1963, **18,** 133–140.
20. Katz, D., & Katz, R. *Gespräche mit kindern.* 1928. Cited in Werner [52].
21. Lee, L. C. Concept utilization in preschool children. *Child Devel.,* 1965, **36,** 221–227.
22. Long, L., & Welch, L. The development of the ability to discriminate and match numbers. *J. Genet. Psychol.,* 1941, **59,** 377–387.
23. Lovell, K. *The growth of basic mathematical and scientific concepts in children.* New York: Philosophical Library, 1961.
24. McCarthy, D. Language development in children. In L. Carmichael (Ed.), *Manual of child psychology.* New York: Wiley, 1954, pp. 492–630.
25. Mead, M. In J. M. Tanner & B. Inhelder (Eds.), *Discussions on child development,* Vol. 2. New York: International Universities, 1954.
26. Meyers, C. E., Dingman, H. F., Orpet, R. E., Sitkei, E. G., & Watts, C. A. Four ability-factor hypotheses at three preliterate levels in normal and retarded children. *Mono. Soc. Res. Child Devel.* 1964, **29:**5.
27. Meyers, C. E., Orpet, R. E., Atwell, A. A., & Dingman, H. F. Primary mental abilities at age six. *Mono. Soc. Res. Child Devel.,* 1962, **27:**1.
28. Miller, W., & Ervin, S. The development of grammar in child language. In U. Bellugi and R. Brown [5], 9–34.
29. Murphy, G. *An historical introduction to modern psychology.* New York: Harcourt, Brace, 1930.
30. Piaget, J. *The language and thought of the child.* New York: Harcourt, Brace, 1926.
31. Piaget, J. *The child's conception of physical causality.* London: Routledge and Kegan Paul, 1930.
32. Piaget, J. Children's philosophies. In C. Murchison, *A handbook of child psychology.* Worcester, Mass.: Clark Univer., 1933.
33. Piaget, J. *The psychology of intelligence.* London: Routledge and Kegan Paul, 1950.
34. Piaget, J. *Play, dreams and imitation in childhood.* London: Heinemann, 1951.
35. Piaget, J. *The child's conception of number.* New York: Humanities Press, 1952.
36. Piaget, J., & Inhelder, B. *The child's conception of space.* London: Routledge and Kegan Paul, 1948.

37. Smart, R. C. The changing composition of "intelligence": a replication of a factor analysis. J. *Genet. Psychol.*, 1965, **107,** 111–116.
38. Smith, M. E. An investigation of the development of the sentence and the extent of vocabulary in young children. *Univer. Iowa Stud. Child Welf.*, 1926, **3**:5.
39. Sontag, L. W., Baker, C. T., & Nelson, V. L. Mental growth and personality development: a longitudinal study. *Mono. Soc. Res. Child Devel.*, 1958, **23**:2.
40. Springer, D. Development in young children of an understanding of time and the clock. *J. Genet. Psychol.*, 1952, **80,** 83–96.
41. Stone, L. J. & Church, J. *Childhood and adolescence.* New York: Random House, 1957.
42. Stutsman, R. *Scale of mental tests for preschool children.* New York: World, 1930.
43. Terman, L. M. *The measurement of intelligence.* Boston: Houghton Mifflin, 1916.
44. Terman, L. M., & Merrill, M. A. *Measuring intelligence.* Boston: Houghton Mifflin, 1937.
45. Thorndike, E. L., *et al. The measurement of intelligence.* New York: Teachers College, Columbia Univer., 1926.
46. Thurstone, L. L. Theories of intelligence. *Sci. Month.*, 1946, **62,** 175–197.
47. Thurstone, L. L., & Thurstone, T. G. *SRA primary abilities for ages 5–7.* Chicago: Science Research Associates, 1950.
48. Vygotsky, L. S. *Thought and language.* Cambridge: Massachusetts Institute of Technology, 1962.
49. Watts, A. F. *The language and mental development of children.* London: Harrap, 1944.
50. Wechsler, D. *Wechsler intelligence scale for children.* New York: Psychological Corporation, 1949.
51. Weir, R. H. *Language in the crib.* The Hague: Mouton & Company, 1962.
52. Werner, H. *Comparative psychology of mental development.* New York: International Universities, 1957.
53. Wohlwill, J. F. A study of the development of the number concept, by scalogram analysis. *J. Genet. Psychol.*, 1960, **97,** 345–377.

The Role of Play in Development

CHAPTER 8

Reporting to the parents of a three-year-old, the teacher said: "Laura works a great deal with water. She and Cindy have been working in the doll corner most of the time during the past week."

To the uninitiated, the word *work* would seem far-fetched in describing anything that Laura, or any three-year-old, did in the nursery school or at home. Understanding the meaning of play in the child's life, the teacher equated it with work. Play is what the preschool child does when he is not sleeping, eating or complying with other such routines or requests. Although to an adult, play may be just a time-filler, to a child play is serious business. Engaging in this serious business, he develops his mind and body, integrating the intellectual functions of thinking, reasoning, problem solving, talking and imagining. Physical environment and guidance are vital influences on the child's development through play. As the last section of this chapter will show, the preschool years are important ones for intellectual growth, even though many people erroneously consider them a time of waiting for education to begin.

PLAY

Differentiation and Integration

The developmental principle of differentiation and integration is illustrated by many sequences observable in play. Just as the newborn baby starts with his reflexive patterns to build a new pattern of grasping an object and bringing it to his mouth, so the two-year-old refines some of his crude coordinations into smaller units which he improves and then combines into complex units. Thus he develops new patterns of thinking and acting which are different from the older, simpler ones and yet include them.

Having only recently progressed from walking to running, the two-year-old runs just for the fun of it. Stepping high and alternating his feet faster than when he walks, he may add little speed. He climbs for the fun of it, too, on stairs, furniture, jungle gym or inclined boards, going up and down, backward, frontward, on his stomach, on his seat, trying out all possibilities enjoying the feel of all. Even after walking, running, and climbing have become integrated into more complex motor patterns, they are still used sometimes by themselves and apparently enjoyed for their own sakes. Similarly, tricycle riding, ball throwing and catching, jumping and cutting with scissors—these are all activities which are used sometimes for themselves and at other times for other ends. As running and climbing become easy and automatic, they are used for other ends, integrated with other actions. The child runs and waves his arms, being a bird; he runs to reach the doll carriage before his sister gets it; he climbs the stairs to get Mommy's knitting for her; he scrambles onto the kitchen counter to find crackers and peanut butter. He modifies walking and running motions to ride a kiddy car and later a tricycle.

By the end of the preschool period, many complex patterns of play have been developed from simple forms of motor play, imagination, manipulation and perception, but growth is merely off to a good start. Mental development goes on, building more and more involved structures through the interaction between child and environment. The coordinations of ball throwing, catching, running, counting, and others, can be integrated into playing basketball, baseball and tennis. Counting may be used eventually in playing bridge. Dramatic play can be integrated into acting and writing.

Persistence of Sensorimotor Play

Infant play is predominately sensorimotor, since intellectual growth has not progressed beyond the sensorimotor level. Although with increasing maturity play becomes more differentiated and parts of it more complex, the child continues to engage in sensorimotor play. So do the adolescent and the adult. Age is no selector of who lingers beside a tidal pool to bathe his senses in sparkles, clarity, colors, undulating form, chill, salt and prickles. Anyone can enjoy making a snowball and throwing it. Preschool play has a large sensorimotor component, as anyone who observes young children will notice. Exploration is one facet of the developing sense of initiative. The young child touches objects eagerly, grasps them, runs his fingers lightly over them, even scratches them with his fingernails. Although he has learned, to a large extent, to keep objects out of his mouth, such inhibitions are not complete and he often finishes an examination with his lips and tongue. Color is important, often featured in his comments and greatly enjoyed in toys, art, clothing and nature. He experiments with sounds, using his voice, musical instruments, and any casual soundmakers which come into his grasp.

Significance and Development of Social Play

Infants show interest and pleasure in the company of other infants. During the preschool years, children seek one another and give evidence of enjoying play together. Parents' usually recognize some of the benefits of social play.

Very often they say, as the reason for sending a child to nursery school: "He needs playmates. We want him to learn to play with other children."

The ordinary course of social play as seen in nursery schools or neighborhood is a progression from simple to complex. Two-year-olds watch others, cooperate momentarily, often engage in the same activity as someone else (parallel play), such as shoveling or sliding, but they play in an essentially solitary style. However, even though they may not appear to be interacting, there seems to be a satisfaction in just being near each other. For instance, a rocking boat is a popular plaything in which a group of young children can be together. They tend to be rough with each other, hitting, pushing, poking, grabbing, often seeming to explore each other as *things* rather than as people. Of course, they recognize each other as people, but they are in a process of finding out the basic characteristics of people, especially of children similar to themselves. Will this person fall over when I push him? What happens when I pull that shiny long hair? How does it feel to hug him? What kind of noise does she make? Egocentric, he seeks information which will eventually help him to grow beyond egocentrism.

At the two-year level pushing or hitting with the apparent intent to hurt is infrequent. The pushing and hitting that does go on is most often for the purpose of getting a toy that someone else has. Sometimes a child hurts others unintentionally because he does not even recognize them as being there, walking into their play, pushing them aside. Such actions are egocentric, since the child has a limited awareness of himself in relation to the rest of the world and is unable to comprehend the situation as it is to someone else.

Gradually interchange grows more frequent, longer, with more cooperation and more conflict. With the development of language, more communication takes place. Two children play together, talking about what they are making in the sand, putting dolls to bed, dressing up, pretending a scene that requires two cooperating characters, such as a mother and a baby. Groups of three children playing together are common between three and six years. While three seems to be the preferred number, groups do increase up to five or six members, especially at the older ages.

In the early stages of group play, children tend to move in and out of the group without changing the content of the play (shifting group play). For instance, Tom, Hal and Barbie were digging and making dribble castles near the water's edge. Barbie took her periwinkles to visit the hermit crab that Tom and Hal were tending in the pool between their castles. Just as Barbie took off to find another hermit crab, Sally settled down beside Barbie's castle to keep the pool from filling in. Later Barbie returned, all four played for a few minutes and then Tom and Hal departed, leaving Barbie and Sally with all three castles, pools and wild life. Play groups are more stable in the older preschool years, as activities become more structured and complex. Conflicts over toys decrease as children learn how to take turns and as their behavior becomes more flexible, with more possibilities for action.

Growth in social behavior comes not from imposing one's will on others or submitting to a stronger person but from perceiving the other person's needs and desires and letting him understand yours; communicating your judgments and values and perceiving his; meeting human needs; discovering common purposes [1]. This statement is reminiscent of Erikson's *sense of intimacy,* a stage which flowers in the late teens and early twenties, but, like all the stages of personality development, has beginnings in childhood. Here, in preschool play, can be seen the beginnings of intimacy with peers, in the integrative behavior that takes place. Several studies have been concerned with the problem of what is constructive or integrative play in the early years and and of how it is influenced. When their playmates show distress, preschool children exhibit some understanding and make some attempts to comfort those in trouble. Sympathetic behavior increases during the preschool years and also shows wide individual differences [22]. An inquiry into conditions of sympathetic behavior showed that it was strongly influenced by what the child was doing, thinking and feeling at the moment. Some of the conditions which enhance basic sympathetic responses between playmates go back to experiences in the family [15]. Preschool children's consideration for others develops most readily when parents do the asserting of power over their children while pointing out the consequences of children's behavior toward other people. (Parent–child relationships are discussed in the following chapter.)

Leadership is integrative, if by leadership is meant the opening up of possibilities for action which others choose to take. A leader in these terms is not always the one in the flashiest role (or even, in later life, the president of the club) but the one who has ideas, skills and resources which facilitate play. Thus leading in one situation does not mean leading in all types of play or with all groups of children.

Compliant behavior was studied in three-to-five-year-olds in a nursery school [2] using time sample observations. *Compliance* was defined as the "frequency and alacrity with which the children acceded to the commands and suggestions of other persons." Degree of compliance with peers was not found to be related to intelligence, nor was there a sex difference. The most compliant children sought more help and more emotional support from other children than did the less compliant children. The most compliant tended to be less aggressive and dominating with their peers than did the least compliant children. The following differences in social behavior between peer-compliant and peer-noncompliant children were found to be statistically significant: opinions are more readily influenced by others; has higher energy level; is more spontaneous and uninhibited; is more distractible; is more suggestible; more often seeks praise and attention from others; is warmer, friendlier; shows more emphatic sensitivity to others' feelings; appears more relaxed and easygoing; is less rigid, less inflexible; is less of a perfectionist; exhibits less self-pity; finds it less difficult to make mistakes. In the nursery school, complying with peers seemed to occur in a give-and-take situation rather than in one of dominance and submission. The child who makes many suggestions for play is likely to be a child who frequently agrees with the suggestions of others. It is noteworthy that the children who showed the greatest degree of compliance with peers were also high in the characteristics of mental health.

While children grow more choosy with age, they do have favorite playmates during the preschool years. They can tell verbally which friends they like best and then proceed to choose desired ones for activities in the nursery school, even showing some consistency over a period of four weeks [14].

Preschool social behavior has also been studied in terms of conflicts, quarreling, fighting and hostility. A certain amount of quarreling is to be expected in any group of young children, simply because they have not yet learned subtler ways of resolving conflicts and differences. Pushing, pulling and hitting are comon types of quarreling behavior [3]. The more social contacts a preschool child makes with his peers, the more he is likely to have quarrels, as well as integrative relationships [11]. Friends were found more likely to quarrel than were children who did not play often together. Most quarrels started over possessions [3]. Older preschool children had fewer quarrels than younger ones, as might be expected with their increasing social skills. However, when the older children had quarrels, the conflicts lasted longer and involved more aggression, retaliation and talking than did conflicts among younger children. Children settled most quarrels by themselves, recovering quickly and showing little resentment [3]. Even so, there are times when children benefit from adult help in preventing or solving conflicts, and there are individual children who need a considerable amount of such help.

Sex differences in quarreling, aggression and hostility have been found in several studies [3, 11, 21]. Common observation also suggests that boys are more quarrelsome, aggressive and more hostile than girls. Boy–boy groups took part in the largest number of quarrels in the nursery school, boy–girl groups the next number and girl–girl groups did the least quarreling. Individual children differ greatly as to how they conflict with each other and as to how often they do so. In one investigation of quarreling, one child took part in 132 aggressive situations, while two children participated in six quarrels each; one child was the aggressor 59 times, while three children started no conflicts at all [4].

Social play becomes more complex as children learn not only more subtle ways of approaching and interacting with each other but also as they develop in motor coordination, language, concepts and imagination. Play is the arena in which all of these behavior patterns are developed, often simultaneously. The various patterns are analyzed and discussed separately only because the whole picture is too complicated to deal with at once.

SIGNIFICANCE OF IMAGINATION

Preschool thinking is "cute" in much the same way that infant proportions are "cute"; preschool imagination is beautiful. Imaginative behavior gives the preschool child a special place in the adult's heart. Adults look wistfully at young children's original interpretations of commonplace events, their fresh, bright paintings, poetry and free-wheeling dramatics. Almost every adult has at least a fleeting memory of being that kind of person himself. "Every child an artist." "The magic years." "The golden years of childhood." What happens to imagination?

Imagination As Part of the Sense of Initiative

Having developed a firm sense of autonomy and a consequent concept of himself as a person, the child wants to find out what he can *do*. To this end, he explores the world through his senses, through thinking and reasoning and through imagination. In most situations, of course, these three instruments of exploration are combined. The essential part played by imagination, however, is probably least understood and appreciated. Through imagination, the young child tries on the roles of the important people in his world, the people who do things which he might some day do. Most vital of all are the roles of his parents, and these are the parts he plays first and most often, especially the part of the parent of the same sex. The child imagines being and/or replacing the parent of the same sex. In doing so, he imitates some of the parent's behavior and thinking, including his standards and goals. His own conscience develops through this activity, modeled upon the parent's, encouraged by his desire to be the parent. Gradually, through interaction with both parents, the youngster faces the facts that he can neither be nor replace his parent and that he himself can one day be a parent through growing up and behaving in grownup ways. He is continually fascinated by the exploration of adult roles, which he does first and foremost through dramatic play, but also through literature and fantasy and even through dancing, painting and other creative media.

Guilt is a necessary product of the developing sense of initiative, as the child changes from a simple pleasure-seeker to a complex self-regulator. Erikson [9, p. 256] expresses it thus:

> Here the most fateful split and transformation in the emotional powerhouse occurs, a split between potential human glory and potential total destruction. For here the child becomes forever divided in himself. The instinct fragments which before had enhanced the growth of his infantile body and mind now become divided into an infantile set which perpetuates the exuberance of growth potentials, and a parental set which supports and increases self-observation, self-guidance and self-punishment.

Through imagination, the child appeases and allays some of the conflicts which arise between these two parts of himself, the part which desires and the part which controls (the conscience). When his conscience punishes him too severely with guilt, he can ease the load through imagination. Not only does expression through some creative medium make him feel better; it is a way of solving problems. Imagination is also a powerful means of pushing aggressively out into the world and incorporating some of it into himself.

If life's problems are solved satisfactorily during the years when imagination predominates, then a residue of imaginative activity and a resource of initiative remain, to enliven, sparkle, inspire and push throughout the rest of life. Such a person will get fresh ideas and will not be afraid to experiment with them. Even though he has attained objectivity, his thinking and feeling will be so flexible that he will be able to take off on flights of imagination. Both creativity and true recreation have their roots in imaginative play.

Imagination As a Part of Intellectual Development

In its simplest form, imagining consists of representing some part of outer reality by an inner image. Without the ability to use images as representations, man would forever stay in the sensorimotor stage of intellectual development. The first indications of imitative and imaginative play occur in babies during the final period of the sensorimotor stage, when the child imitates his own past actions in very simple, concrete ways. Thus he shows that he has mental images of these actions. For instance, he pretends to go to sleep, curling up in the doll bed or on a pillow, shutting his eyes momentarily. He pretends to eat, perhaps taking a real lick of sand or other make-believe food. He imitates the actions of others, especially his mother. He hugs and loves dolls and soft animals, feeds them, washes them and puts them to bed. As he grows older, he uses these incidents in playing house, school or hospital, games that last much longer than the playing of the first simple incidents.

Piaget [26] shows how symbolic games are an important part of the preconceptual period. The transition from the sensorimotor period to preconceptual is marked by using symbolic patterns with new objects. Jacqueline, having pretended to sleep and pretended to cry, made her toys sleep and cry. Later she pretended to play with a cousin (who was not there) and then to be the cousin. Symbolic play represents experiences the child has had and the meaning that they have for him. It also can be what the child wants life to be. Egocentric, the child becomes submerged in action, loses awareness of himself as separate from the play, and lives in the role that he is dramatizing. The very act of living in that other role, however, leads him away from egocentrism, because it lets him see and feel how it is to be that other person or dog or airplane. As mental growth continues through the preconceptual stage, through symbolic play as well as other experiences, egocentrism gives way to objectivity. Piaget calls imaginative play "the purest form of egocentric and symbolic thought" [25, p. 127]. Symbols, he says, are needed as long as egocentric action prevails, since ready-made language is inadequate for the child's purposes. Language, being the product of society, cannot express all the experience and needs of the individual child, nor can the child master the language enough to serve him very flexibly.

TYPES OF IMAGINATIVE PLAY

The major forms of imaginative expression in early childhood are discussed in this section. Anyone who works with young children needs to know a great deal about the development and guidance of imagination. The following comments are intended only as an introduction to the topic.

Fantasy

Everyone does some thinking which is undirected, free, somewhat symbolic and difficult or impossible to put into words. Sometimes it is called daydreaming. Fantasy, imaginative thinking and symbolic thinking all refer essentially to this kind of behavior. Since people engaging in fantasy are not paying attention to the multiplication lesson that may be in progress, teachers have traditionally looked upon daydreaming with disfavor. Research in children's thinking shows, however, that fantasy has an essential role to play. Through her studies on imagination in Australian and English children, Griffiths [12] came to see fantasy and symbolic thinking as useful and adaptive ways of coping with life's problems. Instead of being a waste of time, a blank or a pursuit of pleasure, imagination is a way of dealing with reality which is particularly appropriate for the young child. He can, of course, direct his thoughts to a limited extent, but this free-reining, personal, inner method of symbolic play is his natural medium of action. He makes objective contact with reality and then employs fantasy [12, p. 174].

> Like those simple animalculae that stretch out long pseudopodia into the surrounding water in search of food, retiring afterward into a state of apparent passivity while digestion takes place, so does the child seek experience, and, having come into contact with reality in some form, retires within himself to understand and consolidate what he has acquired. He cannot tackle a problem all at once, immediately, even such problems as seem insignificant to us. This is surely the meaning of childhood; time is needed for adaptation.

Griffiths conducted a series of 20 interviews with each of 50 five-year-olds in situations where the child played freely with drawing materials and was encouraged to say anything he wished. Ink blots and an imagery test were used in addition to the recording of what the child said. For the first few days, comments were controlled and reality-adapted. After three or four days, nearly all children revealed evidence of fantasy. At first, items appeared scattered and chaotic in arrangement, but gradually the elements were linked, themes emerged and the whole content became complex and closely knit. The whole was not static, but constantly developing in relation to the child's problems and experiences [12, pp. 14–31]. Through fantasy, the child moved from a personal, subjective and egocentric point of view to a more socialized and objective attitude. In order to illustrate this process, there follows a rather long, repetitive account from Griffiths [12, pp. 175–177] of stories told by Dick, reflecting on the subject of possessions and the best ways of coming to own the things that he wants. The repetitive nature of this account demonstrates the ways in which fantasy operates, working over and over ideas, varying them, returning to a theme, adapting it and moving on to a solution of the problem.

First phase: Theft

1. (Third day of the work.) "There was an old man and he had some greengages. And there was a great big giant, and he came and pinched all these greengages, and went away to his house. And this man he went to his house too."

2. (Also on third day.) "And once upon a time there was a lady and she had some eggs. And she was eating these eggs, and an old man came along, and he saw her eating them, so he went up to her and pinched 'em all."

3. (Fifth day.) "Once upon a time there was a burglar and he stole something. And so the copper saw him and this copper took him to prison. He stole a watch and the man was hitting him."

The three stories just given represent what may be called the first phase. At first there is the idea of theft successfully carried out. In the third story two days later he is doubtful already of the advisability of the method, for in spite of extenuating circumstances a thief is punished. He hastens to the next phase.

Second phase: Goods purchased

4. (Also on fifth day.) "Once there was a lady and she had some eggs, and a man came down the street, and *he* wanted some. So he went to the stall where the lady bought hers, and he got some and he ate 'em all up."

5. "Some old man had some greengages, and he ate 'em all up, and he said, 'They're good. I think I'll go and buy some more.' "

6. (Sixth day.) "Once upon a time there was a lady running down the street with some apples, and a man wanted some too. And so he asked the lady where she bought 'em. And so *he* went and bought some."

7. (Eighth day.) "Once upon a time there was a lady and a man. So this man he had some apples, and so this lady wanted some. And she asked him where he got his apples so he said out of his garden, and but he didn't. And then the lady found out, and she went to the stall where he bought 'em, and she found out that he was telling lies."

This is the end of the second phase in which the desired article is purchased. In the last story it is interesting to note the emergence of the "garden" idea, anticipating the next phase.

Third phase: Fruit is grown from seeds

8. (Ninth day.) "Once upon a time there was a lady, and she was running down the street, and she had some apples and a man saw them, and so he wanted some. So he planted some apple seeds, and some apples grew. So he

picked 'em up an ate 'em." He adds reflectively, "Yer might see some worms in the mould." He seems in this phase to think the apples grow on the ground.

9. (Tenth day.) "Once upon a time there was a man, and he had some apples, and a man on the roof wanted them so he jumped down off the roof and he got the apples, and there was an aeroplane. So he got in this areoplane and went back up on the roof again."

In the last story there is a serious regression to the phase of theft, but this is probably sufficiently accounted for by the clever method used. The child is not, however, satisfied even here with theft, for in the next story he continues the third phase.

10. (Eleventh day.) "Once upon a time there was a man and he had some pears, and there was a lady and she was running, and she saw these pears and she wanted some. So she got seeds and planted them, and picked all the pears and ate 'em."

11. (Also on eleventh day.) "Once there was a man and he had some apples and he wanted some more apples to grow. And then he planted these and some more apples grew, and then he saw these apples growing, and they were cooking apples, and so he cooked some."

Note here the extension of ideas, first to the planting of seed from one's own apples, and also the added idea of cooking the apples.

12. (Thirteenth day.) "Once upon a time there was a man and he wanted some apples. So he found an apple seed, and he planted this apple seed, and some apples grew on a tree."

In stories 8 to 14 he dwells upon the idea of growing one's own apples. Next he becomes aware of a new difficulty, as the author of these stories: suppose one has no garden.

Fourth phase: Where to plant?

15. (Sixteenth day.) "Once upon a time there was a man and he wanted some plums. And he found a plum seed and so he planted it in another lady's garden. And he went. And the lady said (angrily), 'Where's that plum tree come from?' So she got a chopper, and chopped it down, and it fell right on her head."*

Symbolism

The child's fears and problems are often symbolized by the toys he chooses and by the content of his imaginative games. Discovering an analogy between two objects and situations, he invests one as a symbol for the other. The story

* Reprinted by permission from Ruth Griffiths, *A Study of Imagination in Early Childhood* (London: Routledge & Kegan Paul Ltd., 1935). Copyright © 1935, Routledge & Kegan Paul Ltd.

of five-year-old Joyce illustrates this process [12, pp. 141–148]. Joyce and Dorothy were sisters whose father had died two years earlier. More recently, two neighbor children had died, one of them being their playmate, Dorothy L. Joyce sometimes went on errands for Dorothy L.'s mother, who called Joyce "my little girl" and sometimes acted as though Joyce had taken Dorothy L.'s place. Joyce was rivalrous with her sister Dorothy, a delicate child who received fussing and petting from their parents. Joyce had a china doll which was to her a little girl, and, after Dorothy L.'s death, a dead little girl. When telling the thoughts that came into her mind during a series of play interviews, Joyce disclosed that Dorothy L.'s mother had allowed her to see the dead child in her coffin, where "she was like a china doll." Shortly after this time, sister Dorothy became ill and had to go to the hospital. At this point, her daddy and Dorothy L. disappeared from Joyce's dreams and conversation. She became afraid of her china doll. Instead of taking it to bed with her, she put it on a chair. Waking in the night, she wanted to take the doll into bed, but was afraid that a mouse might get her. "They might get my dolly and get her eyes out with their claws."

Thus Joyce pushed away the reality of her father's death and her sister's frightening disappearance, centering her fears upon an object, the doll, which she used to symbolize all these disturbing occurrences. The doll had formerly been a comforting object. She was still dealing with that object in the daytime, although not at night, when fears were most oppressive. Perhaps she was hanging onto the possibility of getting control of the whole terrifying situation through the doll, which served as such a powerful symbol.

Summarizing the functions of symbolic thinking or fantasy in the life of the child, Griffiths [12, p. 187] makes several points: Fantasy is the normal means of problem solving. Problems are attacked indirectly, often symbolically. The child is only vaguely aware of what he is trying to do. The problem is solved piecemeal, through a series of solutions. The process results in both acquisition of information and a change of attitude. The change of attitude is from personal and egocentric toward socialized and objective.

Dramatic Play

Dramatic play, or pretending, is a kind of symbolism. A child can pretend by himself, on a very simple level, as does the toddler who pretends to eat and sleep. Or a child can carry on dramatic play with other children. The make-believe play of children under three is largely personification, such as talking to dolls and other objects, imitative use of objects such as drinking cups, and taking part in such situations as a bath or a traffic game. Between three and five, children are more active with materials and engage in more frequent, longer and more complex imaginative games [20]. A nursery school or kindergarten is likely to entertain a game of exploring the moon in which several astronauts build with large blocks and packing cases and planks, store much pretend food and drink and go through several days of launching, flying and landing. The following half-hour-long incident is rather typical of four-year-olds in nursery school:

> Bill and Grant were digging with shovels in the dirt in a far corner of the yard. They piled the dirt in a mound against the fence. Both looked excited. Grant said, "We'll have a pile way up to the sky." Bill asked, "How long will it take to get down to the bottom?" Grant replied, "All night and all day and all night."
>
> Bill accepted the answer without comment. Another boy came over to watch the digging. Bill exclaimed in a high voice, "We smell a *bad* bear and a *good* bear here. So it's very *dangerous*. We're going to find the bears in China. I sleep with the bears at night. I lock them in a cage tight. Then I turn out the light."
>
> Bill and Grant went into the building and came out with a small bottle of water. They poured it on the roots which had been exposed by the digging. "Put the poison on my roots, too," Bill told Grant. "Kill them all."
>
> The teacher told the boys it was time for milk. Sitting on the bench in the coat room, Bill leaned towards Kit and told him earnestly, "The *good* bears and the *bad* bears both know me, but only the good bears know you, cause I've known 'em longer than you have. And do you know what happened one night? A *bad* bear visited me [30].

An incident is rarely a pure example of one kind of play or another. In this bit of play, Bill and Grant practice the coordinations of digging, try on the roles of explorers going to China and explore the nature of bears and feelings toward bears. Bill seems to be getting the upper hand of a fear of bears, or perhaps of a less specific fear which he has chosen bears to symbolize. The power of imagination makes water into poison, and the little boys can use that poison to kill roots. Probably the roots symbolized a fear or a threat.

Between two and a half and six and a half, children use increasingly more hostility in their dramatic play. They also use more and more language in these games. A study of 108 children in this age range concluded that dramatic play language and dramatic play hostility were important modes of social intercourse and influence [21]. In other words, the playful expression of anger in make-believe situations, plus imaginative verbal expression, constitute useful social skills for preschool children.

A feeling of pleasure, excitement and satisfaction seems to accompany dramatic play. Observers often comment that two-year-olds laugh when they imitate and pretend. Bill and Grant were noted to be excited. These feelings also accompany new experiences, problem solving and releasing of tensions. In light of children's emotional behavior during dramatic play and from the way they seek this kind of play, its benefits seem obvious. Interacting creatively with his world, a child enjoys the satisfaction that goes along with exploring and finding.

Imaginary Playmates

Imaginary companions of preschool children have long intrigued students of behavior. A frequent production of children in the stage of developing imagination and initiative, imaginary playmates can be human or animal, fleeting or long-enduring, single or multiple, ideals or scapegoats. Studies report a quarter to a third of children as having imaginary companions. The children who create these playmates come in as great a variety as the imaginary creatures themselves, strongly suggesting that the creations serve the needs of the children. Bright children are somewhat more likely to have imaginary companions (or to tell about them) than are children of below-average intelligence. Girls are more prone than boys to create their own playmates [18, pp. 342–344]. A study of college students who had had imaginary companions in childhood showed them to have tendencies toward higher-than-average grades and toward cooperation, friendships and the experiencing of strong feelings and emotions [8].

Creative Language

Stories and poems are imaginative in both the giving and receiving. Symbolism and beauty can be noted in the form as well as the content. Teachers of young children, and sometimes parents, regard their telling of poems and stories as creative activity. Although there is no definite proof that listening and perhaps writing down the story encourages the child to further expression, adults who work with preschool children generally believe that this is so. Rhythm and imagery are apparent in this moon song, chanted and enjoyed by Ellen at two and a half.

> Crescent, crescent, crescent, crescent,
> Crescent goes to sleep, crescent wakes up.
> Ballie, ballie, ballie, ballie,
> Ballie goes to sleep, ballie wakes up.

Sometimes one story will reveal progress in solution of emotional problems. Four-year-old Susan used the following tale with which to struggle symbolically with confusion, fear, good and bad:

> Once Susan was in a theater seeing a grown-up movie. The lady who was giving the movie said, "Our magic fairy who is asleep will have to come out." And so the magic fairy woke up and came out. She chased everybody down the stairs and made everybody dance down the stairs. She chased me down the stairs. When we went out, she spoke to each person as they went out the door and I do not know what she said to the other people, but she said this to me, "You did dance down the stairs but you did not like it." She said that she'd go back in the building and for me to stay there.
>
> She chased me in front of the first car parked outside the theater. Then I

> started to run up across the bridge as quietly as I could. Then I just had time to sneak into a house and hide. When the good fairy came up, pat-a-pat, pat-a-pat, making a funny pat-a-pat, pat-a-pat, pat-a-pat noise. So I just had time to sneak up into my own house on Giles St. and lock the door when the good fairy came up and went ding-dong, ding-dong on my door bell. I would not open it or Mummy or Daddy or my sister, so the fairy could not get in.
>
> Then the fairy went up and down, flying on top of my roof, for she thought that my house would burn down if she did. But it did not. There was a good fairy inside my house. And she, the good fairy, would not let my house burn down, for she took away the bad fairy's wand, and would not return it. So the bad fairy died, because fairies die when their wands are taken away. And so that was the end of the bad fairy and we all lived happily ever after.

Often the expression of fears and problems helps to minimize them. Adults know how much it helps to talk to a friend about a bad experience, past or anticipated. Young children often do not know exactly what is bothering them, or if they do, they cannot express it straightforwardly. To express it in a story or poem or in another artistic medium can relieve tension, clarify the trouble and help the youngster to find solutions.

Sometimes hostility shows through the symbols, even when the comment is understood by all to be imaginary and not a real threat. This five-year-old shows a certain flair for creative imagery, violent as his product is:

> I'll push you out the window and you'll make a mess on the pavement and my Daddy will scrape you up with a knife and spread you on bread and eat you. Then he'll vomit you up.

Humor

Humor is an intellectual process which reduces anxiety. Developmentally, the first joke is the game of peek-a-boo, which dramatizes the baby's anxiety over his mother's disappearance, then presumably reduces his tension. Joking makes psychological pain bearable, expresses fears and wishes which cannot be faced directly and gratifies forbidden desires. One of man's most creative achievements, humor partakes of both language and gesture, with emphasis on gesture during the preschool period. Humor depends on flexibility of thought, which the preschool child possesses to a very limited extent. The punch line, so important to adult jokes, is beyond his cognitive powers. Therefore, his amusements and his attempts to be funny are not amusing but seem silly to an adult. He may actually be funny in the simplicity of his jokes. Although incongruity and surprise are of the essence of grownup jokes, a certain subtlety is usually necessary for adults. Furthermore, preschool humor is too far removed from adult problems to be tension-reducing to adults. Incongruity takes precedence over surprise in preschool humor, although surprise can add to the fun.

Falling down is often hilarious, since it includes both aspects of the joke. The person suddenly gets into the wrong position, in the wrong relationship to the floor. A fillip is added by the involvement of the whole body in the situation. Language jokes tend to be in the form of calling objects or events by inappropriate names, especially forbidden words, such as bathroom terms. Long rambling (pointless to adults) stories may be offered and accepted as jokes, since the surprise element is not essential. These lengthy tales often concern creatures falling down, falling apart and growing together again, getting lost and found, hurt and well, having toilet accidents or performing deliberate excretions. Underlying young children's jokes are their envy of adult size, power and privileges, worries over the wholeness and safety of their bodies, resentment of adult control in the face of their own autonomy strivings, aggressive impulses which frighten them [33].

Music and Dance

Creativity exists both in performance and in enjoying the music and dancing of others. In these areas, as in other parts of the preschool child's experience, exploration is vital. A rich environment offers opportunities to experiment with sound and gesture and with putting them together. Infants enjoy and respond to songs. By two, the child who has had some experience with singing will listen to others and will sing spontaneously as he plays. He likes action songs, in which he responds to words with gestures. He joins in with a few words as others sing. His first efforts to sing with a group will probably not be well coordinated, but they soon lead to his being able to follow along with others' singing. Soon he recognizes and asks for certain songs and recognizes various pieces of music [13, pp. 284–285]. Creative expression flows when the few necessary facilities are present—a chance to listen, a chance to sing, the simplest of instruments to play (easy to make from scrap materials [24, p. 13]) a group with whom to play, sing and dance, experience to play, sing and dance about. In a simpler society, a child can grow into the music and dance of his parents, watching, imitating, being taken through the motions and joining in adult dances and music groups when he is sufficiently grown up. In complex western culture, it often takes an adult with special skill and understanding to appreciate and facilitate the young child's creations in music and dance.

In the machine age many children see little of rhythmic muscular activity which seems to them worth imitating. In contrast, primitive children experience the rhythms of weaving, grinding and chopping. In a preschool day camp dancing grew out of the small happenings of every day, a Moon Time Dance when the children noticed the moon in the daytime sky, The Sunflower Dance, created by a four-year-old and two-year-old who found sunflowers, The Chocolate Sellers, dances of fears, of wonder of God, of cooking [7]. The teacher found that the higher the emotional content in the thought expressed, the more the child seemed to need rhythmic action to express it. With young children, there was rarely dancing without singing or rhythmic language. She told of one child who danced her way out of the fears and obsessions which threatened her health.

With music, as well as dance, young children have potentiality for expression and enjoyment, perhaps even more than that of the average adult. It has been shown that music produces an emotional response in people and a more pronounced response in children than in adults, as measured by the galvanic skin response [34].

Creative Materials

The same statement could be made of young children's expression through *paint, clay, blocks* and other materials. These media offer the same types of benefits that the child gets from fantasy, dramatic play and creative language —increased understanding of the world and his relation to it, expression and understanding of his questions and problems, release of emotional tension, satisfaction from creating beauty and order. Some children get more growth and satisfaction from one kind of creative activity, others from another. It is likely that everybody can derive some benefit from each type of experience. And nobody knows, least of all Johnny, whether painting will be Johnny's forte or whether he will find himself most fully in dramatic arts.

When a child first encounters paint, clay or any other new material, he has to explore it, to find out what it is like and what he can do with it. (Not only children. Watch an African graduate student in the first snowfall of the North American winter!) Set-up and limits are important here—"paint goes on the paper," "blocks are not to throw," "hold the saw this way." The very act of exploring which represents the first stage in his artistic development is satisfying and releasing, especially with tactile materials like clay and finger paint. The second stage, of seeing patterns or meanings, or enjoying patterns from random exploratory activity, is a truly imaginative activity. Whether the long, blobby brush stroke is an elephant's trunk or a cat's tail, whether the tower of blocks is a missile or a chimney, all depends on the child's imaginative use of his own experience and needs. In the third stage of artistic growth, the child will make something, intentionally, not necessarily a recognizable reproduction, but something that symbolizes or represents what he wants. Figure 8–1 shows a developmental sequence in drawing.

ENRICHMENT OF PRESCHOOL LIFE

The tremendous growth potential of young children demands a rich and varied environment in order to be realized. Supplements to the home, in the form of nursery school,* kindergartens, church schools and play groups pro-

* When the first American nursery schools were organized, a distinction was often made between them and day nurseries, the latter being institutions which gave custodial care to the children of working mothers, the former having an educational plan for young children. In recent years the distinction has become largely one of name only since many contemporary day nurseries or child care centers have excellent education programs, and some "nursery schools" do little more than protect children from physical injury. In the material that follows we will use the term *nursery school.*

Figure 8–1. Age changes in artistic expression, from exploration of medium (scribbling) to clear representation. (Reprinted by permission from S. L. Hammond, *et al.*, *Good Schools for Young Children.* New York: The Macmillan Company, 1963.)

vide places where children can reach out to interact with a nurturant world. Although the kibbutzim of Israel and the internat of the Soviets take over some of the functions that American families reserve for themselves, schools for young children in this country are also based on the idea of adding to the child's life opportunities which his family cannot give him.

Even today, many people still hold the view that the preschool years are a time when the child just plays, waiting to be old enough to start learning lessons which really count. Even mothers who spontaneously enhance their children's intellectual and personality development are often surprised when they learn of their own vital influence. Although nursery schools have been operating in the United States ever since 1921, the public has neither understood nor promoted their educational potential. Suddenly, however, new social trends drew attention to what could be accomplished during the preschool years. The problem of poverty and cultural deprivation has highlighted the growth possibilities which exist in all children during their first years of life. Tried-and-true methods of nursery school teaching are being leavened by experimentation and implementation of results from new research. Efforts to help the deprived child are helping all children, by revealing the nature of growth and learning during the preschool years. In this section, we are going to sketch the ways in which an excellent nursery school provides stimulation and learning opportunities for all children. Next, we shall discuss the meaning of cultural deprivation, the significance of preschool education to the disadvantaged child and examples of preschools recently created to meet the challenge of poverty and allied social problems.

Nursery School Education

The preschool child is treated as a whole person who grows through differentiation and integration of body, personality and intellect. Provisions for play, health and growth are carefully planned and maintained. Social growth is promoted by arrangements which facilitate cooperative play and guidance which gives into motivations and feelings of oneself and others. Equipment and program are attuned to the stages of personality growth which dominate the preschool years.

BUILDING THE SENSE OF AUTONOMY. The miniature world which strikes the casual visitor as so cute, is child-sized in order that the child can *do the utmost for himself*. He hangs his snowsuit on the hook that is just the right height; his feet touch the floor when he sits on the toilet. The child-sized world is arranged in such a way that its occupants can *make many decisions for themselves,* decisions which turn out to be right. A child selects a puzzle from the puzzle rack and puts it back before he takes another. An easel with fresh paper, paints and brushes invites him to paint, standing on a floor protector which keeps a spill from being a disaster. The housekeeping corner is full of equipment which children can manage—doll clothes with wide armholes and big buttons, a low bed in which children can snuggle with dolls, a sturdy, stable ironing board with small iron, unbreakable dishes and a place to wash them, grownup purses, shoes and hats, for easy dressing up.

The teachers appreciate what it means to young children to be independent successfully, to make decisions that turn out well and to feel worth while in what they do. In addition to encouraging and facilitating such behavior, teachers also know what not to do, never to use shaming as a way of controlling behavior, never at any age, but especially at this time of life, since doubt and shame undermine the growth of autonomy. Neither is competition used as an incentive, since it too would threaten the child's growing sense of autonomy.

Discipline in the nursery school is not quite the same as the discipline that many students and parents have known in their lives. It is easier to understand in terms of the sense of autonomy. The teacher sets limits on what the child may decide for himself and what he may do. She makes the limits clear and sticks to them firmly, giving him freedom within them. She does not say, "Wouldn't you like to come indoors now?" She says, "Now it's time to go indoors." She does not say, "Nice little boys don't grab toys from little girls." She says, "Jill is using the doll carriage now, Tommy. You may have it when she is finished. Could you use the rocking bed now?" Thus a choice really is a choice and a direction is definite. The teacher understands that the children will often test the limits she sets, as part of their growing up. Because the child knows she respects and accepts him as a person, because he trusts her, he can usually accept the limits she sets for him. Because he likes her and wants to be like her, he often wants to do what he perceives she wants. Thus discipline in the nursery school is carefully planned and carried out in such ways that children can grow in autonomy through successful deciding and doing [27, pp. 222–247].

BUILDING INITIATIVE AND IMAGINATION. Motivational and intellectual aspects of growth are involved here, as this chapter and Chapter 6 have shown. The nursery school's stress on creative activities is one of its most vital ways of contributing to preschool growth. Not only is creativity valuable in itself now and in the future, but imagination is more than a supplement to controlled thought during the preschool years. The young child solves through imaginative processes many problems which he cannot handle by controlled thinking. Setting him free within comfortable limits, the nursery school invites the child to reach out into his world, to explore it vigorously and curiously, to imagine himself in a multitude of roles, to create a variety of beauty. All of this magic is implicit in the combination of children, raw materials, space, some carefully chosen equipment and teachers who love children and know a great deal about them. Dramatic play requires only a few simple props, but it needs a push at the right moment and hands off at other moments. The skillful teacher will suggest straightening the corner block before the whole post office tumbles down. She is quick to produce paper that will do for letters for the postman to carry. She suggests that Ronnie could be a customer at the stamp window after he has hung on the fringes unable to get into the game.

Managing paints, clay, paste and such is so simple that first-time observers often see the teacher doing nothing. It takes real understanding of initiative and imagination, however, to let children create freely, often by keeping quiet and doing nothing. Teachers never "fix up" children's products. They accept them. They never draw models to be copied. They never tell children what to make with materials. They don't say, "What is it?" They listen to what the child spontaneously says about his creations. They show that they realize it meant something to him to do what he did.

Initiative and imagination are stimulated by books, stories, music, trips, pets, plants and visitors with special messages for children. Such experiences provide ideas which are worked over in dramatic play and creative work with materials.

Perhaps it is in the area of initiative and imagination where the nursery school supplements the home most generously. What home can provide such a constant flow of fingerpaint and play dough? What mother can arrange for a group of peers for daily playmates or be on hand constantly to supervise dramatic play constructively? Or to play the piano for a group of elephants who turn into butterflies? Or to take children to see a hive of bees working behind glass? Or to arrange for her child to find out how a pipe organ works? Or to have his teeth cleaned with a group of his friends, attending the dental hygiene clinic after a child-oriented introduction?

FACILITATING INTELLECTUAL DEVELOPMENT. The tremendously rich environment of the nursery school offers never-ending opportunities for building mental structures. The child constantly perceives, integrates his perceptions and integrates sensory experience with verbal. Recent research indicates that nursery schools stimulate mental growth in a variety of ways including the following [17].

Since most preschool children think preconceptually and intuitively, a nursery school curriculum is designed to give them problems which they are capable of solving. Through building with blocks they learn that two of these equal one of those and that a square can be divided into two triangles. Counting may result from figuring out how many blocks to bring from this shelf and how many from that, when blocks are kept sorted according to size and shape. Counting happens in many situations which have real meaning—two cookies for each child at snack time, time before lunch for singing three songs. How many children go home with Peggy's mother? The workbench is a place for dealing with linear measure, roughly, of course, in terms of *longer* or *shorter than* or *about the same size as*. The sink is for learning about volume, if you are allowed to pour water back and forth instead of just washing your hands. Useful equipment includes containers graduated as to size and another series of similar size but different shapes. Clay, sand and mud offer chances to experiment (loosely speaking, not scientifically) with size, shape and volume. So do many other materials found in nursery schools offer opportunities for development of the schemas of cognition—pegs and peg boards, puzzles, shoes to lace, matching games, color sorting games, musical instruments, records, books.

Language is a vital part of the curriculum. The teacher is a model of clear, pleasantly toned, noncolloquial speech. Skilled in understanding baby talk, she replies in speech which the child comes to imitate. She encourages children to talk, to tell her and other children about their experiences and feelings. New words and concepts come from books, stories, songs and the many planned new experiences of nursery school. The beautiful books and satisfying storytimes make children look forward eagerly to learning to read to themselves. Here is preparation for reading—good speech, something to talk about, a love of books. Here also is intellectual development taking place through language, when children communicate with others and acquire symbols with which to think.

Concepts of *time* are part of preschool endeavors, even though young children do not handle chronology very objectively. Many of their comments and questions and much of their play shows efforts to straighten out their ideas of time and to understand how life changes. While educators used to recommend that the teaching of history be delayed until age eight, a recent publication from Teachers College, Columbia University [31], points out that preschool children are deeply concerned with the sweeping changes in life which have occurred with the passage of time. Before they are interested in or able to tell minutes by the clock, they hear about dinosaurs, horse and buggies, steam locomotives. Through play, conversation and thought, children arrange these past events and phenomena into a very rough historical concept. In India we found that relatively uneducated people would often tell us, "It happened in ancient times," meaning that it happened before Independence. It could have occurred any time between 3000 B.C. and 1947. "Ancient times" is probably the way children think of the past before they have had the rigors of history lessons brought to bear upon them. The history lessons will be richer in meaning if they come after the past has content for the children, even though it is content without much chronology.

A recent review of research on teaching in the nursery school [28] yields considerable evidence that nursery school attendance promotes social, language and intellectual growth. The quality of the nursery school seems to make a difference in whether such growth can be demonstrated. Gains are greatest in the children who start with the greatest room for improvement. Those from homes providing meager stimulation are likely to make the greatest intellectual gains.

Cultural Deprivation

The culture of poverty includes restrictions which affect every member of the family in every aspect of life and development. By about two years of age, the child is missing more and more experiences necessary for normal intellectual growth. While it is possible that as a baby, he derived some benefit from the stimulation of close quarters, the drawbacks of slum living soon affect him [16]. Living in a crowded, noisy home, he learns to ignore sounds, since few of them have any relevance for him. When people speak to him, they speak in single words or in short sentences, often in commands. He may not discover that everything has a name. Lacking this powerful piece of knowledge, he does not seek out names, does not add to his vocabulary and hence drops farther and farther behind the average child in thinking as well as in talking and understanding language. Nobody corrects his pronunciation, since the adults and older children articulate poorly. Inaccurate phonetically and grammatically, his speech is not easy for the teacher to understand when he goes to school. The child then has trouble understanding the teacher, because she talks in longer, more complicated sentences than he has heard, she sounds her words differently, she uses words he does not know and she talks about things, places and events which he has never experienced [19].

Slum homes, in contrast to middle-class homes, offer young children few toys and play materials. Deprived children may never have the visual and tactile stimulation which comes from play with color cones, blocks, nests of cubes, puzzles, paints, clay, crayons and paper. They lack the emotional satisfactions of cuddly toys and the imaginative and social possibilities of dolls, housekeeping equipment, costumes and transportation toys. Their motor development is not encouraged, as it would be through the use of climbing apparatus, tricycles and large building materials. Nature is not seen as orderly, beautiful and wondrous, since nature is hardly seen at all. Preschool children in slum areas rarely go more than a few blocks from home. A woman who grew up in a slum recalls that as a child, the only beauty she saw was in the sky.

Upon entering first grade, culturally deprived children are at a severe disadvantage in many ways, but most seriously in the main job of the beginner in school, learning to read. Disadvantaged children differ from middle-class children in how they perceive the world, in what the teacher's words mean to them, in what they know about themselves. First grade is baffling to those who lack meaningful experiences with language and ideas, toys and places, people and other living things. Unable to cope with reading and other school activities, the culturally deprived child falls farther behind in second grade and still farther as he grows older [5, 6]. His IQ declines. Somewhere around third or fourth grade, he feels hopeless and defeated. Intellectually and educationally retarded, he is a serious problem to the school and to himself.

Many children live under conditions which deprive them of opportunities for normal intellectual development. The culture of poverty, according to various estimates, envelopes 20 to 40 percent of the population [5]. Many of these people are Negroes. Others belong to such ethnic groups as Puerto Ricans. Still others are Old Americans, such as the Appalachians. The Civil Rights movement has focused special attention upon the plight of poor Negro children, especially those living in big city slums.

Enrichment Programs for Disadvantaged Children

Basically, the nursery schools for deprived children are like the good nursery school described above, dedicated to providing opportunities for full development. Since the disadvantaged child must catch up with what he has missed, in addition to growing in the regular way, his preschool is necessarily adapted to his special needs. Therefore such schools lay particular stress on teaching verbal and perceptual skills, promoting the child's self-concept and self-confidence, stimulating curiosity and building a need for achievement. These nursery schools, in contrast to those for normally advantaged children, usually structure their programs more, providing for a great deal of adult–child interaction. Already such schools have been successful in raising measured IQ [29, 32], preventing progressive retardation in school [6, 29] and improving children's language, self-expression, attention span, alertness and social behavior [32]. Various projects are experimenting with a variety of techniques. For example, a project at the University of Chicago [29] conducted preschool programs in at least six different patterns, comparing the results as to IQ gain and other changes in the children. (A fairly conventional nursery school did as well as or better than any others.) An example of a Michigan project [32] is given in some detail, so as to show how a successful one is conducted:

Culturally deprived Negro children were selected on the basis of community-wide tests. Experimental and control groups were matched in IQ, degree of cultural deprivation, age, sex and number of working mothers. The control group was left exactly as it had been. The experimental group was given a stimulating educational program which included nursery school and home experience guided by the nursery school teacher. The curriculum was concerned with overcoming deficits in these areas: language, concept formation, use of symbols, learning set, inquiry, attention and focusing, visual awareness and discrimination, environmental knowledge. Techniques of stimulating language development, for example, were planned in order that each area of operation would offer language stimulation. In the music and sound areas, children recorded their speech on a tape recorder and played it back. In the doll corner, they held conversations in dramatic play and over toy telephones. Playing airport, they had to communicate with the control tower. On field trips, teachers encouraged conversation about what they saw. Science experiences stimulated questions and comments.

Results were observable and measurable. Probably the most conclusive change in the experimental group, from fall to spring, was a change in Stanford–Binet IQ from 74 to 92, a highly significant difference. The control group measured 76 in the fall and 81 in the spring, showing no statistically significant change. Qualitative differences in the experimental children were noted. In the beginning, their speech was scant, indistinct and made little sense. By spring, they talked freely, expressing ideas and questions. Books were no longer meaningless objects, but favorite items. Curiosity blossomed and exploration increased greatly. From mechanical manipulation of art materials, the children progressed to creative expression and representation. They grew interested in writing, especially their own names. Increased attention spans were noted, with many hyperactive, distractable children showing greater ability to concentrate.

Each child was visited once a week in his home by his teacher, who brought materials, worked with him and tried to involve his mother in working and playing with him also. Parents, both fathers and mothers, came to group meetings, showing a high level of interest and cooperation. The study yielded findings on parents as well as on children. Most important, the investigators found that it was possible to operate an educational program in the homes of culturally deprived preschool children. The response of the mothers varied from great enthusiasm and cooperation to neutrality. Small discussion groups were possible too, with fathers becoming involved. There was extremely wide variation among lower-class Negro parents in what had been thought to be a homogeneous group. It was found that the factors which correlated most highly with a child's progress in school were the parents' use of ideas and suggestions from the nursery school. Thus the value of the home-based part of the program was established as very significant.

At least one preschool enrichment program [10] includes the mothers in an educational situation during the whole time during which their children are at school. As they learn and develop themselves, the mothers offer more to their children in the way of stimulation, understanding and encouragement. Thus the special enrichment nursery school follows the general principle held by the conventional school, that preschool education is a supplement to the family, not a competitor.

Project Head Start and Related Programs

As a vital part of the war on poverty, the Office of Economic Opportunity established nursery school programs for poor children in all 50 states and Puerto Rico. Day care programs are also being expanded, and more are being established, largely under the auspices of the Children's Bureau. Based on findings from research on cultural deprivation, the Head Start program was planned to promote not only intellectual growth in children but sound physical development, enhanced personality growth and an improved family situation for all children involved [23]. This very ambitious program required a quick mobilization of all the resources which could be brought to bear. The idea caught the public fancy, partly because preschool children are appealing to almost everyone and also because the positive nature of it was heartening. Instead of doing an extensive repair job on the ravages of poverty, it would be *building*. About 550,000 children went to Head Start Schools during the summer of 1965, where they learned to trust teachers and other adults, to use many new words, concepts and play materials, to play constructively with other children and to think of themselves in worthwhile terms. Highly nutritious meals and snacks promoted sound growth. (One little girl gained eight pounds in eight weeks!) Immunizations were brought up to date, including protection against measles. Defects were corrected in eyes, ears, teeth, feet, and so on. Families learned more about their children and themselves, some of them coming to feel comfortable at school.

Some parents gained new strengths, as did the group who, encouraged by their children's teachers and social worker, organized themselves to make a demand upon the school system. In this rural community, the children of the poor had rarely been able to go to kindergarten because transportation was provided in only one direction. The middle-class mothers took their children to school or called for them as necessary, but unless a poor child lived within walking distance, he had to stay home. After four weeks of Head Start, one of the mothers chaired a meeting at which about a third of the mothers and several fathers decided that they must have kindergarten education for their children. Further meetings were held, petitions assembled and orderly pressure brought to bear on the school committee. Transportation was arranged, not only for the children of the poor, but for all children who needed it.

SUMMARY

Play, the main occupation of the young child, is his mode of learning new patterns of thought, feeling and action and of integrating them. While sensorimotor play persists throughout life, social and imaginative play become increasingly influential upon the preschool child's development.

Early social play involves exploration of other children as objects and as persons. Parallel play, typical of two-year-olds, means engaging in the same activity with little interaction other than watching and imitating. Interactions between young children are temporary and fleeting, increasing as children mature. The earliest group play is loosely structured, permitting children to shift in and out of the activity easily. Sympathetic and cooperative behavior occur in young children. Leadership involves opening possibilities for activities to others and integrating their play. Children vary considerably in the degree to which they can and will fit in with the play of others. Quarrels are common when conflicts occur, but most quarrels are settled rather simply, with little aftermath. As children grow older, they tend to quarrel less frequently but more aggressively.

Imagination, the key to preschool personality development, complements controlled thinking. Through mental images, the child represents experiences and objects to himself. He invents symbols to stand for the images and uses those symbols in his thinking. As he acquires language, he is able to think more and more with the words which his culture gives him as representatives of experiences and objects. In imagination, however, he continues to use some of his own private symbols, and to invent more for his own purposes, in fantasy, symbolic thinking and dreams. Other forms of imaginative expression include dramatic play, in which human relationships and roles are explored, creative language, which produces stories and poems and humor, which reduces anxiety. Young children perform and enjoy in all fields of art, music, dance, painting and sculpture. Children use all forms of imagination in solving problems and in expressing their thoughts and feelings.

Schools for young children supplement homes by providing constructive play opportunities. An excellent nursery school (preschool) offers an environment in which the sense of autonomy and the sense of initiative are nurtured.

Guidance and discipline provide limits within which the child can make successful decisions and free choices. Intellectual development is promoted through a rich variety of sensory experiences, available in contexts which lead to conceptualization. The learning of language is encouraged. Preschools have a special contribution to make to culturally disadvantaged children, who are going to school in increasing numbers. Enrichment programs have been successful in raising IQ, improving language, concepts, self-concepts, self-confidence and curiosity, and in preventing progressive retardation in the elementary school. The preschool must work with the family, as well as the child, if the child is to gain maximum benefit from his school.

Federal projects in preschool education, day care, health and family welfare are based on the conviction that the preschool years offer the most promising opportunities for breaking the cycle of poverty. These projects emphasize the promotion of normal, healthy growth before drastic remedial measures become necessary.

REFERENCES

1. Anderson, H. H., & Anderson, G. L. Social development. In L. Carmichael (Ed.), *Manual of child psychology*. New York: Wiley, 1954, 1162–1215.
2. Crandall, V. J., Orleans, S., Preston, A. & Rabson, A. The development of social compliance in young children. *Child Devel.,* 1958, **29,** 430–443.
3. Dawe, H. C. An analysis of two hundred quarrels of preschool children. *Child Devel.,* 1934, **5,** 139–157.
4. Debus, R. L. Aggressive behavior in young children. *Forum of Educ.,* 1953, **11,** 95–105. Cited in A. T. Jersild [18].
5. Deutsch, M. Facilitating development in the preschool child: social and psychological perspectives. *Merrill-Palmer Quart.,* 1964, **10,** 249–263. (a)
6. Deutsch, M. The influence of early social environment on school adaptation. In D. Schreiber (Ed.), *The school dropout*. Washington, D.C.: National Education Association, 1964, pp. 89–100. (b)
7. Dixon, C. M. *High, wide and deep*. New York: John Day, 1938.
8. Duckworth, L. H. The relationship of childhood imaginary playmates to some factors of creativity among college freshmen. Unpublished Master's thesis, Univer. of Alabama, 1962.
9. Erikson, E. H. *Childhood and society*. New York: Norton, 1963.
10. Grams, A. Parent education in the inner city. Merrill-Palmer Inst., 1964. (Mimeo.)
11. Green, E. H. Friendships and quarrels among preschool children. *Child Devel.,* 1933, **4,** 237–252.
12. Griffiths, R. *A study of imagination in early childhood*. London: Routledge and Kegan Paul, 1935.
13. Hammond, S. L., Dales, R. J., Skipper, D. S., & Witherspoon, R. L. *Good schools for young children*. New York: Macmillan, 1963.
14. Henderson, C. G. Companion choice behavior of nursery school children. Unpublished Master's thesis, Univer. of Mississippi, 1962.

15. Hoffman, M. L. Parent discipline and the child's consideration for others. *Child Devel.*, 1963, **34,** 573–588.
16. Hunt, J. McV. The psychological basis for using preschool enrichment as an antidote for cultural deprivation. *Merrill-Palmer Quart.*, 1964, **10,** 209–248.
17. Jensen, A. R. Learning in the preschool years. *J. Nursery Educ.*, 1963, **18,** 133–139.
18. Jersild, A. T. *Child psychology*. Englewood Cliffs, N.J.: Prentice-Hall, 1960.
19. John, V. P., & Goldstein, L. S. The social context of language acquisition. *Merrill-Palmer Quart.*, 1964, **10,** 265–275.
20. Markey, F. V. Imaginative behavior of preschool children. *Child Devel. Mono.*, Teachers College, Columbia Univer., 1935, **18.**
21. Marshall, H. R. Relations between home experience and children's use of language in play interactions with peers. *Psychol. Mono.*, 1961, **75:**5.
22. Murphy, L. B. *Social behavior and child personality: exploratory study of some roots of sympathy*. New York: Columbia Univer., 1937.
23. Office of Economic Opportunity. *Project Head Start Daily Program I*. Washington, D.C.: Government Printing Office, 1965. (a)
24. Office of Economic Opportunity. *Project Head Start Equipment and Supplies*. Washington, D.C.: Government Printing Office, 1965. (b)
25. Piaget, J. *The psychology of intelligence*. London: Routledge and Kegan Paul, 1950.
26. Piaget, J. *Play, dreams and imitation in childhood*. London: Heinemann, 1951.
27. Read, K. H. *The nursery school* (4th ed.). Philadelphia: Saunders, 1966.
28. Sears, P. S., & Dowley, E. M. Research on teaching in the nursery school. In N. L. Gage (Ed.), *Handbook of research on teaching*. New York: Rand McNally, 1963, pp. 814–864.
29. Strodbeck, F. L. The early education of the culturally deprived: an opportunity to rethink older premises. Speech given at Wheelock College Institute for the Exploration of Early Childhood Education, Boston, November 6, 1964.
30. Student observation. Merrill-Palmer Institute (unpublished).
31. Wann, K. D., Dorn, M. S., & Liddle, E. A. *Fostering intellectual development in young children*. New York: Teachers College, Columbia Univer., 1962.
32. Weikart, D. P., Radin, N. L., Aldrich, B., & Bates, P. *Perry preschool project: a progress report*. Ypsilanti, Mich., June 1963. (Mimeo.)
33. Wolfenstein, M. *Children's humor*. Glencoe, Ill.: Free Press, 1954.
34. Zimny, G. H., & Weidenfeller, E. W. Effects of music upon GSR of children. *Child Devel.*, 1962, **33,** 891–896.

Emotions, Character and Self

CHAPTER 9

An increasing complexity of feelings and emotions accompany the child's growing variety of interactions with people and objects. At the same time, he learns to understand and control his emotions, although not completely, of course. He makes a beginning in the long process of learning to behave and to feel in ways which are acceptable to himself and to society. At the beginning of the preschool period, he has some concept of himself as a physical object in space; by the end of this time, he can think of himself as a person-among-persons. He is affected by the religious-philosophical orientation of his family and his culture.

EMOTIONAL DEVELOPMENT

Emotional development in infancy was discussed in Chapter 5, under the headings *love, fear* and *anger*. Since further differentiation of emotions takes place during the preschool period, jealousy, rivalry and aggression also become significant.

Love

The discussion of love in infancy pointed out that love, at all ages, involves delight in being with, desire to be with and desire for contact and response from another person. Early in the course of development, certainly by the time the baby becomes a toddler, love includes another dimension, the desire to give to the other person, expressed in attempts to promote his happiness and well-being. The first dimension, the desire to be with the love object, was explored as *attachment behavior,* an aspect of infant development which has been the subject of research. Preschool love has been studied in terms of the attitudes of adults in the family, especially *nurturant behavior,* and also in terms of *dependent behavior* in children. The child has a variety of love relationships with the individuals who occupy different family positions.

Parental Love

General emotional atmosphere in the family is ordinarily thought to affect the well-being of the young child. A demonstration of this relationship is offered by a study of parental tensions in relation to child adjustment [4]. Seventy-six preschool children were observed and rated on quality of emotional adjustment. Their parents were interviewed about their relationships to each other. Healthy child adjustment was shown to be related to positive husband–wife adjustment in the areas of sex, consideration for one another, ability to talk over difficulties and expression of affection. The data gave some indication that girls were more adversely affected by parental tension than were boys. Corroboration of the importance of general emotional atmosphere comes from a study [27] of two groups of preschool children, one from intact families and one from homes broken by divorce. Matched for IQ and age, the children were drawn from community-supported day nurseries. On a projective test of anxiety, the children from broken homes showed more disturbance than did the controls.

NURTURANCE. Probably the most studied component of love, nurturance is a willingness or even eagerness to promote the well-being and development of the loved one. Parents ordinarily have a large feeling of nurturance for their children. Many, perhaps most, adults feel nurturant toward all children. Erikson [14, p. 97] speaks of the sense of generativity, an essential of the mature personality. "Generativity is primarily the interest in establishing and guiding the next generation. . . ." A high degree of nurturance is involved in generativity.

There is a mutuality to nurturance, the other side of the coin being an acceptance of it. The love that a child feels for a parent has a large measure of this acceptance in it. He counts on the parent's nurturance, expecting it and accepting it as a continuing part of life. The development of the baby's sense of trust was due in large part to the nurturance he received or, in Erikson's terms, to the strengths of his parents' sense of generativity. Having learned to trust his family in this way, the child accepts love as the foundation of his world. Even when parental nurture is not very dependable, some of it is much better than none at all. An authority on mother–infant relationships has written about the nurturing function of mothers in these words [8, p. 68]:

> In no other human relationship do human beings place themselves so unreservedly and so continuously at the disposal of others. This holds true even of bad parents . . . Except in the worst cases, she is giving him food, shelter, comforting him in his distress, teaching him simple skills and above all providing him with that continuity of human care on which his sense of security rests.

We would add that the child's sense of security also requires continuity of the first aspect of love, that his parents will continue to find pleasure in his company. When he acts affectionate, cute, sweet, amusing and otherwise endearing, part of his motivation is doubtless that of making his parents enjoy him. The preschool young child has an extremely rudimentary sense of generativity, and yet he does occasionally show nurturance. Jimmy proudly helps Mother to carry the groceries in from the car. Donald tenderly pats Daddy's head on hearing that he has a headache. Polly carries a mug of coffee to Mommy in bed on Sunday morning. All three children promote their parents' comfort in ways that are simple and temporary yet realistic. And while a pat on the head is rather minute when compared to what Daddy did that day for Donald, it is an act of love, recognized and accepted as such by parent and child.

DEPENDENT BEHAVIOR. Dependency is shown in attempts to secure the presence and nurturance of another person. Degree of dependence is estimated by how hard a child tries to obtain the company and attention of someone else, usually his mother. Children use many different modes of dependent behavior, including crying, following, cuddling, smiling, talking, showing accomplishments, shouting, "Look at me," asking for help. Dependent behavior has been classified into five types: seeking help, seeking physical contact, seeking proximity, seeking attention and seeking recognition [6].

As children grow, they change in their ways of seeking help, contact, proximity, attention and recognition. They are expected to use more mature ways as they get older, ways appropriate to age, stage and sex. For example, crying, the most infantile expression of dependence, is socially acceptable in young children, as long as they do not cry as often as babies do. For school-age children, it is occasionally appropriate for girls, rarely for boys. Adolescent girls and women may properly cry in emotional crises, but adolescent boys and men are not supposed to resort to tears in any but the most extreme situations. Dependent behavior can therefore be classified as to appropriateness or maturity level, as well as according to degree.

Another age change in dependency behavior is in its relation to mutuality. As the person matures he gives more nurturance. Still dependent on others for company and nurturance, he can give as he accepts. The objects of dependency relationships also change. Dependent in the beginning on his mother, the child comes to depend upon other family members, then peers, teachers, other adults, eventually a husband or wife and, perhaps, finally children.

There are wide cultural differences in parental attitudes toward independence. For example, an observer of another culture commented: ". . . it appeared that the child in Brazil is fondled, coddled, hugged more often and to a later age than is general in the United States. There is a strong tendency for parents to be overprotective and indulgent as well, behavior which is reflected in the cultural conception of the child as 'the protected one'—a fragile creature ('his bones are soft') who needs constant warmth, care and protection" [46]. In the United States, observers have noted considerable individual differences in American mothers' attitudes toward dependency [47, p. 143]. For instance, some mothers made comments such as "He's an affectionate child" or "She's such a cuddly baby," while others said, "He's so clingy" or "She's always hanging onto me." Differences have been interpreted in terms of the mothers' own personalities, in terms of sex, social class and occupational orientation.

Many studies have dealt with the effects of mothers' behavior on dependency in children [15, 18]. The availability of the mother has a bearing on the young child's seeking of contact. Two- and three-year-old boys sought more affectionate contact with their female nursery school teachers when they (the children) came from large families where children were spaced close together [53]. There is some agreement that frustration and punishment in infancy and preschool years are associated with dependency in the preschool period. Evidence comes from studies which correlated mothers' feeding practices and discipline practices with later behavior in their children. The preschool child's dependency tended to be greater if his mother used withdrawal of love to discipline him, showed signs of rejection, punished parent-directed aggression and was demonstrative with affection [47]. There is agreement in the literature that maternal rejection is associated with dependency in children. Cross-culture research [56] suggests that frustration and punishment in early childhood may affect adult dependency behavior. In cultures where children are punished severely for dependency behavior, adults show greater dependency than adults do in cultures where children's dependency behavior is indulged.

Overprotection has been related to child dependency. Very indulgent, protective mothers tended to have children who expressed their dependency in negative, aggressive ways, while dominating, protective mothers' children tended to be passive and submissive in their dependency [28]. A study of development from birth to maturity indicated that personality in childhood and adulthood was related to mothers' protective behavior when children were under three [25, pp. 212–214]. The definition of protection was not what many people would think of as an aspect of love or nurturance but was really overprotection. Rather than being a warm, helpful, cherishing pattern, it was rated on "(a) unsolicited and unnecessary nurturance of the child, (b) consistent rewarding of the child's requests for help and assistance, (c) encouraging the child to become dependent on her, (d) overconcern when the child was ill or in danger." A large measure of this kind of "protection" during the first three years in girls' lives was associated with a tendency to withdraw from anxiety-arousing situations in adulthood. In boys' lives, "protection" during the first three years was associated with passivity at the six-to-ten-year age.

A certain amount of protection and nurturance is essential for a child's existence and health. Parents are faced with many decisions as to how to give their children enough response, help, contact, proximity, attention and recognition without forcing or dominating and yet encouraging the child toward independent effort. One student [15] of this problem has concluded that the "spoiled" child, dependent, self-centered and having a weak conscience, was most likely to have a mother who reinforced dependent behavior and failed to be firm; children behaved more independently when mothers were nurturant.

Sibling Love

Sibling love has a large measure of pleasure in being with the other person, and a less important component of nurturance and dependency. Koch [26] has explored the attitudes existing between five- and six-year-olds and their siblings. Since these children are summing up their experiences of the preschool years, and since their younger brothers and sisters are preschoolers, some of the findings are pertinent here. The reasons children gave for wanting to play with their sibs and for not wanting them to leave the family were companionship, protection, general liking for the other child and appreciation of his services. Older children spoke more of personal qualities such as "cuteness" or "niceness," while second-borns mentioned more the sib's services and protection. Girls reported playing more with younger sibs than did boys. Sibs close in age played together more than those with a greater age difference. Second-borns more often stated a preference for play with the sib and at the same time, tended to believe that they played little with the sib. Thus the preschool children did not get all the companionship they sought from their older brothers and sisters.

Grandparent Love

Grandparent love relationships between children and grandparents have qualities different from parent–child and sib–sib love. Anthropological studies show that friendly equality between grandparents and children is a product of a certain kind of social structure [51]. Formality between grandparents and children is related to association of grandparents with family authority, through grandparents' either exercising authority or being the parents of the parent who definitely exercises authority over the children. Indulgent, close and warm relationships are more likely to be built when grandparents have little authority in the family.

Answers to questions put to Americans indicated that parents tended to feel positive and appreciative toward the grandparents of their children [13]. Only seven people out of 1,337 mentioned grandparents as being difficult. Reports from parents suggested that grandparents and children very much enjoyed times they spent together, especially when alone together. Caretaking functions were mentioned secondarily. The thinking seemed to be that grandparents offered uncritical acceptance of the child and an emotional haven.

When grandparents themselves (70 grandfathers and 70 grandmothers) were questioned, it became apparent that the role of grandparent is played in a variety of ways [42]. Grandparenthood was comfortable and pleasant to 59 percent of the grandmothers and 61 percent of the grandfathers but difficult and uncomfortable to 36 percent and 29 percent, respectively. According to the style in which roles were played, there emerged three main types of grandparents and a fourth type, the parent surrogate, which applied to grandmothers only. The *fun-seeking* grandparent (29 percent of grandmothers, 24 percent of grandfathers) is probably the type referred to in the study mentioned above. These grandparents are informal and playful, joining the child for the purpose of having fun and mutual satisfaction. Authority lines are unimportant. The dimension of love featured in this relationship, therefore, is the one of delight in the company of the beloved and desire for response from him. The *formal* grandparent (31 percent of grandmothers, 33 percent of grandfathers) probably represents a more old-fashioned type of relationship. The formal grandparent takes an interest in the child, gives treats and indulgences and occasionally helps the parents, but sees his (or her) role in strict terms. This grandparent does not offer advice and leaves parenting strictly to the parents. Nurturance and pleasure in the child's company are both aspects of the formal grandparent's relationship, with perhaps more emphasis on nurturance, and neither aspect being very strong. The *distant figure* (19 percent of grandmothers, 29 percent of grandfathers) feels remote from the child and acknowledges little effect of the child upon his life. Although this grandparent maintains a benevolent attitude, gives gifts on ritual occasions and goes through certain motions, there is little feeling or response.

The love which a child experiences with his grandparent will, then, depend on the role his grandparent plays in relationship to him. He will most likely establish a mutually joyous relationship with the fun-seeker, where child and grandparent respond to one another, savoring the pleasures of one another's company. From the formal grandparent, the child will derive a certain satisfaction, knowing the nurturance and some response are forthcoming. The distant figure will probably be the object of indifference to the child, just as the child is to him, although the child will perhaps have some pleasant expectations of material benefits on Christmas and birthdays. The surrogate mother, the role played by some grandmothers, takes on many of the emotional characteristics of the mother–child relationship, although if the mother is also in the picture, the three-way relationship is more complex.

Anger and Aggression

As was pointed out in Chapter 5, anger is the distress which accompanies an attack on a frustrating situation. Diffuse and unproductive expressions of anger, such as crying, kicking and throwing, are frequent in late infancy and the early part of the preschool period, when the child's desire for autonomy is strong and when he experiences many frustrations. Aggression is the actual attack behavior which is accompanied by anger. The most common concept of aggression is a hostile attack against another person. Aggression is sometimes conceived as a controlled and productive attack on problems, resulting in increased knowledge, power and/or status for the aggressor. In the latter context, the anger which accompanies aggression is a stirred-up, energized feeling which aids in problem solving and contributes to the development of the sense of initiative. Competition between people can involve either hostile aggression, or controlled and productive aggression. Many practical dilemmas arise from the dual nature of anger and aggression. While a hostile attack is dangerous and destructive, there is great advantage in being able to fend off an attack and in taking the initiative. Some children use aggression very often in order to cope with frustration; others display little aggression but use dependency behavior in the face of frustration. Research is concerned with the question of why some children are more aggressive than others. Some of the answers are to be found in the study of family relationships.

At least two types of parent–child interactions influence children to use hostile aggression as a mode of behavior. When parents themselves use physical punishment on the children, when they approve of suppression and punishment, and when they show hostile aggressive behavior, children are more likely to be hostile and aggressive themselves [47]. Furthermore, in a society where adults are expected to fight aggressively, the child sees this be havior approved in his parents, as well as in other adults [55]. It seems likely that children take parents as models of hostile aggression, when parents behave in ways which illustrate this mode of behavior.

A second type of situation in which the child learns to behave aggressively is when parents permit it, approve it or even instigate it. Parents usually recognize the practical importance of a child being able to defend himself and his possessions. Over half the mothers in Sears' [47] study of five-year-olds believed that a child should defend himself when attacked. Only 4 percent stated that a child should never fight. Since some of the children, in their parents' eyes, did not fight enough to defend themselves adequately, there was actually some parental demand for aggressive behavior and some direct training for it. Parents have also been observed in more subtle encouragement of aggressive acts on the part of their children, encouraging children to act out the antisocial impulses which the parents themselves felt but did not express directly [23]. Children were more openly aggressive when their parents permitted it, but the aggression shown in fantasy was the same for a group of children whose parents did not permit aggressive behavior [47]. The findings from this study and others suggests that the way to produce a nonaggressive child is to make it clear that aggressive acts will not be allowed, to stop such behavior when it starts and to avoid punishing the child for aggression, especially punishing him with physical means.

Practical Application of Research on Anger

Many of the studies mentioned indicate that the results of parental behavior are often unintentional. When one considers that what a mother does in the first three years of life is likely to be reflected in her child's behavior patterns, he is impressed with the complexity of parent–child relationships [25]. Parental action springs from a wide variety of sources other than pure reason and self-control. Even so, there are some steps a parent can take consciously in order to make it easy for a preschool child to do the acceptable thing. Including here the information derived from Goodenough's study of anger, reported in Chapter 5, the following list indicates conditions which encourage the development of self-control:

1. The child is cared for on a flexible routine which provides food, rest and activity before the child is acutely and painfully in need of these things.
2. Parents and other caretakers answer his calls for help promptly.
3. He is offered many opportunities to achieve and decide in approved ways.
4. Parents disapprove of hostile aggression and stop this behavior firmly.
5. Parents clearly express what behavior is permitted and what is not.
6. Physical punishment is avoided.
7. An atmosphere of emotional warmth prevails in the home.

Jealousy and Rivalry

Jealousy is the angry feeling that results when a person is frustrated in his desire to be loved best; rivalry is the angry feeling that results when a person is frustrated in his desire to do best, to win or to place first. Very often an individual feels jealous and rivalrous toward the same person, although sometimes these emotions can be separated. A child is likely to feel jealous of the baby who displaces him as youngest in the family and to feel rivalrous with the older child, who is stronger and abler than he. Parents and children also feel jealousy and rivalry toward one another. The themes of jealousy and rivalry within the family flame in the most ancient literature. Cain and Oedipus symbolize some of the most disturbing situations which exist in family life.

Jealousy of parents and the resolution of that jealousy make up the psychoanalytic story of the preschool period. The play age, the stage when the sense of initiative is developing, is the phallic stage in *psychoanalytic* terms. Almost every little boy says at least once, "Mummy, I'm going to marry you when I grow up," and every little girl has the equivalent plan for the future with her father. Wanting to be first in the affections of the opposite-sexed parent has as its corollary jealousy of the like-sexed parent. How specifically sexual you believe the child's desires to be depends on how analytically oriented you are or on how you evaluate the evidence that the preschool period is a time of active sexuality. In any case, the like-sexed parent represents a powerful, full-blown picture of what the little child hopes to become, even the person who attracts and holds the other parent. As recognition of reality (that he cannot win over the powerful, wonderful parent) helps the boy to give up his attempts to be first with mother, he continues to try to grow more like his father. He identifies with him, feeling less jealous and more affectionate and sympathetic with him. He gains strength by joining with the father. A similar mechanism is thought to work through the girl's attempt to be first with her father.

Jealousy of siblings is usual in western culture, in the typical small family consisting of parents and children. "Let's send the baby back to the hospital" is the classic suggestion of the preschool child who has just lost his place as youngest in the family.

Two or three decades ago, authorities who advised parents placed great emphasis on the value of preparing the child for a new baby. The hope was that jealousy would be eliminated if the young child understood the reproductive process and the characteristics of neonates and if he realized that such a baby was about to enter the family. He was to "help" get clothes and equipment ready and to learn how to share in the baby's care. Attractive books with such titles as "Your New Baby" were read to the young child as preparation.

Modern experience has not shown any of these actions to be wrong or even useless. On the contrary, the most accepted authorities today still recommend them. While we are not aware of studies definitively proving the worth of "preparing for the new baby," common sense and common experience show that the young child feels more loving and less jealous toward the baby who is introduced thus into his family. The difference today is that some jealousy and rivalry are regarded as inevitable in American culture—in fact in most cultures. The reason for it is the same reason which the Book of Genesis puts forth in the story of Cain and Abel. Every child wants to be the best loved by his parents. The first child wants it most deeply, since he once was the only child and knew what it was like to have all the attention, company, endearments and gifts. Interviews with 202 families revealed that the first child was regarded as more selfish and more jealous in families of every size, both white and Negro [12, pp. 119–131]. In studying two-child families, they found that the second was happier and more generous than the first and that on the average the first child was still reported by mothers as being the more jealous and selfish no matter what type of training he had received, no matter whether he was treated more indulgently than the second child. The authors concluded that no type of training whatever, whether severe, moderate or indulgent, is likely to eliminate the first child's sense of having been replaced by the second and of having lost some of his parents' love.

The child's interpretation of the new-baby situation is based on reality, as shown by a study of 46 children and their mothers [2]. The behavior of the mother toward the child was rated before, during and after pregnancy. Substantial and continuing decreases were found in child-centeredness, approval, acceptance, affectionateness and rapport. Declines occurred in duration of contact, intensity of contact, effectiveness of policy and babying (an aspect of indulgence). Increases occurred in restrictiveness of policy and severity of penalties. It is possible that some of these changes would have occurred with increasing age of the child, but since they did occur along with the mother's pregnancy and the birth of a baby, it is easy to understand how the young child would hold the new baby responsible for the unhappy turn of events. In addition, he sees the baby enjoying privileges he would like to have or which he is trying to give up, such as sucking a bottle, wetting his diapers, being carried and fondled, crying. One five-year-old said: "Yes, I would like to change places with my baby brother. Then I could yell my head off and mamma would take care of nobody but me." Another commented, "Sometimes I wish I could tear magazines myself" [26].

Jealous actions include suggestions for getting rid of the baby and attacks on the baby (the most direct) and more devious attacks such as accidents and rough play, acting out aggression with toys, attacking the mother, whining, withdrawing, protesting extreme love and concern for the baby. Later on, jealousy takes such forms as bickering, fighting, teasing, taking toys away. Reasons why parents behave in jealousy-inducing ways are to be found in the culture. In the small American family, there is not enough time and energy to go around after a new baby comes. In contrast, the joint family system provides for several adult women and adolescent girls too who are responsive to all the young children. When a young child's mother is pregnant or busy with a new baby, the child still has the support and attention of women to whom he is attached. The young child's affection and desires for approval are focused less intensively on one person. Therefore one person cannot let him down so severely and even if his mother does disappoint him, aunties and grandmothers are ever ready to care for him and comfort him.

The materialistic and relativistic standards of American society have received some blame for the forms which jealousy and rivalry take [36, pp. 99–114]. Parents' approval and resulting rewards often depend on how the child compares with his siblings, as well as with children outside the family. To look good and thereby be most approved and loved, he has to be better than someone else, often his brother or sister. If he were loved for himself and if his achievements were measured against some absolute standards, he would have less reason to be jealous of his siblings.

Jealous as siblings are, they normally love each other, too. They often feel ambivalent, pulled in two directions. "Sometimes I love you, sometimes I hate you" is a key to understanding many incidents in behavior of siblings (indeed, of most people) toward each other. When questioned about their relationships, 28 percent of 360 five- and six-year-olds said that they quarreled constantly with their sibs, 36 percent reported a moderate amount of quarreling and 36 percent stated that they quarreled rarely [26]. When these children were asked if they would be happier without the sister or brother, about a third of them reported that they would. When the sib was an infant, especially of the same sex, there was less desire to be rid of him than when he was beyond infancy. Apparently infants disrupt their siblings' lives less than do older children. Second-born children, more than first-borns, wanted to be rid of the other children. The wider the age difference between sibs, the more the second-borns wanted to be rid of the first-borns. The second-borns' reasons were largely in terms of the behavior of the sibs themselves, such as, "He always socks me," "She likes to boss me too much," "Sometimes she wishes I were gone." When first-born children wanted younger ones out of the way, their reasons were often in terms of parents' attitudes, especially favoritism toward the other child.

Children often express jealousy and rivalry in play and creative media. The following story by a four-year-old illustrates imaginative expression of these emotions:

> You see, there was a little pussy and do you know, that the little pussy had to go to the bathroom so badly. He couldn't find a place to go. Finally he found a little girl and she said she'd take him into her house and he could go to the bathroom. The kitty said he'd like to be her pet. Where do you think he went to the toilet? In a pot. That little girl had him for a pet and was so nice to him. One day when the little girl's father came home, he brought a dog for a pet. But that dog was mean to the little kitty and hurt him *so* much. So the little girl didn't like the dog and she just had the kitty for a pet.

This little girl had a sturdy, aggressive toddler brother who knocked down her block buildings and spoiled her doll play. Still in diapers, he was a reminder of her rather recent achievements in toileting and other self-care. It seemed to us that the little girl, represented by the kitty, planned to ignore her little brother, represented by the doggie, as a way of coping with her jealousy and anger at him for intruding in her otherwise satisfactory life.

Practical Applications of What Is Known About Jealousy and Rivalry

Jealousy and rivalry are so common in the American family as to be almost inevitable. These feelings can probably be minimized, if not eliminated, by some of the following procedures:

1. Preparing the young child for the birth of a sibling by telling him that the baby is coming, teaching him what babies are like, helping him to understand his own infancy and assuring him of the parents' continued affection for him.
2. Understanding and accepting imaginative expression of jealousy and rivalry, while firmly limiting direct expression.
3. Acceptance and appreciation of each child as an individual.
4. Avoidance of comparisons between children.
5. Avoidance of the use of competition to motivate siblings.

Fear

Fears arise in a variety of ways, as Chapter 5 has shown. Preschool children, as well as infants, are frightened by pain, sudden or intense stimuli, moderately unfamiliar sights. Like infants, preschool children can acquire fears through conditioning. Sometimes one painful experience is sufficient to establish a fear, as when a toddler comes to fear dogs by being pushed over, barked at or bitten. Or a fear can be acquired from another person in as few occasions as one. For example, a young child can become afraid of thunderstorms through an experience of being in a storm with a person who displays fear of the situation. The fears of parents and children show a correspondence as to both kind and number [17]. In Britain, during World War II, children's reactions to air raids were greatly influenced by whether their parents showed calm attitudes or fearful ones [22].

New kinds of fear-provoking situations arise during the preschool years. For example, an overly demanding social situation puts the child into a position where he has no appropriate response at his command, and hence withdrawal is what he attempts. Johnny comes into the living room suddenly to find several strange adults there. Mother tells him to speak nicely to the ladies, but he is shy and silent. He could have spoken to old friends, or he could have spoken to the new ladies too, had he been prepared ahead of time to expect strangers and to say something to them.

Imagination, initiative and conscience contribute to fears at this time of life. Eager to explore and to try out new activities, the child tends to push beyond limits set by his parents. When his budding conscience tells him he is doing wrong, or that he wants to do wrong, he may create imaginative satisfactions, only to have those creations frighten him. He is especially likely to imagine animals which have powers he would like to have and to use, such as great strength for attacking other creatures, biting, kicking or eating them. He may disguise his aggressive wishes quite elaborately, dreaming about such animals instead of telling stories about them or using them in dramatic play. The dream animals sometimes attack their creator, who feels guilty about his destructive wishes and thus suffers punishment. Fear of the dark may accompany fears of imaginary animals and bad dreams. When parents were questioned about the fears expressed by their children between birth and six years, results showed a progressive decrease in fears which were responses to such tangible stimuli as objects, noises, falling and strange people and an increase in fears of intangibles, such as imaginary creatures, darkness, being alone or abandoned, threat or danger of injury and harm [21]. Figure 9–1 depicts some of these feelings.

The answers of 130 children to the question "What are things to be afraid of?" give information on the fears of children five years old and over [35]. Animals were mentioned most often, but less frequently as age increased. Eighty percent of children were afraid of animals at age five and six, 73 percent at seven and eight. Snakes were mentioned more often than any other animals. Then came lion, tiger and bear. A third of children under seven admitted to fear of the dark. Children rarely reported fear of the type which parents try to teach, such as fear of traffic, germs and kidnapers.

An experimental study of children's fears confirmed the finding that expressed fear of tangible situations decreases with age throughout the preschool period [21, pp. 167–296]. Children were carefully observed when left alone, while walking across inclined boards which fell a distance of two inches, entering a dark room, meeting a peculiarly dressed stranger, walking across high boards, hearing a sudden loud sound, picking a toy out of a box containing a live snake and being asked to pat a dog brought in on a leash. Their actions were judged as indicating fear or not. The percentage of children

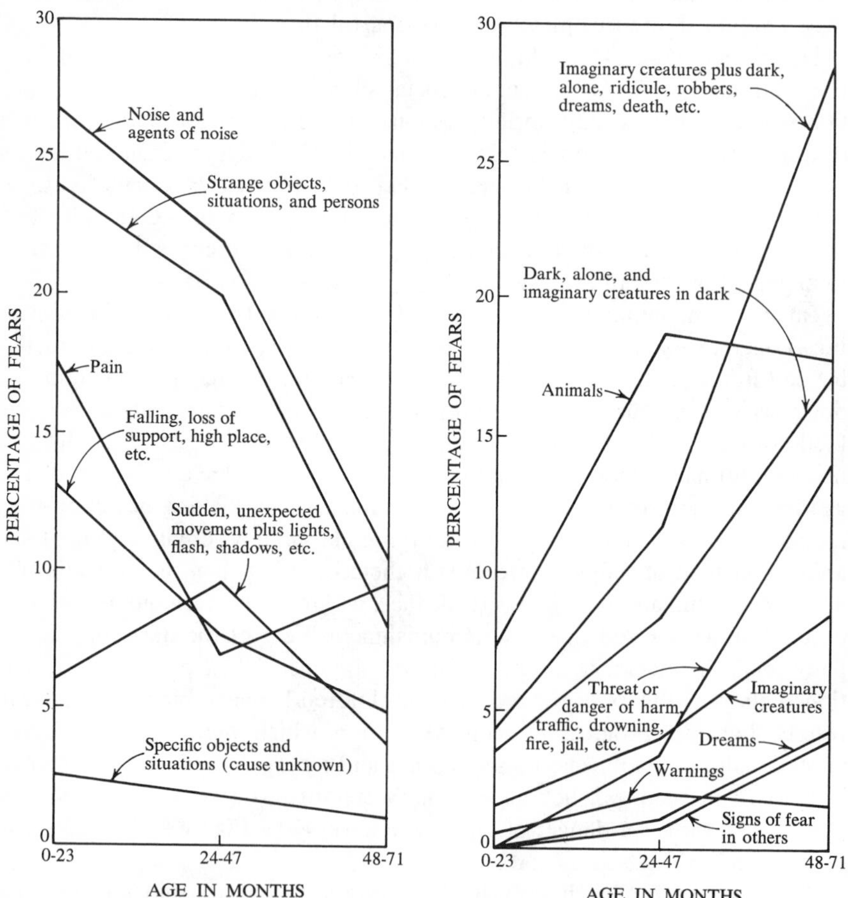

Figure 9–1. Frequency of various kinds of fears at different ages between birth and six years of age, as reported by children or observed in children by parents or teachers. (Figure 3 on page 261 from A. T. Jersild, *Child Psychology,* 5th Edition (Englewood Cliffs: Prentice-Hall, 1960). Adapted from Arthur T. Jersild and Frances B. Holmes, "Children's Fears," Child Development Monographs, No. 20 (New York: Bureau of Publications, Teachers College, Columbia University, 1935. Used by permission.)

showing fear at four different age levels between two and six are shown in Table 9–1.

TABLE 9–1

Fears shown by children age 2 to 6, in several experimental situations.

	Percentage of Children Showing Fear			
Situation	*24–35 months*	*36–47 months*	*48–59 months*	*60–71 months*
1. Being left alone	12.1	15.6	7.0	0
2. Falling boards	24.2	8.9	0	0
3. Dark room	46.9	51.1	35.7	0
4. Strange person	31.3	22.2	7.1	0
5. High boards	35.5	35.6	7.1	0
6. Loud sound	22.6	20.0	14.3	0
7. Snake	34.8	55.6	42.9	30.8
8. Large dog	61.9	42.9	42.9	
Total	32.0	30.2	18.1	4.5

Source: Reprinted by permission from Arthur T. Jersild and Frances B. Holmes, "Children's Fears," Child Development Monographs, No. 20 (New York: Bureau of Publications, Teachers College, Columbia University, 1935), Table 14, page 237.

Fear can be widespread and generalized, in contrast to being focused on a particular object or situation. When fear is widespread, generalized and unfocused, it is called *anxiety*. The preschool child is likely to experience anxiety when separated for a long time from his mother, father or main object of attachment. Considerable research has been concerned with what it means to a young child to be separated from his mother and some research has dealt with the question of separation from the father. Maternal deprivation has already been discussed in Chapter 5, where it was shown that deprivation can be either sensory or emotional or both and that the breaking of established bonds between baby and mother has quite a different result from that of separation when attachment is involved. The effects of partial and complete separation of toddlers from their mothers were explored with children between 16 and 27 months of age [19]. Two groups, carefully equated as to age and sex, were selected, one from each of two nurseries. All subjects were from intact families, without history of separation and with no indications that children had been rejected. No subject had a sibling in the same nursery. The two nurseries were run identically, with one exception. In the first, the children stayed all day but went home at night; in the second, the children lived 24 hours a day in the nursery. The two groups did not differ in behavior for the first two days, but after that, the residential children showed more intense symptoms of anxiety. They sought relations with adults more intensely, sought affection more, cried more, did more thumb and finger sucking, lost sphincter control more often and had more colds. The most striking difference was that the residential children showed more and greater hostility. This study does indicate that although partial separation from parents is not necessarily destructive, *complete* separation is likely to be so.

Maternal employment is a tempting situation to fasten upon when searching for conditions causing anxiety in young children. Public opinion is often expressed against young mothers who hold jobs outside the home. A thorough review of research on this topic concludes that maternal employment is too global a condition to use as a variable in investigating causes of children's behavior [49]. For example, 26 kindergarten children of fully employed mothers were matched in family factors, age and sex with 26 kindergarten children whose mothers had never been employed during the lives of these children. No differences were found between the two groups on the nine personality characteristics investigated [48]. Rather than studying such a general condition as employment of the mother, separation might be understood more clearly in terms of the mother's acceptance of her role, the quality of substitute care provided, the age and sex of the child, the relation of the mother's employment to family functioning and its meaning to husband–wife relations [49].

The question of the presence or absence or the father is likewise a very global condition. Studies of children in father-absent homes have consistently shown boys to be more effeminate, infantile and dependent than boys in father-present homes [11]. These results may be due to not having a chance to envy the father's superior status and privileges. Wanting the status and privileges of the father would spur the boy to try to become like the father, but the boy who had no father to envy would experience no such push toward growing up. In a more positive vein, one study [40] of kindergarten boys found that those with the most masculine interests—that is, those who have most completely adopted the masculine role—have fathers who are warmer and have more affectionate relations with their sons than boys with more feminine interests. The more masculine boys also have fathers who do more caretaking of their sons and who tend to take more responsibility in setting child-rearing policies in their families. It is not, therefore, the mere presence of a father in the family that makes for masculine boys but the presence of a father who is warm, close and involved with his sons. Little has been said or written about the effect of the father's absence on girls.

It is sometimes held that when a parent leaves the family through divorce, death or any other separation, a preschool child is likely to interpret the disruption as due to his own unworthiness. Hence he would suffer a separation anxiety. Since fathers leave households more often than mothers, they are more likely than mothers to cause this kind of fear in preschool children. Definite conclusions about the effects of the father's presence await further research.

Practical Applications of Research on Fear and Anxiety

Although some fears are inevitable and even desirable (caution has survival value), children can learn to deal with frightening situations, and adults can help them to do so. Adults can also arrange and plan so as to prevent the development of extreme fears and anxiety. The following procedures are often valuable:

1. When the child is to be separated from the people to whom he is attached, make the transition gradual.
2. At times of crisis, such as illness, keep the child with a person to whom he is attached.
3. Teach the child techniques for coping with situations in which he is inadequate.
4. Prepare the child for dealing constructively with situations which are about to come up. Talking, stories and dramatic play are useful for this purpose.
5. Use the child's spontaneous expressions of fears, in fantasy, dreams, dramatic play and artistic productions, to gain insight into what he fears and why he does so, in order to help him deal with the fears.
6. Never force a child into a situation he fears. Rather, minimizing the threat, such as by caging the animal which frightens him, encourage him to approach it in such a way that no harm occurs to him.
7. When a child is frightened by bad dreams, comfort him immediately, make sure that he wakens and agrees that the experience was a dream, not real, and put him back in his own bed, with a light if he wishes.

CHARACTER DEVELOPMENT

Both common sense and research show that the American child develops his morality largely through family living. His parents teach him what is right and what is wrong. They push him toward what they consider good behavior and pull him away from the bad. They hold up their ideals for him to see, their inspirations to light the way for him, too. In addition to all this conscious, direct teaching, parents and others exert influences of which they are not aware and which they can turn neither off nor on.

Definition of Character

"Character is the habitual mode of bringing into harmony the tasks presented by internal demands and by the external world" [44, pp. 1–2]. One function of the personality is to find these modes and to carry through the organizing and integrating required. Another function is to determine what demands from the external world shall be heard. Other demands come from the individual's body and some from unconscious parts of his being. For instance, the child, feeling hungry, searches around to get food in a way he feels to be acceptable, such as asking Mother for a cookie and a glass of milk rather than climbing onto the counter or opening the refrigerator.

Sequence of Development

The schemas of character, like all the other behavior patterns of the child, undergo changes with experience and age. Although the preschool child is very different from the infant in his moral behavior, he still has a long way to go in the path toward character maturity. The two-year-old is in the "into-everything" stage. Able to run, climb, manipulate, explore, feed himself and talk, he can get many gratifications for himself. At this point demands from the external world come largely through Mother's voice and hands, supplemented by Father's and other adults. The toddler will pause in what he is doing when someone tells him to stop, or he will do so most of the time. Unless a toy is substituted for the cigarette lighter or the honey pot placed out of reach on the table, the next moment is likely to find the young child once more trying to make fire or to lick and stick.

The next easily observed step in character development occurs when the child obeys rules while watched. Ellen, just under three, was fascinated by Lucy, a doll that belonged to Susan, age five. Susan, knowing Ellen's passion for poking Lucy's blue glass eyes fringed with long black lashes, made a strict rule that Ellen was never to touch Lucy. One day Ellen came home from nursery school to behold Lucy sitting on the sofa. She fell on the doll with cries of joy, began to poke Lucy's eyes and paused when her mother chided her, "Ellen, you know Susie doesn't want you to touch Lucy."

"But Mummy," Ellen said in hurt surprise, "Susie isn't here!"

The voice which commanded Ellen to inhibit impulses toward Lucy was entirely external. When the voice was away at kindergarten, it simply wasn't there, and Ellen felt no restraint.

During the years between three and six, some of the voice of society, via the family, is taken into the child, internalized, made his own, integrated with the rest of his personality. Research shows that internalization takes place most readily when parents are warmly affectionate, firm and consistent [15, 20, 24, 41, 44]. When the love of the parents has become important to the child, then the winning of their approval is also important. Indeed, the child often takes the role of the parents in talking to himself, either aloud or silently, as did the two-year-old who wet her pants and then said to her uncle, who was taking care of her: "Naughty girl! You must come and tell Mommy" [32]. The child was playing the mother role, making comments appropriate to the disciplinary function of the mother. This incident, implied many times in many settings, suggests how the child comes to withdraw approval from himself when he does "wrong" and approves himself when he does "right." Warmly affectionate (nurturant) parents, who have thus been rewarding to the child will be imitated more and their roles learned better and internalized more into the child. Hoffman [20] shows that children whose internalized moral standards are also adaptive and realistic tend to have parents who show disappointment when the child does not live up to their standards. Instead of threatening to withdraw their love or belittling the child, such parents show that they believe the child can live up to the ideal if he would. Thus although the child feels hurt at the time, he too believes that he can do what the parents expect.

Hoffman says, ". . . we may tentatively conclude that an internalized moral orientation is fostered by an affectionate relationship between the parent and child, in combination with the use of discipline, techniques which utilize this relationship by appealing to the child's personal and social motives."

The mechanisms by which a loving, nurturant parent figure becomes the most effective punisher are analyzed by Unger [52], who argues that strong internal controls cannot grow in a child without an adult who combines the nurturing and punishing functions.* Throughout infancy, the parent's presence is associated with comfort, pleasant stimulation, relief of hurts and tensions. Absence or unavailability means the opposite, especially during the time when fear of strangers is dominant. The child learns that certain acts on his part result in withdrawal of the parent and consequent anxiety for him. The parent makes it easier for the child to identify these acts and their results by verbalizing it. "That was naughty. You make Mommy angry when you hit the baby." Sending the child to his room or otherwise isolating him has the same effect. Facial cues and tones of voice associated with these situations become sufficient to induce anxiety over the possibility of parental withdrawal. Thus a parent who has never given spanking or other harsh punishment may be able to control a child by a mere frown or look. This is the foundation of love-oriented discipline. The child regulates his behavior so as not to lose the nurturing presence or approval of a loving adult. The indication that loss of approval is imminent comes first from the parent, either verbally or in gesture, and secondly from the child's own language, aloud in the beginning and silent inner language eventually.

Guilt, according to Unger, is a two-stage process. The first stage is verbal. The child says to himself, "I shouldn't have done that," and the second stage is an autonomic-visceral reaction of fear or anxiety, triggered by the first stage. The second stage is the same reaction which earlier was set off by the with-

* Some critics challenge this theory by citing what happens to children brought up in communal nurseries. In both Russia and Israel, the children who live in nurseries receive little or no punishment from their parents but from the resident nurses and caretakers. Parents and children have companionship and enjoyment for the brief time that they are together. The nursery caretakers do the punishing. However, the caretakers surely also reward the children with affectionate approval as well as tangible rewards. It is hard to believe that these women would be coldly mechanical disciplinarians, since they choose their jobs and are chosen for them on the basis of having some ability with children and desire to be with children. Why, then, would they not have many of the affectional characteristics of foster parents? It may be that the peer group takes a large part of what Americans think of as the parental role, both the rewarding and punishing aspects. Observations in both Russia [9] and Israel [30] indicate that this may be so.

drawal or threatened withdrawal of the nurturing parent but now is activated by the child's own words to himself. The words to himself are, of course, derived from previous situations where the loving and beloved adult expressed disapproval. Now, in order to end the unpleasant autonomic-visceral reaction of fear or anxiety, he must undo the situation which caused his words to himself. If his past experience with the loving adult taught him that a confession or apology would undo or make up for what he did wrong, then he will confess or apologize and will feel better. If he learned that he must pay for wrongdoing by enduring a spanking or giving up a privilege, then he will attempt to find a punishment that represents these punishments. Or he may have learned that wrongdoing cannot be undone and that he must bear a burden of guilt indefinitely. In the meantime as he continues to grow up, he is having more experiences with parental love and punishment, with doing wrong and with reinterpretations of moral behavior.

Knowing all this, can parents control their own behavior so as to produce ideal character in children? Some can more than others, but nobody can behave perfectly with his children or elsewhere. Some acts can be direct and intentional while others cannot. Love or rejection, firmness or vacillation, rigidity or flexibility, emanate from parental personalities with spontaneity. Although much parental behavior springs from unconscious sources and from parts of the personality which cannot be changed at will, there are still parts of parental roles which can be learned and can be consciously controlled. Parents "teach" some of the behavior patterns which constitute character by making their demands clear, consistent, firm and suited to the child's abilities, by showing their pleasure in the child's "good" behavior, by giving understandable reasons but not substituting them for firmness and by avoiding physical punishment.

Role of Intellectual Development in Moral Development

Moral behavior results when a person knows what is right and does it. In other words, knowledge, *judgment* and *volition* are involved. Various cultures give concrete expression to the idea that a certain stage of mental maturity is necessary before the child can exercise either judgment or volition necessary for moral behavior. The Roman Catholic first communion, at age seven, is an example. So is the widespread assumption among tribal people that a child reaches the age of reason and responsibility at about seven. Six or seven is the common age for starting school in earnest. The transition from preconceptual thought to the stage of concrete operations occurs at about the same time when changes occur in character. What precedes these changes?

The earliest judgments about what is good and bad come from what the parents impose in the way of rules and requirements. As a child comes to know the rules, *good,* to him, means following the rules and *bad* means not following them. Moral realism, according to Piaget [45, p. 106] has these features: (1) Any act which shows obedience to a rule or to an adult is good;

a rule is not something thought of by a person, but rather something ready-made, which has been revealed to the adult and is now being imposed by him. (2) The letter rather than the spirit of the law shall be observed. (3) Acts are evaluated according to how well they keep to the rules rather than according to the motives which prompted them. Results, rather than intentions, are what count.

Moral realism is illustrated by two-year-old Jacqueline Piaget, who had been told what would be the results of a laxative which her mother gave to her [45, pp. 177–191]. She nevertheless came close to tears and looked very distressed when she lost control of her sphincters. To Jacqueline, it was bad not to follow the rule about going to the toilet, even though her mother had explained that she was not responsible for the lapse. Another time, Jacqueline broke a fragile shell which Piaget had given her to play with. She was very upset over the breakage, even though her father tried to persuade her that it was not her fault.

By three or four, Piaget says, a child shows that he sees a difference between his own intentional breaking of rules and his unintentional breaches. He will plead "Not on purpose" to excuse himself. With the misdeeds of others, however, his attitude differs. Because of his egocentrism, his inability to see anything from someone else's point of view, he does not understand that another person's breaking of rules could be "not on purpose." He judges the other person's acts by the results, since the results are all that he can perceive.

The next stage of moral judgment, that of evaluating an act in terms of right and wrong intentions, is achieved as the child becomes freed from egocentrism. Piaget believes that this comes about not merely through the passage of time but through certain kinds of interactions with the environment, largely interactions with the parents. A child is helped to grow beyond egocentrism as adults cooperate with him by discussing things on an equal footing, encouraging him to find facts and to analyze them. He is hindered when adults behave authoritatively, especially when they give verbal instructions instead of letting children experiment and figure things out. Speaking of the child whose parents take pleasure in wielding authority, Piaget says, "Even when grown up, he will be unable, except in very rare cases, to break loose from the affective schemas acquired in this way, and will be as stupid with his own children as his parents were with him" [45, p. 19].

Piaget's observations on moral judgment were first published in 1932. The decade of the sixties is seeing an explosion of publications stemming from his conceptions. The question of the timing of processes has been of special interest to Americans. Boehm [7] shows that some American preschool children have developed faster than Piaget's Swiss subjects in being able to distinguish verbally between intentions and consequences of acts. Using Piaget's stories, Boehm tested for maturity of moral judgment 51 preschool children from two socioeconomic levels, middle-class and working-class. She found that more than a third of the children were able to judge intentions in one of the stories, although none of Piaget's had done so. Mental age and cultural background seemed to have some influence on the age of attaining the more mature kind of judgment, with a larger proportion of the more mature children in the middle class and in the Jewish groups. The results of this study are in harmony with Piaget's comments on the role played by parents in helping their children to achieve moral maturity. It is consistent with other studies which indicate that the middle-class families would exceed working-class families in democratic discussion [5, 33] and that the Jewish families would similarly exceed the non-Jewish [31]. The changes which Piaget urged in parental use of authority seem actually to have taken place in the trend toward democratic parent practices noted in America [39]. Perhaps the acceleration of Boehm's sample of American children in regard to moral judgment can be attributed to such changes in parental practice.

What of *willing* to do the right thing, or moral action? The judging and the doing do not necessarily go together. Everyone has had the experience of judging that something was wrong and doing it anyway, or of doing something which he did not know to be wrong even though he later realized that it was. Some people know very well what is right and wrong, but choose to do what gives them the greatest pleasure instead of what is right.

The idea of an age or stage of reason and responsibility comes into the topic of moral action, as well as moral judgment. Nobody expects a newborn baby to choose to do right or wrong, but almost everyone considers a seven-year-old to have some freedom of choice. When and how does the will come to control behavior?

The language development which takes place during the preschool period is fundamental to voluntary behavior and hence to moral action. Luria [29] traces four stages through which speech comes to exercise a regulating influence on behavior:

1. At 18 months to two years, the *initiating function* can be seen. The toddler will clap his hands on command. Instructions will not change an activity that is underway, however. If you tell a child to take off his socks while he is putting them on, or to put rings on a bar while he is taking them off, he cannot change his actions. He only intensifies the efforts he is making.
2. At three to four years, the child can follow both initiating and inhibiting instructions. He can *wait* for a signal, after being told to do so. However, the initiating part of the instruction is stronger and often the child can inhibit only briefly. If he gets continuous verbal instruction, however, he can inhibit more easily.
3. At about four years, when the child's own speech is well developed, he can use it to *start and stop* his own actions. He can follow instructions as to using his own speech for voluntary acts.
4. External regulatory speech becomes internal. The child no longer says it out loud but to himself when he regulates his behavior.

In regard to moral behavior, language has another important function in addition to that of starting and stopping actions. Language is the means by which the child evaluates his actions. "I shouldn't have done that" is the first part of the process of guilt as described by Unger. (See page 287.) There is widespread agreement that signs of guilt in children can be seen first at four or five years of age, the very time when children reach Luria's third stage in the use of speech to regulate behavior. "I shouldn't do that" is avoidance-mediating, anticipating an anxiety reaction. Talking to oneself is thus involved in feeling guilt and in avoiding guilt by means of controlling one's behavior. Since a certain stage of language development has to be reached before speech can regulate behavior, it follows that intellectual growth plays an essential role in moral behavior. Parents and other family members influence the child enormously in helping him to use language in organizing his mental processes and his behavior. Table 9–2 summarizes moral development in childhood.

TABLE 9–2

Summary of developmental changes basic to character.

Age	*Moral Behavior*	*Cognitive and Volitional Behavior*
2	Pauses at *no*. *Good* means following the rule or instruction.	Initiating function of speech. Verbalizes role of parent.
3	Obeys when watched.	Inhibiting function of speech.
4	Begins to internalize demands of parents.	Judges other people by acts, not intentions, but sees difference between his own intentions and unintentional breaking of rules.
	Some feelings of guilt.	Uses his own speech to initiate.
6	Conscience fairly internalized. Definitely feels guilt.	Uses language to evaluate his actions.

THE SELF

An adult knows himself as both subject and object. He feels, he knows, he is; he can stand off and look at himself, his feelings, his actions, his relationships. As far as anyone knows, man is the only creature who can look at himself as an object. It is a viewpoint which begins as the infant distinguishes between his body and the rest of reality and which develops gradually, during the preschool period as the child moves from preconceptual thought toward objectivity. Further elaboration of the self takes place throughout the whole period of development, perhaps throughout all of life.

The development of sense of autonomy means that the child gets a clearer and clearer concept of himself as a person separate from other objects and other people, distinct in body and distinct in actions. With the growth of the sense of initiative, the child enlarges his concept of self by relating it to the world. Having made himself separate and distinct, he integrates his self-concept by trying on different roles (playing fireman, nurse, teacher) exploring and expressing himself in various media.

Investigations of the development of the self-concept have taken two main forms, observing overt actions that have to do with the self and examining evidence from the unconscious. Ames [1] has traced verbalized concepts of self by noting comments made by children of different ages. The two-year-old's typical remarks are about *me* and *mine*. The three-year-old says *me too, we, our, let's, I like you, do you like me?* A typical four-year-old's comment is "I'm bigger than you are." These verbalizations show first a concern with the self, then some thinking of the self along with others, and finally, a comparing of the self with others.

Self Concept in Deprived Children

One of the outstanding characteristics of severely deprived children is lack of self-concept. Such a child may not even realize that he is a person or that he has a name which distinguishes him from others. In Project Head Start and similar programs for poor children, great emphasis is put on teaching the child that he is a distinct individual, important because he is a person. The child is helped to establish self-confidence and self-esteem as he forms a clear and definite idea of himself. Teachers use many methods for promoting self-concepts. They provide mirrors, full-length if possible, in places where children can easily look at themselves. They take pictures of the children, show them and discuss them. They may draw pictures or silhouettes of the children. Songs and games are made up to include the children's names. Feelings of autonomy and worthiness are stimulated by opportunities for successful decisions, achievement and recognition. The teacher's respect for the individual child and her warm response to him are very basic in the development of his self-concept [43].

While Head Start programs varied widely in procedures, quality and scope, due to the haste with which the whole project was begun, the notion of promoting self-concept is one which almost every program implemented carefully. Apparently, professional teachers and volunteers alike found the idea an appealing one. It was easy to understand, when once it had been pointed out, that deprived children were likely to have poor self-concepts and that in order to develop normally, they had to come to regard themselves in clearer, more positive terms.

Body Image

An interesting approach to the study of the self is through the study of body image as conducted by Fisher and Cleveland [16]. The common idea of body image is probably the mental picture of one's body. To Fisher and Cleveland, however, body image includes the images, attitudes toward and feelings about the body, many of them unconscious, which represent the self and summarize the effects of the child's interaction with the world. The relationships a child has with important people, especially the baby with his mother, are internalized as part of the body image. (This idea is similar to the widespread view that the child sees himself as others see him, that his concept of self grows from the roles he takes with other people and his interpretation of their roles).

Fisher and Cleveland measured the clarity of body image in terms of the definiteness with which the person perceives the boundary between his body and the rest of the world.* They have found interesting relationships between methods of childrearing and personality characteristics. Comparing nine cultural groups, they concluded that high boundary scores (definite, clear body image) were associated with permissive acceptance of impulse release in young children. The Bhils, an Indian tribe, who made the highest average score, nurse their children until about three, feed them when they cry, toilet-train them in relaxed style and express feelings freely. The authors theorize that the more a parent inhibits a child, the more antagonistic their relationship becomes, the harder it is to work out close communication between them, the less easily will the child take the parent as a model and the less definite will the child's body image be.

Evidence obtained by Fisher and Cleveland from psychiatric patients suggests that low scorers (indefinite body image) tend to have spent their early years in a family atmosphere of restrictiveness, narrow range of permissible behavior, blocked outlets for relieving tension; they tend to see their parents as threatening, destructive and disrupting. High scorers tend to come from families where expectations of children are clear and firm, modes of controlling them are open and defined and the parents represent devotion to a limited number of primary values and lines of living.

Whether one starts with the concept of *character* or *self* or *body* or *body image,* the research results converge on the topic of teaching and learning within the family during the early years of life. There is agreement about the importance of clarity, firmness, affection and commitment to values on the part of parents. However, it is an open question as to how much parents can purposely and voluntarily influence children's personality growth.

Sex Role

Sex is an inevitable and significant category in which an individual must locate himself. "Are you a little boy or a little girl?" was a question on an old intelligence test which most three-year-olds were expected to answer correctly. In recent years, much effort has gone into finding out how little boys and little girls get to know the answer, what they feel about it and what they do about it. Although the basic knowledge, feelings and action patterns concern-

* Using data from Rorschach tests to give two scores relating to body image.

ing sex role get established in the infant and preschool periods, much learning about his sex role occurs later also.

THE DEFINITION OF MALE AND FEMALE ROLES. Every culture defines the meaning of male and female, basing it somewhat but not consistently on biological characteristics. The variety of definitions is amazing. In Mead's [37] words:

> Now it is boys who are thought of as infinitely vulnerable and in need of special, cherishing care, now it is girls. In some societies it is girls for whom parents must collect a dowry or make husband-catching magic, in others the parental worry is over the difficulty of marrying off the boys. Some peoples think of women as too weak to work out of doors, others regard women as the appropriate bearers of heavy burdens, "because their heads are stronger than men's". . . . In some countries the women are regarded as sieves through whom the best-guarded secrets will sift; in others it is the men who are the gossips.

A study of 110 cultures [3] showed widespread trends in sex role teaching. A majority of societies stressed achievement and self-reliance in boys and nurturance and responsibility in girls. In societies where obedience was required, it tended to be of girls more than of boys. Thus, while certain kinds of work or functions can be assigned to either sex, there is considerable consistency in the personality traits which human beings attempt to encourage in one sex or the other.

Listen in on several informal campus discussions and you are sure to find a group pondering on just what is feminine behavior and what is masculine, or what should they be. You may find every shade of opinion from "Woman's place is in the home" to "There is no difference in what men and women can do, outside of the reproductive role." While a simple, stable society defines sex roles so exactly that everybody knows the score, a complex, changing society such as the American, offers definitions that vary from one family to another, with occupation and social class, with ethnic group religion and with place of residence. What Mr. and Mrs. Jones tell Johnny he must do in order to be a real boy will differ from what their neighbors, Mr. and Mrs. Peabody, tell their Percival about real-boyness. And of course, there is a lot more to the process than just telling.

DIFFERENTIAL TREATMENT OF BOYS AND GIRLS. Once we gave a pink sweater before a baby was born. When the baby turned out to be a boy, the mother expressed regrets that she would have to save the sweater until she had a girl. That little boy's color scheme was to leave no doubt in him or in anybody else as to what sex he was! He soon received a wealth of trucks, cars and erector sets but no dolls. We think he was allowed to keep the teddy bear that an auntie gave him. His father played boisterously with him, stimulating vigorous motor play, acting casual about bumps, discouraging tears. And what happened when someone came along to occupy our pink sweater? She received dolls and homemaking toys. She was held tenderly. Her father stroked her curls, tickled her chin and taught her to bat her long eyelashes at him. Big Brother stroked her curls, tickled her chin and elicited eye-batting too. The mother applauded when Brother was aggressive, active and courageous and when Sister was nurturant, beguiling and sensitive. Often the parents' techniques of influence were subtle—a pat, a shove, a smile, a frown, a tight voice, a song. At other times they were direct—"Don't do that, Brother. Be a big man, like Daddy" or "I was so proud of my girl, acting like a regular little lady."

TEACHING BIOLOGICAL SEX DIFFERENCES. The little boy learns that he is a boy before he realizes that the possession of a penis makes a child a boy. Similarly for the girl. Mead [38] reports some evidence that girl babies a few months old can tell the difference between men and women and they act differently toward men and women. The differential treatment of boys and girls makes it clear to them that they belong to one sex or the other. In a clothed society, especially one which prescribes highly distinctive dress for the sexes, children first express the difference between boys from girls in terms of their outfits and hairdos. Chapter 5 showed that parents often avoid labeling the sexual parts of the body, sex feeling and activities [47, p. 412]. However, when a person knows the name of something, he can discuss it better and reason about it, since labeling is an important aid to learning. Advice to parents from authorities has consistently stated the desirability of telling children the names of their sex organs and of answering their questions directly. Questions during the preschool years are usually first about the names of the sex organs, then about sex differences, such as whether a girl has lost her penis and if not why not. Answers that clarify and reassure are, "A boy has a penis and testicles." "A girl has a vulva and vagina." "Boys grow up to be fathers; girls grow up to be mothers."

Questions about where babies come from are to be expected. "The baby grew inside its mother" is simple and true. The next question, "How did it get out?" is almost inevitable in a preschool child whose questions have been answered in a trust-promoting way. "The vagina stretches to let the baby out. The mother works to push him through." This type of answer is reassuring if it implies that both mothers and babies can cope with the process of birth and if it leaves the way open for more questions. Questions about fertilization and mating rarely come during the preschool period, and if they do, they are simple questions about physiology, not love.

SEX ROLE PREFERENCES. In order to find out which sex role a child actually preferred the *It Test* was devised [10]. "It" is pictured as a child figure which is ambiguous as to sex. Boys and girls were tested with pictures of objects which are sex-typed in our society, asking them whether "It" would rather play with a doll or a tractor, would rather wear trousers or a dress, and so on for 36 items. Boys at all ages who were tested, starting at three and a half, showed a strong preference for the masculine role. Girls between three and a half and six and a half were heterogeneous, some showing a strong preference for the feminine role, some predominantly masculine and some in between. These possible reasons are suggested to explain why role preferences were thus: the anatomical difference (emphasized by Freud), in which boys are seen to have and girls to have not; masculine superiority in this culture, and in most cultures; the greater latitude allowed girls in sex role preference, in contrast to the great pressure put on boys to behave in masculine ways.

SEX ROLE IDENTIFICATION. The process of learning to feel and behave like a member of one sex or the other is known as sex role identification. As mentioned above, parents define sex roles for their children, reward them for playing the appropriate roles and punish, or at least withhold rewards, when the children play the wrong sex roles. Nurturant behavior from a warm adult stimulates the child to imitate the adult [40, p. 306]. These mechanisms are probably basic to sex role identification. Another mechanism may also be at work in promoting sex role identification: because the child wants to have the privileged status of another person, he practices the role of that person in fantasy or play [11]. Since for both boys and girls, the mother is the first person holding a privileged status, she who can give or withhold all that the child desires, it is her role that the young child wants. Although, ideally, girls retain female role identity and boys change over to masculine through learning to want to be like the father, it does not always happen this way.

CONCEPTS OF ROLES OF FAMILY MEMBERS. Concepts of sex role are derived to a large extent from concepts of what fathers, mothers and other family members do. The way in which the child sees the child–father relationship now will also contribute to how he sees it when he plays the father role with his own child. Likewise, his childish observations of the husband–wife roles have implications for his adult life. Tests and anecdotal records of 319 children between three and six give some indication of preschool children's concepts of fathers and mothers [54]. Since several socioeconomic levels were sampled, the results can be considered representative of a large part of the population. Some of the questions asked were these: What are daddies for? What are mothers for? What are families for? Results showed that concepts of fathers were much more limited than concepts of mothers; mothers were seen as busier than fathers, with many of the mothers' activities focused on children, and fathers being more impersonal; mothers were seen as more supporting and more punishing than fathers; fathers' affections were considered to include mothers and children, with mothers occupying a prominent place, but little indication was given that children realized that they shared the mothers' affection with the fathers.

Religion

Religion contributes to understanding of self by placing the self in relation to the rest of reality, past, present and future. While the preschool child is extremely concrete in his concepts of relationships, he does have experiences determined by the religious setting into which he is born.

Parents determine the religious orientation of their child both by uniting him with their religious community, as through circumcision or baptism; by their interpretation of man's relationships to God or gods, to man, to present, past and future; by the expressed thoughts and feelings about beauty, love and truth, animate and inanimate nature. More indirectly, parents' behavior in general is influenced by their religion.

The religious community may have little or no direct bearing on the young child, depending on how it defines him and how it contacts him. Church nurseries and Sunday school groups can be very important in the child's life. He may enter into them eagerly and actively as his only experience with a peer group. A desirable church school takes account of the child's physical and psychological needs just as a nursery school does, although it stresses religious experiences, such as sacred stories and music, enjoyment of creativity, appreciation of beauty and of nature, worship and giving. Symbolic and ritualistic performances appeal to children in the stage of developing initiative and also give them concrete experience of their religion.

The sense of trust developed in the beginning of life is the basis for faith in God or gods or the state or whatever one trusts. Since the mother first and then the father and the rest of the family are key figures in the development of the sense of trust, the family is the primary religious agent. They also play the most important roles, with the young child, in the creation of his sense of autonomy, the development of his self, his character, the standards of right and wrong which he makes his own.

The child begins early to muse upon the religious mysteries of which he becomes aware. "What does God look like?" "Why do the angels just come at Christmas time?" "What does *dead* mean?" "When do the seeds start to grow under the earth and how do they know it's time?" "You won't die before I'm grown up, will you?" "Do you think the astronauts will find heaven?" "Why doesn't God give me the toys I've been praying for?" "Don't you hate the people who killed Jesus?"

Answers to questions such as these depend upon the parent's own religion. What they say or do not say affects their child in a religious way, either helping him to build, restricting him to primitive thinking, or leaving him with gaps. Religious practices in the home can have deeply emotional as well as intellectual effects. Grace before meals, family Christmas dramatics, the seder—each of these events is a scene of family unity in which a little child feels a sense of belonging to his group and to something bigger. A memorable religious occasion often touches many of the senses and thus becomes an allover experience for the child. Consider the variety of experiences during the Hindu celebration of the festival of Ganesh or Gumpati, the god of luck who is a favorite with children. The family brings home a clay model of Gumpati, a fat little boy with an elephant's head and trunk. Placing him on a stand or table in a bare room, they heap flowers, fruit, sweets and incense at his feet. The child has large muscle experience in the walk home. He sees and touches

Gumpati. He smells the flowers and incense. He eats some of the treats. He hears the story of Gumpati's birth and early childhood. After a week or so, there is a parade with music to make and hear. Gumpati in all his glory is transported to the river or lake, where an older boy lets him sink under the waters. The child sees the dramatization of the fact that his Gumpati was only a clay figure and not the real spirit which it represented. He does not *understand* the full meaning of the drama, but he has the picture of it which can later give shape and fullness to the idea.

SUMMARY

Emotions increase in differentiation during the preschool period, as the child takes part in more interactions and more complex interactions with his parents, siblings, grandparents and other people. Nurturance offered by adults to children is an expression of their own personality, indicating degrees of development of the sense of generativity. Children's responses to adults include a small measure of nurturance and a large measure of dependence, which varies with the attitudes and behavior of the adults. Siblings are ordinarily ambivalent to each other, showing nurturance, dependence, jealousy and rivalry, according to the types of experiences they have with one another and to the attitudes and guidance techniques used by adults. Anger, an emotional response to frustration, can be hostile or constructive. Hostile aggression, an angry attack, is often but not always disapproved by parents. The developing imagination of the preschool child contributes to intangible fears, which increase greatly at this time. Concrete fears decrease. As with the infant, the presence of a loved person (attachment object) reassures the frightened child. Research suggests methods of controlling and minimizing anger, jealousy, rivalry and fear in young children.

Character is the characteristic way in which a person harmonizes his own needs and desires with the demands of the outside world. Considerable development of character takes place during the preschool years, when the child increases in knowledge of rules, in his ability to judge right from wrong and in his will to do right. Beginning as a person who requires outer control, he grows toward self-control, internalizing the demands of himself. Parental practices and attitudes are extremely significant in determining the type of character built by the child. The child's intellectual growth is part and parcel of his moral growth.

The young child gradually becomes more and more aware of himself as a distinct body and person, separate from other objects and persons. His increasingly complex interactions contribute to his growing concept of self. Through language and dramatic play, he explores, integrates and expands this concept. His increasing intellectual powers permit greater flexibility of thought, which he eventually uses to view himself as others see him. The establishment and acceptance of his sex role contributes to the concept of self. Male and female roles are outlined by the culture and defined in detail by the family. The family teaches by direct instruction and prohibition, by sex-typing the environment, and by differential treatment of boys and girls. Children respond by identifying with one role or another, by their preference for either role and by the concepts of family members which they build. Religion contributes broadly to the self-concept, by placing the person in a broad orientation to all of existence.

REFERENCES

1. Ames, L. B. The sense of self of nursery school children as manifested by their verbal behavior. *J. Genet. Psychol.,* 1952, **81,** 193–232.
2. Baldwin, A. L. Changes in parent behavior during pregnancy. *Child Devel.,* 1947, **18,** 29–39.
3. Barry, H., Bacon, M. K., & Child, I. L. A cross-cultural survey of some sex differences in socialization. *J. Abn. Soc. Psychol.,* 1957, **55,** 327–332.
4. Baruch, D. W., & Wilcox, J. A. A study of sex differences in preschool children's adjustment coexistent with interparental tensions. *J. Genet. Psychol.,* 1944, **64,** 281–303.
5. Bayley, N., & Schaefer, E. S. Relationships between socioeconomic variables and the behavior of mothers toward young children. *J. Genet. Psychol.,* 1960, **96,** 61–77.
6. Beller, E. K. Dependency and independence in young children. *J. Genet. Psychol.,* 1955, **87,** 25–35.
7. Boehm, L. The development of conscience of preschool children: a cultural and subcultural comparison. *J. Soc. Psychol.,* 1963, **59,** 355–360.
8. Bowlby, J. *Maternal care and mental health.* Geneva: World Health Organization, 1951.
9. Bronfenbrenner, U. Soviet methods of character education: some implications for research. *Am. Psychol.,* 1962, **17,** 550–564.
10. Brown, D. G. Sex-role development in a changing culture. *Psychol. Bull.,* 1958, **55,** 232–242.
11. Burton, R. V., & Whiting, J. W. M. The absent father and cross-sex identity. *Merrill-Palmer Quart.,* 1961, **7,** 85–97.
12. Davis, W. A., & Havighurst, R. J. *Father of the man.* Boston: Houghton Mifflin, 1947.
13. Duvall, E. M. *Inlaws: pro and con.* New York: Association, 1954.
14. Erikson, E. H. *Identity and the life cycle.* New York: International Universities, 1959.
15. Finney, J. C. Some maternal influences on children's personality and character. *Genet. Psychol. Mono.,* 1961, **63,** 199–278.
16. Fisher, S., & Cleveland, S. E. *Body image and personality.* New York: Van Nostrand, 1958.
17. Hagman, R. R. A study of the fears of children of preschool age. *J. Exptl. Educ.,* 1932, **1,** 110–130.

18. Hartup, W. W. Dependence and independence. In H. W. Stevenson, J. Kagan & C. Spiker, *Child psychology*. The Sixty-second Yearbook of the National Society for the Study of Education. Chicago: Univer. of Chicago, 1963, pp. 333–363.
19. Heinicke, C. M. Some effects of separating two-year-old children from their mothers. *Hum. Relat.*, 1956, **9,** 102–176.
20. Hoffman, M. L. Childrearing practices and moral development: generalizations from empirical research. *Child Devel.*, 1963, **34,** 295–318.
21. Jersild, A. T., & Holmes, F. B. Children's fears. *Child Devel. Mono.*, No. 20. New York: Teachers College, Columbia Univer., 1935.
22. John, E. A study of the effects of evacuation and air raids on children of preschool age. *Brit. J. Educ. Psychol.*, 1941, **11,** 173–182.
23. Johnson, A. M., & Szurek, S. A. The genesis of antisocial acting out in children and adults. *Psychoan. Quart.*, 1952, **21,** 323–343.
24. Jones, V. Character development in children—an objective approach. In L. Carmichael (Ed.), *Manual of child psychology*. New York: Wiley, 1954, pp. 781–828.
25. Kagan, J., & Moss, H. A. *Birth to maturity*. New York: Wiley, 1962.
26. Koch, H. L. The relation of certain formal attributes of siblings to attitudes held toward each other and toward their parents. *Mono. Soc. Res. Child Devel.*, 1960, **25:**4.
27. Koch, M. B. Anxiety in preschool children from broken homes. *Merrill-Palmer Quart.*, 1961, **7,** 225–232.
28. Levy, D. *Maternal overprotection*. New York: Columbia Univer., 1943.
29. Luria, A. R. *The role of speech in the regulation of normal and abnormal behavior*. New York: Pergamon, 1961.
30. Luria, Z., Goldwasser, M., & Goldwasser, A. Response to transgression in stories by Israeli children. *Child Devel.*, 1963, **34,** 271–280.
31. Luria, Z., & Rebelsky, F. Ethnicity: a variable in sex differences in moral behavior. Paper presented at the meeting of the *Society for Research in Child Development,* April 1963.
32. Maccoby, E. E. Role-taking in childhood and its consequences for social learning. *Child Devel.*, 1959, **30,** 239–252.
33. Maccoby, E. E., & Gibbs, P. K. Methods of childrearing in two social classes. In W. E. Martin & C. B. Stendler (Eds.), *Readings in child development*. New York: Harcourt, Brace, 1954, pp. 380–396.
34. Marshall, H. Relations between home experiences and children's use of language in play interactions with peers. *Psychol. Mono.*, 1961, **75:**5.
35. Maurer, A. What children fear. *J. Genet. Psychol.*, 1965, **106,** 265–277.
36. Mead, M. *And keep your powder dry*. New York: Morrow, 1942.
37. Mead, M. *Male and female*. New York: Morrow, 1949.
38. Mead, M. In J. M. Tanner & B. Inhelder, *Discussions on child development,* Vol. 3. New York: International Universities, 1955.
39. Miller, D. R., & Swanson, G. E. *The changing American parent*. New York: Wiley, 1958.
40. Mussen, P., & Distler, L. Childrearing antecedents of masculine identification in kindergarten boys. *Child Devel.*, 1960, **31,** 89–100.

41. Mussen, P. H., & Parker, A. L. Mother nurturance and girls' incidental imitative learning. *J. Pers. Soc. Psychol.*, 1965, **2,** 94–97.
42. Neugarten, B. L., & Weinstein, K. K. The changing American grandparent. *J. Marr. Fam.*, 1964, **26,** 199–204.
43. Office of Economic Opportunity. *Project Head Start Daily Program I.* Washington, D.C.: Government Printing Office, 1965.
44. Peck, R. F., & Havighurst, R. J. *The psychology of character development.* New York: Wiley, 1960.
45. Piaget, J. *The moral judgment of the child.* Glencoe, Ill.: Free Press, 1960.
46. Rosen, B. C. Socialization and achievement motivation in Brazil. *Am. Soc. Rev.*, 1962, **27,** 612–624.
47. Sears, R. R., Maccoby, E. E., & Levin, H. *Patterns of child rearing.* Evanston, Ill.: Row, Peterson, 1957.
48. Siegel, A. E., Stolz, L. M., Hitchcock, E. A., & Adamson, J. M. Dependence and independence in the children of working mothers. *Child Devel.*, 1959, **30,** 533–546.
49. Stolz, L. M. Effects of maternal employment on children: evidence from research. *Child Devel.*, 1960, **31,** 749–782.
50. Stolz, L. M. Forty years in the study of children: 1920–1960. Paper presented at the meeting of the *National Association for Nursery Education,* Philadelphia, October 24, 1962.
51. Sweetser, D. A. The social structure of grandparenthood. In R. F. Winch, R. McGinnis & H. R. Barringer, *Selected studies in marriage and the family.* New York: Holt, 1962, pp. 388–396.
52. Unger, S. M. On the development of guilt reactivity in the child. Paper presented at meetings of *The Society for Research in Child Development,* April 1963.
53. Waldrop, M. F., & Bell, R. Q. Relation of preschool dependency behavior to family size and density. *Child Devel.*, 1964, **35,** 1187–1195.
54. Wann, K. D., Dorn, M. S., & Liddle, E. A. *Fostering intellectual development in young children.* New York: Teachers College, Columbia Univer., 1962.
55. Whiting, J. W. M. *Becoming a Kwoma.* New Haven, Conn.: Yale Univer., 1941.
56. Whiting, J. W. M., & Child, I. *Child training and personality.* New Haven, Conn.: Yale Univer., 1953.

Dawn

PART III

The School-Age Child

Introduction

Almost all cultures take some notice of the child's entering a new phase of life at six or seven years of age. Although, as Piaget has pointed out, there are no general stages which are unique wholes, yet age six or seven marks a shift in important processes of development. The fact that formal education is begun at this time in so many different cultures indicates widespread perception of such a shift. Likewise, writers from Shakespeare to Erikson have made use of this age in dividing life into portions that can be studied. We begin our discussion of this segment of life at six or seven years and end it at the point where the pubescent growth spurt starts, an average age of 10, but a point which occurs within a wide range of years.

The loss of his preschool cuteness is not serious to the schoolchild. While an occasional child may mourn the passing of the days when adults thought him perfectly adorable just because he was a young child, most reports of such feelings of regret are from adults looking far backward toward early childhood. By the time he enters first grade, the healthy child has achieved enough trust, autonomy and initiative that he wants to become involved with a private world of children, where adults are often unwelcome. Adults are, of course, necessary at times. He loves his parents and cares what they think, but his appetite for sitting on laps and being petted is definitely diminished. Teachers and club leaders are important too, but in limited time and space. It seems as though the child withdraws most into his private sphere of peers and self at the very time (around 10) when he is least attractive to adults—most gangly, least cuddly, restless, dirty, teeth missing, and speaking a language of childhood that is not completely comprehensible to adults.

Building on all that has gone before, the child interacts with a widening world to create new and more complex behavior patterns. Instead of being confined to family, home and neighborhood, the child is on his own in the school. Warm and acceptant as his teacher may be, he is not special to her, as he is to his mother. He is one of many, and as such, must live with a kind of objectivity which he has not experienced before. Instead of playing with only little boys and girls who are the children of his parents' friends and neighbors, he plays and works with a variety of children. Meeting children from a social class different from his own, he may be surprised to find some of his schoolmates cleaner or dirtier, rougher or gentler, more or less interested in doing well at school than he. Playing in the homes of new friends, he discovers parents, behavior, houses and yards unlike those he has known. Joining Cubs, Brownies, Bluebirds or a similar organized group, the child embraces a new culture of symbolic pins, handclasps and reflecting pools which symbolize his belongingness. His religious connections will expand too. He may make his first communion or begin the study of Hebrew. The public library will enlarge his literary world by conferring the privilege of taking books out. If he lives in a community which sponsors children's concerts, he will be eligible to go to them. Thus he will interact directly with many aspects of the culture which formerly influenced him only through his family.

Privacy is a kind of freedom much enjoyed by the school-age child. Because he is able to take basic physical care of himself and his room, he is often able to keep mother and others out of his room, out of the bathroom, and out of his most secret transactions. Privacy means freedom to take his bath just the way he likes it, to make funny faces in the mirror, to devise messages, signals, codes, club rules, to visit alone with friends. Reading books means freedom to roam in a vast world of thought and imagination. Fast-growing competency in language and thought means greater facility in dealing with all of his private world.

Industry is the name Erikson gives to the stage of personality development of the schoolchild. He has also called it *duty and accomplishment*. This is the time when jobs get done, in contrast to the stage of initiative, when they got started but rarely finished. Having explored all sorts of possibilities for action, the child settles down to learn how to do things and to do them well. He becomes involved in the technology of his culture, whether it stresses fishing and making canoes, or reading, writing and electronics. Withdrawing from home, mother and the emotional situations involved in them, he turns to the objects, tools and techniques of the society in which he lives. Most cultures make provisions for this change-over. Literate societies provide schools where teachers begin the long process of teaching reading and writing. Even in simpler cultures, teachers usually help the children learn the appropriate aspects of technology. Often boys learn farming from their fathers and girls homemaking from their mothers. In American culture, an astonishing number of specialists teach such extracurricular subjects as music, dancing, painting, bird watching, star gazing, first aid, camping and skiing. Recreation workers and youth leaders teach not only these subjects and more but also concern themselves with group dynamics, character, values, leadership, community service, and so on. It is possible for a child to spend all of his hours left over from eating, sleeping and physical care on lessons of one sort or another.

There are aspects of industry and duty which are better accomplished with other children (in the peer group) and alone, however, than in an onslaught of lessons. Take baseball, for instance. To be a real American boy, you practically have to know how to play it. As a girl, you have to know at least the rules of the game and preferably you can play softball. It takes thousands of practice throws to get to be a good pitcher and as many catches to be a baseman. Where could one do all this except in the neighborhood play lot with his friends? There are many more games whose rules and coordinations must be learned. During the school years children are willing, even eager, to practice and practice and practice—batting a ball, jumping, skating, jumping rope, singing and chanting the ditties of childhood, sewing doll clothes, cutting out cookies, playing cards and other games, identifying specimens and arranging collections. There are social skills to develop too, making and keeping close friendships and being a club member.

Success in the stage of industry results in the child's knowing the pleasure and satisfaction of a job well done. He enjoys being a part of a productive situation. He knows that he can produce, achieve and accomplish in certain areas, and in those situations, he feels adequate. There are enough of them that he has a general feeling of being an adequate person. There are some places where he does particularly well and others where he just gets by. This knowledge is incorporated into his picture of himself.

A sense of *inferiority and inadequacy* is the result when development does not go well at this time of life. Since time of entrance to school is usually fixed rigidly, the child who is not ready to enter into the stage of industry is at a great disadvantage in personality development. Failure in the beginning work is disastrous to his concept of himself as an adequate person.

Physical Characteristics and Skills

❧ CHAPTER 10 ❧

Slow growth is typical of the period of middle childhood. In both size and proportions, these children change relatively little from year to year. This statement must be qualified if menarche, and the corresponding point of male sexual maturity, are taken as the end of middle childhood, since a period of very rapid growth precedes these points in time. Although the period of rapid growth, known as the pubescent growth spurt, is discussed in Chapter 14, in regard to adolescence, it is important to realize that some children in the elementary school are already in the pubescent growth spurt. Growth in height begins to pick up speed, on the average, at about age nine in girls and 11 in boys. A few girls, however, begin the spurt as early as age eight and boys at 10. Most girls grow at top speed during their twelfth or thirteenth year, boys during their fourteenth or fifteenth year. A seventh grade classroom is sure to include a wide variety of sizes and stages of maturity. It is safe to generalize that children grow slowly during the early elementary-school years.

The middle years are healthier than the preschool period. With growth needs and the burdens of illness claiming less of his energy than they did in an earlier stage of life, the schoolchild has more of himself to invest in relationships, problem solving and acquiring of skills and knowledge. Now he works to develop and perfect many motor coordinations, enjoying the sense of adequacy which grows from successful performance. His concept of himself and his body reflect the interactions of his body with the world and also reflect his perceptions of people's reactions to him.

PHYSICAL GROWTH

Growth can be described in terms of the large, general measurements of height and weight and also in terms of various parts of the body. A third way of considering it has to do with interrelationships of various aspects of growth.

Growth in Height and Weight

The average six-year-old boy is 46¼ inches tall and weighs 48¼ pounds; a girl the same age measures 45½ inches tall and weighs 46½ pounds [37, pp. 70–73]. Tables 10–1, 10–2, 10–3 and 10–4 show average heights and

TABLE 10–1

Height percentile table for boys age 6 through age 12.

	Height in Inches						
Age	*3%*	*10%*	*25%*	*50%*	*75%*	*90%*	*97%*
6 yr.	42¾	43¾	45	46¼	47½	48½	49¾
6½ yr.	43¾	45	46	47½	49	50	51
7 yr.	45	46	47½	49	50¼	51½	52½
7½ yr.	46	47¼	48½	50	51½	52¾	53¾
8 yr.	47	48½	49¾	51¼	52¾	54	55¼
8½ yr.	48	49½	50¾	52¼	54	55	56¼
9 yr.	49	50½	51¾	53¼	55	56	57¾
9½ yr.	49¾	51½	52¾	54¼	56	57	58¼
10 yr.	50¾	52¼	53¾	55¼	56¾	58	59¼
10½ yr.	51½	53¼	54½	56	57¾	59	60
11 yr.	52½	54	55¼	56¾	58¾	59¾	60¾
11½ yr.	53½	55	56¼	57¾	59½	61	62¼
12 yr.	54½	56	57¼	59	60½	62¼	63¾

Source: From *Growth and Development of Children*, 4th edition, by Ernest H. Watson and George H. Lowrey. Copyright © 1962, Year Book Medical Publishers, Inc., Chicago. Used by permission of Year Book Medical Publishers.

TABLE 10–2

Height percentile table for girls age 6 through age 12.

	Height in Inches						
Age	*3%*	*10%*	*25%*	*50%*	*75%*	*90%*	*97%*
6 yr.	42½	43½	44½	45½	47	48	49½
6½ yr.	43¾	44¾	45¾	47	48¼	49½	50¾
7 yr.	45	46	47	48	49½	50¾	52
7½ yr.	46	47	48	49¼	50¾	52	53
8 yr.	47	48	49	50½	51¾	53	54
8½ yr.	47¾	49	50	51½	53	54	55¼
9 yr.	48¾	50	51	52¼	54	55¼	56½
9½ yr.	49½	51	52	53½	55	56½	57¾
10 yr.	50¼	51¾	53	54½	56	57½	58¾
10½ yr.	51¼	53	54	55¾	57½	59	60½
11 yr.	52	54	55¼	57	58¾	60½	62
11½ yr.	53¼	55	56¼	58¼	60¼	61¾	63½
12 yr.	54¼	56	57½	59¾	61½	63¼	64¾

Source: From *Growth and Development of Children*, 4th edition, by Ernest H. Watson and George H. Lowrey. Copyright © 1962, Year Book Medical Publishers, Inc., Chicago. Used by permission of Year Book Medical Publishers.

weights for boys and girls throughout middle childhood. At age six, 80 percent of boys measure between 45¾ and 48½ inches and weigh between 41 and 56½ pounds. Corresponding figures for girls are 43½ and 48 inches and 39½ and 54¼ pounds. Annual height gain is from two to two and three quarters inches, while weight gain is about six pounds. Girls are slightly

TABLE 10–3

Weight percentile for boys age 6 through age 12.

	Weight in Pounds						
Age	*3%*	*10%*	*25%*	*50%*	*75%*	*90%*	*97%*
6 yr.	38½	41	44½	48¼	52	56½	61
6½ yr.	40¾	43½	47	51¼	55½	60½	65½
7 yr.	43	45¾	49¾	54	58¾	64½	70
7½ yr.	45½	48½	52½	57	62	68¾	74¾
8 yr.	48	51¼	55½	60	65½	73	79½
8½ yr.	50¼	53¾	58¼	63	69	77	84½
9 yr.	52½	56¼	61	66	72¼	81	89¾
9½ yr.	54¾	58¾	63¾	69	76	85½	95
10 yr.	56¾	61	66¼	72	79½	90	100
10½ yr.	59¼	63¾	69	74¾	83½	94½	105¾
11 yr.	61¾	66¼	71½	77½	87¼	99¼	111¾
11½ yr.	64½	69¼	74½	81	91½	104½	118
12 yr.	67¼	72	77½	84½	96	109½	124¼

Source: From *Growth and Development of Children*, 4th edition, by Ernest H. Watson and George H. Lowrey. Copyright © 1962, Year Book Medical Publishers, Inc., Chicago. Used by permission of Year Book Medical Publishers.

TABLE 10–4

Weight percentile for girls age 6 through age 12.

	Weight in Pounds						
Age	*3%*	*10%*	*25%*	*50%*	*75%*	*90%*	*97%*
6 yr.	37¼	39½	43	46½	50¼	54¼	58¾
6½ yr.	39¾	42¼	45½	49½	53¼	57¾	63
7 yr.	41¼	44½	48	52¼	56¼	61¼	67¼
7½ yr.	43¼	46½	50½	55¼	59¾	65½	73
8 yr.	45¼	48½	53	58	63¼	70	79
8½ yr.	47¼	50½	55½	61	67	74½	84½
9 yr.	49	52½	58	63¾	70½	79	90
9½ yr.	51¼	55	60½	67	74¾	84½	96
10 yr.	53¼	57	62¾	70¼	79	89¾	102
10½ yr.	55½	60	66½	74½	84	95	107½
11 yr.	58	62½	70	78¾	89	100½	113
11½ yr.	60¾	66	74	83¼	94	106	120¼
12 yr.	63½	69½	78	87½	98¾	111½	127¾

Source: From *Growth and Development of Children*, 4th edition, by Ernest H. Watson and George H. Lowrey. Copyright © 1962, Year Book Medical Publishers, Inc., Chicago. Used by permission of Year Book Medical Publishers.

shorter and lighter than boys, as they have been ever since birth, until age 11, when they overtake the boys for a brief period. Their earlier entrance into the pubescent growth spurt makes them temporarily taller and heavier. Although the average difference is small (three quarters of an inch at 12 and 13 years), a fast-maturing girl towers above a slow-growing boy, a discrepancy which causes agony if children between 11 and 15 are pushed into dancing, dating and other situations where their heights are compared. At all points in the growth cycle, girls are closer to maturity than boys, since they do not have to grow so far to reach it. For instance, 75 percent of adult height is attained by the average nine-year-old boy and by the average seven-year-old girl.

Height increases more steadily than weight, since it is influenced less by environmental changes. Both measurements are, of course, products of the organism's interaction with the environment, but since height depends almost entirely on the linear measure of skeletal growth, and since length of the skeleton is relatively resistant to environmental pressures, progress in height is quite regular. As was mentioned in Chapter 6 the bones do record such traumas as illnesses and malnutrition, but they do it in terms of bone scars, which can be detected only by X ray. Weight, in contrast to height, is a sensitive indicator of malnutrition or overnutrition. Weight is related to volume, which is the product of three linear measures. All types of body tissue, skeleton, muscles, fat, blood, and all the rest, contribute to weight. Thus although the skeleton is not shortened by illness or malnutrition, the soft tissues of the body may be reduced.

Proportions

Compared with preschool children, school-age children are graceful. With a relatively lower center of gravity, longer legs and slimmer proportions, the older child is steadier on his feet. The photographs on these pages show typical proportions during the elementary-school years as well as preschool and adolescent figures with which to compare the figures of middle childhood. (See Figures 10–1, 10–2 and 10–3.) Each new or refined coordination added to the child's motor schemas increases his poise. He fits better into adult furniture, even though it is still too big for him. He has grown out of a crib. Although his feet dangle at the table, he spurns a high chair. His new proportions make for excellent climbing, since longer arms and legs can reach more distant branches and a lower center of gravity steadies him. Similarly with bicycle-riding. Changes in growth rates also show up in facial changes. Relatively large at birth, the brain case is still large at 5. Then the face begins to catch up. The ratio of face to cranium is about one to three at 6 and one to two at 18 [3, p. 302].

The changes in body configuration which take place during the years from four and a half to seven and a half have been studied in some detail, since this is the period when the child is changing from a preschooler to a school-

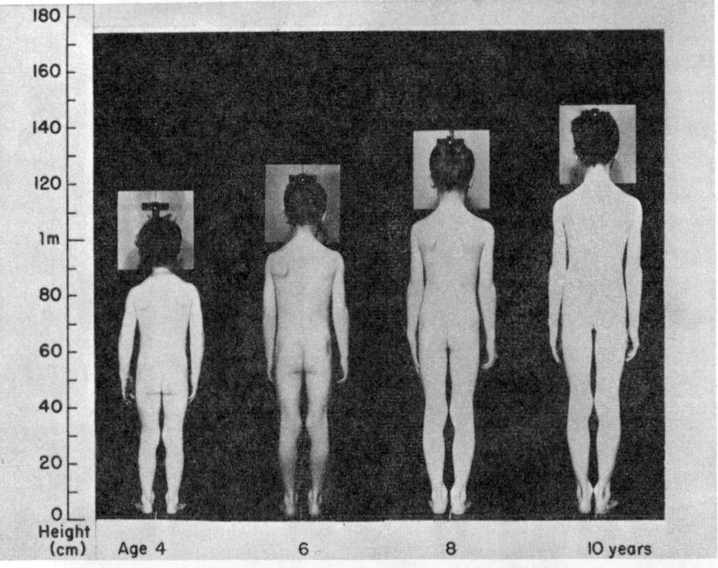

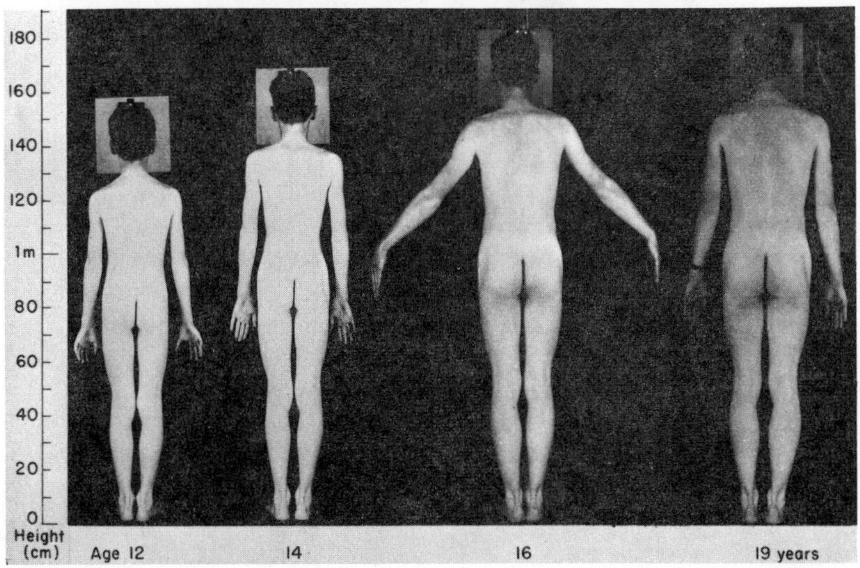

Figures 10–1 and **10–2.** A typical boy's growth from early childhood to adulthood. (Reprinted from *Growth Diagnosis,* by L. M. Bayer and N. Bayley, by permission of The University of Chicago Press. Copyright © 1959, The University of Chicago Press.)

child, from a preconceptual thinker to one who can deal with concrete operations, from one concerned with the sense of imagination to one involved in problems of the sense of industry. In a search for some physical indications of sufficient maturity for assessing school readiness, three types of body configu-

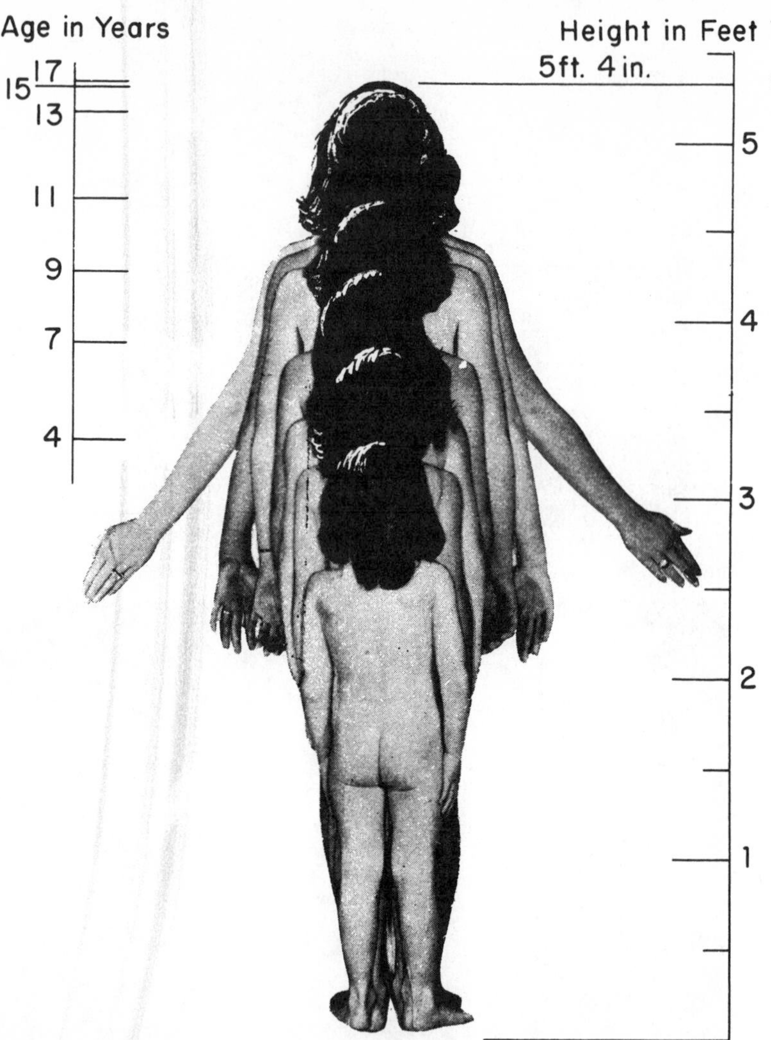

Figure 10–3. A typical girl's growth from early childhood to adulthood. (Reprinted from *Growth Diagnosis,* by L. M. Bayer and N. Bayley, by permission of The University of Chicago Press. Copyright © 1959, The University of Chicago Press.)

ration were distinguished in photographs of boys and girls [30]. Schematic drawings of the figures are shown in Figure 10–4. Judges estimated maturity in terms of both face and body. After the judges of the photographs had agreed on which ones showed the various types of proportions, measurements and relationships between measurements were studied in order to find out which indicated the three stages of maturity. Results showed a general slimming down at the beginning of the middle childhood period, making boys and girls quite similar for a while. Then the girls became more typically

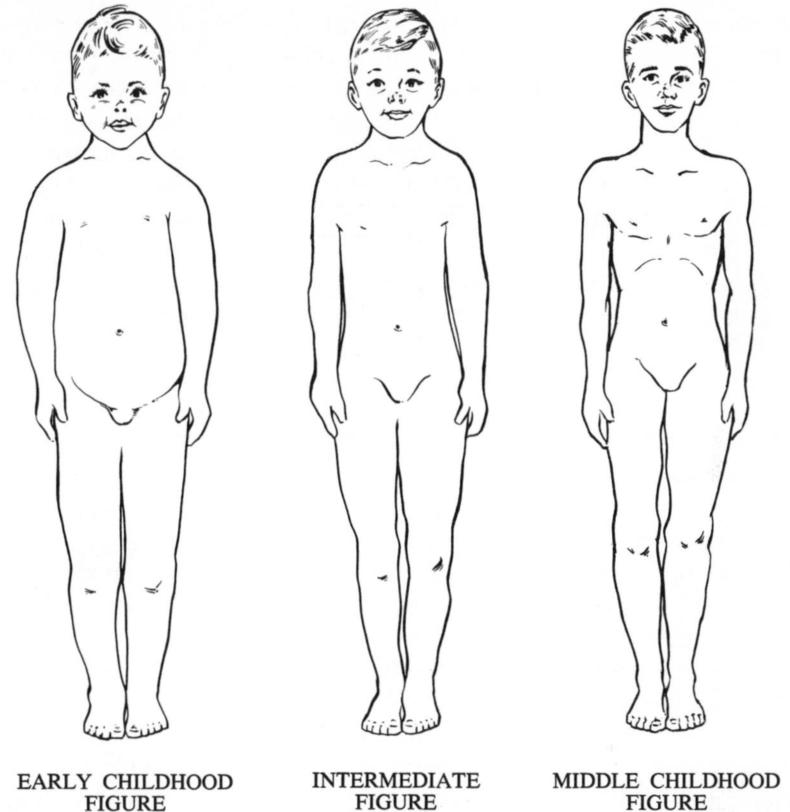

EARLY CHILDHOOD FIGURE | INTERMEDIATE FIGURE | MIDDLE CHILDHOOD FIGURE

Figure 10–4. Three types of body configuration seen in middle childhood. (Reprinted from M. D. Simon, "Body Configuration and School Readiness," *Child Development,* **30,** Figure 1. Copyright © 1959, The Society for Research in Child Development, Inc.)

feminine (rounded). Several indices proved useful in showing increasing maturity: head circumference to standing height (decreasing), waist circumference to height (decreasing) and leg length to height (increasing). Head circumference to leg length (decreasing) was found to be a good indication of maturity of proportions. The typical early childhood ratio was 86 for boys and 85 for girls, intermediate figures were 85 and 81 and middle childhood 81 and 81. Maturity of body configuration was found to be associated with success in first grade and immaturity with failure. Apparently physical maturity, as indicated by proportions, tells something about the child's readiness for meeting the demands of school.

Tissues and Organs

Certain physiological and anatomical characteristics are especially typical of middle childhood. Those mentioned in the following description contribute to his appearance or to his behavior or both. *Fat* diminishes gradually and changes in distribution patterns. School-age children look much thinner than preschool children and adolescents. Girls have more fat than boys and it is placed differently, giving them softer contours at all ages after the first year [8]. The *skin* becomes less delicate. *Hair* may darken. While the *muscles* grow in size and in strength of connections with bones, they are still immature in function as compared with an adolescent's muscles. Muscles of school-age children are more readily injured by strain. For example, Little League pitchers are prey to "Little League Elbow," a muscular injury due to overuse. A brief observation in any first grade classroom will demonstrate how difficult it is for 6- and 7-year-olds—especially boys—to immobilize their muscles.

The *digestive* system shows added maturity by having fewer upsets and by retaining food for a longer time. Thus the school-age child does not have to be fed so carefully, so often and so promptly as the preschool child. Because growth is slow, calorie needs, in relation to the size of the stomach, are not so great as they were earlier and as they will be during the coming growth spurt. The danger at this time is that the child will fill up on empty calories, foods which do not promote growth, such as sugar, starches and excess fats. With relatively low calorie needs, it is important to eat foods which are high in proteins, minerals and vitamins. The combination of freedom to move out from his mother's supervision, plus a bit of money in his pockets, may result in an excessive intake of soft drinks and candy.

Children vary widely in *bladder* capacity, boys having less than girls. There are individual differences in frequency of urination, and difference in one individual from one time to another, due to temperature, humidity, time of day, emotional state, fluids ingested, and so on.

Respiration grows slower, deeper and more regular, changing from 20 to 30 inhalations per minute in the preschool period to 18 to 25 in the school age [21, p. 168]. Infections and disturbances of the respiratory system are fewer and milder than in the early years.

The *heart* grows slowly between 4 and 10 years. During that time it is smaller in relation to the rest of the body than at any other period of life [4, p. 223]. This fact of growth is one of the reasons why strongly competitive sports are dangerous for school-age children. As the child grows toward maturity, his heartbeat slows down and his blood pressure goes up. Between 6 and 12, he reaches the average adult heart rate of 70–100 per minute. Blood pressure, at an average of 105 mm is still below the adult norm.

Ears are less likely to become infected than they were during the preschool years. With the growth of the lower part of the face, the Eustachian tube, leading from the throat into the middle ear, grows longer, relatively narrower and slanted. Thus it is harder for disease organisms to invade. With fewer respiratory infections too there are fewer invading organisms in the child. Hearing acuity probably increases between ages 3 and 13 [38, p. 195].

The *eye* changes shape with growth, resulting in farsightedness until about age six. Studies of visual acuity yield a wide range of results, one showing 20/20 vision to be typical at age seven, another study placing 20/20 vision at age four and yet another at 11 to 13 [5]. Thus there is some doubt as to the age when 20/20 vision is normally achieved. It is after seven when the eyeball gains its full weight and several years later that full development is completed. Binocular vision is usually well developed at six or shortly afterward, although not in all children. Large print is recommended for children throughout the school years [4, p. 355]. A study of elementary-school children showed 59 percent to have visual defects [15]. The defects increased from 17 percent in first grade to 82 percent at the end of the elementary years. Adequate physical care must include attention to signs of visual difficulties and regular eye examinations.

The *skeleton* continues to ossify, replacing cartilage with bone. Since mineralization is not complete, the bones resist pressure and muscle pull less than more mature bones do. Good hygiene includes chairs, desks and shoes that fit, frequent moving around and caution in carrying heavy loads. For example, if a pack of newspapers is to be slung from one shoulder, it should be changed often from one shoulder to the other.

The skeleton is a useful maturity indicator, since its level of development is closely tied to progress toward sexual maturity. A child who is advanced in bone development will reach puberty at an earlier age than the average child. Not only is there this general relationship between the two kinds of development, but individual bones in the hand and wrist have a constant time relationship to sexual maturity. For instance, the sesamoid (a small round bone at the joint at the base of the thumb) appears within two or two and a half years before menarche [7, p. 107]. In the group of normal girls whose skeletal development was studied during puberty, menarche usually occurred soon after fusion of the epiphyses and shafts of the bones at the tips of the fingers [12, p. 11].

These are important years for *teething* since most of the changes from deciduous to permanent teeth take place. At almost any time, a child has a gap or two in his jaw, a loose tooth or one just popping through the gum. Nutrition, oral hygiene and dental care are very important in assuring healthy teeth. Speech, nutrition, appearance and body image are all affected by the soundness of teeth. Figure 10–5 shows the complete set of baby teeth and the complete set of adult teeth, indicating the replacements and additions which transform a young child's jaws into mature jaws. Figure 10–6 shows the two sets of teeth in place, the deciduous ones in the process of losing their roots through resorption, which prepares them to shed, leaving room for permanent teeth, since they exceed the number of baby teeth.

Since first permanent teeth to appear in most children do not replace deciduous teeth, they are likely not to be recognized as permanent teeth. These teeth are the first molars, which appear just behind the second deciduous molars. As in the case with the deciduous teeth, there are some differences in the times of eruption when corresponding teeth in the two jaws are compared. There are also sex differences. The times of eruption of girls' teeth are earlier than those of boys'. This is in line with the faster rate of maturation of girls, but, comparing tooth for tooth, girls are further ahead in the eruption of some teeth than they are for others [35, p. 70].

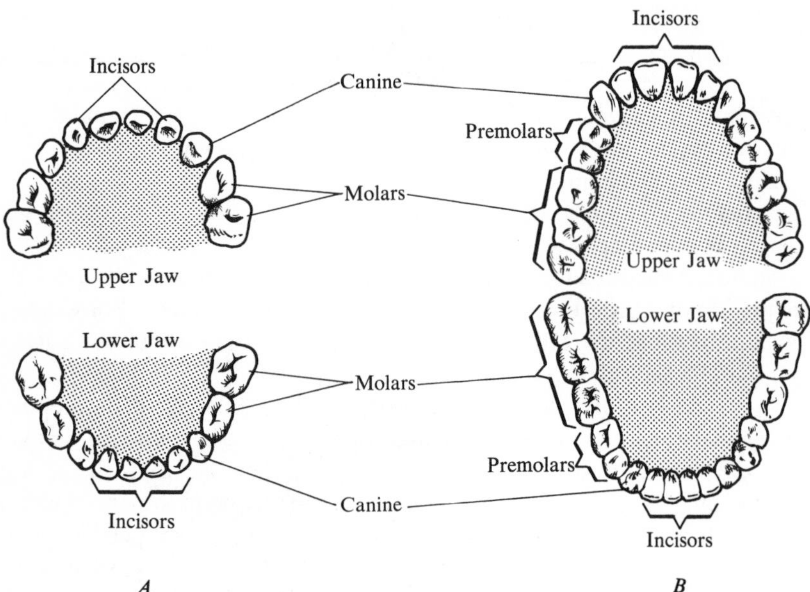

Figure 10–5. *A:* A complete set of deciduous (milk or baby) teeth. *B:* A complete set of permanent (adult) teeth. (Reproduced by permission from Phyllis C. Martin and Elizabeth Lee Vincent, *Human Biological Development*. Copyright © 1960, The Ronald Press Company.)

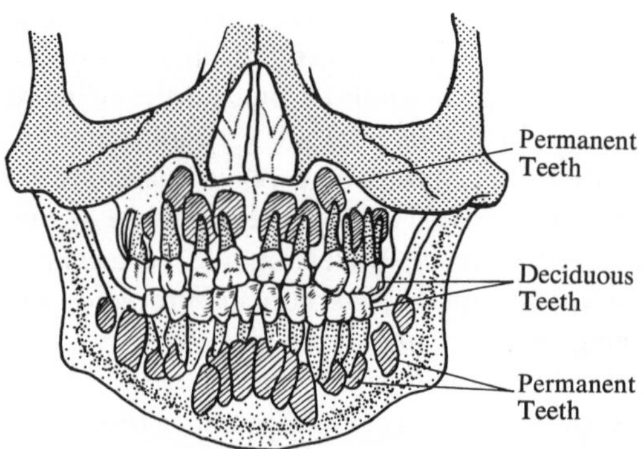

Figure 10–6. Deciduous and permanent teeth, showing preparation of the deciduous teeth for shedding. (Reproduced by permission from Phyllis C. Martin and Elizabeth Lee Vincent, *Human Biological Development*. Copyright © 1960, The Ronald Press Company.)

HEALTH AND SAFETY

Fewer children die than ever before. A recent report on the average annual death rate for children 5 to 14 years of age placed it at less than six in 10,000 for boys and less than four in 10,000 for girls [23]. A comparison of two decades showed a decline in mortality of about one third for school-age children. Although health is improving, from the standpoint of reduction of illness and accident rates, there are several areas in which children's health could be a great deal better than it is at present.

Illnesses

School-age children have fewer illnesses than preschool children do [36]. Respiratory and gastrointestinal upsets decrease considerably although they continue to be the most frequent types of illness, with respiratory the leading cause. After age 10 there is a further decrease in number of illnesses. The variety of major illnesses is greater during age 6 to 10 than during all other ages studied, between birth and 18. The list of illnesses at 6 to 10 includes, for example, nephritis, septicemia, meningococcemia and tuberculosis [36]. Figure 10–7 shows the distribution of the various types of illnesses between ages 5 and 14. According to a national health survey, children in this age group averaged 7.8 days in bed during one year, and 16.4 days of restricted activity, due to illness [20]. Schooldays lost due to illness averaged 5.3 days, with about three fifths of that time due to respiratory diseases [22]. The average number of acute illnesses was three per child. Medical attention was given to children for 54 percent of their illnesses.

The communicable diseases (including measles, chicken pox, mumps, whooping cough and scarlet fever) are much less threatening to children than they were in former years. In a longitudinal study of 67 boys and 67 girls, 50 girls and 45 boys had at least one communicable disease and over half of them had two [36]. No child had more than four. Death rates from these diseases have declined by 70 percent to 80 percent in one decade until they are now at the low figures of between two and seven deaths per million children between 5 and 14 [20].

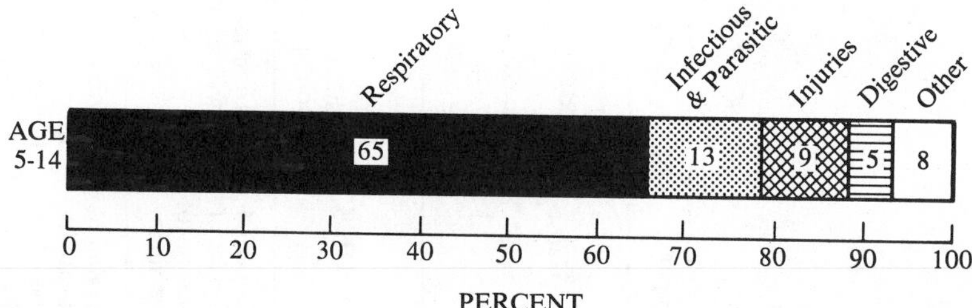

Figure 10–7. Frequency of occurrence of various types of illness in childhood. (From Chart B on page 18, "Problems of Youth," Legislative Reference Service, U.S. Government Printing Office, Washington, 1964.)

TABLE 10–5

Useful facts concerning the main childhood communicable diseases.

DISEASE	*Chicken Pox*	*Diphtheria*	*German Measles*	*Infantile Paralysis*	*Measles*
Cause	A virus: Present in secretions from nose, throat, mouth of infected people.	Diphtheria bacillus: Present in secretions from nose, throat and skin of infected people and carriers.	A virus: Present in secretions from nose and mouth of infected people.	3 strains of polio virus have been identified: Present in discharges from nose, throat, bowels of infected people.	A virus: Present in secretions from nose and throat of infected people.
How spread	Contact with infected people or articles used by them. Very contagious.	Contact with infected people and carriers or articles used by them.	Contact with infected people or articles used by them. Very contagious.	Contact with infected people.	Contact with infected people or articles used by them. Very contagious.
Incubation period (from date of exposure to first signs)	14 to 16 days. Sometimes 3 weeks.	2 to 5 days. Sometimes longer.	14 to 25 (usually 18) days.	About 7 to 21 days.	7 to 14 (usually 12 to 13) days.
Period of communicability (time when disease is contagious)	From about 1 day before, to 6 days after first appearance of skin blisters.	From about 2 to 4 weeks after onset of disease.	From about 4 days after onset of symptoms.	Apparently greatest in late incubation and first few days of acute illness.	From 2 to 7 days after onset of first symptoms.

Most susceptible ages	Common under 15 years.	Common under 10 years.	Young children.	Most common in children 1 to 16 years; prevalent in young adults.	Common at any age during childhood.
Seasons of prevalence	Winter.	Fall and winter.	Spring and winter.	June through September.	Mainly spring. Also fall and winter.
Prevention	No prevention.	Inoculation with diphtheria toxoid (in triple vaccine for babies).	No prevention.	Polio vaccine.	Measles vaccine.
Control	Isolation during period of communicability but not essential to isolate until all skin crusts are gone. Cut child's fingernails short and keep clean. Immunity usual after one attack.	Isolation until 3 cultures from nose and throat taken at 24-hour intervals are free of bacilli. Antibiotics and anti-toxin used in treatment and for protection after exposure. One attack does not necessarily give immunity.	Isolation, when necessary, from first symptoms until 2 days after appearance of rash. No attempt should be made to protect young girls from this disease. No control. Immunity usual after one attack.	Isolation (differs by State law) for about one week from onset, for duration of fever. Immunity to infecting strain of virus usual after one attack.	Isolation during period of communicability. Antibiotics sometimes used in treatment. Immunity usual after one attack.

TABLE 10–5 (*continued*)

DISEASE	*Mumps*	*"Strep" Infections*	*Rheumatic Fever*	*Smallpox*	*Tetanus*	*Whooping Cough*
Cause	A virus: Present in saliva of infected people.	Streptococci of several strains cause scarlet fever, and "strep" sore throats: Present in secretions from mouth, nose, ears of infected people and carriers.	Direct cause unknown. Precipitated by a "strep" infection.	A virus: Present in skin pocks and discharges from mouth, nose, throat, bowels, bladder of infected people.	Tetanus bacillus: Present in a wound so infected.	Pertussis bacillus: Present in secretions from mouth and nose of infected people.
How spread	Contact with infected people and articles used by them.	Contact with infected people and carriers. Also from dust, lint, contaminated food and milk.	Unknown. But the preceding "strep" infection is contagious.	Contact with infected people or articles used by them.	Through soil, street dust, or articles contaminated with the bacillus.	Contact with infected people and articles used by them.
Incubation period (from date of exposure to first signs)	14 to 28 (commonly 18) days.	2 to 5 days.	Symptoms appear about 2 to 3 weeks after a "strep" infection.	8 to 21 (commonly 12) days.	1 day to 3 weeks. Sometimes longer. Commonly 8 to 12 days.	About 5 to 21 (commonly 10) days.
Period of communicability (time when disease is contagious)	Not certain. From about 4 to 7 days before symptoms until swelling of salivary glands subsides.	During period of incubation and illness (about 10 days).	Not communicable. Preceding "strep" infection is communicable.	From first symptoms to disappearance of pocks.	Not communicable from person to person.	From onset of first symptoms to about 4th week of the disease.

Most susceptible ages	Children and young people.	All ages.	All ages. Most common from 6 to 12 years.	All ages.	All ages.	Under 7 years.
Seasons of prevalence	Winter and spring.	Late winter and spring.	Mainly winter and spring.	Winter.	Summer.	Late winter and early spring.
Prevention	No prevention.	No prevention.	No prevention.	Vaccination.	Inoculation with tetanus toxoid (in triple vaccine for babies).	Inoculation with whooping cough vaccine (in triple vaccine for babies).
Control	Isolation until swelling subsides. No attempt should be made to protect boys from this disease before they reach puberty. Immunity usual after one attack but second attacks can occur.	Isolation until recovery. Use of antibiotics. One attack does not necessarily give immunity.	Use of antibiotics. One attack does not give immunity.	Isolation until all pocks are gone. Immunity usual after one attack.	Booster dose of tetanus toxoid for protection after a wound. Antitoxin used in treatment and for temporary protection for child not immunized. One attack does not give immunity.	Special shots can lighten attack or give protection after exposure. Isolation for about 3 weeks from onset of spasmodic cough. Immunity usual after one attack.

Source: Based on *The Control of Communicable Diseases*, American Public Health Association, 1960; and Report of Committee on Control of Infectious Diseases, American Academy of Pediatrics, 1957. Courtesy of the Metropolitan Life Insurance Company.

As Chapter 6 pointed out, many illnesses can be prevented by careful health supervision, carried out under the direction of a physician. Immunizations prevent most of the communicable diseases, as shown in Table 10–5. Optimal nutrition, rest and exercise help the child to build his body's natural resistance to disease. Protection from extreme stress, both physical and mental, prevents the breakdown of the child's own resources for coping with disease. During middle childhood, one of the competencies to be learned is that of self-care, along with some knowledge of basic physiology and nutrition and of how disease organisms operate. Many children receive inadequate care during convalescence from an illness. Certain effects of an illness linger even after the temperature has returned to normal (and some parents do not even realize that the temperature is usually subnormal for a day or so after being elevated). Muscles may be flabby, because they lost some tone during illness. Fatigue and poor posture may result if the convalescent child returns to a normal schedule too soon [4, p. 54]. Since illness may lower the hemoglobin count, the fatigue during convalescence may be partly due to anemia. Appetite is likely to decrease. Lowered emotional control tends to go along with diminished vigor. Therefore, it is wise to arrange a gradual return to normal activity after an illness. Some pediatricians suggest that their patients stay in bed one day after the temperature has returned to normal and that they stay home from school the following day.

SPECIAL HEALTH PROBLEMS. Although certain physical conditions are not considered illnesses, they have harmful long-range effects upon children's health. Dental caries is outstanding as this type of problem. (Many people do not consider it a disease, and since it is not incapacitating, it is rarely accorded the status of illness.) One child in four, at the 5-to-14-year range, has never been to a dentist [22]. A national health survey indicated that about half of the children in this age bracket had had no dental care during the preceding year. When children were divided as to family income, it was found that 5-to-14-year-olds, living in families of less than $4,000 income, averaged 0.8 dental visits annually, and those in families of income above $4,000 went to the dentist 2.4 times. Some progress toward dental health is being made in fluoridation of water supplies and in treating children's teeth with fluoride.

Long-range problems also include nutrition and fitness. Obesity is becoming more frequent among American children, with its prognosis of increasing obesity in adulthood. Although insufficient calories is a problem with only a small percentage of Americans, poor quality of diet is a fairly serious problem, one which will be discussed further in regard to adolescents. Table 10–6 shows the recommended allowances of the various food elements for children during the school years.

Accidents

Accidental injuries account for about half of the deaths of boys between 5 and 14 and for about one third of the deaths of girls the same age [23]. A

TABLE 10–6

Dietary allowances recommended by the Food and Nutrition Board of the National Academy of Sciences, National Research Council.*

	Weight		*Height*		*Calories*	*Protein*	*Calcium*	*Iron*	*Vitamin A*	*Thia-mine*	*Ribo-flavin*	*Niacin Equiva-lents*	*Ascor-bic Acid*	*Vita-min D*
	kg	*lb*	*cm*	*in*										
Children														
1–3 years	13	29	87	34	1300	32	0.8	8	2000	0.5	0.8	9	40	400
3–6 years	18	40	107	42	1600	40	0.8	10	2500	0.6	1.0	11	50	400
6–9 years	24	53	124	49	2100	52	0.8	12	3500	0.8	1.3	14	60	400
Boys														
9–12 years	33	72	140	55	2400	60	1.1	15	4500	1.0	1.4	16	70	400
12–15 years	45	98	156	61	3000	75	1.4	15	5000	1.2	1.8	20	80	400
15–18 years	61	134	172	68	3400	85	1.4	15	5000	1.4	2.0	22	80	400
Girls														
9–12 years	33	72	140	55	2200	55	1.1	15	4500	0.9	1.3	15	80	400
12–15 years	47	103	158	62	2500	62	1.3	15	5000	1.0	1.5	17	80	400
15–18 years	53	117	163	64	2300	58	1.3	15	5000	0.9	1.3	15	70	400

* The allowance levels are intended to cover individual variations among most normal persons as they live in the United States under usual environmental stresses. The recommended allowances can be attained with a variety of common foods, providing other nutrients for which human requirements have been less well defined.

Source: *1963 Recommended Dietary Allowances*, NAS-NRC Pub. No. 1146. Copyright © 1964, National Academy of Sciences, Food and Nutrition Board. Reprinted by permission.

comparison of present rates with those of a decade ago shows a substantial decrease in death rate from accidents (about 20 percent). As Table 10–7 shows, motor vehicles are the leading cause of accidental death, killing about twice as many boys and girls. Many of these fatalities occur when children are playing on streets and when they cross streets and highways. Among boys, drowning is second to motor vehicles as a cause of death. About 6,700 children die from accidents each year in the United States. The number injured is about 12 million. Nearly one third of the people between 6 and 16 years of age are injured seriously enough to require medical attention or at least one day of restricted activity. About two fifths of the nonfatal injuries occur in or near the home.

TABLE 10–7

Children's deaths from different types of accidents.

	Death Rate Per 100,000					
	Males			*Females*		
*Type of Accident**	*Ages 5–14*	*Ages 5–9*	*Ages 10–14*	*Ages 5–14*	*Ages 5–9*	*Ages 10–14*
All Types	25.1	22.9	27.5	10.9	13.1	8.5
Motor vehicle	10.4	10.5	10.3	5.2	6.1	4.3
Drowning†	5.5	4.8	6.3	1.2	1.1	1.3
Firearm	1.8	.9	2.7	.3	.3	.3
Fire and explosion	1.7	2.2	1.1	2.3	3.5	1.0
Falls	.8	.8	.9	.3	.3	.2

* According to rank among males.
† Exclusive of deaths in water transportation.
Source: Basic data from Reports of the Division of Vital Statistics, National Center for Health Statistics. Reprinted by permission from *Statistical Bulletin*, Metropolitan Life Insurance Company, September 1964.

Chronic Illnesses and Impairments

Over 2 million children under 14 years of age must live with disabilities which are permanent or of indefinite duration. Figure 10–8 shows how these defects are distributed, with orthopedic defects most frequent, then speech, then hearing and visual defects, in that order [20]. The Children's Bureau, during a year when its crippled children's program gave aid to nearly 340,000 children under 21, reported that congenital malformations accounted for more than a quarter of these patients. About one fifth of the children under care had diseases of the bones and organs of movement. Cerebral palsy accounted for 8 percent, polio 7 percent, eye conditions 6 percent, impaired hearing 7 percent and impairments from accidents 5 percent [22].

Chronic diseases and long-term disabilities may affect growth adversely. They certainly limit some of the child's activities. Conditions likely to retard growth include chronically infected tonsils and adenoids, syphilis, hookworm,

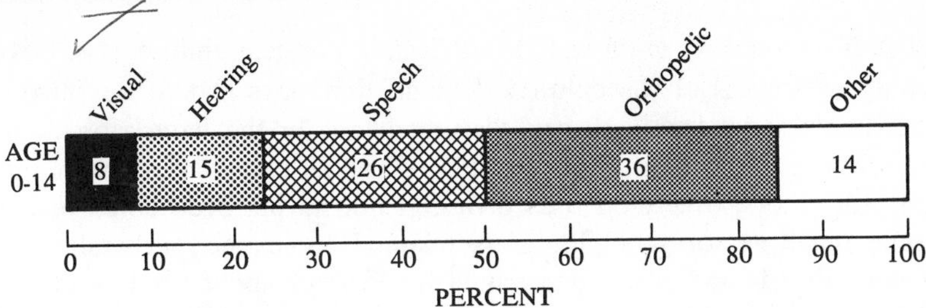

Figure 10–8. Frequency of occurrence of various types of impairments and defects in children. (From Chart C on page 19, "Problems of Youth," Legislative Reference Service, U.S. Government Printing Office, Washington, 1964.)

rheumatic fever and diabetes [4, pp. 53–56]. Good physical care can alleviate some of these conditions and even in cases where the condition cannot be cured, good care may result in normal growth.

Psychological Effects of Handicaps

The disabled child suffers not only the discomfort of diagnostic and treatment procedures. He also misses out on some of the activities which normal children have as part of everyday life. Requiring more physical care, he actually receives more nurturance from his mother and often from the whole family. He has a narrower social and interpersonal experience. Parents and often teachers give him less work to do, less responsibility to carry [27].

Different types of handicaps, of course, produce different reactions in the children burdened with them and in the social environments in which the children live. For example, when asked to rank five disabilities in order of preference, Jewish children judged confinement to a wheelchair as worse than obesity, and obesity as worse than facial disfigurement [11]. The normative group of children, drawn from a wide selection of environments, ranked obesity as most undesirable, facial disfigurement as next to obesity, and confinement to a wheelchair as the least undesirable of these conditions. Italian children ranked the handicaps in another order. Thus it can be seen that a child's handicap is interpreted to him according to the particular value system of the people close to him. The specific restrictions required by various handicaps differ from one to another. For example, the dietary requirements for diabetics are very embarrassing to some children, who often try to hide their condition from other children.

Even though there are some specific reactions to handicaps, certain general effects have been found, too. The self-concepts of a wide selection of handicapped children were investigated in a summer camp situation, by asking these children and a group of normal children to describe themselves and others [27]. The children's conversations were analyzed into categories, so as to find out which topics were important to them and which, of these topics, were most significant. In general the handicapped children showed realistic facing of life by talking more about "handicap" than did the normal children.

The handicapped boys discussed "health" and "physical ability" less, possibly reflecting awareness of the cultural demand that boys should be active and aggressive. "Spatial location" was discussed less by the handicapped, probably because these children had had limited spatial experiences, being unable to move around so freely on their own and not having been taken places by adults as much as normal children are taken. Handicapped girls talked more than normal girls and more than handicapped boys about "giving aid," suggesting the importance to them of receiving aid, as well as the fact that it is easier for girls to accept aid than it is for boys. Comments of the handicapped children indicated that they had fewer interactions with people, with the exception of interactions with mothers. This interpersonal impoverishment probably accounts for their greater use of egocentric comments and expression of self-depreciation and lack of confidence.

As the emotional and developmental situation of the handicapped child becomes understood, it is possible for parents and other adults to help him more effectively. For instance, knowing that handicapped children's spatial experiences are likely to be limited, the adults could plan more carefully to change the child's location and position often and, whenever possible, to take him on expeditions with the rest of the family instead of leaving him home with Mother. Knowing that his feelings of adequacy will be threatened, wise adults will help a handicapped child to develop competencies in the fields where he can operate. The task of broadening his interpersonal contacts is not easy, but constant awareness of it will bring more results than ignoring the matter.

MOTOR COORDINATION

Children's delight in vigorous motor play seems to be universal. Ball games, tag, running, chasing and jumping games are to be found where children are. The motor skills which a society teaches to its children, however, reflect the values and economic level of that culture.

The Influence of Cultural Values on Motor Skills

In order to highlight the affluent American culture, consider the Asian society in which many a boy squats at the far end of a loom, assisting a skilled weaver and gradually acquiring his fine coordinations. Other boys do the rough outlining of ivory figures, which men finish and inlay into boxes and table tops. Little girls struggle to embroider tiny mirrors onto skirts and bags. The aim is excellence in the vocational pursuits of weaving, ivory inlaying and mirror embroidery. In America, vocational excellence has little place in the motor coordinations which children strive to learn. Their parents' aim is more all-round competence than specialized excellence. In fact, as far as girls are concerned, moderate skill may be preferred to excellence. The bureaucratic, other-directed middle-class society described by social observers of the nineteen fifties [24, 28] would logically try to produce children who could fit into whatever kind of athletic recreation their peers were enjoying. These children would be able to make a fourth at tennis, would know an allemande-left from a right-hand-to-your-partner, and a figure eight from an outside edge, would stick on a horse and be able to dive neatly from the low board, if not the high board.

Wanting moderate competence in many coordinations, American society offers many organized learning opportunities to children. Rarely do families teach such skills as dancing and swimming. Of 1,008 parent–child contacts occurring in the water at two beaches, only 82 were instances of parents instructing children in swimming [32, 33]. (Most of the teaching which did occur was in upper-middle-class, rather than lower-middle or lower-class families.) Instead of the informal family instruction of a simpler society, modern arrangements include dancing teachers sponsored by schools, the P.T.A. or community centers, and swimming teachers hired by the state, community or club. Standards for teachers are set and controlled by the Red Cross. The water safety manual delineates levels of achievement in swimming and giving children specific goals for various coordinations. By requiring the child to be 12 years old before trying the Junior Lifesaving examination, the Red Cross implies that children under 12 can pass the beginner's, advanced beginner's and intermediate tests. Thus much of what used to be learned informally, in the way of motor skills, has become formalized, standardized and, in some instances, commercialized. Children still play, however.

Play Activities

The average six-year-old has acquired the motor skills basic to school-age play. He can throw, bounce and catch a ball, although he does not do so very smoothly [14]. For many years, he will practice and seek to perfect games which use balls and similar objects for throwing, catching, hitting, bouncing and carrying. Able to run and climb well, he plays games of chase, such as tag and hide-and-seek, his interest in these games increasing steadily from six to nine [34]. Running is basic to skipping, dancing and skating. Most six-year-olds can skip and jump rope, and seven-year-olds roller-skate [14]. With these skills, as with ball play, the youngster ventures into new games and coordinations, practicing as he goes, in order to achieve competence in a variety of movements. Sometimes he plays follow-the-leader, gaining ideas and courage from a model who knows a little more about the skill than he does. Sometimes he jumps, skates or bounces by himself, apparently thoroughly enjoying the process of developing motor skills.

The average nine-year-old is interested in a greater variety of play activities than he has been before or will be again [34]. When a group of children between 9 and 10 are asked to check their interests on a large list of activities, everything suggested is likely to be checked by someone. Tables 10–8, 10–9 and 10–10 represent a partial list of items which 50 percent or more of a group of fourth, fifth and sixth graders said they liked to do [29]. About 70 percent of these activities are strongly motor, with large muscle coordinations chosen more than four times as often as fine coordinations. Breadth of interest varies from one child to another, some engaging in fewer than ten activities a week and others playing in over 100 different ways [34].

TABLE 10–8

Activities boys reported especially enjoying.

Bandits	Marbles
Bows and arrows	Making model airplanes
Boxing	Shooting
Building forts	Soldiers
Cars	Spacemen
Cops and robbers	Throw snowballs
Darts	Toy trains
Football	Use tools
Hunt	Wrestling

Source: Reprinted by permission from B. G. Rosenberg and B. Sutton-Smith, "A Revised Conception of Masculine-Feminine Differences in Play Activity," *The Journal of Genetic Psychology*, **96**, Table 1, p. 167. Copyright © 1960, The Journal Press.

TABLE 10–9

Activities girls were particularly fond of playing.

Blind man's buff	Jacks
Building snowmen	Jump rope
Cartwheels	Leap frog
Clue	London bridges
Cooking	Mother, may I
Crack the whip	Mulberry bush
Dance	Musical chairs
Doctors	Name that tune
Dolls	Pick up sticks
Dressing up	Puzzles
Drop the handkerchief	Red rover
Farmer in the dell	Ring around the rosy
Follow the leader	Scrapbook making
Fox and geese	See saw
Hide the thimble	Sewing
Hopscotch	School
Houses	Simon says "thumbs up"
Huckle buckle beanstalk	Statues
In and out the window	Stoop tag
I've got a secret	Store

Source: Reprinted by permission from B. G. Rosenberg and B. Sutton-Smith, "A Revised Conception of Masculine-Feminine Differences in Play Activity," *The Journal of Genetic Psychology*, **96,** Table 1, p. 167. Copyright © 1960, The Journal Press.

TABLE 10–10

Play activities enjoyed by both boys and girls.

Basketball	Tug-o-war	I spy
Bowling	Wall dodge ball	Monopoly
Cowboys	Clay modeling	Scrabble
King of the mountain	Draw or paint	Spin the bottle
Racing	Gardening	Tag
Soccer	Hide and seek	Tail on the donkey
Walk on stilts	Fly kite	Make collections
Dominoes	Ghosts	Hiking
Shuffleboard	Black magic	Raise pets
Baseball	Dodgeball	Stunts in gym
Boating	Tiddle di winks	Swimming
Fish	Cards	Horses
Camping	Checkers	Wood tag
Climbing	Pingpong	Kick dodge
Ball tag	Horse shoes	Bingo
Pool	Tennis	Tic tac toe
Post office	Skating	Dog and bone
Chess	Horse riding	Volleyball
Seven up	Bicycle riding	Roller skating

Source: Reprinted by permission from B. G. Rosenberg and B. Sutton-Smith, "A Revised Conception of Masculine-Feminine Differences in Play Activity," *The Journal of Genetic Psychology*, **96,** Tables 2 and 3, p. 168. Copyright © 1960, The Journal Press.

Components of Motor Ability

One analysis of the various kinds of motor abilities yields these classes: strength, impulsion, speed, precision coordination and flexibility [13]. Strength, of course, refers to the amount of force the individual can exert. Impulsion is a measure of the rate at which movements are initiated from stationary positions, whereas speed is the rate of movements which have been begun. Precision is the accuracy with which a position is maintained (static precision) or with which a movement is directed (dynamic precision). Flexibility is freedom to bend and otherwise move the body. These components of motor ability can be studied in relation to different parts of the body, and sometimes in relation to the whole body.

STRENGTH. Although strength can be measured in legs, shoulders and back, or in practically any voluntary muscle, most of the research on increase in strength has been in terms of hand grip. Grip is measured by a dynamometer, an instrument which registers amount of pressure. Boys and girls are quite similar in grip strength throughout the elementary-school years, with boys leading slightly. Both sexes make steady gains in grip strength. The average five-year-old boy can exert about 9.5 kilograms of pressure [26, p. 478]. The average measurements, in kilograms, for boys' grip at each year throughout the school age are as follows: six years, 11; seven years, 12.5; eight years, 14.5; nine years, 17.5; 10 years, 20; 11 years, 22; 12 years, 24. Trunk strength is measured by performance of such exercises as the abdominal pivot (pushing the body around with hands on floor and back arched), push-ups and leg raising while in sitting position [13]. Limb strength is estimated by dips (squatting and rising), chinning, rope-climbing and push-ups.

IMPULSION. Reaction time, or time required to respond to a stimulus, is one measure of impulsion. Reaction time may also be considered a measure of speed. Speed of reaction time increases steadily throughout the school age, with boys reacting slightly faster than girls [10]. Other measures include limb thrust, as shown in jumping, shot-put, short dash and bar vault. A third measure is tapping, turning small objects, removing and placing pegs. Speed of articulation also seems to be a type of impulsion.

SPEED. Speed of movement can be measured for the whole body or for various parts, such as arms, hands and fingers. Such skills as running and hopping show a steady increase in speed throughout the school years, with boys slightly ahead of girls [9, 17].

PRECISION. Balance, steadiness and aiming are all aspects of precision. They are tested by such feats as standing on one foot, walking a line, tracing, threading, jumping and balancing, pursuit aiming and placing dots in circles. Coordination of the whole body and dexterity of hand and fingers can also be considered as precision.

FLEXIBILITY. Ease of moving, bending and stretching contributes to most motor skills. Flexibility is extremely important in dancing and in most sports. Flexibility depends largely on the looseness of the joints and also upon the ease with which the muscles stretch and relax.

Tests of Motor Ability

Two examples of motor tests will be mentioned here, the Lincoln–Oseretsky Motor Development Scale [31] and the Kraus–Weber Test [19]. Additional tests will be discussed in Chapter 14. The Lincoln–Oseretsky Scale is an individual test for children between 6 and 14 years of age. It consists of 36 items, shown in the sample score sheet reproduced in Table 10–11. The test samples a wide variety of motor skills, including gross bodily coordination, activities of trunk, legs, arms and hands, finger dexterity and eye–hand coordination. Although the various components of motor ability, strength, impulsion, speed, precision and flexibility are all called into play by the various items, no separate scores are given. The child's score is for total or overall level of motor development. By means of percentile tables, the child can be compared with all children his age and with children his age and sex.

The Kraus–Weber Test is concerned with flexibility and strength of large muscles. The test will not delineate the upper limits of strength and flexibility. Rather, it was designed in order ". . . to determine whether or not the individual has sufficient strength and flexibility in parts of the body upon which demands are made in normal daily living." Six simple items make up the Kraus–Weber Test. Each of the six items must be passed in order to pass the test as a whole. No score is given other than passed or failed. The results can, however, be broken down into flexibility and weakness failures.

TABLE 10–11

Sample score sheet for the Lincoln–Oseretsky Motor Development Scale.

	Description	*R-L*	*Trials*	*Pts.*	*Notes*
1	Walking backwards, 6 ft.		2		
2	Crouching on tiptoe		2		
3	Standing on one foot	R/L	2/2	/	
4	Touching nose		1		
5	Touching fingertips	R/L	2/2	/	
6	Tapping rhythmically with feet and fingers		1		
7	Jumping over a rope		1		
8	Finger movement		3		
9	Standing heel to toe		2		
10	Close and open hands alternately		3		
11	Making dots		2		
12	Catching a ball	R/L	5/5	/	
13	Making a ball	R/L	2/2	/	
14	Winding thread	R/L	1/1	/	
15	Balancing a rod crosswise	R/L	3/3	/	
16	Describing circles in the air		1		
17	Tapping (15″)	R/L	2/2	/	
18	Placing coins and matchsticks		1		
19	Jump and turn about		1		
20	Putting matchsticks in a box		1		
21	Winding thread while walking	R/L	1/1	/	
22	Throwing a ball	R/L	5/5	/	
23	Sorting matchsticks	R/L	1/1	/	
24	Drawing lines	R/L	2/2	/	
25	Cutting a circle	R/L	1/1	/	
26	Putting coins in box (15″)	R/L	1/1	/	
27	Tracing mazes	R/L	1/1	/	
28	Balancing on tiptoe		1		
29	Tapping with feet and fingers		1		
30	Jump, touch heels		1		
31	Tap feet and describe circles		1		
32	Stand on one foot	R/L	1/1	/	
33	Jumping and clapping		1		
34	Balancing on tiptoe	R/L	1/1	/	
35	Opening and closing hands		1		
36	Balancing a rod vertically	R/L	3/3	/	

Source: Reprinted by permission from William Sloan, "The Lincoln–Oseretsky Motor Development Scale," *Genetic Psychology Monographs*, **51,** Table 5, p. 247. Copyright © 1955, The Journal Press.

The Kraus–Weber Test, from which an excerpt is given in Figure 10–9, was given widely throughout Europe and the United States as a measure of physical fitness. Over 4,000 American children were compared with Austrian, Italian and Swiss children. Figure 10–10 shows the incidence of American failures and European failures at all ages from 6 to 16. The European children show up ever so much better than Americans at all ages. What is more, the Americans gave poorer performances as they advanced in age. The authors attributed the difference in Americans and Europeans to the mechanization of life in America, especially to riding in cars instead of walking. The reports on Kraus–Weber findings stirred up considerable interest in "fitness," even in the

Kraus-Weber Tests for Muscular Fitness

(There should not be any warm-up prior to taking the tests.)

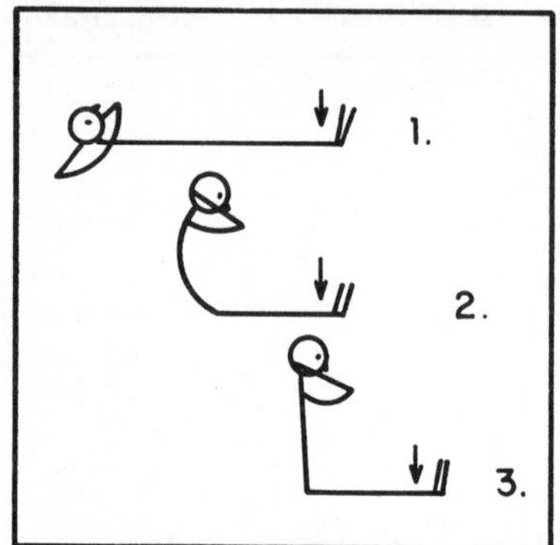

TEST 1.

Purpose: Tests the strength of the abdominals and psoas.

Designation: "Abdominals plus psoas" or A+.

Position of Person Being Tested: Lying supine, hands behind neck. The examiner holds his feet down on the table.

Command: "Keep your hands behind your neck and *try to roll up* into a sitting position."

Precaution: If the person being tested is unable to perform this movement at first try, it may be because he has not understood the directions. Help him a little and then let him try again. Watch for a "stiff back sit-up." This may indicate that either he has not understood you and needs a further explanation with emphasis on "rolling up," or that he has *very* poor abdominals and is doing most of the work with his psoas.

Watch also for a twist of the upper body as he sits up. This may be due to unequal development of the back muscles.

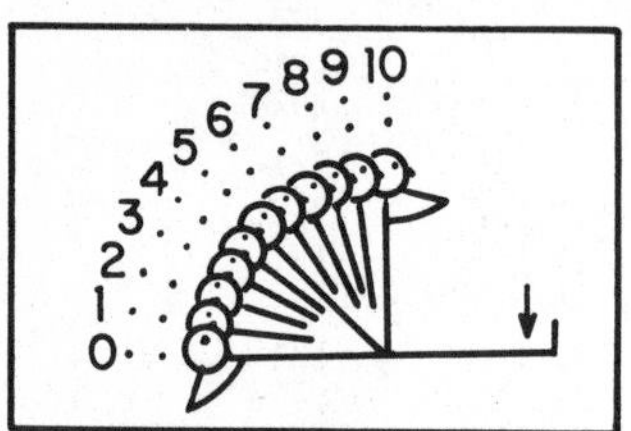

Marking: If the person being tested cannot raise his shoulders from the table, the mark is *0*. If unaided, he is able to reach a sitting position, the mark is *10*. If the examiner must help him halfway to the sitting position, the mark would be *5*. The distance from supine to sitting is marked from *0* to *10*.

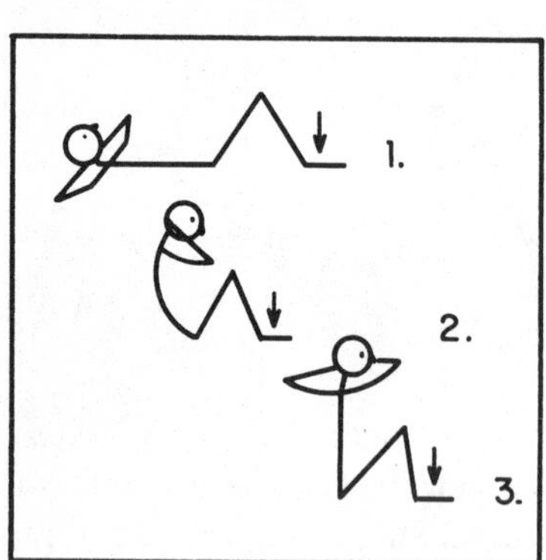

TEST 2.

Purpose: Further test for abdominals.

Designation: "Abdominals minus psoas" or *A*–.

Position of Person Being Tested: Lying supine, hands behind neck and knees bent. Examiner holds his feet down on the table.

Command: "Keep your hands behind your neck and *try to roll up* into a sitting position."

Precaution: The precautions are the same as for Test 1.

Figure 10–9. Two items from the Kraus–Weber Test are given here to illustrate how the tests for muscle strength and flexibility were conducted. (Reprinted by permission from H. Kraus and R. P. Hirschland, "Minimum Muscular Fitness Tests in School Children," *Research Quarterly,* **25,** 178–185. Copyright © 1954, American Association for Health, Physical Education, and Recreation, Washington, D.C.)

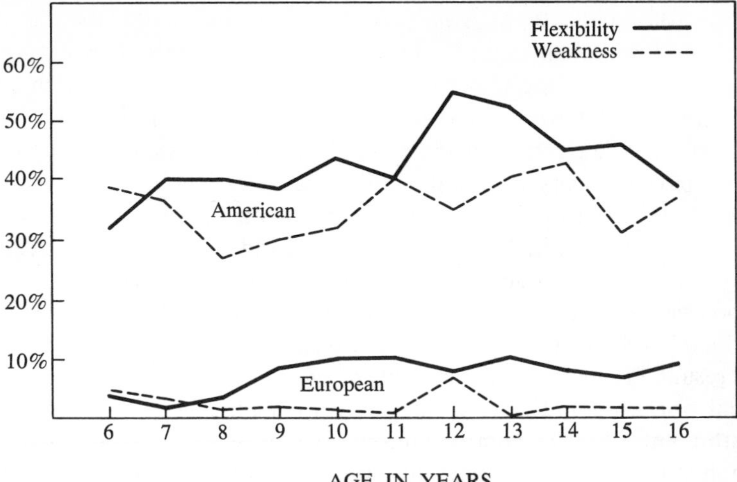

Figure 10–10. American children and youth compared with their European age-mates on tests of strength and flexibility, showing many more failures among Americans. (Reprinted by permission from H. Kraus and R. P. Hirschland, "Minimum Muscular Fitness Tests in School Children," *Research Quarterly,* **25,** 178–195. Copyright © 1954, American Association for Health, Physical Education, and Recreation, Washington, D.C.)

White House. Television programs, community recreation and fitness programs and P.T.A.'s rose to the challenge. There has not been complete agreement as to the meaning of "fitness" and as to how serious a matter it was that American children and youth were outclassed by Europeans on the Kraus–Weber Test. Some constructive steps have been taken to improve American youth. These are described in Chapter 14.

Inhibition of Motor Activity

When a child enters school, the ability to sit down and keep still becomes important. From a practical point of view, it is a great help to the teacher if her pupils can inhibit motor activity sufficiently for her to maintain a quiet, orderly classroom, where she can be heard by all. There has been some difference of opinion on how much physical immobility matters for the child's learning his lessons, some teachers maintaining that children can accomplish more while quiet, others believing that bodily activity is an aid to learning, even though inconvenient for the teacher.

Relationships between motor inhibition and intellectual behavior have been explored in studies of cognitive style, which will be discussed further in the following chapter. It seems worth mentioning these studies in connection with motor control, also, since a relationship has been found between ability to be still and tendency to form analytic concepts [18]. When children were divided into groups, according to the type of concepts which they formed most readily, the analytic children, as compared with nonanalytic, tended to be less impulsive, less distractible, more able to concentrate and more able to inhibit motor acts. Observation suggests that more boys than girls show extremes of motor behavior, including impulsive, disorganized outbursts. In another study adult men were rated for involvement in intellectual mastery [18, p. 109]. An analysis (by another rater) of their childhood records showed that inability to inhibit motor activity during the childhood years was predictive of future avoidance of intellectual activities. Further corroboration came from the ratings on attention span of 46 fourth grade children. For boys, but not for girls, an analytic conceptual style was correlated with attention span. Thus childhood motor control was shown to be related to analytic conceptualization in childhood and intellectual involvement in manhood.

The results of this research are not, of course, an answer to the practical questions of classroom teachers, since they do not tell the teacher how to help the restless little boy to control himself. Nor is it even certain that motor inhibition is basic to the analytic attitude; it may be that the analytic person inhibits motor activity more easily. Restless, impulsive children are often helped by a routine which gives legitimate opportunities for frequent moving around, combined with calm, firm reminders to reflect before answering.

Laterality

The topic of hand preference was considered in Chapter 6, in terms of its establishment during the first years of life. During the elementary-school years, a practical question concerns the changing of a preference already established. Since research possibilities are greater with older children, more data have been collected on school-age children and more is known about the relation of handedness to other questions concerning right and left. Laterality, or sidedness, includes all of the body, feet and eyes as well as hands. Laterality includes the individual's uses, preferences and orientations to his own body and to left and right in other people, objects and situations. Cultures define laterality, through language and customs. For example, consider the implications in the Latin words *sinister* and *dexter* for left and right, the French *gauche,* which means awkward, and the fact that both English and German use the word *right* to refer to hand and to being correct. The custom of shaking hands is rigidly prescribed as for the right hand. A child grows up, therefore, with all sorts of meanings, implications, restrictions and requirements attached to right and left.

Laterality in schoolchildren has been studied in terms of hands, eyes and feet [1]. Preferences were determined by asking the child to show how he would throw a ball, turn a door knob, cut with scissors and write with a pencil. Eye preference was tested by asking the child to look through a kaleidoscope, sight a rifle and look at the examiner through a hole in a paper. Foot preference was determined by noting which foot was used for kicking, estimating which foot kicked more skillfully. Table 10–12 shows lateral preferences for hands, eyes and feet at each year of age from 5 through 11. Note that in each

TABLE 10–12

Laterality patterns for boys and girls.

		Age-Specific Percentages						
Category	*Totals* N = 148	*5–3 to 5–11* N = 23	*6–0 to 6–11* N = 25	*7–0 to 7–11* N = 28	*8–0 to 8–11* N = 20	*9–0 to 9–11* N = 17	*10–0 to 10–11* N = 14	*11–0 to 11–11* N = 18
Handedness								
Right	113 (76%)	87	60	75	75	82	79	83
Left	14 (10%)	5	12	4	10	12	21	6
Mixed	21 (14%)	9	28	21	15	6	0	11
Eyedness								
Right	78 (53%)	44	52	43	60	41	57	78
Left	31 (21%)	31	20	21	15	24	29	6
Mixed	39 (26%)	26	28	36	25	35	14	17
Footedness								
Right	125 (85%)	83	88	89	80	88	79	83
Left	17 (12%)	9	8	7	15	12	21	11
Mixed	6 (4%)	9	4	4	5	0	0	6
Hand-Eye								
Consistent	71 (48%)	39	36	36	50	41	78	67
Crossed	24 (16%)	31	16	14	15	24	8	6
Mixed	53 (36%)	31	48	50	35	35	14	28

Source: Reprinted by permission from L. Belmont and H. G. Birch, "Lateral Dominance, Lateral Awareness, and Reading Disability," *Child Development*, **36,** Table 2, p. 62. Copyright © 1965, The Society for Research in Child Development, Inc.

area, some children made mixed choices, showing that preference was not definitely established. Mixed preferences occurred more often at the younger ages, showing that the development trend toward laterality (mentioned in the discussion of preschool handedness) continues through the elementary-school years. The table also shows that lateral preference was stronger for feet than for hands and weakest for eyes. Twenty-six percent of the children showed no clear-cut preference for eyes, whereas 14 percent showed none for hands, and only 4 percent for feet. Table 10–12 shows that about half the children were consistent in lateral preferences, and the others showed either crossed or mixed preferences. With increasing age, there was increasing use of the hand and eye on the same side.

Awareness of right and left also increased with age. The children were tested to see when they knew right and left on their own body parts. All questions were answered correctly by 70 percent of five-year-olds, by 68 percent at six, 89 percent at seven, 95 percent at eight, 94 percent at 10 and 100 percent at 11. Right–left awareness of own body is achieved about two years before hand preference is established. The authors suggest that the functions of lateral awareness and lateral preference are not closely related to each other.

Further study on the question of lateral dominance, lateral awareness and reading difficulties has been done with 200 boys selected from the total number of 9- and 10-year-old boys in school in one community [2]. One hundred and fifty of these boys were the poorest readers in the age group, the others serving as a control group. Neither left-handedness nor mixed-handedness was found to be related to poor reading, but a definite relationship was found between left–right awareness and reading. Boys who were confused in identifying their own left and right body parts were more likely to be poor readers than boys who showed normal left–right awareness.

Another aspect of laterality is its relation to electrochemical processes in the body. During childhood, the right hand tends to show a higher galvanic skin response (conducts electricity better) than the left [6]. Boys below 11 years of age showed greater sensitivity to touch in the dominant thumb, as contrasted with the opposite thumb.

Practical Significance of Laterality

Parents and teachers have to decide what to do with children who prefer to use their left hands. Some left-handed children have been taught to use their right hands skillfully without the appearance of any behavior problems or emotional tensions [25]. It is easy to understand, though, how a child would become upset when nagged or shamed about using his left hand, especially if he were not given real help in learning how to use his right. If it is decided that the child shall be allowed to continue to use his left hand, then he is likely to need help in arranging his environment suitably. A survey of practices of 19 commercial systems of handwriting gives a summary of present-day techniques for teaching the left-handed child to write [16]. The companies were concerned most with the position of the paper and the position of the arm, hand and writing instrument. Figure 10–11 shows the recommended positions

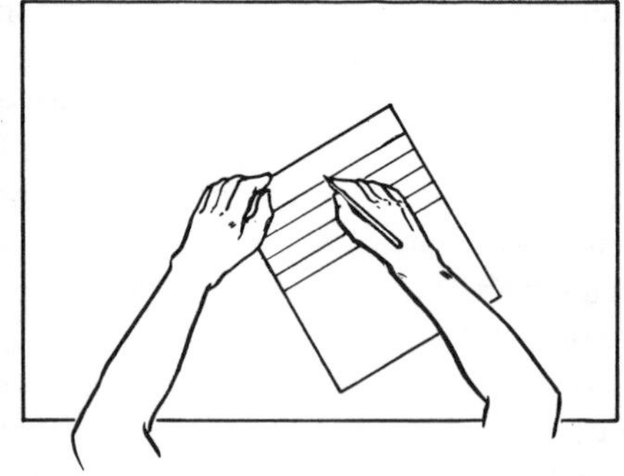

Figure 10–11. Recommended writing positions for left-handed and right-handed children. (Reprinted by permission from G. Hildreth, "The Development and Training of Hand Dominance: I. Characteristics of Handedness," *Journal of Genetic Psychology*, **75,** 197–220. Copyright © 1949, The Journal Press.)

for right-handed and left-handed children. The left-handed child was thought to profit from help in assuming a certain position at the blackboard and a position while seated.

The left-handed child can use adult help in other situations too, although probably none are so important as that of writing. He can be placed at the dinner table in such a way that his hand preference will not interfere with other people. He will need certain kinds of special equipment, such as left-handed scissors. If adults accept his special laterality casually, he will most likely avoid being embarrassed over it himself and hence will be less inclined to be awkward. Advantages can be appreciated, too, such as those accruing on the baseball diamond and tennis court.

SUMMARY

Growth is relatively slow during middle childhood. Wide individual differences exist at the end of the elementary-school period, however, since the onset of the pubescent growth spurt occurs then in some children and not in others. Boys are, on the average, slightly taller and heavier than girls, except for the years from 11 to 13, when girls are bigger because of being farther along in the pubescent growth spurt. Height increases more steadily than weight, since weight is more responsive to environmental changes. School-age children's bodily proportions contribute to their growing grace and agility. Facial proportions change, too, with the lower portion of the face growing more rapidly than the upper part. Different stages of bodily maturity can be distinguished during the middle years.

Certain aspects of physiological and anatomical maturing are especially significant. Fat decreases and changes somewhat in its distribution pattern. Muscles, although more firmly connected than in the preschool child, are still immature and easily strained. The digestive system is less prone to upsets than in a younger child. In relation to the size of the stomach, calorie needs are small. Bladder capacity varies, girls having a greater average capacity than boys. Respiration becomes slower and deeper. The heart is small in relation to the rest of the body. Growth of the face results in a change in the orientation of the Eustachian tube, which becomes more resistant to invasion by disease organisms. Visual defects increase throughout the school years. The skeleton matures, replacing cartilage with bone. As revealed by X rays, the skeleton is a useful maturity indicator. The baby teeth are replaced by permanent teeth, and additional permanent teeth erupt, the jaw growing to accommodate them.

Mortality has declined and health improved. Respiratory disturbances are the most frequent type of illness. The communicable diseases have declined in seriousness and incidence, due largely to immunization. Illness is prevented also by good nutrition, rest, exercise, protection from physical and mental stress and cleanliness. Health is promoted also by good convalescent care and by teaching children principles and practices of self-care. Special health problems include dental caries and malnutrition, both of which are related to poverty.

Accidents are an important cause of death and injury of children, affecting more boys than girls. Chronic illnesses or impairments affect over 2 million children under 14. Growth is sometimes but not always adversely affected by chronic diseases and long-term disabilities. Certain activities are limited, resulting in handicapped children growing up in environments which differ significantly from those of normal children. Psychological effects of handicaps vary with the type of handicap and with the cultural and family environment of the child.

Many kinds of vigorous motor play, such as ball games, running, chasing and jumping, are almost universal. Special motor skills reflect the values of the culture in which the child grows up. American parents tend to want their children to be moderately competent in many areas, often turning to experts for instruction for their children. School-age children build upon the basic motor skills learned in preschool years, practicing diligently and achieving a variety of competencies and interests.

The components of motor ability include strength, impulsion, speed, precision coordination and flexibility. Various tests can be employed to measure these components, either as overall characteristics or as characteristics of certain parts of the body. General motor ability can be measured by a test which places the child in relation to other children his age. A test which measures flexibility and strength, used to compare Americans with Europeans, indicated that American children are inferior in these aspects of motor coordination. The ability to inhibit movement is important for getting along well in school. Impulsive movement is related to style of thinking.

Laterality includes preference for using one hand rather than the other, preference for one eye or for one foot. Cultures define laterality as right or wrong, good or bad, acceptable or not. Certain functions are reserved for one hand or the other. The child who does not fit into such rules and customs is handicapped, both through the attitudes of other people and because tools and arrangements are awkward for him. With some children, the nonpreferred hand can be brought into dominant use, often without noticeable harmful effects. When the child persists in using the unconventional hand, he needs special help in writing and other manual skills. Reading difficulties seem to be associated more with left-right confusion than with lateral dominance.

REFERENCES

1. Belmont, L., & Birch, H. G. Lateral dominance and right-left awareness in normal children. *Child Devel.,* 1963, **34,** 257–270.
2. Belmont, L., & Birch, H. G. Lateral dominance, lateral awareness and reading disability. *Child Devel.,* 1965, **36,** 57–71.

3. Breckenridge, M. E., & Murphy, M. N. *Growth and development of the young child* (7th ed.). Philadelphia: Saunders, 1963.
4. Breckenridge, M. E., & Vincent, E. L. *Child development* (5th ed.). Philadelphia: Saunders, 1965.
5. Eichorn, D. H. Biological correlates of behavior. In H. W. Stevenson, *Child psychology.* The sixty-second yearbook of the National Society for the Study of Education, Part I. Chicago: Univer. of Chicago, 1963, pp. 4–61.
6. Fisher, S. Developmental sex differences in right-left perceptual directionality. *Child Devel.,* 1962, **33,** 463–468.
7. Flory, C. D. Osseous development in the hand as an index of skeletal development. *Mono. Soc. Res. Child Devel.,* 1936, **1:**3.
8. Garn, S. M. Fat weight and fat placement in the female. *Science,* 1957, **125,** 1091.
9. Glassow, R. B., & Kruse, P. Motor performance of girls age 6 to 14 years. *Res. Quart.,* 1960, **31,** 426–433.
10. Goodenough, F. L. The development of the reactive process from early childhood to maturity. *J. Exptl. Psychol.,* 1935, **18,** 431–450.
11. Goodman, N., Richardson, S. A., Dornbusch, S. M., & Hastorf, A. H. Variant reactions to physical disabilities. *Am. Sociol. Rev.,* 1963, **28,** 429–435.
12. Greulich, W. W., & Pyle, S. I. *Radiographic atlas of skeletal development of the hand and wrist* (2d ed.). Stanford, Calif.: Stanford Univer., 1959.
13. Guilford, J. P. A system of the psychomotor abilities. *Am. J. Psychol.,* 1958, **71,** 164–174.
14. Gutteridge, M. V. A study of motor achievements of young children. *Arch. Psychol.,* 1939, No. 244.
15. Harmon, D. B. Some preliminary observations on the developmental problems of 160,000 elementary school children. *Woman's Medic. J.,* 1942, **49,** 75–82. Cited in Breckenridge [4].
16. Herrick, V. E. *Comparison of practices in handwriting advocated by nineteen commercial systems of handwriting instruction.* Madison: Committee on Research in Basic Skills, Univer. of Wisconsin, 1960. (Mimeo.)
17. Jenkins, L. M. A comparative study of motor achievements of children at five, six and seven years of age. *Contributions to Education.* New York: Teachers College, Columbia Univer., 1930, No. 414.
18. Kagan, J., Moss, H. A., & Sigel, I. E. Psychological significance of styles of conceptualization. In J. C. Wright & J. Kagan (Eds.), Basic cognitive processes in children. *Mono. Soc. Res. Child Devel.,* 1963, **28:**2, 73–111.
19. Kraus, H., & Hirschland, R. P. Minimum muscular fitness tests in school children. *Res. Quart.,* 1954, **25,** 178–185.
20. Legislative Reference Service. *Problems of youth.* Washington, D.C.: Government Printing Office, 1964.
21. Martin, P. C., & Vincent, E. L. *Human development.* New York: Ronald, 1960.
22. Metropolitan Life Insurance Company. Health of the school-age population. *Stat. Bull.,* 1961, **42:**8, 1–3.
23. Metropolitan Life Insurance Company. Accident hazards of school-age children. *Stat. Bull.,* 1964, **45:**9, 3–5.

24. Miller, D. R., & Swanson, G. E. *The changing American parent.* New York: Wiley, 1958.
25. Morsh, J. E. The development of right-handed skill in the left-handed child. *Child Devel.,* 1930, **1,** 311–324.
26. Olson, W. C. *Child development* (2d ed.). Boston: Heath, 1959.
27. Richardson, S. A., Hastorf, A. H., & Dornbusch, S. M. Effects of physical disability on a child's description of himself. *Child Devel.,* 1964, **35,** 893–907.
28. Riesman, D., Glazer, N., & Denny, R. *The lonely crowd.* New Haven: Yale Univer., 1950.
29. Rosenberg, B. G., & Sutton-Smith, B. A revised conception of masculine-feminine differences in play activities. *J. Genet. Psychol.,* 1960, **96,** 165–170.
30. Simon, M. D. Body configuration and school readiness. *Child Devel.,* 1959, **30,** 493–512.
31. Sloan, W. The Lincoln-Oseretsky motor development scale. *Genet. Psychol. Mono.,* 1955, **51,** 183–251.
32. Smart, S. S. Personal communication, 1964.
33. Smart, S. S. Social class differences in parent behavior in a natural setting. *J. Marr. Fam.,* 1964, **26,** 223–224.
34. Strang, R. *An introduction to child study* (4th ed.). New York: Macmillan, 1959.
35. Tanner, J. M. *Growth at adolescence* (2d ed.). Oxford: Blackwell, 1962.
36. Valadian, I., Stuart, H. C., & Reed, R. B. Studies of illnesses of children followed from birth to eighteen years. *Mono. Soc. Res. Child Devel.,* 1961, **26:**3.
37. Watson, E. H., & Lowrey, G. H. *Growth and development of children* (4th ed). Chicago: Year Book, 1962.
38. Zubeck, J. F., & Solberg, P. A. *Human development.* New York: McGraw-Hill, 1954.

Intellectual Development

CHAPTER 11

The central problem of the school age, the development of the sense of industry, requires the child to solve intellectual problems and to develop intellectual skills, along with the motor coordinations and social skills which also contribute to his adequacy. As Chapter 7 showed, intellectual development proceeds through growth in three main modes, thinking, imagination and language. These three activities are intimately related and dependent on one another.

CHARACTERISTICS OF THINKING DURING MIDDLE CHILDHOOD

As was true during the preschool period, an important part of cognition is the taking in of information and processing it into meaningful and useful form. Information and experience are stored as memories, to be tapped when needed. When memories are in the form of words, they are likely to be more easily available. The outstanding cognitive developments during this period are increased freedom and control in thinking and increased understanding of relationships between events and/or symbols. The child takes satisfaction in his feeling that there exists a systematic, productive way of thinking about experience and in his conviction that he can think thus [23, p. 139].

Flexibility of Thought

While the preschool child reacts rather promptly to his perceptions of the moment, the school-age child can delay his response while he takes several aspects of the situation into account. His thoughts range back and forth in various directions, dealing with more than one perception at a time, comparing them, considering them in relation to past experience and knowledge. Thus he shows more control, as well as flexibility. With his increasing store of memories, his past becomes more and more useful for evaluating and interpreting the present. The preschool child is egocentric or centered in his thinking, limited in such a way that he cannot consider and weigh several pertinent factors at one time; the school-age child is less egocentric or more decentered in his thinking. Another aspect of the immobility of preschool thinking is that the child is centered on his own point of view. With his growing flexibility of thought, the older child can look at situations from the points of view of other people.

The child's increasing mobility of thought enters into everything that he does, his classifying, ordering and dealing with numbers, his language, his social relationships and self-concepts. His thinking is limited in flexibility, however. He tends to think about concrete things rather than about abstractions.

Reversibility is one aspect of the flexible and controlled thinking which emerges during middle childhood. Reversibility has two meanings, both of which apply. First, the child can think an act and then think it undone. He can think himself part way through a sequence of action, return to the first of it and then start out in another direction. In contrast to thoughts, motor acts and perceptions are irreversible, since they cannot be undone. Reversibility is one of the most important differences between thought and action. When the child can try out different courses of action mentally, instead of having to touch and see in order to believe, he has the advantage of a quicker and more powerful control over his environment and himself.

The second meaning of reversibility is that any operation can be canceled by an opposite operation. For example, the operation of subtracting three from five is canceled by the operation of adding three to two. $5 - 3 = 2$ is canceled by $2 + 3 = 5$. Another example is this: all children minus all girls equals all boys; all boys plus all girls equals all children. Also: hemisphere minus torrid zone minus frigid zone equals temperate zone; temperate zone plus frigid zone plus torrid zone equals hemisphere. The child learns that there are certain kinds of things which can be taken apart and put back together again into their original form and that he can do this dissembling and reassembling in his thoughts.

Concrete Operations

The name that Piaget gives to the stage of cognition which lasts from about 7 to 11 is the period of concrete operations. At this time, the child understands and uses certain principles of relationships between things and ideas. In this understanding and using, he operates on (does something to) objects, ideas and symbols. He adds and subtracts. He classifies and orders. He applies rules to social situations. Each operation fits into a system and the systems fit together. The operation two-plus-two-equals-four fits into a system of addition, which is part of a system of arithmetic.

The infant's cognitive behavior is sensorimotor, concerned with simple adjustments to the immediate present, symbolic behavior being completely absent. The preschool child begins to use symbols in some kinds of representational thought. Beginning at around seven years, children can use symbols consistently to perform acts of cognition which are abstracted and freed from complete dependence on sensory stimulation. The adolescent can think in more abstract terms than the child, however. During the years between 7 and 11, the child makes great strides in understanding principles of relationships and in his use of symbols for manipulating or operating on experience. Developing certain logical rules in dealing with his experiences, he performs two important operations, classifying and ordering.

CLASSIFYING. Although children in the preoperational period are dominated by their immediate perceptions in their grouping of objects, children in the stage of concrete operations can reflect upon and choose the qualities by which they group. From the experience of picking out a group of objects with something in common, the child internalizes (creates a mental structure of) the common quality into a concept of a class. Strolling along the beach, he collects small, hard objects into his pail, squats down and sorts them into a pile of shells and a pile of stones. From these activities, he comes to think of shells and of stones. He builds a concept *shell* and a concept *stone*. From more experiences on the beach, he can build concepts of bivalves and univalves, of clams and scallops, of marine life and terrestrial life. An important aspect of his understanding of classes is that he can also think of subclasses. Suppose our shell collector, in the stage of concrete operations, has his bivalves sorted into a pile of six scallop shells and ten clam shells. Ask him, "Do you have more clam shells or more shells?" He will know that he has more shells. His preschool brother, however, who knows full well the difference between clams and scallops, will most likely answer, "More clam shells." The younger child cannot compare a part with the whole which includes the part; the older child can. When the younger child thinks of the clam shells (the subclass), it seems as though he takes them out of the shells (the class), leaving the scallop shells (the other subclass), with which he then compares the clam shells. In order to appreciate the achievement of the older child, then, it is necessary to understand the limits of the younger one. It is indeed an indication of cognitive growth when the child is able to deal simultaneously with more than one order of classes.

A very cherished activity of children in the elementary-school years is collecting. Children collect stamps, butterflies, coins, match books, trading cards, evergreen cones, rocks, and so on. Although some of the motivation for collecting may be imitation of peers or receiving a stamp book for Christmas, the main push comes from classifying as an emergent ability. Just as the youngster thrilled to riding his tricycle after he mastered the pedals, he now enjoys collecting for the sake of collecting. And just as he first splashed colors onto his nursery school easel without planning ahead, he starts out as a rather indiscriminate collector. Any stamps—any cones—will do. Crude classifying is satisfying at first. Then finer classifications are made as the child grows in his ability to conceptualize more and more complicated classificatory systems. As the child matures, he classifies more and more on the basis of abstract ideas and less on the basis of perception or personal experience. The results from a test of sorting objects, given at several age levels from kindergarten through college, and also to adult scientists, proves these points [10]. Figure 11–1 shows the prevalence of three different bases for classifying, as they occurred at the various levels of maturity. Classifying on basis of perception is illustrated by the line for color, which drops sharply between kindergarten and first grade and remains fairly constant after second grade. Situation, as a basis for classifying, represents personal experience, as, for example, when the subject explains his selection by saying, "You buy them all in a hardware store." This rationale for sorting is high in the early grades, dropping

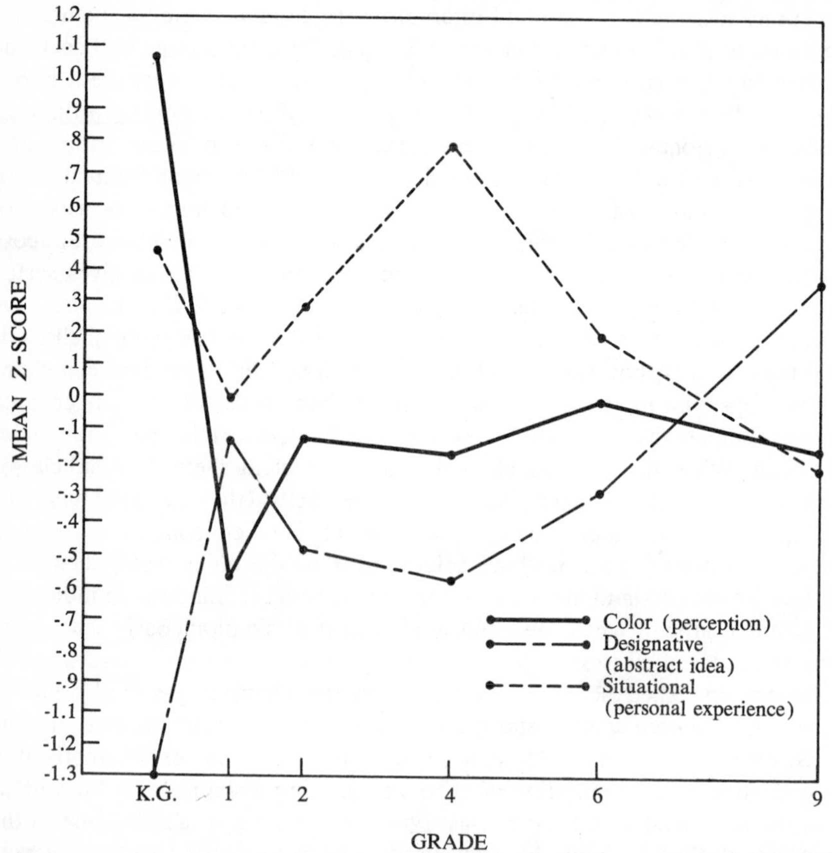

Figure 11–1. Age changes in the use of three different bases for classifying objects. Younger children use personal experience and perception more and abstract ideas less than older children. (Adapted from A. E. Goldman and M. Levine, "A Developmental Study of Object Sorting," *Child Development,* **34,** Figures 3, 4, and 5. Copyright © 1963, The Society for Research in Child Development, Inc.)

steadily after fourth grade. Classification in terms of an abstract idea occurs seldom in the kindergarten and frequently in the higher grades.

RELATIONS AND ORDERING. From the experience of arranging things in order, the child internalizes concepts of relations. A little girl arranges her dolls so that they can watch her dance for them, the tallest doll on the bottom step, the next tallest on the second step, and so on up to the shortest doll on top. The child's activities are preparing her to have concepts of decreasing and increasing size, concepts of relations. The place where the term *relations* is commonly used, in regard to family members, is a true example of concepts of relations. Many experiences must go into building the concepts on which family trees hang.

Ordering activities occur often in children's play. Objects collected can be ordered inside their classes—all the coins arranged in order of their minting dates, the evergreen cones according to length. Children may line each other up, using height as a criterion, for the purpose of taking turns. Just as they enjoy using their newly developed ability to classify, so do they enjoy ordering the world in terms of various relations.

Children find the world ordered for them, too. The kindergarten teacher lines them up for going to the bathroom and getting morning milk. Perhaps she helps them to order sounds in terms of high to low or colors from light to dark. Early in the school career, the child meets that remarkable ordering device, the alphabet. An ever-widening collection of symbols called words, he finds, can be ordered in terms of their structure and its relation to the alphabet. He learns that many other kinds of relations and orders exist and that it is his job to learn them. Relations of events in time are called history. Relations of places in space are called geography. (Relate time relations and space relations and you get geology and astronomy, but these come later in school. The child in the stage of concrete operations is aware of them, however.)

Numbers are concepts derived from the operations of classifying and ordering. A cardinal number is a class. *Four* means a group of four apples or four automobiles or four abracadabras. An ordinal number is a relation. Fourth is related to third and fifth in size and position. A real understanding of *four* requires an understanding of *fourth,* and vice versa. Thus classifying and ordering are interlocking and essential processes in the development of number concepts.

Conservation

As cognitive structures develop, the child builds a more and more permanent, stable and inclusive picture of the world, the people in it, himself and their interrelationships. As a baby, he learned about the permanence of objects, that things continued to exist even when he could not perceive them. As a preschool child, he began to form concepts of space, relations, time and number, but he was dominated by his perceptions. As concepts become more organized the child achieves the idea of constancy. Substance, quantity and number are seen as permanent. Conservation of number, for example, means that the child realizes that seven is always seven, whether it consists of 3 + 4, 5 + 2, : : :., . . : . :, $\substack{*\,*\,*\,*\\ *\,*\,*}$, or any other arrangement.

Conservation of substance means that the child realizes that the amount of material stays the same if nothing is added or taken away, even though the shape and/or position of the material change. One of Piaget's methods of exploring a child's conservation of substance is with two equal balls of clay. After the child has agreed that they contain equal amounts, the examiner rolls one ball into a sausage and asks, "Which has more clay?" The child in the stage of concrete operations will say that they are the same, while the child who has not achieved conservation of substance will reply either that the ball is larger (because it is fatter) or the sausage is larger (because it is longer). A variation on this test is to break one ball into little bits and ask whether the ball or the heap of bits contains more clay. If the child cannot conserve, he will say that the bits contain less (because they are smaller) or that they contain more (because there are more pieces). Conservation of substance can be demonstrated with liquid, starting with the same amounts of lemonade in two identical glasses and then pouring the contents of one glass into a thinner or a fatter glass. Or liquid from one glass can be poured into two and questions asked about whether the amount is the same. When the clay ball and sausage test was given to 322 English children between 7 and 12, results showed how conservation ability was distributed [20]. In stage 1, nonconservation, the child denied conservation. In stage 2, he sometimes admitted it, sometimes denied it. In stage 3, he was firmly convinced of conservation.

The idea of conservation is by no means an all-or-none notion which the child either has or does not have. As can be seen by Table 11–1, there is a transition stage for the specific experiment mentioned. Research shows that for different situations that have to do with *amount,* conservation is achieved at different times [19]. For example, many children recognized that there was

TABLE 11–1

Percentage of children at each year in the junior school (ages 7 through 11) in various stages of understanding conservation of amount.

No. of Children	*Stage 3 Conservation %*	*Stage 2 Transition %*	*Stage 1 Non-Conservation %*
1st year (83)	36	33	31
2nd year (65)	68	12	20
3rd year (99)	74	15	11
4th year (75)	86	9	5

Source: Reprinted by permission from K. Lovell, *Growth of Basic Mathematical and Scientific Concepts in Children* (New York: Philosophical Library, Inc., 1962), Table 1, p. 63.

the same amount of rubber in a rubber band before and after stretching before they appreciated conservation in the clay ball and sausage experiment. Furthermore, some of the nonconservers of the ball and sausage situation were able to conserve when liquid was poured into a glass of different shape. Conservation is not achieved at the same time for the different ways of ordering, as, for example, amount and weight. The children who were tested for conservation of amount were tested for conservation of weight also [20]. They were shown two balls of clay, the smaller one weighted so as to make it heavier. After the child had agreed that the smaller ball was heavier than the larger one, the latter was rolled into a sausage and questions asked about the weights of the sausage and ball. Table 11–2 shows the distribution of children at each

TABLE 11–2

Percentage of children at each year in the junior school (ages 7 through 11) in various stages of understanding conservation of weight.

Year	*Stage 3 Conservation* %	*Stage 2 Transition* %	*Stage 1 Non-Conservation* %	*No. of Children Tested*
1st year	4	5	91	57
2nd year	36	36	29	73
3rd year	48	20	32	66
4th year	74	13	13	168
				364

Source: Reprinted by permission from K. Lovell, *Growth of Basic Mathematical and Scientific Concepts in Children* (New York: Philosophical Library, Inc., 1962), Table 2, p. 71.

stage of conservation. Comparing it with the previous table, it can be seen that weight conservation, as shown by this experiment, developed more slowly than conservation of amount. Conservation of volume is acquired after conservation of weight. No matter which material was used for testing, conservation of amount, weight and volume were achieved in that order [31]. However, the times at which the child went through the amount-weight-volume sequence varied from one material to another.

That conservation develops at different times in regard to different situations is an argument for the importance of experience in building mental structures. As the child interacts with his environment, he learns first here, then there, and finally everywhere, that substance, weight, length, area and numbers remain the same throughout changes in arrangement and position. The following investigation underlines the role of practical experience in the speed with which weight conservation is learned [19]. Children who were not conservers in regard to amount of sausages and balls of clay were asked, "What would happen to the weight of a piece of butter if it hardened?" and "What would happen to the weight of a lump of clay plasticine if it got harder?" Many more children conserved with the weight of butter than the weight of plasticine. These children had had frequent experience in shopping for butter by weight and in seeing it soften and harden under different conditions at home. They knew from many experiences that the weight of the butter stayed the same under varying conditions of shape and texture. With plasticine, though, the weight had rarely if ever been a matter of any practical importance.

Attempts to teach children conservation have generally met with indifferent success, especially when children were younger than the age at which it is normally learned. Using subjects between six years five months and seven years eight months, with an average age of six years eleven months, a successful experiment was carried on [33]. Children who failed tests of conservation were divided into two groups, one of which received instruction and the other of which did not. The instruction was based on the idea that the concept of reversibility contributes heavily to the concept of conservation. Using dolls and doll beds, the experimenter and child went through a standard series of situations in which the child put the dolls into the beds and took them out with, for example, the dolls close together, the dolls closer together and a bed removed, the dolls farther apart, and the dolls farther apart and a bed added. The experimenter would question the child each time in such ways as, "Do you think we can put a doll in every bed now?" Each situation was repeated until the child predicted correctly and confirmed his prediction. All subjects but one succeeded, after training, in demonstrating conservation, and the whole control group showed no change. What is more, the trained children transferred the notion of conservation to a test which used checkers and cards instead of dolls and doll beds.

Conservation has been found to be related to other cognitive measures. Among young children who were developing conservation, there was a tendency for those with higher IQs to achieve conservation earlier [1, 8]. The complexity of the task also made a difference as to whether young children conserved amount [8]. Success in conservation tests was somewhat related to success on a stencil design test, picture vocabulary, reading and measurement [1]. Transitivity tests might be expected to correlate more highly with conservation tests, and this was indeed the case [25]. (Concrete transitivity was shown when a child, after seeing that stick *A* was longer than stick *B* and that stick *B* was longer than stick *C*, concluded that stick *A* was longer than stick *C*.) Among children 4 to 10 years of age who were tested for both conservation and transitivity, most of those who showed transitivity also showed conservation, and most of those who did not show transitivity did not show conservation [25].

Cognitive Style

Children use their mental structures in a variety of ways. To say that two children have the same IQ or the same mental age is not to imply that they think in the same ways or that they will achieve the same products. Nor does it mean similarity of cognitive behavior if two children develop conservation and transitivity at the same time. To get at some of the differences in the ways in which children behave intellectually, the concept *cognitive style* is useful.

There are different ways of organizing perceptions and classifying and finding solutions to problems. The particular ways preferred by an individual are called his *cognitive style*. Kagan and associates [14] have found that some children analyze the environment much more minutely than do others in forming concepts and producing answers. "Some children are splitters, others are lumpers," they say. The tendency to differentiate the stimulus environment, in contrast to responding to the stimulus-as-a-whole, they call "an analytic attitude." To test cognitive style in children, they used a set of stimuli, each containing three drawings. The child was asked to select two figures which "were alike or went together in some way." Since the drawings could be grouped in two or three ways, the child's first choice was considered his preference. An analytic response would be choosing the two figures holding knives in Figure 11–2. A relational response would be choosing the hunter and the dead deer. Other tests used were word association tests, word lists to be learned and figure sorting tests, all of which gave indications as to the child's preference for conceptualizing by analytical, relational or inferential concepts. (Inferential concepts involve making an inference about the items grouped together, not on objective description. For instance, the two figures would be chosen not as holding knives but as killers.)

An analytic style is based on two fundamental tendencies, both of which are quite stable in the individual, the tendency to analyze visual presentations and reflectivity [15]. Reflectivity refers to one of the characteristics of school-age thought which was discussed in the first part of this chapter, under the heading "Flexibility of Thought," the delaying of a response while considering various aspects of the situation, mentally trying out different solutions before

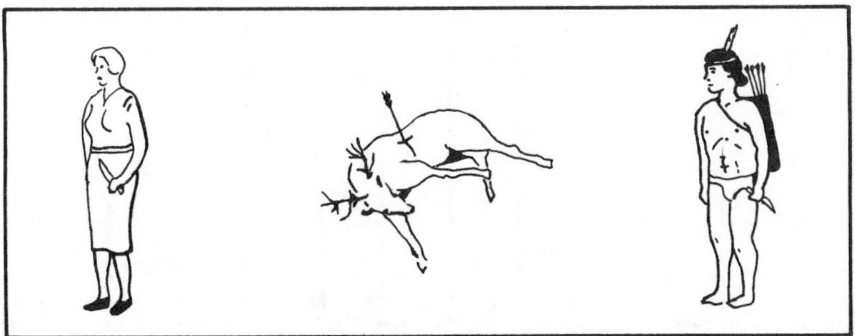

Figure 11–2. An example of the stimuli used in the test for conceptual style for children. The child was asked to choose two figures which "were alike or went together in some way." (Adapted from J. Kagan, H. A. Moss, and I. E. Sigel, "Psychological Significance of Styles of Conceptualization," *Monographs of The Society for Research in Child Development,* **28,** Figure 2. Copyright © 1963, The Society for Research in Child Development, Inc. Used by permission.)

deciding on the answer. Reflectivity does *not* mean the delaying of response because of fear or inability to think of solutions. The opposite of reflectivity is impulsivity, which involves responding quickly, without first thinking of alternative solutions. The relationship between reflectivity and analytic concepts is stronger in boys than in girls.

Children tend to become more reflective and more analytic as they grow older [14]. Figure 11–3 shows the increase in analytic responses from grade one through grade six. Although there is, on the average, no sex difference in reflectivity, the extremes do show a difference between boys and girls [13]. There are more very reflective boys than girls and more very impulsive boys than girls. Impulsivity is expressed in motor behavior as well as in cognitive behavior. Perhaps the motor impulsivity is basic to the cognitive impulsivity, but in any case, there are more boys than girls who show extreme lack of motor inhibition. The student can easily verify this statement by observing a few times in a kindergarten or grade school, where he will be almost sure to see one or more little boys unable to sit still for more than a few moments. These youngsters wriggle in their chairs, sharpen their pencils often, throw things in the waste basket, get frequent drinks of water, drop things on the floor, poke their neighbors and pay attention to all sorts of extraneous stimuli.

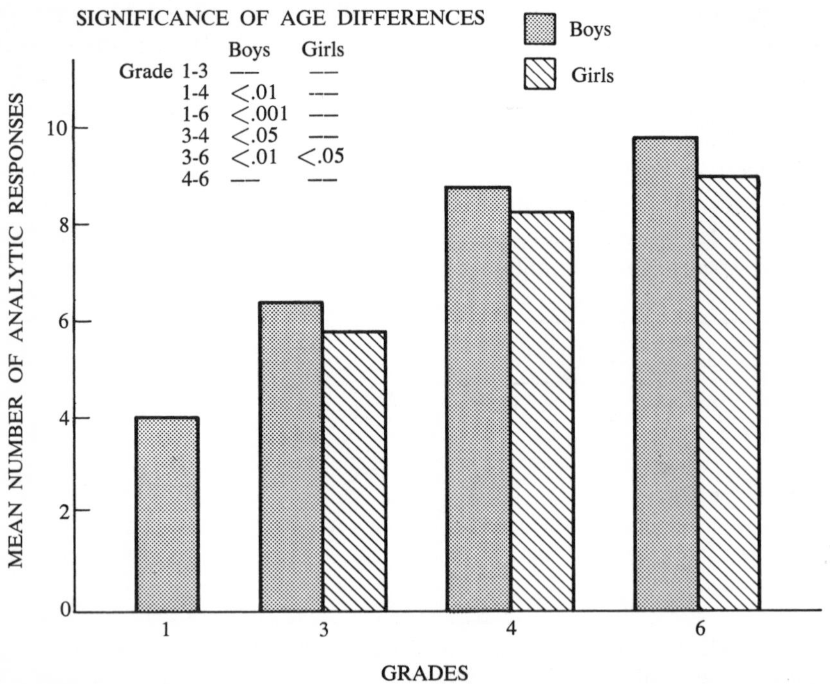

Figure 11–3. Analytic responses of boys and girls to conceptual style test, grades one through six. (Reprinted by permission from J. Kagan, H. A. Moss, and I. E. Sigel, "Psychological Significance of Styles of Conceptualization," *Monographs of The Society for Research in Child Development,* **28,** Figure 3. Copyright © 1963, The Society for Research in Child Development, Inc.)

Understandably, it is likely to be hard for very impulsive children to learn to read. Not only does their motor activity preclude sitting still long enough to concentrate; the beginning reader who responds very quickly is likely to give the wrong answer. Without pausing to reflect on whether the letter is *b* or *d* or *p,* for example, the child encounters many sources of error. It has been found that the impulsive child is more likely to make a mistake in the latter part of the word rather than the first part [14].

Now let us examine the other of the two fundamental tendencies which contribute to analytic style, the tendency to analyze visual presentations. A significant sex difference is usually found when this area is investigated, with boys and men superior [14, 21, 35]. For example, in Kagan's previously mentioned study, boys would be more likely than girls to group the two figures holding knives, while girls would be more likely than boys to place together the hunter and the deer. There are, of course, girls and women who are analytic in their concept formation, and there are boys and men who prefer relational concepts. Differences exist between individuals, regardless of sex.

The sources of differences in regard to analytic thinking have been sought by Maccoby [21], who attributes an important role to the child's assumption of initiative, responsibility and independence. Since analytic concepts are important for success in mathematics and of less use in language tests, it is pertinent to investigate the childrearing methods of mothers of analytic and nonanalytic children, and of children with high or low mathematical ability. Overprotected boys, whose mothers babied them at age 10 or 11 by taking them to school and helping them to dress, were very poor in math but good in language [18]. A comparison of girls who were high in math and low in verbal, with girls whose talents were the opposite, showed that the mothers of the former tended to leave their daughters alone to solve problems. Girls who were high in verbal tests and low in math were likely to have mothers who intruded when their daughters worked on problems, praising, criticizing and offering suggestions [3]. Further evidence comes from a study in which boys were tested for whether they saw visual presentations as wholes or whether they easily analyzed for details. Interviews with the mothers of these children revealed that the analytic youngsters had been given considerable freedom to explore the environment and to use their initiative, while the nonanalytic children had been kept closely tied to their mothers who were intolerant of self-assertion and who often talked about the dangers of the environment.

More detailed studies of analytic, differentiated children have confirmed earlier findings in regard to the mother's influence on the cognitive development of her child [7]. The investigators were interested in children who had distinct self concepts and who structured and analyzed their experiences. They found a relationship between these characteristics in children and tendencies in the mothers to permit or encourage their children in responsible activities, such as walking to school alone, going to camp, doing homework, keeping appointments and taking care of pets. Children tended to see mothers with these characteristics as supportive to them.

ADVANTAGES OF ANALYTIC AND NONANALYTIC STYLES. While the analytic style is more useful in certain fields, such as mathematics and physics, other styles can be more productive in other areas. A very strong reflective attitude may be a disadvantage in the humanities, arts and social sciences [15]. It has been suggested that good memory for faces is more common among people who experience situations globally than among those who react analytically [37, p. 121]. Research [17] shows that while an analytic style is efficient in learning analytic concepts, a different approach gives quicker results with relational concepts. Third grade boys were tested to see how quickly they learned, for example, that *ces* (a nonsense syllable) stood for objects with a missing leg, as shown by pictures of a table, boy and bird, and that *hib* (another nonsense syllable) meant objects related to school, as shown by teacher, crayons and globe. Boys with analytic style learned the first concept more quickly. To learn analytic concepts, the analytic boys took an average of 20.3 trials, while the nonanalytic boys required 38.7 trials. For the relational concepts, analytic boys had 35.4 trials and the nonanalytic boys 27.9. Thus the speed with which concepts were learned was related to the cognitive style of the subjects, with each style having an advantage and a disadvantage in the array of tasks presented.

LANGUAGE

Intimately associated with cognitive development, language is both a product of intellectual growth and a contributor to it. The school-age child masters more of the mechanics of his language, articulating more clearly, using longer and more complicated sentences and doubling his vocabulary, both spoken and understood, between first and sixth grade [26].

Normative Examples

Level of abstraction and facility in using *words* can be traced in intelligence tests. To give an idea of the average abilities at each year, the following examples are presented from the Stanford–Binet test [27].

Year 6. Defines six words such as *orange, envelope, puddle.*
Opposite analogies. ("A bird flies, a fish . . .)
Describes or interprets a picture.

Year 7. Tells what is foolish in an absurd picture.
Tells how two things are alike (an apple and a peach).
Answers questions of comprehension. (What makes a sailboat move?)
Opposite analogies. (The rabbit's ears are long; the rat's ears are . . .)

Year 8. Defines eight words, such as *gown, roar, eyelash.*
Recalls a story.
Explains verbal absurdities.
Gives similarities and differences. (A baseball and an orange.)

Year 9. Makes rhymes. (A color that rhymes with head.)

Year 10. Defines 11 words, such as *juggler, scorch, lecture.*
Defines two of: pity, curiosity, grief, surprise.
Gives reasons. (Why children should not be too noisy in school.)
Names 28 words in a minute.

Year 11. Explains absurdities.
Defines three of: *connection, compare, conquest, obedience, revenge.*
Gives similarities between three things. (Snake, cow, sparrow.)

Socialized speech becomes more frequent as the child grows beyond egocentrism into the stage of concrete operations. More able to look at situations from another person's point of view, he tries to convey meaning, to understand what the other person is telling him and to give and take through words. (In egocentric speech, the child is not concerned with exchanging meaning with someone else but only with expressing himself.) Through socialized speech, he checks his perceptions and interpretations of reality with other people's. Egocentric speech decreases in observable form (see pages 233–234) as the child learns to speak to himself silently. Egocentric speech thus becomes the tool of thinking, problem solving and self-regulation. Freed from the dominance of moment-by-moment experience, the child can sit back and reflect. He has many more real choices of behavior open to him, since he can delay action while thinking. Having more possibilities for different kinds of action means that he is a more differentiated person, more of an individual. And because of being more truly an individual, there are more ways in which he can relate to other people. Thus the development of speech and thought contribute to the child's development as an individual and a social being.

Language and Concept Formation

The formation of a concept does not take place by memorizing a word and attaching it to objects. Rather the formation of a concept is a creative process which solves a problem [32, pp. 54–58]. A word is the mediating sign for the concept, helping in its formation, and then coming to stand for it. When a child first uses language, he employs words which stand for concepts, words given him by adults. He communicates with adults using these words which stand for approximations of the concepts for which adults use them. For Bobby, *teacher* means any one of the four ladies who run the four-grade school that he attends. For Bobby's father, *teacher* means any person who stands in an educational relationship to another person, in the past, present or future, anywhere in the universe. As children progress toward the stage of formal operations, they become capable of forming concepts which are more and more abstract.

The ways in which children learn words through verbal context were examined by Werner and Kaplan in one of the first studies to deal with this process [16, 34]. They show how concepts emerge as products of problem solving, whereas words come to stand for the concepts gradually, during their emergence. The subjects ranged in age from 8½ to 13½. The task was to find the meaning of 12 artificial words each of which appeared in six different contexts. For example, *lidber* (gather) was presented thus:

1. All the children will lidber at Mary's party.
2. The police did not allow the people to lidber on the street.
3. The people lidbered about the speaker when he finished his talk.
4. People lidber quickly when there is an accident.
5. The more flowers you lidber, the more you will have.
6. Jimmy lidbered stamps from all countries.

Under 10 or 11 years of age, children often indicated that they did not differentiate between the word and its context. Word–sentence fusion was apparent in their answers, as where one little boy said that Jimmy collected stamps from all countries, and then stated, "The police did not permit people to collect stamps on the street." The word *collect* had fused with a word from sentence 6, to make *collect stamps* instead of *collect.*

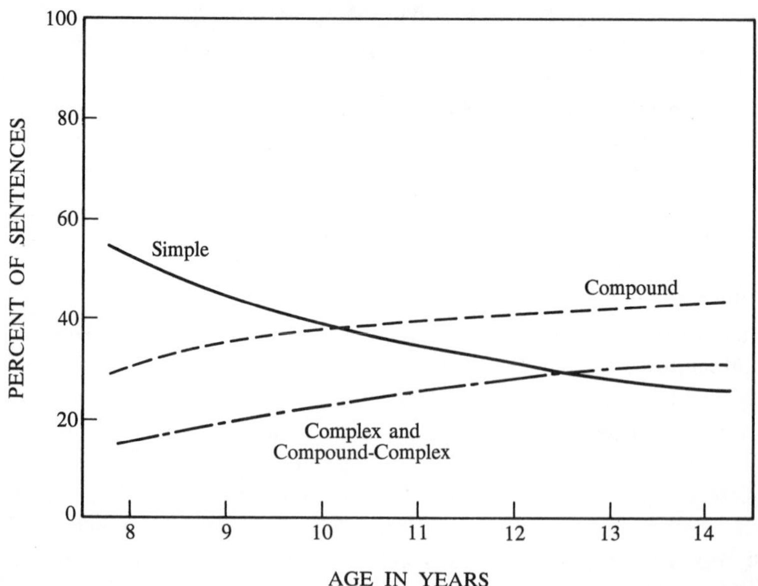

Figure 11–4. Frequencies of simple, complex, compound and complex-compound sentences in written compositions of children ages 8 through 14. (From G. A. Miller, *Language and Communication,* 1951. Used by permission of McGraw-Hill Book Company.)

The younger children's responses often showed a tendency to include more in a word meaning than an older person does and also to perceive a sentence as an undifferentiated whole. For instance, a child of 9½ responded to the sentence *People talk about the bordicks* [faults] *of others and don't like to talk about their own.* He said, "People talk about other people and don't talk about themselves, that's what bordick means." Then, when trying to fit his interpretation of bordick into the sentence *People with bordicks are often unhappy,* he said, "People that talk about other people are often unhappy . . . because this lady hears that someone is talking about her and she'll get mad." Thus he took more meaning from the first sentence than an adult would ascribe to *bordick* and tried to fit almost all of the context of the first sentence into the second. He could not isolate the meaning of *bordick* out of the first sentence in order to fit it into the second.

The nine-year-olds gave correct responses to only 6.7 percent of the sets of sentences, whereas the 13-year-olds succeeded with 47.7 percent. The younger children tended not to see the necessity for integrating the cues of all six contexts, but with increasing age, children tried harder and more successfully to integrate. Younger children tended to change the context of sentences to fit in with their solutions, whereas older ones showed more respect for the context as given. Throughout the age range studied, there was a growing appreciation of the sentence as a stable grammatical structure.

Throughout the childhood years the use of compound and complex sentences increases in relationship to the use of simple sentences. Figure 11–4 shows the frequencies of various types of sentences between ages 8 and 14, as calculated from children's written compositions.

IMAGINATION

The school-age child can and does use all the modes of imaginative expression in which the preschool child engages—fantasy, dreams, the performing arts and the producing arts. As it does throughout life, imagination is linked with controlled thinking and language to form the complex system with which human beings think, communicate, solve problems and create. The balance of these three links is, in middle childhood, a little different from what it was during the preschool years. Controlled thought and language have become more powerful instruments for dealing with the environment. Perhaps there is less need to solve problems through the use of fantasy, symbolism and other such imaginative means. On the other hand, it may be that the increased complexity of demands upon the child requires full use of all means at his disposal, including imaginative ones. Some students of creativity [30] have noted regretfully that in third and fourth grade certain tests show a drop in creativity. Although it may be, as is often claimed, that school practices discourage originality in children, there may be a more basic reason why the young grade-school child cuts down on some of his creative activity. Developing his sense of industry, he feels impelled to learn the accepted practices of his culture, the tried-and-true ways of producing, the techniques of work which adults and older children offer to him.

Since Chapter 8 is devoted to all forms of preschool imaginative behavior and Chapter 11 deals further with creativity, this section includes only two aspects of imaginative behavior, word magic and humor. In these two areas of behavior, middle childhood has a very distinctive flavor. In fact, it has been said that childhood has its own culture, consisting of behavior patterns which are passed from one generation of children to the next, without benefit (or contamination) of adult intervention. An extensive collection [22] of English children's language humor traces jokes and stories historically and geographically, revealing some connections with European and Middle Eastern children's language productions. Children's humor is shown to have broad, deep and ancient sources, connecting each generation of children with the past. Children apparently teach their rhymes and riddles to one another, initiating the younger ones, leaving the treasure with them and then almost forgetting it.

Word Magic

Words give power over reality. (The power of names is mentioned briefly on page 232.) To know a person's name is to have some control over him. In fact, to know the name of anything is to have some control over it. To label something—for example, an "inferiority complex"—gives one a feeling of understanding and control, albeit superficial and even handicapping to true understanding and control. The chants of childhood combine names with other magic-making words in order to induce certain feelings or behavior in playmates. For example:

Cry, Billy, cry
Stick your finger in your eye
And tell your mother it wasn't I.

The name-calling of childhood is half in earnest, half in play. Sometimes it is an imaginative attempt to produce a new verbal pattern, sometimes an effort to control or change reality. Mike, in a burst of annoyance at Chris, shouted, "You're a cringing crustacean." The result, a cowed and silent Chris, strengthened Mike's belief in word magic, for had not his words changed his friend?

Word magic, the power of words to change reality, is used more by children than adults, but it is not the exclusive property of children.

Star light, star bright
First star I've seen tonight
I wish I may, I wish I might
Have the wish I wish tonight.

What goes up the chimney?
Smoke.
May your wish and my wish
Never be broke.

If you say RABBITS for your first word on the first morning of the month, you'll have good luck all month. If two people say the same word together spontaneously, each will get a wish if he keeps quiet until asked a question. This is the simple word magic of childhood, so appealing that adults often engage in it "just for fun." (Our family says RABBITS.) Having only recently discovered the very real power of words, it is understandable that children attribute even more power to them than they actually have. It is hard to check reality in this respect. How can we possibly know that it did no good to say RABBITS this month? We have had pretty good luck. It surely did no harm. It was no trouble to say. We'll continue to say RABBITS when we remember. Eventually, of course, the educated person develops intellectually to the point where he rejects word magic from most of his life. Not in his grade school years, however. The less sophisticated person may continue to use word magic often throughout his life.*

Humor

Characteristic of the very creative human being, humor is the joint product of thinking, language and imagination, but especially of imagination. Since humor is a way of solving problems and reducing tensions, it is functionally related to each stage of life. A new phase in humor begins with the beginning of the school age, in keeping with the *industry* stage of personality development and the *concrete operations* of cognitive development. Long, rambling stories are no longer extremely funny. A joke has to be concise, with a surprise ending or punch line. Children use ready-made jokes or invent jokes similar to them [36]. With more realistic, objective thinking, the child does not permit himself the free-flowing fantasy of his preschool days, his stage of developing initiative and imagination. Although he still expresses his wishes, fears, aggression and anxiety, they are further down in his unconscious. They appear in more stylized form, like other people's, as the standard jokes of childhood. The "little moron" jokes are especially appropriate to the school-age child [36]. These children, concerned with industry, duty and accomplishment, with being smart, with adequacy, find the stupid behavior of the moron tension-relieving. The moron in their jokes is definitely not a child like themselves. He is an older person. The jokes disparage parents, teachers and the silly answers they give children. They reassure children that it is all right not to know the things they do not know and cannot find.

The following selection of typical American jokes comes from a book [11, p. 229]† on middle childhood. Too crude to amuse adults and yet possessing the surprise which a real joke requires, these examples show what is funny and tension-releasing to someone halfway between the preschool age and adulthood.

> What is black and white and read all over?
> A newspaper.
> No. A sunburned Zebra.

* A highly sophisticated person, too, may use word magic throughout life if he is a very creative person. Such people have extremely complex and flexible cognitive powers [2, p. 193]. An extremely creative adult can assume a childlike viewpoint temporarily, giving his imagination rein to work naïve magic, as did Lewis Carroll.

† From *Behavior and Development from Five to Twelve* by Glenn R. Hawkes and Damaris Pease. Copyright © 1962 by Glenn R. Hawkes and Damaris Pease. Reprinted by permission of Harper & Row, Publishers.

What was the president's name 35 years ago?
Calvin Coolidge.
No. Lyndon B. Johnson. His name doesn't change just because he is older.

What do ghosts eat for breakfast?
Ghost toasties and evaporated milk.

What does the mother ghost say to the baby ghost?
Don't spook until spooken to.

TEACHER: How would you punctuate this sentence: *I saw a five-dollar bill in the street.*
JIMMY: I would make a dash after it.

LINDA: Do you know I don't have all my toes on one foot?
DEBBIE: No! How did it happen?
LINDA: I have five on one foot and five on the other.

What did one eye say to the other?
Just between you and me something smells.

What's twelve and twelve?
Twenty-four.
Shut your mouth and say no more.

What's eight and eight?
Sixteen.
Stick your head in kerosene, wipe it off with ice cream
And show it to the king and queen.

INTELLIGENCE AND ACHIEVEMENT AS REVEALED THROUGH TESTS

Most schoolchildren are tested many times as part of academic procedure. Teachers give tests or examinations in order to see how much children have learned and, upon this basis, to give them grades or credits. Intelligence tests, achievement tests and diagnostic tests are given in various contexts, in order to achieve a variety of aims.

Several intelligence tests for children were mentioned in Chapter 7. The Stanford–Binet and the Wechsler Intelligence Test for Children were pointed out as those used most often for individual examinations. Both tests yield IQ's. The Wechsler also gives a percentile rating, showing how the child stands in relation to a representative 100 children. Verbal and nonverbal scores are a further advantage of the Wechsler, which is the test most often used with school-age children. When an individual test is administered, a qualified psychologist carries out carefully designated procedures in a room alone with the child. In addition to giving the items in standardized ways, the psychologist pays special attention to the child's comfort, alertness, motivation and any other such factors which might conceivably contribute to his doing the best he is capable of. The psychologist makes and records observations on the total behavior of the child, in addition to recording passes and failures on tests. Thus an individual intelligence test can yield valuable qualitative information, as well as scores.

For every individual test given, many group tests are administered. Teachers give the informal tests, quizzes and exams which they themselves make up as well as standardized tests which are made up and sometimes scored by nationwide test bureaus. A group test is a rough instrument, as compared with an individual test. When a child is one of a group, his own particular feelings, attitudes and needs cannot be taken into consideration to any degree. No qualitative observation can be made. The result is only a score which is an indication of how one child stands in relation to the group. Such tests are useful for revealing characteristics of the group and for pointing out children who need further study.

Prediction of Success

Intelligence tests correlate significantly with success in school, as measured by grades. Third and fourth grade children, tested on the Stanford–Binet test and on the California achievement tests, showed these correlations: IQ and arithmetic, 0.59 for girls and 0.50 for boys; IQ and reading, 0.57 for girls and 0.66 for boys [6]. Table 11–3 consists of correlations between Stanford–

TABLE 11–3

Correlations between ninth grade IQ and scores on achievement tests taken one year later.

Subject	*r with S-B*
Reading Comprehension	.73
Reading Speed	.43
English Usage	.59
History	.59
Biology	.54
Geometry	.48

Source: From E. A. Bond, *Tenth Grade Abilities and Achievements* (New York: Bureau of Publications, Teachers College, Columbia University 1940), p. 29. Reprinted by permission.

Binet IQ's and school grades in the tenth grade. Since the correlations are far from perfect, this table shows that academic success is based upon more than IQ but that IQ is an important factor. The Stanford–Binet and most other intelligence tests are adaptations and refinements of Binet's original procedures, which were devised in order to predict academic success.

There are many different ways of judging success. If the criterion of originality, or production of new ideas is considered, then IQ tests are of limited usefulness. Correlations between IQ and some tests of creative thinking are fairly high (from 0.11 to 0.73) if the subjects have a wide range of IQ's [24]. For a group of uniformly low, average or high IQ's, however, correlations with tests of creative thinking are generally low (0.00 to 0.45). For a group above 120 IQ, the correlation between creativity and IQ was positive but low [9]. Intelligence tests tend to sample the kinds of intellectual processes which produce *the* right answer to each question, whereas creativity tests sample processes which produce unusual, new, original, often multiple answers. The former type of thinking is called convergent, the latter divergent. It is reasonable, then, that if success is being defined in terms of creative production, IQ tests will not be used to predict it.

Success in adult life is more difficult to define than success in school, where grades are easily used as a measure. Many adults can point to at least one former schoolmate who has achieved status and success in business, a profession or the arts and who used to be a poor student in school. There is, however, some relation between intelligence at school age and performance as an adult. Children who tested at the low and high ends of the scale and a group of average scorers have been studied as adults. The various criteria of their success include earnings, status, degrees, publications, family behavior and survival rates. All criteria are shown to have some relation to childhood IQ by the two studies which follow.

Terman and his associates [28] have published four volumes of *Genetic Studies of Genius* in which over 1,000 gifted children were studied, between 1921 and 1945. The distribution of Stanford–Binet IQ's was between 135 and 200, with a mean of 151. Various criteria of success were used to appraise the subjects 25 years after their selection as gifted children, showing the widespread superiority of these people as adults. Half the men and over half the employed women were in professional occupations. This ratio was nine times the proportion of professional men in the general Californian population. Eighty percent of the men were in the two highest groups, as contrasted with 14 percent in the general professional population. Seventy percent were college graduates, as contrasted with 7 percent for the population of corresponding age. Twenty-five percent of the college graduates were elected to Phi Beta Kappa or Sigma Xi. Twenty-nine percent took graduate degrees. A random selection of people would probably contribute less than 5 percent of the doctors and lawyers produced by the gifted group. The subjects received a proportionately large number of scholarships, assistantships and fellowships. The gifted group earned significantly more money than the average, even though they were below the age for maximum earning capacity. The group had published 90 books and 1,500 articles. Nearly 100 patents had been granted.

Marriage and divorce rates and age at marriage were the same as in the general population, but for the gifted college graduates, as compared with all college graduates, incidence of marriage was higher, age of marriage lower, and the divorce rate lower. The married gifted group showed a slightly higher score on a marital happiness test than did a group of less gifted subjects. The mean IQ of the 384 offspring tested was 128, with fewer than expected below 80 IQ and those above 150 being 28 times as numerous as in the general population. The death rate was 4.0 percent, significantly lower than that of the general population the same age.

At the other end of the distribution of IQ's were 151 adults who had, as schoolchildren, been judged mentally deficient, because of IQ's below 70, placement in special classes for a year or more and teachers' and psychologists' evaluations [4]. The subjects' average age was 42. Only nine of them were institutionalized. All but seven of those not in institutions had at least part-time jobs. About 83 percent were self-supporting part of the time. The range of occupations included all categories from managerial to unskilled labor. The most common occupations were laborer for males and housekeeper for females. The higher-placed subjects included a business manager and a bookkeeper. The subjects were tested with the Wechsler Intelligence Test, on which scores are expected to be a little higher than on the Stanford–Binet. The results, however, averaged 23 points higher, an increase greater than the difference in the two tests would explain. IQ's ranged from 56 to 104. Improvement in performance scores was greater than in verbal scores.

About a third were entirely self-sufficient, less than half had some assistance from public relief funds and the remainder lived in institutions or with their parents. Types of dwellings ranged from filthy shacks to costly new houses. Eighty percent of the group were married, with a marriage rate slightly below the general population. Divorce rates were about average. About 80 percent of those married had children, most of whom were making average progress at school. The children's average IQ was 95, with a range from 50 to 138.

Higher than the national average, the death rate was 15 percent, with twice as many males as females deceased. Nearly a third of the deceased had died violently, a much greater percentage than the national average for violent deaths.

In all these measures of success, even in the global one of staying alive, the high IQ group greatly exceeded the low IQ's. And while the low IQ's did better than might have been expected in several measures, they were below average in most criteria. Overwhelming evidence points to the lifelong advantages of having a high IQ. Table 11–4 summarizes the comparison between the groups.

Adult outcomes of average childhood IQ's are rather surprising. Twenty-five subjects who had tested average (a mean IQ of 100) at age six were retested at an average age of 33, when the mean IQ of the group was 107 [5].

TABLE 11–4

Comparison of high and low IQ groups on criteria of success in life.

Success Criterion	*Terman's Gifted Group*			*Charles' Retarded Group*		
	Above Average	*Same*	*Below*	*Above Average*	*Same*	*Below*
Occupational status	X					X
Education	X					
Income	X					X
Publications	X					
Marriage rate		X				X
Divorce rate		X			X	
Marital happiness	X					
Children's intelligence	X				X	
Height & weight	X					
Death rate			X	X		

At age six, the range of IQ's was 96 to 104; at age 33, IQ's ranged from 90 to 132. Changes in IQ ranged from −8 to +29. Thus, a group of children who had tested average at age six were scattered all the way from the lower end of the average category to the superior level. In occupational classification, the subjects ranged from unskilled labor to professional, with a wide variety of jobs represented. Educational attainment ranged from eighth grade to graduate school. The results of the study suggest that IQ in the early elementary-school years is an inadequate basis on which to predict future achievement and from which to make educational plans for children who test average.

Estimating Readiness for Educational Experiences

Although IQ accounts in part for academic success, another important influence is the child's readiness to learn from the situation presented. Readiness is a function of the child's stage of maturation and of his "set" or motivation toward the particular kind of learning involved [12, p. 392]. Maturation is tested by physical-motor tests, most of which are appropriate for the infant and preschool child. The Lincoln–Oseretsky test (mentioned in the previous chapter) is an example of a physical-motor test designed for the school-age child. Subject-matter-readiness tests are often used upon school entrance and during the early grades, in order to place the child in a class or group where the level and type of work are suited to his maturity and interests. The most frequently used readiness tests are those of reading readiness, which correlate highly (around 0.75) with progress in first grade reading [12, p. 424]. Arithmetic readiness tests are also used. Tests for aptitudes, such as artistic and musical talent, are readiness tests in the sense that they predict whether the child will profit greatly from education in these fields. Aptitude tests do not imply that everyone will eventually reach a state of readiness, however, since specialized talents are distributed quite unevenly throughout the population.

Reading tests correlate highly with intelligence tests. It is estimated that a mental age of six and a half, as measured by the Stanford–Binet, is necessary for learning to read [12, p. 420]. Reading tests typically explore the following: visual discrimination of differences and similarities in letters, words, phrases or pictures; auditory discrimination of words, linking them to pictures; motor control in such activities as maze tracing, placing dots in circles and drawing lines; understanding numbers and relations; remembering and reproducing a story; vocabulary, naming objects and classifying; reproducing pictures; giving information, by answering questions of common knowledge; laterality, through hand- and eye-preference tests.

Measuring Achievement Level and Diagnosing Deficiencies

Measures of achievement show what a child has learned and what he can do in the field in question. The ordinary classroom tests and examinations are usually achievement tests, used as a basis for giving marks and grades. Standardized achievement tests are used quite widely, often to reveal how a particular class, school or area stands in relation to children throughout the country as a whole. The California Achievement Tests [29] are an example of this type of test. Through their use, a child can be compared with a large, carefully selected sample of children. Weaknesses, as well as strengths, can be diagnosed through the use of achievement tests, especially standardized ones. The California Achievement Tests, for example, can serve as a rough diagnostic test, since they consist of a battery. The arithmetic section includes four groups of tests, addition, subtraction, multiplication and problems. A deficiency in any particular area can point to the need for further diagnostic study and then to definite remedial measures.

Research

All types of tests are used for research purposes. Sometimes research programs require the giving of tests which are valuable to the individuals involved. Often, however, the investigator has to get information which benefits neither the child nor his parents. The experimenter may be developing his own tests, using the children's performances as the basis of standardizing tests, which will eventually be useful for individual diagnosis. Or he may be testing theories and generating hypotheses. Research can also be done on test data which was originally collected in order to give information about children as individuals.

SUMMARY

The school-age child feels a necessity to develop intellectual skills as part of a whole network of competencies which contribute to his sense of industry. His thinking increases in both flexibility and control. He can delay his response to the experience of the moment, taking account of several aspects of the situation, weighing them, bringing in past experience and even considering the future. The points of view of other people are realities which enter into his deliberations and influence his actions. While considering which response to make, the child can think and act and think it undone, thus trying out various courses of action mentally. He also learns that there are certain kinds of processes or operations of thought and of nature which can be done and undone, or reversed.

The child thinks about experiences and symbols in systematic ways. He is not likely to think about pure abstractions, however. In his classifying, he can understand relations between classes and subclasses and between parts and wholes. He relates objects to each other, ordering them in terms of size, age, sound or some other criterion. Number concepts are built from the combined operations of classifying and ordering. During this period of cognitive development, the child becomes convinced of certain constancies in the environment. He comes to realize that substance, weight, length, area, volume and numbers remain the same (are conserved) even when changes are made in arrangements and positions. The notion of conservation, like other cognitive achievements, is built through interaction with the environment.

Cognitive style refers to the ways in which an individual characteristically perceives, organizes his perceptions and seeks solutions to problems. Some children analyze experiences minutely; others respond more to the event-as-a-whole or to the object-in-relation. An analytic style is based on two fairly stable characteristics, the tendency to analyze visual arrays and the tendency to reflect before responding. At both extremes of reflectivity, very reflective and very impulsive, there are more boys than girls. Analytic thinking seems to be related to childrearing practices, especially to the promotion of independence, responsibility and initiative.

Language develops in intimate relationship with thought and with social interaction. The ability to talk silently to oneself increases, contributing to problem solving and self-regulation and opening more avenues of behavior from which to choose. Language development and concept formation contribute to one another. Concepts, and the words attached to them, emerge gradually, as the words become differentiated from the context in which they appear. As the child matures, he shows increasing understanding of the sentence as a stable grammatical structure.

Imagination continues to be used in problem solving and self-expression although there is some indication that the school-age child uses imagination less than does the preschool child. A large part of the imaginative expression of middle childhood is through language and humor, which create the distinctive culture of childhood. Language play takes the form of magic-making formulas, verses and chants which are handed down from one generation of children to another. Jokes and riddles reflect the child's preoccupation with adequacy.

Intelligence, achievement and special abilities are often tested and measured at this time of life. Most testing is done in groups, at school, in order to assign credit for what the child has learned. The child may be compared with his classmates or with a broader group, even a national sample. Intelligence tests correlate with achievement in school and with success in later life, as measured by many criteria. Although group performance can be predicted fairly well from intelligence tests, such tests tell little about what a given child will achieve. IQ tests and creativity tests tap different intellectual functions. Readiness tests are used to explore various aspects of maturity which are necessary before a child can profit from certain educational experiences. Reading readiness tests are widely used. Diagnostic tests reveal areas where children need remedial help. All types of tests are used for research purposes.

REFERENCES

1. Almy, M., & Chittenden, E. Young children's thinking: understanding the principle of conservation. Paper presented at Society for Research in Child Development, April 13, 1963.
2. Barron, F. *Creativity and psychological health.* Princeton: Van Nostrand, 1963.
3. Bing, E. Effect of childrearing practices on development of differential cognitive abilities. *Child Devel.,* 1963, **34,** 631–648.
4. Charles, D. C. Ability and accomplishment of persons earlier judged to be mentally defective. *Genet. Psychol. Mono.,* 1953, **47,** 3–71.
5. Charles, D. C., & James, S. T. Stability of average intelligence. *J. Genet. Psychol.,* 1964, **105,** 105–111.
6. Crandall, V., Dewey, R., Katkovsky, W., & Preston, A. Parents' attitudes and behaviors and grade school children's academic achievements. *J. Genet. Psychol.,* 1964, **104,** 53–66.
7. Dyk, R. D., & Witkin, H. A. Family experiences related to the development of differentiation in children. *Child Devel.,* 1965, **36,** 21–55.
8. Feigenbaum, K. D. Task complexity and IQ as variables in Piaget's problem of conservation. *Child Devel.,* 1963, **34,** 423–432.
9. Getzels, J. W., & Jackson, P. W. *Creativity and intelligence.* New York: Wiley, 1962.
10. Goldman, A. E., & Levine, M. A developmental study of object sorting. *Child Devel.,* 1963, **34,** 649–666.
11. Hawkes, G. R., & Pease, D. *Behavior and development from five to twelve.* New York: Harper, 1962.
12. Horrocks, J. E. *Assessment of behavior.* Columbus, Ohio: Merrill, 1964.
13. Kagan, J. Development and personality differences in problem-solving. Paper presented at Wheelock College Institute for the Exploration of Early Childhood Education. Boston, November 6, 1964.
14. Kagan, J., Moss, H. A., & Sigel, I. E. Psychological significance of styles of conceptualization. In Wright [37], pp. 73–111.
15. Kagan, J., Rosman, B. L., Day, D., Albert, J., & Phillips, W. Information-processing in the child: significance of analytic and reflective attitudes. *Psychol. Mono.,* 1964, **78:**1.

16. Kaplan, E. The acquisition of word meanings: a developmental study. *Mono. Soc. Res. Child Devel.*, 1952, **15:**1.
17. Lee, L. C., Kagan, J., & Rabson, A. Influence of a preference for analytic categorization upon concept acquisition. *Child Devel.*, 1963, **34,** 433–442.
18. Levy, D. M. *Maternal overprotection.* New York: Columbia Univer., 1943.
19. Lovell, K. *The growth of basic mathematical and scientific concepts in children.* New York: Philosophical Library, 1961.
20. Lovell, K., & Ogilvie, E. A study of the conservation of substance in the junior school child. *Brit. J. Educ. Psychol.*, 1960, **30,** 109–118. Cited in [19].
21. Maccoby, E. E. Woman's intellect. In S. M. Farber & R. H. L. Wilson (Eds.), *The potential of woman.* New York: McGraw-Hill, 1963, pp. 24–39.
22. Opie, I., & P. *The lore and language of school children.* Oxford: Clarendon, 1959.
23. Piaget, J. *The psychology of intelligence.* London: Routledge and Kegan Paul, 1950.
24. Ripple, R. E., & May, F. B. Caution in comparing creativity and IQ. *Psychol. Reports,* 1962, **10,** 229–230.
25. Smedslund, J. Development of concrete transitivity of length in children. *Child Devel.*, 1963, **34,** 389–405.
26. Smith, M. K. Measurement of the size of general English vocabulary through the elementary grades and high school. *Genet. Psychol. Mono.*, 1941, **24,** 311–345.
27. Terman, L. M., & Merrill, M. A. *Stanford–Binet intelligence scale.* Boston: Houghton Mifflin, 1960.
28. Terman, L. M., & Oden, M. H. *The gifted child grows up, Vol. IV.* Genetic studies of genius series. Stanford, Calif.: Stanford Univer., 1947.
29. Tiegs, E. W., & Clark, W. W. *California achievement tests.* Los Angeles: California Test Bureau, 1934.
30. Torrance, E. P. *Guiding creative talent.* Englewood Cliffs, N.J.: Prentice-Hall, 1962.
31. Uzgiris, I. C. Situational generality of conservation. *Child Devel.*, 1964, **35,** 831–841.
32. Vygotsky, L. S. *Thought and language.* Cambridge: Massachusetts Institute of Technology, 1962.
33. Wallach, L., & Sprott, R. L. Inducing number conservation in children. *Child Devel.*, 1964, **35,** 1057–1071.
34. Werner, H., & Kaplan, E. Development of word meaning through verbal context: an experimental study. *J. Psychol.*, 1950, **29,** 251–257.
35. Witkin, H. A., Dyk, R. B., Faterson, H. F., Goodenough, D. R., & Karp, S. A. *Psychological differentiation.* New York: Wiley, 1962.
36. Wolfenstein, M. *Children's humor.* Glencoe, Ill.: Free Press, 1958.
37. Wright, J. C., & Kagan, J. (Eds.) Basic cognitive processes in children. *Mono. Soc. Res. Child Devel.*, 1963, **28:**2.

The Development of Competence As a Learner and Doer

CHAPTER 12

Ever since birth, or even earlier, the child has been bringing more and more of his environment under control, through his exploration, manipulation, thinking, talking, imagining and producing changes. Much of the satisfaction he has experienced has been the product of these activities. He has indeed been competent in many ways, including sucking milk, shaking a rattle, creeping, filling a basket with toys, riding a kiddy car, climbing the jungle gym and playing store. All of these achievements brought joy in the process of mastery. For the most part, these activities were undertaken for themselves, because they were intrinsically interesting, not because anyone urged or rewarded the child to explore, learn and perform [74].

As the child becomes concerned with developing a sense of industry, a new dimension is added to his efforts to explore and control the environment. He becomes much more interested in operating in socially accepted ways. In order to behave thus, it is necessary to learn just what those patterns of thought and action are, to learn the rules of the game. As the previous chapter showed, increasing intellectual maturity results in socialized thinking, whereby the child delays responses while he checks his conclusions and decisions with those of other people, instead of jumping quickly to his own. Some of his satisfaction now comes from measuring up to standards outside himself, from fitting into a bigger and broader world. He is willing to work to learn the basic skills of his culture, the patterns of thinking and doing which mark the difference between being a little child and being a big child on the way to adulthood. He is getting ready to be a producer [25, p. 259].

The child goes about the business of learning his society's skills and rules in style which grows out of his own personality. His performance depends, for example, on how strongly he wants achievement and recognition, how anxious he feels over succeeding, and upon his tendency to reflect before responding. The cultural and social settings within which he interacts will be discussed in the next chapter. In this chapter, the child's development as a learner and producer will be considered in relation to the school, the institution designed especially for teaching him the fundamentals of knowledge.

AREAS OF COMPETENCY

Academic skills figure largely in this picture. Competencies include motor coordinations, skills as a worker at home, knowledge of games and various areas of interest and knowledge of a religion and of a system of morals and values. In all such areas, the child takes over the patterns of his culture and while making them his own, makes himself a functioning member of his society. The child benefits greatly from having a wide choice of opportunities for adequacy in order that there will be a goodly number of places in which he really does succeed. A healthy environment therefore includes broad academic areas, a variety of play activities and chances to work at different jobs and to know many people, places and objects.

Academic Skills

Our purpose here is not to describe the development of knowledge of the various elementary-school subjects, but rather to point out the significance of these areas of learning to the child. We shall take for example, the three R's, the basic tools of academic learning.

READING. A special kind of cognitive and linguistic skill, reading expands the child's experiences enormously. His success at school depends largely on his ability to read. The teaching and learning of reading are so complicated and of such vast importance for educators that they have been the subject of much discussion, study and publication. Opinions have fluctuated widely on when children should learn to read. At mid-century, the dominant educational philosophy in America held that reading was generally bad for children under seven. To teach them to read earlier was to crowd out imaginative and motor activities. Early reading also might damage their eyes. A few children taught themselves to read anyway, and a few others wheedled enough help out of their parents in order to learn to read. With the demand for stiffer school curricula, which Sputnik stimulated, some parents began to demand earlier teaching of reading. Special methods were used to teach more preschool children to read. One author advocates teaching babies to read and tells how to do it [19].

Much remains to be discovered about the levels of cognitive and linguistic maturity which favor learning to read, and also about the impetus to intellectual development which the acquisition of reading skill might be expected to give. Much is known, on a practical level, of the feeling of inadequacy engendered by failure in reading and resulting general academic failure. Such failure produces a feeling of inferiority and inadequacy, the opposite of a sense of industry and its accompanying feeling of adequacy. Although nobody ever feels completely adequate, the overwhelming inferiority resulting from reading failure can seriously block a child in his efforts toward competency. The problem, therefore, is threefold: to arrange for each child to learn to read at the time most appropriate for him; to let him proceed at full speed for him; and to have him feel right about himself, whether he learned early or late, quickly or slowly.

The study of reading disorders is a specialized field. Causes of disorders reach into almost every facet of the child's development and relationships, to include basic physical disorders, such as paranatal brain injury, social deprivation in the form of impoverished family background and lack of early stimulation, emotional disruptions, lack of establishment of lateral dominance and preference, motor disturbances and upsetting educational experiences.

WRITING. The development of skill in writing involves eye–hand coordination perceptual and conceptual activity. Aims, values and practices in teaching handwriting are often rather confused [33]. For instance, if it is important for the child to learn to write in a standard style, then precise coordination is at a premium, and the child who lacks such control must work very hard, with much frustration. When handwriting style is considered an expression of individual personality rather than a standard product, the teacher will help the child to develop his own style within certain limits of legibility. If the main purpose of writing is conceived of as communication, then a high standard of legibility is in order. If writing is done mainly for the individual himself, in order to express his thoughts or take notes for himself, then speed, not legibility, is the prime essential.

Since motor control plays such a large part in learning to write neatly, according to a standard form, and since motor control is not highly correlated with IQ, reading and other academic achievement, high skill in handwriting may be possible for many children who do not have widespread academic success. This is not to say that a very adequate student might not also write well, but only that chances to be good writers are distributed on a different basis from chances to excel in other subject matter areas. Handwriting, then, might serve some children as a much-needed source of feelings of adequacy and thus aid in development of a sense of industry.

Rarely, if ever, does handwriting express thoughts quickly enough to be efficient and satisfying. The first grader, just learning to write, would be completely frustrated if he wanted to record his thoughts. If an adult will occasionally take dictation from him, he can thus "write" stories and letters which will give him satisfaction and adequacy and which will also develop his ability to communicate through writing. Another effective aid to written expression is the typewriter. After the initial stages of learning to type, which can be done early in this stage of life, or even before, the individual can communicate and record his thoughts ever so much more quickly, efficiently and legibly by typewriter than by hand.

Writing can be considered in a context quite different from that of making representational marks. Writing is also linguistic expression. In this sense, it shares some characteristics with thought or inner speech and some with socialized speech. A comparison of oral and written language reveals some similarities and differences [31]. The subjects were 320 children, ages 9, 11, 13 and 15, who told and wrote stories. The stories were analyzed for length, type of clauses and unrelated words used. The findings included these: no tendency for girls to excel boys, excepting in length of written compositions; more subordinate clauses used in writing than in speaking, increasingly so with advance in age; more adjective and adverb clauses in writing, more noun clauses in speaking; positive correlations between subordinate clauses in writing and age, mental age, IQ and occupational status of father; no indication that a mature level had been reached in either oral or written stories by age 15. Writing in this sense, then, is an academic skill with its own distinctive characteristics, a skill which shows continuous development throughout the school years.

MATHEMATICS. Based on the cognitive activities of classifying, abstracting, ordering and relating, the learning of number concepts is influenced by the experiences the child has had at home, at nursery school and at kindergarten. His cognitive style makes a difference, too. The tendency to analyze visual arrays is helpful in abstracting numbers out of groups of objects. Spatial imagery and discrimination are probably quite important to success. Reflectivity, rather than impulsivity, is understandably an aid in problem solving. Thus the intellectual and personality development of the child have a direct bearing on the ease or difficulty he experiences in his first encounters with arithmetic in school. He soon feels adequate or inadequate in regard to mathematics, often reinforced by family or friends. Since mathematical ability is often considered appropriate for men and not for women, many girls inhibit their growth along these lines in order to fit into the sex role, which they feel required to assume.

Like the teaching of reading, instruction in mathematics has undergone a revolution since mid-century. The old methods relied heavily upon rote memory and drill. In former times teachers tried to build mathematical concepts by having the child manipulate spoken and written symbols. Most likely, the children who made good progress with these methods were the ones blessed with stimulating environments, in which they had and continued to have rich opportunities for arranging, ordering, grouping and discriminating. The "new math" incorporates knowledge about concept formation. Number concepts are built with the aid of visual perception and imagery and often other sensory experiences as well. Books and pictures are planned and arranged so as to use visual perception and imagery. Objects such as blocks, rods, beads and cards are employed not only to provide tactile perception, but to permit the child to arrange, group and order objects. This type of apparatus has been designed in such a way as to give insight into counting, grouping, addition, subtraction, multiplication, division, measurement, fractions, ratio, decimals, percentage, square measure and cubic measure. Eventually, of course, the child must free himself of dependence on concrete objects if he is to go very far in mathematics.

"The new math" holds a promise of success for more children. Under the old methods, many children, especially those with limited backgrounds, experienced early failure and discouragement. Now, if a child is allowed to progress at his own rate, the school can offer him materials and experiences with which to build useful concepts. It is theoretically possible for all children (except the severely brain-damaged and ill) to be successful with mathematics in the elementary school. As a child sees himself mastering this important cultural tool, his sense of industry is enhanced, and he enjoys healthy personality growth.

Performance As a Worker

Development of the sense of industry hinges largely on feeling and being successful as a worker. Some of such feeling and being comes when the child does well in reading, writing, arithmetic and all the other academic skills. Although school is indeed his job, he knows too that school is not identical with the work world, in which his parents and other adults earn their living. The child needs some success in that real work world too. Significant work experience adds greatly to his sense of adequacy, contributes to his understanding of adults, his family and society, and gives him experience which can help him in later choice of a vocation. When he does a good job, he wins recognition and respect, giving him a toehold in the work world.

Whereas simple agricultural or hunting societies offer children easy access to important work, a complex technological society provides severely limited work opportunities. Many of the jobs available both at home and otherwise are in the realm of cleaning and tidying. While necessary and useful, this type of work does not give the child the feeling of being a producer, nor even of being necessary in earning the family living. For instance, after milking the cow, collecting the eggs and picking the strawberries, the youngster joins with his family in eating the fruits of his labor plus the contributions of other family members. There is no comparable integrating and satisfying experience for the child who straightens up his room, empties the waste baskets and carries the empty pop bottles out to the car. Kitchen, basement, garage and garden do, of course, offer some opportunities for children to contribute constructively to the home. Job possibilities outside the home are probably more curtailed, as compared with those in a simpler society. Newspaper delivery is one of the very few ways in which a child can work steadily. Even though they cannot find real jobs in the market place, many children get valuable work experience in the organizations for children, such as Boy Scouts, Girl Scouts, 4H, Rainbow, Demolay, Future Farmers of America, Future Homemakers of America and church clubs. In cooperation with adult leaders and his own peers, the child takes part in service projects and money-making projects, joins in consuming the profits made by the group and thereby enjoys many of the benefits of being a real producer. When leaders and peers judge his performance good, especially when they give unmistakable signs of approval and recognition (badges and pins), the youngster's feeling of adequacy are enhanced and he makes progress in the development of a sense of industry.

Recreational Activities and Interests

Children's play activities are the means by which they develop competency on many different levels and in several senses. Already discussed in Chapter 10, motor skills contribute greatly to effectiveness and adequacy. During the school age, many basic motor coordinations are integrated into games which have social meaning as well. Such games—for example, baseball—involve not only the coordinations of hitting, throwing and running but also knowing a set of rules which tell exactly how to play and also how to feel about the game (being a good sport, competing, team spirit and such). Performing well in such situations brings recognition, approval and a sense of mastery over some of the complexities of the social and physical environment. Similarly, intellectual games integrate recently learned skills with social behavior, in a framework of rules. Checkers, Monopoly and other table games are examples, along with thinking games, such as Twenty Questions and Coffee Pot.

Self-mastery, with little or no reference to other people, is the objective of certain types of games [5]. This type includes the ancient, widespread games which appear spontaneously in the early school years and then disappear just as spontaneously. For example, the game of not stepping on cracks, in which the rule is self-set and is thought to work magic. Through this game, the child controls his own actions and controls the world. In the same way, a child sets himself an obstacle to overcome, such as hopping a certain distance on one foot or holding his breath for a given length of time. Or he seeks a certain form of anxiety in order to master it, as he does in walking on a high place or riding on a roller coaster. Imaginative play is also used in the service of self-mastery. Expressing fears, hostility or fantasies of grandeur through dramatic play, he gains control through expressing these disturbing feelings and through distinguishing between imagination and reality.

A variety of purposes are served by the individual activities of making collections, reading, watching TV and creating in art media, all of which the child does for pleasure and recreation. Through these means, he extends his concepts and knowledge. Reading, of course, contributes to competency in almost everything a child does, in addition to giving him enjoyment. Children read a wide range of materials, if they have chances to do so. They especially like stories which get off to a fast start, probably because of the influence of TV and the generally fast pace of modern life [43]. Books of wide appeal include historical stories (because they are full of action), plots with well-sustained suspense, animal stories, humorous tales, informational books and books in series (because they are collections, as well as books). Although most children enjoy fantasy stories, some children are very particular about the type of fantasy which they will accept [43]. Most children read comic books. In a recent year, 30 million of them were sold in this country [43]. It is estimated that each comic is read by three children. The satisfactions from comic books include quick action and adventure, short episodes, very easy reading, availability everywhere and being an activity which other children share. Many children have nothing else to read. When the reading behavior of 323 seventh grade children was related to other aspects of their behavior, several interesting findings resulted [8]. There was no relationship between reading ability and amount or type of comic books read. Neither school adjustment nor achievement nor intelligence was related to amount and type of comic books read. The children who read comic books read more library books than did children who did not read comics.

Watching television is an important childhood activity (or perhaps it could be called passivity!). Some children spend many hours a day viewing. The ways in which children use television vary with the children themselves, their needs and problems, their opportunities for other kinds of recreation. One of the most serious threats of television is the likelihood of its crowding out other kinds of activities. The sitting child is not practicing motor skills, which he needs in order to be physically competent; he is not playing games with other children; he is not creating. Some of the effects of television on children have been studied in both England and the United States [34, 63]. In both countries, television had a leveling effect, intellectually, stepping up the information obtained by duller children and younger children and reducing the amount of information which older, bright children could have been expected to obtain without television. Comparing children's behavior before and after the families own TV sets, the English investigation found that children went to bed about 20 minutes later on the average when they owned a set. There was no evidence of harmful physical effects, nor was there any indication that television caused fears or aggression. Rather, the results of television were results of interaction of the individual child with television. It mattered what kind of child he was. The research does not rule out the possibilities that television can magnify disturbances in disturbed children and that it can suggest modes of procedure to budding criminals. (The dangers have long been considered as inherent in comic books, fiction and films.) The problem of addiction to television is a real one. A study of kindergarten children and their family relationships showed that the time spent viewing television increased as the middle-class child's frustrations increased [49]. Middle-class children who were treated coldly by their mothers watched TV 50 percent more than those who were warmly treated. Probably the middle-class child turned away from his parents and their activities to TV for solace when family relationships were frustrating, whereas the lower-class child (whose frustration showed no relation to TV viewing) found himself in the bosom of the family when he turned to TV. It was their recreation as well as his. Television, as well as other forms of individual recreation, serves the child in intellectual, social and/or emotional contexts, depending upon the ways in which he chooses to use it.

Moral Knowledge and Judgment

The rules governing right and wrong behavior are among the important guides to thought and action which a child seeks to master in his efforts to become a functioning member of his society. He realizes that rules and laws extend beyond his family and that he has obligations and privileges outside the family. In fact, many of the basic rules about how one ought to behave can be stated fairly early in this stage of life although reasons behind them are not understood. For example, the average seven-year-old can give appropriate answers to these questions: "What's the thing for you to do when you have broken something that belongs to someone else?" and "What's the thing for you to do if another boy hits you without meaning to do it?" [73]. Although they show some relation to conduct, moral knowledge scores also indicate intelligence [75], cultural background and the desire to make a good impression [42].

LEARNING THE RULES. Being able to state the rule governing behavior is only an early stage in a long process of development which continues throughout the age span under discussion. At first, rules are by definition. They cover limited situations, without reasons or explanations. Gradually the child comes to understand the involvement of more and more people and viewpoints. This process was illustrated in a study of children's concepts of money and of the relations between storekeepers, customers, clerks and manufacturers [70]. The rules which govern buying and selling are based on complicated relationships involving arithmetic, monetary value, profit, ownership, distribution and the roles which people play. The ways to which children between 4½ and 11½ grasped this network of rules and relationships are organized into a sequence of stages of broader and broader understanding. Some of the stages given with the median ages are as follows:

Five years eight months: Rules exist by definition. You need money to buy with. You just can't take goods without paying. In the first of this period, any coins buy any goods. The storekeeper also gives coins. Later, a coin buys objects of certain value, coin and object being matched exactly.

Six years four months: Rules cover indirect but imprecise relations. The child knows that a certain amount of money is necessary for a certain purchase and that the amount of change is systematically related to price and amount paid, but he cannot figure out the amounts. He understands that work is worth paying for. He begins to understand that goods cost the storekeeper something and that he pays his helper.

Seven years ten months: The value and relations of coins are understood precisely. The children make change exactly.

Eight years seven months: He realizes that it does not matter whether the storekeeper gives the goods first or whether the customer pays first.

Eight years nine months: He understands more of the impersonal rules which govern buying and selling, that retailers properly charge more than wholesalers, who are too far away to be able to sell directly to the consumer.

Nine years nine months: He has impersonal, interconnected concepts of profit, credit, storekeeper, worker, customer, factory owner and helper.

Eleven years two months: He knows that in spite of the impersonal system of profit making, personal, immoral motives sometimes prevail. The existence of a rule does not assure its being obeyed.

MORAL JUDGMENT. Moral thought and judgment, in contrast to knowledge of the rules, continue to develop throughout the school years. Although the first or second grader knows fairly well what he is supposed to do, his reasons for doing it or not doing it change as he matures. Cognitive growth is basic to the growth of moral thought and judgment. Interaction between people is a fundamental factor in both cognitive and moral development, since the child checks his ideas, beliefs and interpretations against those of other people, modifies them in accordance with discrepancies he finds and attempts to justify his thinking to people who disagree with him. In this give and take of social relationships, he shapes his own beliefs within the social and cultural context in which he is growing up. Six aspects of moral judgment have been demonstrated as defining moral development during the elementary-school years. Evidence from many different studies is in essential agreement on the development of the following attitudes and viewpoints:*

INTENTIONALITY IN JUDGMENT. Young children usually judge an act by its consequences, older children by the intentions which prompted it. This tendency has been tested by Piaget's [58] story of the boy who broke up 15 cups while trying to help his mother, in contrast to the boy who broke one cup while trying to steal jam. Almost all four-year-olds say that the boy who broke the large number of cups was worse. About 60 percent of six-year-olds agree. The majority of nine-year-olds say that the other boy was worse [9, 44, 46, 58].

RELATIVISM IN JUDGMENT. There is only one way in which to judge an act, according to the thinking of young children, either right or wrong. If a child and an adult conflict in judging an act, then the adult is right. To illustrate this way of thinking, children were told a story in which a friendly classmate helped a lazy pupil to do his homework, even though the teacher had forbidden the pupil to receive help. The children were asked whether the teacher thought the friendly classmate's behavior right, whether the lazy pupil thought it right and whether the friendly classmate thought himself right. Most six-year-olds gave only one judgment, on which all three characters were supposed to agree; most nine-year-olds realized that there were different points of view from which to make this judgment [44, 46].

INDEPENDENCE OF SANCTIONS. An act is bad if it elicits punishment, ac-

* This account follows Kohlberg [42].

cording to many children of four or five. Between five and seven, most children change this point of view to believe that an act is bad because it does harm or breaks a rule. The test story was about a child who obediently watched a young sibling while the mother was away, only to have the mother spank him when she returned. The younger children said that the babysitting child must have been bad, because his mother spanked him; most seven-year-olds said that the child was good, because he had done good.

USE OF RECIPROCITY. Several steps can be distinguished in the process of accepting the idea of doing as you would be done by. Four-year-olds rarely use the concept at all. Between 7 and 10, children usually employ it in a concrete, utilitarian way, avoiding retaliation and courting return of favors. After 10 or 11, children show more feeling about how it would be in someone else's place [21, 42].

USE OF PUNISHMENT AS RESTITUTION AND REFORM. Younger children believe that retribution should be the main basis for punishment and that severe punishment will reform the wrongdoer. Older children advocate milder punishment, with restitution rather than retribution as the aim [36, 58].

NATURALISTIC VIEWS OF MISFORTUNE. At six or seven, children are likely to see accidents and misfortunes as punishment for their misdeeds. This confusion diminishes with age, as the child builds more mature concepts of causality [44, 46].

Further discussion of stages and types of moral judgments occurs in Chapter 18, where some growth trends are traced through childhood and adolescence.

Moral Behavior

Since the elementary-school child is quite limited in his understanding and application of moral principles, he can hardly be expected to be extensively guided by them in his behavior. Rather, he is guided more by the rules of his family, peers, school and community. While there seems to be a general factor resulting in individual difference in honesty, a large determiner of whether a child cheats or not is the situation in which he is tempted [10]. When a child cheats in one situation, it does not mean that he will do so in another, since cheating in one context has only a low correlation with cheating in another [32, 59]. In experimental testing of cheating, most children do some, a few a great deal and a few only a little [32]. In other words, cheating scores were distributed normally. Cheating was also found to depend upon the ease of doing so and upon the risk of detection. No age changes in cheating and stealing have been found experimentally during the school years, although according to parents' reports, stealing and lying decreased after age six to eight [29, 65].

Knowledge of rules and the ability to make moral judgments are important in the production of moral behavior, but they do not determine it entirely. A control or will factor also goes into behaving or not behaving in certain ways. Several other aspects of behavior have been found related to moral behavior. General intelligence has been shown to contribute to moral behavior [32, 57]. So does the tendency to look into the future and to delay immediate satisfaction for the purpose of greater gain at a later time [54]. The ability to maintain stable, focused attention also contributes to moral conduct [42]. Probably related to this factor is the ability to control aggressive fantasy [57]. Moral development, then, is an extremely complex process which can be viewed in different ways and which is inextricably bound up with the child's psychological development and with the various relationships through which he grows.

Religious Concepts

Children search for meaning in life, for explanations of the great mysteries which puzzle all human beings, for unifying concepts. A sense of adequacy is enhanced by some success in asking questions, being able to discuss them and finding answers which give some satisfaction. Although religion and philosophy do not occupy the school-age child as much as they do the adolescent, yet the child lays a foundation for his adolescent enquiries.

Religious concepts, like other concepts, are the products of cognitive development and social interaction. Some children receive direct teaching in the form of religious instruction carried on by their church or temple. A series of studies on denominational concepts shows age-related steps in the child's progress toward an adult understanding of his religion [22, 23, 24]. Each child was asked a series of questions about his own denomination: Is your family Protestant (Catholic, Jewish)? Are you a Protestant? Are all boys and girls in the world Protestants? Can a dog or a cat be a Protestant? How can you tell a person is a Protestant? How do you become a Protestant? What is a Protestant? Can you be a Protestant and an American at the same time? After answering *yes* or *no,* the children were asked to explain their answers.

Four aspects of denominational conception could be distinguished: knowledge of characteristics common to all members of the denomination, knowledge of class membership compatible or incompatible with membership in the denomination, knowledge of how membership in the denomination is gained or lost and knowledge of the signs by which a member of a denomination can be recognized. With Jewish and Catholic children, each of these types of knowledge could be seen developing in three stages. With Protestant children, only the first two types of knowledge developed in three stages. The stages were:

1. At about six years, the child had a *global, undifferentiated concept.* "What is a Catholic?" JAY: "A person." How is he different from a Protestant? "I don't know." "What is a Jew?" SID: "A person." How is he different from a Catholic? " 'Cause some people have black hair and some people have blonde."

2. From seven to nine, concepts were *differentiated* but *concrete*. "He goes to Mass every Sunday and goes to Catholic School." "He belongs to a Protestant family." Jewishness was understood both as a group of actions and as a family quality, leading to some contradictory answers. Can a dog or a cat be a Jew? STAN: "No." Why not? "They are not human." What difference does that make? "They can't go to the Synagogue or say the prayers . . . but I guess if it belonged to a Jewish family, it could be Jewish."
3. Children between 11 and 14 had a *differentiated* and *abstract* concept of their denomination. The child realizes that his religion is one religion among others. What is a Catholic? BILL: "A person who believes in the truths of the Roman Catholic Church." What is a Protestant? FAITH: "A faithful believer in God and doesn't believe in the Pope." Can a dog or a cat be Jewish? SID: "No . . . because they are not human and would not understand a religion." Gaining membership involves learning and believing. Religion is recognized as a way of categorizing people which is different from other ways, such as by nationality. Can you be an American and a Jew at the same time? "Yes . . . because Jewish is a religion and American is a nationality."

This demonstration of the growth of religious concepts with increasing age is one more illustration of how development is the result of interaction between the child and his environment. In the first stage, cognitive maturity is such that the five- or six-year-old can form only a global concept of being a Catholic, Protestant or Jew. The global concept he forms, however, depends on the religion which is offered to him. Without the religious environment with which to interact, religious concepts would not come into being.

Another aspect of the exploration of the religious institution's impact on children's concepts was concerned with the understanding of causality [26]. The subjects were 153 Protestant, Jewish and Roman Catholic boys, between six and eight years of age. A rating as to the degree of religious devoutness was obtained through a questionnaire sent to the families and by rating the type of school attended. The solutions given by the subjects to problem situations were classified as animistic, anthropomorphic and scientific. While there were no differences between the three religions, differences were significant in terms of devoutness. Children from very devout homes gave more animistic and anthropomorphic responses and fewer scientific responses than did children from less devout homes. Similarly, children attending religious schools gave more animistic and anthropomorphic responses and fewer scientific responses than did children attending public schools. Thus it could be concluded that the religious institution tended to retard the development of scientific thinking in six-to-eight-year-old boys. *Some* of the subjects from devout homes and religious schools did give scientific answers. The author pointed out that this could mean that religion and science are not inevitably incompatible. It could also mean that these youngsters, although from devout homes, were not themselves devout, and had, in opposition to their environment, developed modes of scientific thinking.

A philosophical question, fourth graders' interest in living a good life, was examined by having children write about their interests [1]. The 10 schools used were all private ones probably Catholic. Among nine interest categories, the good life, or living a good life, ranked second. One eighth of all interests listed pertained to it. The order of interests was thus: possession of objects, good life, pets, vocation, travel, relatives, money, school and education. Under interest in good life were items pertaining to living a good life, but an even larger number of items concerned the ultimate purpose of life.

COMPETENCY AND RELATED ASPECTS OF PERSONALITY

Although skills, abilities and talents make their contributions to success, other facets of the child have their parts to play in determining the quality of his interactions. The strength of his desire for achievement and recognition will affect his striving for success. His curiosity, the degree to which he seeks new experiences, will make a difference in the breadth and depth of his interactions. His attack on problems and challenges will vary with the extent to which he feels self-confident and adequate or anxious and inferior.

Need for Achievement and Recognition

There are two standpoints from which to consider achievement—the strength of the need or desire for it and the behavior oriented toward it. Basic to achievement motivation, or the need for achievement, is the child's application of a standard of excellence to the performance he is judging and a feeling tone which goes along with that judgment [47]. In other words, he says, "I did well" or "He did a good job" or "He did a poor job," while having a pleasant or unpleasant feeling about the situation. The goal of achievement behavior is the attainment of approval and avoidance of disapproval, either one's own or somebody else's [16]. Achievement, then, is of the essence of the period of the development of a sense of industry. In order to become a successful learner of the ways of the culture and to become a productive member of society, thus assuring a sense of adequacy, the child must want to achieve and must, in fact, achieve.

STABILITY OF ACHIEVEMENT OVER TIME. Both need for achievement and achievement behavior were studied over a period of 18 years at the Fels foundation. Both types of measurements showed some consistency from one age level to another. Need for achievement was tested at eight years, by asking children to tell stories in response to pictures* and analyzing for achievement themes. Retesting the children at 11 and 14, moderate correlations were

* Thematic Apperception Test.

found with the need for achievement at eight years [38]. A similar study on 8-to-10-year-old boys, retested after six years, showed similar results [27]. Achievement behavior, as shown by ratings and interviews at the Fels foundation, showed some consistency from nursery school age to young adulthood. Low but significant correlations were found between ratings during preschool and elementary-school years and between elementary-school age and early adolescence. Girls' preschool achievement behavior was related to their adult achievement behavior, but boys' was not. By middle childhood, however, achievement striving was related to adult achievement behavior. During early adolescence, intellectual achievement behavior was predictive of adult behavior, but athletic and mechanical achievement efforts were not related to adult behavior.

STABILITY OF ACHIEVEMENT ACROSS SITUATIONS. During the early elementary-school years, a child's expectations of himself tend to be consistent between intellectual, artistic, mechanical and athletic areas [14]. If he did well in one area, he expected to do well in the others. If he held high standards in one, he was likely to hold high standards in all. However, actual achievement behavior did not show so much consistency across situations. With slightly older children, a relationship was shown between intellectual and mechanical achievement behaviors, but not between intellectual and athletic [56].

SEX DIFFERENCES. Achievement motivation is not the same for girls as it is for boys. Boys' achievement need and behavior has been studied much more extensively than has girls', perhaps reflecting the general attitude that it is more important for boys to achieve than it is for girls to do so. The difference is, of course, closely related to sex role. Achievement for the sake of achievement seems to motivate boys more than girls, while the seeking of approval and affection is often bound up with the achievement efforts of girls [40]. The boys' achievement behavior was more autonomously motivated, in a sample of early-grade schoolboys and girls who were tested for achievement and whose parents were interviewed. For boys, but not for girls, belief in self-responsibility was correlated with scores on academic achievement tests. When academic achievement test scores were correlated with tests of achievement need, a significant relationship was found for boys but not for girls [64]. The girls' achievement was found to relate instead to their desire for affection and approval.

The standards of excellence which boys set for themselves tend to be more realistic than those of girls, or at least such was true for 40 day camp children from the first three grades [17]. The boys held standards which corresponded with their performances on intelligence and achievement tests. The opposite was true of girls, whose expectations of success were negatively correlated with their intelligence scores. The sexes also differed in their beliefs about personal responsibility for success. Among the boys but not girls, the more capable ones were strongly convinced that they themselves were responsible for their own achievements. Thus the boys were practical and realistic in their attitudes toward achievement, whereas the girls were more influenced by their wishes and values. Sex role expectations probably account for the differences. Perhaps boys are criticized more than girls when their stated expectations do not fit their performances. It may be that incompetent girls are praised for saying, "I'll try," while very able girls are scolded for being boastful when they predict high success for themselves. At any rate, sex is an important determiner of achievement orientation.

SOME CORRELATES OF ACHIEVEMENT. High-achieving children are distinguished from average and low achievers by certain characteristics which suggest that in the early years of life, high achievers accept and internalize adult middle-class values. A group of gifted third-grade children, studied through tests, observations and parent-and-teacher interviews, indicated that superior academic achievers are likely to be independent, asking for little help from adults. These children persisted longer at problems, competed more with their peers, expressed less warmth toward their siblings and had more guilt feelings than average children [18]. Information obtained about the same children, four years later, showed them as persistent, competitive, still mastering and striving, but sometimes aggressive and destructive in order to win, often antagonistic and belittling to adults, more anxious than formerly and less creative than they used to be [30]. High academic achievement, then, is likely to exact a price, even during middle childhood.

Anxiety

Anxiety, to most people, means a stirred-up, unpleasant, tense feeling, focused only vaguely or generally. Fear indicates the same type of feeling state but with accompanying attention focused on a specific situation or problem. In childhood, according to Erikson [25, p. 408], it is difficult or impossible to distinguish fear from anxiety. Whether fear or anxiety, this unpleasant tension affects the ways in which the child approaches and deals with his job of learning and producing. Some of the tests devised to measure anxiety deal with general situations and others with particular situations, especially school. The type of statements used to test general anxiety are illustrated by the following: "I feel I have to be best in everything." "I notice my heart beats very fast sometimes." "I worry about doing the right things." "It is hard for me to go to sleep at night" [11]. Anxiety over tests is examined by means of questions such as these: "When the teacher wants to find out how much you have learned, do you get a funny feeling in your stomach?" "Do you worry a lot before you take a test?" "While you are taking a test, do you usually think you are not doing well?" [60].

Girls have been found to be higher than boys in both types of anxiety, general and text anxiety [61]. Since this finding fits in with cultural expectations of boys and girls, it may be that the difference is partly due to youngsters trying to live up to ideal sex roles. Another contributing factor may be girls' tendency to care a great deal about approval and affection and to try to win these prizes through their achievement efforts. Boys, with their more internalized standards of excellence, would understandably worry less about what people thought of them.

Both types of anxiety tests correlate negatively with IQ [61]. A stronger negative relationship has been found between anxiety and achievement than between anxiety and IQ [62]. Although these correlations are small, they tend to increase with grade level. Probably interaction is reciprocal. Suffering more and more defeats as he went through school, a child of low intelligence would feel increasingly inferior, anxious and reluctant to get into the situation of being tested. Learning and achievement show complicated relationships to anxiety. Both the level of anxiety and the difficulty and type of task must be taken into account. While moderate anxiety may help the child in performing fairly easy tasks, anxiety, especially high anxiety, is likely to interfere with success on difficult tasks. To show the significance of type of task, high-anxious and low-anxious children were tested for achievement in reading and arithmetic [13]. The low-anxious group was definitely superior in arithmetic. For reading, there was a slight but insignificant difference in favor of the high-anxious group. Another study, however, a longitudinal one, found anxiety related earlier and more strongly to reading than to arithmetic [62].

The definition of success and failure will vary from one child to another, depending upon what he and others expect of him. To one person a grade of C means success, while to another, anything short of A is a failure. The aspirations of children who achieve on a low level in the class are, on the average, above the level at which they achieve. Therefore, they usually experience failure. In contrast, children who achieve on the highest level tend to pitch their aspirations lower than their achievement level. Therefore, they usually experience success. Success and failure in school are so very public, as compared with success on the job. It is impossible to hide from teachers, classmates or parents, and even neighbors and grandparents, the exact marks or grades obtained, and just how those grades compare with Betty's, Tommy's and Jonathan's grades. Contrasting the aspiration level of children who had chronic failure in reading and arithmetic with children who had a history of success, the successful children were seen as aspiring to levels where they succeeded, while the chronically unsuccessful ones set their aspirations with little regard for achievement [3]. Some set extremely high goals which they could never reach, as though a mere gesture would substitute for realistic action.

It seems reasonable that a very mild degree of fear or anxiety would help a child in problem solving, as long as the resulting tense feeling served to focus his attention squarely on the task at hand. A greater degree of fear would immobilize his resources, freezing them instead of energizing them. Repeated experiences with failure would lead to expectation of more failure, a feeling of worthlessness, inferiority, and inadequacy, all of which constitute the opposite of a sense of industry.

Curiosity

A curious person seeks new experiences and new answers to problems. Insufficient new experience leads to boredom and restlessness; too great an environmental change is either shocking or frightening or both. Curiosity is aroused by appropriate degrees of unusualness and incongruity. Children vary in how much new experience they seek, how many new answers they try to find and how great an environmental change is satisfying rather than frightening [48]. During the preschool years, when the sense of initiative is developing fast, satisfying experiences with exploration lead to a lasting interest in reaching out and discovering. The richer the environment, the more curious the child can become; the more curious he is, the more he can discover in his environment. Curiosity can be both a help and a hindrance in the tasks of middle childhood. In situations where adults demand high conformity, as in schools where routines are sacred, or in homes where privacy, quiet and order are greatly cherished, a very curious child will be too disruptive. The advantages of curiosity outweigh these small liabilities, however, as various studies show.

Healthy psychological adjustment was associated with high curiosity in sixth grade children [48]. Teachers' ratings of overall psychological health correlated positively with scores on tests in which children manipulated objects, examined them freely and commented on them. Low-anxious children preferred more novelty than high-anxious children [53]. A sex difference was demonstrated in first grade children's and younger children's curiosity and seeking of information and experience. Boys were more curious than girls [53, 67]. Desire for novelty seems to increase with age, at least during the early years [53].

Intellectual competence is related to curiosity, as might be expected. One piece of evidence comes from a comparison of children whose IQ's rose with those whose IQ's fell during the years between the ages of 6 and 10 [39]. Responses to a projective test indicated that children with rising IQ's were more curious and less passive than those with falling IQ's. Another type of evidence is furnished by fifth grade children whose curiosity was judged by ratings of teachers, peers and selves. A child was called curious to the extent that he moved toward, explored or manipulated new, strange or mysterious elements of his environments; showed a need or desire to know about himself and his environment; scanned his surroundings, seeking new experiences; persisted in examining and exploring. A week after hearing a story read, the children were tested for memories of it. The children with high curiosity remembered significantly more than did those with low curiosity [50, 51]. In a third study, tasks were arranged in such a way that some children experienced more curiosity than others during the problem-solving process [55]. The high-curiosity group learned more efficiently (made fewer errors) than the low-curiosity group.

Both research and common sense indicate the importance of curiosity in stimulating intellectual functioning and development. Can curiosity, then, be encouraged and nurtured in grade school children? Recent experiments, using a method called *Inquiry Training,* show that children can learn to use curiosity for solving problems [71]. After viewing films of simple physics experiments, fifth and sixth grade children asked questions which could be answered by *yes* or *no.* The children learned to formulate, use and test hypotheses. The process of discovery through questioning was made more real and functional by a discussion of each session, based on a tape recording of the session.

THE ROLE OF THE SCHOOL

Schools and the sense of industry are made for each other. It is no accident that children are sent to a special institution which imparts the wisdom of the culture at just the age when they become interested in learning it and in becoming producing members of society. Young children usually look forward greatly to entering first grade and usually they like it very much [68, 69]. At this point, their behavior begins to improve in responsibility, helpfulness, good humor and independence.

Multiple Values of Schools in the United States

As an agent of the broad community, the school reflects the values of the community. In those cultures where the state is more important than the individual, the school stresses preparation of contributing citizens; when the individual is valued highly, then the school is concerned with his development and fulfillment. Much of the American confusion and disagreement over purposes and methods of education stem from the holding of both sets of values, individual and collective. Shall schools try to turn out well-trained scientists who can develop theories and practices which will benefit America and possibly mankind? Shall they aim toward producing graduates who can realize their potential as individuals? Can they do both? And what about educating the child of superior ability while giving average and retarded children every opportunity for growth?

Another set of confusions stems from the role of the child in society. Is he important and valuable as a child or as a potential adult or as both? Americans pay more attention to the child as a child than do most other cultures. Here, again, the tendency is to try to do both, to make childhood happy and good and at the same time to prepare the child for adulthood.

Disagreement on school policy also arises from different people holding different beliefs about learning and development, and everyone tends to consider himself an expert since *he* was once a child. Mrs. Newman commented approvingly on her Freddie's teacher: "She had drilled and drilled those children for the play they put on at the P.T.A. Each child knew his lines perfectly. I was so proud of Freddie, but then it was really because he has such a good teacher."

Mrs. Brower, discussing the same event, complained: "Those poor children were just like puppets on the stage. It broke my heart to see Janet learning all that stuff by rote and spending hours practicing for such a sterile performance."

AN EXAMPLE OF RESULTS OF DIFFERENT VALUE SYSTEMS. Two schools in New York City were studied through their first- and second-graders' answers to questions about pictures [7]. The questions elicited feelings about trouble, happiness, good and bad behavior, punishments and anger. The majority of children in the North School (a public school) showed that they felt they must obey blindly, that "goodness" meant obeying and sitting quietly with folded hands; South School (a private school) children defined goodness more in terms of social responsibility and good relationships. In the North School, punishment was expected to be angry and violent. In the South School, punishment was never violent, but more likely to be deprivation. In the latter, children expected warmth, comfort and interest when they were in trouble. Thus the first school emphasized conformity to tradition, while the second promoted responsibility, communication and understanding.

Increased Expectations of School

When a society is as complex as American society, the job of transferring the accumulated knowledge and technology to the next generation is a big one. The three R's have long been considered the fundamentals or tools which make possible the more involved learning. As the nature and development of children has been explored scientifically, the school has been required to expand its role. Schools are expected increasingly to safeguard and promote the child's physical well-being, to arrange for learning to take place in research-proven ways, and to take healthy personality development into account [6]. The teachers' jobs and the physical plant of the school have had to elaborate in order to achieve these goals. A new expansion is in the making, due to the recent discovery of the preschool years as a time for crucial intellectual development and a time when millions of children suffer from limited learning opportunities [35].

The Teacher's Role

When the child enters school, his teacher is largely a mother substitute. He may even call her "Mother" by mistake and may do the reverse at home, calling his mother "Mrs. Jones." The attitudes toward authority he learned at home will probably carry over to school. Since nearly all first grade teachers are women, the child will most likely expect his teacher to be like his mother. His trust or mistrust, his hostility or acceptance, his dependency or autonomy will largely reflect what has gone on at home with mother. Gradually he learns the differences between teacher and mother, both role differences and personality differences. Gradually the teacher differentiates herself more and more from mother. Moving up the grades, teachers become more subject-matter-oriented and less concerned with the "whole child" and his adjustment in general. The child comes to see his teacher as the key person in his development of essential competencies.

The teachers from two large communities, 280 in number, answered questions about how they conceived the teacher's role and goals [2, pp. 189–191]. They agreed strongly that the teacher should stimulate thinking and interest, guide and help students in their learning and be a personal character model for pupils. Responsibility for evaluating students and motivating them was accepted more by the elementary-school teacher than the secondary teacher. The teachers disliked the idea that they should have to *control* pupils. When asked about educational goals, the teachers rated intellectual ones highest. They placed the goals in this order: developing love of and interest in learning, teaching knowledge and skills in subject matter, developing intellectual ability, character formation, promoting emotional maturity, transmitting cultural values.

The teacher's role varies with the sex of the teacher and sex of the child, as well as with age. There is widespread agreement that boys present more problem behavior in school than girls do [4]. Men and women teachers differ somewhat in their interpretations of what is problem behavior and how serious it is.

Not only does the teacher present material to be learned and problems to be solved; she rewards some behavior and punishes other. Through words, smiles, frowns, attention and ignoring, even more than through marks, displays or gold stars, the teacher makes it plain, over and over and over again, what kind of behavior she wants from children and what she does not want. She also serves as a model of behavior, especially to those children whose needs she satisfies and who like and love her.

Nothing idealizes the teacher's role more beautifully than Erikson's concept of generativity, the seventh stage in personality development. In his words, "Generativity is primarily the interest in establishing and guiding the next generation or whatever in a given case may become the absorbing object of a parental kind of responsibility" [25, p. 231].

The teacher's work is one way of achieving normal adult personality development, since everyone who is not to stagnate must have a stake in the next generation. The teacher chooses to nurture intellectual development in growing human beings. Thus she grows at his level while her students grow at theirs.

Some Factors Influencing the Interaction of School and Child

CULTURAL LEVEL. Success in school depends heavily upon intellectual and social learning at home. The tremendous advantage of belonging to a family of high cultural level is illustrated by the distribution of merit scholars: among professors' families there was one merit scholar for every 540 families; laborers produced one merit scholar in 3.5 million families [66]. Another way of measuring results of cultural differences is in terms of IQ. A difference of about 20 points in average IQ has been found in several comparisons of highest and lowest socioeconomic groups [37]. The disadvantages of cultural deprivation weigh upon the child long before he starts school, causing him to begin his formal education with a limited store of memories and concepts, a small, inadequate vocabulary, inability to understand connected sentences, limited concepts of time and causality, restricted experience with books and other school materials. Piled upon the cognitive disadvantages are emotional burdens: low self-concept, feelings of worthlessness, guilt and shame, little trust in adults, hyperactivity, impulsivity, apathy and lack of responsiveness to people [72].

The material and social resources of the family determine the world in which the child grows. The intelligence he brings to school has been built through interacting with what that world offered. The language he has heard is the language with which he communicates and thinks. If it is not the language of the school, then he is at a disadvantage. For example, in Scotland schools discourage the use of dialect which many of the poorer people use exclusively. A first-grader, seeing the word *cap* for the first time and required to sound it out looked at the picture which accompanied it and said, *"c-a-p, c-a-p, c-a-p, Bonnet!"* [20].

Socioeconomic factors make a difference in many forms of intellectual nurture. Compare the opportunities of a child whose home contains no reading materials to that of one who grows up surrounded by books and magazines. Suppose, also, that the first child rarely, if ever, goes far from home. The second goes on trips with his family and visits many local points of interests, expanding his vocabulary and getting first-hand information on geography, history, science, nature and technology. While movies and television are available to nearly all children, the child who has books and trips is also likely to be exposed to a variety of art forms—theater, concerts, exhibits, often in a show designed for children. In addition to enjoying what others have created, he often has chances to create himself, using the paints, violin and dancing lessons which middle-class parents are able to provide. Such parents also teach the values, motivations, social behavior and techniques for learning which fit their children for academic success. They help their children with homework, show them how to look up answers in the library and offer discriminating praise and evaluation.

Money and social position may determine even the school to which the child will go. The child who lives in a slum goes to school with other poor children, often in an old school building. Upper-middle-class neighborhoods tend to offer bright, spacious, well-equipped buildings and classmates who enjoy rich opportunities for growth. Upper-class children are often sent to private schools which offer opportunities for achieving excellence. Small wonder, then, that socioeconomic status correlates with IQ and with academic success!

SOCIAL POSITION IN THE CLASSROOM. The child has his own social position, as a member of his school class, a position which is not necessarily the same as the social position held by his family in the community. His own position is both product and cause of his behavior and of how children and teachers feel and behave toward him. Many socioemetric studies have shown that each classroom has its own social structure and that each child in it has his own place and relationships. Children in the lower positions have more difficulties than higher-status children. They are less able to cope with frustration; their teachers see them as showing more behavior problems, poorer social adjustment and more emotional instability; they feel more disliking for other children and this increases as the year goes on; they show more aggressive–assertive or passive–hostile activity, as observed and measured on behavior schedules [45]. The interactions of children and teachers were recorded by observers who did not know the children's sociometric positions. Results yielded these insights into child–teacher interaction: teachers noticed the social behavior of low-status children more than they noticed that of high-status children; low-status boys received more criticism than high-status boys; low-status girls received more affectionate support than did other girls. The teachers were responding to the girls' seeking of affection from them, while being relatively passive in the classroom; they were responding to the boys' typical aggressive, disruptive behavior.

Relationship between individual child and type of school program. Different programs and styles of teaching suit different children, according to the children's various cognitive and personality characteristics. For example, one child works well by himself, pursuing a topic for a long time, concentrating on it and resenting interruptions. Another child accomplishes more when small tests are set for him and when he can change often from one activity to another. Visual aids, teaching machines and role playing are especially appropriate for children from low socioeconomic backgrounds, since they are likely to do better with visual than with verbal materials [59].

Different methods of teaching reading have been demonstrated to be differentially suited to children according to certain personality characteristics [28]. One system used the phonics method, which provided a maximum of structure, rules, systematic arrangements and definiteness of directions and expectations. The other used the whole-word method, which gave a minimum of structure, because of its encouragement of intelligent guessing and its lack of rules. The children, all third-graders, were rated as to compulsivity (wanting neatness, order and certainty, conforming, perfectionist, rigid, not spontaneous) and anxiety (response to a perceived threat). Compulsive children achieved at a higher level than less compulsive children in the structured classroom, but in the unstructured classroom, there was no significant difference between compulsive and noncompulsive children. The highly anxious children were at a real disadvantage in the unstructured school, where they were excelled by nonanxious children. In the structured school, there was no significant difference between anxious and nonanxious children. Therefore, unless children were assigned to a reading program on the basis of personality tests, some children would be at a disadvantage in either type of program.

Textbooks

Books and other teaching materials are instruments through which the school affects the competence of its pupils. Textbooks, however, are more than this, since they reflect the values of the whole culture, chosen by the community or even by the state, as compulsory reading for its children. Textbooks hold up the virtues and behavior which adults want children to attain. Because they are chosen by committees and the choice is influenced by additional people, the behavior exalted tends to be conventional and stereotyped. The values extolled change as the culture changes, as can be seen in Figure 12–1, which shows the frequency of three themes—achievement, affiliation and moral—as they appeared in children's readers over a 60-year period. Even before the Sputnik-inspired revolution in American education, critics were expressing dissatisfaction with textbooks. A review and analysis of third-grade readers pointed out that the picture of life presented was often unrealistic [12]. Friendly and helpful behavior was almost always rewarded, for instance, while problems of aggression and greed were handled by pretending that children did not have such problems. Autonomy and initiative were usually discouraged, while skills, enjoyment, optimism and cooperation were approved. Very conventional sex roles were upheld.

More recently, problems of civil rights, poverty and cultural deprivation have focused criticism upon textbooks which present only a white, middle-class way of life. A demand has arisen for books for urban children of lower socioeconomic status who belong to minority groups. Their problems and their ways of life are to be handled in such a way that the reader can identify with the characters. In these ways and in other ways, modern textbooks are planned with more insight than were textbooks of former years.

SUMMARY

The child now feels a need to learn the rules of the game, as they pertain to many aspects of life, as he looks forward to taking his place as a producing member of society. His approaches to learning skills, rules and various competencies grows out of his motivations and out of the social and cultural settings in which he grows up.

A wide choice of activities assures each child a good chance for success in one or more areas of competency. While academic excellence is out of reach for most children with limited background experience, motor skills and play activities offer them chances to excel. Reading, the key to success in school, is influenced by a multitude of physical, emotional and experimental factors. Writing, a psychomotor skill, serves the purpose of communication and self-expression. Mathematics, an area in which many children have experienced inferiority, can be taught on a broad base of experiences with manipulating, grouping, arranging and ordering.

The sense of industry grows upon success as a worker at home, as well as

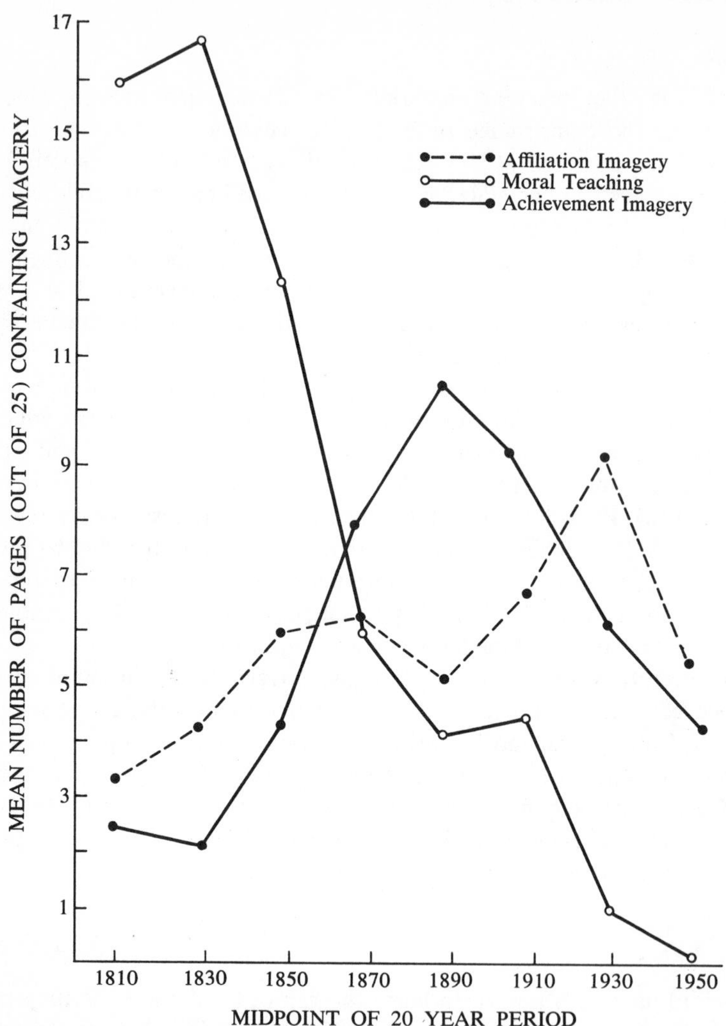

Figure 12–1. Values extolled by children's textbooks over a period of a century and a half. (Adapted from R. deCharms, and G. H. Moeller, "Content Analysis of Children's Readers," *Journal of Abnormal and Social Psychology*, 1962, **64,** 136–162. Used by permission of the American Psychological Association and Richard deCharms.)

at school and in the community. Since meaningful jobs are not always easy to find, group leaders and recreation workers often supplement the home in this important area. Play activities also contribute competencies in physical, intellectual, social and emotional fields.

The learning of society's rules is a long process which begins by being able to state what people are supposed to do and which progresses by grasping more and more of the abstractions involved and by understanding the complicated interweaving of social roles. Moral judgment, involving evaluation of actions, matures along with cognitive and social growth. Moral behavior depends upon will and control, in conjunction with moral knowledge and judgment. Religious and philosophical concepts also develop through cognitive and social growth, guided by the type of concepts to which the child is exposed.

Success in development of the sense of industry is strongly influenced by the child's desire for achievement and recognition. Applying standards of excellence to himself, he and others judge his performance. A feeling tone results from that judgment, a happy feeling from approval, or an unpleasant feeling from disapproval. Both the need for achievement and achievement behavior show some consistency over time across situations and in sex differences. Boys apparently have more internalized standards and more realistic goals, whereas girls are more likely to seek approval and affection through their achievement efforts. Characteristics of high-achieving children include independence from adults, persistence and competitiveness.

Anxiety has been studied as general anxiety and as anxiety in the situation of taking tests or examinations. Learning and achievement show complicated relations to level of anxiety. In general, low or moderate anxiety may aid or not deter a child in performing fairly easy tasks, and high anxiety is likely to reduce his competency. Fear of failure is a common type of anxiety of schoolchildren. Failure itself depends upon the relationship of achievement level and aspiration level.

Curiosity determines the vigor with which a child seeks new experiences. New experiences contribute to further curiosity and to cognitive development. Curiosity can be stimulated by educational techniques.

The American educational system is dedicated to a number of values, some of which conflict with each other. The complexity of the culture requires that the school perform many functions, including the promotion of health and personality development along with the teaching of traditional academic skills and knowledge. The child's success at school is influenced by his cultural level, which strongly determines his preparation for school, his social position in the classroom and the fit between his personality and the style and philosophy of his school. Educational materials, especially textbooks, strongly reflect cultural values and concerns.

REFERENCES

1. Amatora, M. Expressed interests in later childhood. *J. Genet. Psychol.*, 1960, **96,** 327–342.
2. Allinsmith, W., & Goethals, G. W. *The role of schools in mental health.* New York: Basic Books, 1962.
3. Barker, R. G. Success and failure in the classroom. *Progressive Educ.*, 1942, **19,** 221–224.
4. Beilin, H. Teachers' and clinicians' attitudes toward the behavior problems of children. *Child Devel.*, 1959, **30,** 9–25.

5. Bettleheim, B. What children learn from play. *Parents',* 1964, **39:**7, 48 ff.
6. Biber, B. Integration of mental health principles in the school. In G. Caplan (Ed.), *Prevention of mental disorders in children.* New York: Basic Books, 1961, pp. 323–352.
7. Biber, B., & Lewis, C. An experimental study of what young children expect from their teachers. *Genet. Psychol. Mono.,* 1949, **40,** 3–98.
8. Blakely, W. P. Study of seventh-grade children's reading of comic books as related to certain other variables. *J. Genet. Psychol.,* 1958, **93,** 291–301.
9. Boehm, L., & Nass, M. L. Social class differences in conscience development. *Child Devel.,* 1962, **33,** 565–575.
10. Burton, R. V. The generality of honesty reconsidered. *Psychol. Rev.,* 1963, **70,** 481–500.
11. Cantaneda, A., McCandless, B. R., & Palermo, D. S. The children's form of the manifest anxiety scale. *Child Devel.,* 1956, **27,** 315–326.
12. Child, I. L., Potter, E. H., & Levine, E. M. Children's textbooks and personality development: an exploration in the social psychology of education. *Psychol. Mono.,* 1946, **60,** 1–7, 43–53.
13. Cox, F. N. Test anxiety and achievement behavior systems related to examination performance in children. *Child Devel.,* 1964, **35,** 909–915.
14. Crandall, V. J. Parents as identification models and reinforcers of children's achievement behavior. Progress report, NIMH Grant M-2238, January 1961. (Mimeo.) Cited in Crandall [15].
15. Crandall, V. J. Achievement. In H. W. Stevenson, J. Kagan & C. Spiker (Eds.), *Child psychology.* The sixty-second yearbook of the National Society for the Study of Education, Part I. Chicago: Univer. of Chicago, 1963, pp. 416–459.
16. Crandall, V. J., Katkovsky, W., & Preston, A. A conceptual formulation for some research on children's achievement development. *Child Devel.,* 1960, **31,** 787–797.
17. Crandall, V. J., Katkovsky, W., & Preston, A. Motivational and ability determinants of young children's intellectual achievement behaviors. *Child Devel.,* 1962, **33,** 643–661.
18. D'Heurle, A., Mellinger, J., & Haggard, E. Personality, intellectual and achievement patterns in gifted children. *Psychol. Mono.,* 1959, Whole No. 483.
19. Doman, G. *How to teach your baby to read.* New York: Random House, 1964.
20. Donaldson, M. Class lecture. Kingston: Univer. of Rhode Island, 1963.
21. Durkin, D. Children's concepts of justice: a comparison with the Piaget data. *Child Devel.,* 1959, **30,** 59–67.
22. Elkind, D. The child's conception of his religious denomination. I: the Jewish child. *J. Genet. Psychol.,* 1961, **99,** 209–225.
23. Elkind, D. The child's conception of his religious denomination. II: the Catholic child. *J. Genet. Psychol.,* 1962, **101,** 185–194.
24. Elkind, D. The child's conception of his religious denomination. III: the Protestant child, *J. Genet. Psychol.,* 1963, **103,** 291–304.
25. Erikson, E. H. *Childhood and society.* New York: Norton, 1963.
26. Ezer, M. The effect of religion upon children's responses to questions involving physical causality. In J. Rosenblith & W. Allinsmith (Eds.), *The causes of behavior.* Boston: Allyn and Bacon, 1962, pp. 481–487.

27. Feld, Sheila. Need achievement and test anxiety in children and maternal attitudes and behaviors toward independent accomplishments: a longitudinal study. Paper read at meeting of *American Psychological Association,* Cincinnati, 1959. Cited in Crandall [15].
28. Grimes, J. W., & Allinsmith, W. Compulsivity, anxiety and school achievement. *Merrill-Palmer Quart.,* 1961, **7,** 247–271.
29. Grinder, R. E. Relations between behavioral and cognitive dimensions of conscience in middle childhood. *Child Devel.,* 1964, **35,** 881–891.
30. Haggard, E. Socialization, personality and academic achievement in gifted children. *School Rev.,* 1957, 388–414.
31. Harrell, L. E. A comparison of the development of oral and written language in school-age children. *Mono. Soc. Res. Child Devel.,* 1957, **22:**3.
32. Hartshorne, H., & May, M. A. *Studies in the nature of character. Vol. I: studies in deceit; Vol. II: studies in self-control; Vol. III: studies in the organization of character.* New York: Macmillan, 1928–1930.
33. Herrick, V. E., & Okada, N. The present scene: practices in the teaching of handwriting in the United States—1960. From V. E. Herrick (Ed.), *New horizons for research in handwriting.* Madison: Univer. of Wisconsin, 1963.
34. Himmelweit, H. T., Oppenheim, A. N., & Vince, P. *Television and the child.* London: Oxford, 1958.
35. Hunt, J. McV. The psychological basis for using preschool enrichment as an antidote for cultural deprivation. *Merrill-Palmer Quart.,* 1964, **10:**3, 209–248.
36. Johnson, R. A. A study of children's moral judgments. *Child Devel.,* 1962, **33,** 327–354.
37. Jones, H. E. The environment and mental development. In L. Carmichael (Ed.), *Manual of child psychology* (2d ed.). New York: Wiley, 1954, pp. 361–696.
38. Kagan, J., & Moss, H. Stability and validity of achievement fantasy. *J. Abn. Soc. Psychol.,* 1959, **58,** 357–364.
39. Kagan, J., Sontag, L. W., Baker, C. T., & Nelson, V. L. Personality and I.Q. change. *J. Abn. Soc. Psychol.,* 1958, **56,** 261–266.
40. Katkovsky, W., Preston, A., & Crandall, V. J. Parents' attitudes toward their personal achievements and toward the achievement behaviors of their children. *J. Genet. Psychol.,* 1964, **104,** 67–82.
41. Kohlberg, L. The development of children's orientations toward a moral order. I: sequence in the development of moral thought. *Vita Humana,* 1963, **6,** 11–33.
42. Kohlberg, L. Development of moral character and moral ideology. In M. L. Hoffman & L. W. Hoffman (Eds.), *Review of child development research.* New York: Russell Sage Foundation, 1964, pp. 383–431.
43. Larrick, N. *A parent's guide to children's reading.* New York: Doubleday, 1964.
44. Lerner, E. Perspectives in moral reasoning. *Am. J. Sociol.,* 1937, 249–269.
45. Lippitt, R., & Gold, M. Classroom social structure as a mental health problem. *J. Soc. Issues,* 1959, **15,** 40–49.
46. MacRae, R. A test of Piaget's theories of moral development. *J. Abn. Soc. Psychol.,* 1954, **49,** 14–18.

47. McClelland, D. C., Atkinson, J. W., Clark, R. A., & Lowell, E. L. *The achievement motive.* New York: Appleton-Century, 1953.
48. McReynolds, P., Acker, M., & Pietila, C. Relations of object curiosity to psychological adjustment in children. *Child Devel.,* 1961, **32,** 393–400.
49. Maccoby, E. E. Why do children watch television? *Pub. Opinion Quart.,* 1954, **18,** 239–244.
50. Maw, W. H., & Maw, E. W. Establishing criterion groups for evaluating measures of curiosity. *J. Exp. Educ.,* 1961, **29,** 299–306. (a)
51. Maw, W. H., & Maw, E. W. Information recognition by children with high and low curiosity. *Educ. Res. Bull.,* 1961, **40,** 197–201, 223–224. (b)
52. Maw, W. H., & Maw, E. W. Selection of unbalanced and unusual designs by children high in curiosity. *Child Devel.,* 1962, **33,** 917–922.
53. Mendel, G. Children's preferences for differing degrees of novelty. *Child Devel.,* 1965, **36,** 453–464.
54. Mischel, W. Delay of gratification and deviant behavior. Paper read at meetings of *Society for Research in Child Development,* Berkeley, Calif., April 1963.
55. Mittman, L. R., & Terrell, G. An experimental study of curiosity in children. *Child Devel.,* 1964, **35,** 851–855.
56. Moss, H., & Kagan, J. Stability of achievement and recognition-seeking behaviors from early childhood through adulthood. *J. Abn. Soc. Psychol.,* 1961, **62,** 504–513.
57. Peck, R. F., & Havighurst, R. J. *The psychology of character development.* New York: Wiley, 1960.
58. Piaget, J. *The moral judgment of the child.* Glencoe, Ill.: Free Press, 1948.
59. Riessman, F. Low-income culture: the strengths of the poor. *J. Marr. Fam.,* 1964, **26,** 417–429.
60. Sarason, S. B., Davidson, K. S., Lighthall, F. F., & Waite, R. R. A test anxiety scale for children. *Child Devel.,* 1958, **29,** 105–113.
61. Sarason, S. B., Davidson, K. S., Lighthall, F. F., Waite, R. R., & Ruebush, B. K. *Anxiety in elementary school children.* New York: Wiley, 1960.
62. Sarason, S. B., Hill, K. T., & Zimbardo P. G. A longitudinal study of the relation of test anxiety to performance on intelligence and achievement tests. *Mono. Soc. Res. Child Devel.,* 1964, **29:**7.
63. Schramm, W., Lyle, J., & Parker, E. B. *Television in the lives of our children.* Stanford, Calif.: Stanford Univer., 1961.
64. Sears, P. S. Correlates of need achievement and need affiliation and classroom management, self-concept, achievement and creativity. Unpublished manuscript, Laboratory of Human Development, Stanford Univer., 1962. Cited in Crandall [15].
65. Sears, R. R., Rau, L., & Alpert, R. *Identification and child-rearing.* Stanford, Calif.: Stanford Univer. Press, 1965.
66. Sexton, P. *Education and income.* New York: Viking, 1961.
67. Smock, C. D., & Holt, B. G. Children's reactions to novelty: an experimental study of curiosity motivation. *Child Devel.,* 1962, **33,** 631–642.
68. Stendler, C. B., & Young, N. The impact of beginning first grade upon the socialization as reported by mothers. *Child Devel.,* 1950, **21,** 241–260.

69. Stendler, C. B., & Young, N. Impact of first grade entrance upon the socialization of the child: changes after eight months of school. *Child Devel.*, 1951, **22,** 113–122.
70. Strauss, A. L. The development of conceptions of rules in children. *Child Devel.*, 1954, **25,** 193–208.
71. Suchman, J. R. Inquiry training: building skills for autonomous discovery. *Merrill-Palmer Quart.*, 1961, **7,** 147–170.
72. Taba, H. Cultural deprivation as a factor in school learning. *Merrill-Palmer Quart.*, 1964, **10,** 147–159.
73. Terman, L. M., & Merrill, M. A. *Stanford-Binet Intelligence Scale*. Boston: Houghton Mifflin, 1960.
74. White, R. W. Motivation reconsidered: the concept of competence. *Psychol. Rev.*, 1959, **66,** 297–333.
75. Whiteman, P. H., & Kosier, K. P. Development of children's moralistic judgments: age, sex, IQ and certain personal-experiential variables. *Child Devel.*, 1964, **35,** 843–850.

Social Development and Interpersonal Relationships

CHAPTER 13

In his fast-expanding world, the child interacts with a greater and greater variety of teachers and influences. Relationships with peers grow more extensive and complex. While his family continues to be essential for protection, love and teaching, the school, church and other institutions play more and more important roles in his life. Through mass media, he contacts thoughts and events originating far from his own neighborhood.

SOCIAL AND CULTURAL SETTINGS

A child is born into a community, a nation, a social class, a racial group and other such divisions of mankind to which his parents belong. Even before he is aware of these classifications of people, he is affected by his memberships in them. As a preschool child, he is influenced largely through his family, but as a school child, he makes many direct contacts.

Community

While community is often understood as neighborhood, or town, it can also be taken to mean the whole wide world. It can include all the people of whom one is aware. During the school years, many children do reach out beyond the confines of face-to-face contacts to relate to distant people. The newly acquired skills of reading and writing are keys to expanded relationships. A letter to Grandpa and Grandma may go right across the United States or into another country. Cousins known during vacation visits remain real throughout the year. Through pen pals, many children travel to the other side of the world to build warm friendships. The integrating experience of really helping other children is now a possibility for almost all American children at Halloween. Then they can give up their right to demand treats for themselves in order to collect for the United Nations Children's Fund. Boy Scouts and Girl Scouts spell out ways of learning about the rest of the world and facilitate the making of meaningful contacts and contributions. Schools open up vistas in time and space.

The world is indeed one level of community with which the child interacts. World concern for children is expressed through the United Nations, especially through its health and educational agencies. The federal government is another level of interaction. Here, responsibility for all children is a matter of increasing interest, with more agencies and more money being devoted to child and family welfare. Every state performs some functions for its children, dealing with such matters as health, education and protection with more or less adequacy. Cities, towns and sometimes townships have their special areas of responsibility too.

National

Differences in social behavior have been reported by cultural anthropologists, who have investigated what is important to the Balinese and Alorese, contrasted East and West and looked behind the Iron Curtain. The material collected on this topic is vast. Students of family life and childrearing have compiled descriptions of many different parental practices [48, 50, 60, 73].

One extensive series of studies by two psychologists will serve as an example of the impact of national value systems upon the school-age child. Harold and Gladys Anderson [1, 2] collected data in seven languages from 9,546 children in grades four, seven and ten. Through a projective method using incomplete stories, they studied the effects of democratic and authoritarian cultures upon children's interpersonal relations. England and the United States represented the democratic nations, Mexico and Germany the more authoritarian ones.

Using a story about the teacher's money disappearing from her desk, children's responses in a democratic country showed more expressions of confidence and trust in the children by the teacher. In the authoritarian countries, responses showed more frequent assumptions of theft and fewer expressions of confidence in the child. Another story, dealing with a lost composition, produced in democratic countries higher frequencies of responses in which the teacher believed the child, and in authoritarian countries, more instances where the teacher did not believe the child. The Andersons suggest that democratic countries promote integrative social relationships through their values of confidence in, trust and respect for the individual, respect for property, responsibility, honesty, social invention in interpersonal relations and social creativity. On the other hand, authoritarian cultures restrict creativity and stifle originality and social problem solving.

On the other side of the ledger of American national values are materialism and the exalting of mediocrity. Materialism is expressed in many ways which impinge upon the child, most notably through the advertising industry. Exploiting everyone's childish fantasies, it promotes immaturity, urging impulse gratification and avoidance of reality by travel, changing one's looks or buying status symbols. Mediocrity is nurtured by the entertainment industry, which pitches to the lowest common denominator of taste and understanding.

Racial and Ethnic

As a member of a minority group, the school-age child directly experiences the particular attitudes and actions which other people customarily direct toward his group. If he is a member of a group which is easily distinguished by physical characteristics, then his experiences as a member are likely to be more intense and extensive. For many years, Negro Americans, who are fairly distinctive in appearance, have occupied a subordinate social and economic position. Their experience is probably representative of any group so situated. While a thorough discussion of it is impossible here, something of what happens to the schoolchild is pertinent.

Studies of Negro education have overwhelmingly proven its inferiority. One example from the South and one from the North will suffice. In Tennessee, Negro students were found to be a year and a half to two years retarded in grade level when they were transferred to white schools [76]. The same report revealed that only 49 percent of qualified Negro teachers passed the National Teacher's Examination, while 97 percent of qualified white teachers passed it. In New York City, time sampling of activities in the elementary schools indicated that in classrooms where Negro children predominated, 50 percent to 80 percent of the time was spent on disciplining and other nonacademic tasks. Where class membership was predominantly white, although of the same socioeconomic level, 30 percent of the time was spent on disciplining and nonacademic tasks [20].

Desegregation, while intended as a means to justice, brings many problems for the Negro child. The social threat of hostile, powerful white children can provoke great anxiety, impairing the child's problem solving and learning and even causing him to lower his achievement efforts so as not to compete with the whites [43]. If, however, the Negro child encounters friendly, acceptant white children and teachers, he is likely to feel encouraged and to raise his achievement efforts. If the academic standards are so high that he sees little chance of success, though, he is likely to become too discouraged to try hard. As probability of failure increases, likelihood of disapproval from parents and teachers also increases. As the child realizes the increasing danger of adult disapproval, he grows more fearful and hostile. Unable and/or afraid to express his hostility against adults, he turns it against himself as self-derogatory attitudes, increased expectation of failure and desire to escape. These attitudes can be expected to weaken his performance in school [43]. Competence and the sense of industry, then, are likely to be severely handicapped by membership in a subordinate minority group.

Parental teaching and expectations are known to vary with race and ethnic group. When the child first contacts the attitudes of outsiders toward himself as a minority group member, the parents interpret those attitudes toward him and tell him how he is to think and behave. Parents are faced with the dilemma of explaining hostility, exclusion or mere condescension while protecting their child's sense of adequacy. The wife of the executive director of the National Urban League tells of her own interpretation to her nine-year-old daughter, while the two of them watched a television program on the trials and tribulations of being a Negro [78]. They had listened to a description of the unemployment crisis, ghetto living, police brutalities and inferior schooling. Mrs. Young asked her daughter if she minded being a Negro. She answered, "No, I don't mind."

Her answer to her daughter was, "I'm glad you don't mind. There are many groups of people all over the world who have not been treated fairly. In Germany, it was the Jews; in some parts of Europe, it was the Catholics; in Viet Nam, it was the Buddhists. Some people are mistreated because of color or religion and some because they are poor or blind or crippled. You should be especially proud of being Negro because, in your lifetime, you will enjoy a better America, knowing that we are the ones who helped our country to meet her commitment to all of her peoples."

Mothers in six different ethnic groups were interviewed to explore their attitudes and practices in regard to their sons' achievement [63]. The boys were between 8 and 14 years of age. The ethnic groups included were French-Canadian, Italian, Greek, Jewish, Negro and white Protestant. When the mothers were questioned about how they trained their sons for independence and what they demanded in the way of achievement, results showed that Protestants, Jews and Greeks placed greater emphasis on independence and achievement than did Italians and French-Canadians. Negroes often trained children early in independence, but tended to do little achievement training. Differences between Protestants, Jews and Greeks were not statistically significant. Roman Catholics did significantly less achievement training than did non-Roman Catholic whites. A college education was intended for their sons by 96 percent of the Jewish, 88 percent of the Protestant, 85 percent of the Greek, 83 percent of the Negro, 64 percent of the Italian and 56 percent of the French-Canadian mothers. Vocational aspirations were explored by asking the mothers which occupations (for their sons) would satisfy them. Negro mothers obtained the lowest score here, showing that they would be content with less than all the other mothers, probably a realistic reflection of the vocational opportunities which they knew existed. The order of the ethnic groups in vocational aspirations was Jewish, Greek and Protestant, Italian and French-Canadian, Negro. This research points up the influence of ethnic group membership on a child's training in independence and achievement and the values and standards held for him in regard to education and vocation.

Social Class

Behavior and outlook on life vary considerably with the social position occupied by a family. American middle-class and lower-class behavior has been studied extensively [10]. Less is known about the upper class, since its members are more elusive as subjects for research. Class values and behavior patterns are transmitted from parents to children through their childrearing practices.

The cognitive behavior patterns transmitted by the lower class have been described elsewhere in this book in the context of cultural deprivation. To mention it only briefly here, the lower-class child is relatively reluctant to explore and to ask questions. His mother most likely discourages assertiveness, curiosity and imagination, encouraging him to wait to be told, to receive, to be acted upon [62].

Values. The basic values of the upper class include respect for families and lineage; a belief that money is important, but only as a means to an end; contempt for pretense, striving, status symbols and conspicuous consumption [5]. The upper-class child enjoys the care, education and privileges that money will buy, but he has little realization that money is involved. In contrast, the middle-class child is keenly aware of what money will buy and how striving to achieve will bring money. The upper-class child does not learn social striving nor does he experience social anxiety, since his family is already at the top, relaxed and poised, exercising quiet good taste. The middle-class child learns that he could rise socially by behaving in certain ways.

Middle-class values are achievement and status improvement, respectability and morality, property, money, organizations, self-improvement through the church, school and civic organizations [18]. Lower-class values include security and getting by rather than getting ahead; traditional, patriarchal education; traditional, clearly differentiated sex roles; pragmatism, anti-intellectualism; such excitement as news, gossip, sports and gadgets; physical expression and power [61].

Several observers [16, 17] see traditional middle-class values of competition and self-improvement being tempered by an increased desire for cooperation, conformity, fitting in and popularity. Parents thus affected want their children to be fairly good at everything but not extreme in anything.

These value systems operate not only through parental influence but also through teachers, other children, club leaders, librarians, clergymen, policemen, doctors and everybody else who contacts children. Although a middle-class child is likely to have predominantly middle-class values held up to him, he will meet few conflicting values. A lower-class child, in contrast, faces a bewildering mixture of value systems when he enters school [20, 43]. His teacher's values conflict with those of his family and friends; verbal achievement versus physical; self-control versus frank expression; self-improvement versus unself-conscious acceptance; equalitarianism versus patriarchy; femininity versus masculinity; tomorrow versus today. It is hard to live up to the teacher's expectations of manners, quiet, orderliness, respect for property, thinking out instead of acting out.

Interaction of class and family in value transmission. Not only do values vary from class to class, but the behavior which transmits the values also varies. Child-training practices and philosophy of the middle and lower classes have been contrasted in many studies. Table 13–1 shows some of the important areas of difference indicated in a summary of this research [16].

TABLE 13–1

Behavior and philosophy of parents of two classes.

	Working Class (Lower Class)	*Middle Class*
Behavioral requirements	Specific	Internalized standards
	Obedience, neatness, cleanliness	Honesty, self-control
	Qualities assuring respectability	Boys, curiosity; Girls, considerateness
Concept of good parent	Elicits specific behavior	Promotes development, affection, satisfaction
Response to misdeed	Focus on immediate consequences of child's actions	Takes into account child's intentions and feelings
Discipline techniques	More physical punishment	More reasoning, isolation, appeals to guilt
Role differentiation	More rigid. More paternalistic	More flexible, more equalitarian
Father as companion to child	Less	More
Permissiveness	Less to infant and young child More to older child	More to infant and young child Less to older child
Achievement demands	Less	More

Source: Data from Clausen & Williams [16].

The transmission of values and behavior patterns is complicated. A study of boys' acquisition of achievement orientation illustrates the complex ways in which only a few variables interact [64]. Drawn from diverse social strata, 122 boys and their mothers were interviewed. Results showed middle-class mothers and sons to be more similar in value than lower-class mothers and sons. Among lower-class pairs, values were more similar if the mother was older rather than younger. Small- and medium-sized families produced more similarity in mother–son values than did large families.

RELATIONSHIPS WITH PARENTS

Earlier chapters of this section have dealt with changes in children between 6 and 12. To the extent that these changes give the child a different repertory of behaviors they make him a different person vis-à-vis members of his family.

Because, for instance, at the end of the period a child is moving out of the stage of concrete operations into the stage of formal operations, his conversations with adults may at times take on a flavor and substance of which he would have been incapable at the age of six. Because of the increase in muscular skills and coordinations, children at the end of the elementary-school years can take part with parents and adolescent siblings in household tasks and athletic games with fewer allowances made for his immaturity.

"The Changing American Parent"

However cloudy and distorted the picture, any individual beyond the late teens or early twenties has some memories of what he was like at younger ages and some recollections of the expectations parents then held for children. Comparing his memories with what he sees today, he will probably notice the trend for parents to be more permissive, less authoritarian in dealing with children; to give freer expression to affection; and to use psychological rather than physical techniques in discipline. Families have been concurrently tending away from father-centered control toward a sharing of control and decision making by both parents. As fathers have become less the wielders of control and power, they have become, for the children, sources of affection and nurturance. Not all individual families show this trend, but there is evidence that more families recently fit the description than families in preceding generations [51].

Indication of changes in parent–child relationships comes from the child-development research literature [10, 11] and from a review of advice given to parents through the years by the United States Children's Bureau [75]. The Children's Bureau does not change its mind arbitrarily from one edition of *Infant Care* to the next. Rather, it reflects trends in American society, changes which have not yet run their course [51]. Although changes are slow in relation to the life span of any individual, they are rapid from the point of view of society. While a parent may not be very aware of these trends while taking care of children, he is very much affected by them. In a stable or rigid society, parents can look back to their own childhood and then treat their children in the same ways in which their own parents took care of them. In a changing society, each generation has to work out its own style of family life, in accordance with the larger social scene. Parents seek help from science, from literature on child guidance and from one another, instead of depending upon tradition and grandparents.

Children's Perceptions of Parents

Most of the information available about the functioning of American families has been obtained by family members' reports. Direct observation of how families operate, especially within the walls of their homes, is frowned upon not only because of the American value of individual privacy but also because a nonfamily member introduced into the family group changes behavior to such an extent that the observations of such a person bear little relation to run-of-the-mill occurrences. There are several studies which have collected information from school-age children as to how their families operate and how they feel about it. These studies are all cross-sectional. The summary of age differences is therefore of statements true about children of different ages at the same point of time. If fewer 10-year-olds than six-year-olds say that their fathers do most of the punishing, we may or may not be correct in assuming that four years from now, the fathers of the current six-year-olds will be doing less punishing.

CLASS DIFFERENCES IN PERCEPTION OF PARENTS. When lower-class boys' perceptions of their parents were compared with those of middle-class boys, the differences corresponded with what is known about behavior of lower- and middle-class parents [65]. The differences in their perceptions were greater in regard to fathers than to mothers. Middle-class boys' perceptions of fathers were more favorable than those of lower-class boys. The former saw their fathers as more successful, ambitious and smart, as more secure (less nervous, shy and worried), as more acceptant of their sons and more interested in their sons' behavior and needs. Differences in the two groups' perceptions of mothers were in the same direction as differences in perception of fathers.

PARENTAL AUTHORITY. The traditional pattern of authority in the American family, as in families in most of the world's cultures, was for the father to be considered the head of the household by all the members. All important decisions and all decisions basic to the countless choices that have to be made from day to day were made by the husband and father. In colloquial terms, the man of the household was the boss. Recent studies reveal a different picture in modern family life.

When wives were asked to tell whether they or their husbands usually made decisions in each of eight areas of family living, they were given five alternative answers, ranging from "Husband Always" through "Wife Always." Differential weights were given the answers at each point, and the scores summed across the eight areas. The scores at the ends of the resulting scale were called "Husband Dominant" and "Wife Dominant." Two out of eight of the families fell into the "Wife Dominant" group; another two out of eight were "Husband Dominant;" the remaining four were equal or showed "Balance of Power" [7, p. 45].

When children were given only two alternatives (Mother or Father) in answering a question concerning who was boss at home, about two out of eight children answered "Mother" [24, 38]. In answering the question many of the children hesitated before replying and then explained that they answered "Father" because he was the economic supporter of the family. The hesitation may have occurred for some of the children because they actually perceived their parents as having equal power but, forced to choose between only two alternatives, gave an answer which they knew agreed with the cultural expectation and justified it in the traditional way.

When three alternatives were permitted to the question as to power, 40 percent of children between 7 and 15 said that their parents were equal [31]. The opinion that power was shared equally was held more often by older youngsters than younger ones and more often by girls than by boys. Perhaps children's reports reflect an actual decline in the father's power as the family gets older. The highest paternal power was reported by eight-year-olds [21]. Children's views in this respect agree with findings from interviews with wives, where fathers of oldest children were seen as less powerful than fathers of youngest children [7].

Perhaps the most significant generalization to be drawn from this wealth of data is that about half of American families carry on a democratic form of life in the home. Or so it appears to their children. Authority is shared and decisions made jointly by husband and wife in 50 percent or more of families studied. It is possible that the figure is greater, since children are more likely to make all-or-none choices than to see and describe relationships in all their subtleties. Another indication that a balance-of-power, or cooperative partnerships, may exceed dominated families is that older children, more than younger children, see their fathers as having less absolute authority and sharing more with their wives. Older children would be more likely to perceive the complex relationship which cooperation involves, while younger ones might not notice it or might not be able to express it in words.

PUNISHMENT. Another source of information on children's perceptions of parental power is from asking children "Who punishes you?" Some age changes can be seen in the reports on punishment. Sex differences would be expected, and these have been found. Answers from a group of fourth and fifth grade children indicated 29 percent of fathers usually punished, 30 percent of mothers and 33 percent of both [24]. (Eight percent of the group did not answer this question.) However, more boys than girls reported that their fathers usually punished them, and more girls than boys reported that the mother usually punished. First-to-third-graders, when asked a question as to who would punish if both parents were present when a misdeed occurred, indicated that the father would be the probable punisher about twice as often as the mother, the girls reporting this fact less often than the boys [38]. More of the third grade than of first and second grade girls reported the mother as punisher, but fewer of the older grade boys reported so. In a study of boys and girls in grades three through six both the boys and the girls said that their fathers punished more than their mothers did, but the boys reported receiving more punishment from their fathers than the girls did [32].

When asked questions as to the mode of punishment usually meted out to the boys and girls, fourth and fifth grade children reported that fathers used physical punishment more often than mothers, and that they used it more often with their sons than with their daughters [24]. Fathers equally often used physical and verbal punishment with their daughters. Mothers used physical punishment with boys as often as they used verbal punishment with girls, each slightly less than half the time. Both parents used deprivation as punishment least often, about one quarter of the time.

To generalize about punishment as experienced by children, there are important sex differences as to who gives and who receives punishment. Fathers punish more than mothers, especially where boys are concerned. Fathers use physical punishment more than mothers, especially with boys. Boys receive more physical punishment, girls more verbal.

NURTURANCE. Results of research on children from preschool age to preadolescence agree that the mother is perceived as more nurturant than the father [24, 38, 39, 40]. A comparison of boys' and girls' perceptions of their parents revealed girls as not only viewing the father as more punitive than the boys did but also as seeing him as more nurturant than the boys did [40]. (These children were between four and eight, but there were no age differences.) The greater ambivalence toward the father on the girls' part is explained as due to their acceptance of the two aspects of the fathers' role, whereas the boys, in the process of identifying with the father, tend to repress parts of both. The children's answers to their questions probably reflected not only the child's perceptions of his parents derived from the experience of living in the family but also from the cultural stereotype of men as competent, aggressive and powerful and women as loving, weak and subordinate. The child thus has his experience in the home tempered by communications from sources other than his family.

Liking for Parents

If children distinguish between the power of their parents, they tend to see the father as more powerful. They report that punishment, particularly physical punishment, is more often given by the father. They see their mothers as nurturant, helpful and lenient. It is not surprising that children more often like their mothers better than their fathers. Direct questioning of children as to preference for one parent or the other may yield only stereotyped results which are socially approved. Culturally approved answers may also show up as a result of indirect questioning, but there is more likelihood of the child's true feelings showing up in this kind of inquiry.

Attitudes toward parents have been examined by asking children to complete a series of sentences [26]. The responses were scored as being favorable, unfavorable or neutral. For example, "My mother . . . is a teacher" was scored neutral, whereas "My father . . . is the best father in the world" was scored positive. Children's attitudes toward both parents were more favorable than unfavorable, with the mother receiving more favorable responses than the father. Neutral responses increased sharply from grade three to grade four. Unfavorable responses constituted less than 10 percent of responses at all ages. Figure 13–1 shows the proportions of favorable, neutral and unfavorable responses of boys and girls toward parents during middle childhood. While the increasing number of neutral responses shows growing objectivity of the older children, the change could also be explained as occurring because the older children are more unwilling to express their feelings even in such an indirect measure of feelings.

Identification with Parents

Identification is the process by which one person tries to become like another person in one or more ways. Identification with the parent of the same sex is, according to psychoanalytic theory, an important factor in the personality development of children from 6 to 12. Social psychologists have also been interested in the process of identification with parents. It probably rarely if ever happens that a child identifies only with one parent to the exclusion of

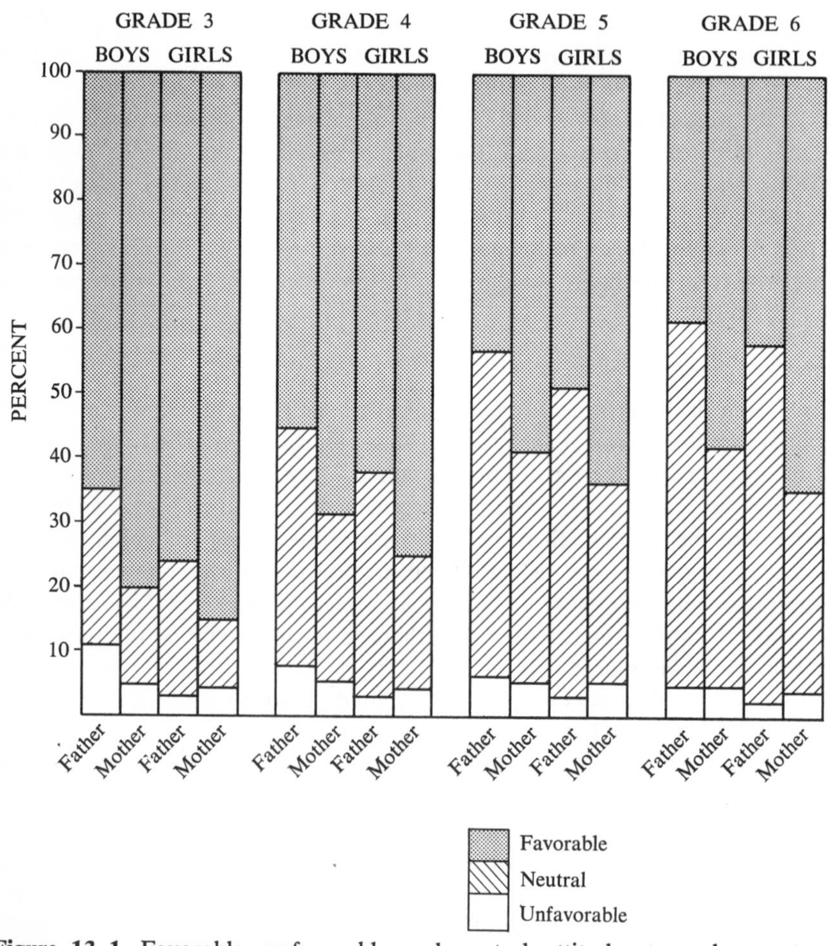

Figure 13–1. Favorable, unfavorable and neutral attitudes toward parents, by age and sex. (Adapted from D. B. Harris and S. C. Tseng, "Children's Attitudes Toward Peers and Parents as Revealed by Sentence Completions," *Child Development,* **28,** Figures 5 and 6. Copyright © 1957, The Society for Research in Child Development, Inc. Used by permission.)

the other, nor is it likely to be true that identification goes on only during a limited period of time.

How does a child select certain characteristics with which to identify, and not other characteristics? An interplay of many factors, at least some of which will not be conscious, will be involved in making such choices. Some research has been done on the influence of sex of child and sex of parent on the child's patterning of identification. The different roles played by mother and father call for different behaviors and learnings in children. One way of systematizing the resulting relationships is by the concepts of *expressive* and *instrumental* roles [58]. Playing an expressive role in a group means being sensitive to the feelings, thoughts and needs of the other people, aware of their relationships with each other, devoted to promoting their happiness and well-being, understanding them, pleasing them and enjoying them. Within the family the person having the main responsibility for the care and emotional support of the children is therefore playing the main expressive role. To play an instrumental role is to be responsible for solving the problems facing the group and to assume authority for making decisions. The person playing the instrumental role is the final court of appeals, the punisher, the family member with the primary responsibility for the discipline and training of children. The person in the instrumental role settles disputes between members, deciding on the basis of issues involved; the person in the expressive role smooths them over, comforting and consoling the members concerned.

Parental identification of boys and girls can be explained in terms of the instrumental and expressive roles played by parents [37]. A mother plays a family role which is largely expressive, while a father plays both roles, instrumental and expressive, with emphasis on the instrumental role. One piece of evidence for the expressive nature of mothers' roles is that they were more accurate than fathers in perceiving anxiety in their daughters [25]. (Parents were equally perceptive in estimating anxiety levels of sons.) It is not hard to think of exceptions to the expressive-instrumental dichotomy, such as those which occur in one-parent families and in families where mothers earn income and play important community roles. However, let us see what happens when the mother is the expressive leader in the family and the father the instrumental.

During infancy and the early preschool years, both boys and girls are more closely attached to their mothers than to their fathers. Thus both sexes first relate to a person playing a largely expressive role. In this relationship boys and girls are exposed to love-oriented discipline and take their basic steps toward internalizing conscience. In this relationship, boys and girls learn to be expressive. The next step toward maturity for both boys and girls is to become attached to the father, outgrowing some of the infantile dependence upon the mother. The father represents the reality of the outside world to his children. The father tends to react expressively with his daughters, enjoying, praising and appreciating them as feminine creatures, while with sons he is more demanding, exerting pressure and discipline, insisting upon successful interaction with the world. The salience of the father in the family has been shown to have a vital effect on the boys' assumption of his sex role [53]. The more the son interacts with a powerful father, a man who does both punishing and rewarding, the more masculine the boy will be. Girls' sex role learning has been found to be enhanced by fathers who encouraged their daughters to take part in feminine activities and by mothers who were warm and self-confident and with whom the daughters had satisfying relationships [54].

While mothers make little difference in the demands they place on boys and girls, they tend to go along with the fathers in expecting more aggression from boys. Thus according to this theory, it is the father more than the mother who teaches boys and girls to play their sex-appropriate roles. The mother supplements his teaching, especially in defining him to the children as a worthy person, and also in choosing the children's clothing, assigning their jobs and telling them "boys do this and girls do that." It tends to be the father, however, who has the stronger feelings and reactions about sex-inappropriate activities, especially boys engaging in feminine ones. While mothers sometimes consider it all right for boys to knit or play with dolls, fathers are usually disturbed by such activities. The mother, realizing the father's feelings, sees that the boys do behave appropriately.

It would be hard to find a family in real life where the roles were played with the clarity implied in the theory. Women do play instrumental roles. They do some disciplining of children. They make some decisions in the family. They take jobs and earn money. A woman often takes an active part in defining her family's status in the community. Some women operate on the level of groups higher and larger than their own communities. There are women executives, politicians and club women holding high offices. Men vary in the ways in which they combine expressive and instrumental roles. Even so, this description of roles points up essential differences between mothers and fathers and the ways in which they act with boys and girls. This theory is consistent with the results of studies of children's perceptions of parents summarized earlier. Children see the father as having more power, as doing more punishing, as being more distant, while the mother is seen as being warmer, better liked and more nurturant.

Discipline

When parents are brought together in child-study groups by nursery schools or P.T.A.'s, a topic almost always chosen for discussion and learning is that of discipline. Parents report that discipline is the most difficult aspect of child-rearing and that it is the largest source of their feeling ineffective as parents [30]. Most parents equate discipline and punishment. When asked to think it over, however, most will agree that discipline can be a scheme for regulating children's behavior, teaching them self-control through reward *and* punishment, and helping them to internalize moral standards. When parents ask for discussions of discipline, they usually are asking for ways of getting their children to behave acceptably without the necessity of frequent and drastic punishment. They tend to see their own behavior or attitudes as the cause of the necessity for discipline, although a sizable number evidently consider that it is inescapable, due to the nature of children, that parents must mete out some punishment [30].

When parents of children in the elementary grades in a Southern city were asked to tell what method of punishment they usually used with their children, corporal punishment headed the list, with 46 percent of the mothers and fathers reporting this as their usual method. About a fifth of the parents reported withdrawal of privileges and another fifth confinement as their usual punishment, while about a tenth said they usually gave verbal punishment [30]. (These ratios agree quite closely with those reported in the studies concerning children's perceptions of parents, reported earlier.)

When the parents were asked to tell what their children did to incur punishment, half of the respondents gave disobedience as the misdeed. Between 10 and 20 percent of the parents said that their children had been aggressive or insolent or careless prior to the punishment, while 3 percent said the child had been untruthful and 2 percent reported unkindness or unfairness.

These figures on parental practices regarding discipline can be taken as fairly representative of parents in the United States. They were gathered as a pretest for a study of the effectiveness of changing parental attitudes through group discussion. After the series of discussions the parents who had attended them were interviewed again and asked the same questions. Fewer parents used corporal punishment (37 percent), while more used withdrawal of privileges and confinement. The same number used verbal punishment. Significant increases occurred in the parents' confidence in themselves as parents, acceptance of the child's behavior as opposed to inherited factors and rigid causal determinism. Therefore, parents can learn and improve in their child guidance, through a process of parent education.

An earlier study of discipline came out of an investigation of about 400 "well-adjusted" children [45]. Well-adjusted children were defined as those who, according to teachers and school principals, were getting along well with their peers, were working up to their capacity and had control over their emotions. The children were between 5 and 20 years of age. Their parents were interviewed to find out what, in the child's home life, had caused his good adjustment. Every parent in the study mentioned discipline, although the group showed a wide variety of ways of behaving with children and ways of interpreting children's behavior. It is quite evident that most of the parents saw discipline as including more than punishment, and punishment as including more than corporal punishment.

Love came first in importance, with a quotation from one father summing up the general belief: "But most important of all is loving them and letting them know it, thinking of them as people and treating them so, appreciating what they do and trusting them and telling them so, and above all letting them know they are wanted" [45, p. 221]. This statement suggests that the enjoyment-companionship aspect and the nurturing aspect of love are both essential. There was general consensus among the parents on all of these statements about discipline.

There are so many things to learn—for all of us. Children and parents grow and change, making constant learning and readjustment necessary. Standards change. Children grow in self-direction.

The question of punishment always comes up. They tried to punish without threatening loss of love and to give punishments appropriate to the deed and age. Punishment can often be avoided by explanation, discussion and good planning.

What we do in discipline depends on how we feel about many things. Obedience, trust and confidence are necessary.

It takes understanding and compromise. Fun and friends, understanding of feelings promote cooperation and give-and-take.

Children need bringing up—they can't just grow. Children are the parents' responsibility. Parents must tell them right and wrong, set limits, face them with responsibility and hold up goals for them.

You have to keep busy at it but it does not have to be a big problem. Being busy and active is good for both parents and children. These parents took an interest in their children's affairs and backed them up. Pets are worthwhile.

It must all be built on a happy, wholesome home life. Parents agree and work together. Children feel that they belong and are needed. Families do things together, often including grandparents and other relatives.

The parents' views of punishment as a part of discipline are interesting. They used the word with a variety of meanings—as only something physical, as any penalty imposed on the wrongdoer, whether dispensed by a person or the natural consequence of doing something wrong, or as all of these plus the awareness that follows a misdeed. Most of the parents agreed that they had to impose punishment on their children, but they also agreed that "one has to give thought to what punishment is best" [45, p. 66]. Many were quite clear that they had not used physical punishment, but had used deprivation of privileges or curtailment of freedom. An important element in the punishment used, of whatever kind, was the way in which it was given and the way in which it was received. Many parents told of gradual shifts in punishment as their children grew up, leading to the complete elimination of parent-imposed punishment, even talking and reasoning, which may have a punishing tone. One mother gave an explanation for eliminating punishment by saying, "Learning what to do is the only reason for punishing anyway" [45, p. 71]. The parents agreed that punishment can often be prevented and gave many examples of ways in which parents, by being aware of the trend of events, can forestall the development of situations in which the child will be prone to do wrong, especially fatigue and anger. But whether or not punishment was a part of the home life of these well-adjusted children, it is quite clear that discipline was, in the sense of conscious effort on the part of the parents, meant to help the children to learn to behave in acceptable ways.

A review of parental practices and their pertinence to child behavior comes to a conclusion which is consistent with the general findings of the study on well-adjusted children [33]. Despite the diversity of methods and findings, there is a common core of agreement in the results. The type of discipline which tries to use the child's internal forces to induce his compliance seems to foster understanding and adoption of appropriate behavior. By *using the child's internal forces* is meant appealing to his need for affection, his self-esteem and his concern for others. Psychological, or love-oriented, discipline uses the child's affectionate relationship with his parents. Here, then, is corroboration of the importance which the well-adjusted children's parents placed on love—"but most important of all is loving them and letting them know it." The review also concludes that the use of physical coercion and other forms of direct power assertion of parent over child promotes a moral orientation based on fear of external detection and punishment [32].

Stimulation of Cognitive Development and Need for Achievement

Families promote intellectual growth in two main ways; by stimulating the child's desire for achievement and by offering experiences through which the child can grow mentally. The desire for achievement is highlighted during these years, as being an essential in the development of the sense of industry. Normal personality development centers around becoming competent in the basic skills of the culture. Since the academic skills are a vital part of those basic skills, the encouragement of intellectual development is also the encouragement of personality development.

When a parent, especially a father, has a strong desire for intellectual competence for himself, he is likely to stimulate such achievement in his children [42]. The higher value the father placed on intellectual achievement, the more likely he was to share intellectual activities with his children, to encourage children to engage in such pursuits and to show great interest in the children's achievements. The mothers behaved similarly, except that they were more likely to show such reactions with daughters than with sons.

The aspirations which parents hold for their children apparently affect the ways in which parents interact with children, often producing the desired effects. Boys with high-achievement needs tend to have mothers who expected them to be self-reliant at an early age, who gave them freedom to learn and who rewarded their independent efforts [74]. When observed working together at home, boys with high-achievement aspirations were found to have parents who held high standards for them and who gave them autonomy in working out problems. The mothers of these boys treated them warmly, freely giving both approval and criticism. The fathers showed considerable interest in and involvement with their sons [66].

Rising IQ's were found to be associated with certain personality characteristics in children and with certain kinds of parental behavior which most likely had been instrumental in producing the personality characteristics [69]. As might be expected from other studies already mentioned, the children whose

IQ's rose were, on the whole, independent children who ventured forth curiously, explored freely, competed and showed high need for achievement. The mothers of these children took considerable interest in their children's achievements and encouraged them to master the environment [41].

AN ANALYSIS OF A FAMILY TEACHING SITUATION. How does a family teach its children what to expect of themselves, how to behave, how to think and feel? In many ways and places, of course. One of the most educational interaction situations in middle-class families is the family dinner table. An observer [8] of family behavior has described the learning which goes on during family table talk. A summary of his account goes thus:

The family dinner is a regular and frequent occurrence of family interaction under circumstances favorable to communication. Each person's role is clearly defined through many devices—where he sits, what and when he is served, what duties and rituals he performs and how others listen to him. The family is an audience for each member. An individual can try out ideas and performances on this audience and mold his future behavior accordingly. It is easier to take and to give criticism in the protected family setting than in most outside situations. Therefore a person is likely to learn more quickly at the family table than in many social situations away from home.

Through the free verbal activity, children (and sometimes parents) learn new words, thus increasing their language and cognitive powers. They give and take new concepts and ideas, sparking curiosity and increasing knowledge. With some competition for the role of speaker, verbal facility and quickness of expression are encouraged. Warmed by the satisfactions of eating, and the intimate setting, family members are likely to be at their most tolerant and democratic, permitting maximum freedom of speech.

Interests are developed or quashed at the family table. Jim's baseball talk may find a kindred spirit in father and produce an animated discussion, or it may be received with polite boredom. A lucky bird-watching enthusiast will elicit reports of others' avian observations combined with interest in how his year's list and life list are growing.

Table talk transmits culture, connecting and extending to each family member some of the broader contacts of each individual. The children tell news from school, father from the business and political world, and mother from the standpoint of her job or other interests. Some events and comments strike interest in others and a discussion ensues on the church supper, the new tax law, Friday's movie, the changing length of skirts or the price of school lunches. Children learn how to feel about minority religions and whether to be Democrats, Republicans or Communists. They learn not only that they should be honest, truthful and sexually controlled, but the behavior is spelled out in detail, through discussion and criticism of specific events.

This kind of parental teaching, the reasonable, rational conversation at the dinner table, is a middle-class custom. It is important to note that studies of slum children indicate that dinnertime is rarely used for talking over what has happened to family members as persons. Rather, when parents and children are together at dinner, the time tends to be used for giving punishments and assigning chores. They talk about the most immediate concerns, not about the past and future. Discussions of concepts, causal relationships and logical consequences are almost entirely lacking [70]. Dinnertime conversation is a specific area where cultural deprivation takes place, with many middle-class children having opportunities to grow in thoughtful self-direction while many, perhaps most, slum children deal with little beyond the pressures of the moment.

RELATIONSHIPS WITH PEERS

Friends of the same age are important to children in the United States, not as important as they are to Russians [12] and Israelis [49], but more important than they are to Hawaiian Chinese [35]. The peer group is a socializing agent to the degree that a culture stresses the importance of the age group rather than the family. In the United States, as in most places, the peer group plays a bigger and bigger role in the child's life as he grows older and more independent of his family. The elementary-school child wants very much to be one of the gang. To be isolated or rejected is devastating. The companionship and affection offered by peers are very satisfying and growth-promoting. Rebelling against adults, especially in the later years of this period, say from 9 to 11, the youngster feels a bulwark in his gang. The gang's parents and teachers do the same awful things to them that his do to him. Similar questions and fears plague them. As one of a group, the individual child gains courage to stand up to the threats of other children, too. Speaking a common language [57], they explore many questions together. They explore the physical world too, as well as the universe of ideas. Often parents will give permission for children to go on hikes or expeditions together which they would not permit a child to undertake alone. Children give each other ideas as to what to do next.

In the early elementary grades the cultural patterns represented by the other children in his classroom may closely resemble that of the child's family if he goes to a neighborhood school which draws on a homogeneous population. But whether or not he is exposed to new ideas of accepted ways of behavior, he is brought in contact with larger numbers of people his own age than he has known before, all of them more or less confined within the limited area of a classroom. These are his peers, with some of whom, if his family does not move from the community, he will progress from grade to grade in the school system and graduate from high school 12 years hence. With some of them he will go to Sunday school and Scout troop meetings. One of them may be his (or her) first date and even, though this is less likely, his (or her) marriage partner.

The social skills which a child has at the beginning of his school life, and his rejection, suspicion, cooperation, acceptance and outgoingness with his peers are based on his previous experience, which is largely within the family or very strongly influenced by his family. As new experiences happen to him and as he continues to grow and develop, his social skills and attitudes will change, sometimes slowly, sometimes rapidly, sometimes not at all.

Learning of Values, Behavior and Attitudes

Children expose one another to a variety of sets of values which stem from memberships such as those of family, class and ethnic origin. The values of a peer group are especially compelling, since a youngster has to accept them in order to be accepted as a member. If the peer values are not too different from those of his family and teachers, a mild conflict between them only serves to differentiate him from adults and to give him a feeling of belonging to the gang. He will suffer if values differ greatly, as when his peers idealize the member who pilfers successfully, while his family requires honesty. Peers reinforce many values which adults approve sincerely but less enthusiastically. Physical bravery in boys is an example. Most parents make some effort to discourage crying and fussing over hurts and dangers, but the group may insist upon bravery, with expulsion the penalty for being a "sissy."

The peer group teachers its members how to act and how to think. Skills are learned through imitation and practice, coordinations, games, the arts, humor, language. Some of the behavior is childhood ritual, which is passed from one generation of schoolchildren to the next and almost forgotten by adults [57]. It includes the chants used with jumping rope and bouncing balls:

One, two, three O'Leary
I spy Miss McGary
Sitting on a huckleberry
Reading a dictionary.

Down in the valley where the green grass grows
There sat Helen as sweet as a rose
She sang and she sang and she sang so sweet
Along came her fellow and kissed her on the cheek.

It includes wishing on white horses and "stamping" the first robins of spring (not literally, just touching one thumb to the tongue and pushing it into the other — open — palm).

The group may require certain modes of speech, a secret language such as Pig Latin or simply modified English, tending toward toughness and crudity through dropping G's and mixing up rules about plurals and tenses. Most boys and girls learn vulgar words for sex and elimination processes. It is very exciting and status-defining to use the four-letter words and some swear words, too.

Matters of taste and fashion come strongly under peer influence. It becomes essential to wear woolen knee socks, white ankle socks or nylon stockings according to what the other girls are wearing, regardless of the weather or of what Mother thinks. One winter everybody slides down the hill on sleds, but the following winter the only vehicle worth sliding on is a tray. The next year, trays are out, but one must buy a gadget which manufacturers have thoughtfully designed to be almost like trays. The group even has strong opinions as to the best kind of candy and gum, opinions which change rapidly.

CONFORMITY. The extent and nature of children's conformity to group pressure has been investigated in classroom situations, using children from 7 to 13 [6]. The subjects were asked to estimate the lengths of line, compare lines and match lines. Unknown to the subject, eight of his brightest classmates had been instructed to give wrong answers on certain of the questions before he had a chance to answer them. After the subject responded, he was questioned about why he answered as he did. The results showed younger children following the wrong group responses more than older children. There was no difference in the following of average and bright children. The more ambiguous the material, the more likely were children to follow the wrong responses of their peers. The experience of group pressure to give a wrong answer was a difficult one, whether the child gave in to the pressure or not. Subjects made comments such as "I felt like my heartbeat went down," and "I wanted to be like the rest, but then I thought it was correct to say the right answer. It would have been easier to give the same but then it didn't look right."

Another investigation of peer influence on judgment analyzed some of the factors determining whether a child shifts his judgments in the direction of those of peers [29]. The subjects were 405 children in grades 3, 6, 9 and 11. After choosing which of two pictures he liked, the child heard a story about which pictures were liked by a high-status, popular child and which by a low-status, unpopular child. The subject again chose which he liked better. The results showed: older children tended more than younger ones to shift toward the preferences of high-status children; girls shifted preferences more than boys; low-status children shifted more than high-status children.

SELF-CONCEPT. A child's self-concept of himself is built partly through seeing himself as others see him. As a person who belongs to a peer group, liked and accepted by them, he feels himself to be a worthy person. (And, if he is not accepted, he feels unworthy.) If his friends laugh at his jokes and call him amusing, he sees himself as a wit. If they call her "Fatso," she believes that she is *too* fat.

Measuring himself against the standards of peers is another way in which a person's self-concept is built. Age-level segregation plus great emphasis on competition make American childhood a very competitive time. Even though peers cooperate in their play, they owe each other nothing in the sense that family members have obligations to each other. Group loyalty is comparatively ephemeral, depending on continuing to meet competitive standards of behavior. The feeling which a youngster gets from successful competition with his age mates is *adequacy*. Since these years are most critical for development of a sense of adequacy, this aspect of peer influence is a vital one.

Position in the Group, Acceptance and Rejection

Children vary in how much they are liked by other children and in how many other children like them. Sociometry is a way of finding out where each child in a group stands in relation to the other children in it, who likes him, who does not like him and who is indifferent or mild in attitudes toward him. When these data are collected for each child, a picture of relationships within the group can be drawn. By means of sociometry, group relations can be measured and described [52]. Each child is asked to name one or more group members with whom he would like to engage in one or more activities (to sit beside, to go to the movies with, to work with, and so on). The choices are then represented by symbols on a diagram, using conventions for indicating various choices. Figure 13–2 is an example of a sociogram which shows the friendships of a group of 11 girls. Two subgroups can be seen. Five of the six girls at the top of the diagram chose each other mutually. Dotty was chosen by two of this group (Beryl and Inez), but she chose only Inez, giving her two other choices to two girls in the other subgroup. Jewell was chosen by none of the other 10, while she gave her first choice to a boy, something which only Ruth, of all the others, did, although Joy gave a third choice to a boy.

Other procedures have been developed measuring the interrelationships within groups. For instance, every child is asked to make a choice between every possible pair of the others in his group [44]. If the group consists of more than a very few individuals, the paired comparison method involves so many pairs that motivation of the children to finish becomes a matter of some importance. An easier procedure asks each child to rate his acceptance–rejection of every other child on a series of rating scales [71]. The ease with which it is done may actually be deceptive as to the results which are obtained. For instance, the activity for which the child is asked to choose a companion influences his choice, as shown when the children were asked to choose a companion of the same sex, of the opposite sex, or no companion at all for each of three different situations—eating, taking a walk and going to a movie [9]. The percentage choosing a companion of the opposite sex differed in the three activities. If only one of the activities had been specified, a different picture would have emerged. Incidentally, inviting someone for a meal at home or to a party may have very different meanings for children from different backgrounds. For some children it may be a realistic possibility, for others an experience they have never had. A brief guide for doing sociometric testing in schools, as well as in other kinds of groups, is available [56].

The characteristics of children who are accepted or rejected have been assessed by many investigators, using a variety of measuring devices. Friendliness and sociability are, not surprisingly, associated with acceptance, whereas rejection or nonacceptance are associated with hostility, withdrawal and similar negative social attitudes. Greater intelligence and creativity, if they are not too far above the level of the group are typical of popular children.

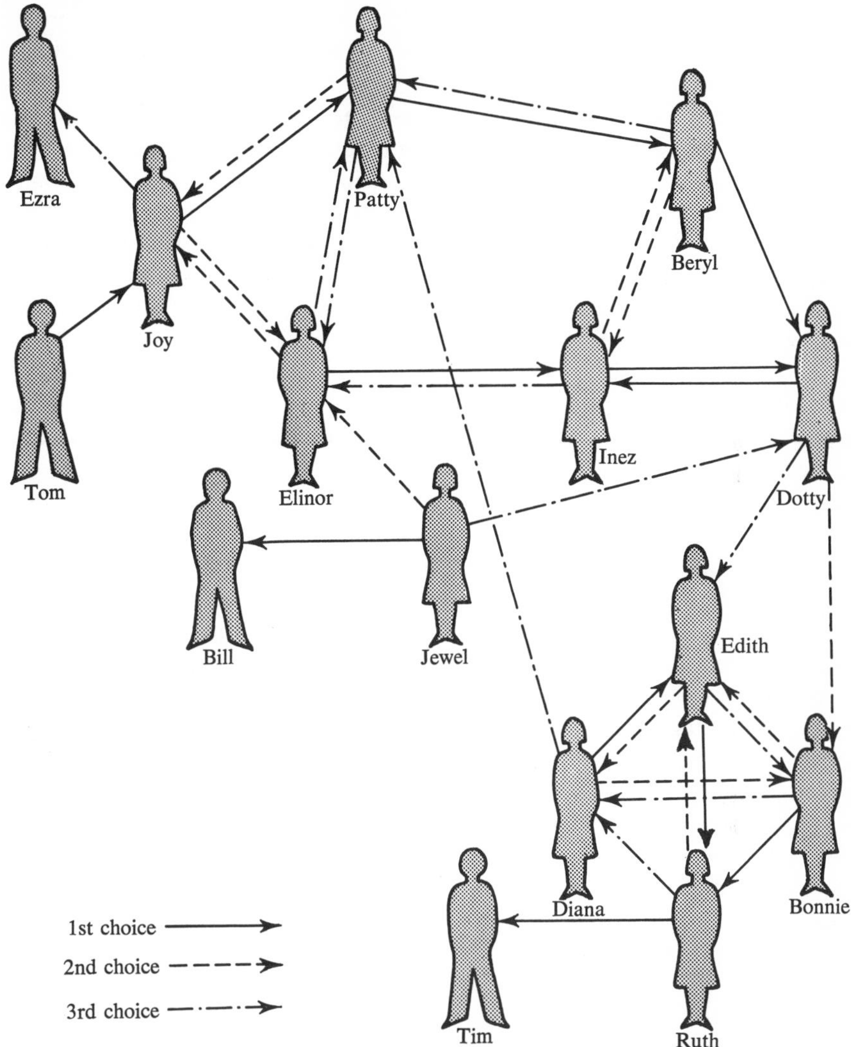

Figure 13–2. A sociogram showing friendship choices of eleven girls in fourth and fifth grade. (Reprinted by permission from Ruth Cunningham, *Understanding Group Behavior.* New York: Bureau of Publications, Teachers College, Columbia University, 1951. Figure 16, p. 168.)

Boys are accepted by other boys if they have athletic ability, muscular strength and above-average size. Socioeconomic class also makes a difference, since children tend to choose friends of their own class or a higher one [15]. Older preadolescents fluctuate less than younger ones over a two-week period in their choices of friends [34]. This age trend continues on into adolescence, and is evident from the experience of adults, most of whom recognize that their friendships change slowly over a period of years.

PERSONAL CHARACTERISTICS AS SEEN BY OTHER CHILDREN. An approach to the topic of peer acceptance started with the question "How do children perceive one another?" [77] The subjects were 267 white and Negro children, 8 to 13, living in a summer camp. Strangers to each other at the beginning, they lived in groups of eight for two weeks. Each child was asked to choose a child whom he knew most about and to tell all about him. Adults made systematic behavior observations of the camp life. In telling about each other, children showed two strong tendencies: they made broad positive or negative judgments; the judgments were mainly in terms of actions that had direct interpersonal consequences. Individuals showed consistency in the ways in which they described others, whether they described the same child twice or a different child. Within this consistency, there were changes over the two-week period in increasing emphasis on interaction between persons and in giving more organized descriptions. There were some sex differences. Girls emphasized nurturing behavior, boys nonconforming and withdrawn behavior. Older children evidenced a slight tendency to give more complex reports. When children were divided into categories according to the adults' observations, these results were found: active and friendly children gave more complex descriptions of peers than did withdrawn or hostile children; active children were more explicit than withdrawn; friendly children made more inferential statements than hostile children; there was a consistent but nonsignificant tendency for friendly children to describe others in a more organized fashion than hostile children. These results suggest that those who take an active part in social relationships perceive other people more sharply than do those who are less active.

Socioempathic ability, the ability to perceive one's own status in a group and the statuses of others tends to increase with age [3]. Children from grade three through grade 12 were asked to rate all of their classmates as to acceptability as friends, and to predict how each of the classmates would rate them and be rated by the group. True sociometric status was calculated for each child from the first rating. Accuracy of perception of sociometric status was calculated by correlating the mean predicted statuses with the sociometric statuses. Figure 13–3 shows the correlational scores for accuracy of perception (socioempathic ability) at each age between 8 and 17.

PERSONAL CHARACTERISTICS AS REFLECTED BY TESTS. The behavior characteristics valued by low- and high-socioeconomic groups of 12-year-olds were studied by using a Guess-Who test [59]. Results showed definite socioeconomic and sex differences in the prestige value of various clusters of behavior patterns. Fighting ability was important to all boys in determining leadership position, but more important to low-socioeconomic boys. Restlessness was less acceptable to High Boys than to Low. An eminent fighter among Low Boys was likely to be also a ladies' man, but among High Boys, the friendly, conforming, "little gentleman" had success with the girls. Among High Boys, the classroom intellectual was not a leader but was not rejected. Such a person among Low Boys would be considered too effeminate and yielding to deserve

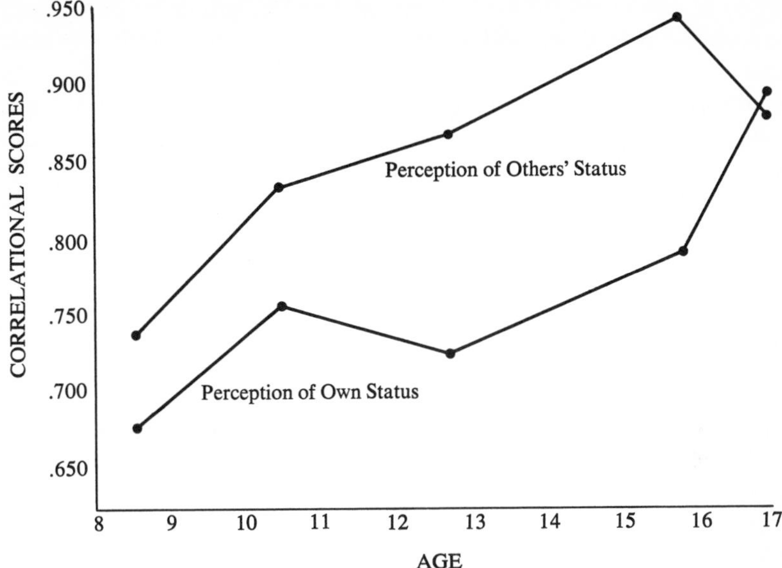

Figure 13–3. Age changes in the ability to judge one's own sociometric status and to judge the status of another person. (Reprinted by permission from D. P. Ausubel, H. M. Schiff, and E. B. Gasser, "A Preliminary Study of Developmental Trends in Socioempathy: Accuracy of Perception of Own and Others' Sociometric Status," *Child Development,* **23,** Figure 1. Copyright © 1952, The Society for Research in Child Development, Inc.)

any recognition. Low Girls were more sharply differentiated as to aggressiveness than were High Girls. Among Low Girls, the fighting tomboy was the one who went out with boys, while among High Girls, the "little lady" was more interested in and successful with boys. The tomboy was unpopular with High Girls, but had considerable prestige with Low Girls. High Boys and Girls value some conformity to adult standards in the classroom and at parties, while low groups did not.

Personalities of very popular, average and unpopular children were studied with the Rorschach test among other tests [55]. The very popular children showed great sensitivity to the social situation, conventional interpretations of social situations, little originality, strong need for affection and a conscious striving for approval. The least popular children showed less emotional control, appeared to be more self-centered, moody and impulsive and were often unable to react to a situation even though they desired to participate.

Although popular children differed from one another in many ways, all of them had two characteristics in common: they put forth a great deal of energy and they used their energy for purposes approved by the group. The popular child was likely to be a conformist. He was likely to be conventional rather than creative. He tended to be sympathetic to the needs and wants of others. Some unpopular children were simply unliked, and others actively disliked.

They had in common a lack of energy directed to group purposes, but the disliked child used his abounding energy in ways which conflicted with the interests of other children.

Children at both extremes of popularity showed more emotional disturbance than did the average children. Great striving for popularity may be due to feeling a lack of love. The very popular child may pay a severe price in energy expenditure and anxiety. Some children were, of course, both popular and well-adjusted.

Boy–Girl Relationships

Boys and girls are friendlier toward one another than they used to be. When such relationships were first studied systematically, in the 1930's boys and girls showed strong antipathy toward the opposite sex during the latter half of the elementary-school years [14, 23]. Children excluded one another from activities which were strongly labeled as sex-inappropriate. Not only did they shun the activities of the opposite sex but they also avoided physical contact with peers of the opposite sex [14]. Adults considered the aversion of the sexes to each other as necessary for personality development during childhood. In the process of solidifying their understanding and acceptance of membership in their own sex, children were helped by participating in like-sex group activities [46]. Teachers and parents of elementary-school children expected and planned for cleavage between the sexes until after puberty.

Twenty to 30 years later, parents and teachers became concerned because boys and girls were attracted to each other at younger and younger ages. At the same time, the median age for marriage was declining. The 1950 census showed it to be below 20 years for women, for the first time. The average age for menarche (first menstruation) was also declining steadily. Presumably, boys too were reaching sexual maturity earlier. Three conditions, earlier boy–girl attraction, earlier marriage and earlier sexual maturity, may be related. Possibly the earlier sexual maturity is the independent factor which causes the other two conditions.

A United States Office of Education report documented teachers' observations [47]. Boys and girls were getting along better with each other in school, showing less antagonism and a greater spirit of friendliness. Some teachers reported children in fourth, fifth and sixth grades asking for activities together and showing little tendency to separate into like-sex groups. Boys were cleaner and better groomed, girls more adorned with lipstick and nail polish than children of former years. Some fifth graders dated and wore "steady" rings. The results of this study were corroborated by a report on middle-class fifth-to-seventh-graders, ages 9 to 14, in a Southern urban community [9]. Cross-sex best friend choices ranged between 15 and 20 percent in the three grades, a strong contrast to the situation in the 1930's, when no cross-sex friendships were reported in these grades. When the children were asked to list three other good friends in addition to the "best friend," between a third and a half chose at least one cross-sex friend. Eight out of 10 boys and 9 out of 10 girls admitted to having a sweetheart, a relationship observed only very rarely by the authors of the earlier studies.

Positive, negative and neutral attitudes of boys and girls toward one another were measured by means of a sentence-completion test, similar to the one mentioned earlier, in which attitudes toward parents were measured [26]. As can be seen from Figure 13–4, boys give more favorable responses to boys than to girls at all age levels, showing little change in types of responses throughout the elementary-school years. The girls show quite a different pattern. More differentially positive toward their own sex than boys are, they change their minds more than boys do. Favorable attitudes toward girls decrease rather steadily; favorable attitudes toward boys decrease from grade three to grade six and then increase to grade nine. Unfavorable attitudes also show more changes in girls than in boys. Boys' negative responses increase between third and fourth grade, with little change during the remaining years of elementary school. Girls' negative responses rise steadily from third to sixth grade and then decrease to ninth grade.

Sex-Role Differentiation

Boys make progress toward thinking, feeling and acting like men, girls like women. There are great variations in how these processes occur, however, and variations in the end results. In the section on parent–child relations, the influence of each of the parents on sex-role learning was discussed. Children also teach each other sex-appropriate attitudes and behavior. The sex-role preferences established between 6 and 10 years of age tend to be fairly stable into adulthood [41].

American girls are allowed greater latitude in sex-appropriate behavior than are boys. Girls incur little or no censure for being tomboys, whereas a boy is severely frowned upon for being effeminate. These statements are borne out by test findings which showed that second, third and fourth grade girls made many choices of masculine activities, whereas boys showed a strong preference for masculine activities [13]. Girls show a wider range of play preferences than boys, girls taking in many masculine activities along with feminine ones, boys sticking largely to masculine games [67]. Certain playthings are established as appropriate for boys at an earlier age than are corresponding appropriate toys designated for girls [27]. Not only are boys' play roles defined earlier [19], but they are defined more strictly [27]. It seems likely that boys learn their roles as much by avoiding feminine behavior as by acquiring masculine patterns ("Don't be a sissy!"), even when offered a choice between old, dilapidated neutral toys and new, attractive "female" playthings [28]. The same is true of the books which girls and boys choose to read. Boys tend to read boys' books only, while girls read girls' books and boys' books. It is likely that over the years the cultural definition of the girl role has expanded, whereas that of the boy's role has not. Table 13–2 shows the

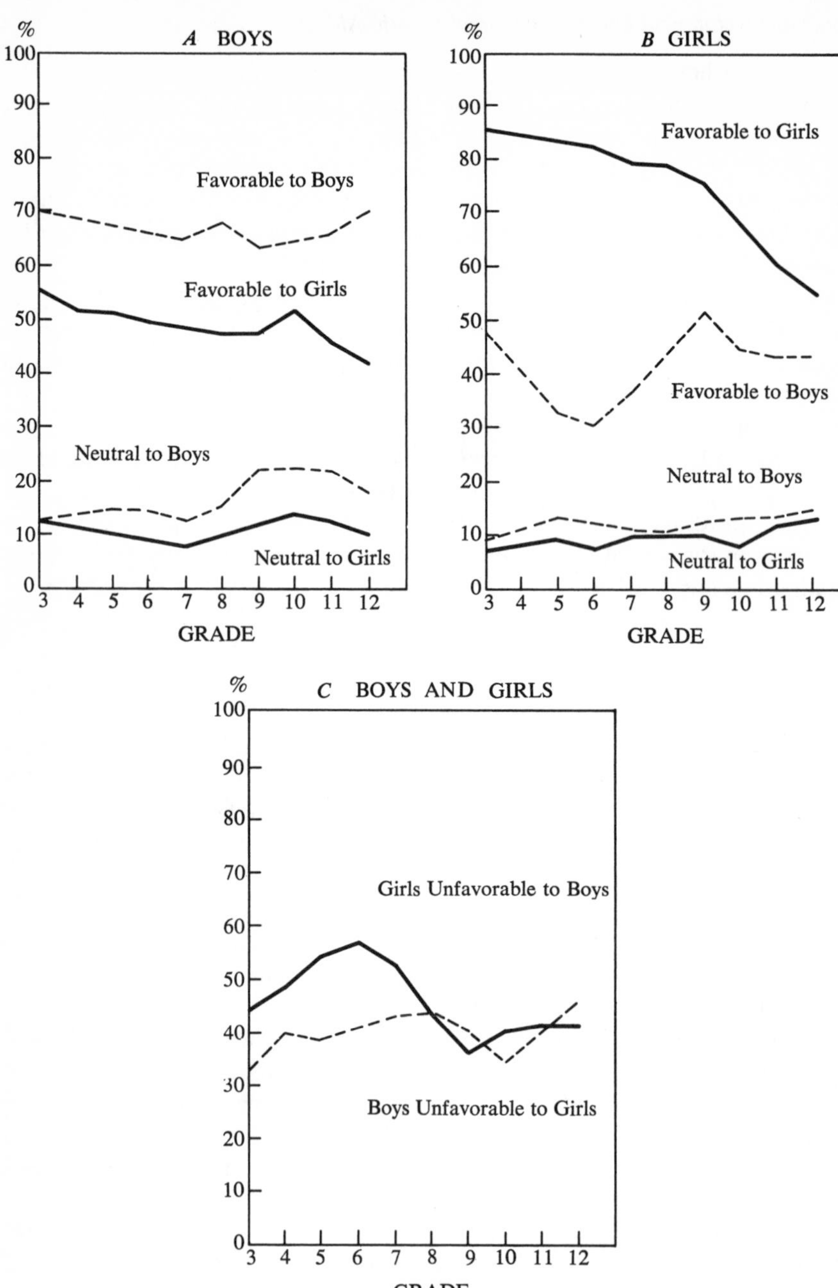

Figure 13–4. Boys' and girls' responses to incomplete sentences, indicating favorable and unfavorable attitudes toward peers. *A:* Boys' favorable and neutral attitudes. *B:* Girls' favorable and neutral attitudes. *C:* Unfavorable attitudes toward the opposite sex. (Reprinted by permission from D. B. Harris and S. C. Tseng, "Children's Attitudes Toward Peers and Parents as Revealed by Sentence Completions," *Child Development,* **28,** Figures 1, 2, and 4b. Copyright © 1957, The Society for Research in Child Development, Inc.

TABLE 13–2

Percentages of boys and girls seeing various activities as being either masculine or feminine.

Item	Description of Activity	Percentage of Attribution: Female Sample	Percentage of Attribution: Male Sample
	A. Implemented mostly by girls		
53	plays with doll carriage	100.0*	100.0*
40	plays with toy sewing machine	98.9*	97.5*
43	plays with toy dishes	96.7*	100.0*
46	plays with toy carpet sweeper	95.6*	92.5*
47	plays with toy pocketbook	94.4*	97.5*
49	plays with toy electric mixer	91.0*	87.5*
29	helps mother hang clothes	90.0*	82.5*
37	plays with little girl	88.8*	90.0*
14	cares for baby when parents away	87.8*	85.0*
35	dusts table	86.7*	72.5†
56	plays with jump rope	81.1*	90.0*
33	dries dishes	78.9*	68.4‡
23	washes dishes	77.8*	80.0*
25	clears table	73.3*	72.5†
16	takes dancing lessons	65.6†	70.0‡
51	plays with jacks	64.4†	72.5†
	B. Implemented mostly by boys		
38	plays with toy air-rifle	94.4*	95.0*
32	hitches ride on back of truck	91.1*	82.5*
52	plays with toy trucks	91.1*	90.0*
55	plays with fort and soldiers	90.0*	97.4*
21	helps man fix ceiling	86.5*	92.5*
45	plays with ball and bat	81.1*	92.3*
13	carries wood into house	80.0*	90.0*
27	climbs trees	80.0*	90.0*
54	plays with toy tool bench	80.0*	92.5*
24	plays with little boy	79.5*	77.5*
50	plays with drums	78.9*	77.5*
57	plays with jack-knife	78.7*	95.0*
39	plays with erector set	76.7*	82.5*
15	goes with man to ballgame	76.4*	70.0‡
10	plays in messy empty lot	75.6*	72.5†
8	plays in street	74.7*	77.5*
42	plays with electric train	73.3*	85.0*
17	shovels snow off walk	66.7†	75.0†
44	plays with marbles	66.7†	72.5†
2	plays on roofs	63.3‡	70.0‡
	C. Implemented by both sexes		
5	plays at beach	84.4*	94.5*
12	plays in country fields	72.2*	72.5†
1	plays on playground	69.2*	75.0†
48	owns and takes care of puppy	65.2†	56.4‡
7	plays in park	63.7†	72.5‡

* Probability is beyond the .001 level.
† Probability lies between the .01 and the .001 levels.
‡ Probability lies between the .05 and the .01 levels.
Source: Reprinted by permission from R. E. Hartley and F. P. Hardesty, "Children's Perceptions of Sex Roles in Childhood," *Journal of Genetic Psychology*, **105**, Table 2, p. 48. Copyright © 1964, The Journal Press.

activities which were attributed to girls, boys and both sexes by children 8 and 11 years old [27]. The percentage of attribution by boys and by girls is shown with each activity listed. For instance, all boys and all girls agree that playing with a doll carriage is a female activity, while 80 percent of girls and 90 percent of boys say that climbing trees and carrying wood into the house are male activities. Concepts of the feminine role, as revealed by this study, seemed to parallel traditional adult female activities to a greater extent than did childhood concepts of the male role parallel adult male activities.

By sixth grade, sex roles begin to have a different look [36]. Girls are not so free after all. At least for the culture of one sixth grade class, there was a real difference in the way sex roles were defined, as determined by using personality and sociometric tests. Boys who were active initiators and organizers enjoyed wide acceptance by classmates, while girls with these qualities were more rejected by classmates and felt more anxious than the other girls. In generalizing about the American middle-class culture this study concludes, "Boys are expected to be somewhat aggressive, direct and analytic, while girls are taught more submissive, conforming, 'ladylike' type of behavior. The girl who identifies with this role gains acceptance and is subjectively aware of fewer discomforts. . . ." In other words, the sixth grade boys were rewarded for playing instrumental roles, and the girls were rewarded for playing expressive roles. The instrumental role requirement for boys was laid down earlier than the requirement for girls.

A study of creativity demonstrated the restriction of sex role by pressures in the classroom [72]. Boys and girls gave ideas and solutions to problems which contributed to the success of the groups for which they were working. Then they were asked to rate themselves and the others on value of contribution. The whole group ranked the boys' contributions ahead of the girls. The objective reality was that boys and girls were equal in contributions. Thus both boys and girls considered that what boys had done was better than what girls had done when both sexes actually had done the same.

Growth of Understanding Between Peers

As the child grows less egocentric, he is more able to see another person not as an object but as a person like himself, with thoughts and feelings which relate that person to him and to others. He can take the other person's point of view without losing his own. The ability to understand and appreciate the feelings and thoughts of another person in this way is called *empathy*. Because the cognitive development of the period of concrete operations makes for a great increase in empathy, the school-age child can have deeper and more intimate friendships than can the preschool child. The development of empathy was studied in children 9 to 12, using drawings showing family life situations [68]. Results showed that empathy tended to increase with age, but that there were wide individual differences within each age level. Although there were no sex differences in general, the spurts in growth of empathy came at different times for boys and girls. Empathy related to general intelligence and to cognitive awareness of the social and emotional environment. Empathy varied inversely with the size of the child's family and depended somewhat on his ordinal position.

As the child grows more adept at shifting back and forth between his own position and those of others, he can sustain conversations more adequately. When a child talks egocentrically, he expresses himself, but he does not develop a topic. Now he takes on more responsibility of trying to understand what others are communicating to him and of speaking in such a way that they will understand him. This is not to say that all talking is going to be true conversation when once a child can appreciate another viewpoint. Far from it. Even adults are known to engage in egocentric speech. Table 13–3

TABLE 13–3

Related and unrelated contribution to class discussions in elementary grades.

Contribution	*Grade 2 (62 Pupils)*	*Grade 4 (54 Pupils)*	*Grade 6 (45 Pupils)*
New Topic, not obviously related to what earlier speaker had said	87%	33%	23%
New Topic, but apparently suggested by something said by a previous contributor	8	24	33
Logical Continuation of a topic previously introduced	4	43	44

Source: Table adapted by A. T. Jersild, *Child Psychology*, Fifth edition (Englewood Cliffs: Prentice-Hall, 1960), p. 354, from H. V. Baker, *Children's Contributions in Elementary School General Discussion.* Child Development Monographs No. 29, pp. 32–33. Copyright Teachers College, Columbia University, 1942. Reprinted by permission.

shows how gradual is children's increase in ability to sustain a discussion. Note that even in grade six, 23 percent of the comments made in the discussion period were not related to the topic which had been introduced and developed [4].

Verbal communication skills have been investigated in terms of the child's ability to understand the other person's role and capacities, and the child's ability to use that understanding as a tool in communicating with other persons [22]. Adult *A* taught the child to play a parchesilike game. Then the child was asked to teach the game to blindfolded Adult *B*. As might be expected, children increased in communicating ability as they increased in age from grade 2 through 12. Some of the youngest children were almost entirely indifferent to the blindfold, making comments such as "Pick up this and put it in there." None of the oldest group failed to take some account of the blindfold. This experiment illustrates the child's gradually increasing capacity to put himself in the place of the other person and to use his mobility of thought for improved interpersonal communication.

Through play with peers and its resultant social insights, children gain increasing understanding of social organization. The nature of rules and moral order is clarified gradually through playing games with peers (in addition to experiences with parents and others). The following example shows two boys experimenting with lawmaking.

During a quiet hour at camp, a counselor noticed an eight- and a nine-year-old playing checkers. After some moments of orderly play, Jake made an extremely irregular move. Steve, watching intently, said nothing. A little later, when Steve broke the rules flagrantly, Jake was silent. "Don't you know you can't do that, Steve?" the counselor broke in. "And, Jake, you made a mistake, too."

"That was no mistake," Jake explained. "We made a rule that each person can cheat once during each game. I cheated and Steve cheated. Now we have to finish without cheating."

Although Steve and Jake were in the stage of cognitive development where they generally considered rules as *given* by a vague authority, their cooperative play was the means by which they found that man, even middle-sized boys, can make rules. They learned that by coming to an agreement with each other, they could play satisfactorily within limits which they created.

SUMMARY

The elementary-school years bring a great expansion of environment and resulting experiences for the child. His experiences are determined and limited by the different social and cultural settings into which he is born. His nation affects his values, especially in regard to the value placed upon the individual in contrast to the group and also in regard to materialism and standards of excellence. Racial and ethnic memberships determine many of the prejudices and hostilities which the child encounters, as well as the attitudes, practices and aspirations of his parents. Social class membership is related to values, parental behavior and resulting cognitive stimulation for children.

A modern trend in parental behavior seems to be a change away from paternalistic authoritarianism toward cooperative families where both parents are affectionate and nurturant. Reporting on the location of authority in their families, children place it more often in the father than in the mother, but they tell increasingly of equality between parents. Children see fathers as doing more punishing than mothers, especially to boys. Boys receive more physical punishment than girls. Mothers often are seen as more nurturant than fathers and are frequently liked better, according to children's reports. Children learn to play adult roles by identifying with their parents. Mothers and fathers demonstrate different roles, both of which contribute to the development of boys and girls. Discipline, an important parental function, includes the regulation of behavior, the teaching of self-control and the imparting of moral standards. Parents vary in their disciplinary methods, using various combinations of corporal and verbal punishment, withdrawal of privileges, acceptance of the child's behavior and feelings, understanding, trust and rewards. Parents of well-adjusted children stressed the value of love-oriented discipline. Parents promote intellectual growth in their children by holding aspirations for them by caring of them in ways which promote independence and the building of desire for achievement and by giving them experiences which are stimulating, especially conversations.

Children gain much from friends in the way of knowledge, experience and satisfaction. Values learned in the family are modified through peer interaction. New behavior patterns, learned from peers, promote growth in various areas, especially a conviction of competence. Children often bow to group pressures, even when exerted against their standards and beliefs. A youngster's concept of himself is strongly influenced by the ways in which his peers regard him. Popularity and social position in the group can be tested and measured. The ability to perceive one's own status and the statuses of others increases with age. While different characteristics may be appealing in different groups, in general, popular children tend to be those with abundant energy, who use their energy for group-approved purposes. The very popular child may pay a price, psychologically, for his extended efforts to adjust to the needs and wishes of others.

Boy–girl relationships, like parent–child relationships, have changed over the decades. A friendlier, more cooperative spirit seems to have arisen between boys and girls, in contrast to the extreme antipathy which used to exist during part of the elementary-school years. Girls' attitudes toward the opposite sex change more during this period than boys' do.

Peers grow in understanding of each other through this period. Increased cognitive growth is both cause and result. With increased flexibility of thought, the child can take and hold the point of view of another person. Thus he can understand, accept, communicate and cooperate increasingly. Through these interactions with peers, he deepens his understanding of the whole social group to which he belongs.

REFERENCES

1. Anderson, H. H., & Anderson, G. L. Culture components as a significant factor in child development. *Am. J. Orthopsychiat.*, 1961, **31,** 481–492.
2. Anderson, H. H., & Anderson, G. L. Social values of teachers in Rio de Janeiro, Mexico City, and Los Angeles County, California: a comparative study of teachers and children. *J. Soc. Psychol.*, 1962, **58,** 207–226.
3. Ausubel, D. P., Schiff, H. M., & Gasser, E. B. A preliminary study of developmental trends in sociempathy: accuracy of perception of own and others sociometric status. *Child Devel.*, 1952, **23,** 111–128.
4. Baker, H. V. Children's contributions in elementary school discussion. *Child Devel. Mono.* No. 29. New York: Teachers College, Columbia Univer., 1942.
5. Bell, R. R. *Marriage and family interaction.* Homewood, Ill.: Dorsey, 1963.

6. Berenda, R. W. The influence of the group on the judgments of children. In M. L. Haimowitz & N. R. Haimowitz (Eds.), *Human development.* New York: Crowell, 1960, pp. 327–339.
7. Blood, R. O., & Wolfe, D. M. *Husbands and wives.* Glencoe, Ill.: Free Press, 1960.
8. Bossard, J. H. *The sociology of child development* (3d ed.). New York: Harper, 1960.
9. Broderick, C. B., & Fowler, S. E. New patterns of relationships between the sexes among preadolescents. *Marr. Fam. Living,* 1961, **23,** 27–30.
10. Bronfenbrenner, U. Socialization and social class through time and space. In E. R. Maccoby, T. M. Newcomb & E. L. Hartley (Eds.), *Readings in social psychology.* New York: Holt, 1958.
11. Bronfenbrenner, U. The changing American child—a speculative analysis. *Merrill-Palmer Quart.,* 1961, **7,** 73–84.
12. Bronfenbrenner, U. Soviet methods of character education: some implications for research. *Am. Psychol.,* 1962, **17,** 550–564.
13. Brown, D. G. Sex-role development in a changing culture. *Psychol. Bull.,* 1958, **55,** 232–242.
14. Campbell, E. H. The social-sex development of children. *Genet. Psychol. Mono.,* 1939, **21,** 461–552.
15. Campbell, J. D. Peer relations in childhood. In M. L. Hoffman & L. W. Hoffman (Eds.), *Review of child development research.* New York: Russell Sage Foundation, 1964.
16. Clausen, J. A., & Williams, J. R. Sociological correlates of child behavior. In H. W. Stevenson, J. Kagan & C. Spiker (Eds.), *Child psychology.* The Sixty-second Yearbook of the National Society for the Study of Education, Part II. Chicago: Univer. of Chicago, 1963, pp. 62–107.
17. Coleman, J. S. *The adolescent society.* Glencoe, Ill.: Free Press, 1961.
18. Davis, A. *Psychology of the child in the middle class.* Pittsburgh: Univer. of Pittsburgh, 1960.
19. DeLucia, L. A. The toy preference test: a measure of sex-role identification. *Child Devel.,* 1963, **34,** 99–106.
20. Deutsch, M. Minority group and class status as related to social and personality factors in scholastic achievement. *Soc. Appl. Anthropol. Mono.* No. 2, St. Louis, Mo., Washington Univ., Social Science Institute, 1960.
21. Emmerich, W. Family-role concepts of children ages six to ten. *Child Devel.,* 1961, **32,** 609–624.
22. Flavell, J. H. Role-taking and communication skills in children. *Young Children,* 1966, **21,** 164–177.
23. Furfey, P. H. *The growing boy.* New York: Macmillan, 1930.
24. Gardner, L. P. An analysis of children's attitudes toward fathers. *J. Genet. Psychol.,* 1947, **70,** 3–28.
25. Grams, A. Child anxiety: self-estimates, parent reports and teacher ratings. *Merrill-Palmer Quart.,* 1965, **11,** 261–266.
26. Harris, D. B., & Tseng. S. C. Children's attitudes toward peers and parents as revealed by sentence completions. *Child Devel.,* 1957, **28,** 401–411.
27. Hartley, R. E., & Hardesty, F. P. Children's perceptions of sex roles in childhood. *J. Genet. Psychol.,* 1964, **105,** 43–51.

28. Hartup, W. W., Moore, S. G., & Sager, G. Avoidance of inappropriate sex-typing by young children. *J. Consult. Psychol.*, 1936, **27,** 467–473.
29. Harvey, O. J., & Rutherford, J. M. Status in the informal group: influence and influencibility at different age levels. *Child Devel.*, 1960, **31,** 377–385.
30. Hereford, C. F. *Changing parental attitudes through group discussion.* Austin: Univer. of Texas, 1963.
31. Hess, R. D., & Torney, J. V. Religion, age and sex in children's perceptions of family authority. *Child Devel.*, 1962, **33,** 781–789.
32. Hoffman, L. W. The father's role in the family and the child's peer-group adjustment. *Merrill-Palmer Quart.*, 1961, **7,** 97–105.
33. Hoffman, M. L. Childrearing practices and moral development: generalizations from empirical research. *Child Devel.*, 1963, **34,** 295–318.
34. Horrocks, J. E., & Buker, M. E. A study of the friendship fluctuations of preadolescents. *J. Genet. Psychol.*, 1951, **78,** 131–144.
35. Hsu, F. J. K., Watrous, B. G., & Lord, E. M. Culture pattern and adolescent behavior. *Int. J. Soc. Psychiat.*, 1960–61, **7,** 33–53.
36. Iscoe, I., & Carden, J. A. Field dependence, manifest anxiety and sociometric status in children. *J. Consult. Psychol.*, 1961, **25,** 184.
37. Johnson, M. M. Sex-role learning in the nuclear family. *Child Devel.*, 1963, **34,** 319–333.
38. Kagan, J. The child's perception of the parent. *J. Abn. Soc. Psychol.*, 1956, **53,** 257–258.
39. Kagan, J., Hosken, B., & Watson, S. Child's symbolic conceptualization of parents. *Child Devel.*, 1961, **32,** 625–636.
40. Kagan, J., & Lemkin, J. The child's differential perception of parental attributes. *J. Abn. Soc. Psychol.*, 1960, **61,** 440–447.
41. Kagan, J., & Moss, H. A. *Birth to maturity*. New York: Wiley, 1962.
42. Katkovsky, W., Preston, A., & Crandall, V. J. Parents' attitudes toward their personal achievements and toward the achievement behaviors of their children. *J. Genet. Psychol.*, 1964, **104,** 76–82.
43. Katz, I. Review of evidence relating to effects of desegregation on the intellectual performance of Negroes. *Am. Psychol.*, 1964, **19,** 381–399.
44. Koch, H. L. Popularity in preschool children: some related factors and a technique for its measurement. *Child Devel.*, 1933, **4,** 164–175.
45. Langdon, G., & Stout, I. W. *The discipline of well-adjusted children.* New York: John Day, 1952.
46. Levy, J., & Munroe, R. *The happy family*. New York: Knopf, 1938.
47. Lewis, G. M. *Educating children in grades four, five and six.* Washington, D.C.: Government Printing Office, 1958.
48. Lewis, O. *The children of Sanchez*. New York: Random House, 1961.
49. Luria, Z., Goldwasser, M., & Goldwasser, A. Response to transgression in stories by Israeli children. *Child Devel.*, 1963, **34,** 271–280.
50. Mead, M., & Wolfenstein, M. *Childhood in contemporary cultures.* Chicago: Univer. of Chicago, 1955.
51. Miller, D. R., & Swanson, G. E. *The changing American parent.* New York: Wiley, 1958.
52. Moreno, J. L. *Who shall survive?* Washington, D.C.: Nervous and Mental Disease Publishing Company, 1934. Also, New York: Beacon, 1953.

53. Mussen, P., & Distler, L. Child-rearing antecedents of masculine identification in kindergarten boys. *Child Devel.,* 1960, **31,** 89–100.
54. Mussen, P., & Rutherford, E. Parent-child relations and parental personality in relation to young children's sex-role preferences. *Child Devel.,* 1963, **34,** 589–607.
55. Northway, M. L. *What is popularity?* Chicago: Science Research Associates, 1955.
56. Northway, M. L., & Weld, L. *Sociometric testing.* Toronto: Univer. of Toronto, 1957.
57. Opie, I., & P. *The lore and language of school children.* Oxford: Clarendon, 1959.
58. Parsons, R., & Bales, R. F. *Family, socialization and interaction process.* Glencoe, Ill.: Free Press, 1955.
59. Pope, B. Socioeconomic contrasts in children's peer culture prestige values. *Genet. Psychol. Mono.,* 1953, **48,** 157–220.
60. Queen, S. A., Habenstein, R. W., & Adams, J. B. *The family in various cultures.* Philadelphia: Lippincott, 1961.
61. Riessman, F. *The culturally deprived child.* New York: Harper, 1962.
62. Riessman, F. Low-income culture: the strengths of the poor. *J. Marr. Fam.,* 1964, **26,** 417–429.
63. Rosen, B. C. Race, ethnicity and the achievement syndrome. *Am. Soc. Rev.,* 1959, **24,** 49–60.
64. Rosen, B. C. Family structure and value transmission. *Merrill-Palmer Quart.,* 1964, **10,** 25–38. (a)
65. Rosen, B. C. Social class and the child's perception of the parent. *Child Devel.,* 1964, **35,** 1147–1153. (b)
66. Rosen, B. C., & D'Andrade, R. The psychosocial origins of achievement motivation. *Sociometry,* 1959, **22,** 185–218.
67. Rosenberg, B. G., & Sutton-Smith, B. A revised conception of masculine-feminine differences in play activities. *J. Genet. Psychol.,* 1960, **96,** 165–170.
68. Ruderman, L. An exploration of empathic ability in children and its relationship to several variables. Unpublished doctoral dissertation, Teachers College, Columbia Univer., 1961.
69. Sontag, L. W., Baker, C. T., & Nelson, V. L. Mental growth and personality development: a longitudinal study. *Mono. Soc. Res. Child Devel.,* 1958, **23:**2.
70. Taba, H. Cultural deprivation as a factor in school learning. *Merrill-Palmer Quart.,* 1964, **10,** 147–159.
71. Thompson, G. G., & Powell, M. An investigation of the rating-scale approach to the measurement of social status. *Educ. Psychol. Measmt.,* 1951, **11,** 440–445.
72. Torrance, E. P. Changing reactions of preadolescent girls to tasks requiring creative scientific thinking. *J. Genet. Psychol.,* 1963, **102,** 217–223.
73. Whiting, B. B. *Six cultures: studies of child rearing.* New York: Wiley, 1963.
74. Winterbottom, M. The relation of need for achievement in learning experiences in independence and mastery. In J. Atkinson (Ed.), *Motives in fantasy, action and society.* Princeton: Van Nostrand, 1958, pp. 453–478.
75. Wolfenstein, M. The emergence of fun morality. *J. Soc. Issues,* 1951, **7,** 15–25.

76. Wyatt, E. Tennessee. In *U.S. commission on civil rights, civil rights, U.S.A.—public schools, southern states*. Washington, D.C.: Government Printing Office, 1962, pp. 105–130.
77. Yarrow, M. R., & Campbell, J. D. Person perception in children. *Merrill-Palmer Quart.*, 1963, **9,** 57–72.
78. Young, M. B. A Negro mother speaks. *Parents'*, 1964, **39:**7, 50–51, 78.

PART IV

The Adolescent

Introduction

Pubescence, the period surrounding the peak of velocity in physical growth, is only the beginning of a long critical period in personality growth. Here the problem is posed, "Who am I?" All of adolescence involves finding the answers. As is true of trust, autonomy, initiative and industry (which have their growth periods earlier), the sense of identity is built throughout life, but it too has its special time of growth. The personality with which the child begins pubescence is the product of all his past interactions with the world.

The more slowly maturing children in grades seven, eight and nine are still in the stage of developing a sense of industry, busy with basic school subjects, perfecting motor skills, earning merit badges, active in like-sexed peer groups. Nearing the completion of this particular stage of development, the successful ones are good at many activities. The unsuccessful ones have a proportionate sense of failure and inferiority by now. Many feel inferior because of poor performance and poor grades at school. Some have found themselves awkward and outclassed in games and sports. Others are unwanted as friends. Some suffer tragically from all kinds of inferiority. Thus, some junior high school youngsters are unready to deal with the crucial question of identity simply because they have not lived through the previous stage, while others are unready because they have not been adequate in the previous stage. Eventually, ready or not, questions of identity will be forced upon them, but the junior high, in its ideal form, is a flexible place where children in different stages of development can find what they need to help them grow.

Even though a new critical phase is entered upon, the sense of industry continues to be strained and tested. Further development is required of it, in intimate association with the sense of identity. The adolescent must *do well* in many new areas. He has to develop new competencies, intellectual, social and moral, and competency in school and on the job. The way in which his childhood sense of industry comes into play is in making him feel that he is adequate or inadequate, likely to be successful or unsuccessful. Erikson underlines the importance of the sense of industry throughout life by repeating Freud's answer to the question "What should a normal person be able to do well?" Freud said, "Lieben und arbeiten." ("To love and to work.") He meant productiveness balanced and integrated with the capacity to be a sexual and a loving being [3, p. 96].

As a time of rebirth into an almost-new body and rapidly expanding mind and world, adolescence is a period of shakeup and testing of all that has gone before. The adolescent's psychological structure is fluid [2]. The stages of developing trust, autonomy and initiative, as well as the most recent stage of industry, all come in for questioning and reorganization. Problems of trust and mistrust come to the fore in religious upheavals. Questions of autonomy versus shame and doubt most likely enter into parent–adolescent struggles. The relationship of initiative and guilt is pertinent to the moral development of adolescence.

"The sense of ego identity, then, is the accrued confidence that one's ability to maintain inner sameness and continuity . . . is matched by the sameness and continuity of one's meaning for others" [3, p. 89]. Thus does Erikson summarize the role of other people in the growth of an individual's sense of identity. The "other people" include the whole culture, since the person's concept of himself has to be one which is acceptable in his culture. The most important people, as far as "one's meaning for others" is concerned, are those individuals who play important parts in his life, family, friends, sweethearts, teachers, employers. The adolescent sees himself partly through reflections mirrored by all the significant people in his life (the old concept of "the looking-glass self"). He also models his self-concept on the ways in which he sees other people, identifying with some pictures, rejecting others. Part of his problem is to hang onto a feeling of being the same person, a person who is changing but who is still continuous and identifiable as the person he has always been and always will be.

Adolescence brings greater differentiation between boys and girls than has existed before. Sex factors elaborate physical, physiological and personality differences. Social roles become more clearly delineated along sex lines. The establishment of the sense of identity is understandably different for boys and girls. Using the data from two national sample surveys of boys and girls between 14 and 16, Douvan [1] comes to some conclusions about sex differences in identity. A boy is more concerned with establishing personal controls and standards, and this is more crucial to his identity than it is to a girl's. Boys with well-internalized standards were found to be also high in achievement striving, independence of judgment, energy level in work and play, self-confidence, self-criticism and organization of thought. The boy who had not internalized controls tended to be poorly integrated, demoralized and deficient in the qualities in which the highly internalized boy excelled. Girls who had well-internalized controls did not show the pattern of high-level functioning showed by boys. Rather, the critical achievements in girls seemed to be interpersonal skills and sensitivity. Girls high in these qualities were also high in energy level, self-confidence, time perspective, organization of ideas and positive identification.

Establishing independent standards and controls is part of the identity crisis in Western culture. Social and personal forces push the boy to take this step earlier than the girl. Perhaps American culture influences girls to stay malleable in personal identity until they have found husbands. A very clear self-definition in adolescence would limit the choice of marital partners and might interfere with adapting to the needs of the husband after marriage.

The first chapter in this section deals with the rapid physical growth and genital maturity, which launch the adolescent into questioning his sameness and continuity. The second chapter is concerned with intellectual maturing, which facilitates deeper thinking and questioning. Caused by his new body and new questions, disturbances in the sense of identity are resolved through successful peer relationships, maturing of relationships with parents, satisfactory vocational, moral and religious development. The final chapters examine these avenues to a firm sense of identity.

REFERENCES

1. Douvan, E. Sex differences in adolescent character processes. *Merrill-Palmer Quart.*, 1960, **6**, 203–211.
2. Eisenberg, L. A developmental approach to adolescents. *Children,* 1965, **12,** 131–135.
3. Erikson, E. H. *Identity and the life cycle.* New York: International Universities, 1959.

Physical Growth, Health and Coordination

CHAPTER 14

A child changes into an adult during *adolescence,* a period lasting from about 11 to about 18 years of age. The changes which take place during adolescence include not only physical events but also psychological and social ones.

Puberty is the time when sexual maturity is reached. *Pubescence* is the period of time encompassing the physical changes which lead to puberty. Two years is the average length of time for pubescence, although the span is shorter in fast-maturing adolescents and longer in slow-maturers.

Bodily Changes During Pubescence

The child's body changes into an adult's through an almost invariable sequence of events. A person familiar with pubescent growth could tell from a physical examination what change could be expected next and how far the youngster had progressed toward puberty. The following list of changes in boys and girls shows the normal sequences for development during pubescence [3, p. 94]. Note that the age of most rapid growth comes not at the very end of pubescence but before menarche (first menstruation) for girls and before certain adult characteristics in boys.

Girls	*Boys*
Initial enlargement of breasts.	Beginning growth of testes.
Straight, pigmented pubic hair.	Straight, pigmented pubic hair.
	Early voice changes.
	First ejaculation of semen.
Kinky pubic hair.	Kinky pubic hair.
Age of maximum growth.	Age of maximum growth.
Menarche.	
Growth of axillary hair.	Growth of axillary hair.
	Marked voice changes.
	Development of the beard.

Puberty

It is difficult to pinpoint the achievement of sexual maturity, the capacity for reproduction. Menarche is often assumed to be the time when a girl becomes able to have babies, but a sterile period of a year or more probably occurs in most girls after menstruation [25]. Menarche is usually considered the point of sexual maturity, however, since it is a definite event which is easy to remember. There is no corresponding definite event for boys, although a criterion sometimes used is the production of spermatozoa. In research studies on growth in adolescence, the various growth events in the sequence of pubescence are often used, rather than one point such as menarche.

The menarche occurs at different average ages in different times and places. To judge the normalcy of an individual girl's menarche, one would have to compare her with a suitable group. For example, for girls in the south of England from 1950–60, the average age at menarche was 13.2 [33, p. 154]. In Jerusalem, in 1958–59, the average menarche came at 13.9, but for girls of occidental origin at 13.5, for girls of oriental origin at 14.0 and for girls of Israeli-born fathers at 13.8 [29]. The average for American white girls was between 12.5 and 13.0, on the basis of data collected between 1940 and 1955 [33, p. 154]. About two thirds of all girls achieved menarche within the time span a year before to a year after the average. Almost all menstruated within the period of three years before to three years after the average. A very few menstruated before 10, and a very few did not reach menarche until after 16.

A criterion of puberty which has been found useful for both boys and girls is that of maximum yearly increment in height. Shuttleworth [30] in his classic research on adolescent growth, found the average for boys to be 14.8 and for girls 12.6. The normal range for age at puberty is large, however—10 to 16 in girls and 12 to 18 in boys [3, p. 92].

Growth in Height

Growth speeds up during pubescence, becoming faster as the child moves through the sequence of events which leads to puberty. As was noted above, the period of fastest growth comes before menarche, about six months before. Figure 14–1 shows height increment curves for boys and girls who reached the peak velocity of growth at the average times, the girls between 12 and 13, the boys between 14 and 15. When increment curves are plotted for early or late maturers, the curves show essentially the same shape, with a rise and then a sharp drop which starts just before puberty.

While everybody expects a youngster to spurt in height, the spurt is still an amazing and often mysterious phenomenon to family, friends and most of all to the person experiencing it. It is amazing because the middle years of childhood are so stable and uneventful from the standpoint of growth. Then suddenly, velocity picks up and the child seems to grow overnight. (The average boy grows eight inches between ages 13 and 15½; the average girl, three and a quarter inches between 11 and 13½). Families often discuss and

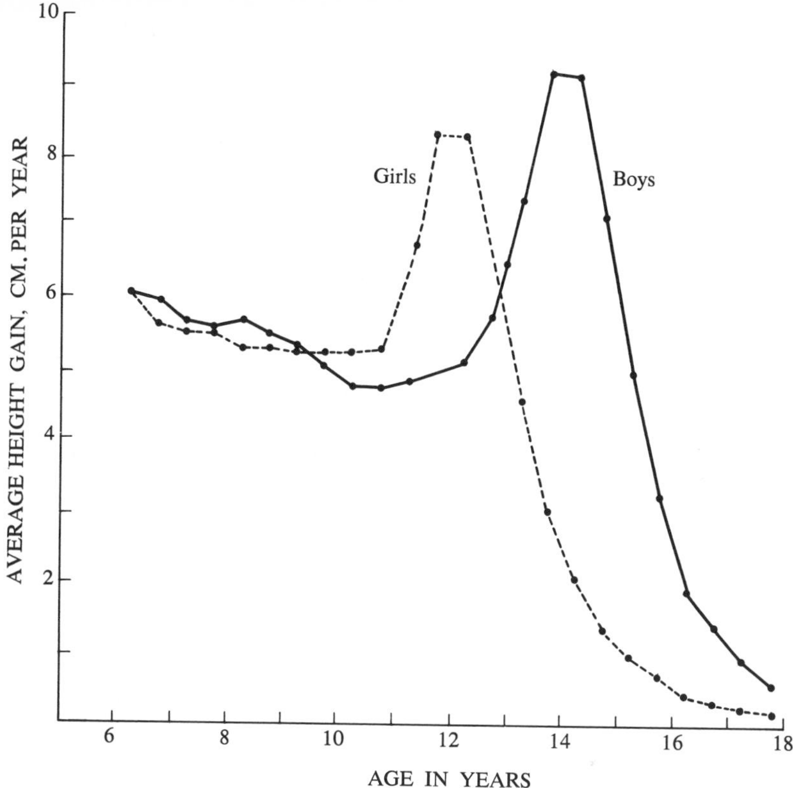

Figure 14–1. Adolescent increment growth curves in height for boys and girls who reached puberty at the average times. (Reprinted by permission from J. M. Tanner, *Growth at Adolescence,* 2nd edition. Oxford: Blackwell Scientific Publications Ltd., 1962. Copyright © 1962, Blackwell Scientific Publications Ltd.)

wonder about the spurting child's eventual height, how long he will grow so fast and when he will stop. The factors behind each child's peculiar style of growth are so complex and interwoven that parents have little success in prediction.

The taller the child, the taller he can expect to be as an adult. At each age from infancy to the onset of pubescence, height correlates increasingly with adult height. Mary Jane, at age seven, is tall for her age, while Phyllis, at seven, is short. The chances are that Mary Jane will grow to above-average height for women, while Phyllis will be petite.

The wide normal range in the age at which puberty is reached means that children vary widely in when they begin the growth spurt, when they reach the peak and when they finish. John and Bill, the same height at age 13, will be inches apart as adults because John has been rapidly increasing in height for the past year while Bill has not grown noticeably. John will soon shoot ahead of Bill, but Bill will eventually overtake him.

The velocity and duration of the growth spurt vary from one individual to another. When the spurt occurs early, it tends to be more intense but to last over a shorter period than when it occurs at a later age. Early maturers tend to be shorter than late maturers because the longer duration of the growth period in late maturers more than makes up for the brief advantage which more intense velocity gives to the early maturers. This factor accounts for most of the difference in height between men and women. Men have a longer time in which to grow.

Linear people, as contrasted with people of rounded shape, tend to be late maturers. Only a small part of their linearity is due to their late maturing, which allows a greater time for growth of the legs than an early maturer has. From the age of two, people who will mature late weigh less for their height than do those who will mature early. Figure 14–2 shows the weight per centimeter of height for early, average and late-maturing boys and girls.

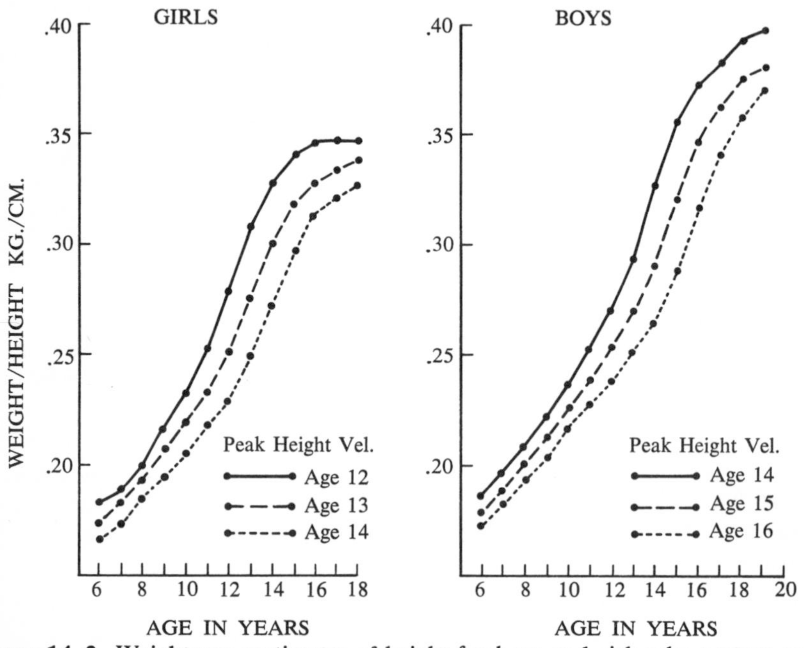

Figure 14–2. Weight per centimeter of height for boys and girls who mature early, late and at the average time. (Reprinted by permission from J. M. Tanner, *Growth at Adolescence,* 2nd edition. Oxford: Blackwell Scientific Publications Ltd., 1962. Copyright © 1962, Blackwell Scientific Publications Ltd.)

Because of the wide variation in both height and weight during adolescence, percentile tables are not so useful at this time as they are earlier. However, for what they may be worth, height and weight percentiles are included here, as they are in the other sections of the book which have to do with physical growth (Tables 14–1, 14–2, 14–3 and 14–4).

*Endocrinology of Growth**

Besides stature and weight, other dimensions of the human body have been studied in similar ways. These include sitting height, and dimensions of the chest and head. Even diameters of the head show increments which follow

TABLE 14–1

Height percentile table for boys age 12½ through 18.

	Height in Inches						
Age	*3%*	*10%*	*25%*	*50%*	*75%*	*90%*	*97%*
12½ yr.	55¼	57	58	60	62	63½	65¼
13 yr.	56	57¾	59	61	63¼	65	66¾
13½ yr.	56¾	58¾	60¼	62½	64¾	66½	68¼
14 yr.	57½	60	61½	64	66¼	68	69¾
14½ yr.	58¾	61	62¾	65	67¼	68¾	70¾
15 yr.	59¾	62	64	66	68	69½	71½
15½ yr.	60¾	63	64¾	66¾	68¾	70¼	72¼
16 yr.	61½	64	65¾	67¾	69½	70¾	73
16½ yr.	62	64½	66¼	68	69¾	71	73¼
17 yr.	62½	65¼	66¾	68½	70	71½	73½
17½ yr.	62¾	65¼	67	68½	70¼	71½	73¾
18 yr.	62¾	65½	67	68¾	70½	71¾	74

Source: From *Growth and Development of Children*, 4th edition, by Ernest H. Watson and George H. Lowrey. Copyright © 1962, Year Book Medical Publishers, Inc., Chicago. Used by permission of Year Book Medical Publishers.

TABLE 14–2

Height percentile table for girls age 12½ through age 18.

	Height in Inches						
Age	*3%*	*10%*	*25%*	*50%*	*75%*	*90%*	*97%*
12½ yr.	55½	57½	58¾	60¾	62½	64	65½
13 yr.	56½	58¾	60	61¾	63¾	65	66¼
13½ yr.	57½	59½	60¾	62½	64	65¼	66¾
14 yr.	58¼	60¼	61½	62¾	64½	65¾	67¼
14½ yr.	58¾	60¾	61¾	63	64¾	66	67½
15 yr.	59	61	62	63½	65	66¼	67½
15½ yr.	59¼	61¼	62¼	63¾	65	66½	67¾
16 yr.	59½	61½	62½	64	65¼	66½	67¾
16½ yr.	59½	61½	62½	64	65½	66½	67¾
17 yr.	59½	61½	62½	64	65½	66¾	67¾
17½ yr.	59½	61½	62½	64	65½	66¾	67¾
18 yr.	59½	61½	62½	64	65½	66¾	67¾

Source: From *Growth and Development of Children*, 4th edition, by Ernest H. Watson and George H. Lowrey. Copyright © 1962, Year Book Medical Publishers, Inc., Chicago. Used by permission of Year Book Medical Publishers.

* This account follows Tanner [32, pp. 30–31].

the same kind of pattern of increments, although the curve for each dimension is unique in some way. Although all the details are not understood, it is pretty well agreed that the underlying factor of the spurt in growth that occurs around pubescence is the complicated but interrelated ebb and flow of endocrine substances in the blood stream.

TABLE 14–3

Weight percentile table for boys age 12½ through 18.

	Weight in Pounds						
Age	*3%*	*10%*	*25%*	*50%*	*75%*	*90%*	*97%*
12½ yr.	69½	74½	80½	88¾	102	116½	131
13 yr.	72	77	83¾	93	108	123¼	138
13½ yr.	76	82¼	89½	100¼	115½	130	144¼
14 yr.	79¾	87¼	95½	107½	123	137	150½
14½ yr.	85½	93¼	102	114	129	142½	156
15 yr.	91¼	99½	108¼	120	135	147¾	161½
15½ yr.	97½	105¼	113½	125	139¾	153½	166
16 yr.	103½	111	118¾	129¾	144½	157¼	170½
16½ yr.	107	114¼	121½	133	148	161	173
17 yr.	110½	117½	124½	136¼	151½	164½	175½
17½ yr.	111¾	118¾	125¾	137½	153½	166¾	177¼
18 yr.	113	120	127	139	155¾	169	179

Source: From *Growth and Development of Children*, 4th edition, by Ernest H. Watson and George H. Lowrey. Copyright © 1962, Year Book Medical Publishers, Inc., Chicago. Used by permission of Year Book Medical Publishers.

TABLE 14–4

Weight percentile table for girls age 12½ through 18.

	Weight in Pounds						
Age	*3%*	*10%*	*25%*	*50%*	*75%*	*90%*	*97%*
12½ yr.	68	74¾	83¾	93¼	105	118	135
13 yr.	72¼	80	89½	99	111	124½	142¼
13½ yr.	77¾	85½	94½	103¾	115½	129	146½
14 yr.	83	91	99¾	108½	119¾	133¼	150¾
14½ yr.	86	94¼	102½	111	121¾	135¾	153
15 yr.	89	97½	105	113½	124	138	155¼
15½ yr.	90½	99¼	106¾	115¼	125½	139½	156½
16 yr.	91¾	101	108½	117	127¼	141	157¾
16½ yr.	92¾	102	109½	118	128½	142¼	158½
17 yr.	94	102¾	110½	119	129½	143¼	159½
17½ yr.	94¼	103¼	110¾	119½	130¼	144	160
18 yr.	94½	103½	111¼	120	130¾	144½	160¾

Source: From *Growth and Development of Children*, 4th edition, by Ernest H. Watson and George H. Lowrey. Copyright © 1962, Year Book Medical Publishers, Inc., Chicago. Used by permission of Year Book Medical Publishers.

During the childhood years before pubescence, growth is stimulated and controlled by phyone, a hormone secreted by the pituitary gland, which lies in the center of the head. From birth to pubescence, the velocity of growth decreases steadily. The pubescent phase of growth is initiated by the hypothalamus, a small area in the base of the brain. When the hypothalamus reaches a certain stage of maturity, its anterior portion releases its restraint on the posterior portion, which then secretes a certain chemical. This chemical acts upon the pituitary gland, triggering its release of trophic hormones. The trophic hormones stimulate the ovaries, testes and adrenal glands to produce their hormones. Androgens, secreted by the adrenals, and testosterone, from the testes and perhaps in small amount from the ovaries, are the agents which cause pubescent growth.

The different timings of the adolescent growth spurts of the various organs and tissues can be explained by differential sensitivity to the androgens. For instance, the sequence of appearance of pubic, axillary and facial hair is probably due to different thresholds to stimulation and reactivity to either adrenal or testicular androgens [33, p. 130]. The skin of the pubis thus responds to the smallest increase of androgen, growing hair in early pubescence. The skin of the axilla requires a larger amount of androgen before it produces hair and the skin of the face an even larger amount.

The differences between early and late maturers are in part differences in the timing of the beginning of the adolescent growth spurt. These are probably genetic in origin since the spurt is related to the age of sexual maturity, which is known to be strongly hereditary. (The age at menarche of identical twin sisters is highly correlated, that of fraternal twins and siblings is lower and that of mothers and daughters lower still, but even so, greater than chance.) Environmental factors also influence pubescent growth, as will be shown in the section on nutrition at adolescence.

Growth in Weight

The curve of increments of weight begins to rise earlier than does the curve of increments of height. This can be accounted for in part by the earlier increase in the width and depth measurements of the chest and hips. It is also partly due to the preadolescent increase of subcutaneous fat and muscle.

Unlike muscle and bone, *fat* has periods of decreasing in width as well as of increasing during the growth span. Fat thickness increases from birth to nine months, decreases to about six years, increases slowly until about a year before the height spurts start. In boys, fat has a growth spurt lasting about two years. Then, when the height spurt has been going for about a year, fat decreases until the height spurt ends. Fat then increases until it reaches a level at least as great as the preadolescent level. Girls increase more steadily than boys in growth of fat [33, pp. 19–25].

Fat thickness throughout childhood is closely related to weight at maturity [14]. By measuring fat thickness semiannually, it was shown that between

1.5 and 12.5 years of age, children in the top 14 percent in fat were advanced by about half a year's growth. Fat thickness was associated with skeletal maturity. The authors suggest that overnutrition or supernutrition results in speeded maturation, and general dimensional growth, in addition to subcutaneous fat. A series of studies on obesity in adolescents [8, 18, 31] revealed activity level as a crucial difference between obese adolescents and normal ones who ate about the same number of calories. The level of activity affects metabolic rate and hence the rate at which calories are used. These results

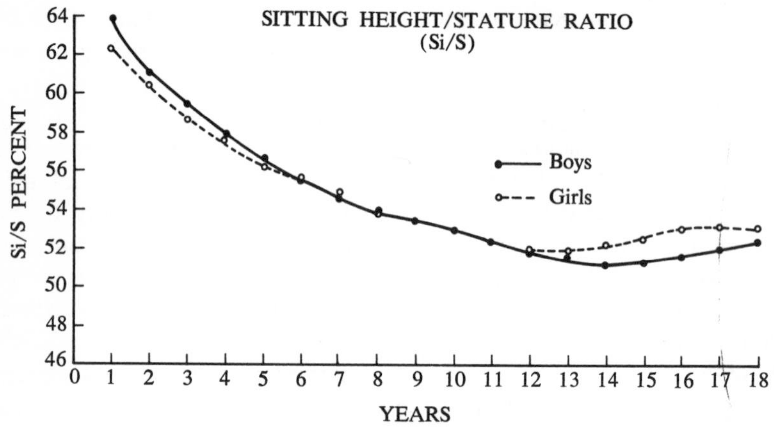

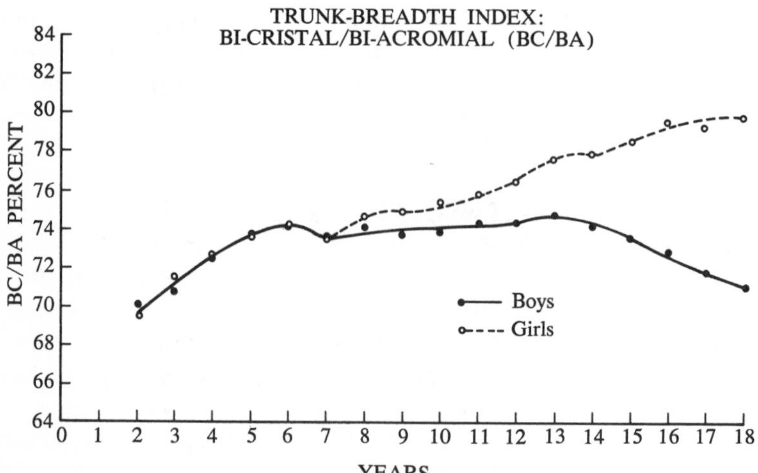

Figure 14–3. These ratios, the ratio of sitting height to total height (above) and the ratio of hip width to shoulder width (below), are shown for each year from birth to 18, indicating average changes in proportions as children mature. (Reprinted from *Growth Diagnosis* by L. M. Bayer and N. Bayley, by permission of The University of Chicago Press. Copyright © 1959, The University of Chicago Press, Chicago.)

raise the question of whether inactivity is related to early maturity, as well as to fat.

Changes in Proportions

The changes in average proportions can be seen in Figure 14–3, which uses the Sitting Height/Stature Ratio and the Trunk-Breadth Index. The former is the percentage of total height that is contributed by sitting height. According to the diagram (see Figure 14–3) at one year sitting height is about 64 percent of total height for boys and about 62 percent for girls. From ages 5 to 12 the girls' and boys' ratios are the same (on the average), but the ratios decrease throughout the age range up to 12 since the legs are growing faster than the trunk, neck and head. From 12 to 15 for girls and from 14 to 18 for boys the ratio increases slightly as the trunk grows more rapidly than the legs.

The Trunk-Breadth Index is the ratio of hip width to shoulder width. Hip width is the distance between the crests of the pelvis. Shoulder width is the distance between the outer ends of the acromium, at the ends of the clavicles. The higher the Index, the wider the hips are in relation to the width of the shoulders. Up to about the age of eight, on the average, the Index for boys and girls is the same. From 8 to 18, girls' average Index increases steadily, as the hips increase faster in width than do the shoulders. The average Index for boys stays at the same amount from 7 to 13, then drops as boys' shoulders increase faster than do their hips. Pubescent changes can be seen in every part of the body except the brain and eyeball, where there are no easily-measured growth spurts. The growth spurts of the various parts of the body do not coincide exactly with one another but are spread throughout the pubescent period. Figure 14–4 shows the timing of the spurts of several different body measurements. Notice that the peaks for growth in weight and head circumference come after the peaks for growth in height and hand length.

If a child grew in the way that a balloon blows up, he would keep the same proportions all the way along, but he does not. Spurting now in one measurement, now in another, he often looks different from the way he looked just a short time before. Spurts in head length and breadth make the eyes look smaller. The nose and lower jaw grow more than other parts of the face, changing its proportions from childish toward adult. The ways in which a boy grows out of his suits are predictable, since the spurts of the various parts of the body follow a sequence. First the trouser legs become too short. If his mother can lengthen them, they will last for another four months until his hip growth makes the trousers too tight. Since chest breadth increases at the same time as hip width, a new suit is in order. It is a good idea to buy it wide in the shoulders, since the spurt in shoulder breadth comes just a few months after the spurts in chest and hip width. This suit will become too short in the jacket with the peak of growth in trunk length which comes about a year after the peak of growth in leg length. A filling-out process will make the

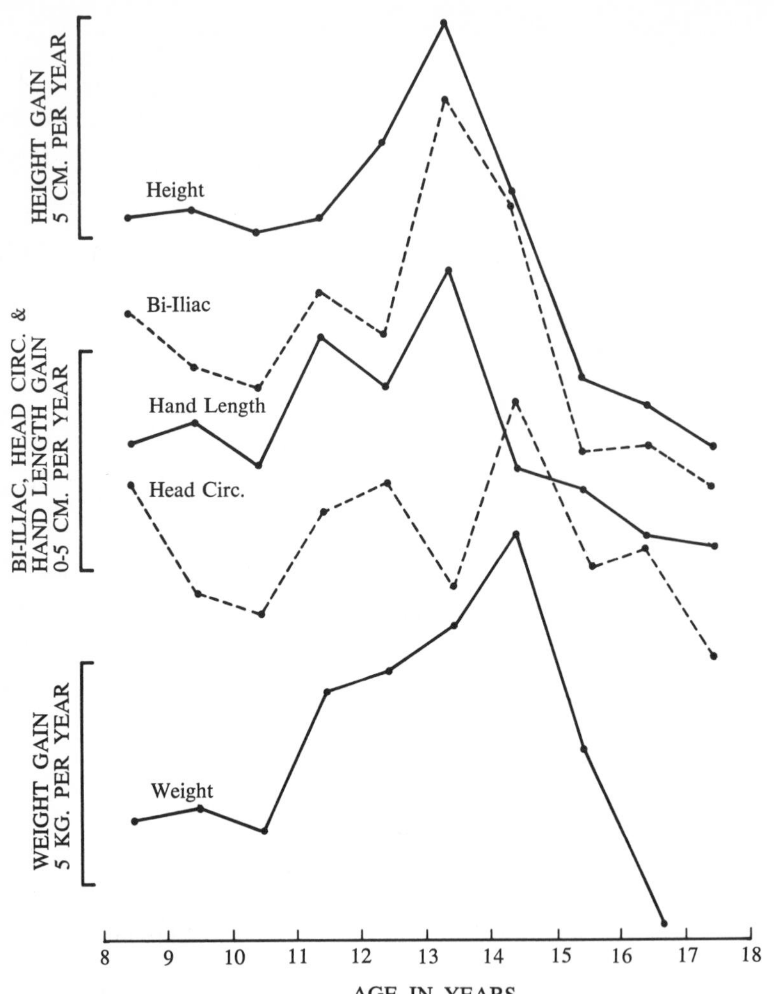

Figure 14–4. Adolescent increment growth curves, showing spurts and peaks for various body measurements. (Reprinted by permission from J. M. Tanner, *Growth at Adolescence,* 2nd edition. Oxford: Blackwell Scientific Publications Ltd., 1962. Copyright © 1962, Blackwell Scientific Publications Ltd.)

jacket too tight just after it becomes too short, since the peak in muscle growth comes soon after the peak in trunk length. (Although boys' suits illustrate these changes better than girls' clothing, the same sequence of changes takes place in girls.)

Both boys and girls tend to worry as their feet spurt in growth. This spurt happens when the height spurt gets under way or before it [23]. The earlier it happens, of course, the larger the youngster's feet seem to him and to his family, who tend to be concerned about the frequent need for new shoes as well as about what looks like awkwardness.

Changes in Organs

The *viscera* undergo pubescent growth spurts [33, p. 18]. Most data on visceral growth are cross-sectional, and therefore the nature of their spurts has not been so clearly demonstrated as with outer body measurements. The cardiovascular system has been studied in terms of blood pressure, pulse rate, capacity for athletic and work effort and recovery from work. Since the heart is relatively small during childhood, undergoing a growth spurt in pubescence, there is always the question for an individual as to how mature his heart is in relation to the rest of his body. Breckenridge and Vincent [6, p. 223] among others, point out that children and young adolescents should be protected from physical overexertion. A rise in blood pressure and a drop in pulse rate begin with puberty, with boys exceeding girls in both [3, p. 98]. Chest cavity and lungs increase, while rate of breathing decreases. In relation to the size of the body, however, pubescence brings a steady decrease in volume of air taken in. The sex difference grows in favor of boys, who develop a much larger lung capacity than girls.

The *nervous system* matures during the adolescent period, but the exact nature of the changes has not been mapped in much detail. The intellectual changes at adolescence must have their counterparts in the nervous system. Tanner [33, p. 15] states that there is some evidence for a small growth spurt in the brain at adolescence. Physical measurements of heads indicate that there may be some brain growth along with growth in bone and membranes. While the study of brain waves has not yet produced much practical information about the behavior of normal children, it does show that changes in the brain take place as the child grows up. An adult type of brain wave pattern becomes established during adolescence [35, p. 134]. Figure 14–5 shows the average proportions of delta, theta and alpha rhythms from birth to about 18. Between 10 and 15, the proportion of alpha waves increases, delta decreases and theta almost disappears. This diagram is a representation of averages. Individual patterns do not look just like it, nor do they look alike.

Development of the Primary and Secondary Sex Characteristics

The organs of reproduction grow enormously. Although only cross-sectional data are available for the growth of the uterus and ovaries, they show these organs as increasing in weight between ages 10 and 20. The male primary reproductive organs have been studied longitudinally. The stages of genital development are numbered according to the advancement of the primary and secondary sex characteristics. Stages of hair growth, for example, are:

1. Prepubescent. About the same as in early childhood.
2. Sparse, long, slightly pigmented, downy hair.
3. Darker, coarser, curlier, spread over small area, but larger area than in 2.

4. Hair resembles adult hair but covers smaller area.
5. Adult quantity, quality and distribution.

The average time to go from stage 2 to stage 5 is four years, but it may be done in as short a time as two years or as long as six.

Axillary hair usually appears when pubic hair is reaching stage 4, but it may come earlier. Circumanal hair appears just before axillary. Boys' facial hair comes at about the same time as axillary hair, developing through a sequence, as does pubic and axillary hair. Body hair develops for some time after puberty, with hair on the chest appearing last.

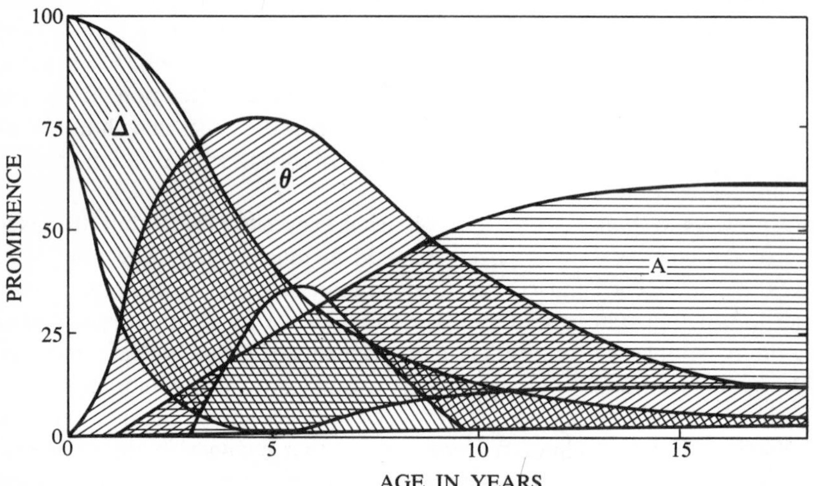

Figure 14–5. Diagram of brain waves during childhood and adolescence, showing changes in frequency of occurrence of three types of waves. (Reprinted by permission from W. G. Walter, "Electroencephalographic Development of Children," in J. M. Tanner and B. Inhelder (Eds.), *Discussions on Child Development,* I. New York: International Universities Press, Inc., 1953. Copyright © 1953, International Universities Press.)

The voice change takes place throughout pubescence, sometimes continuing for years afterward. The spurt in growth of the larynx takes place at about the same time as the spurt in trunk growth. Figure 14–6 shows the tones typically produced by both sexes at various ages. Note the nine low notes added to the boy's voice between age 10 and adulthood, while the girl added only three low ones. The boy lost four high notes, and the girl gained one.

The apocrine sweat glands of the axillary and genital regions enlarge and secrete sweat, which has a strong odor. The sebaceous glands enlarge and secrete more oil. Their ducts, which do not enlarge correspondingly, are likely to become plugged with the secretion, causing or contributing largely to the skin difficulties so frequent at this age.

Breast changes occur in boys as well as in girls. About a half of boys have some enlargement of the breasts at about stage 4 of genital development and lasting from a year to 18 months. Breast development in girls has been outlined in five stages:

1. Prepubescent. Elevation of papilla only.
2. Breast bud. Small mound of papilla and breast. Enlargement of areola.
3. Breast and areola enlarge further.
4. Areola and papilla project to form mound above level of breast.
5. Mature stage. Areola recedes to general contour of breast. Papilla projects. The breast bud tends to appear about a year and a half before the menarche. Breast bud and pubic hair usually occur within a year of each other.

The growth spurt of the ovaries probably begins about a year before the breast bud, the uterus and vagina, at about the time the breast bud appears. Early menstrual cycles tend to be irregular. Ovulation probably does not occur often. Full fertility is probably not reached until the early or middle twenties.

Sex Feelings and Desires

The dramatic development of the reproductive system, culminating in sexual maturity, implies sexual activity or at least the desire for it. While some

AGE	TONES
2 years	D E F G A
3 years	*C* D E F G(A)[1]
4 years	B *C* D E F G A B C
5 years	A B *C* D E F G A B C D
6 years	A B *C* D E F G A B C D E F G
7 years	A B *C* D E F G A B C D E F(G)[2]
8 years	G A B *C* D E F G A B C D E F G
9 years	F G A B *C* D E F G A B C D E F G
10 years	[3](F)G A B *C* D E F G A B C D E F G
Boys	f g a b c d e f g a b c d e f g
Girls	g a b c d e f g a b c d e f g a
Men	[4](D)E F G A B C D E F G A B *C* D E F G A B C[5]
Women	C D E F G A B *C* D E F G A B C D E F G A

[1]Sung by 49 percent of the children.
[2]Sung by 48 percent of the children.
[3]Sung by 48 percent of the children.
[4]Sung by 49 percent of the men.
[5]Includes the falsetto.

Figure 14–6. Notes sung at various ages from early childhood to adulthood. Note additions and subtractions to and from the repertories of boys and girls at adolescence. (Reprinted by permission from A. T. Jersild and S. F. Bienstock, "A Study of the Development of Children's Ability to Sing," *Journal of Educational Psychology,* **25,** 481–503. Copyright © 1934, Abrahams Magazine Service, Inc.)

children are capable of true sexual response [21, p. 103], sexuality is heightened at puberty, especially for boys. Boys frequently experience sexual arousal and tension which they urgently desire to discharge through orgasm. By counting frequency of sexual "outlets," which include masturbation and nocturnal emissions, Kinsey [22] concludes that males are most active sexually during their teens and that the mid-teens are the most sexually active years of life. While there is some question as to whether sex desire is adequately measured by frequency of outlets [5, pp. 67–68], Kinsey has shown that in regard to number of orgasms of all kinds, adolescent boys greatly exceed adolescent girls. The 15-year-old boys reported an average of five orgasms per two-week interval, while only 23 percent of girls that age had experienced orgasm, and of those, the average frequency was less than one in two weeks. When sex feeling or arousal is taken into account, adolescent girls appear more sexually responsive than when orgasm is the criterion. By age 13, 34 percent of girls, by 15, 53 percent, and by 20, 89 percent experienced sexual arousal [21, pp. 512–513].

These figures are given only to show that the average adolescent has had sex feelings and desires, the boy more frequently and acutely than the girl. There are wide individual differences in frequency and intensity of desire and in how it is satisfied. In a following chapter, we shall discuss the role of sex in the development of personality and in interpersonal relationships.

PHYSICAL CARE AND HEALTH

Since any period of rapid growth is a time of vulnerability to certain deprivations or noxious influences, adolescence, especially pubescence, must imply important physical needs. Extra food and rest for fast growth stand out as important. Because the adolescent is declaring his independence, *how to* meet his physical needs is often as problematic as knowing what he needs. Health is important at any age, but at this time, when a youngster has such a confusion of problems to cope with, it is especially helpful for him to feel well and to have maximum energy.

Illnesses

Adolescents are more free from illness than children are. A study of children from birth to 18 [34], where illness scores included both frequency and severity, showed lowest scores in the 14–18 bracket, with scores almost as low in 10–14. Greater than in any other period of childhood were the numbers of children who suffered no illnesses other than respiratory. The number of communicable diseases dropped sharply in early adolescence and continued to decrease in the later period. Most of the cases of communicable disease were of moderate severity. Accidents and surgery decreased through the 10–18 period.

Sex differences appeared in most categories. Boys exceeded girls in number of total illnesses. Boys had about three times as many gastrointestinal upsets as girls. Accidents and surgery were much alike for the sexes. Figure 14–7 shows the number of illnesses in each category for boys and girls. The differences between categories are much greater than the sex differences. Note the high frequency of respiratory difficulties as contrasted with the other types of illness.

The study quoted above dealt with illnesses. While the investigator recorded health problems not classified as illnesses, such as eye difficulties or teeth requiring dental care, those conditions are not included in the report. Certain physical conditions threaten the young person's self-concept. Acne, for example, the skin ailment so typical of the teen years, has vast psychological significance. The young person trying to build an acceptable body image suffers acutely when he beholds his pimply reflection in the mirror and when he imagines how he looks to other people. Adolescents so afflicted often spend many hours fussing and agonizing and many dollars in the search for a cure. Figure 14–8 shows the relatively enormous incidence of skin difficulties occurring in the second decade of life. Diseased teeth and tonsils, while not actually illnesses, can cause lowered resistance to disease and fatigue and possibly emotional upset.

Sensory Handicaps

The incidence of eye difficulties rises in the teens, as shown in Figure 14–9, which shows the number of eye examinations given in 9,000 families. You can see that there is a peak of eye trouble in adolescence which is not exceeded until the decade of the forties. While adolescents may not have worse vision than younger children and adults, their need for accurate eyesight is probably greater since good vision is important in academic success. Eye defects have their psychological impact, just as acne does. Many people feel that glasses spoil their appearance and adolescents feel it most keenly since their appearance is so significant. Contact lenses are a happy solution for some youngsters, but not for others, since some individuals cannot adjust to them, some cannot afford them and some deficiencies cannot be corrected by them.

Accidents

Accidents are the greatest single cause of death in the second decade. The years from 15 to 24 are the most vulnerable period, according to the Metropolitan Life Insurance Company [24]. During this age period 61 percent of deaths of boys and 39 percent of deaths of girls were caused by accidents. Motor vehicle accidents were responsible for 39 percent of the deaths of 15-to-24-year-old males and for 22 percent of deaths of females that age. Here, then, are some of the figures behind the fact so unpopular with young men, that they must pay higher insurance rates on their cars than do girls the same age.

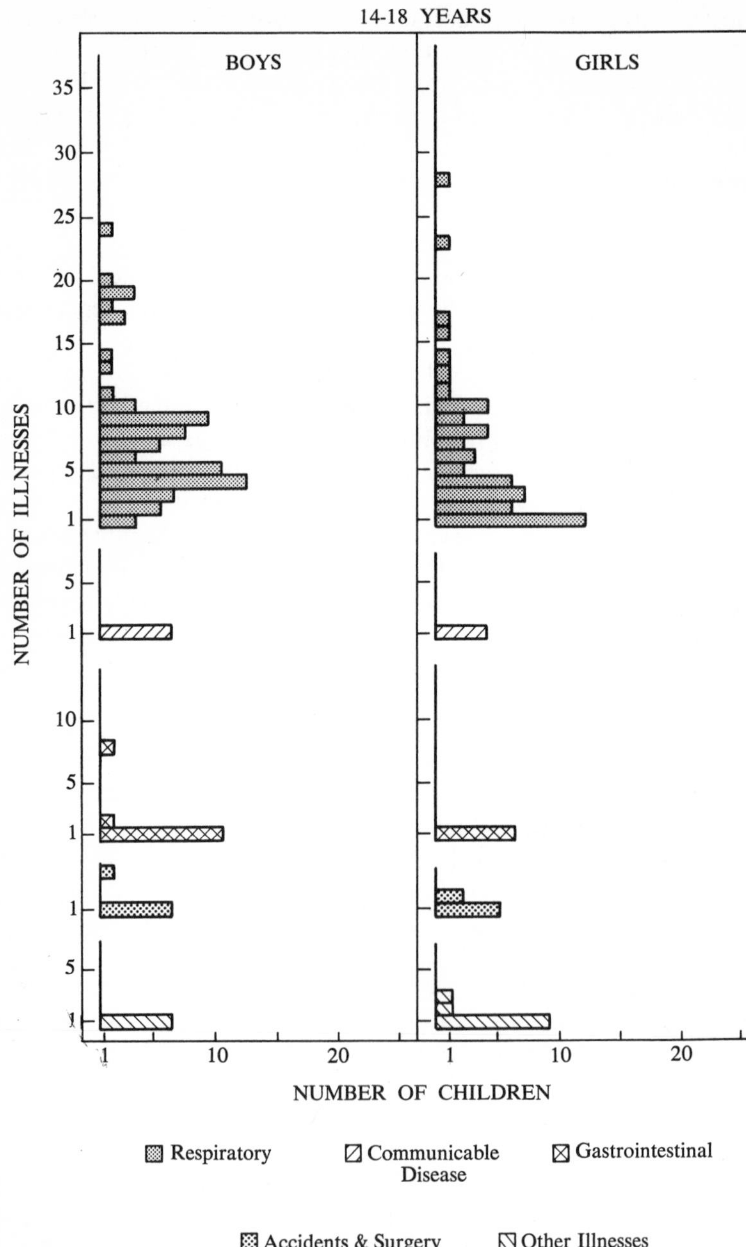

Figure 14–7. Frequency of various types of illnesses suffered by adolescents. (Reprinted by permission from I. Valadian, H. C. Stuart, and R. B. Reed, "Studies of Illnesses of Children Followed from Birth to Eighteen Years," *Monographs of The Society for Research in Child Development,* **26,** Figure 25. Copyright © 1961, The Society for Research in Child Development, Inc.)

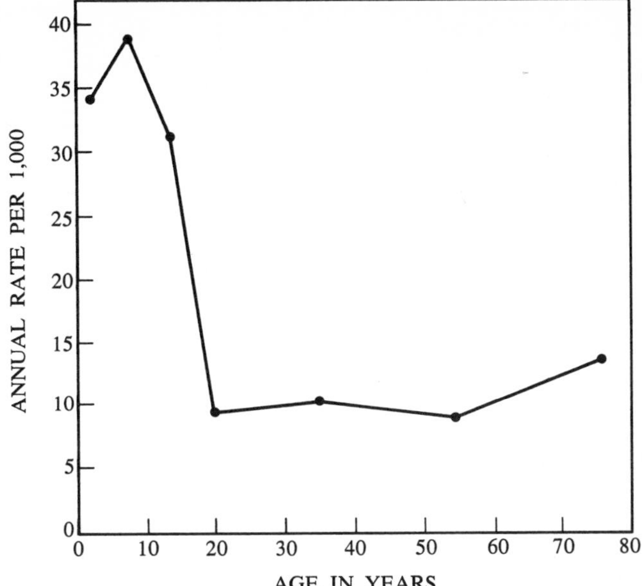

Figure 14–8. Frequency of diseases and defects of the skin. (Adapted from F. K. Shuttleworth, "The Adolescent Period," *Monographs of The Society for Research in Child Development,* **3,** Figure 181. Copyright © 1938, The Society for Research in Child Development, Inc. Used by permission.)

Other kinds of accidents and injuries are also of concern in the adolescent years. We have already mentioned that in the early part of this period, the heart may be relatively small and therefore inadequate for a strain imposed by highly competitive athletics. Rapid growth in bones, muscles, joints and tendons makes them especially vulnerable to unusual strain. The increase of strength and vigor in adolescents, especially in boys, may tempt them to over-exertion, especially if their teammates and coach egg them on and their girl friends admire from the sidelines.

Nutrition

Studies on the effects of wartime famine have shown that malnutrition in childhood delays the onset of the pubescent growth spurt [33, pp. 83–87]. The body has great recuperative powers, which result in a speed-up of growth when nutrition returns to a higher level. Tanner reports that there is little evidence as to whether malnutrition alters proportions of the human body, but says that if it does, the parts growing fastest at the time probably suffer the most.

Malnutrition does not have to be at the starvation level, however, to affect the bodies of adolescents. Evidence from the Harvard–Florence research project shows the influence of socioeconomic factors on age of menarche. In

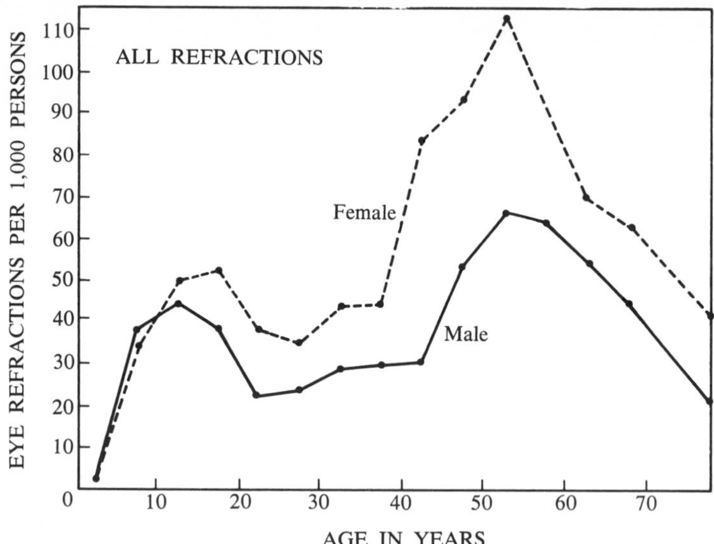

Figure 14–9. Incidence of eye refractions at each age. The peak of examinations required during the teen years is exceeded only in later adulthood. (Reprinted by permission from F. K. Shuttleworth, "The Adolescent Period," *Monographs of The Society for Research in Child Development,* **3,** Figure 217. Copyright © 1938, The Society for Research in Child Development, Inc.)

Florence, Italy, girls whose families had moved up in socioeconomic status reached menarche a year earlier than their mothers did. Girls whose families had moved down were a year later than their mothers in reaching menarche [36].

Deficiencies in any of the elements required for growth—vitamins, minerals and proteins—can have adverse effects on energy level, resistance to disease, behavior, emotions and appearance. Adolescents are all too likely to eat empty calories, foods which contain mostly sugar, starch and flavorings, and perhaps fats, such as soft drinks, pastries, potato chips and candy. If the empty-calorie foods are added to a wholesome diet, the result is too many calories and a fat adolescent. If they are substituted for it, the result is dietary deficiency. This is not to say that some empty-calorie foods cannot be eaten with impunity during the teen years. At the peak of the pubescent growth spurt, calorie needs are enormous. The average boy between 16 and 19 needs 3,600 calories, more than he has ever needed before or will again. The average girl between 13 and 15 needs 2,600 calories, an amount exceeded only by the lactating mother. These figures do not accurately indicate the caloric needs at the peak of the growth spurt, since they are derived from age groups rather than on groups based on physiological maturity. The actual number of calories needed is greater than these figures. A fast-growing boy may literally never get filled up. His stomach may be too small to hold as many calories as his body can use unless he eats at very frequent intervals, or what seems like all the time to his mother. The calories used for energy can, of course, be empty ones, since sugar and starch are converted into fuel. Obesity is a problem of nutrition as well as a problem of exercise. Many adolescents, especially girls, are bothered by real or fancied obesity. A study of teen-age girls whose heights and weights placed them in the obese channel of the Wetzel grid (see page 186) showed that they ate poorer diets and fewer calories than did the other girls in the same school [15]. These results are confirmed by other studies of obese girls [18] and boys [31]. The first study indicated that the girls lacked adequate information as to how to select adequate diets and that their parents could help, if they would, by providing a cheerful, relaxed atmosphere for meals.

Rest

For many youngsters, pubescence ushers in the desire to sleep on Saturday mornings and on other mornings, as well. Their rapid growth requires more rest than did the quiescent growth of the elementary-school years. Adolescents tend to stay up later at night than they did as children, because of pressures of school work, visiting with friends, especially over the telephone, more attention to appearance, particularly in girls, and resistance to parental control. When growth slows down, they can and do get along with less sleep than they needed as children.

Supervision of Adolescent Health

It takes the combined efforts of home, school and community to see that adolescents get even a minimum of health protection. Schools and other community agencies usually offer something in the way of screening for sensory defects and certain gross physical defects. Immunizations may be given on a community basis. The school lunch program is effective in raising the nutritional level of some youngsters, but is not generally appreciated for its potentially great contribution. A good physical education program can contribute enormously to sound health and growth. Many responsibilities are left to the home—providing regular medical and dental care, giving an adequate diet, planning for rest, seeing that clothing is not only warm enough but that it protects growth, such as bras and shoes that fit. Here, as in other areas, the adolescent's search for independence often collides with parents' duties as protectors.

MOTOR DEVELOPMENT

"One mark of childhood is a strong desire to be active. One sign of maturity is a strong inclination to sit down" [17]. Jersild's observation sums up the course of motor activity in many American adolescents. Jersild goes on to say that if maturity consists of sitting down, then girls achieve it earlier than boys. The quality and quantity of motor activity during adolescence, however, is a complex story which, even though it ends in relative quiet, adds to one's understanding of human development. A more widespread and thorough understanding of its significance could lead to improvement in the physical condition of Americans.

American Youth Compared with Others

In Chapter 10, we mentioned the Kraus–Weber test of minimum muscular fitness, by which American children and adolescents were demonstrated to be inferior to their age mates in Europe. Four years later, in 1957, over 8,000 American youngsters between 10 and 17 were examined for physical fitness on a much more thorough battery of tests and compared with over 10,000 British boys and girls [9]. Figure 14–10 shows some of the results of this comparison. British boys are consistently superior to American boys and British girls to American girls. What is more, British girls make some improvements during the teen years, while American girls make almost none. Similar results come from a Japanese study [27], which shows Japanese youth to be superior to American in endurance, strength and flexibility. Swedish children were found to have a higher work capacity (demonstrated by oxygen-intake capacity) than American children [2, 28].

Since these discoveries were made public, efforts to improve the physical condition of Americans have been considerable and have met with some success. The few American children who attended excellent fitness programs scored just as high as Europeans [11, p. 139]. Physical education research centers and laboratories have demonstrated methods of improving physical structure and function. Some of this work is reported in a monograph based on research done in the Sports-Fitness School of the University of Illinois [11]. The research proves that physical education can improve boys in physique and in specific skills, as well as in balance, flexibility, agility, strength, power and endurance. American physical education, according to the director of this research, has been particularly deficient in training for endurance, since the emphasis has been largely on play and games, with little attention to sustained exercise. Nor has there been much systematic development of strength in various sets of muscles, through exercises designed for the purpose.

Strength

Longitudinal studies on increase of strength have shown boys making gains throughout adolescence, while girls tend to taper off after pubescence. Figure 14–11 shows four measures of strength for boys and girls. Tanner points out that in all four of the boys' curves a marked spurt can be seen between ages 13 and 16 and a less definite spurt in the girls' hand grip curves between 12 and 13½. A sex difference in strength of arm thrust arises at puberty, and the small difference in arm pull increases then. Boys also show spurts in strength of back and legs and in strength per pound of body weight [11]. The pubescent growth spurt in boys is closely associated with a spurt in strength, while in girls it is not. It is probably pertinent that the increase in vital capacity which

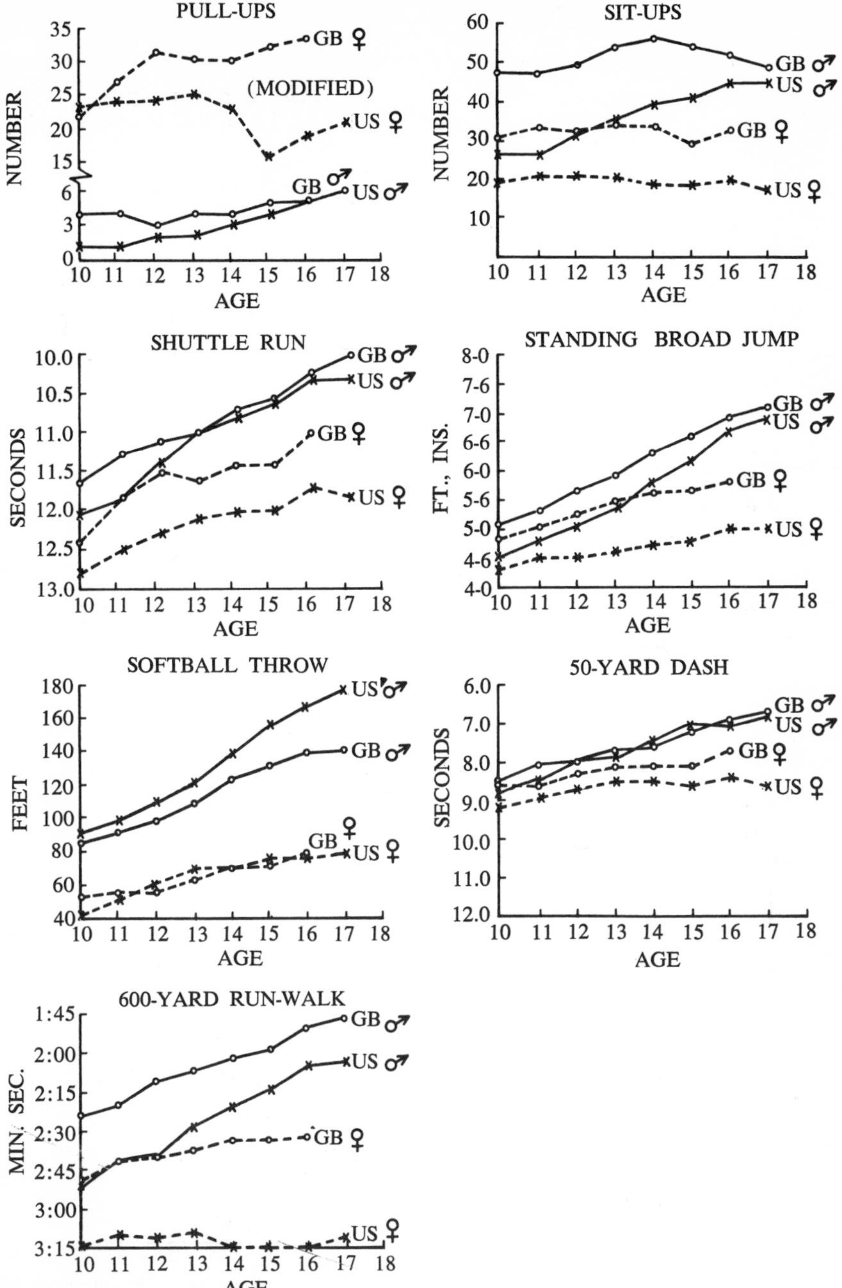

Figure 14–10. Comparisons between American and British youth on several athletic events. (Data from W. R. Campbell and R. H. Pohndorf, "Physical Fitness of British and United States Children," in *Report of Conference on Health and Fitness in the Modern World* (Chicago: Athletic Institute, 1961), pp. 8–16. Reprinted by permission from T. K. Cureton, "Improving the Physical Fitness of Youth," *Monographs of The Society for Research in Child Development,* **29,** Figure 1. Copyright © 1964, The Society for Research in Child Development, Inc.)

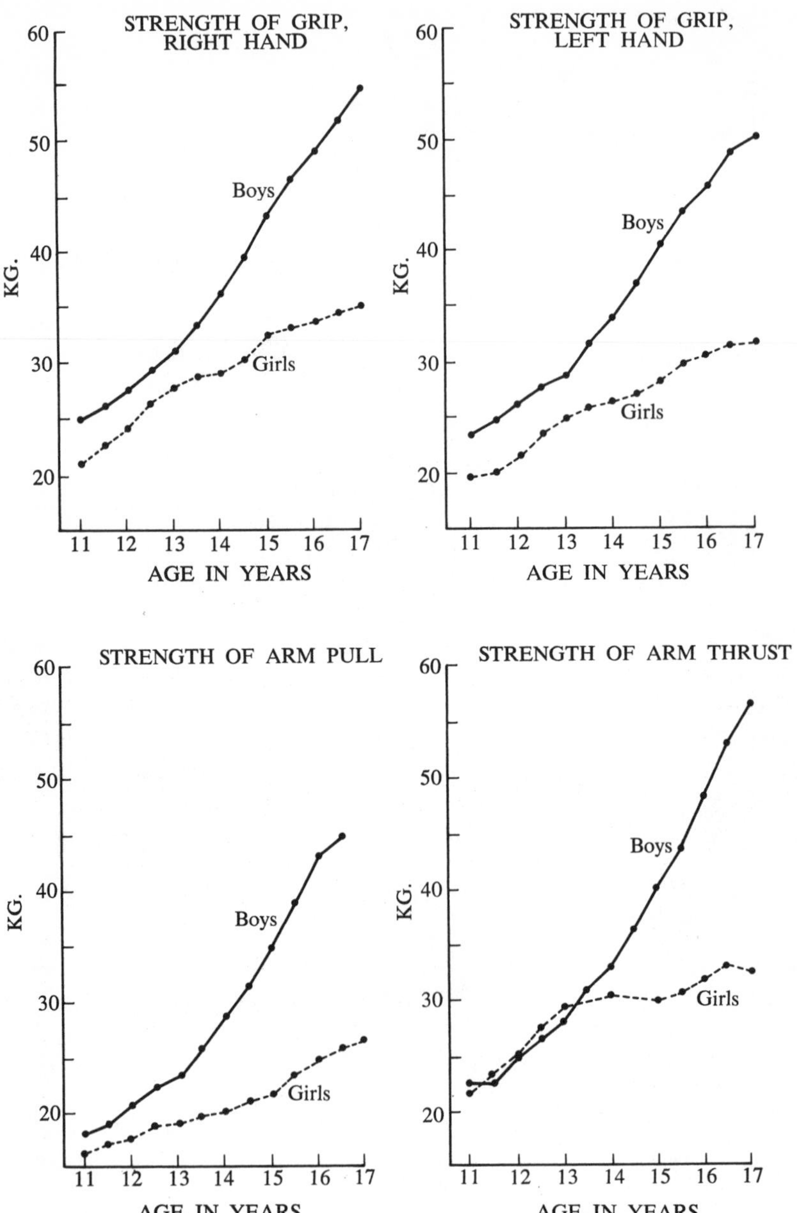

Figure 14–11. Measures of strength in boys and girls throughout adolescence. (Reprinted by permission from J. M. Tanner, *Growth at Adolescence,* 2nd edition. Oxford: Blackwell Scientific Publications Ltd., 1962. Copyright © 1962, Blackwell Scientific Publications Ltd.)

occurs in boys at this time is not matched by such an increase in girls [33, pp. 133–135]. These very real differences in strength are basic to the fact that boys excel girls in athletics during late adolescence. However, the girls' lack of increase in strength cannot be dismissed as genetic when we have the contrast of girls in other countries who do improve in strength throughout their adolescence.

Coordination

Several investigators have studied motor coordination by means of the Brace test, which may tap basic, generalized motor factors. It consists of a series of tests of agility and balance, such as jumping up, clapping feet together and landing with feet apart [12]. The Brace test was used along with other tests of basic athletic performances on 165 boys and girls, repeating them on the same subjects over a period of four years. Boys increased steadily in all measures throughout the whole period. After 14 years, girls showed a gradual decline in dash and broad jump, little if any change in distance throw and Brace test and an increase in jump and reach scores. While sex differences existed at all ages, boys gained marked superiority from 14 onward. Figure 14–12 shows the results from these tests.

ADOLESCENT AWKWARDNESS—FACT OR FANCY? Ever since it was found that boys steadily improve in the Brace test and that girls do not change for the worse, students of adolescence have thought that adolescent awkwardness might be just a myth. If the average trend is steadily toward greater balance and agility, or no less of either, how, then, can the adolescent be more awkward than the child? The answer may be that adolescents show increased self-awareness and frequent uncertainty as to how to play the new roles required of them. Indecision and lack of self-confidence rather than neuromuscular inability are reflected in jerky or obvious movements. There is still the fact that different parts of the body grow at different rates, especially the reality of feet growing long before full height is reached. Do adolescent boys trip over their feet more often than younger boys or men? The Brace test might not reveal it. (It does not.) Observations in natural settings may be the only way to reach a definite answer to such a problem!

Speed

Between the years of 7 and 13, the average boy cuts 2.4 seconds off his time for the 60-yard dash and 8.2 seconds off his time for the 600-yard run [11, pp. 19–22]. In speed involving large muscles, boys improve throughout the teen years. Girls show little or no gain in speed, when judged thus. When speed of manual tasks is measured, differences tend to be in favor of boys, but not always. Reaction time, measured by the time it takes to respond to a sound, probably reaches a maximum at 13 or 14, with little sex differences. Tests of simple eye–hand coordination usually show little improvement after 14 or 15, with boys somewhat superior. The development of these abilities is charted in Figure 14–13.

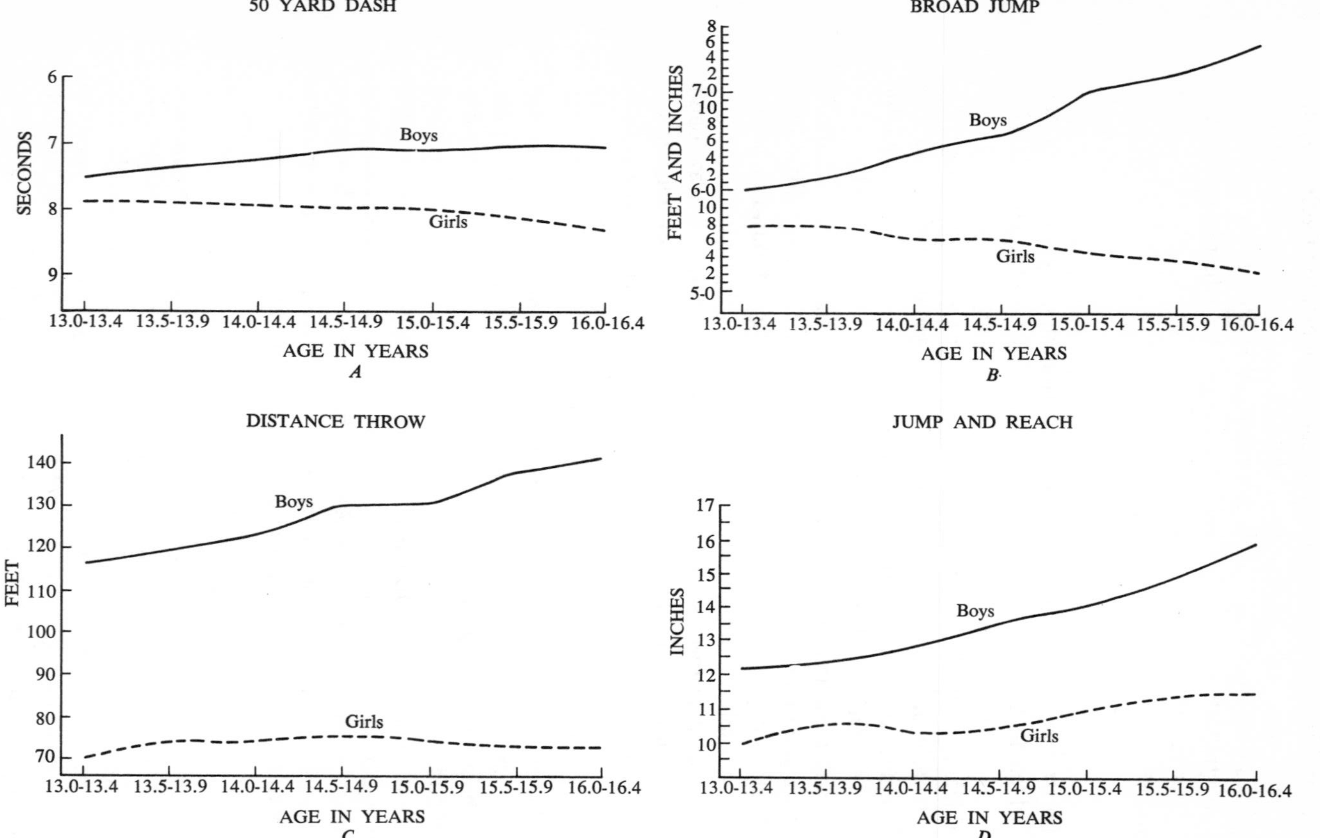

Figure 14–12. Sex differences in American youth are illustrated by these records of performance in athletic events during the years from 13 through 16. (Reprinted by permission from A. Espenschade, "Motor Performance in Adolescence," *Monographs of The Society for Research in Child Development,* **5,** Figure 8. Copyright © 1940, The Society for Research in Child Development, Inc.)

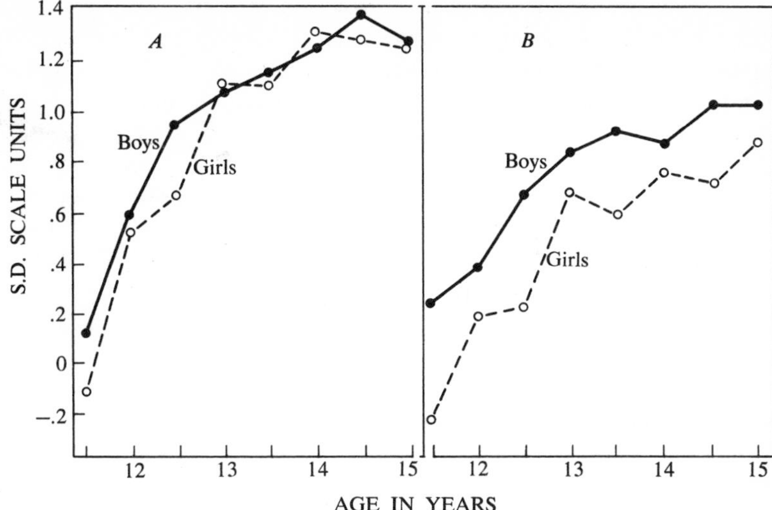

Figure 14–13. *A:* Reaction time to sound, by age and sex. *B:* Speed of eye-hand coordination. (From R. H. Seashore and H. E. Jones, "Development of Fine Motor and Mechanical Abilities," *Yearbook of the National Society for the Study of Education,* Forty-third Yearbook, Part I, p. 127. Used by permission of the National Society for the Study of Education.)

Endurance

Endurance or stamina refers to being able to keep up an activity for a considerable length of time. Endurance is developed by muscles and also by the circulatory system. For example, hopping tests the endurance of feet and leg muscles, while running a mile requires considerable endurance from the circulatory and respiratory systems, as well as from feet and leg muscles and other muscles [11, p. 90]. Analysis of cardiovascular endurance has shown that at least eight measurable factors are involved, including such conditions as velocity and force of heart ejection stroke, vagus tone, by pulse rate in the quiet state and after moderate exercise, and blood pressure adjustment to hard work. Thus stamina and its improvement can be measured not only by noting how long a boy can keep at a given activity but by making a large number of laboratory measurements.

The following methods of developing endurance have been proved successful at the University of Illinois Sports-Fitness School [11, pp. 92–93]:

1. Adjustment to the full program is expected to take several weeks, even up to eight.
2. Activities are cycled and paced to permit continuous activity over a long period, such as by alternating walking and running, by cross-country running, long cycling trips, canoe trips, long hikes and by gradually working at a faster pace.

3. Rest intervals are planned also, with provision for a mid-day rest and for a longer night sleep than boys usually take.
4. Deep breathing is taught and emphasized.
5. Careful attention to motivation includes participation and demonstration by instructors, use of standards and records and inspirational stories of athletes.
6. Nutrition is planned and supervised and moderation required. Emphasis is placed on the use of vegetables, fruits, lean meats and whole-grain cereals. Skim milk is preferred to whole milk and real fruit juices to imitation. Animal fats, chocolate, soda and fried foods are curtailed.
7. The best activities for developing circulatory-respiratory endurance include steeplechase running, continuous muscular exercise for 30 minutes, interval training (cycles of fast and slow) in running, skating, swimming, cycling, rowing and taking tests in endurance runs.

Influence of Training on Physical Fitness and Physique

Youngsters who have had good physical education show up consistently as superior to those who have had poor programs or none [11, pp. 142–145]. The Cureton Test of Motor Fitness, shown in Figure 14–14, measures balance, flexibility, agility, strength and endurance, thus sampling fitness more broadly than do the Kraus–Weber and Brace tests. Table 14–5 gives the average improvement from year to year on the Cureton Test, while Table 14–6 shows the difference in scores between pupils who had had fitness training and those who had not. Improvements after training have been shown in many different motor activities, including balancing, flexibility tests, agility tests, strength, power and endurance tests and also in such specific performances as hopping, dipping, rope skipping and chinning [11].

TABLE 14–5

Average scores for Cureton Motor Fitness Test, by age.

	Average Score	*N*	*Range*
7 years	5.40	10	3– 9
8 years	5.36	22	2–12
9 years	6.09	36	2–12
10 years	7.05	77	2–13
11 years	8.43	82	3–14
12 years	9.21	134	1–16
13 years	10.00	107	3–17
14 years	11.22	137	2–17
15 years	11.79	29	5–17
		634	

Source: Reprinted by permission from T. K. Cureton, "Improving the Physical Fitness of Youth," *Monographs of The Society for Research in Child Development*, **29**: 4, Table 46, p. 143. Copyright © 1964, The Society for Research in Child Development, Inc.

MEASURE YOUR OWN PHYSICAL FITNESS

	YOUR SHOWING	
	PASS	FAIL

BALANCE

1. Hold diver's stance (on toes, arms outstretched, eyes closed) for 20 seconds.

2. Squat and balance on hands for 10 seconds, toes off ground, knees outside elbows.

3. With one finger on floor, take 10 turns around finger, then walk a 10-foot line in 5 seconds.

FLEXIBILITY

4. Bend at waist and touch floor, keeping knees stiff. (Women touch palms.)

5. From sitting position with knees held down, bend forward slowly until forehead is 8 inches from floor.

6. Lie face downward, with back held down and hands behind neck; raise chin 18 inches from floor.

AGILITY

7. Kneel so that insteps are flat on floor; spring to feet and balance 3 seconds.

8. Spring up from floor and touch hands to toes while in air. Do 5 times.

9. Squat; extend legs backward (hands to floor); extend legs forward; turn over; return to squat; stand. Do this 6 times in 20 seconds. (Women squat, extend legs backward, return to squat, stand—6 times in 10 seconds.)

STRENGTH

10. Pick up partner your own weight and place on shoulders in 10 seconds.

11. With heels on floor, head on partner's knee and hands on hips, hold body rigid for 30 seconds.

12. Lie face downward. With arms extended—and without using elbows—press up until body balances on hands and toes. (Women do forearm press-ups and hold for 20 seconds.)

POWER

13. Do standing broad jump, the distance of your height plus one foot.

ENDURANCE

14. Do 15 full-length push-ups from floor. (Women do 30 from knees.)

15. Lie on floor, straddled by standing partner. Grab his hands and pull yourself up until your chest strikes his legs, 20 times. (Women do 10.)

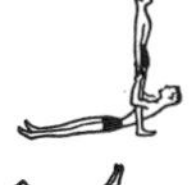

16. Sit in V-position with legs and back off floor. Hold for 60 seconds.

17. Run in place for 2 minutes at 180 steps per minute. Then hold breath for 30 seconds.

18. In succession, do 200 two-footed hops, 200 straddle jumps (jumps from I to inverted-Y position), 200 alternate-stride hops, 50 hops on each foot, and as many squat-jumps as possible.

TO HELP YOU JUDGE your own performance, here's what happens to the majority of normal young adults who take these tests at the University of Illinois' Physical Fitness Research Center:

MEN: 1—pass; 2—fail; 3—fail; 4—pass; 5—pass; 6—fail; 7—pass; 8—fail; 9—fail; 10—pass; 11—pass; 12—fail; 13—pass; 14—pass; 15—pass; 16—pass; 17—fail; 18—fail.

WOMEN: 1—pass; 2—fail; 3—pass; 4—pass; 5—pass; 6—fail; 7—pass; 8—pass; 9—pass; 10—pass; 11—fail; 12—pass; 13—fail; 14—pass; 15—fail; 16—fail; 17—fail; 18—fail.

Figure 14–14. Test of motor fitness devised by T. K. Cureton. (Reprinted by permission from T. K. Cureton, "How to Keep Your Family Young," *Redbook,* April 1955. Copyright © 1955, McCall Corporation, New York.)

TABLE 14–6

Scores of trained and untrained pupils in motor fitness tests.

	Percentage of Failures		
	New Pupils (*N* = *51*)	*Experienced Pupils* (*N* = *53*)	*% Gain*
1. Balance 1	72.5	24.5	48.0
2. Balance 2	82.4	22.6	59.8
3. Balance 3	55.0	22.6	32.4
4. Flexibility 1	13.8	9.4	4.4
5. Flexibility 2	25.5	11.3	13.2
6. Flexibility 3	21.6	5.7	15.9
7. Agility 1	53.0	13.2	39.8
8. Agility 2	78.4	20.8	57.6
9. Agility 3	100.0	67.9	32.1
10. Strength 1	27.5	5.7	21.8
11. Strength 2	25.5	7.5	18.0
12. Strength 3	23.5	15.1	8.4
13. Power 1	47.0	17.0	30.0
14. Endurance 1	45.0	3.8	41.2
15. Endurance 2	33.3	5.7	27.6
16. Endurance 3	58.8	17.0	41.8
17. Endurance 4	70.6	32.1	38.5
18. Endurance 5	56.9	15.1	41.8

Source: Reprinted by permission from T. K. Cureton, "Improving the Physical Fitness of Youth," *Monographs of The Society for Research in Child Development*, **29**:4, Table 47, p. 145.

Fat, muscles and even bones change during the course of a good fitness program. A special program for boys with underdeveloped upper bodies resulted in significant increases in biceps, chest, abdomen and shoulders [1]. Both structural and functional improvement occurred in the feet of boys who had foot defects [11]. Well-functioning feet, of course, are basic to good posture.

Relation Between Motor Coordination and Maturity

Boys' spurts in strength of grip, arm pull and arm thrust occur as part of the sequence of pubescence, in connection with the growth of the shoulder, back and pectoral muscles [33, pp. 133–137]. Other motor spurts can be similarly related to bodily growth. Early-maturing boys spurt early in strength, late-maturing boys are late in strength spurts. The peak of the strength spurt occurs about a year and a half after the peak height velocity and a year after the peak weight velocity. The menarche marks approximately the end of the girls' spurt in strength. There is evidence to show that male hormones are involved in development of male strength.

"To him that hath shall be given" holds true for the physical endowments of boys. The slow-maturing, childish-looking boy is also weak and poor in athletics, as compared with the fast maturer, who looks like a man and can throw strength as well as bulk into a competition. Even so, the boy who will put forth enough effort can improve his appearance and physical status, provided he has access to good physical education.

Significance of Motor Coordination to Adolescents

Athletic prowess is a social asset to boys, as well as a source of experiences of physical mastery and adequacy. Boys, girls and adults admire the athlete, the strong, able, masculine-looking male. While girls may get direct satisfaction from motor adequacy, they lack the added fillip of widespread social acclaim for athletic performance. There may indeed be mild approval for winning the girls' badminton tournament, but in most American high schools, such approval is mild indeed. It might work up to a higher pitch in a private girls' school, where the athletic tradition is stronger than in the public schools. In other cultures, even in such closely related ones as Canadian and English, the ideal woman is more athletic than she is in America, and the adolescent girl receives much more recognition for athletic achievement than she does here.

Even in the area of male athletics the American emphasis has been largely on the doings of a few experts which other people watch. The newer trend in physical education is, however, to encourage adolescents to learn coordinations which they will use throughout life for recreational, social and health purposes. Swimming, tennis and dancing are therefore more valuable than basketball, football and track. When a motor pattern has meaning for the person and when it fits into his cultural role, it becomes worth while to learn it well. Witness girls dancing! They dance as well as boys, if not better.

SOME RELATIONSHIPS BETWEEN PHYSICAL DEVELOPMENT AND PSYCHOLOGICAL DEVELOPMENT

Like the change from tadpole to frog or from caterpillar to butterfly, the change from child to adolescent brings an essentially new body into existence. The person has to come to terms with his new body in many ways. Updating his body image, he includes in it the revised notions of where he stops and the rest of the world begins, what his body can do, how to control it, whether it looks beautiful or ugly, good or bad to him, and how it appears to everybody else in the world. A strong sense of identity requires that the adolescent see himself as the same person who used to have a childish body.

Physical appearance is a matter of real concern to most adolescents, to younger ones more than to older ones [16]. A teenager is likely to look into a mirror and wish for something different from what he sees. Applying tape measure to bust, waist and hips, she sadly notes discrepancies from the measurements of the reigning Miss America. In the process of getting used to his new face and physique, he compares them with those of his peers and also with currently popular movie stars, TV personalities and models. Nobody wants to be too different from the peer group, an understandable attitude when identity is still shaky. During the flapper era, a full-bosomed girl often felt impelled to slouch, while in the age of the padded bra she could more easily hold herself proudly. Beauty is defined variously in different ages. So are masculine and feminine appearance. But whatever the current definition of a beautiful girl, that's what a girl wants to be. Likewise for a handsome, masculine man, with more emphasis on the *masculine* than on the *handsome*.

While some desired physical features can be achieved through art and science, such as blond hair and straight teeth, height and body build are stubbornly resistant to willful interference. Since a common ideal for femininity is a small, dainty body and for masculinity, a large, strong body, many girls would like to be smaller, while many boys wish they were larger [10]. Because the timing of the pubescent growth spurt plays such an important part in determining a young adolescent's size, it is evident that early maturers differ from late maturers in what influences their personality growth.

The relationship between physical maturity and personality development has been considered in several studies. One approach [19] was to contrast the experiences, behavior and attitudes of early maturers with those of late maturers. Physically accelerated boys at 17 years were found to receive general acceptance and to be treated as older, able people. They were rated as above average in physical attractiveness, grooming, matter-of-factness and relaxation. Often successful as student leaders and athletes, they showed little striving for status. The contrasting boys, maturing late, were treated more as little boys than as men. They were rated as significantly less attractive than the early maturers, but exceeded the first group in eagerness, initiative and sociability. Disadvantaged by small physical size, they apparently tried to compensate by striving for attention and status. Further study of the personalities of early and late maturers [26] yielded a picture of the former as self-confident, independent and socially capable while the latter often had negative concepts of themselves, feelings of inadequacy, rejection and dependency, and felt rebellious toward their parents.

Considering the question of effects of the timing of maturity on girls' personalities, it was surprising to find results similar to those of the study on boys [20]. Early-maturing 17-year-old girls too had more favorable concepts than did late-maturing girls, even though they must have been bigger than their classmates during early adolescence. The late maturers showed a greater need for recognition, somewhat more dependency and slightly poorer relationships with parents than did the early maturers. Apparently being closer to adulthood had outweighed the supposed disadvantage of being big in a culture where attractive females are supposed to be small.

Another approach was from the point of view of peers [13]. Girls in grades six through nine were tested to determine the effect of physical maturity on prestige. Sixth graders received high prestige ratings more frequently when they were in the same developmental phase as their classmates. That is, they had not reached menarche. In the following three grades, however, physical acceleration was an advantage in receiving prestige ratings. Here, then, is some explanation of the results of the study mentioned above, where physically accelerated 17-year-old girls had favorable self-concepts. Their peers likewise held favorable concepts of such girls.

Relationships have been found between physical characteristics and various kinds of mental functions, although usually no causal relationship between the two is made clear. For example, height and weight are correlated with intelligence [4, 30, 33]. One aspect of cognitive style seems to be related to physical development in college men and high school boys [7]. The aspect of cognitive style investigated was *automatization,* the ability to perform well on simple repetitive tasks. Various body dimensions were taken and the men rated for amount of body hair. The thickset, hairy, masculine-looking boys and men tended to do better than their opposites in tests of automatization. The strong automatizers must have had higher androgen levels than the men whose bodies were farther away from the extreme of masculinity, since androgens stimulate the development of male characteristics. This research gives no indication of whether the strong male physical characteristics cause strong automatizing or whether a more basic condition (such as a large androgen supply) is responsible for both the physical and mental characteristics.

These studies deal with only a few of the ways in which physical development can and might affect and be affected by an adolescent's attitudes toward himself and the world. The developmental factors, of course, interact with other events and conditions. For example, very creative people often have a history of a long illness during childhood (see page 554). They also have such background factors as educated mothers who pursue interests of their own, leaving children free to think their own thoughts. A child socially isolated by physical illness, surrounded by cultural opportunities, mentally and emotionally free, would understandably experiment intellectually and imaginatively. Other examples can be drawn from the area of motor coordination. The social success of a football player is legendary, while the awkward boy shrinks from the dance floor to find solace as a ham radio operator.

SUMMARY

Adolescence, the period of changing from child to adult, is physical, psychological and social. The sequence of physical changes which result in puberty (sexual maturity) takes place during pubescence. The timing and duration of pubescence varies between individuals and between the sexes, with girls, on the average, two years ahead of boys. Growth speeds up during pubescence, the peak in height velocity occurring about six months before puberty. Early maturers have a shorter, faster growth spurt than late maturers. Linear people tend to be late maturers, rounded people early maturers. The pubescent growth spurt and the developmental sequence of sexual characteristics are triggered and controlled by hormones from the pituitary, hypothalamus and gonads. The timing of puberty and its antecedent changes seems to be largely genetic, although somewhat influenced by environmental factors.

Changes in proportions occur in a predictable sequence, since different parts of the body, including the viscera, reach their peak velocities at various times during the pubescent growth spurt. Various sex differences increase, such as that of lung capacity. The primary and secondary sex characteristics develop in a sequence. Definite stages have been outlined for both sexes. Sexual feelings, especially those of boys, are heightened at puberty.

Physical needs include large amounts of food and rest, since this period is a time of rapid growth. The meeting of such needs is often inadequate because of the adolescent's insistence upon making his own decisions. Adolescents are relatively free from illness, although they suffer from many health problems, such as acne, eye troubles and diseased teeth. Accidents, especially motor vehicle accidents, cause a large proportion of the deaths and injuries during this time of life. Calorie needs are very large during adolescence. Nutritional problems include dietary deficiencies and obesity.

American children and adolescents were, and probably still are, inferior to European and Japanese in almost all tests of physical fitness. An outstanding lack in American physical education is in the area of endurance training. Good physical education has brought some youngsters up to the level of Europeans and has demonstrated methods of meeting the needs of Americans.

During the adolescent years, strength increases in all boys but tapers off in American girls. A general test of motor development showed steady increases in boys and little change in girls. While boys are superior in speed of large muscle movements, such as running, a sex difference is not clear in manual speed. Athletic prowess is a great social asset to the boy and of minor importance to the girl.

Physical and psychological growth are interrelated in many ways. Physical phenomena interact with social, intellectual and personality development. Physical appearance and adequacy are of great concern to the adolescent, since he is involved in building a sense of identity. Early maturers differ from late maturers in personality characteristics, as rated by others and as reported by boys and girls themselves. The former are more likely to have favorable self-concepts.

REFERENCES

1. Araki, C. T. The effects of medicine ball activity on the upper body development of young boys. Unpublished Master's thesis, Univer. of Illinois, 1960. Cited in Cureton [11].
2. Astrand, P. O. Experimental studies of physical working capacity in relation to sex and age. Copenhagen: Munksgard, 1952. Cited in Cureton [11].

3. Ausubel, D. P. *Theory and problems of adolescent development.* New York: Grune & Stratton, 1954.
4. Bayley, N. Individual patterns of development. *Child Devel.,* 1956, **27,** 45–74.
5. Blos, P. *On adolescence.* Glencoe, Ill.: Free Press, 1962.
6. Breckenridge, M. E., & Vincent, E. L. *Child development* (5th ed.). Philadelphia: Saunders, 1965.
7. Broverman, D. M., Broverman, I. K., Vogel, W., & Palmer, R. D. The automatization cognitive style and physical development. *Child Devel.,* 1964, **35,** 1343–1359.
8. Bullen, B. A., Monello, L. F., Cohen, H., & Mayer, J. Attitudes toward physical activity, food and family in obese and nonobese adolescent girls. *Am. J. Clin. Nutr.,* 1963, **12,** 1–11.
9. Campbell, W. R., & Pohndorf, R. H. Physical fitness of British and United States children. In *Report of conference on health and fitness in the modern world.* Chicago: Athletic Institute, 1961, pp. 8–16. Cited in Cureton [11].
10. Cobb, H. V. Role-wishes and general wishes of children and adolescents. *Child Devel.,* 1954, **25,** 161–171.
11. Cureton, T. K. Improving the physical fitness of youth. *Mono. Soc. Res. Child Devel.,* 1964, **29:**4.
12. Espenschade, A. Motor performance in adolescence. *Mono. Soc. Res. Child Devel.,* 1940, **5:**1.
13. Faust, M. S. Developmental maturity as a determinant in prestige of adolescent girls. *Child Devel.,* 1960, **31,** 173–184.
14. Garn, S. M., & Haskell, J. A. Fat thickness and developmental status in childhood and adolescence. *Am. J. Dis. Child.,* 1960, **99,** 746–751.
15. Hampton, M. C., Shapiro, L. R., & Huenemann, R. L. Helping teen-age girls improve their diets. *J. Home Econ.,* 1961, **53,** 835–838.
16. Jersild, A. T. *In search of self.* New York: Teachers College, Columbia Univer., 1953.
17. Jersild, A. T. *The psychology of adolescence.* New York: Macmillan, 1957.
18. Johnson, M. L., Burke, B. S., & Mayer, J. Relative importance of inactivity and overeating in the energy balance of obese high school girls. *Am. J. Clin. Nutr.,* 1956, **4,** 37–44.
19. Jones, M. C., & Bayley, N. Physical maturing among boys as related to behavior. *J. Educ. Psychol.,* 1950, **41,** 129–148.
20. Jones, M. C., & Mussen, P. H. Self-conceptions, motivations and interpersonal attitudes of early- and late-maturing girls. *Child Devel.,* 1958, **29,** 491–501.
21. Kinsey, A. C., Pomeroy, W. B., Martin, C. E., & Gebhard, P. H. *Sexual behavior in the human male.* Philadelphia: Saunders, 1948.
22. Kinsey, A. C., Pomeroy, W. B., Martin, C. E., & Gebhard, P. H. *Sexual behavior in the human female.* Philadelphia: Saunders, 1953.
23. Meredith, H. V. Human foot length from embryo to adult. *Human Biol.,* 1944, **16,** 207–282.
24. Metropolitan Life Insurance Company. The causes of premature death. *Stat. Bull.,* 1961, **42:**5, 9–11.
25. Montagu, M. F. A. *Adolescent sterility.* Springfield, Ill.: Charles C Thomas, 1946.

26. Mussen, P. H., & Jones, M. C. Self-conceptions, motivations and interpersonal attitudes of late- and early-maturing boys. *Child Devel.,* 1957, **28,** 243–256.
27. Noguchi, Y. A comparative study of motor fitness between Japanese and American youth. Tokyo: Ministry of Education, 1960. Cited in Cureton [11].
28. Rodahl, K., Astrand, P. O., Birkhead, N. C., Hettinger, T., Issekutz, B., Jones, D. M., & Weaver, R. Physical work capacity. *Arch. Environ. Health,* 1961, **2,** 499–510. Cited in Cureton [11].
29. Shilo, I. Seker al hathalat haveset ben benot batey hasefer birushalayim. [Survey on the age of menarche in school pupils in Jerusalem.] *Harefual,* 1960, **59,** 305–307. *Psychol. Abs.,* **37:**952.
30. Shuttleworth, F. K. The physical and mental growth of girls and boys age six to nineteen in relation to age at maximum growth. *Mono. Soc. Res. Child Devel.,* 1939, **4:**3.
31. Stefanik, P. A., Heald, P. F., & Mayer, J. Calorie intake in relation to energy output of obese and nonobese adolescent boys. *Am. J. Clin. Nutr.,* 1959, **7,** 55.
32. Tanner, J. M. *Education and physical growth.* London: Univer. of London, 1961.
33. Tanner, J. M. *Growth at adolescence* (2d ed.). Oxford: Blackwell, 1962.
34. Valadian, I., Stuart, H. C., & Reed, R. B. Studies of illnesses of children followed from birth to eighteen years. *Mono. Soc. Res. Child Devel.,* 1961, **26:**3.
35. Walter, W. G. Electroencephalographic development of children. In J. M. Tanner & B. Inhelder (Eds.), *Discussions on child development,* Vol. I. New York: International Universities, 1953.
36. Young, H. B. Biological and chronological age. Paper presented at meeting of the Society for Research in Child Development, April 12, 1963.

Intellectual Development

CHAPTER 15

Psychological growth is just as dramatic as physical growth at the beginning of adolescence. Between 12 and 14 years, on the average, thought processes are reorganized on a higher level, making the adolescent as different from the school-age child as the school-age child is different from the preschool child. The new level of thinking, formal thought, is not the automatic result of accumulated years any more than the transition from sensorimotor to preoperational intelligence is automatic. New schemas result from the child's using what he has already to interact with the environment. His achievements depend upon his own resources and what the environment offers. Some adolescents, therefore, go farther than others in building and using the structures of formal thought. Some individuals never achieve formal thought.

CHARACTERISTICS OF ADOLESCENT THINKING

Increased Mobility and Flexibility

Each new stage in thinking brings greater freedom and stronger control in intellectual operations. The stage of formal thinking carries the greatest mobility of all the stages. The infant is confined to his own sensory perceptions and motor acts of the immediate present. The preschool child uses words and symbols to represent actions and perceptions, thus speeding up his dealings with the world, but he is still confined largely to individual objects and events. Egocentric in that he is tied to one perception or another, his thought is not free and mobile enough to weigh and balance various aspects of an experience with each other and with other knowledge. The school-age child's thought is free in that he can delay response while considering and judging much information. He can also think and act and then think it undone, since thought is reversible at this age. The adolescent excels him, however, in freedom of thought.

Flexibility and control of intellectual operations increased between ages 12 and 14 in an experiment on concept formation [26]. Each problem, consisting of a series of slides, required an answer of a single attribute, such as *black* or *cross*. It was possible to get the right answer after the first four slides. Each successive cycle of three slides gave enough information for solution. Results showed significant differences between the 12-year-olds and 14-year-olds, but not between the 14-year-olds and 16-year-olds. The 12-year-olds gave answers not in accord with the immediately previous slide, showing that they were less efficient than the older subjects in dealing with information given directly. The younger subjects were less able to remember their previous guesses in order to check them with current information. They were less able to maintain their guesses when current information confirmed them and less able to change their guesses when current information did not confirm them. The older subjects, both 14-year-olds and 16-year-olds, more readily held or changed their guesses in the light of all previous information.

Another aspect of mobility of thought in adolescence is that thinking can go on without using real objects or events. In contrast, the school-age child thinks about things even when he reasons. The adolescent can range over the universe in time and space, entertaining concepts which cannot be tied to concrete experience, such as infinity.

Consideration of What Is Possible

"The adolescent is the person who commits himself to possibilities . . . who begins to build 'systems' or 'theories' in the largest sense of the term" [10, p. 339]. The child is concerned with *what is,* the adolescent with *what is plus what could be.* The relationship between the real and the possible is new in adolescent thinking, as compared with childish thinking. In formal thinking, the individual uses a system to discover all possible combinations or relationships and to make sure that he *has* found them all. He uses a system to establish a rule, from which he can make predictions. By 14 or 15, according to Inhelder and Piaget, the adolescent can use the combinatorial system. That is, he varies one factor at a time, keeping all other things equal, and determines the effect of one factor. This method, of course, is the essence of research.

The following account of one of Piaget's experiments [4] demonstrates the difference between a 7-year-old and a 13-year-old in tackling a problem in chemistry. The younger child's approach was relatively unsystematized. He took the perceptually salient element and combined it successively with each of the other elements. The older child set about systematically to try all possible combinations of elements.*

> In experiment I, the child is given four similar flasks containing colorless, ordorless liquids which are perceptually identical. We number them: (1) diluted

* From Flavell's *The Developmental Psychology of Jean Piaget,* Copyright 1963, D. Van Nostrand Company, Inc., Princeton, N.J. Reprinted by permission.

> sulphuric acid; (2) water; (3) oxygenated water; (4) thiosulphate; we add a bottle (with a dropper) which we call *g*; it contains potassium iodide. It is known that oxygenated water oxidizes potassium iodide in an acid medium. Thus mixture $(1 + 3 + g)$ will yield a yellow color. The water (2) is neutral, so that adding it will not change the color, whereas the thiosulphate (4) will bleach the mixture $(1 + 3 + g)$. The experimenter presents to the subject two glasses, one containing $1 + 3$, the other containing 2. In front of the subject, he pours several drops of *g* in each of the two glasses and notes the different reactions. Then the subject is asked simply to reproduce the color yellow, using flasks 1, 2, 3, 4 and *g* as he wishes (Inhelder and Piaget, 1958, pp. 108–109).

The two behavior protocols which follow illustrate the kinds of concrete formal differences we have been discussing:

> Ren (7;1) tries $4 \times g$, then $2 \times g$, and $3 \times g$: *"I think I did everything . . . I tried them all."*—"What else could you have done?"—*"I don't know."* We give him the glasses again: he repeats $1 \times g$, etc.—"You took each bottle separately. What else could you have done?"—*"Take two bottles at the same time"* [he tries $1 \times 4 \times g$, then $2 \times 3 \times g$, thus failing to cross over between the two sets (of bottles), for example, 1×2, 1×3, 2×4, and 3×4].—When we suggest that he add others, he puts $1 \times g$ in the glass already containing 2×3 which results in the appearance of the color: "Try to make the color again."—*"Do I put in two or three?* [he tries with $2 \times 4 \times g$, then adds 3, then tries it with $1 \times 4 \times 2 \times g$]. *No, I don't remember any more,"* etc. (*ibid.*, p. 111).

> Cha (13;0): *"You have to try with all the bottles. I'll begin with the one at the end* [from 1 to 4 with *g*]. *It doesn't work any more. Maybe you have to mix them* [he tries $1 \times 2 \times g$, then $1 \times 3 \times g$]. *It turned yellow. But are there other solutions? I'll try* [$1 \times 4 \times g$; $2 \times 3 \times g$; $2 \times 4 \times g$; $3 \times 4 \times g$; with the two preceding combinations this gives the six two-by-two combinations systematically]. *It doesn't work. It only works with"* [$1 \times 3 \times g$].—"Yes, and what about 2 and 4?"—*"2 and 4 don't make any color together. They are negative. Perhaps you could add 4 in $1 \times 3 \times$ g to see if it would cancel out the color* [he does this]. *Liquid 4 cancels it all. You'd have to see if 2 has the same influence* [he tries it]. *No, so 2 and 4 are not alike, for 4 acts on 1×3 and 2 does not."*—"What is there in 2 and 4?"—*"In 4 certainly water. No, the opposite, in 2 certainly water since it doesn't act on the liquids; that makes things clearer."*—"And if I were to tell you that 4 is water?"—*"If this liquid 4 is water, when you put it with 1×3 it wouldn't completely prevent the yellow from forming. It isn't water, it's something harmful"* (*ibid.*, p. 117).

Sticking to the Premises in Solving a Problem in Logic

Formal thought involves starting with what is given, neither adding to it nor substracting from it, and reasoning with that information. For example:

> Blonde hair turns green on St. Patrick's Day.
> Bertha has colored her hair blonde.
> It will turn green on St. Patrick's Day.

When asked if the last statement is true, the person employing formal thought would say *yes*. The person not thinking formally would probably say, "Blonde hair does not turn green on St. Patrick's Day. I've never seen it happen," or perhaps, "Bertha's wouldn't turn green, anyway, because it isn't really blonde." Piaget [16] places the change to formal thinking at around 11 or 12. Below 12, he says, children rarely solve this problem:

Edith is fairer than Susan.
Edith is darker than Lily.
Who is the darkest of the three?

Until then, they give such answers as, "Edith and Susan are fair, Edith and Lily are dark; therefore Lily is darkest, Susan is fairest and Edith in between."

In her study of children's thinking, Donaldson [2] found that between 12 and 14, children increased sharply in being able and willing to accept the given conditions and to reason within them, but even the sharp increase did not mean that a child *always* reasoned formally. She tells of Robin, when faced with this problem:

> Five boys, Jack, Dick, James, Bob and Tom go to five different schools in the same town. The schools are called North School, South School, East School, West School and Central School.
> Jack does not go to North, South or Central School.
> Dick goes to West School.
> Bob does not go to North or Central School.
> Tom has never been inside Central School.
> What school does Jack go to? What school does Bob go to?
> What school does James go to?
> What school does Tom go to?

Robin eliminated North, South and Central to deduce that Jack went to East or West. He then apparently could not see how to combine the negative information about Jack with the positive statement about Dick. "You would have to find out the district he was in," Robin suggested. Unable to deal with the problem as stated, he added his own experience. He knew that children usually went to schools near their own homes and so pulled in this information with disregard for the premises as given. Donaldson says that difficulty in solving a problem increases the tendency to ignore premises.

An Abstract Attitude

Formal thinking requires strict control of thought. Similar to the child's achievement of considering more than one perception before acting, but much more complex, the adolescent's achievement includes: keeping himself from being distracted by irrelevant thoughts, taking account of all premises or pertinent information, holding all aspects in mind while considering one, organizing information, relating it and reflecting on all aspects of the situation before concluding. The experiment previously quoted in order to show increased flexibility between 12 and 14 years also shows increased ability to control thought [26].

One particular facet of the abstract attitude which distinguishes the stage of concrete operations from formal operations is this: the adolescent can think about his own thinking; the child cannot. Here, then, is another step away from egocentrism and toward mobility of thought, to be able to stand off and reflect upon one's own intellectual activity. This is to be truly self-conscious, a complex, differentiated being.

Prevalence of Formal or Abstract Thinking

Nobody performs constantly at his highest level. An adolescent who is capable of formal thought does not apply it at all times and in all places.

Even though a person can think logically, there is no guarantee that he will do so. Grandparents notoriously stray from the facts when describing their grandchildren. An overweight person is all too likely to draw unwarranted conclusions about why his diet did not work. A study of thinking in adults [25] demonstrated flights from logic among a group of people who might be expected to respect premises more than the average person. The subjects were professors and other highly educated men. They were asked to draw conclusions from a set of statements and to discuss the compatibility of the statements. The answers revealed many instances of men telling what they thought about the statements themselves. The tendency to stray from the premises increased in men over 35 years of age, suggesting that this aspect of logical thinking is not stable after being established.

Abstract thinking is not achieved in all areas by all adolescents. For example, an investigation [3] of concepts of mass, weight and volume in American high school students showed that not all of the subjects had abstract concepts of volume. Although the test was similar to Piaget's, using the clay ball and sausage (as described in Chapter 11), it was given as a group test instead of as an individual test. After testing for conservation of mass and weight, the experimenter showed the two balls of clay, explaining that they were identical in volume, which meant, he said, that they took up the same room or space. After rolling one into a sausage, he asked if they still had the same volume, still took up the same amount of room or space, and also what would happen if the two pieces of clay were put into identical glasses of water. At age 11–12, only 27 percent succeeded, and for the total group of high school students, only 47 percent succeeded. (Of these significantly more were boys). An example of an unsuccessful subject is the 16-year-old girl who wrote that mass and weight were conserved because nothing was taken away or added, but in regard to volume she wrote, "The molecules may be more compressed in one object (the ball) than in the other (the sausage); although it (the sausage) has the same number of molecules and the same weight, its volume is not the same."

Two points of interest concern this study. First, an abstract concept, as shown by conservation, is not an all-or-none achievement but is easier or harder to achieve according to the way it is presented. Second, it is noteworthy that only about half of the high school students achieved a highly abstract concept of volume. Speculating on why this was so, the author used Piaget's ideas on roles as a way of explaining it. Interest in and effort toward developing abstract concepts probably depends upon how much the adolescent feels he needs these ways of thinking. The role he hopes to play as an adult, therefore, affects the mental structure he builds. The college-bound youngster, especially if headed for science and mathematics, will probably seek and find more abstract concepts than the one who plans to tend store or keep house.

Limitations of Adolescent Thinking

Each age and stage has its own way of being constricted in thinking. While the adolescent is freer intellectually than the child, he still has his limits. He tends to have grand ideas about how society should be improved, which he fuses vaguely with his own plans for the future. He does not distinguish between his own point of view as a person organizing his future, and the point of view of the social group to which he belongs [19, pp. 343–345].

The mobility of thought achieved in the formal period is what empowers the adolescent to think of many possibilities for his own future and for transforming society. Instead of being tied to the concrete aspects of reality, to *what is,* he can soar out into the realm of the possible. Thus an adolescent is able to fuse (or confuse) two viewpoints *because* a new level of thinking has been achieved. The confusion disappears gradually as the young person assumes adult roles, especially the work role in a real job. When he meets the realities of dealing with the society which he has considered reforming, he learns the difference between what he can actually do, what he wishes could happen and what society wants.

This special kind of adolescent thinking is very enduring in Western culture. Adults expect young people to be idealistic and impractical in their dreams of remaking the world. There is general belief that this type of thought has value for both the adolescent and society, in opening up possibilities for his future development and for social innovations.

Self-cognition

The growth of thought and language during adolescence facilitates a self-awareness which is not possible for the child. The mobility and flexibility of thought allows the adolescent to stand off and look at himself as a person. He can consider himself as a physical specimen, as a person-among-persons, as an intellectual being or as a person in any one of the numerous roles he plays —son, friend, sweetheart, student, and so on. He sees himself as a person-in-relation.

The discovery of oneself, as a person to be thought about objectively, may come rather suddenly. A psychiatrist's study of Vassar girls [13] showed a crisis of self-discovery to be common between the years of 15 and 18. A crisis of independence was often closely related to the crisis of self-discovery. The former had to do with emancipation from parents and getting established in adult roles, the latter with revelations about identity. Often involved were feelings about parents, siblings, peers, self and sexuality. One girl likened her self-discovery to the appearance of a third eye, with which she could see herself. Another could remember not thinking about herself in this way and then becoming able to do so when she was in junior high school. The girls showed an urgency to grow psychologically and made rapid progress in solving their problems.

Self-cognition makes it possible for the adolescent to see himself as continuous with the child he once was, how he differs and how he is the same. He can see his continuity with the adult that he is becoming. He can look at himself in the ways in which other people and the community see him. Integrating all of this informaiton and all of these points of view, he strengthens his sense of identity. At the same time, he begins to grow beyond the limits of adolescent thinking as he differentiates between his own plans and hopes and those of his social group.

LANGUAGE DEVELOPMENT

Used for both communication and thinking, language power expands with growth of vocabulary, facility in expression and understanding, elaboration of concepts and adoption of the symbolic organization which the culture offers.

Increase in Vocabulary

The number of words understood far exceeds the number used in speech. When children were given a recognition vocabulary test, the average number of words understood in grade one was 23,700, with a range from 6,000 to 48,000, and in grade 12, 80,300, with a range from 36,700 to 136,500. Figure 15–1 shows results of this study for grades two through 11, indicating the steady rise in number of words understood. In a study which dealt with university students, their recognition vocabulary was estimated at 156,000 words [18].

To figure out how many words an adolescent actually uses is an almost impossible task. An estimate of the average English child's vocabulary at age 14 is between 8,000 and 10,000 words, a number similar to estimates made for American children [24]. Between 7 and 14, the English child is judged to increase his vocabulary by about 700 words a year. The increase from 14 to 20 averages about 10,000 words, resulting in an adult vocabulary of 18,000 to 20,000 words.

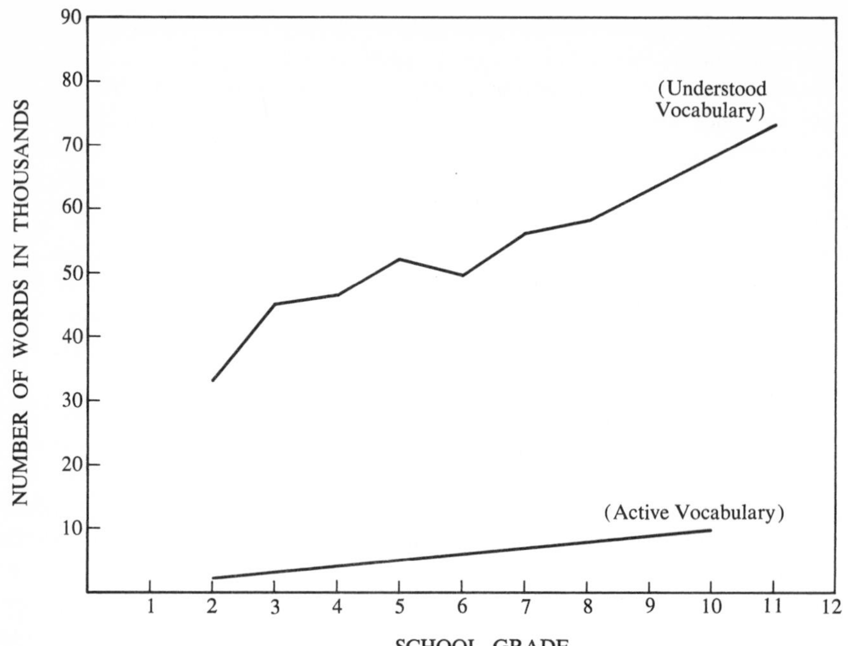

Figure 15–1. Average sizes of understood vocabulary and estimates of active vocabulary at various ages. (Adapted from M. K. Smith, "Measurement of the Size of General English Vocabulary Through the Elementary Grades and High School," *Genetic Psychology Monograph,* **24,** 311–345. Copyright © 1941, The Journal Press, Inc. Used by permission. Also from A. F. Watts, *The Language and Mental Development of Children.* London: Harrap, 1944.)

Relation of Language to Thinking

Through language, experience is put into symbolic form, in which it can be manipulated and processed by methods which other people use. The individual gets from his social group these methods of dealing with his experience. He gets them through the use of language, and he uses language to check back on his experiences, their results and meanings. While most people are capable of taking methods of thinking from their culture, few contribute new methods to their fellow men. For example, many students are capable of understanding and using calculus, but few will invent a comparable method of organizing data.

The relationship between thought and speech which adolescents achieve includes three functions: external speech, inner speech and thought, according to Vygotsky, the Russian authority on thought and language. External speech is usually interwoven with thought although it can occur without thought. Inner speech, derived from both external speech and thought, can be simply silent reciting, but rarely is just that. It can be largely thinking in pure meanings, but is not just that. "It is a dynamic, shifting, unstable thing, fluttering between word and thought . . ." [23, p. 149].

Thought itself does not have to be put into words. Sometimes a thought cannot be put into words. There are no units of thought, unlike speech, which has words as units. A thought is global, present at one time, but to be expressed in speech, it has to be developed in a succession of words. Vygotsky has likened a thought to a cloud shedding words. Words rarely express the whole thought, since a thought has a feeling and willing part to it. These subtle aspects are communicated somewhat through words, but largely through gesture, intonation and context.

CREATIVITY

Just as inner speech flutters between word and thought, so does thought itself shift and flutter between controlled thinking and fantasy or imaginative thinking. Having greater control over his intellectual processes, the adolescent can move more rapidly and easily between purposeful thinking and fantasy. Unlike the preschool child who loses himself in a dramatic role, the adolescent can imagine himself into a role and then stand off to observe himself in it.

Adolescence sees a resurgency of creativity in many forms. While creativity is the breath of life to the preschool child, the school age is concerned with industry, duty and accomplishment, with matters of fact, with learning what reality is and how to cope with it. While recognizing that all creative activities bring satisfaction, development and personality integration, we are here particularly concerned with creative thinking and production.

Creative Thinking

Creative thinking produces new, original and unusual ideas, products and solutions. One way of judging creativity is to measure what a person has produced and to compare it with what others have done. One might, for example —as did one investigator [12]—identity creative architects by asking for nominations and judgments from professors of architecture, editors of architectural journals and architects themselves. To measure creative thinking in children and adolescents is quite another problem, since practically none of them have produced ideas that can be rated in the work world. Consequently, psychologists have turned to tests as a method of measuring creativity. For many years, cognitive functioning was measured by standardized intelligence tests and the results taken as a measure of what the child could do. Some very creative people did not measure unusually high on the tests, however, and some people who measured very high did not produce anything original or remarkable. From a series of studies where both IQ and creativity were measured in large numbers of children, Torrance [20] concludes, "Whatever the measure of intelligence used, we would miss about 67 percent of the upper

20 percent on creativity if we were to rely upon the IQ metric alone for selecting the top 20 percent as a gifted group for any purpose."

Flexibility of thinking is generally thought to have a great deal to do with creativity. It is logical that new productions would come from an individual who can easily tap a variety of experience and then combine it in many fresh and different ways, shifting easily from one class to another. Guilford has suggested that uncreative people, who think rigidly and routinely, suffer from "hardening of the categories" [9]. Guilford distinguishes divergent thinking from convergent thinking. The first produces new answers, selecting them from an indefinite number of answers which might fit; the second finds the one right answer. Although much of creative thinking is divergent, some convergent thinking is necessary, too. Sometimes in the course of producing an original solution, one has to ask and answer a question which has only one right answer. Factors in divergent verbal thinking include fluency, flexibility and elaboration. Fluency includes easy recall of information, words that fit certain classes, words or phrases that make certain relationships (such as opposites) and producing connected discourse in phrases or sentences. One type of flexibility, called adaptive flexibility, involves turning old interpretations into new ones, such as thinking up a number of clever titles. For example, a clever title for "The Fox and the Grapes" was "The Fox Griped About the Grapes." Elaboration means building up or rounding out what is given.

The flexibility, fluency and elaboration factors just mentioned had to do with verbal information. Other parallel factors, according to Guilford, pertain to visual and symbolic information. Some people are creative verbally, others artistically and still others mathematically.

Another characteristic associated with originality is independence of judgment [23]. College students were tested for readiness to yield to group pressure in abandoning evidence from their own senses. Those who yielded most easily were compared with those who stuck most firmly to their judgments. The latter scored significantly higher on tests of originality.

Testing Creativity

Guilford and others have devised a goodly number of tests of creativity. What results from testing a person for creativity is more vague, however, than the results of a conventional intelligence test [19]. It is difficult, if not impossible, to find a general creativity factor. Although research on creativity is in a preliminary, exploratory stage, it is full of promise.

An example of a test of originality comes from the study [1] in which this characteristic was shown to be associated with independence of judgment. The answers of the more original subjects are given:

1. I like to fool around with new ideas, even if they turn out later to be a total waste of time. (True)
2. The best theory is the one that has the best practical applications. (False)

3. Some of my friends think that my ideas are impractical, if not a bit wild. (True)
4. The unfinished and the imperfect often have greater appeal for me than the completed and the polished. (True)
5. I must admit that I would find it hard to have for a close friend a person whose manners or appearance made him somewhat repulsive, no matter how brilliant or kind he might be. (False)
6. A person should not probe too deeply into his own and other people's feelings but take things as they are. (False)
7. Young people sometimes get rebellious ideas, but as they grow up, they ought to get over them and settle down. (False)
8. Perfect balance is the essence of all good composition. (False)

These questions, and the answers to them, give some idea of the characteristics of the students who were the most original. The tests which follow will give further insight into some of the characteristics investigators are seeking when they study creativity. These tests are selected from those used in a project at the University of Minnesota, where tests were applied throughout the age range from kindergarten through college [20].

1. *Nonverbal tasks.* Incomplete figures, picture construction, circles and squares, creative design. For the picture construction test, the subject is given a blank piece of paper and a piece of glued, colored paper in the shape of a triangle or a curved jelly bean. He is told to glue the shape wherever he wants on the paper and to add lines to it with a pencil to make a picture that nobody else will think of making. He is to keep adding to it and then to think of a name for it. The time limit is 10 minutes. Responses are scored for originality, elaboration, sensitivity, communication and activity.
2. *Verbal tasks using non-verbal stimuli.* Ask-and-Guess test, product-improvement tasks, unusual uses test. For the product-improvement test, the child is given a toy (a nurse kit, fire truck, toy dog and toy monkey have been used) and asked to think of clever, interesting and unusual ways of changing the toy so that boys and girls will have more fun playing with it. Scoring included measures of ideational fluency (a count of all responses), flexibility (number of approaches used), originality (how seldom response occurred) and "inventivlevel."*
3. *Verbal tasks using verbal stimuli.* Unusual uses, impossibilities, consequences, just purpose, situations, common problems, improvements. In the first of these, subjects were to think of unusual uses of tin cans, the cleverest and most interesting they could think of. Responses are scored for fluency, flexibility and originality.

* The criteria used by the U.S. Patent Office: a stride forward, newness, challenging and thought-provoking.

Age-Level Differences

Using the Ask-and-Guess test, Torrance [20] shows development from first grade to adult. (See Figure 15–2.) In this test, the subject must look at a picture and ask questions about it which cannot be answered by looking at it. (The pictures were mostly from Mother Goose and included *Ding Dong Bell* and *Little Boy Blue.*) Then the subject is asked to make guesses about the causes and results of the behavior portrayed. From the Ask-and-Guess test and others which he used on 70 to 200 children at each educational level, he found a general pattern of development. Creative thinking increased steadily from the first through the third grade. With one exception, there was a sharp decrease between third and fourth grades, and then an upswing toward adulthood. Other studies likewise show that a slump in imaginative activity has frequently been found during the middle school years. In terms of Erikson's

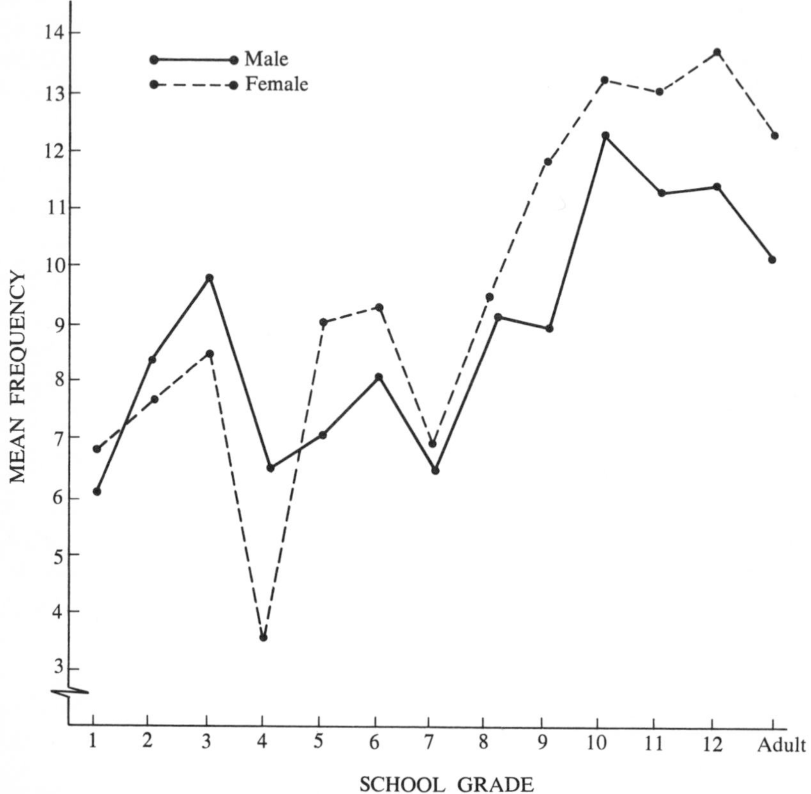

Figure 15–2. Increases and decreases in creative thinking, as measured by the *Ask* part of the *Ask-and-Guess* test. (Reprinted by permission from E. P. Torrance, "Factors Affecting Creative Thinking in Children: An Interim Report." *Merrill-Palmer Quarterly,* **7,** 3, 171–180. Copyright © 1961, The Merrill-Palmer Institute.)

theory of personality development it seems very understandable that the child should decrease his creative thinking while he strives to master the rules, facts and basic techniques of his culture.

Sex Role and Creativity

Nobody needs research studies to prove that the great creative achievements in science and the arts have been made chiefly by men, not by women. In Chapter 11, evidence was quoted to show that boys are given more experiences that promote independent, analytic thinking and that creative behavior is probably related to this kind of thinking. Overemphasis on conforming to sex role depresses creativity in both sexes and creates serious problems of adjustment [21, pp. 111–114]. Creative behavior requires both sensitivity and independence. Sensitivity is feminine and independence masculine, according to cultural definitions of sex role. Therefore, the creative boy is likely to seem feminine and the creative girl masculine. In his studies on creative children, Torrance finds children who sacrifice their creativity in order to play the sex roles expected of them. For instance, on the test requiring thinking of ways to improve a nurse's kit, some boys refused to try, saying: "I'm a boy. I don't play with things like that."

A Comparison of High IQ and High Creativity

Getzels and Jackson [5, 6, 7] did a series of studies using a group of subjects with very high IQ's but not-so-high creativity scores and a group with high creativity and not-so-high IQ's. They were drawn from the total population of one high school of 449. The high IQ's were the top 20 percent in IQ but below the top 20 percent on the tests of creativity. Their average IQ was 150. The High Creatives were the top 20 percent on the creativity test but below the top 20 percent in IQ. Their average IQ was 127. Thus there was a difference of 23 IQ points in the averages of the two groups. A remarkable finding was that the two groups, as measured by standard school achievement tests, were equally superior to the other students in the school. Since the mean IQ of both groups combined was 132, perhaps their equally superior achievement was not so remarkable after all. Probably everyone had a sufficiently high IQ to enable him to cope quite easily with the academic demands placed on him.

In intellectual functioning, the two groups were very different. For example, in stories, the High Creatives made significantly greater use of stimulus-free themes, unexpected endings, humor and playfulness. In defining values for themselves, the Creatives were rebellious or autonomous in respect to adult standards, while the High IQ's were compliant or realistic. Table 15–1 shows how the Creatives took little interest in adopting traits which they believed teachers liked. The High IQ's, in contrast, went along with what they thought would bring success and teacher approval. In both cognitive and social problems, the two groups were consistent. The Creatives produced new forms,

TABLE 15–1

Correlations showing differences in conformity between High IQ's and High Creatives.

Components of Correlation	*Subject*	
	IQ	*Creative*
Personal traits believed predictive of success and personal traits believed favored by teachers	.62	.59
Personal traits preferred for oneself and personal traits believed predictive of adult success	.81	.10
Personal traits preferred for oneself and personal traits believed favored by teachers.	.67	−.25

Source: Reprinted by permission from J. W. Getzels and P. W. Jackson, "Occupational Choice and Cognitive Functioning: Career Aspirations of Highly Intelligent and Highly Creative Adolescents," *Journal of Abnormal and Social Psychology,* **61**: 1, Table 2, p. 122. Copyright © 1960, American Psychological Association.

taking the risk of joining elements ordinarily considered independent and even inappropriate. The High IQ's focused on the usual, the standardized, the accepted and the socially acceptable answers.

Perhaps the most outstanding cognitive difference between the two groups was in their use of humor and their evaluation of it. All the students were asked to rank eight qualities in which they would like to be outstanding and to rank the qualities also in order of what they thought teachers preferred in students. The Creatives ranked sense of humor second, while the High IQ's ranked it eighth. Both groups gave it rank 7 for what they thought teachers liked. The humor in their stories showed the swiftness, freedom and flexibility of thought which is associated with high levels of cognitive development. The contrasting pictures on this page and the following examples of stories from Getzels and Jackson [5] show the contrast between the two groups in sense of humor. (See Figure 15–3.)

The picture stimulus was one usually seen as a man sitting in an airplane in a reclining seat.

The High IQ subject:

Mr. Smith is on his way home from a successful business trip. He is very happy and he is thinking about his wonderful family and how glad he will be to see them again. He can picture it, about an hour from now, his plane landing at the airport and Mrs. Smith and their three children all there welcoming him home again.

The High Creative subject:

This man is flying back from Reno where he has just won a divorce from his wife. He couldn't stand to live with her any more, he told the judge, because she wore so much cold cream on her face at night that her head would skid across the pillow and hit him in the head. He is now contemplating a new skidproof face cream.

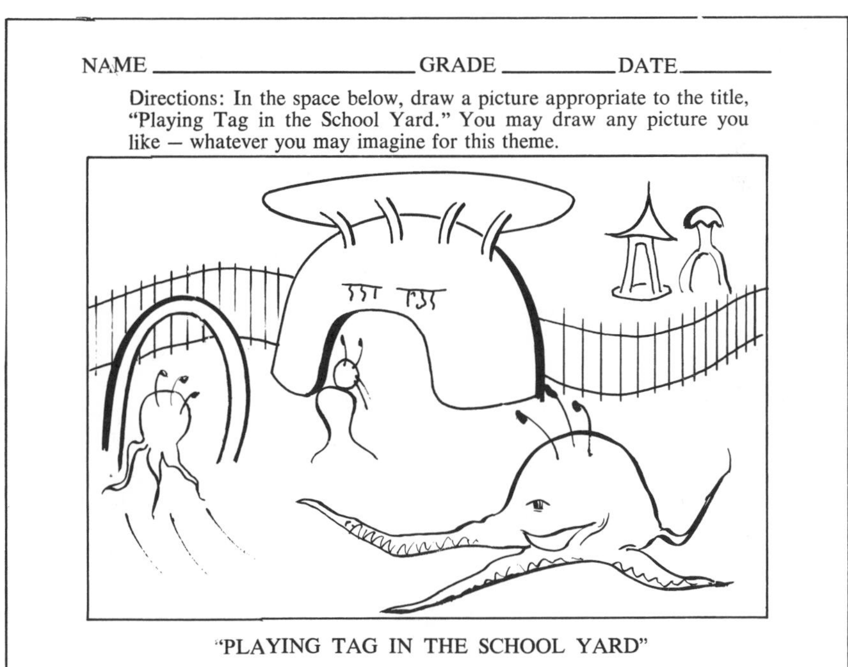

Figure 15–3. *A:* Drawing by a High-IQ student. *B:* The same topic, drawn by a High Creative student. (Redrawn by permission from J. W. Getzels and P. W. Jackson, *Creativity and Intelligence*. New York: John Wiley & Sons, Inc. 1962. Copyright © 1962, John Wiley & Sons, Inc.)

A personality difference between the two groups was in their need and desire for closeness to other people. The High Creatives tended to be independent and solitary, finding resources within themselves. The High IQ's sought and found more interaction with parents and friends and did less on their own. In this characteristic, the High Creatives resemble the scientists, whose development is described in Chapter 17. This finding is not surprising since outstanding scientists are highly creative.

The Families of Creative Individuals

The similarities in family backgrounds of Getzels' and Jackson's High Creatives and MacKinnon's [12] creative architects are striking. Their mothers, in comparison with the mothers of the respective contrasting groups, were more highly trained and more likely to have careers outside the home. Their homes were less child-centered; the children were granted autonomy earlier, trusted to do the right thing without a great deal of supervision. Both sets of homes differed from their neighbors' as to conventional standards of cultural, artistic and intellectual matters. Thus the children felt a certain sense of aloneness because of estrangement from the people near them. MacKinnon's architects also reported moving frequently, an experience which would add to the feeling of being apart. Table 15–2 summarizes some differences between the families of highly creative people and people who measured high in IQ.

A Description of Creative Artists

A summary of the characterisics of creative artists, and also perhaps of creative scientists, comes from a study done at the University of California [1]. Careful observers who value accurate observation, creative people often see

TABLE 15–2

A comparison of background factors in high IQ and high creative subjects.

Condition in Home	*High Creatives*	*High IQ's*
Parents' ages	Similar	Different
Father's education	High	Higher
occupation	Professional and business	Mostly professional
Mother's education	High	Higher
career	More likely	Less likely
Child rearing: center of home	Adult	Child
autonomy	Much	Granted later
trust	Much	Less
parent satisfied with	Less	More
Emphasis on finances	Little	Much
Magazines in home	Fewer	More
Parent sees unfavorable qualities in child	Fewer	More
Mother prefers in child's friends	Internal, general, e.g., sense of values	External, specific

Source: Getzels and Jackson [5]; Roe [17]; and MacKinnon [12].

what other people do not observe, in addition to what people ordinarily see. They often call attention vividly to unnoticed phenomena, using their powers of accurate observation not only for their own satisfaction but also for the benefit of mankind. With their greater mental capacity, creative people can hold many ideas at once, compare more ideas and hence synthesize more than the ordinary person. Often extremely vigorous, both mentally and physically, they lead complex lives, in touch with a complex universe. They contact and use the unconscious life liberally, with broad and flexible self-awareness. They can easily regress to primitive fantasies, naive ideas and tabooed impulses and then return to rationality and self-criticism. "The creative person is both more primitive and more cultured, more destructive and more constructive, crazier and saner, than the average person."

Application of Knowledge about Creativity

Both parents and teachers may wonder if they can purposefully promote creativity in children. Research on family background and relationships has shown that the parents' personalities and background are significant. The likelihood of producing a creative child is increased when parents are active in intellectual, cultural matters; when parents guide the child while recognizing him as an active, able, trustworthy person; if parents do not mind being unconventional and different from their neighbors. This is hardly a blueprint for parental procedure, since nobody can turn on such global conditions at will.

Many authorities have given advice to teachers on nurturing creativity in their students. There is a question as to how great a factor is the teacher's own personality. How creative must a teacher be in order to perceive and promote creativity in students? Research indicates that highly creative teachers stimulate more originality in their students than do less creative teachers [22]. Since teachers are less globally involved with their pupils than are parents with offspring, the former can often control their interactions more objectively and hence use "methods" more effectively than can parents.

Consider the findings on creativity together with what is known about adolescence. Intellectually, adolescents are able to think more freely and flexibly than are children. Although originality is related to firmness in sticking to one's judgments, adolescents often need the support of their peers in order to feel a sense of identity. Being different from the group involves some disapproval from both peers and teachers. The most creative adolescents, however, seem to care relatively little about approval. Their values differ from those of more ordinary peers and teachers. Inner satisfaction seems to matter more than marks, prizes, money and praise. Perhaps adults can do some deliberate promotion of creativity by encouraging youngsters to think and act independently. If unusual ideas and products are valued, then perhaps approval-dependent adolescents will feel freer to create.

Psychologists and educators are working on various ways of promoting creativity. The method of "inquiry training" has already been described in

Chapter 12, where curiosity of elementary-school children was considered. Courses in creative problem solving have been developed by several people in various institutions. An example is the course taught by Parnes [14] at the University of Buffalo. Here students are helped to overcome various kinds of blocks to thinking, such as overemphasis on competition and fear of failure. They learn to defer judgment (not to criticize) while they are producing ideas —to wait until later, when the ideas are formed. (This method of thinking is also called *brainstorming.*) Different ways of finding and solving problems are taught. Social settings are relaxing and confidence-promoting. Students who had taken such a course produced significantly better ideas and more ideas than other students [15]. In general, results from various kinds of creativity training have been encouraging. When teachers appreciate the creative process and when they direct students' interest toward being original and clever, their students tend to produce more ideas and unusual work [8].

Creative methods of teaching, such as the discovery method, will not have the same success with all students. Age, intelligence level, creativity level and personality characteristics will all interact with the methods used. For example, the discovery method is much more attractive to children over 12 years of age than to those under seven, since the 12-year-old is much more capable of appreciating the nature and limits of the problems to be solved [11]. More intelligent youngsters get along better with the discovery method than do less intelligent ones. Reflective people do better than those who answer quickly and impulsively. High motivation also facilitates use of discovery [22].

SUMMARY

A reorganization of thought processes results in a new level of intellectual activity, formal thought, which is logical and abstract. Thinking becomes more mobile and flexible, less egocentric. Contrasted with the child in the stage of concrete operations, the adolescent can consider and make use of a greater amount of information, delaying his conclusions and responses while weighing and judging. The adolescent can think without using concrete objects or events, while concrete thinking is the essence of the intellectual operations of childhood. The adolescent uses and builds systems of thought, by which he searches for possible combinations and relationship and by which he determines whether he has found all combinations and relationships. Formal reasoning means accepting the conditions given and keeping to those conditions while solving the problem. Formal thought requires a high degree of control. Another characteristic of this stage of intellectual development is the ability to think about one's own thinking, an achievement which results in a highly complex person.

Individuals vary in the degree to which they think formally. An individual may achieve abstract concepts in one area and not in another. Logical thinking depends upon the young person's opportunities for developing it, upon the demands made upon him and upon the roles he wishes to play in.life.

Concerned about how society could and should be improved, the adolescent is likely to make grand plans for his own role in transforming society. He grows more realistic as he becomes an adult, especially as he works at an adult job. Thus he comes to differentiate more accurately between what might be and what is, between his own needs and those of his society, further differentiating himself as a person. Thus he can reflect upon his own thinking, and he can see himself as a person-in-relation.

Language development includes not only increases in vocabulary, but increased processing of experience into symbolic form. The forms thus used are taken from the culture, socializing the individual's thinking according to reality as interpreted by his fellow men.

Due to his increased intellectual complexity, the adolescent can control his thinking in order to consider his imaginative and creative behavior. Creative thinking results in new ideas, products and solutions. Although conventional intelligence tests do not measure original thinking, tests for creativity have been devised. Such tests include measures of verbal fluency, flexibility of thought, elaboration of ideas and independence of judgment. Men have created more in art and science than have women. Boys are given more experiences in independent, analytic thinking, to which creative behavior is probably related. Restrictive sex role training is likely to curtail creativity in both sexes. When adolescents scoring high on IQ tests are compared with those scoring high on creativity tests, the former are found to be more socially interactive and the latter more solitary and independent in their thinking. Background differences between such groups are distinguishable, especially differences promoting autonomy and independence in the highly creative people. Psychologists and educators are trying to promote creative behavior by approving independent thinking, by courses in creative problem solving and by setting up courses in ways which require children to seek and find answers for themselves.

REFERENCES

1. Barron, F. The psychology of imagination. *Sci. Am.,* 1958, **199:**3, 150–166.
2. Donaldson, M. *A study of children's thinking.* London: Tavistock, 1963.
3. Elkind, D. Quantity conceptions in junior and senior high school students. *Child Devel.,* 1961, **32,** 551–560.
4. Flavell, J. H. *The developmental psychology of Jean Piaget.* Princeton: Van Nostrand, 1963.
5. Getzels, J. W., & Jackson, P. W. Occupational choice and cognitive functioning: career aspirations of highly intelligent and highly creative adolescents. *J. Abn. Soc. Psychol.,* 1960, **61,** 119–123.
6. Getzels, J. W., & Jackson, P. W. Family environment and cognitive style. *Am. Soc. Rev.,* 1961, **26,** 351–359.
7. Getzels, J. W., & Jackson, P. W. *Creativity and intelligence.* New York: Wiley, 1962.

8. Guilford, J. P. Creativity: its measurement and development. In S. J. Parnes & H. F. Harding (Eds.), *A source book for creative thinking.* New York: Scribner's, 1962, pp. 151–168.
9. Guilford, J. P. Potentiality for creativity and its measurement. Proceedings of the 1962 Invitational Conference on Testing Problems. New Jersey: Educational Testing Service, 1963, pp. 31–39.
10. Inhelder, B., & Piaget, J. *The growth of logical thinking.* New York: Basic Books, 1958.
11. Kagan, J. Personality and the learning process. *Daedalus,* 1965, **94,** 553–563.
12. MacKinnon, D. W. The nature and nurture of creative talent. *Am. Psychol.,* 1962, **17,** 484–495.
13. Nixon, R. E. An approach to the dynamics of growth in adolescence. *Psychiatry,* 1961, **24,** 18–31.
14. Parnes, S. J. The creative problem-solving course and institute at the University of Buffalo. In S. J. Parnes & H. F. Harding (Eds.), *A source book for creative thinking.* New York: Scribner's, 1962, pp. 307–323.
15. Parnes, S. J., & Meadow, A. Effects of "brainstorming" instructions on creative problem-solving by trained and untrained subjects. *J. Educ. Psychol.,* 1959, **50,** 171–176.
16. Piaget, J. *The psychology of intelligence.* London: Routledge & Kegan Paul, 1950.
17. Roe, A. *The making of a scientist.* New York: Dodd, Mead, 1952.
18. Smith, M. K. Measurement of the size of general English vocabulary through the elementary grades and high school. *Genet. Psychol. Mono.,* 1941, **24,** 311–345.
19. Thorndike, R. L. Some methodological issues in the study of creativity. Proceedings of the 1962 Invitational Conference on Testing Problems. New Jersey: Educational Testing Service, 1963, pp. 40–54.
20. Torrance, E. P. Factors affecting creative thinking in children: an interim report. *Merrill-Palmer Quart.,* 1961, **7,** 171–180.
21. Torrance, E. P. *Guiding creative talent.* Englewood Cliffs, N.J.: Prentice-Hall, 1962.
22. Torrance, E. P. Scientific views of creativity and factors affecting its growth. *Daedalus,* 1965, **94,** 663–681.
23. Vygotsky, L. S. *Thought and language.* Cambridge: Massachusetts Institute of Technology, 1962.
24. Watts, A. F. *The language and mental development of children.* London: Harrap, 1944.
25. Welford, A. T. *Ageing and human skill.* London: Oxford Univer., 1958.
26. Yudin, L., & Kates, S. L. Concept attainment and adolescent development. *J. Educ. Psychol.,* 1963, **54,** 177–182.

Parent–Adolescent Relationships

❧ CHAPTER 16 ❧

Parent–child relationships change during adolescence from protection–dependence to affectionate equality, or so they do in the ideal American situation. The change involves turmoil in parent and child, as they learn to play new roles and feel new feelings as the child establishes a mature sense of identity.

CULTURAL PERSPECTIVE

Many observers have noted that American parents and children have more trouble with each other than do their counterparts in other cultures. Some of the conditions basic to this situation are these:

1. AMERICAN IDEALS. Where every individual has a right to life, liberty and the pursuit of happiness, the attempt to establish a distinct identity is going to be pretty vigorous. Not only does the individual have the right to be himself, but he has a heritage of go-getters—explorers, colonists, pioneers, inventors—young people, full of initiative, not doing what their parents told them, but out on their own, improving on what their parents did. These ideals result in continual social changes, making parents and adolescents unsure of their roles in regard to each other.

2. THE NUCLEAR FAMILY. Father, mother and children make up the typical American family. The two-generation family is the norm, even though in actual practice many families have additional members living with them, and many also are minus a parent. Children are expected to grow up, move out and start their own two-generation families. A rupture in parent–child relationships is implicit in this expectation where parents and children intend to be quite independent of each other after the children reach adulthood.

In contrast, in some cultural settings in the United States and in other cultures, the joint family or the stem family, may be typical.* Both types see

* There are in the United States over 29,000 families in which four generations live in a single dwelling. Younger marriages and longer life spans contribute to this situation.

generations as connected intimately, expect no break between children and parents. As parents grow old, children take more and more responsibility for them instead of pushing off on their own. Children are not encouraged to develop distinct identities as individuals, but to feel a family identity. An adolescent does not have to work so hard to achieve a sense of identity because it is already partly built for him. Therefore, he stays *with* his family psychologically as well as physically. Even if he goes away for a while to be educated, as many Indian youths do, he still belongs deeply to his whole family and returns to them when he can. This is not to say that Indian adolescents live in complete harmony with their parents but only that they conflict less than do Americans.

Americans usually believe that you have only one life to live. It's not so with over half of the world's people. A belief in reincarnation usually exists in cultures which have joint family, stem family or any kind of extended family. An individual's sense of identity is thus part of an identity which extends into the infinite past and future. His religion most likely involves ancestor worship, or at least a duty toward ancestors, with the assurance that his decendants will be obligated to him in the same way. Thus a person is not alone, to find himself. He *belongs,* in time and space. He therefore feels no necessity to cut himself off from his parents or from the other people who are part of his identity.

3. A FAST-CHANGING SOCIETY. "Everyone over twenty is an immigrant in the nuclear age," said Mead [19]. The rapid pace of science and technology tears an ever-widening gap between generations. From the time when technology produced the automobile, America has seen continuing changes in behavior patterns and values, especially regarding sex. Society is becoming less work-oriented, more leisure-oriented. Although less socialistic than many countries, the United States continues to legislate for social welfare, while rugged individualism is favored less than it used to be. Bureaucratic businesses and government have replaced many small, independent operations.

Adolescents feel that parents are hopelessly old-fashioned. Parents know that they are. Parents are often not sure what is right and what standards to insist upon. Here is one of the sources of the loss of moral authority suffered by parents, their uncertainty due to a youth which differed from their children's experience of today.

4. MASS MEDIA AND THE SHRINKING WORLD. It used to be that learning to read opened a child's eyes to the existence of standards and authorities which differed widely from those of his parents. Now television assaults him in infancy. Children as well as parents are at the mercy of the advertising octopus which exploits childish fears and fantasies, and the entertainment industry, which reduces man to the lowest common denominator. Insofar as parents' values and standards differ from those promoted by mass media, conflict with adolescents is generated. Easy communication and travel bring youngsters into contact with different worlds of discourse. Middle-class Christian

parents seem small-town and narrow-minded to Jane who wants to bring a dark-skinned friend home for vacation, to Ken who writes that he is dating a Jewish girl, and to Walter, when he reports an exciting time working for civil liberties.

CONFLICT

Different Interpretations of Parent–Adolescent Conflict

The psychoanalytic point of view is that conflict is a necessary part of growing up. If an adolescent does not battle his parents in one area, he will in another.

"I take it that it is normal for an adolescent to behave for a considerable length of time in an inconsistent and unpredictable manner; to fight his impulses and accept them; to ward them off successfully and to be overrun by them; to love his parents and to hate them; to revolt against them and to be dependent on them; to be deeply ashamed to acknowledge his mother before others and, unexpectedly, to desire heart-to-heart talks with her; to thrive on imitation of and identification with others while searching unceasingly for his own identity; to be more idealistic, artistic, generous and unselfish than he will ever be again, but also the opposite: self-centered, egotistic, calculating" [11]. These are the words of Anna Freud. She goes on to say, "There are few situations in life which are more difficult to cope with than an adolescent son or daughter during the attempt to liberate themselves." Levy and Munroe [17] also extend sympathy: "I wish I could offer a pain-dispelling drug to mothers during this second birth, this delivery of children into the adult world." They hold that an adolescent has to fight his parents in order to grow up. Not only does he reject his parents, but also his baby-self, with whom parents are intimately associated. While rejecting childhood and parents, in order to strive toward identity as a distinct and independent being, he still wants the love, comfort and protection which parents gave him. Thus parents are wrong no matter what they do, and children have to pick fights. This point of view is often comforting to bewildered parents, since it helps to allay their guilt and feelings of inadequacy. If adolescents have to go through a difficult stage then parents simply have to wait patiently, confidently and lovingly until the young people grow out of it into civilized adulthood!

Another point of view is this: While conflict often occurs, it is neither essential nor inevitable. Adolescents mature most easily when parents place reasonable limits on their behavior and when they are affectionate, interested and active with their children [14, 21]. Research gives considerable evidence to show that this is so. For example, when college students were asked to recall how they felt toward their parents before they were 15 years old, approximately half of them reported that they had felt very close to both parents [16]. Compared with a group who had not been close to both parents, these students had more positive ratings on several personal and family characteristics. They were more likely to be virgins, to have received sex information from parents and from it to have developed healthy attitudes toward sex in marriage, giving family training as their reason for refraining from premarital sex relations. They tended to evaluate themselves more highly on personal attractiveness, to be satisfied with their sex, to have little trouble making friends with the opposite sex and to have confidence in their chances for successful marriage.

Problems with parents are important, but not the most important problems, from the adolescent's standpoint. School problems were of much greater concern than parent problems, to 4,000 adolescents who were asked to report the biggest personal problem that was causing difficulty [1]. Personal problems (usually relationships with peers) were equally troublesome with parent problems, and for boys, financial concerns also ranked equal with parental and personal. Other difficulties plagued the subjects of this inquiry, also. Family problems made up only 10 per cent of the most pressing difficulties reported by boys and 22 percent of those of girls. Family problems tended to decrease with age, while school problems did not but even increased somewhat for boys. Boys' financial problems also increased. These facts put adolescent–parent conflicts into perspective as real aspects of adolescent life, but not dominant. (See Figure 16–1.)

Parents' Feelings about Adolescents

The parents' feelings and personal development also have some bearing on the production of conflict. Even though children are a burden and annoyance, they also give joy and satisfaction. Most adults who reach the stage of developing a sense of generativity are launched into it and propelled along in it by their children. It is hard to switch from the kind of nurturing role required by offspring into other forms of generativity such as being on the board of education or collecting money for crippled children. While a few parents have nurtured and created in situations other than their child-raising roles, many have not. Most parents, if not all, feel ambivalent about seeing their children become adults. This is what they have been working toward. For many years they tried to prepare their children for independence. Success, however, means the end of the job of parenthood. Viewing the almost-finished product, at 18 or so, it occurs to many a parent that the job is not perfect. The impact of this realization is twofold. First it seems as though a little more control and direction might improve the son or daughter to the point where future success would be assured. The parent then continues to try to make decisions which the youngster knows he himself must make in order to establish his identity firmly.

Second, the imperfection of the child may reactivate the parent's own adolescent feelings, the fears and pains he knew, his unsolved problems which were almost forgotten until now. Mr. Jenks relives his sorrow over missing college when Freddie gets a low score on college entrance examinations. Contemplating Gladys' generous proportions, Mrs. Kaufman plumbs the de-

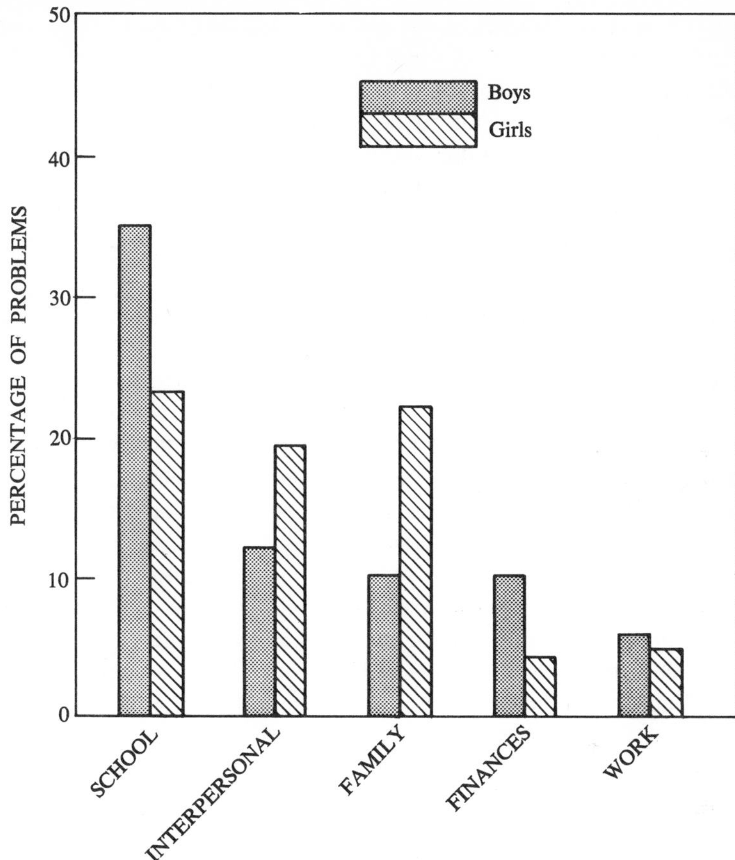

Figure 16–1. Extent of adolescents' concern with various types of problems, by sex. (Adapted from J. F. Adams, "Adolescent Personal Problems as a Function of Age and Sex," *Journal of Genetic Psychology,* **104,** 207–214. Copyright © 1964, The Journal Press, Inc.)

spair she felt over her own bulk at 16. The shame and guilt which accompanied youthful sex behavior generate the parental explosion which greets Helen's appearance in a new bathing suit which leaves practically nothing to the imagination. In all these situations, parents seem to their children to be overreacting. To themselves, they are simply trying to protect their children from dangers they know to be much more serious than the children realize.

The real essence of the sense of generativity is wanting the child (or creature or project) to grow in the way that is best for him. Not only does the parent have to let him go on his own at the right point, but the parent also has the problem of knowing what way *is* best, and where to compromise with reality while aiming toward perfection. Sometimes only the threat of disaster will move a parent from a rigid insistence upon making decisions for the adolescent whose growth depends upon making his own. Larry's parents permitted him to drop out of college for a year only when a psychiatrist told them that he was in danger of an emotional breakdown. Janet's parents stopped criticizing her boyfriend when they realized that, if she married him, the breach they were creating would probably be permanent.

It is also possible for parents to be too laissez-faire with adolescents. A hands-off policy can give too little guidance and support to the youngster who needs and wants to stand on his own and yet at the same time needs and wants the security of being held to standards of behavior in which his parents truly believe. Parents who have read about adolescents' need for independence may grant more freedom than their children can profitably use. Some parents are so uncertain about their own beliefs and standards that they cannot be firm in setting limits for adolescents. And some parents don't care enough. They may give up the struggle from fatigue, pressures from other areas of life or a feeling of hopelessness, as did one divorced mother who moved away, leaving two teen-age girls at home with plenty of money, one to go to high school, the other to college. Perhaps the most sophisticated parents of all, appreciating the need for a delicate balance between freedom and control, will agonize over achieving that balance.

Quite aside from the annoyance of adolescent ambivalence, negative parental feelings are engendered from the financial burden which adolescents place upon parents. Probably this feeling is confined to middle-class parents. In lower socioeconomic levels, adolescents are expected to earn money as soon as they can and even to contribute to family support. While middle-class children often earn money, they are still expensive to keep. Costing more than adults to feed and clothe, adolescents represent a large cash outlay even before they go to college, that fabulously costly place where expenses grow every year. Upper-middle-class parents find that scholarship aid is unavailable or present in such minute quantities as to make little difference in the great drain which education represents. As adolescent children go about their business of athletics, cheer-leading, dating, fraternities, telephoning, joyriding, beach parties and shopping, hard-working parents sometimes resent these noncontributing consumers.

POSITIVE INTERACTIONS

Much of what parents and adolescents do together is a give and take. Much of it is growth-promoting in the children and often in the parents, too.

Communication

Any human relationship is enhanced by mutual understanding. Conflicts are stimulated and increased by not seeing one another's point of view. Sometimes it is hard for parents and children to put themselves in each other's shoes, but having lived together for between one and two decades, a parent and child know many ways of letting each other know what they are thinking and feeling. Facial expressions, posture, silences, tones of voices—all have meaning and add to the meaning of acts and spoken words. "Sorry, but you can't take the car tonight" may be interpreted as hostility, punishment, parental wisdom or sincere regret, according to how it is said. A youngster's sudden seeking of a parent's company may tell the parent, without words, that the son or daughter has been rebuffed by friends.

Talking together is very necessary too, even though nonverbal communication may be quite meaningful. One would expect adolescents to be able to express themselves better than children, since they have more words at their command and a greater flexibility of thought. Why, then, do some parents and adolescents have great difficulty in understanding each other through talking? This question was approached with 100 college students, 99 of whom indicated some trouble in communicating with their parents [8]. These subjects said that lack of words had nothing to do with any difficulties they experienced in talking with parents. When asked which subject was most difficult to discuss with parents, boys and girls replied that sex was hardest to discuss, with mothers as well as with fathers. Girls had trouble talking with mothers about marriage and about misbehavior. Boys found it especially hard to talk about misbehavior and about failures and defeats. When asked why they found it hard to talk about these topics, the girls indicated that they often did not get enough opportunities to talk to their mothers or their fathers. Guilt too held them back. Both boys and girls were affected by fear of mothers nagging and fear that their mothers might not keep secrets.

Children's understanding of parents' motives was considered in a study [22] of 656 Swedish boys and girls, ages 11 through 15. As the children grew older, they were less acceptant of parental restrictions that stemmed from authoritarian attitude and more acceptant of rationally or altruistically motivated restrictions. As the children increased in verbal intelligence, with age factor eliminated, they also were less acceptant of authoritarian-motivated restrictions. This study may indicate either that greater maturity brings increased understanding of parents' motivations, or greater maturity brings less tolerance for authoritarian restrictions, or both.

Searching for broad, general conditions which would lead to good communication in a family, parents' satisfactions with their children were compared with the ways in which children perceived the parents' satisfactions [10]. The subjects were boys and girls between 11 and 16 and their parents. A high level of accuracy in communication between parent and adolescent was found to exist in families where husband and wife communicated well with each other. That is, when the husband and wife agreed well on domestic values and on which roles they expected one another to play, then their children tended to understand clearly how well-satisfied their parents were with them. High socioeconomic status was associated with good communication between parent and adolescent. (This finding is consistent with the fact that high socioeconomic status is associated with happy marriages and hence with good communication between husband and wife.)

The practical significance of these research results is varied. It does not help parents and children much to know that high socioeconomic status predicts good communication. Nor can children do a great deal about the clarity with which their parents understand each other. Parents can, of course, work to build a sound marriage which will serve as a foundation for communication with their children. Some of the more detailed research results could prove worthwhile in day-to-day family relationships. Realizing that their children may feel they have not enough chances to talk, parents could plan their time so as to make regular and frequent opportunities. Adolescents, too, could point out to their parents that they need more time together in order to understand one another. If mothers realized how important it is to keep confidences in order to continue to receive them, then surely they would be more reluctant to gossip and to share private information with friends. Both parents might try to be more acceptant and less critical of their children as persons, while still making clear their own values and standards of behavior. Can a parent change in the direction of being more rational and understanding with his child? Yes indeed, according to results from a study on changing attitudes through group discussion [13]. Not only did these parents change their attitudes toward their children, but the children also changed their behavior.

Feelings of Love and Closeness

A previously mentioned study [16] of adolescents' feelings of closeness to parents revealed that 47 percent of the men and 58 percent of the women reported feeling very close to both parents before the age of 15. Similar findings on sex difference occurred in a study [7] of boys and girls from seventh to eleventh grades, in which girls reported receiving more love, affection and nurturance from both parents than boys reported receiving. Boys saw themselves as being treated in more hostile, negative ways by both parents. Even though there is a statistically significant sex difference in this area, it is noteworthy that about half of the men and over half of the women did feel very close to their parents. Only 13 percent of the men and 7 percent of the women reported having felt neutral toward both parents. The remainder were close to one parent, more to the mother than to the father.

Further indication of love and parents by adolescents is from a study [12] of attitudes in which children from third grade through twelfth grade were asked to complete sentences beginning with "My father—" and "My mother—." Answers were classified into favorable, unfavorable and neutral. While a favorable attitude may not be exactly the same as love, at least it is an indication of some sort of positive relationship. Figure 16–2 shows that adolescents held many more favorable than unfavorable attitudes toward their parents. Both sexes were more favorable to the mother than to the father, a fact compatible with the finding mentioned above, that adolescents were more likely to feel close to the mother than to the father. During the high school years, boys' attitudes grew more favorable toward both the mother and father, while girls showed a larger increase in positive statements about

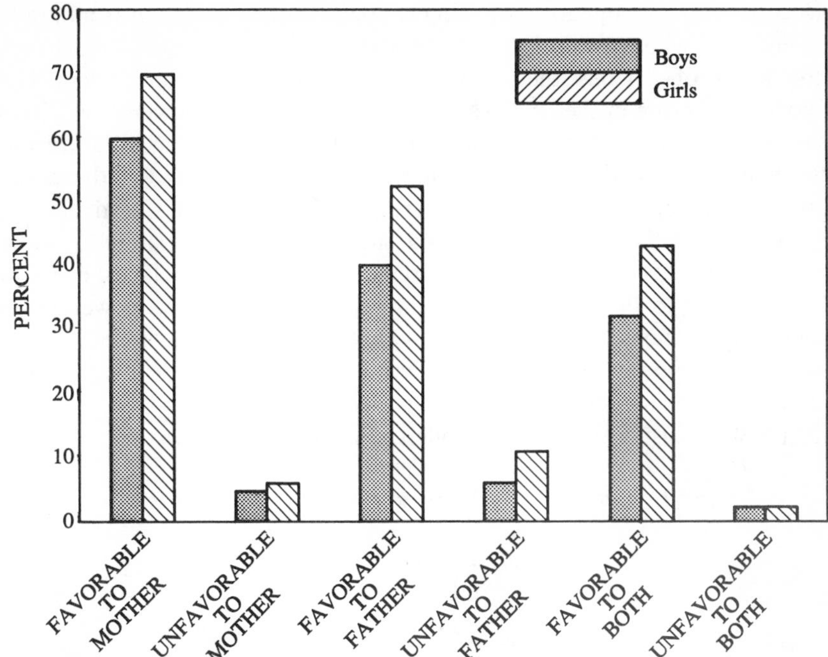

Figure 16–2. Responses of boys and girls to incomplete sentences, revealing attitudes toward parents. Favorable attitudes far outweigh unfavorable ones. Mothers receive a few more positive responses than fathers, from both boys and girls. (Adapted from D. B. Harris and S. C. Tseng, "Children's Attitudes Toward Peers and Parents as Revealed by Sentence Completions," *Child Development,* **28,** Figures 5 and 6. Copyright © 1957, The Society for Research in Child Development, Inc. Used by permission.)

the father than they did in regard to the mother. Considering the high level of acceptance of both parents by both sexes along with the increases in favorable attitudes as the adolescents grew older, it does not look as though the adolescent search for independence requires hostility toward parents.

Identification

Identification has been discussed in earlier chapters as a way in which children model their own thinking and actions upon those of their parents and others. By the time a child reaches adolescence, his personality has been deeply affected by identification. The question of his own identity comes to the fore, and he becomes more concerned with and more conscious of its sources. He notes his similarities to parents and differences from them, convincing himself of his separateness as a distinct individual, even though modeled after his parents and other people important in his life.

The ways in which parents guide and discipline adolescents have a relationship to the degree to which the children identify with their parents [9]. The subjects for this investigation were almost 10,000 students, drawn from grades 7 through 12, who answered questions about how much they would like to be the kinds of persons their mothers and fathers were and about how decisions were made in their homes. Three levels of parent power were distinguished—autocratic, where the parent just tells the child what to do; democratic, where the child has many chances to make decisions but the parent has the last word; and permissive, where the child makes his own decision either with or without the interest and suggestions of the parent. Another aspect considered was how much the parent explained rules, policies, decisions and suggestions to the child. Results showed that at all three power levels, frequent explanations were associated with the child wanting to be like the parent. Taking power level into consideration, the democratic parents were most attractive as models to their children, permissive parents next and autocratic parents least attractive as models. Figure 16–3 shows the extent to

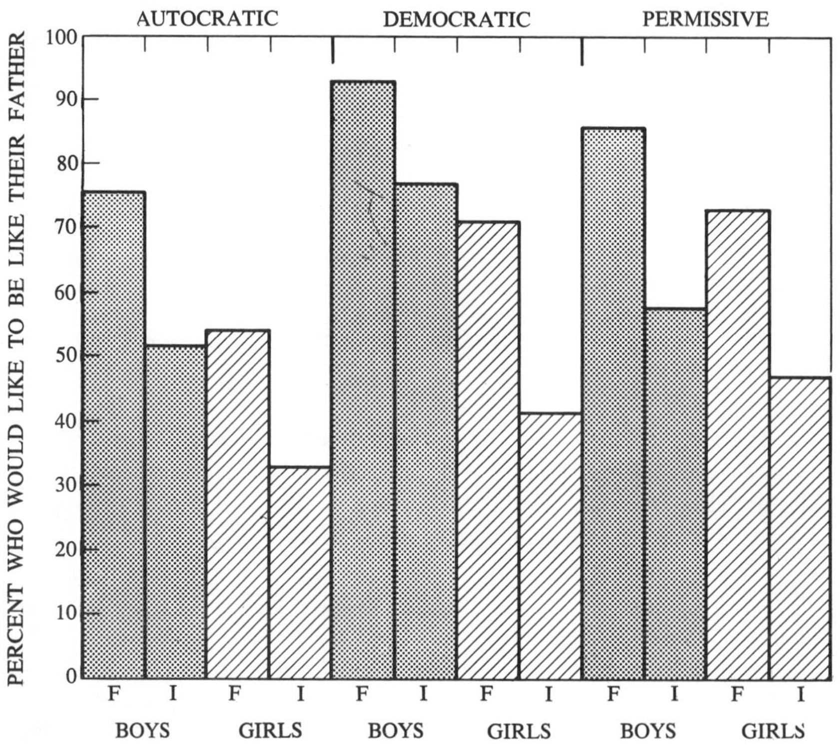

F = Frequent parental explaining

I = Infrequent parental explaining

Figure 16–3. (*Above and facing page*) Strength of boys' and girls' desires to be like their parents, for three levels of parental power, taking amount of parental explaining into account. (Adapted from G. H. Elder, "Parental Power Legitimation and Its Effect Upon the Adolescent," *Sociometry,* **26,** 50–65. Copyright © 1963, The American Sociological Association.)

which boys and girls wanted to be like parents at the three power levels, with amount of explaining taken into consideration.

Perceived similarity to parents has been shown to have some correlates in adolescent adjustment. Positive personality characteristics in both young men and women are associated with their seeing themselves as similar to their fathers [15]. Studies [20, p. 254] contrasting normal and neurotic subjects demonstrated that normal young men identified more with their parents than did neurotic young men. The normal men saw their fathers as being closer to their ideals than did the neurotics. In another study [25] college students filled out a personality test (Minnesota Multiphasic Inventory) for themselves; again, as they thought their fathers would respond; and again, as they thought their mothers would respond. The results showed that for both men and women normal personality characteristics were associated with seeing oneself as similar to one's father. This association was most clearly shown in women in the masculinity–femininity scale, while masculine women were less similar to their fathers than were feminine women.

Adolescents' acceptance of parents' values may take place through identification or through such other means as study and criticism. When two generations hold the same values, however, it indicates harmony and positive

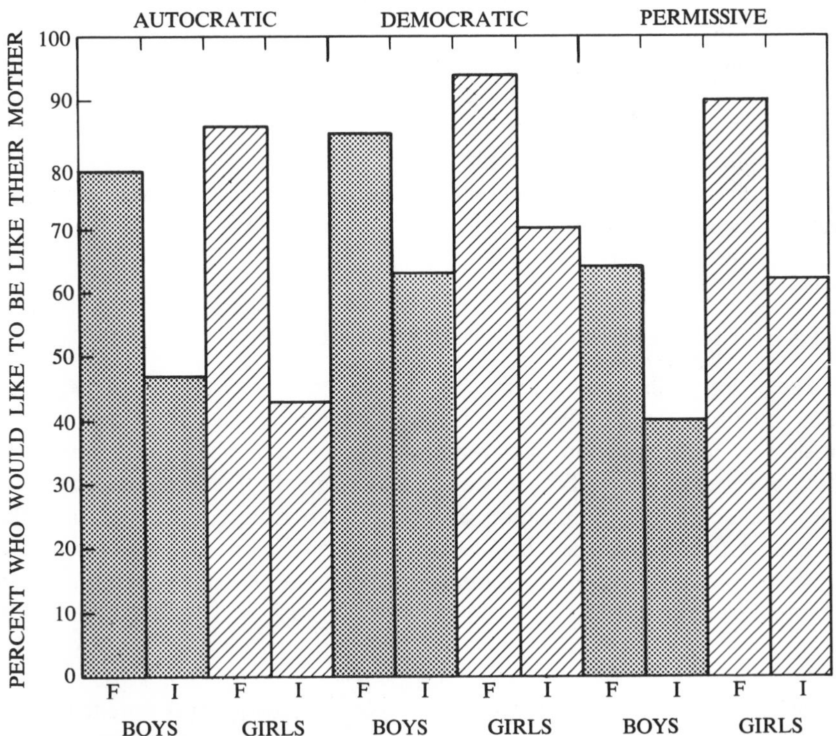

F = Frequent parental explaining
I = Infrequent parental explaining

interaction between them. Although a study of conflicts may give the impression that adolescents usually reject their parents' values, there is much evidence to show that parents and teenagers are more alike than unlike in values [3]. For example, first-voters are likely to vote as their fathers do [18, p. 212]. When parents agree with each other on religion, most of their children, especially girls, follow the same ideology. A survey of college students' religion in relation to that of their parents showed only 17.8 percent disagreeing with parents, and many of the disagreements were minor [23]. Vocational ambitions and efforts are strongly affected by parents, as shown in an investigation of parental and peer influences on social mobility. While most working-class boys did not aspire to go to college, a minority of boys from blue-collar homes were in the college preparatory course, headed for middle-class occupations. Forty-three percent of these boys had been advised by their parents to enter professions, whereas of the remainder of the working-class boys, only 16 percent had been advised by parents to enter professions. A similar contrast was shown for middle-class boys. Of those planning to enter professions, 53 percent had received such advice from parents, but only 21 percent in noncollege preparatory courses had been so advised [24]. While this research shows that adolescents' ambitions are affected by factors other than parents, it does indicate that parents have considerable influence on their sons' vocational values.

Even though teenagers disagree on values with their parents, there is evidence that as the children grow into adulthood, they tend to adopt the same attitudes toward adolescent behavior which their parents held toward them [2]. The areas in which 103 college girls conflicted most with their parents were discipline, responsibilities and family rules and regulations. These girls were planning to bring up their own daughters in ways very similar to the methods their mothers had used.

PARENTS VERSUS OTHER INFLUENCES

The many pulls upon adolescents include those exerted by their parents. Some conflicts are frankly between parents and children. Other problems are created by the opposition of parental and other influences, most importantly the influences of peers. Teachers and other adults in the community may also put adolescents into the position of having to choose between them and their parents. Other adults also can be very influential on the adolescent while reinforcing values held by the parents or opening new vistas which the parents then endorse.

Parents and Other Adults

There is little to show the relative importance of parents and teachers in helping adolescents to establish the sense of identity and to grow up in general. Generalizations do not mean a great deal anyway, since such a wide variety of relationships and circumstances are possible. Almost everyone knows at least one case where a teacher had a significant lifelong influence on an adolescent. Ellen's third grade teacher channeled her sensitivity to nature into careful observation. Her tenth grade biology teacher refined and deepened her knowledge and enjoyment with the result that she has become a botanist. Almost everyone knows at least one case of a child modeling himself after a teacher in direct contrast to the models available at home. Stan, a big, socially awkward boy, identified strongly with the high school football coach and rejected his librarian father. He is majoring in physical education. For many youngsters, a teacher or youth leader provides a welcome and healthy chance to explore a new identity and then to adopt it if it fits. With the variety of personalities, relationships and situations possible in American life, parents cannot possibly open up to an adolescent sufficient choices of identity for him to be sure of finding what he needs. Part of the letting-go process which many parents find difficult is the acceptance of these other adult influences as essential relationships for their children.

Studies comparing the importance of parents and teachers in adolescence have generally awarded parents the first place. Coleman [6, p. 5] asked his subjects, "Which one of these things would be hardest for you to take—your parents' disapproval, your teacher's disapproval, or breaking with your friend?" The results were thus:

	Boys	*Girls*
Parents' disapproval	53.8%	52.9%
Teacher's disapproval	3.5	2.7
Breaking with a friend	42.7	43.4
Number of cases	3,621	3,894

Apparently the teacher's approval counted for very little if matched against that of parents and friends.

Another comparison of adolescents' concepts of teachers and parents indicated that adolescents considered teachers to be more clever, skillful, persevering, rich and knowledgeable than parents [27]. Parents were seen as more easygoing, trustful, happy, popular and peaceful than teachers. The boys rated the teachers as less calm, strong, successful and patient than their parents. A personality test (Cattell) showed that both boys and girls tended to be more strongly identified with parents than with teachers.

Peck and Havighurst [21] found in their case studies a number of clear-cut instances in which an adult outside the family who had a close relationship with the subject had served as a model. It happened as often with adolescents of low morality as with those of high. Using an Adult Guess-Who Test, the subjects were asked to write names of adults in the community who were community-minded, friendly to young people, trustworthy, good looking or carefully dressed. The morally mature adolescents tended to name solid, reputable people in their neighborhoods. The low group gave more scattered responses, including some teachers but also some young adults of questionable reputation. Clergymen were almost never mentioned.

Parents and Peers

Peers are of tremendous importance in the lives of adolescents, indeed so important that the entire next chapter is devoted to peer relationships. But at this point, what of their influence as compared with that of parents? Coleman's subjects were almost equally divided as to which would be worse, disappointing a parent or breaking with a friend.

In some ways, adolescents become closer to their peers as they grow up; in other ways they remain fairly close to their parents. They want to spend more and more time with their friends and less at home. They often feel that friends understand them better and that they are more like their friends than they are like parents. However, parents are still recognized as sources of guidance and authority.

Changes between the fourth and tenth grades are shown in an investigation of family and peer orientation [4]. The subjects were asked three types of questions. To find out which group they identified with most, they were asked whether friends or family understood them better and whether they wanted to be more like their parents or more like their friends when they grew up. Questions to explore association orientation were about which group they most enjoyed being with. Norm orientation was studied by asking whose ideas were more like theirs in regard to right and wrong, activities that are fun and the importance of school. Table 16–1 shows family and peer orientation at the various grade levels for the three different areas. The trend is clearly from family to peer orientation. Although the family loses and peers gain in regard to identification, there are twice as many tenth graders with a family orientation as with a peer orientation. As for spending time with friends or family, three prefer friends to the one who prefers family. As for values and norms, peers made steady gains, ending in tenth grade with 50 percent of choices as compared with 30 percent for the family.

Studies on guidance and acceptance of authority show adolescents behaving realistically. The influence of parents was compared with that of peers by asking boys aged 14 to 16, in a national survey [26, p. 31], "Would you take the ideas of people your own age, or the ideas of your parents, on—?" On the question of what time to be in at night, 95 percent would pay attention to their parents, 1 percent to peers; on personal problems, 76 percent to parents, 8 percent to peers; on how to act with the gang, 62 percent to parents, 23 percent to peers; on joining clubs, 47 percent to parents, 34 percent to peers; on personal grooming, 45 percent to parents, 30 percent to peers. These answers give a rather surprising weight to parents' influence.

Another attempt to assess the relative influence of parents and peers used a method that was more subtle than simply asking [5]. Girls in grades 9, 10 and 11 read stories about adolescent girls trying to solve conflicts in which one solution was favored by parents, another by peers. Then the subjects made their own choices as to solutions. The experimental group was then given a second form of the test, in which parents were credited with the solutions offered in the first test by peers, and vice versa. Thus a measure

TABLE 16–1

Orientation to family and peers in children from fourth through tenth grade.

Orientation Toward	Grade in School						
	4th	*5th*	*6th*	*7th*	*8th*	*9th*	*10th*
Combined Orientation							
Family	87.1	80.5	80.2	66.7	41.7	44.7	31.6
Neutral	6.9	12.2	11.2	9.3	18.3	22.4	20.2
Peer	5.9	7.3	8.6	24.1	40.0	32.9	48.1
Normative Orientation							
Family	82.2	64.6	69.8	51.9	33.0	42.4	30.4
Neutral	5.9	12.2	12.1	13.9	14.8	16.5	19.0
Peer	11.9	23.2	18.1	34.3	52.2	41.2	50.6
Association Orientation							
Family	75.2	65.9	62.1	51.9	20.9	21.2	15.2
Neutral	15.8	24.4	25.0	22.2	39.1	37.6	29.1
Peer	8.9	9.8	12.9	25.9	40.0	41.2	55.7
Identification							
Family	81.2	79.2	77.6	72.2	57.4	62.3	51.9
Neutral	13.8	18.3	18.1	18.5	24.3	24.7	21.5
Peer	5.0	2.4	4.3	9.2	18.2	13.0	26.6
N	101	82	116	108	115	85	79

Source: Reprinted by permission from C. E. Bowerman and J. W. Kinch "Changes in Family and Peer Orientation of Children between the Fourth and Tenth Grades," *Social Forces*, **37**, Table 1, p. 208. Copyright © 1959, University of North Carolina Press.

of shifting to parent or peer was obtained. Results indicated that the girls tended to see parents and peers as differing as to the areas where they were competent guides to behavior. In other words, the girls consistently chose parents' advice in any areas concerned with the larger society, such as jobs. They tended to take peers' advice in areas where peer conformity was important, such as how to dress for a party or football game. In consulting peers as to which course to take in school, they were not seeking vocational advice, but information which would prevent them from being separated from friends.

Where adolescents perceived themselves as more like peers than parents, they chose the peers' solutions, as in taste in clothes and feelings about school. Where they perceived themselves as more like parents, they chose parents' solutions, as in questions of moral behavior. Other data from the study suggested that the more difficult the choice, the more the girl referred to the parents' solution. Also, the girls often dealt with parent–peer cross-pressures by not communicating with their parents.

SUMMARY

American parents and adolescents are likely to have considerable trouble with each other as the child, in accordance with cultural demands, establishes his independence and sense of identity. Some of their conflicts are intensified by the emotional concentration of the nuclear family, rapid social changes and the impact of mass media and easy travel. Some authorities consider conflict inevitable, while others, noting the existence of many harmonious parent–adolescent relationships, doubt the necessity of conflict. Problems with peers and self rank high among adolescent concerns, often higher than problems with parents.

Parents usually have complex feelings about their teenage children, often with considerable ambivalence. Not only do they worry about the child's adequacy in coping with his life but they also relive some of their own adolescent feelings and problems. Parents often find it difficult to achieve a satisfactory balance between controlling their almost-grown children and allowing them sufficient freedom.

Most adolescents have some trouble in communicating with parents, finding certain topics, such as sex, misbehavior and failure hard to discuss. When husband and wife communicate well with each other, then parent–child communication tends to be satisfactory, as well. From studies on feelings of closeness and on attitudes towards parents, it seems that the search for independence does not require most adolescents to feel hostile. The extent to which adolescents want to be like their parents is affected by the family power structure, or the ways in which decisions are made. Normal personality characteristics have been found related to adolescents seeing themselves as similar to their fathers. Parents have considerable effect upon their adolescents' values. The effect is more obvious when the children become adults.

While adolescents are usually influenced more by their parents than by any other adults, youngsters often use several adults for models. Teachers, youth leaders and such people may build relationships which are important in adolescents' development. Although teenagers move from family orientation toward peer orientation, the family retains strongest influence in certain areas, while peers become stronger in places where adolescents see them as knowing more than parents.

REFERENCES

1. Adams, J. F. Adolescent personal problems as a function of age and sex. *J. Genet. Psychol.*, 1964, **104,** 207–214.
2. Bath, J. A., & Lewis, E. C. Attitudes of young female adults toward some areas of parent-adolescent conflict. *J. Genet. Psychol.*, 1962, **100,** 241–253.
3. Bealer, R. C., Willits, F. K., & Maida, P. R. The rebellious youth subculture—a myth. *Children,* 1964, **11,** 43–48.

4. Bowerman, C. E., & Kinch, J. W. Changes in family and peer orientations of children between fourth and tenth grades. *Soc. Forces,* 1959, **37,** 206–211.
5. Brittain, C. V. Adolescent choices and parent-peer cross-pressures. *Am. Soc. Rev.,* 1963, **28,** 385–391.
6. Coleman, J. S. *The adolescent society*. Glencoe, Ill.: Free Press, 1961.
7. Droppelman, L. F., & Schaeffer, E. S. Boys' and girls' reports of maternal and paternal behavior. *J. Abn. Soc. Psychol.,* 1963, **7,** 648–654.
8. Dubbe, M. C. What teen-agers can't tell parents and why. *The Coordinator,* 1956, **4**:3, 3–7.
9. Elder, G. H. Parental power legitimatization and its effect upon the adolescent. *Sociometry,* 1963, **26,** 50–65.
10. Farber, B., & Jenne, W. C. Family organization and parent-child communication: parents and siblings of a retarded child. *Mono. Soc. Res. Child Devel.,* 1963, **28**:7.
11. Freud, A. Adolescence. *Psychoan. Stud. Child.,* 1958, **13,** 255–278.
12. Harris, D. B., & Tseng, S. C. Children's attitudes toward peers and parents as revealed by sentence completions. *Child Devel.,* 1957, **28,** 401–411.
13. Hereford, C. F. *Changing attitudes through group discussion.* Austin: Univer. of Texas, 1963.
14. Hoffman, M. L. Childrearing practices and moral development: generalizations from empirical research. *Child Devel.,* 1963, **34,** 295–318.
15. Johnson, M. M. Sex-role learning in the nuclear family. *Child Devel.,* 1963, **34,** 319–333.
16. Landis, J. T. A re-examination of the role of the father as an index of family integration. *Marr. Fam. Living,* 1962, **24,** 122–128.
17. Levy, J., & Munroe, R. *The happy family*. New York: Knopf, 1949.
18. Lipset, S. M. *Political man*. New York: Doubleday, 1960.
19. Mead, M. Symposium: the American family—a profile in three dimensions. Child Study Association of America Annual Conference, March 4, 1963.
20. Osgood, C., Suci, G., & Tannenbaum, P. H. *The measurement of meaning.* Urbana: Univer. of Illinois, 1957.
21. Peck, R. F., & Havighurst, R. J. *The psychology of character development.* New York: Wiley, 1960.
22. Pikas, A. Children's attitudes toward rational versus inhibiting parental authority. *J. Abn. Soc. Psychol.,* 1961, **62,** 315–321.
23. Putney, S., & Middleton, R. Rebellion, conformity and parental religious ideologies. *Sociometry,* 1961, **24,** 125–135.
24. Simpson, R. L. Parental influence, anticipatory socialization, and social mobility. *Am. Soc. Rev.,* 1962, **27,** 517–522.
25. Sopchak, A. L. Parental "identification" and "tendency toward disorders" as measured by the MMPI. *J. Abn. Soc. Psychol.,* 1952, **47,** 159–165.
26. Survey Research Center. *A study of adolescent boys.* Ann Arbor: Univer. of Michigan, 1956.
27. Wright, D. S. A comparative study of the adolescent's concepts of his parents and teachers. *Educ. Rev*. 1962, **14,** 226–232.

The Quest for Identity Through Social Interaction

CHAPTER 17

Much of social and emotional growth in adolescence takes place with contemporaries of both sexes. The sense of identity includes a firm concept of where one fits with other people, especially people of his own generation. The young person's image of himself is built partly on his interpretations of the ways in which others regard him. Is he seen as bold or timid, witty or tongue-tied, handsome or funny-looking? Is she considered artistic or all thumbs, steady or flighty, intelligent or stupid? The reputation will influence behavior as well as self-concept. Friendships and love relationships enhance self-concepts and promote constructive behavior and personality growth. Failure to find friendship and love can be threatening. In this chapter, social relationships are discussed under two main headings, "The Peer Group" and "The Opposite Sex." The peer group, of course, is made up of members of both sexes, but under it is included friendship and popularity. Relationships with the opposite sex are considered as those which progress toward and include love, sex and marriage.

THE PEER GROUP

For most adolescents, peers (age mates) play an even more important part in life than they did during childhood. A few adolescents remain outside the social swim from preference, pursuing studies, hobbies or athletics, perhaps with one or two friends. Some youngsters, rejected by the peer group, exist in isolation or with other isolates in twos or threes. Among peers, there are two main kinds of groups, crowds and cliques.

The Crowd

Both boys and girls belong to "the crowd," but there are occasions when one sex gets together. The like-sex crowd is not always identical with the group of boys or girls which participates in the boy–girl crowd. Especially at the younger ages, late-maturers and certain nonconforming, independent individuals are unacceptable or uninterested in boy–girl affairs, but they may be cherished members of a like-sex group. Within the crowd are cliques, small groups of close friends, and pairs of best friends.

The crowd is usually based on the school, although neighborhood has some influence. School is the place where most social interaction takes place, in the classroom and library, at basketball and football games, clubs, interest groups, parties, in the corridor and yard (or campus, as it is sometimes called).

One of the basic functions of the crowd is to provide a group identity which separates adolescent from parent, a "we" feeling apart from the family. Thus the adolescent strengthens his own sense of identity by being a member of a group which defines his difference from his parents. Joe gets his hair cut (or not cut) like the other boys do, but different from Dad's. The girls wear pretty much the same shade of lipstick and nail polish, as well as standardized coiffures, but if adults adopt those fashions, they are soon dead and replaced. Signs known to the crowd tell whether you are going steady, looking for a new steady, interested in playing the field or not interested. As adults catch on, the signs change. Language, music and dancing are also exclusive as regards the older generation. While embracing the latest dance fashion, teenagers are likely to register disgust when their parents do the same dance, even if they do it rather well. It is quite acceptable, even cute, for parents to do a similar dance, however, as long as it comes from their own adolescent days. In these and a thousand other ways adolescents reject their parents and their parents' generation. The crowd gives them strength for self-assertion and a new frame of reference from which to reject the old.

Sociologists debate the question of how distinctly the youth subculture is defined and separated from the rest of American culture and whether it is accurate to call it a "youth subculture." The sharpness with which youth is cut off from childhood and adulthood doubtless varies from one American situation to another. Conclusions from investigations of adolescents in a Canadian suburban community suggest that sociological literature has overemphasized the gap between generations [14]. Perhaps a difference between the United States and Canada was indicated, or more likely, the community was one in which generations articulated more smoothly than in the average American situation. Since there are few discernible differences between this Canadian suburb and typical American ones, the study suggests at least that a definite youth subculture is not essential for the socialization of adolescents today.

The crowd is also for fun and comfortable feelings, for doing things together like bowling and strolling, for hanging around the soda fountain, for just talking and talking and talking. And giggling and shouting. The output in decibels is very large in comparison with the intellectual content of conversation, but with good reason. Everybody is trying out a variety of roles, uncertain and tentative as to what kind of person he can be. There is security and warmth in the company of people who face the same problems, feel the same way, behave the same way and wear the same symbols of belonging. It feels good to giggle and shout, to be silly and to stand together against those who do not understand.

Table 17–1 shows how high school boys and girls say they like to spend their leisure time. Table 17–2 reveals the ways in which friends spend their

TABLE 17–1

Percentage of high school boys and girls reporting pleasure in various activities.

	Boys (%)	*Girls (%)*
1. Organized outdoor sports—including football, basketball, tennis, etc.	22.0	6.9
2. Unorganized outdoor activities—including hunting, fishing, swimming, boating, horseback riding	14.7	11.3
3. "Being with the group," riding around, going up town, etc.	17.2	32.5
4. Attending movies and spectator events—athletic games, etc.	8.5	10.4
5. Dating or being out with opposite sex	13.6	11.6
6. Going dancing (girls only)		12.0
7. Hobby—working on cars, bicycles, radio, musical instruments, etc.	22.5	20.1
8. Indoor group activities—bowling, playing cards, roller skating, etc.	8.0	8.1
9. Watching television	19.4	23.6
10. Listening to records or radio	11.2	31.7
11. Reading	13.7	35.5
12. Other, e.g., talking on telephone	7.1	9.3
13. No answer	8.1	3.7
Number of cases	(4,020)	(4,134)

Source: Reprinted with permission of The Free Press from *The Adolescent Society* by J. S. Coleman. Copyright © 1961 by The Free Press Corporation.

time together. It is based on answers to the question "What do you and the fellows (girls) you go around with here at school have most in common—what are the things you do together?

Both tables point up the boys' greater participation in athletics and the greater variety of activities and interests which boys have as compared with girls. Girls reported "just being with the group," rather than specific activities, almost twice as often as boys.

The Clique

Smaller and more intimate than the crowd, although often called "the crowd" by its members, a clique is a highly selected group of friends. Usually alike in social background, interests and experience, they are emotionally attached to each other. Members' feeling for one another is the basic factor holding them together. Some cliques become formalized into clubs, even fraternities and sororities, but most adolescent cliques remain informal and small. Just as the adolescent generation differentiates itself from adults by many

TABLE 17–2

High school boys and girls report on how they spend time with their friends.*

	Boys (%)	*Girls (%)*
1. Organized outdoor sports—including football, basketball, tennis, etc.	34.5	8.2
2. Unorganized outdoor activities—including hunting, fishing, swimming, boating, horseback riding	11.7	6.6
3. In-school activities, interests, clubs	8.9	19.2
4. Attending spectator events		
(a) School-related games and events	5.4	22.1
(b) Out-of-school—movies, etc.	17.8	33.0
5. Eating together at lunch or taking classes together	9.1	13.7
6. Dating together or going to dances together	19.7	39.6
7. Having parties together (girls only)		10.6
8. "Hanging around together," "going uptown"	13.4	26.8
Number of cases	(4,020)	(4,134)

* Listed in the table are all the categories of activities or interests mentioned by at least 10 percent of the boys or girls.

Source: Reprinted with permission of The Free Press from *The Adolescent Society* by J. S. Coleman. Copyright © 1961 by The Free Press Corporation.

symbols, and one crowd from another, so a clique is likely to have ways of proclaiming its difference from others and solidarity within itself. "Everybody" wears blue on Tuesdays. A fraternity pin. The turn of a phrase. A food fad.

Research substantiated the common observation that girls are more cliquish than boys [2, p. 353]. Since cliques are instruments of status achievement, and girls have fewer opportunities to earn status than do boys, it may be that clique activity attracts them for status reasons as well as for emotional response. (They seem to feel a greater need for close friendships than boys do.) Struggling for a sense of identity, the adolescent is looking for ways of achievement status, of looking important and worthwhile to himself and to everybody else. By belonging to a high-status clique, he (or, more likely, she) derives status from it. High status is relative. Other people's positions must be lower if yours is to be higher. Therefore, high-status cliques look down upon others and guard admission to their own jealously.

Erikson [15, pp. 92–93] tells how clique members can be petty, cruel and intolerant in order to defend themselves against a sense of *identity diffusion.* By excluding others who are "different" in skin color, religion, class, abilities or even such trivialities as dress and appearance, the youngster gains some sense of identity from the group to which he belongs. Erikson stresses the importance of understanding this mechanism without condoning the behavior. Adolescents have to be helped to grow beyond the point where they feel the necessity for defending themselves by these cruel methods. (These are the methods of totalitarian systems.) Erikson implies that it can be done by adults living so as to demonstrate "a democratic identity which can be strong and yet tolerant, judicious and still determined."

Dominant Values in the Peer Culture

In every one of the 10 high schools (chosen for diversity and representing the United States), boys chose the role of famous athlete as more desirable than jet pilot, with atomic scientist third and missionary far down at the bottom [10]. Girls chose in this order: model, nurse, schoolteacher, actress (or artist). When asked how they would like to be remembered in high school, boys chose first athletic star, then brilliant student and last, most popular. Girls preferred being a leader in activities, with popularity a close second and scholarship last. When asked about dating preferences, girls ranked brilliant students below athletic and good-looking boys, while boys registered even less desire to date brilliant girls, strongly preferring best-looking girls and preferring cheer leaders. Apparently, certain values have been stable since a generation ago when a popular song summed it up thus: "You gotta be a football hero, to get along with a beautiful girl."

Although the study does not yield information on what happened to individuals' values over the high school years, it does show group changes throughout the academic year based on questionnaires answered by 8,000 youngsters. Although the shifts are small, the image of the athletic star for boys becomes even more attractive, and for girls, the activities leader becomes more attractive. For both, the scholarship value loses appeal.

A very different picture of adolescent values emerges from a longitudinal, intensive study of character development in adolescence [34]. Of all the children born during one year in a carefully selected city, a third of these cases, selected to be representative, were studied in greater detail. When these youngsters evaluated one another, their judgments could be checked against the elaborate findings of the research staff. In judging and rewarding peers, the adolescents took into account both moral values and social skill values. They tended to reward peers who were honest, responsible, loyal, kind and self-controlled. They also rewarded geniality and skill in games. Peers and research staff had high agreement on which adolescents showed the most desirable social behavior. As they grew older, the youngsters weighted character values more heavily in relation to surface values. Here is an example from this study, [34, p. 136]:

> "Earl Eddy" could do practically no wrong when he and his peers were in the early teens. He was highly active, socially visible, and good at games and dancing, well before most of the group had mastered these skills. This is a vivid illustration of the way somewhat superficial values can sometimes outweigh the virtues of good character in the eyes of uncertain adolescents, until they themselves have achieved solid competence. However, at the time he was seventeen, he was still relying on his old techniques. The group had mastered and outgrown these social and athletic skills as a primary basis for judging personal worth. At that point, they dramatically lost respect for him. He did not change, but the group outgrew his adolescent "techniques."

The results of these two studies do not conflict. Each touches upon peer group values from its point of view. Together, they give a more rounded picture than either yields by itself. They show adolescents saying they care more about looks, athletics and activities than they do for academic achievement, and yet demonstrating respect for moral values and mature social behavior.

Values vary from one peer group to another. Coleman shows distinctive differences in the ways in which the various schools emphasized the values investigated. For instance, in Elmtown and Maple Grove, scholastic interests were combined with others, while Green Junction focused on the athletic and Marketville gave independent status to the athlete and scholar [10, p. 196]. The intensive longitudinal study indicated that the moral values held by deviant groups can result in rewards for stealing or cruelty [34, p. 139]. The values which an adolescent accepts as his own will come partly from his own crowd and the other groups he contacts (See Figure 17–1). The local variation of the general picture is the environment with which he will

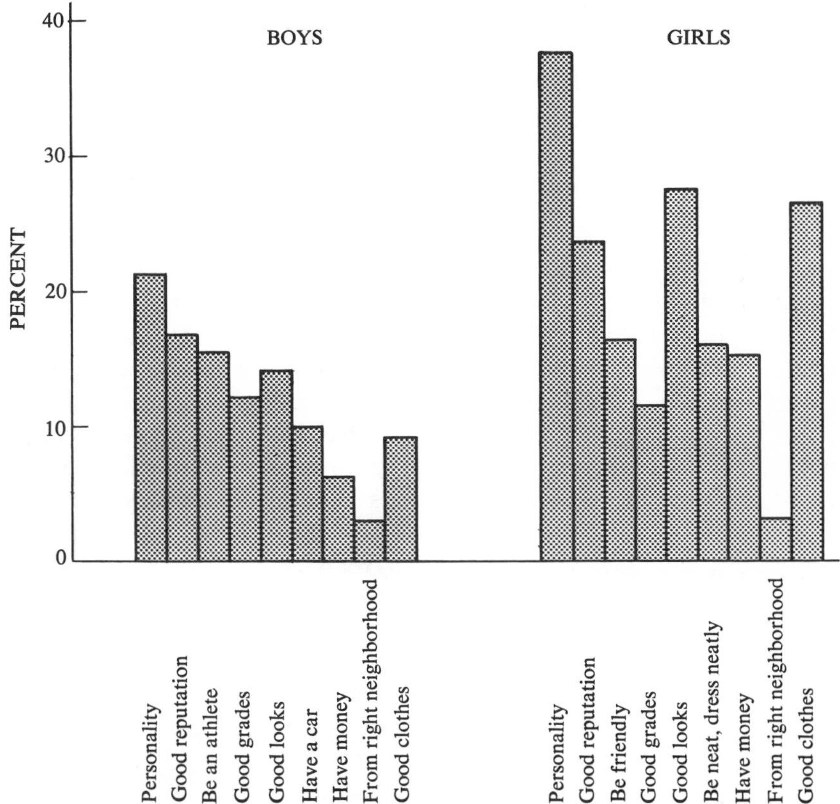

Figure 17–1. Categories of responses of high school students to the question, "What does it take to get into the leading crowd in this school?" (Reprinted with permission of The Free Press from *The Adolescent Society* by J. S. Coleman. Copyright © 1961 by The Free Press Corporation.)

interact. What of the value system he makes his own will depend on many factors, such as his position in the peer social system, his own personality and his family. The study of character development suggested that the family is on the average a more potent force than the peer group, which reinforces and crystallizes tendencies already present. It is possible, however, for peer group values to become the most important ones for an adolescent [34, pp. 140–141].

With increasing age, adolescents pay more attention to adult values. Distinctions along class lines become more obvious. "With his and their increasing age, it becomes decreasingly possible for a child with a winning personality to gain acceptance from his economically more favored contemporaries if he happens to come from 'the wrong side of the tracks.' " [2, pp. 347–348] The increasing acceptance of adult values is shown further as older adolescents grow less slavish in conforming to peer group practices and more tolerant of deviations in others.

A leading sociologist sees a recent change in the youth culture, especially as represented by college students [33]. Emphasis on irresponsibility, pleasure seeking and athletics has declined in favor of political activity, concern with such moral problems as race relations, civil rights and war, and involvement with problems of meaning and identity. He finds the present youth culture better integrated into the adult culture and less antagonistic to adult culture.

Friends

"Best friends are members of the same sex." Thus indicated adolescents in grades 8 through 12 when they were asked to write down the names of their best friends [24, p. 298]. The best-friend relationship is an important one for the sense of identity, as anyone who shares a telephone with an adolescent will testify. The long conversations are between like-sex friends, especially best friends, and longer for girls than for boys. (The best-friend relationship tends to be more important to girls.) A best friend is the best audience on whom to project all the roles and identities that you want to test as possibilities, since this audience is just as concerned with testing and trying. A pair may try a role together. "We'd both look better minus 10 pounds. Let's go on the same diet! We just won't let each other eat more than eleven hundred calories a day." They may play at building a common identity, each gaining security from feeling stronger as a pair than as an individual. "Edna is part of me and I'm part of her. We think the same things. Each of us knows what the other one is thinking. We wear the same kind of clothes and we trade clothes." Communication is easy with someone who faces the same succession of disequilibria—fluctuations in physical balance, emotional upsets, new mental powers, problems with parents, and all the rest. Sometimes the communication is only partial, in that each is a sounding board for the other, not unlike the egocentric conversations of preschool children.

Best-friend relationships have been shown to be more stable with increasing age, from 11 to 18 as seen in Figure 17–2. In these studies [20, 36], it is implied, although not specifically stated, that the best friends chosen were members of the same sex. The increasing possibility for intimacy is probably an important factor in making these relationships more permanent. Erikson's sixth stage of personality development, the growth of the sense of intimacy, follows the stage of identity. ". . . the condition of a true twoness is that one must first become oneself" [15, p. 95]. Just as all the senses have early beginnings before their periods of critical growth, so we would expect the sense of intimacy to show some expression in childhood and adolescence. In its fullest meaning, intimacy between two people exists on all planes of contact, including sexual, but here, in its beginning stage, it is largely a meeting of minds. Bob tells Tom what he thinks and feels, trying to express it in ways that Tom will understand. Tom listens carefully to Bob and asks pertinent questions, trying to put himself in Bob's place. Each tries to understand and

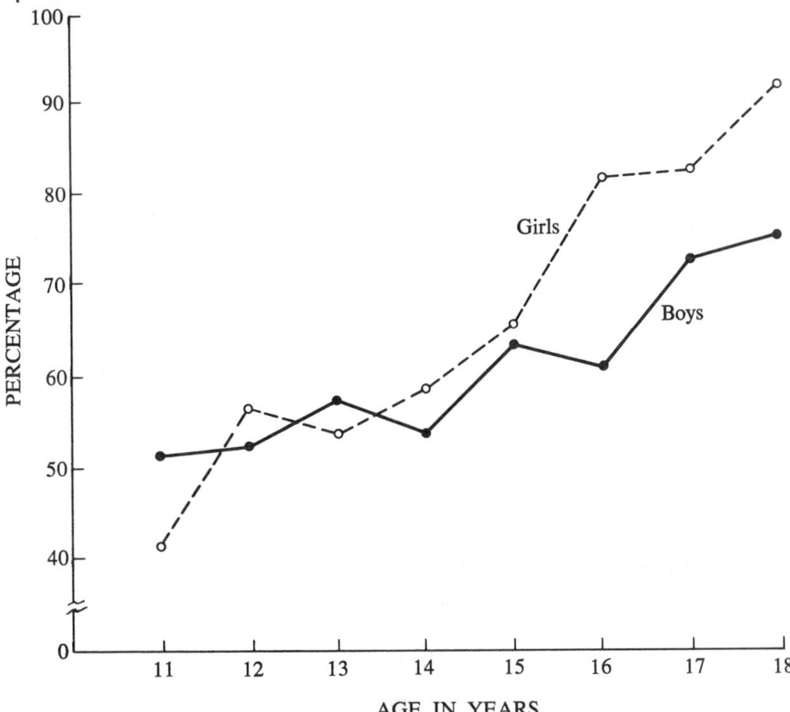

Figure 17–2. Increasing stability of friendships, as shown by percentages of boys and girls choosing the same person as "best friend" on two occasions two weeks apart. (Reprinted by permission from G. G. Thompson and J. E. Horrocks, "A Study of the Friendship Fluctuations of Urban Boys and Girls," *Journal of Genetic Psychology,* **70,** 53–63. Copyright © 1947, The Journal Press.)

to make himself understandable. Each cares what the other thinks and feels. The stronger a person's sense of identity, the more he can care about the other person's thoughts and feelings. Released from the constant necessity of searching for his identity, he is free to enter into an intimate relationship. Since identity develops slowly throughout the period of adolescence, it is reasonable that it should gradually make way for intimacy.

The years 1946 and 1947 were the dates of the studies showing that the best-friend relationship became more stable through the teen years. If the studies were to be repeated today, we wonder (1) would best friend still continue through the teens to mean a member of the same sex? and (2) would friendships with the same sex show increasing stability? Adolescents have less time and energy for like-sex best friends because they are turning increasingly to the opposite sex for companionship. Comparing adolescents of 1942 with those of 1963, a recent study shows an increase in the choice of cross-sex companions for 9 activities, such as studying and going to the movies [25]. Mead [30] points out that earlier dating, earlier going steady and earlier marriages have shortened the period when adolescents can form deep friendships within their own sex. Very early, they come to compete with one another for dating partners, thus lessening the trust they can put in each other. At the age when dating begins, the junior high school age, boys are, on the average, two years behind girls in physiological maturity. Boys and girls of the same age are less suited to be together at this time than at any other time of life. Thus neither can grow at his own pace, in the way that a boy could in male society and a girl in female. The recent increase in identity diffusion, the failure to develop a healthy sense of identity, is attributable to a complex of factors. This could be one of them, the deprivation of a period dominated by strong, deep friendships with members of the same sex.

Popularity. A popular person is one who is chosen or liked by many peers. A youngster may achieve popularity at some expense to his integrity since he may have to make many concessions in order to please a variety of people. He does not necessarily have a deeply satisfying "best friend" with whom he develops intimacy and strengthens his identity. Popularity is a strong value, however. We have already discussed some of the ways in which it is achieved. The study of 10 high schools gives some insight into the average criteria for popularity [10, pp. 43–50]. Boys see being an athlete, being in a leading crowd and being an activities leader as important criteria. Scholarship, while relatively unimportant, appears to boys as even less important in their popularity with girls, while having a nice car becomes more important in relation to girls. From the feminine point of view being a leader in activities and being in a leading crowd and cheer-leading are consistently important. Grades and family background are less important in popularity with boys than with girls. Nice clothes are more so. Since popularity with boys is important in the status system of girls, the importance of personal attractiveness is increased.

To the extent that success is measured by popularity and membership in the leading crowd, there is widespread threat to the sense of adequacy of many youngsters. There are not enough places at the top. Nor is there free access to the top for anyone who is willing to work hard for it. The system does have its democratic aspects, however. Social position of families counts for considerably less than athletic achievement. Motor skill is distributed much more evenly throughout the socioeconomic hierarchy than is scholarship. If scholarship and class position were more important than athletics, then the youngsters from more privileged families would have a greater advantage than they do.

THE OPPOSITE SEX

Patterns of Association

In the 1930's and 40's, research [9, 16] revealed the pubescent child as standing on the brink of heterosexual relationships. He was at the end of preadolescence, the time of life when boys and girls said they hated each other, when they played sex-appropriate games in like-sex groups, shunning the opposite sex vociferously. Preadolescent boys proclaimed their masculinity by being loud, aggressive, dirty and rejecting of feminine values, many of which coincided with adult values. With pubescence came covert interest in the opposite sex, expressed by taking a quick look when others were not noticing, and by hostile, provocative and teasing behavior. Groups of boys and groups of girls engaged in such exciting and enticing activity. The group hostility phase gradually gave way to group activities and group dating. After group dating came double dating and eventually pair dating.

This situation changed at mid century, as described on pages 422–423. Predictions from recent research include continued increases in cross-sex friendships and romantic attachments, increased early cross-sex experimentation, more early marriages and more confusion in sex role definition [6].

A study on dating practices in a Midwestern high school [8] used the reports of seniors on their dating experience through high school. While their reports showed lower percentages dating in the seventh grade (49 percent of girls and 36 percent of boys at age 13) than did the study mentioned above, they still indicated considerable boy–girl activity at the age when boys and girls used to be apart or only beginning tentative approaches to each other. Dating during the three years was thus: tenth grade, girls 85 percent, boys 71 percent; eleventh grade, girls 94 percent, boys 72 percent; twelfth grade, girls 89 percent, boys 85 percent.

Several important questions arise from the fact that dating begins earlier and happens more frequently than it used to do. First, what is the result in terms of personality development in both sexes? Second, what is happening to sex and love relationships of adolescents? These topics have been discussed at length by members of the clergy, sociologists, newspaper columnists, parents and adolescents. Research sheds some light on these questions but does not answer them clearly.

Personality Development and Dating

We have already mentioned Mead's concern over the detrimental effect of shortening the period of exclusive like-sex association. The education editor of the New York *Times* has registered disapproval of early dating, after pointing out that some children are dating at nine years of age [19]. The Roman Catholic Church has taken a strong stand against early dating. A recent church-approved book for adolescents, *Dating for Young Catholics* [23, pp. 20–21], stresses the importance of learning appropriate sex-role behavior (which of course contributes to the sense of identity) through like-sex associations through adolescence. ". . . boys and girls who date too early and who spend a lot of time with the other sex, sometimes do not develop the characteristics of their own sex as fully as they should. They don't have as good an understanding as they might have of what will be expected of them as men or women for the rest of their lives."

Erikson's theory does not preclude the possibility of developing the sense of identity through association with the opposite sex. In fact, he describes such a boy–girl relationship: ". . . such attachment is often devoted to an attempt at arriving at a definition of one's identity by talking things over endlessly, by confessing what one feels like and what the other seems like, and by discussing plans, wishes and expectations" [15, p. 95]. The danger implied in a boy–girl relationship of this sort is not that it is inadequate for promoting identity, but that it may come to involve a sexual relationship before the pair are ready for intimacy. That is, before the sense of identity is sufficiently established.

Another point of view, one which has been widespread in textbooks on family relationships, is that dating is educational, giving adolescents experience in human relationships, promoting social skills and enhancing their ability to choose a mate wisely [29]. If indeed variety in dating partners and a large number of dates actually do promote personality development and wise mate selection, then early dating is desirable, since it has been shown that early-daters (beginning under 13) delay going steady for a longer time than do late-daters [29]. Early-beginners tend to play the field, have a try at going steady and then return to playing the field before going steady again. Thus they have considerable experience with the opposite sex before choosing a marriage partner and getting involved in a situation where a sense of intimacy is required for success. It may be inaccurate to think of early dating as a causal factor here, however. Early daters tend to be early-maturers. Early-maturing boys enjoy more favorable self-concepts and other positive personality attributes than do late-maturers [22, 32]. While early-maturing girls do not evoke the social esteem or popularity granted to early-maturing boys, they still have favorable self-concepts, as compared with late-maturing girls. It is likely that the youngsters with the most favorable personality characteristics have the most opportunity for dating, both in regard to early dating and number of partners throughout the dating period. (See pages 418–422 and Figure 17–1 for importance of personality factors in popularity.)

Romantic Love

One of the effects of love is an emphasis on the loved one's favorable qualities and a playing down of his faults. Romantic love makes this emphasis to an extreme degree. Romantic love is embedded in a complex of beliefs and ideals in Western culture: for every individual, there is an ideal mate; love hits suddenly, even at first sight; when ideal mates marry, they live happily ever after; nothing matters but love; fidelity is a natural part of love; moonlight, roses, music and perfume symbolize and promote love. Large parts of the American economy reinforce these beliefs and ideals through advertising, movies, songs and magazine stories.

Adolescents are fertile ground for the seeds of romance, although it is likely that some recent cultural developments are causing a decrease in romantic love. In spite of its potential danger, that of leading to a marriage without a realistic basis, romantic love offers opportunities for personality growth, along with a deeply beautiful experience which is worth while in itself. Tom sees Alice, the girl of his dreams, as a perfect woman and a perfect person, embodying the qualities which he, in his imperfection, would like to achieve. And Alice loves him! To be loved by such a marvelous creature proves that he is more worthy than he had thought possible. What's more, since they are a pair (unique and perhaps predestined), he derives some good qualities from her. The qualities which Tom sees in Alice and then makes his own are his own ideals. His identity becomes firmer as he projects his ideals and then incorporates them, with Alice playing an essential reciprocal role. With Alice, of course, the same process can take place, resulting in a stronger sense of identity for her, too.

Tom's and Alice's relationship may develop into one where the sense of intimacy is promoted. Tom may share thoughts and feelings with Alice as he does with Bob, in a search for real understanding of the other person. If Tom and Alice communicate realistically, they will discard some of their romantic patterns, but *after* romantic love has served its identity-building function. If their love affair does grow into a permanent one, they may retain some romantic patterns which can continue to serve each one's sense of identity. After all, none of the crises of personality growth is ever completely solved, and identity, like the other senses, continues to need strengthening throughout life.

Sex and Love

Since American adults have a hard time telling how sex and love are the same and how they are different, it is no wonder that adolescents are often bewildered in this context. American sex mores are not extreme (Scandinavians are more permissive, Indians less) but they are extraordinarily varied and complex. The incidence of adolescent premarital intercourse is increasing, much of it expressing feelings, urges and needs which cannot be called "love" [17].

CULTURAL INTERPRETATIONS. In order to put love and sex in the broad cultural framework which permits consideration of the many influences on behavior, Ausubel* uses some of Mead's findings. The way in which a culture defines and relates sex and love will determine a large part of what people think, feel and do about them. Mead's studies of the South Seas show the relation between certain practices and beliefs. Parallels can be seen in America. When a culture denies the existence of a sex drive in women, most girls grow up without experiencing sex desires. This is what happens among Manus girls and puritanically reared American girls. The physiological equipment for sex functioning and sex desire is there, but it is not activated because the society interprets women as unconcerned with sex. Samoans see both men and women as having physiological sex urges which are natural and pleasurable, although women are considered to react more slowly than men. Adolescents are expected to carry on casual sexual relationships of a sensuous nature with no deep affection involved. Middle-class American youth tend to look enviously upon Samoan sex life when first they hear about it, since it looks delightfully gratifying. Lower-class Americans actually do approach the Samoan attitudes and practice, although they have hostile elements of the larger culture directed against them which do not exist in the South Sea paradise. A cover story in *Time* magazine [37], reporting on sex mores and morality, suggests that the casual attitude toward sex is being held more widely. The author points to a Broadway musical which includes, without reference to love or passion, this song:

> Drinks are okay, they break the ice
> Dancing this way is also nice
> But why delay the friendliest thing two people can do?
> When it can be the sweetest and,
> Let's face it, the completest and friendliest thing
> Two people can do!

Middle-class American have partially adopted the rationale which the Arapesh have developed to an advanced state of integration—sexual intercourse is an ultimate expression of a deep affectional relationship, made permanent by marriage. This is the point of view sanctioned by the Judeo-Christian religion and also supported by Erikson's theory of personality development. A person with a well-established sense of identity can become truly intimate because he is not afraid of losing himself [15, p. 125]. True

* This account of cultural influences on love and sex draws heavily on Ausubel's [2, pp. 390–436].

intimacy is a necessary condition for genitality. Genitality is the capacity for a complete and mutual sex relationship. As each partner gives of himself unselfishly, the two enter into a wholeness which Erikson says, "in some way appeases the potential rages caused by the daily evidence of the oppositeness of male and female, of fact and fancy, of love and hate, of work and play" [5, p. 96].

This point of view is also the conclusion of the *Time* reporter, after his research into sex attitudes and behavior. He expresses it movingly: "But many do feel the need for a reaffirmation of the spiritual meaning of sex. For the act of sex is above all the supreme act of communion between two people, as sanctified by God and celebrated by poets. 'Love's mysteries in souls do grow, but yet the body is his book,' wrote John Donne. And out of this come children, who should be a responsibility—and a joy. . . . the Victorians, who talked a great deal about love, knew little about sex. Perhaps it is time that modern Americans, who know a great deal about sex, once again start talking about love."

Since the whole Arapesh society treats sex expression as the natural culmination of a couple's deepening, loyal affection, neither boys nor girls experience sex urges apart from marital love. American middle-class youth have a very different experience with sex desire. While they hold the ideal of sex integrated with love and marriage, they feel urgent, sometimes overwhelming, sex desires. Boys do so very much more than girls. Early-maturing boys feel sex desire for more of the teen years than do late maturers.

Instead of the consistent picture of love and sex absorbed by the Arapesh child, the American child learns from many different points of view. Mass media promote romantic concepts and also pour out a flood of sexually exciting sights, sounds and ideas which stimulate Samoan-type sensuousness. The *Time* article [37] calls this phenomenon "spectator sex." Parents, often bewildered by discrepancies between what their own parents did to them and modern recommendations for frankness, may operate according to the idea that the less said, the better. Or they may do a good job of telling where babies come from and even how they got there, but bog down when the youngster wants to know how sex feelings work and what they have to do with love. A conscientious parent may manage to say, "Sex is beautiful in marriage but not before" without being able to marshal much convincing evidence. After all, it is not easy to explain Erikson's theory! The culture gives little help. The peer group, with its emphasis on popularity and physical attributes, stimulates physiological excitement. Middle-class boys, ranging more freely for friends and activities than do girls, contact youngsters who take part in casual sex relationships without emotional involvement. The ugliness of sex is pointed out by parents, teachers and mass media. While it is hard to explain why full mutuality with a loved partner is sublime, it is easy to recite the shocking statistics on venereal disease and to underline the heartbreaks resulting from premarital pregnancy. Thus sex is often put in a framework of physiological desire, frustration, guilt and fear. The rationale behind this treatment is that adolescents must be frightened into controlling their physical urges.

RESULTING BEHAVIOR. Sexual tensions are very real to American boys in general and to some American girls, because the culture has interpreted sex in such a way that these feelings are stimulated and easily recognized. There is even explicit statement of the naturalness of sex in the sex education literature. Since boys and girls are permitted to associate freely, with little supervision, opportunities abound for satisfying sex urges on a sensory level. At the same time, the sex-and-love ideal acts as a deterrent to casual sex, while fears may be a general deterrent. The American middle-class boy who is caught in a dilemma of conflicting desires and ideals tends to use masturbation and petting as solutions. The majority of American males do not experience this conflict and accept premarital intercourse as natural.

MASTURBATION. Cultural interpretations of masturbation have followed such a confusing course that neither parents nor children know what to think about this common adolescent practice. While the old idea that masturbation is a shame and a sin is not outmoded, contemporary sex guides to youth still hint that it is not quite nice or at any rate, something to be indulged in as seldom as possible. Even while fully accepting the fact that masturbation has never been known to cause physical harm, many people have a nagging idea that there is something wrong with it psychologically. Blos [5, pp. 159–169] gives the psychoanalytic point of view that masturbation plays a necessary but temporary role in psychosexual development. Through masturbation, the adolescent integrates his childhood sex experience with his present and future. Infantile sexual pleasures become not ends in themselves but part of the mature heterosexual act, in foreplay. Through fantasy during masturbation, the adolescent connects the solitary sex experience with heterosexual acts. In this way, masturbation promotes development. If it becomes indispensable for releasing tension, then development has gone wrong and masturbation is pathological.

In addition to its function of integrating the total sex experience, masturbation helps to relieve the sexual tendencies of individuals who are denied heterosexual outlets. Among such individuals are those who hold the ideal of love integrated with sex and who wish to avoid sexual intercourse until they can have it with a deeply loved, permanent partner. The effect of masturbation on these people is probably determined largely by whether they consider it shameful, sinful and injurious or a natural, neutral substitute for a necessarily postponed activity.

PETTING. Tender touching means love as well as the stimulating and releasing of sexual tension. From a light kiss or the stroking of a hand to sexual intercourse itself, touch can symbolize the closeness of people who love each other. As a love symbol, the more intimate the touch, the deeper the love indicated. To adolescents, experimenting with symbols, not knowing for sure how deeply they care or how much they dare reveal, sexual excitement can well up in response to the tender touch, turning the encounter into sensual pleasure rather than communication. It sometimes happens that one of the partners is symbolizing love in her caresses while the other is seeking stimulation and tension release for himself. In these two situations, communication fails, destroyed by sensuousness. No doubt most petting fuses love and sensual pleasure, even when confusion also results. The same thing holds true for petting as for sexual intercourse, that true intimacy cannot be achieved until the sense of identity is fairly well established. For the person who is striving hard to find himself, symbols of love will have to remain at the light-touch level, since he has only a light love to give. If sensory gratification is his purpose in petting, however, he can go as far as he may. And if he is overwhelmed by sexual stimulation and carried along to an intimate level of gesture, then, if he holds the sex-with-love ideal, he will feel wrong and guilty.

Petting is generally accepted in American middle-class culture as a natural expression between a couple in love, and often as a desirable substitute for premarital intercourse. A study of several hundred college students indicated [13, p. 63] that petting occurred on 73 percent of the dates of males and 71 percent of the dates of females, while sexual intercourse occurred on 12 percent of the men's dates and 2 percent of the women's. This study and others have corroborated the commonly held opinions (1) that the girl usually defines the level at which petting shall stop, but that when a couple are in love, couples tend more to decide the stopping point by mutual agreement, and (2) that girls are motivated more by love and men by sensory gratification but that being in love draws them closer together in motivation.

SEX ROLE AND SEX IDENTIFICATION. A strong sense of identity includes the conviction that one is feeling, thinking and behaving appropriately as a man or a woman. A complex, fast-changing society presents the child with the formidable task of figuring out just what *is* expected of men and women. We have just sketched America's varied assortment of prescriptions for sex behavior, which is only one facet of the sex role. Although men's and women's roles will necessarily vary with each other, the bulk of publications on sex role feature the uncertainty of what is expected of women. One never sees a book title such as *Modern Man: The Lost Sex,* but libraries abound in such volumes as: *Modern Woman: The Lost Sex, The Modern Woman's Dilemma, The Second Sex, How To Be a Woman, Her Infinite Variety, The Feminine Mystique, American Women: The Changing Image.* The first of these urges woman to a fully sexual being, the last two spank her for wasting her intellect. Although adolescents will not derive their concepts of sex role from such learned sources as these books, the books illustrate the variety of concepts which will affect the youngsters. Chapters 9 and 13 have discussed the learning of sex roles and sex identification within the family. The process continues in adolescence, of course, but now it becomes influenced more strongly by experiences outside the family. The peer group definitions (discussed on pages 516–517, in terms of popularity) are largely for the present.

In the long gab sessions of best friends, however, the kind which stimulate the sense of identity, the future is considered too. Other sources of sex role concepts are teachers, other adults and mass media and literature.

The likely reason for the printed stress on woman's role rather than man's is that woman plays a series of quite disconnected roles, while man's roles are much more continuous, even though he does make adjustments to the changes of the women in his life. This is not to say that woman's roles are clear-cut within each stage, even though the biological events which punctuate a woman's life are definite and irreversible. The adolescent girl role lays heavy stress on being physically attractive, socially active and popular with boys. Intellectual achievement is a minor theme which occasionally swells to take precedence over the major theme, such as when college entrance is in the offing. Overdevelopment of the minor theme is thought to endanger the major ones. In other words, girls won't be popular if they appear too smart. The two themes continue to conflict in the girls who go to college and to some extent in those who take jobs right after high school. At their peak of beauty and attractiveness (as defined by American society), these are glamor girls, women drinking the heady wine of general admiration and power over men. A full sense of identity requires work and achievement too. The role which follows glamor girl, wife for most women and career girl for some is sharply different from glamor girl. She gets little reward for being young, beautiful and female. She has to work.

Men realize, of course, that the roles played by women affect profoundly the roles of men. Rejection of the role of American husband was shown by many men who married European and Asian women. The same attitude is related in magazine articles, aptly expressed by Hunt [21, p. 149].

> Today's young neotraditionalist doesn't want a girl just like the girl that married dear old Dad, for she was probably a hell-for-leather feminist. What he does want is a good, old-fashioned girl of the kind they still have in Europe, where women are said to be truly feminine. Depending on who tells the tale, European women are chic, sexy, intriguing, adorable, and let their escorts talk while they tinkle with appreciative laughter; or are sturdy enough to rise at 6 A.M., scour the markets for bargains, carry staggering loads home, and bear babies without a whisper; or can simultaneously turn the cuffs on a man's shirt, whip out *truite amandine* for dinner, and keep four children silent and neat, all without any sense of strain. It is not quite clear whether all these traits are to be found in one and the same woman, but it *is* absolutely clear that the neo-traditional man thinks the European woman knows her place—and allows him *his* place, without any contest.

The adolescent boy knows and has known from early childhood that he must achieve and produce. Even though the high school peer group in general rewards athletes more than it does scholars, the adult male's vocational role is that of breadwinner, both before and after marriage. This fundamental is clear, even though expectations of husbands are not so definite. Also, there is continuity between the two roles. Research shows that husband–wife relationships are strongly influenced by the husband's vocational role. Men who were successful and competent in the work world exert more power in making decisions at home than did men who were less adequate vocationally [4, p. 31]. The very importance of work as part of a man's role makes vocational decisions serious and problems anxiety-producing [35].

There is evidence that the ideal male role is changing from the picture of a man as a go-getter, a competitive individual who initiates, invents, saves for the future and pushes ahead. Modern bureaucratic society seems to influence men to be cooperative, relaxed group members, enjoying the present and letting the company take care of the future [31]. Mead [30] decries the shift from longtime goals to immediate gratification which means early marriage and early forcing into a pattern of domestication, focusing on earning a living instead of on ambitions for the future, curtailing the period of freedom in which a youth can dream.

The adolescent asks, "Just what does it mean to be an adult of my sex and what sort of acceptable adult am I capable of becoming?" Since the cultural prescription is not clear-cut and, in fact permits many different interpretations, each young person has to select from the variety of possibilities, without the certainty of knowing that his choice is right. While freedom of choice is a cherished democratic right, it does carry the disadvantage of uncertainty and anxiety. College students reflect the strain of this burden in their current practice of dropping out for a semester or a year or two in order to "find themselves." About 25 percent of Harvard students, for example, drop out at some point during their undergraduate years, many to return and do well. About 90 percent of those admitted to Harvard eventually receive degrees. An exploration of this situation at Harvard revealed a deep understanding on the part of the faculty and administration as to the difficulties their students experience in establishing a sense of identity [38]. The Dean of Freshmen wrote to parents, "For those who cannot find a field that really interests them, or who find that their motivation is at a low ebb, I have no hesitation in recommending a year's leave to think things over."

Marriage

Americans marry relatively young, as Figure 17–3 will show. Average age at marriage gradually decreased from 1890 to 1950 while social change has been speeding up and the complexity of life increasing. Early marriage is a problem insofar as the participants who are not mature enough to cope with the demands of marriage. The number of teenage marriages has increased since mid-century, because the number of teenagers has greatly increased. While the nationwide average age of marriage has not decreased since 1950, as can be seen from Figure 17–3, the problems of youthful marriages are serious to the people involved and to society.

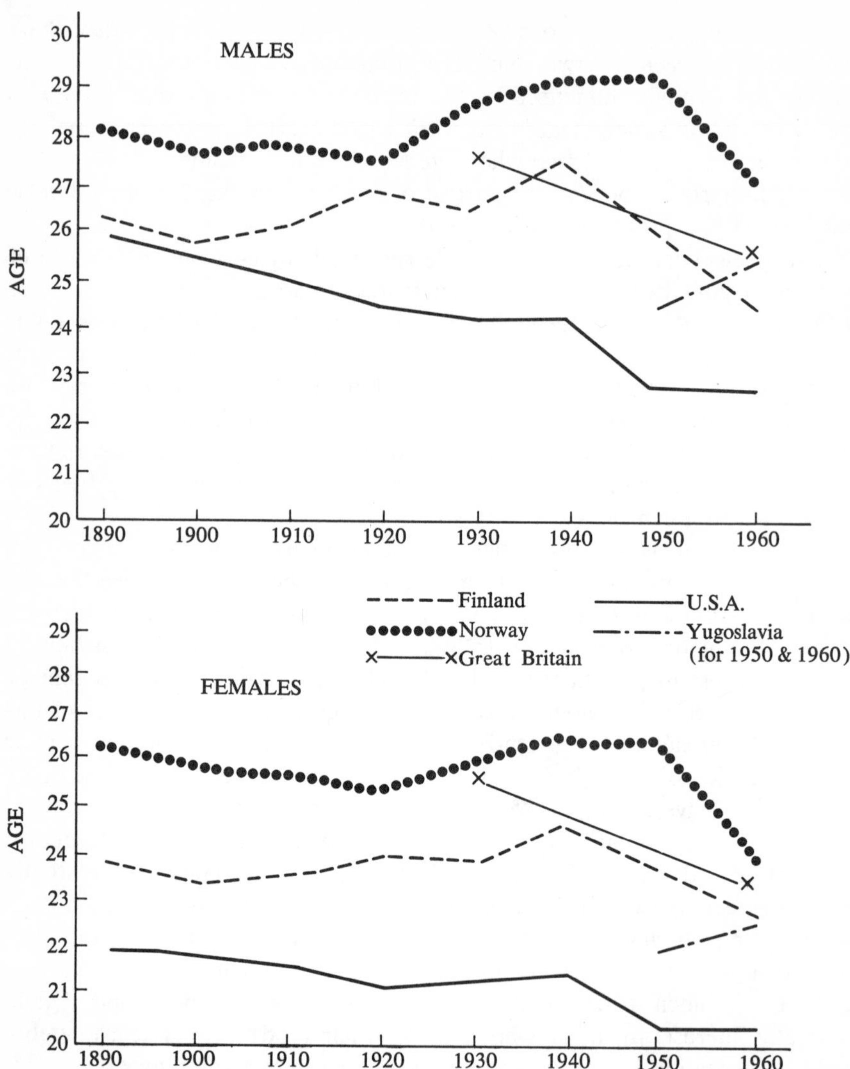

Figure 17–3. Average age at marriage over seven decades. (Reprinted by permission from J. Moss, "Teen-age Marriage: Cross-National Trends and Sociological Factors," *Journal of Marriage and the Family,* **27,** 2, 230–242. Data on Britain from E. Venables, "Proposed Affinities in British-American Perspectives of Adolescence," *Journal of Marriage and the Family,* **27,** 2, 148–170. Copyright © 1965, National Council on Family Relations.)

From the standpoint of personality development, one would expect adolescent marriages to be less satisfactory than those between adults. With one partner or both in the crisis of developing a sense of identity, the relationship cannot be one of mutuality and intimacy, which is the essence of the ideal American marriage. Both partners expect happiness from marriage, and yet their own immaturity prevents the establishment of the relationship which yields lasting happiness. The theory is borne out by statistics. A study [27, p. 130] of 1,425 high school marriages showed that 20 percent of those occurring three years previously had already ended in annulment, divorce or separation. This figure is nearly three times as large as the marriage dissolution rate for the general population for the first three years of marriage [3, p. 94]. Further evidence comes from census data on age at marriage and remarriage. Women still in their first marriage in a given year had been married at an average age of 21, while those already in their second marriage had contracted the first at 19 [18]. A study of divorced couples and happily married couples showed that as contrasted with the happily married, more of the divorced women had married before 18 and the men before 21 [28, pp. 101–102].

Conclusions from extensive research on young marriages indicate the factors contributing to early marriage [7]. The insecurity of modern life leads to a desire for loyalty, warmth and affection which adolescents hope to find in marriage. Personal happiness is understood as inherent in family life. Sometimes marriage is used for avoiding the draft. A bandwagon effect may operate, as friends marry young. Marriage is overevaluated due to the romantic, glamorous image promoted by mass media. Economic restraints are reduced by prosperity, employment of wives, contribution of parents and occupational fringe benefits. Increased heterosexual behavior at younger years, earlier dating and going steady, plus increased stimulation of sex drives by mass media, leads to increased premarital sexual intercourse, pregnancy and forced marriages. Some early marriages are precipitated by the desire to escape from unhappy situations in home, school, or community or to solve other emotional problems.

Some of the outstanding characteristics of young marriages are as follows [7]. Most of them involve young brides and older grooms. Only 10 percent of high school brides marry high school students. High school students who marry are mostly juniors and seniors. One third to one half of high school brides are pregnant. One half to three quarters of high school grooms are involved in a premarital pregnancy. Premarital pregnancy rates are highest among couples where both are still in high school, lowest where both have finished high school. Most weddings are performed by clergymen. Young marriages involve more crossing of religious lines than do older marriages. Brides tend to come from lower- or working-class families.

PROBLEMS RESULTING FROM EARLY MARRIAGE. In addition to the disasters of marriage dissolution and the hazards to personality development already mentioned, young marrieds face curtailment of education and reduction of level of aspiration. (This problem is a serious one from the standpoint of society, as well as for the individuals involved, since it results in individuals less able to do society's productive and creative work.) Not only do married high school students face restrictions and some hostility from teachers and principals, but economic pressures may force them out of school. An analysis of 765 Pennsylvania high school marriages showed that two thirds of the married high school boys remained in school, while 90 percent of the girls dropped out [11]. A Minnesota study on teenage marriages showed that 69 percent of these brides were pregnant and that most of them were required to drop out of school [1]. A more liberal policy exists in California, where only 9 percent of high schools reported that they suspended a married pregnant girl as soon as the pregnancy was known [26]. Even when pregnant teenage brides are allowed to stay in school, they must stop to have their babies, and few ever return. Limited in education, and needing to take any sort of a job in order to make ends meet, the married adolescent may have to settle for a vocational identity which is a far cry from his dreams.

Most obvious of problems is children. The higher instability of teenage marriages implies that they will involve more children in divorce than will other marriages. Thus the average adolescent is two stages behind the stage of maturity required by parenthood. Since most teenagers are deeply involved in the identity crisis and barely started on the problems of intimacy, the sense of generativity is far beyond them. One has to grow far beyond mutual give and take, understanding and communicating in order to nurture a completely dependent being, to fit one's own existence in with his, to enjoy giving without receiving immediate understanding and appreciation.

MARRIAGE EDUCATION FOR ADOLESCENTS. Many high schools and colleges try to prepare their students for marriage through courses, as well as through lecture series and individual lectures, films and discussions. The objectives of marriage education include giving adolescents knowledge of facts, behavior, development and social norms, attitudes towards the self and other people, competence in interpersonal skills and values in human development and relationships. Evaluations of the results of marriage and family living courses have shown considerable benefit to those students who have taken them, in terms of added knowledge, understanding, attitudes and abilities [12]. Marriage courses are not available to many American young men and women. A study of the recent history of marriage courses in California shows that opportunities for marriage education increased after World War II until 1954, when such courses were cut back. At present, the teaching of marriage and family living is again on the increase, with 67 percent of the California high schools queried offering at least one unit in this area [26]. The figure for the whole United States is probably considerably lower than that found for California.

SUMMARY

The sense of identity grows through interactions with peers of both sexes. The crowd provides a group identity which helps the adolescent to separate himself from his family, drawing a distinct line between generations. He feels comfortable when identified with the crowd, and therefore able to try out a variety of roles. The clique is a small, select group of close friends, usually alike in interests and background, giving one another security and status, often behaving cruelly to outsiders.

A large survey by questionnaire indicated that dominant values for boys are athletic, for girls, social, with scholarship not only low on the list but actually losing value over time. A longitudinal study demonstrated adolescents' respect for moral values and mature social behavior. Adult values are accepted increasingly with age.

Friendship contributes to the sense of identity, especially close relationships such as "best friends" enjoy. When the sense of identity has reached a certain level of strength, friends can achieve true intimacy. It is easier and safer to develop the first intimate friendship with members of the same sex.

Greatly valued by many adolescents, popularity may exact a price of those who achieve it. Popularity, along with other attributes, gives high status. Many adolescents feel inadequate and inferior because they are assigned low or moderate statuses in systems which offer little room at the top.

Cross-sex friendships occur at earlier ages today than they did formerly. Earlier dating, going steady and marriage also occur, threatening to restrict personality development.

Romantic love is an aspect of American culture which sometimes confuses adolescents and yet also strengthens and beautifies their relationships with the opposite sex. Romantic love can promote the development of the sense of identity.

Adolescents have difficulty in achieving a satisfactory philosophy of sex and love and in integrating their behavior with it. Confusions result from a wide variety of values and behavior within the culture and from the rapid social changes which are taking place. Parents can offer little help. Sexually expressive acts have various interpretations, sometimes making communication difficult between members of a couple. The establishment and acceptance of a sex role is also difficult, especially for women.

Adolescent marriages have a poor chance for success, posing threats to the participants, their families and the children who result from them. Personality immaturity, including educational and vocational immaturity, makes it difficult to achieve the high level of satisfaction which Americans demand of marriage. Education for marriage and family living has been found helpful to those adolescents who have such courses. Unfortunately, this type of education is not available to all.

REFERENCES

1. Anderson, W. J., & Latts, S. M. High school marriages and high school policies in Minnesota. *J. Marr. Fam.*, 1965, **27,** 266–270
2. Ausubel, D. P. *Theory and problems of adolescence.* New York: Grune & Stratton, 1954.

3. Bernard, J. Divorce and remarriage—research related to policy. In E. M. Duvall & S. M. Duvall (Eds.), *Sex ways—in fact and faith*. New York: Association, 1961.
4. Blood, R. O., & Wolfe, D. M. *Husbands and wives*. Glencoe, Ill.: Free Press, 1960.
5. Blos, P. *On adolescence*. Glencoe, Ill.: Free Press, 1962.
6. Broderick, C. B., & Fowler, S. E. New patterns of relationship between the sexes among preadolescents. *Mar. Fam. Living,* 1961, **23,** 27–30.
7. Burchinal, L. G. Young marriages—what we know about them. In E. M. Duvall & S. M. Duvall (Eds.), *Sex ways—in fact and faith*. New York: Association, 1961, pp. 69–83.
8. Cameron, W. J., & Kenkel, W. F. High school dating: a study in variation. *Mar. Fam. Living,* 1960, **22,** 74–76.
9. Campbell, E. H. The social-sex development of children. *Genet. Psychol. Mono.,* 1939, **21,** 461–552.
10. Coleman, J. S. *The adolescent society*. Glencoe, Ill.: Free Press, 1961.
11. de Lissovoy, V., & Hitchcock, M. E. High school marriages in Pennsylvania. *J. Marr. Fam.,* 1965, **27,** 263–265.
12. Duvall, E. M. How effective are marriage courses? *J. Marr. Fam.,* 1965, **27,** 176–189.
13. Ehrmann, W. Changing sex mores. In Ginzberg, E. (Ed.), *Values and ideals of American youth*. New York: Columbia Univ., 1961, pp. 53–70.
14. Elkin, F., & Westley, A. A. The myth of adolescent culture. *Am. Soc. Rev.,* 1955, **20,** 680–685.
15. Erikson, E. H. *Identity and the life cycle*. New York: International Universities, 1959.
16. Furfey, P. H. *The growing boy*. New York: Macmillan, 1930.
17. Glassberg, B. Y. Sexual behavior patterns in contemporary youth culture—implications for later marriage. *J. Marr. Fam.,* 1965, **27,** 190–192.
18. Glick, P. C. *American families*. New York: Wiley, 1957, pp. 56–58. Also, Stability of marriage in relation to age at marriage. In R. F. Winch, R. McGinnis & H. R. Barringer, *Selected studies in marriage and the family*. New York: Holt, 1962, pp. 622–626.
19. Hechinger, G. Slowing down the social pace. *New York Times Magazine,* April 14, 1963, p. 99.
20. Horrocks, J. E., & Thompson, G. G. A study of the friendship fluctuations of rural boys and girls. *J. Genet. Psychol.,* 1946, **69,** 189–198.
21. Hunt, M. M. *Her infinite variety*. New York: Harper, 1962.
22. Jones, M. C., & Mussen, P. H. Self-conceptions, motivations and interpersonal attitudes of early- and late-maturing girls. *Child Devel.,* 1958, **29,** 491–501.
23. Kelly, G. A. *Dating for young Catholics*. New York: Doubleday, 1963.
24. Kuhlen, R. G. *Psychology of adolescent development*. New York: Harper, 1952.
25. Kuhlen, R. G., & Houlihan, N. B. Adolescent heterosexual interest in 1942 and 1963. *Child Devel.,* 1965, **36,** 1049–1052.
26. Landis, J. T. High school student marriages, school policy and family life education in California. *J. Marr. Fam.,* 1965, **27,** 271–280.

27. Landis, J. T., & Landis, M. G. *Building a successful marriage.* Englewood Cliffs, N.J.: Prentice-Hall, 1963.
28. Locke, H. J. *Predicting adjustment in marriage.* New York: Holt, 1951.
29. Lowrie, A. H. Early and late dating: some conditions associated with them. *Marr. Fam. Living,* 1961, **23,** 284–290.
30. Mead, M. The young adult. In E. Ginzberg (Ed.), *Values and ideals of American youth.* New York: Columbia Univer., 1961, pp. 37–51.
31. Miller, D. R., & Swanson, G. E. *The changing American parent.* New York: Wiley, 1958.
32. Mussen, P. H., & Jones, M. C. Self-conceptions, motivations and interpersonal attitudes of late- and early-maturing boys. *Child Devel.,* 1957, **28,** 243–256.
33. Parsons, T. Youth in the context of American society. *Daedalus,* 1962, **91,** 97–123.
34. Peck, R. F., & Havighurst, R. J. *The psychology of character development.* New York: Wiley, 1960.
35. Strodbeck, F. L. Family interaction, values and achievement. In R. F. Winch, R. McGinnis & H. R. Barringer, *Selected studies in marriage and the family.* New York: Holt, 1962, pp. 355–376.
36. Thompson, G. G., & Horrocks, J. E. A study of the friendship fluctuations of urban boys and girls. *J. Genet. Psychol.,* 1947, **70,** 53–63.
37. *Time* Magazine, January 24, 1964, **83:**4, 54–59.
38. Wertenbaker, W. A problem of identity. *The New Yorker,* December 1, 1962, **38,** 68 ff.

Growth in Self-Direction

CHAPTER 18

A crucial difference between adolescence and adulthood is in the taking of responsibility. An adult is expected to be on his own in many ways, not completely, but more so than an adolescent. Looking forward to being grown up, the young person expects to make more and more decisions independently and to receive less help and direction from parents and other sources. Self-reliance, responsibility and achievement behavior during adolescence have roots in childhood experience and in background factors. This chapter examines some of these relationships as well as the adolescent's present interactions. Growth in self-direction is traced in several different areas of life, vocational, moral and religious.

RESPONSIBILITY, SELF-RELIANCE AND ACHIEVEMENT

Responsibility

A responsible person is one who can be counted on to do his work, contribute his share and carry his load and to do it on his own, without being coerced or watched by someone else. Research shows that although this characteristic is begun early in life, it develops throughout childhood and adolescence and into adulthood [14, 15]. Responsibility in tenth graders was shown to be positively associated with having companionship with their parents, and negatively associated with parental rejection and neglect [2]. This does not say what caused children to be responsible, or that rejecting, neglectful parents caused irresponsibility. More likely, a certain quality of interaction between parent and child builds companionship, mutual involvement and responsibility.

A sex difference in responsible behavior showed up when teachers' ratings of tenth grade boys and girls were compared [2]. Teachers considered girls more responsible than boys, although they rated boys higher in leadership. The parents of these girls had given them more affection, praise and companionship than they had given their sons. In matters of discipline, they were more love-oriented with girls, using more reasoning, appealing, showing disappointment and threatening to withdraw love, while with boys they tended more toward physical punishment. Here then is further evidence that companionship and loving concern are related to the development of responsibility in adolescents.

Although parent attitudes and family relationships have much to do with it, the giving of specific jobs by parents was not found to be associated with responsibility in the child. Social responsibility on the part of the parents was, however, related to socially responsible attitudes in the children [13]. Probably the meaning of his work to the adolescent has a great deal to do with the responsibility he feels and shows. A serious, significant and demanding job is likely to evoke more responsible effort and more satisfaction than is a simple routine task. Compare lifeguarding with tidying the garage, or making a wedding cake with doing the week's ironing! Paid work outside the home tends to give a youngster a greater feeling of responsibility than does working for his family, since in the former situation, he is judged entirely on his own performance, whereas his family has to keep him anyway. Responsibility is shown also in school, with friends and in community work and play. This topic will be touched upon again under the heading "Moral Development."

Independence

Independence or self-reliance is a characteristic which can be seen early in life, probably in infancy. From preschool years through adolescence, it is a fairly stable characteristic, more so for girls than for boys [22]. The investigators who studied independency defined its opposite, dependency in terms of passive behavior in the face of obstacles or stress; seeking support, nurturance and help when under stress; seeking affection and emotional support from female adults; seeking help with specific problems. Dependency in adults was rated on seeking dependent gratifications in choice of an occupation; dependent behavior toward a love object (sweetheart, husband, wife); dependent behavior with parents; dependent behavior with nonparents; withdrawing in face of failure; conflict over dependent behavior. Relating childhood behavior to adult behavior, results showed that girls who were generally dependent as children tended to be dependent adults, but boys often changed during childhood. Probably these findings reflect the pressure that is placed upon boys to become more and more independent as they grow up. College freshmen's capacity for autonomous behavior has been found to be related to their parents' behavior as autonomous people with inner-directed standards of action [30].

Achievement

Children develop standards of performance for themselves from their parents' expectations of them, depending on the ways in which parents make demands. Different levels of achievement motivation occur in different environmental situations, presumably because of the parent–child interaction which takes place. Success or failure at school doubtless contributes also to aspirations. By the time a child reaches adolescence, he has many experiences which affect his desire for excellence and his definition of it. What happens during adolescence also contributes in an important way to ambition. The stability of achievement behavior has been studied at the Fels Foundation, where 71 subjects were followed from birth to early adulthood [29]. Ratings of achievement behavior at age 10 to 14 showed significant relationships to ratings of adult achievement behavior, particularly in the intellectual sphere. In this area, ratings at 10–14 accounted for at least a quarter of the variation in ratings in adulthood. In other words, taking the group as a whole, childhood experiences determined 25 percent or more of the striving for intellectual achievement in early adulthood. The true figure may be greater than 25 percent, since other kinds of observations, interviews and ratings might reveal more. Even if childhood experience determined as much as half of the adult achievement behavior, there is still room for the adolescent years to be extremely important in the development of achievement motivation.

When parent–adolescent relationships are studied for the light that they shed upon achievement behavior, one has to consider that some of the measured results will be due to past parent–child relationships rather than to only the present situation. With this limitation in mind, let us see what is offered by some research on parents and adolescents. In general, when parents demand high achievement, adolescents, as well as children, are likely to deliver it [3]. This statement is deceptively simple. If it were that easy to build achievement motivation, the world might be overrun with eager beavers. Many other influences interact with parental demands.

Achievement motivation is closely related to independence. The settings in which parents communicate their expectations make a difference in children's reactions to those expectations. Children tend to develop high levels of aspiration when their parents make appropriate demands at appropriate times, rewarding success liberally, and holding standards of excellence for them while also giving them freedom to work out their own problems in their own ways [47]. Both of these conditions seem to be necessary for high achievement motivation, a demand for achievement and plenty of opportunities for independent work and decision making. Parental faith is implicit. The youngster and everyone else must realize that if a parent expects his offspring to do well, while giving him autonomy within wide limits, then the parent believes strongly in the child. Such a relationship has meaning for an adolescent's sense of identity, as well as for his desire to excel. He is faced with the problem of believing in himself, his abilities and potential, with the questions of whether he will be able to play the roles in life that he wants to play and of what *are* the roles he would like to play. The demonstrated faith of parents shows him that significant people are sure he can accomplish what he must.

Background Factors

What kinds of settings produce the types of parent–child relationships which lead to high-achievement motivation? Research shows that culture, class, family size, position in the family and family structure all have some bearing on the question.

Cultural differences in training for independence and achievement were found in a study which compared six racial and ethnic groups [37]. The groups differed in social mobility and achievement motivation. High-achievement motivation was more characteristic of Greeks, Jews and white Protestants than of Italians, French-Canadians and Negroes. A comparison of English and American parents showed the former as giving children more training for self-reliance [7].

Class comparisons show the middle class to be most concerned with achievement and most intent upon training its children thus. One investigator [2] compared upper-middle-class parent–adolescent relationships with those in the lower-middle class and commented on the results in both boys and girls. Independence training was greater for upper-middle-class girls than for lower, with the former showing more initiative. For boys, the reverse was true, with lower-middle-class boys being controlled less by their parents and showing more achievement aspiration.

The joint effects of social class and family size have been studied for boys only [38]. Although the middle class averaged the highest achievement scores, scores within a given class varied greatly with the sizes of the families. The lowest aspiration levels were seen in large, lower-class families, the next lowest in large, upper-class families. Medium-sized upper-class families produced about the same aspiration levels as middle-class families. Tables 18–1 and 18–2 show the contrasts and similarities between the different classes and family sizes.

Position in the family makes a difference in achievement orientation. The popular notion is that eldest children are most ambitious. When class and family size are also taken into account, the eldest child does not always show up as the one most interested in achievement although he often does. The study from which these tables come indicates that the highest achievement scores of all belong to children born into intermediate positions in large families of the upper and middle classes. Eldest children score high in medium-sized families in the upper and middle class. The youngest child in a small upper- or middle-class family is likely to be just as achievement-oriented as the eldest. Least ambitious of all is the eldest in a large, lower-class family. Second place for lack of achievement motivation goes to the youngest in a large, upper- or middle-class family.

TABLE 18–1

Achievement aspiration scores of boys, according to family size and social class.

	*Sample A**				*Sample B†*			
	Family Size				*Family Size*			
Social Class	*Small*	*Medium*	*Large*	$\bar{x}$	*Small*	*Medium*	*Large*	$\bar{x}$
I–II	5.20	6.41	2.33	5.46	7.28	7.93	2.25	7.11
III	6.49	6.14	5.83	6.28	7.67	7.36	6.13	7.32
IV	5.06	3.40	2.82	4.00	6.33	6.15	7.29	6.29
V	4.57	3.67	1.48	3.31	4.15	5.00	2.00	4.69
$\bar{x}$	5.43	4.64	2.48		6.61	6.57	6.22	
N	178	193	54		155	166	45	

* Information lacking for two cases.
† Information lacking for one case.
Source: Reprinted by permission from B. C. Rosen, "Family Structure and Achievement Motivation," *American Sociological Review*, **26**:4, Table 1, p. 585. Copyright © 1961, American Sociological Association.

TABLE 18–2

Achievement aspiration scores of boys, according to birth order, family size and social class.

	Social Class I–II–III			*Social Class IV–V*		
	Family Size			*Family Size*		
Birth Order	*Small*	*Medium*	*Large*	*Small*	*Medium*	*Large*
Oldest	5.82	7.52	5.75	4.31	2.86	1.00
Intermediate	*	5.44	10.00	*	3.43	1.96
Youngest	5.94	5.21	2.00	5.93	3.90	2.84

* There are, of course, no intermediate children in a two-child family.
Source: Reprinted by permission from B. C. Rosen, "Family Structure and Achievement Motivation," *American Sociological Review*, **26**:4, Table 3, p. 578. Copyright © 1961, American Sociological Association.

The effect of power structure on achievement motivation is interesting. Power structure can be described in terms of who dominates the family, who makes most of the decisions and whether and how people cooperate. In a study [40] of aspiration and actual school achievement of urban high school boys, families were classified into four types, father-dominant, mother-dominant, conflicting and autonomic (cooperating smoothly). Scholastic achievement was about the same for boys from mother-dominated and autonomic families, lower for those from father-dominated and lowest for those from conflicting families. There was a difference in the emotional patterns of the first two groups, even though they achieved about the same. The boys from mother-dominated families showed much more anxiety and tension than did their scholastic equals from autonomic families. When the subjects were compared in level of aspiration, those from conflicting families were considerably lower than the rest. The other three groups did not differ greatly, although the highest average score came from the autonomic group. In this respect, the lowest socioeconomic group differed from the whole group, in that mother-dominated families produced the highest levels of aspiration, father-dominated next and autonomic third highest. Thus it can be seen that the relationships between husband and wife create a family atmosphere which affects the children's aspirations and their actual achievements. This study suggests that the democratic, equalitarian family is just as efficient as a mother- or father-dominated family in producing go-getters and that the democratic family is best of all in building healthy personalities at the same time.

While the family is extremely influential in childhood achievement motivation, with the school the second important factor, the adolescent interacts with a wider world of which family and school are only parts. He has a broader base on which to build his level of aspiration, since it is part of the identity which he is working to achieve. He seeks this part of himself through relationships with peers, while he works and earns money, when he tastes the pleasures of recreation and acquisition which achievement makes possible, when he reads about heroes and failures, when he creates and enjoys the arts, when he contemplates good and bad in the world. (See Figure 18–1.)

VOCATIONAL DEVELOPMENT

A major concern of adolescents is the choosing of a vocation and getting established in it. A firm sense of identity requires successful working and producing in a role acceptable to the young person and to the adults and peers important to him. In contrast to the situation in simple societies, where there is little choice of occupation, modern youth is faced with a bewildering array of possibilities. Even though his parents may be ready with advice or even urging, the young person feels the necessity for self-direction in choosing his occupation. To be adequate and successful in an acceptable work role is usually a requirement of adulthood. In actually doing adult work, a young person learns to distinguish between what he thinks and hopes he might become, and what he hopes and thinks he could do in order to make a better world [20, pp. 335, 336].

To achieve a satisfactory work role one must choose it and prepare for it. Much as adolescents desire to take on the role that will give them adult status, they are often at a loss to know how to choose and how to prepare. The puzzling facts revealed in one study [28] were that high social status in high school was closely associated with both high interest in going to college and low interest in scholastic achievement. How could adolescents who wanted to

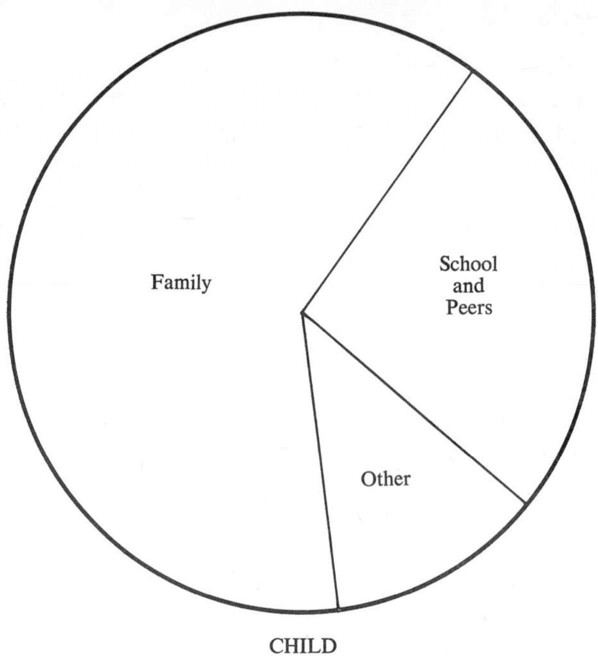

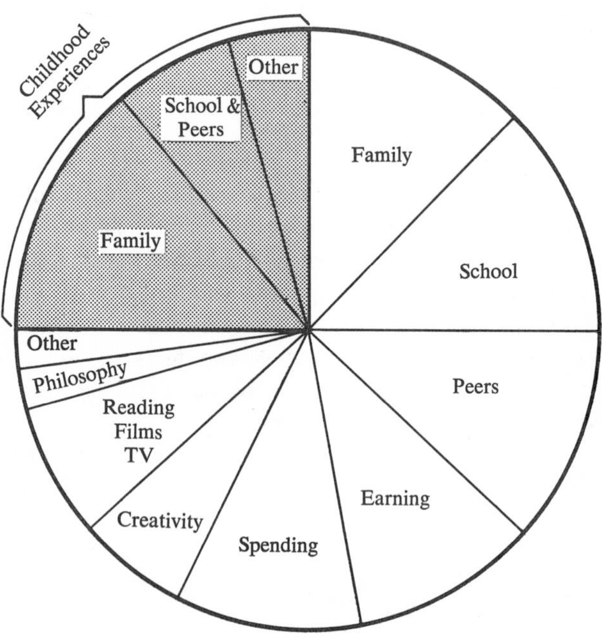

Figure 18–1. Schematic representation of interactions influencing achievement motivation.

go to college be disinterested in academic achievement during high school years? Perhaps school achievement symbolizes subordination to adults, a status which teenagers are trying to escape. Perhaps it is associated with gold stars, good grades, doing what the teacher wants. College, on the other hand, symbolizes adult status, "sophisticated" activities, freedom from parental control, choosing for oneself. Although desirous of assuming adult roles, these adolescents seem unrealistic in regard to preparing for those roles. Although the majority of the adolescents in this study evidenced this lack of realism, some avoided the paradox.

Vocational guidance means helping with both the choosing and the preparation. In a broad sense, all of education is preparation for work roles. The youngster's interaction with his school depends upon many influences, including the important ones of his desire for achievement and his intellectual resources. Educational achievement and vocational preparation depend also on the opportunities offered.

Opportunities for Education

A society expresses important beliefs and values in the educational system it maintains. In a project sponsored by UNESCO and the International Association of Universities [1] educational selection processes in 12 countries were studied. About three quarters of the world's educational systems, which enroll about half of the world's students, follow the European plan. The other quarter, enrolling the other half of the students, uses the American plan, or what the Russians call the Russian plan. The European system channels children at 10 to 12 years into those who may go to university and those who will not. The former are permitted to study in preparation for higher education. The latter receive a different kind of education, with emphasis on the vocational. Further selective processes operate on the first group. Eventually, 1 to 8 percent of an age group go to university, having passed a final examination which makes them eligible.

The American plan permits everyone who wishes to do so to take a college preparatory course in secondary school. Completion of such a course does not grant automatic entrance to college. The institutions of higher learning apply their own systems of selection. About 35 percent of an age group goes to college. In other countries using this system, 15 to 20 percent go to college. The American plan also includes terminal education for those electing it in high school, with preparation for some vocations possible. The junior high school is an American invention designed to accommodate to the variety of physical, intellectual and emotional growth encountered in people between about 11 and 15. Criticized severely by Conant in 1960, the junior high school's virtues are still being debated by education authorities [19]. Ideally, the junior high provides a time and a place where the young adolescent can explore vocational identities and find at least the broad outlines of one that fits, if not the exact form. Guided by teachers and counselors, he tests himself as to interests, talents and achievements. With basic self-knowledge in these areas, he is helped to choose the high school course which will lead him to an appropriate work role. Whether the junior high school is fulfilling its obligations or not, some sort of system like this is required by the basic values in American democracy.

Does extending high school education to a larger proportion of the population lower the average intellectual level of the students? One student of this matter [21, pp. 278–280] quotes research to show that it does not. Not only is there a larger potential of intellectual ability in the population than was inferred from tests of 40 years ago, but intellectual growth continues for a greater number of years than early students of intelligence thought.

Education Required by Various Occupations

Educational level is related to occupational level. As one ascends the occupational scale, more and more years of academic achievement are required, with the professions necessitating education that extends into adulthood. A college education has become almost essential for success in the professions and management occupations. In one study, 84 percent of 9,000 college graduates were professional people or proprietors, managers and executives, while only 16 percent of noncollege graduates were such [17]. Although the labor force is growing rapidly and openings for technical and professional workers are increasing, openings for unskilled labor remain about the same and employment for farmworkers is decreasing [33]. Figure 18–2 shows the level of education of young people entering the labor force. Table 18–3 shows the educational level of the adult men who are now in the labor force. Vocational and technical education are required by most occupations. The average professional or technical worker has had more than four years of college. In some jobs, the worker can learn while doing, through an apprenticeship, an in-service training program or a probationary period after an appropriate amount of formal education. Such jobs include many skilled crafts, sales clerk, policeman and college professor. For other jobs, especially those where licensing is required, an institutional training period and examination are required before the worker is allowed to operate. Examples of these occupations are hairdresser, optometrist, schoolteacher and physician. The increasing technological complexity of the modern world creates an increased demand for workers who are competent in using various scientific techniques. Many technicians are trained by the companies who need them, others by educational institutions. In addition to finding out which work roles he wants and which he could achieve, the adolescent has to find and obtain the education necessary for the job.

Intellectual Factors

Intelligence as measured by IQ tests is positively related to occupational level, but correlations between intelligence and job success are quite low, as

Educational level of men now in the labor force.

Occupation Group	Percent Distribution by Highest Educational Attainment																				
	Ages 25 and Over			25–29			30–34			35–44			45–54			55–64			*65 and Over*		
	Less Than 1 Year of High School	*1–3 Years of High School*	*At Least High School Graduate*	*Less Than 1 Year of High School*	*1–3 Years of High School*	*At Least High School Graduate*	*Less Than 1 Year of High School*	*1–3 Years of High School*	*At Least High School Graduate*	*Less Than 1 Year of High School*	*1–3 Years of High School*	*At Least High School Graduate*	*Less Than 1 Year of High School*	*1–3 Years of High School*	*At Least High School Graduate*	*Less Than 1 Year of High School*	*1–3 Years of High School*	*At Least High School Graduate*	*Less Than 1 Year of High School*	*1–3 Years of High School*	*At Least High School Graduate*
	1960*																				
All Occupations‡	36.4	20.1	43.5	19.4	20.6	60.0	23.1	22.9	54.0	27.8	21.5	50.7	42.5	20.7	36.8	57.3	16.6	26.1	63.4	12.6	24.0
Professional, technical, and kindred workers	3.6	5.6	90.8	1.0	3.6	95.4	1.3	4.4	94.3	2.0	4.7	93.3	4.8	7.5	87.7	9.7	9.0	81.3	12.7	7.9	79.4
Managers, officials, and proprietors	18.8	17.5	63.7	6.0	12.8	81.2	7.1	15.8	77.1	9.9	15.8	74.3	19.6	19.8	60.6	34.0	19.8	46.2	45.1	16.4	38.5
Clerical and kindred workers	18.1	20.7	61.2	6.0	15.4	78.6	8.7	19.7	71.6	11.0	19.7	69.3	21.8	24.1	54.1	37.5	23.9	38.6	43.6	19.6	36.8
Sales workers	17.2	18.3	64.5	4.9	13.3	81.8	6.6	15.5	77.9	9.1	16.5	74.4	18.9	22.1	59.0	34.7	22.4	42.9	47.0	18.4	34.6
Craftsmen, foremen, operatives, and kindred workers	43.8	25.9	30.3	24.8	28.3	46.9	30.8	31.4	37.8	35.4	28.7	35.9	52.1	24.9	23.0	68.4	17.7	13.9	74.9	12.8	12.3
Farmers and farm managers	58.6	14.3	27.1	26.4	14.9	58.7	33.2	18.0	48.8	45.3	15.4	39.3	60.6	15.8	23.6	73.8	12.9	13.3	78.5	9.9	11.6
Service workers	49.5	22.1	28.4	21.3	26.3	52.4	25.9	29.8	44.3	33.5	27.3	39.2	53.8	22.9	23.3	71.2	15.7	13.1	78.4	11.1	10.5
Laborers	68.4	17.1	14.5	47.5	24.8	27.7	56.4	24.4	19.2	62.7	20.4	16.9	76.4	13.7	9.9	85.3	9.0	5.7	87.5	6.6	5.9
	1950†																				
All Occupations‡	47.1	17.9	35.0	27.1	22.3	50.6	31.4	21.6	47.0	42.5	20.3	37.2	56.5	16.0	27.5	65.7	12.2	22.1	70.6	9.7	19.7
Professional, technical, and kindred workers	6.6	5.9	87.5	2.6	4.4	93.0	3.1	4.4	92.5	5.1	6.2	88.7	9.5	7.1	83.4	13.0	7.1	79.9	14.0	6.3	79.7
Managers, officials, and proprietors	28.3	17.5	54.2	9.5	16.5	74.0	11.4	17.2	71.4	20.3	19.4	60.3	34.0	18.1	47.9	44.8	15.4	39.8	51.9	13.7	34.4
Clerical and kindred workers	23.2	19.5	57.3	8.0	16.8	75.2	10.9	17.7	71.4	19.6	21.5	58.9	33.0	22.2	44.8	41.3	19.4	39.3	48.2	14.5	37.3
Sales workers	22.1	18.1	59.8	8.1	15.8	76.1	10.1	16.9	73.0	17.1	19.9	63.0	30.2	19.8	50.0	40.9	17.3	41.8	47.9	15.3	36.8
Craftsmen, foremen, operatives, and kindred workers	52.3	22.8	24.9	29.8	29.9	40.3	35.6	28.6	35.8	49.9	25.5	24.6	66.3	18.0	15.7	74.9	12.8	12.3	77.5	10.4	12.1
Farmers and farm managers	71.1	12.7	16.2	49.9	16.6	33.5	56.3	16.3	27.4	65.6	14.8	19.6	76.9	12.3	10.8	80.9	9.8	9.3	84.0	7.9	8.1
Service workers	58.7	18.5	22.8	29.7	26.6	43.7	34.3	25.6	40.1	48.1	23.7	28.2	66.8	17.2	16.0	76.9	11.3	11.8	79.8	9.6	10.6
Laborers	74.7	13.7	11.6	55.5	22.0	22.5	62.6	19.6	17.8	74.0	15.1	10.9	84.2	9.3	6.5	88.3	6.5	5.2	89.2	5.6	5.2

* Data relate to the experienced civilian labor force. † Data relate to employed civilians with education reported. ‡ Includes persons with occupation not reported.

Source: Basic data from 1960 Census, PC(2)-5B, Table 8, and 1950 Census, P-E, No. 5B, Table 11. Reprinted by permission from *Statistical Bulletin*, Metropolitan Life Insurance Company, June 1965.

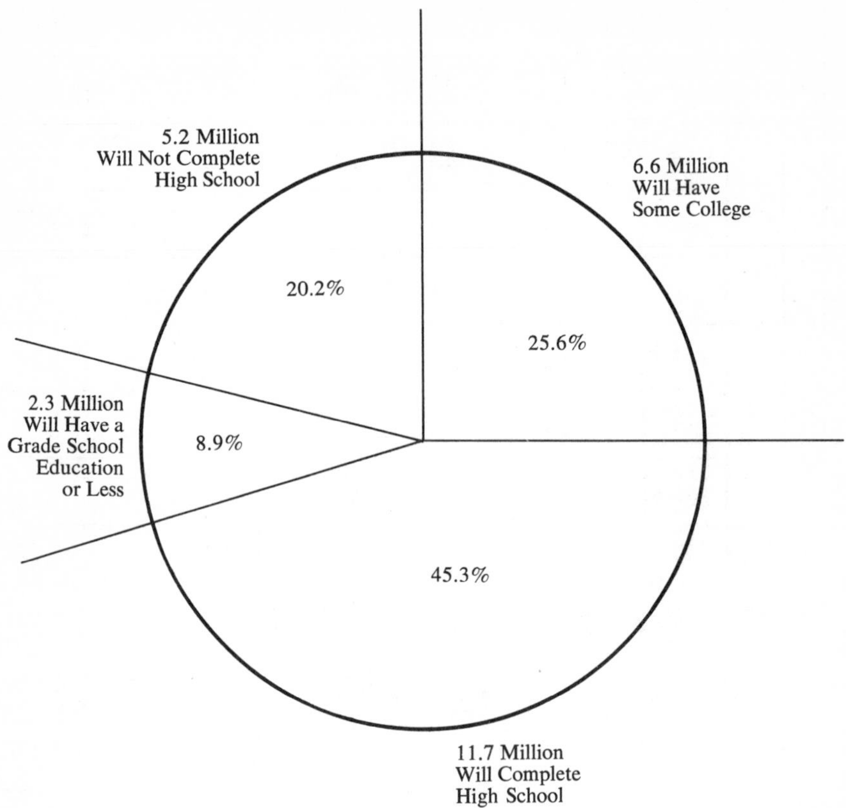

Figure 18–2. Educational level of young people entering the labor force. (From page 3, President's Committee on Youth Employment, "The Challenge of Jobless Youth," U.S. Department of Labor, U.S. Government Printing Office, Washington, 1963.)

can be seen in Table 18–4. The occupations can be arranged in a hierarchy according to average intelligence of those following them, but with each occupation, there is a wide range of intelligence scores, with considerable overlapping between levels [45]. Table 18–5 shows how recruits in both world wars scored on the Army General Classification Test, where the average is 100. Percentiles for various occupations are shown. For example, a teacher with a score of 110 scored higher than 10 teachers out of 100, while a lumberjack with a score of 60 scored higher than 10 lumberjacks out of 100. The top 10 percent of lumberjacks, however, scored higher than the bottom 10 percent of teachers.

An analysis of test scores of 10,000 people in 22 occupations yields Figure 18–3 [44]. Arrangement along the quantitative axis shows the relative requirements of the various occupations for quantitative and mathematical performance. The horizontal axis shows relative requirements for mechanical and verbal skills and knowledge. The diagram suggests how requirements are

TABLE 18–4

Relationships between measured intelligence and job success.

Type of Job	*Median Correlation with Job Success*	*Percent Significantly Positive Correlations**	*Number of Coefficients*
Clerical workers	.35	70	84
Supervisors	.40	78	9
Salesmen	.33	100	4
Sales clerks	−.09	6	18
Protective services	.25	33	6
Skilled workers	.55	100	6
Semiskilled workers	.20	47	45
Unskilled workers	.08	31	13

* Significant at 5 percent level.

Source: Adapted from E. E. Ghiselli and C. W. Brown. Reprinted by permission from R. L. Thorndike and E. Hagen, *Measurement and Evaluation in Psychology and Education* (New York: John Wiley & Sons, Inc., 1961), Table 9.4, p. 249. Copyright © 1961, John Wiley & Sons, Inc.

combined in various jobs. It is easy to pick out each type of combination by quadrants. Occupations placed near one another are close in requirements. See Figure 18–3.

Occupational choice was found to be related to style of cognitive functioning in high school students. When the occupational aspirations of highly creative adolescents were compared with those of highly intelligent (high IQ) adolescents, [9] striking differences occurred between the two groups in both quantity and quality of vocations which appealed. The Creatives mentioned significantly more occupations, apparently having mobility of thought which permitted considering many possibilities. The Creatives also mentioned more unconventional occupations, such as veterinarian and entertainer, and unresolved combinations, such as "law or music" and "teaching or art." Answers to the parents' questionnaire about children's occupational interests showed 75 percent of the high IQ's interests falling into five categories: engineering and architecture, science, medicine, law and teaching. Only 35 percent of the Creatives' choices fell into those categories. Creatives chose many of the expressive occupations, such as writing and dancing, while High IQ's did not mention expressive careers.

There is then a fundamental consistency in both groups of gifted adolescents. Their cognitively oriented and socially oriented behaviors *fit*. The high IQ's selected stereotyped meanings, judged success by conventional standards, accepted models provided by teachers and planned for careers that conform to what other people expected. The Creatives diverged from stereotyped meanings, rejected the models provided by teachers, sought careers which did not conform to expectations of others. Thus cognitive style makes a difference not only in the occupations adolescents choose but in the way in which they define success.

TABLE 18–5

Percentiles for measured intelligence as they occur in various occupations.

	Percentile				
Occupational Groups	10	*25*	*50*	*75*	*90*
Accountant	114	121	129	136	143
Teacher	110	117	124	132	140
Lawyer	112	118	124	132	141
Bookkeeper, general	108	114	122	129	138
Chief clerk	107	114	122	131	141
Draftsman	99	109	120	127	137
Postal clerk	100	109	119	126	136
Clerk, general	97	108	117	125	133
Radio repairman	97	108	117	125	136
Salesman	94	107	115	125	133
Store manager	91	104	115	124	133
Tool maker	92	101	112	123	129
Stock clerk	85	99	110	120	127
Machinist	86	99	110	120	127
Policeman	86	96	109	118	128
Electrician	83	96	109	118	124
Meat cutter	80	94	108	117	126
Sheet metal worker	82	95	107	117	126
Machine operator	77	89	103	114	123
Automobile mechanic	75	89	102	114	122
Carpenter, general	73	86	101	113	123
Baker	69	83	99	113	123
Truck driver, heavy	71	83	98	111	120
Cook	67	79	96	111	120
Laborer	65	76	93	108	119
Barber	66	79	93	109	120
Miner	67	75	87	103	119
Farm worker	61	70	86	103	115
Lumberjack	60	70	85	100	116

Source: Adapted from N. Stewart. Reprinted by permission from R. L. Thorndike and E. Hagen, *Measurement and Evaluation in Psychology and Education* (New York: John Wiley & Sons, Inc., 1961) Table 9.3, p. 248. Copyright © 1961, John Wiley & Sons, Inc.

Special Abilities

In addition to intelligence tests, occupational aptitude tests are used for occupational selection. A factor analysis of 59 different tests given to 2,156 subjects yielded these factors as pertinent in the various occupations [36, pp. 73–74]: verbal meaning, number, manipulation of spacial relations, general intelligence, perception of geometric forms, perception of words and numbers, aiming, accuracy or precision of movement, speed, finger dexterity, manual dexterity and logic. Vocational guidance includes measuring such abilities and matching the individual to the requirements of the occupation. A given ability can be desirable, undesirable or neutral for a certain job.

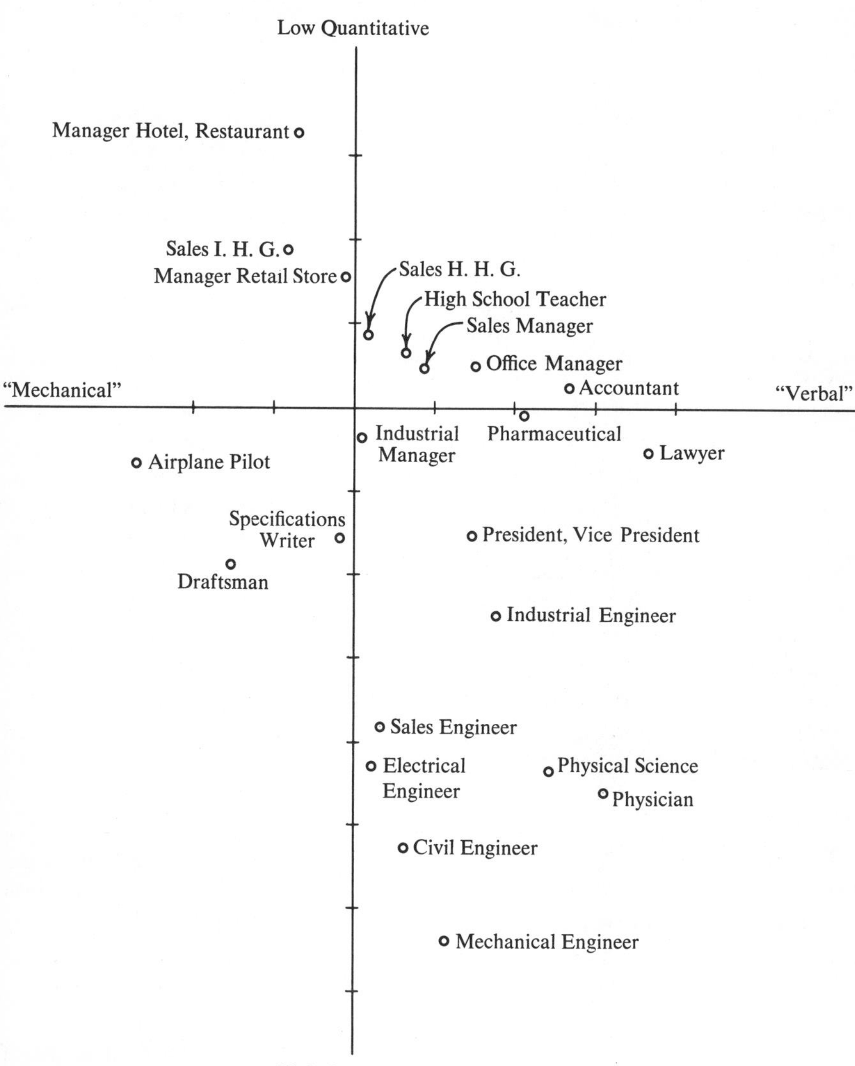

Figure 18–3. Quantitative, mechanical and verbal requirements of various occupations, shown by the location of the occupation in the quadrants. The quantitative dimension is represented by the vertical axis, the mechanical-verbal dimension by the horizontal. (Reprinted by permission from R. L. Thorndike and E. Hagen, *Ten Thousand Careers*. New York: John Wiley & Sons, Inc., 1959. Copyright © 1959, John Wiley & Sons, Inc.)

Social ability, for example, although not listed in the factors above, is very valuable to an insurance salesman, of indifferent use to a fireman and possibly distracting to a theoretical physicist.

Personality Factors

Personality factors contribute to choice of occupation as well as to achievement in the work role selected. Insofar as interests are considered an expression of personality, then a great deal of research has been done in this area. Interest inventories are questionnaires which reveal a pattern of interests. The pattern is then matched to the interest pattern of people engaged in a certain occupation. In the Strong Vocational Interest Test, for example, occupations are grouped by similarity of interest pattern, and the individual's test results are examined to see which group or groups they fit. Thus a person may find that his pattern fits that of Group IX, consisting of sales manager, real-estate salesman and life insurance salesman. Or he may go into Group II, mathematician, engineer, chemist, physicist. When the results of interest tests are factor-analyzed, these broad types of interests show up as distinct: scientific, linguistic, social and business [36, p. 86]. Interests in children are quite unstable. Interest patterns increase in permanence as adolescents progress through high school and college. A longitudinal study concludes that the interests characteristic of scientists become crystallized in boys between ages 10 and 14, but that the temperamental pattern basic to the interests becomes established much earlier. Girls who are interested in careers, as contrasted with those who are not, show certain characteristics. The career girls scored higher on scales measuring responsibility, self-control and achievement. Their career interests began to take shape at or before the age of 14 [46].

Background Factors

The higher the socioeconomic level of the family, the better are the children's chances of going to college, graduating from college, achieving high-level occupations and achieving eminence. The reasons for these conditions are complex. They include differences in all sorts of opportunities as well as the personality structure produced by middle- and upper-class families and the values held.

Work adjustment of men between 16 and 36 has been studied in terms of family background. Adjusting well to the demands of the job was related to these aspects of early family life: closely knit, unified, affection for father, little sibling rivalry, independence, little ambivalence [8].

Studies of eminence and achievement at high levels usually show a larger-than-chance proportion of first-borns and only children. The same is true in studies of gifted children and children with high IQ's [36].

The effects upon adult roles of experiences with siblings has been explored by using a vocational interest test (Strong) with 20-year-olds [43]. A child's sex and ordinal position influence not only the ways in which his parents treat him but also the interactions between him and his siblings. What is more, these interactions continue to occur while the nuclear family lasts. They are not merely a matter of infancy and early childhood. In this article, only twosomes are considered, the effect of the relationship on each member of the pair being considered. The analysis of interest patterns as related to role situation led to these conclusions:

First-borns, especially girls, tended to choose teaching occupations more than did second-borns. This finding fits with other research which suggests that they have higher responsibility training, being more often put in charge of younger children and playing adult surrogate roles.

The all-boy twosome had the most masculine scores and preferred the conventional economic activities of producing, buying and selling: life insurance salesman, buyer, real-estate salesman, banker, purchasing agent, production manager, farmer, accountant, sales manager and president of a manufacturing company. Of all the girls, the girl with the older brother showed the highest interest in the economic activities of buyer and life insurance salesman.

In the all-boy pair, the first-born tends to choose occupations where achievement is by strategy, the second-born achievement by power. Jobs involving strategy are production manager, personnel director, public administrator, YMCA secretary, school administrator, social worker, CPA, accountant, office man, purchasing agent, banker, sales manager, lawyer, president of manufacturing concern. Occupations requiring applications of physical power to persons, animals and things are physician, osteopath, dentist, veterinarian, farmer, policeman, mortician and YMCA physical director.

The all-girl pair did not show such definite trends as the all-boy. Preferences as to power strategy were the reverse of the boys, the first-born girls preferring occupations involving physical power and the second-borns preferring strategic jobs. The authors suggest that the first-born girl is encouraged and approved by her mother when she takes physical care of her siblings and acts as a parent surrogate. Therefore, she has little need to develop strategic ways of coping with siblings.

Two-sex twosomes preferred the most expressively creative occupations of artists, music performer, author and architect. The highest-scoring boy was the boy with a younger sister, while the highest-scoring girl was the one with an older brother. This twosome, older boy, younger girl was therefore the most creative. When the technically creative professions were considered —psychologist, physicist, mathematician, engineer and chemist—it was found that the older brother of a girl tended to express greatest interest.

This study is significant in its illumination of the processes by which people come to assume the great variety of work roles offered in a society. The number of reciprocal roles which siblings can play is large, and this research is only beginning in delineating their influence upon the adult work roles which the individual chooses.

Vocational Maturity

Based on the idea that growth occurs through solving certain problems at each age, a project called The Career Pattern Study is concerned with finding out what is appropriate vocational behavior at various ages. Selecting and preparing for an occupation is one of the essential tasks of adolescence. In order to understand better how this task is achieved, and thus to know better how to help adolescents with it, the investigators started with the handling of the task in early adolescence, using boys entering the ninth grade [42]. They were concerned with the competence of these adolescents as to making important decisions about their vocational futures. From analyses of tests and interviews and a factor analysis, the following vocational maturity in ninth grade was defined. The essence of vocational maturity was *planfulness,* a looking ahead in preparation for vocational choice. Planfulness was the general factor in the four kinds of behavior which indicated vocational maturity, planning orientation, and taking the long view ahead, the short view ahead and the intermediate view. Wisdom of choice was not characteristic of boys this age. Almost half the subjects had vocational preferences which were inappropriate for their intelligence levels. Almost half chose vocations which did not agree with their interest patterns as shown on a standard vocational interest test.

Those who did express wise preferences, however, were more likely to be among the more successful young men at age 25, as shown by a follow-up study of the ninth grade boys [41]. Other ninth grade predictors of success at age 25 were concerned with education and vocational choices, acceptance of responsibility for choice and planning, planning itself, consistency of field preferred, parental occupational and educational levels, cultural stimulation, out-of-school activities and high school grades.

This research shows, then, that at the beginning of adolescence, vocational maturity is an expression of the whole personality rather than a narrow part of it. Preparation for taking adult roles has a broad base. The study also yields evidence that it is unwise to let boys this age make vocational choices which will limit their experience and education, since they tend not to choose appropriately.

Another study of vocational choice dealt with 929 high school students [32]. Questionnaires were administered to the tenth, eleventh and twelfth grades. Although this inquiry was neither as deep nor as thorough as the one described above, its conclusions give some information about the problems adolescents face in trying to find suitable occupations. The subjects did not know enough about the various vocational possibilities to be able to choose wisely. They often did not know why they chose certain work roles. They received little useful guidance from adults. The authors concluded that these facts were the reasons why the subjects had not gone far in developing long-range vocational objectives.

An Example of Vocational Development: The Growth of Scientists

A study [35] of the development of scientists offers insight into the making of a scientist but also into some of the ways in which background, experiences, relationships and abilities influence the adolescent's work roles. Sixty-four eminent scientists were chosen for careful individual study on the bases of membership in learned societies and ratings by scientists in important positions. The subjects were biologists, physicists and social scientists (psychologists and anthropologists). Although the report goes into what the scientists were like as adults, our interest here is in how they came to be scientists.

Most of the families were upper-middle-class, with an economic range from relatively poor to very well-to-do and none extremely wealthy. Fifty-three percent of the fathers were professional men. In most of the homes, learning was valued for its own sake, and the interests of many of the subjects took an intellectual form at an early age. Many were first-borns or only children, and many of those who had siblings were in positions similar to those of first or only children.

Certain home situations occurred more often in this group than in the normal population. One such event was the early death of a parent. Fifteen percent lost a parent by death before the age of 10, whereas of a group of 624 college students, only 6.3 percent had lost a parent by age 10. There were significant differences between the three groups. Twenty-five percent of biologists, 13 percent of physicists and 9 percent of social scientists had lost a parent by age 10. The author mentions a corroborating study which showed that 25 percent of mathematicians and physicists lost a parent before age 10. The author suggests that the effects of parental death included stimulating the boys to greater independence. She also tries to explain the differential effects. The problem of facing death, she speculates, turned the boys to a deep concern with the mechanisms of life, and for some, this concern developed into a generalized interest in biology.

Social isolation and some disinterest in persons was often felt by the physicists and to a slightly lesser extent by the biologists. These men had tended to have cordial but rather distant relationships with their fathers, apparently identifying comfortably with them, respecting them and not being pressured by them. They tended not to have close relations with siblings and to have only a few friends rather than a crowd or gang. They were slow in dating, often starting in the later years of college. They found satisfaction in things outside the human realm. The social scientists, in contrast to the others, were more involved with family relationships and pressures. They more often conflicted with their fathers and found their fathers unsatisfactory persons with whom to identify. Their families tended to feel superior, and to strive to isolate themselves from other families. Boys growing up in such families would understandably place great importance on interpersonal relationships and, if they acquired a scientific attitude, would generalize the problems they encountered and try to solve them as social scientists. Half of them started dating in high school. They dated more extensively than did the other two groups.

A number of the scientists had unusual physical conditions which may have contributed to feeling isolated. There were extremes of height, a few were abnormally small and a few unusually weak. Only three of the 12 theoretical physicists had generally good health and normal physical development. Such physical difficulties probably helped to make these boys avid readers.

The majority went to public schools, although all but two of the anthropologists went to private schools. Most of them liked school, got along well with teachers and did a great deal of reading. The different subgroups had different reading patterns, the theoretical physicists being very omnivorous readers. The physicists, and not the others, carried on great activity with gadgets, radio, meccano sets, and such. Half of the biologists showed interest in natural history as children, the other half becoming interested during adolescence in chemistry, agriculture and what science their schools offered. The social scientists showed early interest in literature and the classics.

The decision to become a certain kind of scientist was made by a few in childhood, by over half during the junior and senior years in college and by some in the second year of graduate school. The social scientists were most often late in choosing, often because they did not know enough about their fields to have become interested in them earlier. Several social scientists switched from English because they became disillusioned with it as a way of understanding human behavior. Although physicists found out early about the possibilities of research, the others often came upon it as an exciting discovery when they did their own first research. One of them expressed it thus: "One of the professors took a group of us and he thought if we wanted to learn about things, the way to do it was to do research. My senior year I carried through some research. That really sent me, that was the thing that trapped me. After that there was no getting out."

Curiosity was always characteristic of the scientists. Instead of losing their childish curiosity as many people do, they developed it into a system of thinking in a question–answer way. They settled upon their particular fields as objects of curiosity. The experience of doing research showed them how to spend their lives finding out the things they wanted to know.

Opportunities for Solving Identity Problems Through Vocational Means

The problem of insufficient and inadequate education has already been touched upon. Education is assuredly necessary for getting and holding a good job. Education and a good job are not always enough, however, to make the adolescent sure of his identity in the work world. Evidence of this fact is the feeling of uncertainty and the lack of direction which many college students express, even when they are doing well in their studies and perhaps holding good part-time jobs. On the brink of adulthood, many a person wants to assume an adult work role while trying to transform society, "to make a better world."

Some cultures require service to society at this point of life. Military service is such a requirement. Or a society may offer a choice or an honor which some of its youth are privileged to receive, such as service in the Peace Corps or VISTA, where the volunteer has a real chance of effecting changes in the conditions of men. While holding a job, he can come to terms with the difference between what he can really achieve and what he would like to do about changing the world.

The director of training for the Peace Corps has pointed out that today's college student is placed in a position of being preoccupied with his own advancement [23]. For an earlier generation, he says, college offered a moratorium from occupational responsibility, whereas today even high school, as well as college, is oriented toward getting ahead. The student is urged to score high on many tests, to engage in strategic extracurricular activities and to make the right contacts. During high school, he must work, plan and strive to get into the right college. During college, he must do the same to get into graduate school or the right job. Thus for many years, he is involved in doing for himself. These years are, however, the time when his personality development demands that he relate himself to the rest of mankind. This is the time to dream about what he might do to improve the world and to try out some of his ideas. If he is selfishly preoccupied with his own progress, then he misses important chances for growth. The Peace Corps supplies those opportunities which have diminished in the high schools and colleges. At least 36 other countries, recognizing the potentiality of the Peace Corps idea, either have organized or are initiating their own Peace Corps [4].

Similar opportunities are available within the framework of various religious and charitable organizations, many of them established long before the Peace Corps. The American Friends Service Committee has long worked at home and abroad, alleviating pain and poverty. The Red Cross brings comfort to disaster victims throughout the world. The Mormon church sends all of its young men as missionaries to bring enlightenment to others. Civil rights organizations offer chances for idealistic and selfless work. The sense of identity can be enhanced through working in one of these areas. The opportunities which are optional, however, are sought by only a few of the total number of young people, those who have already achieved a fairly high level of personality development and self-direction. (See Figure 18–4.)

MORAL DEVELOPMENT

Increasing self-direction is possible through the development of moral judgment and moral action. The sense of identity includes a concept of oneself as a moral person, behaving responsibly and acceptably in his own eyes

Figure 18–4. Volunteer George Kroon is a member of a community development project in Colombia. Here he and two young friends set off to work. (Courtesy Ray Witlin from BLACK STAR.)

and in the eyes of his fellow men. The adolescent, then, is concerned with what is right and with doing right. Moral knowledge and moral actions are not the same, although both are essentials of morality.

Moral Knowledge and Judgment

Intellectual growth and broader experience make possible a more comprehensive kind of thinking about morality. The adolescent can think more objectively than the child, influenced by his own needs and desires. His greater flexibility of thought makes it possible to go beyond the immediate situation to consider many factors that might have bearing on the question. Therefore he can judge an act right or wrong or in-between in terms of the intentions and the setting in which it happened, whereas a child is more likely to judge in terms of results and to declare it good or bad rather than shaded. An adolescent can accept, understand and invent flexible rules because he is flexible in thought. His potential for independence in moral thinking (as in all thinking) contrasts with the dependency of the child, who thinks that rules are unchangeable, given by adults or by God, or by some obscure and rigid agent. An adolescent can understand duty and obligation as based on reciprocal rights and expectations which people have of one another, whereas the childish concept of duty is as obedience to a rule or to an adult. Children are likely to believe in eye-for-an-eye, tooth-for-a-tooth type of justice, in which people must pay for their misdeed by enduring inevitable punishment given by some authority. Adolescents can grasp a concept of justice based on making amends for misdeeds, repairing, restoring what has been spoiled or taken away by the wrongdoing. They can conceive of individual responsibility, equality before the law and impartiality in justice [26].

This is not to say that all adolescents think in the most mature ways possible at their age, nor to say that children do not occasionally think on the levels designated as adolescent. Everyone has heard of a little child making an extraordinary sage moral comment and everyone knows that adolescents (and adults) sometimes think childishly. Rather, there are typical levels of moral judgment at different ages. There are also wide individual differences at each age.

Sequential Development of Moral Judgment

Kohlberg's studies [24, 25] show growth trends from childhood well into adolescence. In intensive interviews with 100 boys, he discussed 10 stories about moral conflicts. Analysis showed a definite sequence of stages in individual development. Kohlberg concluded that the level of morality a boy accepted was closely related to his level of understanding of moral concepts. Moral internalization was not to be considered simple cognitive learning of cultural norms, however, nor only a matter of mental age, as defined by intelligence tests. Level of moral judgment was found to be related to IQ, but even more to chronological age, or to age-linked experience. Peer-group participation and social class were also related to moral development. Kohlberg maintains that moral development is the product of continuous reaction to the whole social world. When a child moves from a lower type of moral thinking to a higher type, he does it through a transformation of his system of thought, a reorganization, not a simple addition of new thoughts.

Six types of moral judgment were distinguished. Each of the moral ideas expressed by every boy was designated as one of the six types. Then it was possible to show proportions of various kinds of moral thinking for each subject and for each age level. Growth trends could thus be plotted. In order to understand Figure 18–5, which shows those trends, it is necessary to define the six types of moral judgment. They are grouped in twos, making three general levels of moral development, thus:

I. Premoral level, on which impulse gratification is modified by rewards and punishments.

Type 1. Punishment and obedience orientation. The reason for doing anything or for not doing something is to avoid punishment. "Being right" means obeying an authority. There is no concept of *a* right.

Type 2. Naive instrumental hedonism. The reason for behavior is to get pleasure for oneself, often in the form of rewards from another person. Every-

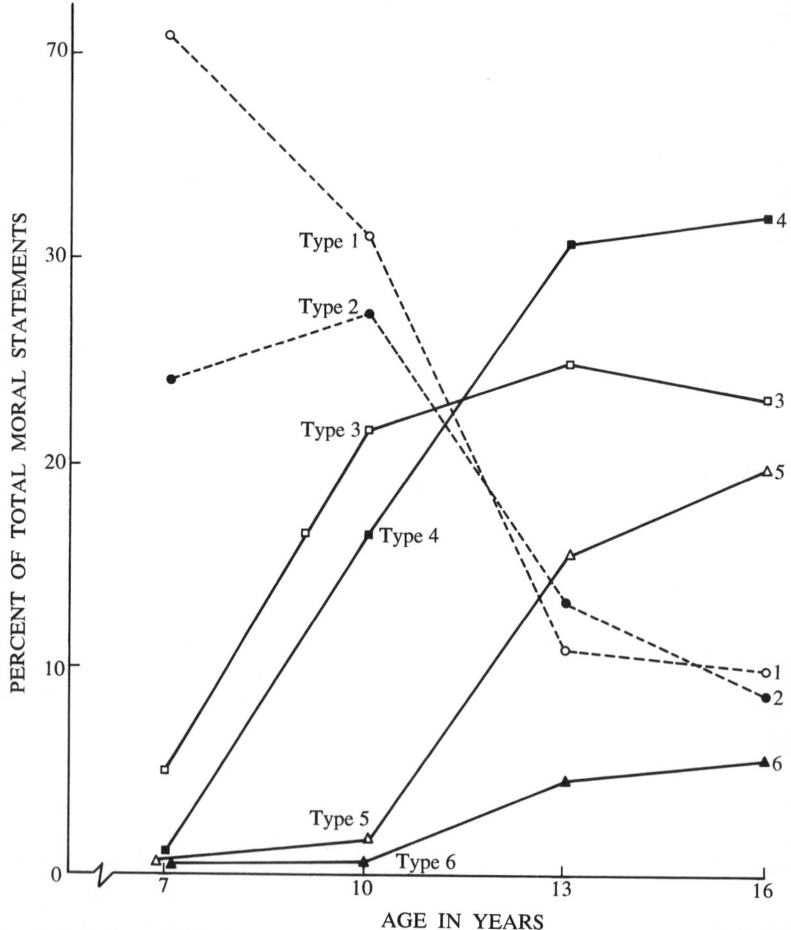

Figure 18–5. Frequency of use of six types of moral judgment by boys at ages 7, 10, 13 and 16. (Reprinted by permission from L. Kohlberg, "The Development of Children's Orientations Toward a Moral Order: I. Sequence in the Development of Moral Thought," *Vita Humana,* **6,** 11–33. Copyright © 1963, S. Karger, Basel/ New York.)

one has a right to do what he wants with himself and his possessions, even though his behavior conflicts with the rights of others.

II. Conventional role conformity, where conduct is controlled by the anticipation of social praise and blame.

Type 3. Good-boy morality, of maintaining good relationships and the approval of other people. The concept of everyone's rights is the same as in Type 2, with the addition that nobody has the right to do evil.

Type 4. Authority maintaining morality. When legitimate authorities disapprove or punish, the youngster feels guilty. A right is a claim on the actions of others, usually an earned claim, such as payment for work.

III. Morality of self-accepted moral principles, in which the person regulates his behavior by an ideal which he holds, regardless of immediate social praise and blame.

Type 5. Morality of contract and of democratically accepted law. Community respect and disrespect are powerful motivators. The concept of human rights emerges here. There are rights linked to role and status and also unearned, universal, individual rights as a human being.

Type 6. Morality of individual principles of conscience. Motivation is feeling right with oneself. The idea of rights includes all that expressed in Type 5 plus the notion that the life and personality of every individual is to be respected.

Turning to Figure 18–5 note that every type of moral judgment existed at each age examined. See the changes in each type of moral judgment between ages 7 and 16. The rank order of types of moral judgment changes at the beginning of adolescence. Premoral thinking, shown by Types 1 and 2, decreases rapidly after age 10, leveling off after 13, to constitute about 20 percent of moral judgments at age 16. Moral level II, conventional role conformity, rises rapidly in childhood to become the most frequent kind of judgment at adolescence and to remain the most frequent throughout the adolescent years studied. At 16, then, the predominant type of moral judgment is made in order to maintain good social relationships, to receive social praise, to avoid censure by authorities and its resultant guilt. A goodly number of responses occur on the highest level, however, where moral principles regulate behavior and human rights are highly respected.

Consistency of Moral Development Through Time

Although an individual grows more mature in moral judgment as he progresses through childhood and adolescence, he is likely to remain in about the same position relative to his age mates. Thirty-four children, studied intensively between the ages of 10 and 17, showed early evidence of their patterns of moral development [31]. This is not to say that the child remained the same, but that he was likely to continue to be high, average or low in moral development as compared with the rest of the subjects. These results are consistent with the idea that moral development results from the child's interactions with his environment, within the limits of his intellectual development. Since the subjects in this study had lived all their lives in the same Midwestern community and in the same families, it is not surprising that there had been few changes in the relative level of any individual's moral development.

Studies of specific kinds of moral acts, however, have not shown much consistency between different measures [16, p. 287]. Since these studies and others on specific moral conduct have focused more on children than on adolescents, it is not clear as to how consistent adolescents tend to be in specifics of moral conduct.

Moral Behavior

Doing is not the same as thinking. Everyone occasionally does a deed which he believes to be wrong and more often fails to do something which he values as right and good. How great a relationship is there between moral knowledge or judgment and moral conduct? Kohlberg has considered this question with the boys whose moral judgment he traced from ages 7 to 16. An experimental measure of cheating showed that those high in moral judgment cheated significantly less than those who were lower. (Also, delinquents scored lower in moral judgment than did normal working-class boys.) When teachers were asked to rate Kohlberg's subjects on conscience and on fairness with peers, the boys' moral judgment correlated .31 with conscience and .51 with fairness. An older study [16, pp. 116, 399] showed a correlation of .43 between moral knowledge and character ratings by teachers and peers, and a correlation of .46 between moral knowledge and tests of honesty. Thus there is some experimental and statistical evidence that moral judgment and moral behavior are related to each other but that the relationship is not a simple one.

Correlates of High Moral Development

Since moral judgment involves more and more flexible and abstract thinking as higher levels are attained, it seems reasonable that intelligence should be correlated with moral judgment. Kohlberg [26] found a correlation of .31 between intelligence and stage of moral development. A higher correlation (.59) appeared between age and moral development with mental age controlled, suggesting the great importance of age-linked experience in making moral judgments. These findings support a concept of moral development as taking place through not only cognitive learning but also social learning.

Insight into such cognitive and social learning comes from a comparison of high school students who were judged to be high in moral behavior and judgment with a group judged high in adjustment [9]. (Those high in both were eliminated from the comparison.) Although the two groups were about the same in IQ, the first did significantly better on achievement tests, both numerical and verbal. They were less satisfied with their performance, however, than the second group. The high moral group was also less satisfied with the school and the teachers. When they thought about school, they reflected on its intellectual aspects in contrast to the highly adjusted group, who thought first of social and personal aspects. Learning, to the high moral adolescents, was a personal, serious, individual experience, in which the learner attacked a problem and with which other people tended to interfere. To the others, learning was more a shared enterprise than a solitary one, and other people often helped. Socially, the high moral people were on the fringe, having placed other values ahead of success and popularity.

Family Influences

As cognitive and social interactions permit continuous reorganizing of moral judgments and moral actions, certain kinds of experiences stand out as particularly significant. Family relationships are, of course, one of the important areas of experience. How do families influence moral development?

In the longitudinal research mentioned previously, Peck and Havighurst were concerned with the family relationships of the boys whose character development was followed and analyzed [31]. Each subject was assigned a character type (which was really a description of his moral judgment and conduct), on the basis of ratings, interviews and tests. Peck and Havighurst found that some of their subjects remained at immature levels, some showed mixed behavior, typical of two levels, and some reacted fairly consistently at the highest level. The different character types distinguished are quite similar to the levels of moral development found by Kohlberg. Family correlates are given for each of the character types (levels of moral judgment and behavior):

Type 1 (similar to Kohlberg's Type 1): The *amoral* person acts largely on impulse, motivated by immediate rewards and punishments. . . . Egocentric, he sees other people as means to ends. He is unsuccessful and ineffectual because of inability to set realistic goals, to adapt his behavior and to control his impulses. This type did not occur in pure form in any of the 34 subjects, but mixed with other kinds of moral behavior.

Amoral adolescents' families were chaotically inconsistent, rejecting the children, giving them neither gratification nor any rules or principles to guide them. With no chance of gaining pleasure through pleasing his parents, the child used impulse gratification. Sometimes he was punished for it, sometimes not. Therefore he never learned behavior which was acceptable and useful for carrying on in the outside world.

Type 2 (similar to Kohlberg's Type 2): The *expedient* person considers other people's welfare and reactions only in order to gain his own ends. He is more successful than the amoral type in understanding other people and hence more successful in gratifying himself through others. He fits in when he has to do so in order to gain his ends, but takes the easiest way in avoiding as many demands as possible. He respects the reward–punishment power of adults and behaves correctly in their presence, as does a three-year-old. He is often tense from suppressing impulses and seeking the human warmth that he cannot find.

Expedient adolescents' families were mostly lenient, giving indiscriminate freedom and unthinking, inconsistent approval. One different pattern was high consistency, high severity and autocratic control by mistrustful parents. Consistency without affection and affection without consistency were equally ineffective. The child who had had superficial success at home approached the world sensitive to approval, but placing his own desires above everything else. Since his parents had neither demanded from him nor controlled him, he did not internalize rules, nor did he learn to adapt to other people's points of view.

Level II (similar to Kohlberg's Level II, including types 3 and 4): The *conforming* person follows rules rather than principles. He plays the role assigned to him by his society, says and does what others want and expect of him. A variation at this stage of development is the *irrational-conscientious* person, who follows rules compulsively. He does not realize that rules are man-made to serve human purposes, and he follows them without regard for feelings and motivation.

Conforming adolescents' families were largely consistent, autocratic and severe punishers. Mutual trust existed in some, mutual distrust and disapproval in others. Consistent authoritarianism seemed to be the key factor in producing conforming adolescents. It provided the children with stable behavior patterns which they used unquestioningly and fairly successfully as long as they could remain in a similar community. These adolescents tended to feel positively towards their parents and to like their family life. Irrational-conscientious adolescents' families were severe to extremely severe in their discipline.

Level III (similar to Kohlberg's Level III, including types 5 and 6): The *rational-altruistic* person is spontaneous, friendly, perceptive and concerned with the well-being of other people. His impulses are usually in accord with his own principles and with what society approves. He feels little hostility and guilt. This type of person matches Erikson's concept of an individual with firm identity, well-developed intimacy and a strong sense of generativity. About a quarter of the subjects in the study showed a considerable component of rational-altruistic character.

Rational-altruistic adolescents' families were consistent, strongly trustful, loving, democratic and lenient. They encouraged their children to make an increasing number of decisions as judgment matured, but reserved the right to decide what they considered necessary. Mature parental love and rational discipline seemed to be interrelated and overlapping. Both appeared to be essential, joint determinants of good character.

Peck and Havighurst found significant relationships between personality and family relationships in four areas: mutual trust and approval, consistency of family life, democratic control and severity of punishment. They concluded that the child learned to feel and act morally as just the kind of person his mother and father had been in their relationships with him.

Civic Responsibility

Successful growth in self-direction includes making and taking a place for oneself in the community. A child is given a place in a family when he is born and a place in school when he reaches the legal age for school. He makes his own way to a certain extent in a peer group. To belong firmly as a citizen, however, requires moral judgment and behavior, along with other contributions. Juvenile delinquency is a very serious kind of failure to assume civic responsibility. Because of the threat to society which it poses, juvenile delinquency has been studied more than has its opposite. Delinquents usually begin to behave illegally before adolescence. More boys than girls are involved, about four or five times as many. Boy delinquents are more likely to commit aggressive acts; girls are more likely to be apprehended for sexual acts.

A low level of moral development is typical of delinquents. A vast amount of effort has gone into finding out what causes delinquency and how to change low moral judgment and conduct into high moral judgment and conduct [10, 34]. Results show many influences interacting with each other and with the delinquent youngster. Geographic area is one such factor, which is related to other contributors such as crowding, poor economic conditions, ethnic segregation, minority group segregation, rapid population turnover. Adolescents are affected directly by these conditions and also by their parents and peers who are also affected by the same conditions. Peers often exert enormous pressure toward antisocial behavior, especially through gangs. In extreme situations, an adolescent may have to belong to a delinquent gang in order to avoid being beaten up or even killed.

The family has already been shown to be very influential in moral development, with low-moral children often coming from low-moral families. Personal inadequacy in parents is likely to be reflected in the children. For example, delinquent boys are more likely to have emotionally disturbed fathers than are normal boys. An investigation of this question showed 44 percent of delinquent boys, as contrasted with 18 percent of a normal group, to have disturbed fathers [12].

A scale of parental behavior revealed significant differences between the parents of a group of normal boys and girls and a group of 81 institutionalized delinquent 12 to 18-year-old boys [39]. The parents of delinquents were more likely to grant extreme autonomy and to provide lax discipline. Delinquent boys' fathers were less positive and less loving, while mothers were more positive and more loving than those of normal youngsters.

If the family is so important an influence, how can one family produce both a delinquent and a civically responsible adolescent? The answer is twofold. Siblings do not have identical experiences with their family, nor with any situation. Siblings are different individuals, different in physical constitution as well as in life experience. A classic [18] study on delinquent and nondelinquent pairs of brothers concludes that the delinquent boy had had little satisfaction from his family relationships, while his brother had had a much more fulfilling family life. The former was likely to feel rejected, unloved, deprived, insecure, blocked, jealous, guilty and confused. He was often intensely unhappy over family shortcomings, such as lack of harmony and parental mistakes and misconduct.

Physical constitution has been found to have a bearing on delinquency in boys [3, 11, 12]. Delinquents were more likely to be solid, muscular, closely knit, rather than linear and fragile. The interplay between physical, social and psychological factors is shown in the series of studies from which this information comes. For example, linear and fragile boys tended to be more sensitive and responsive to the environment than did chubby types, who were more stolid and matter-of-fact. When a linear boy had an emotionally disturbed father, he was more likely to be delinquent than was a chubby boy with an emotionally disturbed father.

Poor moral development, as expressed in delinquency, is the result of a complex of interactions between the individual and the environment. This topic constitutes a whole area of specialized study.

RELIGIOUS DEVELOPMENT

Just as increased cognitive and social growth underlie the moral development of adolescence, so they also contribute to religious and philosophical development. The adolescent, in his urge for self-direction, tries to find out for himself the meaning of life. To find his identity involves placing himself in new relationships. What eventually results from a successful search is called by Erikson the sense of integrity [6, pp. 268, 269].

Studies on children of three denominations have already been reported (pages 379–380). Adolescents between 11 and 14 showed differentiated and abstract conceptions of their denominations, seeing them as systems-among-systems. Such concepts were seen as typical of Piaget's stage of formal operations. Changes and progression in certain religious beliefs from age 12 to 18 are apparent in Table 18–6 [27]. Adolescents were asked to indicate agreement with statements of religious belief. With increasing age, there was a marked discarding of specific, concrete beliefs, such as, "Every word in the Bible is true" and "God . . . punishes you if you are not good." About two thirds of 12-year-olds believed such statements, in contrast to about one third of 18-year-olds. Tolerance of various beliefs and practices was greater in older adolescents than in younger. The 18-year-olds agreed more with "Catholics, Jews and Protestants are equally good" and "It is not necessary to attend

TABLE 18–6

Differences in religious beliefs at three age levels during adolescence.*

Statement	"*Believe*" 12	15	18	"*Not Believe*" 12	15	18	"*Wonder About*" 12	15	18
God is a strange power working for good, rather than a person.	46	49	57	31	33	21	20	14	15
God is someone who watches you to see that you behave yourself, and who punishes you if you are not good.	70	49	33	18	37	48	11	13	18
I know there is a God.	94	80	79	3	5	2	2	14	16
Catholics, Jews and Protestants are equally good.	67	79	86	9	9	7	24	11	7
There is a heaven.	82	78	74	4	5	5	13	16	20
Only good people go to heaven.	72	45	33	15	27	32	13	27	34
Hell is a place where you are punished for your sins on earth.	70	49	35	16	21	30	13	27	34
Heaven is here on earth.	12	13	14	69	57	52	18	28	32
People who go to church are better than people who do not go to church.	46	26	15	37	53	74	17	21	11
Young people should belong to the same church as their parents.	77	56	43	13	33	46	10	11	11
The main reason for going to church is to worship God.	88	80	79	6	12	15	4	7	6
It is not necessary to attend church to be a Christian.	42	62	67	38	23	24	18	15	8
Only our soul lives after death.	72	63	61	9	11	6	18	25	31
Good people say prayers regularly.	78	57	47	9	29	26	13	13	27
Prayers are answered.	76	69	65	3	5	8	21	25	27
Prayers are a source of help in times of trouble.	74	80	83	11	8	7	15	10	9
Prayers are to make up for something that you have done that is wrong.	47	24	21	35	58	69	18	17	9
Every word in the Bible is true.	79	51	34	6	16	23	15	31	43
It is sinful to doubt the Bible.	62	42	27	18	31	44	20	26	28

* Discrepancies between the totals of "Believe," "Not believe," and "Wonder About" and 100 percent represent the percentages who did not respond to the statements. Differences of 8 or 9 will ordinarily yield a *CR* of 2.0, depending upon the magnitude of the percentages involved.

Source: Reprinted by permission from R. G. Kuhlen and M. Arnold, "Age Differences in Religious Beliefs and Problems during Adolescence," *Journal of Genetic Psychology*, **65**, 291–300.

church to be a Christian." Of the 52 statements, 36 showed significant differences in the answers of the youngest and oldest groups.

Some differences in religious experience between honor students and average students emerged in the study of adolescent religious experiences [5]. An analysis of the compositions written by 144 ninth-graders showed that the honor students (with presumably higher intelligence) had more experience of feeling close to God when alone than did the average students. The average ones had more experiences than the honor students of feeling close to God when in church. The authors suggest this explanation of the result: because of higher intelligence and the ability to think more abstractly, the honor students could conceive God in broader terms and in more situations than could the average students. Since curiosity and independence were most likely more characteristic of the honor students than of the average, the former would be expected to resist the conformity required by church. Resisting church and conceiving God broadly, they would experience Him more in solitary situations than would the average adolescent.

Some sex differences in adolescent religious experience were also reported. Girls were much more likely than boys to experience God in solitary situations. For example, "I think the time when I feel closest to God is at night when my brothers and sisters are sleeping and the house is quiet. . . ."

Girls were more likely than boys to experience God when they were feeling anxiety of fear. "I feel close to God when someone I love is in danger."

Boys more often than girls felt that they contacted God in situations involving moral action. "I feel closest to God whenever I do something for someone else. I don't need any reward; the feeling I get is all I need."

In the type of religious experiences called *acute,* there were no significant differences between honor and average students, nor were there between boys and girls. Although the study did not show whether these experiences distinguished between adolescents and younger children, we could expect at least two of them, meditation and initiation, to be typically adolescent. Meditation experiences which brought an acute awareness of God were occasions of quiet, solitary thinking, often with heightened awareness of self and surroundings. They sound much like the self-cognition described in Chapter 15 as an essential in the establishment of the sense of identity. This example is given: "I had gone into the woods as I often did, but for some reason, I felt more alone. I began to think of what had brought me back to camp that year and my motives and how right and wrong they were. The way in which I answered my own questions seemed to go deeper than my own personal thoughts. . . . I felt He had been a guiding influence in my decision."

Initiation experiences typically take place at adolescence, in order to establish the individual as an adult in his own eyes and in those of God and society. Apparently some initiation ceremonies do bring the adolescent into contact with God. "I think the day of my Bar Mitzvah I felt closest to God. During the ceremony, when I became an adult according to Jewish law, I felt a holiness and closeness to God which I never felt before."

SUMMARY

Individuals of any age differ among themselves in responsibility, self-reliance and achievement, but these characteristics develop during childhood and adolescence and into adulthood. Assuming responsibility in adolescence seems to be related to warmth, friendliness and companionship of the home in which the adolescents grew up. Girls have been found to be rated as more responsible than boys and to be given more love-oriented discipline. Girls tend to maintain about the same level of dependency on others as they grow up, but boys often change, probably because the culture calls for more independence from adolescent and adult males.

Adolescents' motivation to achieve is related to the extent to which parents have expected achievement from their children and given them chances to achieve on their own. Cultural background and class position of the family are related to adolescents' measured need for achievement. Democratic, equalitarian families tend to produce children with a high need for achievement. Factors which help to build a strong sense of identity also bring about the building of independence, responsibility and drive for achievement because of the relationship of the latter characteristics to a sense of identity.

In the American culture adolescents are expected not only to prepare for a vocation, as is true in all cultures, but to decide from a vast array of vocations which one to prepare for. Because some vocations demand education beyond high school, vocational choice and preparation are related to educational achievement and aspirations. Although individuals in any occupation differ widely in intellectual capacity, it is possible to arrange occupations from low to high as to average level of intelligence of people engaged in them.

Intellectual level therefore is one of the factors involved in occupational choice. Cognitive style, particularly creativity, is another such factor. Specific abilities are required in differing degrees in various occupations. Not only are specific interests important in occupational success, but patterns of interests have been found to be so related. These patterns of interests are unstable in childhood, but are very stable from late adolescence onward through adulthood.

Family background is related to vocational success, not only because of differences in wealth and prestige, but also because of differences in personality of the children. One study has shown interesting differences in the interest patterns related to vocational success between children who occupied different positions among their siblings.

Many adolescents state vocational choices which are inappropriate for them as to their intelligence level or interest patterns. The earlier a wise choice is made, the more likely the adolescent is to become successful in his vocation in young adulthood. The wisdom of choice can be increased by greater knowledge of vocational possibilities and greater insight into one's own abilities. Adolescents can be helped to achieve both of these by sympathetic guidance from adults.

Background and personality characteristics of groups of eminent biologists, physicists and social scientists were found in one study to differ among the three groups and from more unselected groups of individuals. This study shows not how to bring about eminence in these fields, but the fact that the development of personal characteristics is a dynamic, coherent process.

One of the important parts of a developing sense of identity is the vocational role that the individual is looking forward to playing. Another is the offering of service or betterment to the world around one. The American culture offers several different institutional means for combining these aspects of the sense of identity. The Peace Corps is an example.

Moral judgments made by individuals are related to the level and kind of intellectual processes of which they are capable. The development of flexibility of thought during adolescence makes possible the holding of relative standards of morality and the recognition of extenuating circumstances. Although individuals of all ages make some moral judgments at all levels of thought, older people give more judgments which show the development of and adherence to individual standards. Moral judgment and moral behavior are positively related to each other, but it is obvious that people behave immorally even when they "know better." The general level of moral development of adolescents is related to the kind of family in which they have grown up. Lack of moral development, as shown in juvenile delinquency, is related not only to family but to broader social environment and to the kind of relationships with others which have occurred.

Religious development, akin to the development of the sense of integrity, is related to intellectual ability, to rigidity or flexibility of thinking. Since it is an expression of relatedness of oneself to one's environment, individual and environmental factors are important.

REFERENCES

1. Bowles, F. *Access to higher education.* Paris, United Nations Educational, Scientific and Cultural Organization and the International Association of Universities, 1963.
2. Bronfenbrenner, U. Some familial antecedents of responsibility and leadership in adolescents. In L. Petrullo & B. M. Bass (Eds.), *Leadership and interpersonal behavior.* New York: Holt, 1961, pp. 239–271.
3. Clarke, H. H., & Olson, A. L. Characteristics of 15-year-old boys who demonstrate various accomplishments or difficulties. *Child Devel.,* 1965, **36,** 559–567.
4. Coleman, J. G. Volunteerism: a constructive outlet for youthful energy. *J. Marr. Fam.,* 1965, **27,** 171–175.
5. Elkind, D., & Elkind, S. Varieties of religious experience in young adolescents. *J. Sci. Stud. Religion,* 1962, **2,** 102–112.
6. Erikson, E. H. *Childhood and society.* New York: Norton, 1963.
7. Farber, M. L. English and Americans: values in the socialization process. *J. Psychol.,* 1953, **36,** 234–250.
8. Friend, F. G., & Haggard, E. A. Work adjustment in relation to family background. *Applied Psychol. Mono.* No. 16. Stanford, Calif.: Stanford Univer., 1948.
9. Getzels, J. W., & Jackson, P. W. *Creativity and intelligence.* New York: Wiley, 1962.
10. Glueck, S., & Glueck, E. *Unraveling juvenile delinquency.* New York: Commonwealth Fund, 1950.
11. Glueck, S., & Glueck, E. *Physique and delinquency.* New York: Harper, 1956.
12. Glueck, S., & Glueck, E. *Family environment and delinquency.* Boston: Houghton Mifflin, 1962.

13. Harris, D. B. Work and the adolescent transition to maturity. *Teachers College Record,* 1961, **63,** 146–153.
14. Harris, D. B., Clark, K. E., & Rose, A. M. The measurement of responsibility in children. *Child Devel.,* 1954, **25,** 20–28. (a)
15. Harris, D. B., Clark, K. E., & Rose, A. M. The relationship of children's home duties to an attitude of responsibility. *Child Devel.,* 1954, **25,** 29–33. (b)
16. Hartshorne, H., May, M. A., & Shuttleworth, F. K. *Studies in the nature of character: Vol. III. Studies in the organization of character.* New York: Macmillan, 1930.
17. Havemann, E., & West, P. S. *They went to college.* New York: Harcourt, Brace, 1952.
18. Healy, W., & Bronner, A. F. *New light on delinquency and its treatment.* New Haven: Yale Univer., 1936.
19. Hechinger, F. M. The junior blues. *New York Times,* July 28, 1963.
20. Inhelder, B., & Piaget, J. *The growth of logical thinking from childhood to adolescence.* New York: Basic Books, 1958.
21. Jersild, A. T. *The psychology of adolescence.* New York: Macmillan, 1957.
22. Kagan, J., & Moss, H. A. The stability of passive and dependent behavior from childhood through adulthood. *Child. Devel.,* 1960, **31,** 577–591.
23. Kaufman, J. F. Youth and the Peace Corps. In E. H. Erikson (Ed.), *Youth: change and challenge.* New York: Basic Books, 1963.
24. Kohlberg, L. The development of children's orientations toward a moral order: I. Sequence in the development of moral thought. *Vita Humana,* 1963, **6,** 11–33. (a)
25. Kohlberg, L. The development of children's orientations toward a moral order: II. Social experience, social conduct and the development of moral thought. *Vita Humana,* 1963. Cited in [24]. (b)
26. Kohlberg, L. Moral development and identification. In H. W. Stevenson, J. Kagan & C. Spiker (Eds.), *Child psychology.* The Sixty-second Yearbook of the National Society for the Study of Education. Chicago: Univer. of Chicago, 1963, pp. 277–332. (c)
27. Kuhlen, R. G., & Arnold, M. Age differences in religious beliefs and problems during adolescence. *J. Genet. Psychol.,* 1944, **65,** 291–300.
28. McDill, E. L., & Coleman, J. High school social status, college plans and interest in academic achievement: a panel analysis. *Am. Soc. Rev.,* 1963, **28,** 905–918.
29. Moss, H. A., & Kagan, J. Stability of achievement and recognition-seeking behaviors from early childhood through adulthood. *J. Abn. Soc. Psychol.,* 1961, **62,** 504–513.
30. Murphey, E. B., Silber, E., Coelho, G. V., Hamburg, D. A., & Greenberg, I. Development of autonomy and parent-child interaction in late adolescence. *Am. J. Orthopsychiat.,* 1963, **33,** 643–652.
31. Peck, R. F., & Havighurst, R. J. *The psychology of character development.* New York: Wiley, 1960.
32. Powell, M., & Bloom, V. Development of and reasons for vocational choices of adolescents through the high school years. *J. Educ. Res.,* 1962, **56,** 126–133.
33. President's Committee on Youth Employment. *The challenge of jobless youth.* Washington, D.C.: U.S. Printing Office, 1963.

34. Robison, S. M. *Juvenile delinquency: its nature and control.* New York: Holt, 1960.
35. Roe, A. *The making of a scientist.* New York: Dodd, Mead, 1953.
36. Roe, A. *The psychology of occupations.* New York: Wiley, 1956.
37. Rosen, B. C. Race, ethnicity and the achievement syndrome. *Am. Soc. Rev.,* 1959, **24,** 47–50.
38. Rosen, B. C. Family structure and achievement motivation. *Am. Soc. Rev.,* 1961, **26,** 574–585.
39. Schaefer, E. S. Children's reports of parental behavior: an inventory. *Child Devel.,* 1965, **36,** 414–424.
40. Straus, M. A. Conjugal power structure and adolescent personality. *Marr. Fam. Living,* 1962, **24,** 17–25.
41. Super, D. E. Ninth grade vocational maturity and other predictors of career behavior and occupational criteria at age 25. Paper presented at American Psychological Association, August 30, 1963.
42. Super, D. E., & Overstreet, P. L. *The vocational maturity of ninth-grade boys.* New York: Columbia Univer., 1960.
43. Sutton-Smith, B., Roberts, J. M., & Rosenberg, B. G. Sibling associations and role involvement. *Merrill-Palmer Quart.,* 1964, **10,** 25–38.
44. Thorndike, R. L., & Hagen, E. *Ten thousand careers.* New York: Wiley, 1959.
45. Thorndike, R. L., & Hagen, E. *Measurement and evaluation in psychology and education.* New York: Wiley, 1961.
46. Tyler, L. E. The antecedents of two varieties of vocational interests. *Genet. Psychol. Mono.,* 1964, **70,** 177–227.
47. Veroff, J. Theoretical background for studying the origins of human motivational dispositions. *Merrill-Palmer Quart.,* 1965, **2,** 3–18.

AUTHOR INDEX

SUBJECT INDEX

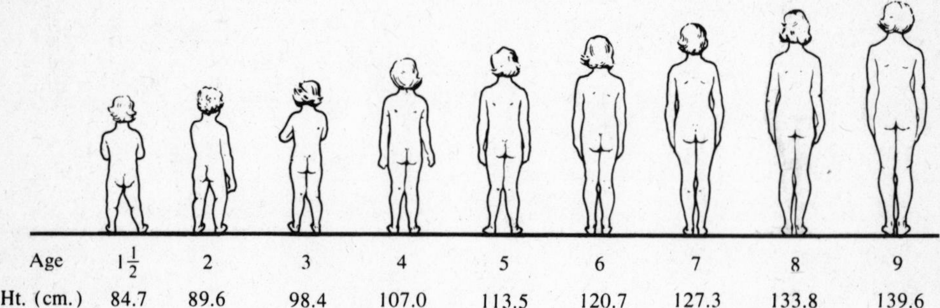
Age 1½ 2 3 4 5 6 7 8 9
Ht. (cm.) 84.7 89.6 98.4 107.0 113.5 120.7 127.3 133.8 139.6

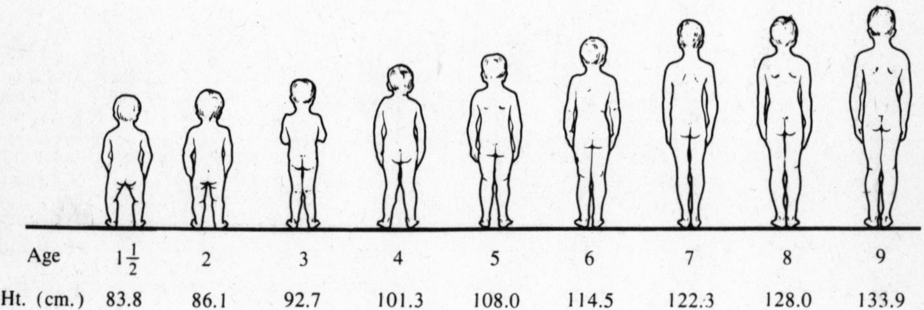
Age 1½ 2 3 4 5 6 7 8 9
Ht. (cm.) 83.8 86.1 92.7 101.3 108.0 114.5 122.3 128.0 133.9